A GUIDE TO STATE SUCCESSION IN INTERNATIONAL INVESTMENT LAW

ELGAR INTERNATIONAL INVESTMENT LAW

Series Editors: Andrea K. Bjorklund, *McGill University, Montreal, Quebec, Canada* and August Reinisch, *University of Vienna, Austria*

This monograph series provides a point of convergence for authoritative, original works focused specifically on international investment law in all its forms. Works will be single or co-authored, theoretically rigorous and analytically precise, often considering the intersection of investment law with other fields of law such as trade, intellectual property, environment or public international law. The series will comprise works from established authors as well as from younger scholars whose work is genuinely innovative and challenging. Proposals are encouraged that primarily engage with new and previously under-developed themes in the field, draw on other disciplines in order to further thinking in the field, or alternatively attempt to offer a definitive statement on areas of uncertainty in the existing law.

The development of original thinking in international investment law and research of the highest quality is the main emphasis of the series. Both international and comparative in its approach, it aims to include some of the best theoretical and empirical work from both well-established researchers and the next generation of scholars.

Titles in this series include:

International Investment Law and the Environment
Saverio Di Benedetto

Intellectual Property Rights as Foreign Direct Investments
From Collision to Collaboration
Lukas Vanhonnaeker

Performance Requirements and Investment Incentives Under International Economic Law
David Collins

The ASEAN Comprehensive Investment Agreement
The Regionalisation of Laws and Policy on Foreign Investment
Julien Chaisse and Sufian Jusoh

Non-Discrimination and the Role of Regulatory Purpose in International Trade and Investment Law
Andrew D. Mitchell, David Heaton and Caroline Henckels

Regulatory Autonomy in International Economic Law
The Evolution of Australian Policy on Trade and Investment
Tania Voon, Andrew D. Mitchell and Elizabeth Sheargold

Proportionality, Reasonableness and Standards of Review in International Investment Law and Arbitration
Valentina Vadi

A Guide to State Succession in International Investment Law
Patrick Dumberry

A GUIDE TO STATE SUCCESSION IN INTERNATIONAL INVESTMENT LAW

PATRICK DUMBERRY

Professor, Faculty of Law (Civil Law Section), University of Ottawa, Canada

ELGAR INTERNATIONAL INVESTMENT LAW

Edward Elgar PUBLISHING

Cheltenham, UK • Northampton, MA, USA

Published by
Edward Elgar Publishing Limited
The Lypiatts
15 Lansdown Road
Cheltenham
Glos GL50 2JA
UK

Edward Elgar Publishing, Inc.
William Pratt House
9 Dewey Court
Northampton
Massachusetts 01060
USA

A catalogue record for this book
is available from the British Library

Library of Congress Control Number: 2018931789

This book is available electronically in the **Elgar**online
Law subject collection
DOI 10.4337/9781788116619

MIX
Paper from
responsible sources
FSC® C013604

ISBN 978 1 78811 660 2 (cased)
ISBN 978 1 78811 661 9 (eBook)

Typeset by Columns Design XML Ltd, Reading
Printed by CPI Group (UK) Ltd, Croydon CR0 4YY

CONTENTS

PART F GENERAL CONCLUSION

EXTENDED CONTENTS

4 Different forms of consent by States for the continuation of BITs

5 Critical analysis of the solutions adopted by the Vienna Convention

6 BIT arbitration cases involving State succession issues

PART C STATE SUCCESSION TO MULTILATERAL TREATIES

PART D STATE SUCCESSION TO STATE CONTRACTS

PREFACE

Why write a book on the question of State succession in the context of international investment law? My first international law *coup de foudre* was regarding issues of State succession. I did my Ph.D. thesis more than 10 years ago (from 2000 to 2006) at the Graduate Institute for International Studies, in Geneva, on the (then) obscure question of State succession to State responsibility. At the time I wrote my thesis, there were only five published articles that focused on this issue. I decided to tackle this question because I believed that the manner in which (almost) all published international law textbooks addressed the issue was unsatisfactory. Indeed, their answer to the question of whether the successor State should be held responsible for internationally wrongful acts committed by the predecessor State was invariably in the negative. At the time, I thought that the answer should be context-dependent in that the answer could not realistically always be negative in all circumstances. In any event, I believed that the question was much more complex than the two sentences which were typically devoted to the topic. It turned out that I was right. My comprehensive analysis of State practice and international and municipal case law has shown that the solution to the problem first depends on the type of succession involved. Thus, there is not one solution that will apply to all cases. The answer to the question simply cannot be the same considering that in some cases the predecessor ceases to exist (dissolution) and in others it does not (secession). Second, the solution to the problem depends on a number of factors and circumstances (including who committed the wrong, the need to avoid any unjust enrichment, etc.) that should be taken into account by a tribunal. My findings were published in a book.[1] The new framework of analysis I have provided and the conclusions I reached in this book have since then been endorsed by other scholars, including former ILC Special Rapporteur James Crawford (now judge at the ICJ) in a recent book,[2] the Institut de droit international in a 2015 Resolution on the matter,[3] and, finally, by the preliminary work of the ILC Special Rapporteur Šturma.[4]

In the years that followed the publication of my book, I became more interested in another field of law: international investment law. I was very fortunate to work in Geneva (while doing my Ph.D. thesis) with one of the greatest international arbitration lawyers: Professor Pierre Lalive. At Lalive and Partners, I was given the opportunity to work on a number of investor-State arbitration cases with him, Michael Schneider and Veijo Heiskanen. In 2006, I

1 Patrick Dumberry, *State Succession to International Responsibility* (M. Nijhoff, 2007).

2 James Crawford, *State Responsibility: The General Part* (CUP, 2013) 437ff.

3 Institut de Droit international, *State Succession in Matters of State Responsibility*, 14th Commission, (Rap. M.G. Kohen), Resolution, 28 August 2015.

4 ILC, Report of the International Law Commission, Official Records of the General Assembly, 71st session, Supplement No. 10 (A/71/10), recommendation of the Working-Group on the long-term programme of work, Annex B: 'Succession of States in respect of State responsibility', Syllabus by Pavel Šturma. See also: Pavel Šturma, 'State Succession in Respect of International Responsibility', (2016) 48 *Geo Wash. Int'l L Rev* 653–78. ILC Special Rapporteur recently issued his 'First report on succession of States in respect of State responsibility' (69th session, 2017, A/CN.4/708, 31 May 2017).

came back to Montreal to work at Ogilvy Renault (now known as Norton Rose Fulbright) and was again tremendously privileged to assist another giant and emblematic figure in the field of investment arbitration: Me Yves L. Fortier. Finally, I also worked with an amazing team of lawyers at Canada's Ministry of Foreign Affairs (Trade Law Bureau) where I was involved in investor-State NAFTA Chapter 11 cases. Based on my ten years of experience working as a lawyer involved in these cases, I started focusing on investment arbitration questions when I became Professor at the University of Ottawa in 2009. I have been pursuing research in that field ever since.

Three years ago, I started exploring the impact that events of State succession could have in the context of investment arbitration. The interaction between these two distinct fields of law was a perfect mix between past and new 'loves'. I first assessed the question of State succession to BITs. I was surprised to find out that almost nothing had been written on the general question of succession to bilateral treaties. Moreover, the specific topic of succession to BITs had never been addressed by scholars. My initial reaction was to think that this was probably because the subject matter was not worthy of any analysis! Yet, I found many investment cases where the issue arose, but had been barely noticed (let alone discussed) by arbitral tribunals. The only exception was the *Sanum Investments Ltd. v. Laos* award, a case that only dealt with a very specific question (succession to a BIT in the context of a transfer of territory) in rather unique circumstances (the special status of Macao within China).[5]

I also started investigating the work of the ILC on the question of succession to treaties and, I must admit, the results were very disappointing and, frankly, slightly disturbing. As further explained in this book, the conclusion reached by the ILC in the 1978 Vienna Convention that a new State (in the context of secession and dissolution) *automatically* succeeds to bilateral treaties which were signed by the predecessor State is illogical considering the particular nature of these instruments. Moreover, the outcome is contrary to all the work that had been conducted on the matter by the Commission itself for many years. This discovery confirmed my earlier impression that this was, after all, a topic worthy of further investigation. After writing two articles on the question in 2015,[6] I worked as counsel to Kazakhstan in the *WWM v. Kazakhstan* case which (as further discussed in this book) involved State succession issues.[7] This is when I truly discovered the complexity of the issue which had been so far unexplored by scholars.

When I started conducting research on this under-investigated 'open field', I must confess that I felt the same kind on enthusiasm (and sometimes anguish ...) that I first encountered when I commenced working on my Ph.D. thesis. For instance, I soon realised that nothing had been published on the question of succession to State contracts since the work of O'Connell in the 1960s and 1970s.[8] It seems that no one had given any thought to the question whether a new State should be bound by State contracts which had been signed by the predecessor State. This was surprising given the fact that the problem was not uncommon and had often occurred

---

5 *Sanum Investments Ltd. v. Laos*, UNCITRAL (PCA Case No 2013–13), Award on Jurisdiction, 13 December 2013.

6 P. Dumberry, 'An Uncharted Question of State Succession: Are New States Automatically Bound by the BITs Concluded by Predecessor States Before Independence?' (2015) 6(1) *J Int Disp Settl* 74–96; P. Dumberry, 'State Succession to Bilateral Treaties: A Few Observations on the Incoherent and Unjustifiable Solution Adopted for Secession and Dissolution of States under the 1978 Vienna Convention' (2015) 28 *Leiden JIL* 13–30.

7 *World Wide Minerals Ltd. and Mr. Paul A. Carroll, QC v. Kazakhstan*, UNCITRAL, Award, 19 October 2015.

8 D.P. O'Connell, *State Succession in Municipal Law and International Law* vol I (CUP 1967); D.P. O'Connell, 'Recent Problems of State Succession in Relation to New States', (1970–II) 130 Rec des Cours.

in the past. Using both classic material[9] and new research tools,[10] I reassessed old examples of State practice and case law which had been discussed by scholars in the past in other contexts to determine whether they could be relevant to the issue of succession to contracts. I found a number of old and new examples which were indeed very pertinent to my analysis. I also examined all existing (and publically-available) arbitration cases involving succession to BITs. I found 46 publicly-known investor-State arbitration cases dealing with the issue.

This book offers the first comprehensive analysis of State succession issues arising in the context of international investment law. Specifically, this book examines two fundamental questions:

- is a successor State bound by investment treaties (including BITs) entered into by the predecessor State with other States?;
- is a successor State bound by the obligations contained in State contracts (including arbitration clauses) which had been signed by the predecessor State with foreign companies before the date of succession?

The book answers the question for each type of State succession. The answer is in part based on the work of the ILC on succession to treaties and the (very limited) scholarly analysis which has been conducted in the past by authors. The analysis is for the most part based on my own investigation of State practice and the review of judicial decisions from international and domestic courts. Based on my previous work on other issues of State succession, I developed a novel comprehensive framework of analysis which takes into account a number of factors and circumstances. The solution I have put forward in this book for each type of succession is ultimately the one which I believe to be the most logical and appropriate given the specific circumstances of each situation. The questions that were at the heart of my reflection throughout this book were the following: What should be the logical solution to this specific problem?; what would be a fair and just outcome to solve that problem? Another concern was to assess whether any given solution takes into account the interests of the different actors involved, that is, not only the successor State and the predecessor State (if it continues to exist), but also the other State party to a BIT or the other non-State party to a State contract. In that sense, some of the findings contained in this book should be considered as a 'progressive development' of rules rather than a codification of existing practice. This is particularly the case given the fact that some of the questions examined in this book have simply never been addressed by tribunals. For instance, what happens when an event leading to a State succession occurs *during* the arbitration proceedings? This is an important question given the fact that such changes may affect the identity of the respondent State in the proceedings. For example, in the context of the dissolution of a State, the respondent will cease to exist during the proceedings. An event of succession may also affect the home State of the claimant investor and result in changes of nationality during the proceedings.

This book aims to offer guidance to actors on how to solve issues of State succession in the field of investor-State arbitration. It will provide States, investors and arbitrators with

9 I systematically examined all cases dealing with State succession issues published in law digests, including Annual Digest of Public International Law Cases, United Nations Reports of International Arbitral Awards, International Legal Materials, International Legal Reports.

10 I have examined all cases dealing with State succession in databases, including Oxford Public International Law, Oxford Reports on International Law in Domestic Courts, Kluwer Arbitration Law, ITAlaw, Investor-State Law Guide, Investment Claims, etc.

indispensable (yet currently scarcely available) tools to enhance their ability to solve disputes between foreign investors and States involving the phenomenon of State succession. It should be recalled here the critical comments made by O'Connell almost 50 years ago, on the 'practice' of States regarding succession issues:

> The truth of the matter is that this 'practice' is likely to consist of decisions taken by public officials who have not achieved the necessary intellectual penetration of the problem to perceive the true issues, who may be more influenced by political or other ephemeral considerations than by juristic logic, who may even be ignorant of the nature of the problem, or of its ramifications, or who may be equipped with obsolescent literature, or even no literature whatever. Some of the processes of decision-making respecting matters of State succession that have occurred in recent years can hardly be dignified as significant contributions to the elaboration of the law.[11]

This remark is rather crude and certainly unfair to the difficult tasks undertaken every day by thousands of civil servants and bureaucrats working in foreign and justice ministries throughout the world. Yet, the truth of the matter is that new States (but also 'old' ones) generally have few resources and little experience concerning complex questions of international law, such as those relative to State succession. Furthermore, these questions are generally not considered to be the priorities in the context of the process leading to independence of the new State. The goal of this book is to provide States (and also foreign investors) with guidelines to help them address succession issues in the context of investment disputes.

11 O'Connell (n 8) 117.

ACKNOWLEDGMENTS

This book is the result of more than two years of research. I would like to thank the Faculty of Law (Civil Law Section) at the University of Ottawa, my colleagues and members of the administrative staff for their support throughout the years. I am especially indebted to several bright and talented students from the University of Ottawa who have assisted me over the last several years with research and editing. Their assistance was invaluable to the completion of this book. I want to sincerely thank Nicolas Karsenti, Jessica Provencher-Garand, Corey Spector, and Evan Bernstein. All of them have done an amazing job.

I would furthermore like to thank to all the people at Edward Elgar Publishing (Stephanie Tytherleigh, Luke Adams, Sally Philip, Sarah Brown, etc.) for their patience and support in the revision process for the publication of this book. More particularly, I would like to express my gratitude to Professor Andrea Bjorklund and Professor August Reinisch for agreeing to publish my book in the *Elgar International Investment Law* series.

Most importantly, I would like to dedicate this book to my parents and my children. I would like to first express my gratitude to my parents for their unconditional support and love throughout my life. I also wish to thank my beautiful, funny and bright children, Ophélie and Florent. Your love and affection have given me the strength to write this book. I hope that one day you will read this book and fully understand the extent to which this whole odyssey would have simply been impossible (and really pointless) without your constant love and support. You have been there for me through thick and thin. My daughter (who is now nine years old) told me a few years ago 'Daddy, I personally don't really care what your books are all about, what I am happy about is that you like to write them so much.' That is exactly the kind of support that I needed when I wrote this book. Ophélie, your interests have changed so much over the years: astronaut, doctor, teacher, etc. Recently, after watching the movie *Gandhi* you said 'I think I want to be a lawyer like him.' Well, needless to say that it would make me very proud! In any event, your current plan to become a professional Bolshoi ballerina is also quite awesome! Florent (now seven years old), in my last book published in 2016, I promised you that one day I would write an international law book involving Ninja Turtles! Well, I must admit that I'm still struggling to figure out the proper angle to touch up the controversial question of their (limited, yet unquestionable ...) impact on contemporary international law! Nowadays, your love has turned to football, and more specifically to the player Cristiano Ronaldo. I fully support your on-going plan to become as good as him! Yet, you may want to consider continuing your school career for a (little) while in the (unlikely) event that you don't quite get there! Merci à vous deux mes amours! Finally, a very special thanks to Christina in the last miles of this journey: you have been amazing!

Patrick Dumberry
Montréal, Canada
October 2017

ABBREVIATIONS

ABDI	Anuario Brasileiro de Direito Internacional
AEI	Annales d'études internationales
AFDI	Annuaire français de droit international
AJIL	American Journal of International Law
Am J Comp L	American Journal of Comparative Law
Am Rev Int'l Arb	American Review of International Arbitration
Annuaire IDI	Yearbook of the Institut de Droit international (Institute of International Law)
Annual Digest	Annual Digest of Public International Law Cases
Arb Int	Arbitration International
Arbitration & ADR	Arbitration & Alternative Dispute Resolution
ARCS	American Review of Canadian Studies
ASA Bull	Bulletin of the Association Suisse de l'Arbitrage
ASDI	Annuaire suisse de droit international
ASIL Proc	American Society of International Law Proceedings
Australian YIL	Australian Yearbook of International Law
Austrian RIEL	Austrian Review of International & European Law
Baltic YIL	Baltic Yearbook of International Law
BIICL	British Institute of International and Comparative Law
BITs	Bilateral investment treaties
British YIL	British Yearbook of International Law
Cal W Int'l L J	California Western International Law Journal
Cambridge JICL	Cambridge Journal of International and Comparative Law
Canadian YIL	Canadian Yearbook of International Law
Cardozo JICL	Cardozo Journal of International and Comparative Law
CIS	Commonwealth of Independent States
Columbia JEL	Columbia Journal of European Law
Colum J Transnat'l L	Columbia Journal of Transnational Law
Colum L Rev	Colombia Law Review

Comp & Int'l L J S Afr	Comparative & International Law Journal of Southern Africa
Cornell LQ	Cornell Law Quarterly
CSFR	Czechoslovak Socialist Federal Republic
CUP	Cambridge University Press
Czech YPPIL	Czech Yearbook of Public & Private International Law
Denver J Int L	Denver Journal of International Law & Policy
EJIL	European Journal of International Law
EJIL Talk!	European Journal of International Law: Talk!
FET	Fair and equitable treatment
FRG	Federal Republic of Germany
FRY	Federal Republic of Yugoslavia
FTA	Free Trade Agreement
GDR	German Democratic Republic
Geo Wash Int'l L Rev	George Washington International Law Review
German LJ	German Law Journal
German YIL	German Yearbook of International Law
GPO	Government publication office
Howard LJ	Howard Law Journal
ICC	International Chamber of Commerce
ICJ	International Court of Justice
ICJ Rep	International Court of Justice Reports of Judgments, Advisory Opinions and Orders
ICJ Statute	Statute of the International Court of Justice
ICLQ	International and Comparative Law Quarterly
ICSID	International Centre for Settlement of Investment Disputes
ICSID Rev	International Centre for Settlement of Investment Disputes Review – Foreign Investment Law Journal
IDI	Institut de Droit international (Institute of International Law)
IISD	International Investment Law and Sustainable Development
ILA	International Law Association
ILC	International Law Commission
ILC Articles on State Responsibility	Titles and Texts of the Draft Articles on Responsibility of States for Internationally Wrongful Acts Adopted by the Drafting Committee on Second Reading, 26 July 2001

ILC Commentaries	Commentaries to the Draft Articles on Responsibility of States for Internationally Wrongful Acts Adopted by the International Law Commission at its Fifty-Third Session (2001), November 2001
ILM	International Legal Materials
ILR	International Legal Reports
Indon. J Intl & Comp L	Indonesian Journal of International and Comparative Law
Int'l L	International Lawyer
Int'l L Stud	International Legal Studies
Italian YIL	Italian Yearbook of International Law
JDI	Journal du droit international
J East Asia & Int'l L	Journal of East Asia & International Law
J Hist Int'l L	Journal of History & International Law
J Int Arb	Journal of International Arbitration
J Int Disp Settl	Journal of International Dispute Settlement
J Int'l Econ L	Journal of International Economic Law
J Int'l L	Journal of International Law
J Int'l L & Pol	Journal of International law and Politics
J World Invest & Trade	Journal of World Investment & Trade
J World Trade	Journal of World Trade
Korean JCL	Korean Journal of Comparative Law
L & Bus Rev Am	Law and Business Review of the Americas
La L Rev	Louisiana Law Review
Leiden JIL	Leiden Journal of International Law
LGDJ	Librairie générale de droit et de jurisprudence
Loy LA Int'l & Comp L Rev	Loyola Los Angeles International Law and Comparative Law Review
McGill LJ	McGill Law Journal
Mealey's IAR	Mealey's International Arbitration Report
MFN	Most-Favored-Nation
Michigan JIL	Michigan Journal of International Law
Michigan State JIL	Michigan State Journal of International Law
Mich St Int'l L Rev	Michigan State International Law Review
Mil L & L War Rev	Military Law and Law of War Review
MST	Minimum standard of treatment
MTF	Moving Treaty Frontier
NAFTA	North American Free Trade Agreement

NEICLA	New England International and Comparative Law Annual
Netherlands ILR	Netherlands International Law Review
Nordic JIL	Nordic Journal of International Law
NYUJ Int'l L & Pol	New York University Journal of International Law and Politics
OECD	Organisation for Economic Co-operation and Development
Oxford J Legal Stud	Oxford Journal of Legal Studies
OUP	Oxford University Press
özörv	Austrian Journal of Public and International Law
Palestine YIL	Palestine Yearbook of International Law
PCA	Permanent Court of Arbitration
PCIJ	Permanent Court of International Justice
Penn State ILR	Penn State International Law Review
PUF	Presses universitaires de France
PU Montréal	Presses de l'Université de Montréal
Queen's LJ	Queen's Law Journal
Questions Int'l L	Questions of International Law
Rec des cours	Collected Courses of the Hague Academy of International Law
RBDI	Revue belge de droit international
Rev Arb	Revue de l'arbitrage
Rev crit d i privé	Revue critique de droit international privé
RGDIP	Revue générale de droit international public
RHDI	Revue Hellénique de Droit International
RQDI	Revue québécoise de droit international
SCR	Supreme Court of Canada
SFRY	Socialist Federal Republic of Yugoslavia
Singapore YBIL	Singapore Yearbook of International Law
SSRN	Social Science Research Network
St. Antony's Int Rev	St. Antony's International Review
Sw J L & Trade Americas	Southwestern Journal of Law and Trade in the Americas
TDM	Transnational Dispute Management Journal
U Cin L Rev	University of Cincinnati Law Review
UKTS	United Kingdom Treaty Series
UN	United Nations
UNCC	United Nations Compensation Commission

UNCITRAL	United Nations Commission on International Trade Law
UNCTAD	United Nations Conference on Trade and Development
Univ Illinois LR	University of Illinois Law Review
UNRIAA	United Nations Reports of International Arbitral Awards
UNTS	United Nations Treaty Series
US	United States
USSR	Union of Soviet Socialist Republics
VCLT	Vienna Convention on the Law of Treaties
VCST	Vienna Convention on Succession of States in Respect of Treaties
Virginia JIL	Virginia Journal of International Law
World Arb & Med Rep	World Arbitration and Mediation Review
Yb Int'l Invest L & Pol	Yearbook of International Investment Law and Policy
Yearbook ILC	Yearbook of the International Law Commission
ZaöRV	Zeitschrift für ausländisches öffentliches Recht und Völkerrecht

TABLE OF CASES

1. INVESTOR-STATE ARBITRATION ARBITRAL AWARDS

2. ICJ AND PCIJ CASES

3. OTHER ARBITRAL AWARDS

4. DOMESTIC COURT DECISIONS

5. OTHERS

TABLE OF TREATIES AND LEGISLATION

TREATIES

Multilateral and bilateral treaties

Exchanges of notes and letters

Others

REPORTS OF THE IDI, ILA, ILC, OECD AND UNCTAD

International Law Commission, 'Fifth Report on Succession in Respect of Treaties', by the Special Rapporteur, Sir Humphrey Waldock, A/CN.4/256 and Adds.1–4, 10 April, 29 May and 8, 16 and 28 June 1972, A/8710/Rev.1, in (1972) II Yearbook ILC 5.03

International Law Commission, 'First Report by the Special Rapporteur V. Mikulka on State Succession and Its Impact on the Nationality of Natural and Legal Persons', UN A/CN.4/467, (1995) II(1) Yearbook ILC 16.05, 16.10

International Law Commission, 'First Report on Diplomatic Protection, by John Dugard', 52nd Sess., UN Doc. A/CN.4/506, 2000 .... 16.32, 16.39, 16.40

International Law Commission, 'First Report on Succession of States and Governments in Respect of Treaties', by the Special Rapporteur, Sir Humphrey Waldock, A/CN.4/202, 15 March 1968, A/7209/Rev.1, in (1968) II Yearbook ILC 5.03, 5.04

International Law Commission, 'First Report on Succession of States in Respect of Rights and Duties Resulting from Sources other than Treaties', by Mr. Mohammed Bedjaoui, Special Rapporteur Topic: Succession of States in respect of matters other than treaties, A/CN.4/204 and Corr.1 (French only), in (1968) II Yearbook ILC 94 ...... 10.08, 13.64, 13.77, 13.79, 13.80, 13.81, 13.86

International Law Commission, 'First Report on Succession of States in Respect of Treaties', by the Special Rapporteur, Sir Francis Vallat, A/CN.4/278 and Adds.1–6, 19 and 22 April, 8, 24 and 31 May and 10 and 21 June 1974, reproduced in A/9610/Rev.1, in (1974) II(1) Yearbook ILC 5.03

International Law Commission, 'Fourth Report on State Responsibility' by Mr. F.V. Garcia-Amador, Special Rapporteur, A/CN.4/119, in (1959) II Yearbook ILC 10.09, 10.10, 12.08

International Law Commission, 'Fourth Report on State Responsibility of the Special Rapporteur', Mr Roberto Ago, 24th session of the ILC, 1972, UN Doc. A/CN.4/264 and Add.1, ILC Report, A/8710/Rev.1 (A/27/10), 1972, chp. IV(B) [72–73] in: (1972) II Yearbook ILC 71 .... 14.32

International Law Commission, Fourth Report on Succession in Respect of Treaties, prepared by the Special Rapporteur, Sir Humphrey Waldock, A/CN.4/249, 24 June 1971, A/8410/Rev.1, in (1971) II(1) Yearbook ILC ... 4.03, 4.04, 4.05, 4.28, 4.39, 4.43, 4.44, 4.45, 5.03, 5.55, 5.57, 5.58, 5.59, 5.60, 5.61, 5.69, 5.73, 7.09

International Law Commission, 'Guiding Principles Applicable to Unilateral Declarations of States Capable of Creating Legal Obligations With Commentaries Thereto', in: (2006) II(2) Yearbook ILC 4.10

International Law Commission, 'Ninth Report on Succession of States in Respect of Matters Other Than Treaties', A/CN.4/30111981/Add.l, in (1981) II Yearbook ILC 14.21

International Law Commission, 'Report of the International Law Commission on the Work of its 21st Session', 2 June–8 August 1969, Official Records of the General Assembly, 24th Session, Supplement No. 10 (A/7610/Rev.1), A/CN.4/220, in (1969) II Yearbook ILC 228 .... 5.03, 5.40, 10.01

International Law Commission, Report of the International Law Commission on the Work of its 24th session, 2 May–7 July 1972, A/8710/Rev.1, in (1972) II Yearbook ILC ... 4.04, 4.05, 4.28, 5.03, 5.50, 5.71, 7.07

UN DOCUMENTS

DOMESTIC LAW INSTRUMENTS AND DOCUMENTS

Part A
GENERAL INTRODUCTION

1

CONCEPTS

1. THE ISSUES ADDRESSED IN THIS BOOK

Until recently, investment arbitration lawyers and scholars did not pay much attention to the question of the interaction between the different fields of State succession and international investment law. The same was true for specialists of State succession. While scholars in the field of State succession have spent an incredible amount of time and energy in the last decades examining the practice of States and numerous theoretical aspects regarding the question of succession to treaties in general, they have barely noticed the particularities of bilateral investment treaties for the promotion and protection of investments ('BITs'). Similarly, while epic battles were fought decades ago amongst scholars on the controversial question of the survival of acquired rights, there seems to be a lack of interest in the rather basic issue of succession to State contracts. This is very surprising considering the fact that questions about the nature and effect of State contracts have been fiercely debated in international law throughout the last 30 years. More than one generation of investment arbitration specialists have analysed questions related to, for instance, the law applicable to such contracts, the effect of stabilization clauses, and even more esoteric topics such as the 'internationalization' of these instruments. Yet, none of the investment arbitration specialists seem to have been concerned about the fate of these contracts in the event of State succession. **1.01**

1.02 In sum, until very recently, both fields of law seemed to have been isolated from one another given the fact that specialists in each discipline are consistently reading different books from different shelves of the law school libraries. There was little, if any, interaction between these two areas. Such a segregation was, of course, always illusory. Thus, both fields have the same common heritage: public international law. Readers of each discipline may have used different shelves, but they were nevertheless always in the same library. Thus, it is rather uncontroversial to affirm today that the solution to specific problems in the field of investment arbitration must necessarily be found under general international law. This is due to the fact that investment arbitration is part of public international law.[1] It is not a self-contained regime.[2] The same is true for solutions to State succession questions which are, by definition, grounded in public international law. The aim of this book is to apply the existing rules of State succession to problems arising in the specific context of international investment law.

1.03 To the best of the present author's knowledge, the first article to fully address the specific question of State succession to BITs was one published in 2015 by myself.[3] As noted by Tams, 'in fairness, until recently, State succession to investment treaties may not have seemed a topic worthy of detailed analysis'.[4] This is indeed true since the question had not arisen in arbitration cases. In fact, to be more precise, as explained in my article, the issue of the successor State's continuation of the treaties to which the predecessor State had been a party before the date of succession was at the heart of several cases in the context of the dissolution of Czechoslovakia. Yet, the matter was hardly addressed by tribunals (and therefore not noticed at all by investment arbitration scholars) since the respondent States in these proceedings (the new States of Slovakia and the Czech Republic) did not object to the jurisdiction of these

1 C.J. Tams, 'The Sources of International Investment Law' in T. Gazzini and E. De Brabandere (eds), *International Investment Law: The Sources of Rights and Obligations* (Brill 2012) 320; M. Forteau, 'La contribution au développement du droit international général de la jurisprudence arbitrale relative aux investissements étrangers', (2009) 4(1) ABDI 14; Jose E. Alvarez, 'Bit on Custom', (2009–2010) 42 *NYUJ Int'l L & Pol* 76; C. McLachlan, L. Shore and M. Weiniger, *International Investment Arbitration: Substantive Principles* (OUP 2007) 15.

2 *Archer Daniels Midland Company and Tate and Lyle Ingredients Americas, Inc. v. Mexico*, ICSID Case No. ARB(AF)/04/05, Award, 21 November 2007 [195].

3 P. Dumberry, 'An Uncharted Question of State Succession: Are New States Automatically Bound by the BITs Concluded by Predecessor States Before Independence?' (2015) 6(1) *J Int Disp Settl* 74–96. Around the same time, another article was published by A. Genest, 'Sudan Bilateral Investment Treaties and South Sudan: Musings on State Succession to Bilateral Treaties in the Wake of Yugoslavia's Breakup' (2014) 3 TDM. Another article examining only partly the question of succession to BITs is: Justin A. Fraterman, 'Secession, State Succession and International Arbitration' (paper, SSRN, 2013). More recently, see: Raúl Pereira Fleury, 'State Succession and Bits: Challenges for Investment Arbitration', (2016) 27 *Am Rev Int'l Arb* 451.

4 C.J. Tams, 'State Succession to Investment Treaties: Mapping the Issues' (2016) 31(2) *ICSID Rev.* 315.

tribunals over cases that were brought under BITs to which Czechoslovakia was a party before its break-up.

The question of State succession to BITs has since gained some attention from scholars. This is because the issue has been featured centre stage in a number of recent awards. Thus, in the *Sanum v. Laos* case, the tribunal addressed in its 2013 award the controversial question of whether the China-Laos BIT extended to Macao after the cession of territory in 1999.[5] The award was later set aside by a judgment of the High Court of Singapore in 2015.[6] That judgment was subsequently overturned by the Singapore Court of Appeal in its 2016 judgment, which held that the BIT does apply to Macao and that the tribunal had jurisdiction over the claim brought by Sanum.[7] The *Sanum v. Laos* saga (examined in some detail in this book) provides the first comprehensive analysis of succession issues regarding BITs, albeit in the specific context of a cession of territory. The fact that Brigitte Stern, a specialist of both investment arbitration and State succession,[8] was one of the arbitrators on the tribunal explains the in-depth analysis of the succession issues contained in the award. Since then, many other awards have examined complex questions of State succession. These awards are examined in this book. For instance, the *WWM v. Kazakhstan* case involves a Canadian investor filing a claim against Kazakhstan invoking a breach of the 1991 Canada-USSR BIT. The question at the heart of this case was whether or not Kazakhstan is bound by this BIT.[9] In its 2015 award, the tribunal held that the Canada-USSR BIT was binding on Kazakhstan. The award is confidential.[10] A number of arbitration claims have been recently filed by Ukrainian investors against Russia under the Ukraine-Russia BIT following the annexation of Crimea by Russia in 2014. These cases are currently pending. As examined in some detail in this book, these claims involve very complex and unprecedented questions of State succession. At the time of writing this book (May 2017), issues of State succession had arisen in no less than 46 publically-known BIT arbitration cases. All these cases will be discussed in this book. 1.04

According to Tams, 'investment tribunals have so far done relatively little to clarify the law of State succession: they have tended to be receivers of general 1.05

5 *Sanum Investments Ltd. v. Laos*, UNCITRAL, PCA Case No 2013–13, Award on Jurisdiction, 13 December 2013.

6 *Lao People's Republic v. Sanum Investments Ltd.*, Judgment [2015] SGHC 15.

7 *Sanum Investments Ltd v. Government of the Lao People's Democratic Republic* [2016] SGCA 57.

8 See, for instance, Brigitte Stern, 'La succession d'États' (1996) 262 Rec des Cours.

9 *World Wide Minerals Ltd. and Mr. Paul A. Carroll, QC v. Kazakhstan*, UNCITRAL, Award, 19 October 2015 [hereinafter '*WWM v. Kazakhstan*'].

10 Disclaimer: the present author acted as a counsel for the respondent in this case.

rules, not shaped them'.[11] For him, 'an area of law rather in need of clarification remains in many ways obscure: the potential of arbitral awards to consolidate and develop the law has so far not been realised'.[12] This assessment is generally correct (although the *Sanum* award would be an exception). One reason why tribunals may have been reluctant thus far in examining relevant questions of succession in great detail is because the matter was largely considered to be 'obscure' and unsettled. The issue was, until recently, never addressed by public international law specialists. The enthusiastic specialist of investment arbitration who would have been intrepid enough to venture into the different sections of the library to closely examine books on State succession would have certainly come back disappointed and rather lost from his/her journey. He/she would have thus found very few clear-cut answers to his/her questions. For instance, any person keen on solving a problem related to State succession to a BIT would have been quite surprised to discover that the question of succession to bilateral treaties has been the object of a mere handful of publications in the last 50 years, the most famous having been published in the 1960s![13] Thus, while State succession scholars have (unnecessarily) ravaged many acres of forests when compulsively addressing every angle and facet of the fate of *multilateral* treaties, they have surprisingly had very little interest regarding *bilateral* instruments.[14] This lack of interest was undoubtedly reflected in the way the ILC would end up analysing such instruments in the final phase of the adoption of the 1978 Vienna Convention on succession to treaties.[15] Similarly, any person interested in knowing what should happen to a State contract in the event of State succession would have found it rather strange to discover that the last survey of the issue has been conducted by O'Connell in his monumental 1967 two-volume book.[16] Thus, not a single publication (in French or English) has focused on this rather straightforward question in the last 50 years!

1.06 In sum, apart from the fact that the issue of State succession had not arisen frequently in the past, investment tribunals may have been reluctant to venture

11 Tams (n 4) 342.

12 Ibid.

13 K.J. Keith, 'Succession to Bilateral Treaties by Seceding States', (1967) 61(2) AJIL 521: A.P. Lester, 'State Succession to Treaties in the Commonwealth', (1963) ICLQ 475–507.

14 The only articles which addressed the topic in recent years are: P. Dumberry, 'State Succession to Bilateral Treaties: A Few Observations on the Incoherent and Unjustifiable Solution Adopted for Secession and Dissolution of States under the 1978 Vienna Convention', (2015) 28 *Leiden JIL* 13–30; Qerim Qerimi and Suzana Krasniqi, 'Theories and Practice of State Succession to Bilateral Treaties: The Recent Experience of Kosovo' (2013) 14(9) *German LJ* 1359; Genest (n 3).

15 Vienna Convention on Succession of States in Respect of Treaties, signed on 23 August 1978 and entered into force on 6 November 1996, 1946 UNTS 3, in: (1978) 17 ILM 1488 [hereinafter 'Vienna Convention on Succession to Treaties'].

16 D.P. O'Connell, *State Succession in Municipal Law and International Law* vol I (CUP 1967).

into such unknown territory without being equipped with the necessary investigation skills and the proper theoretical background. Having observed this phenomenon, Tams published a groundbreaking article in 2016 entitled 'State Succession to Investment Treaties: Mapping The Issues'.[17] He described his paper as 'a bird's eye account of questions of State succession that arise in relation to investment treaties'.[18] He, however, added that the article was not intended to provide readers of any 'in-depth discussion of particular problems', but rather to 'inform debate about a particularly tricky area of public international law now confronting investment lawyers'.[19] Tams is evidently too modest with regards to what was achieved with his paper. In fact, he has offered readers much more than a mere *tour d'horizon* of the legal issues that are relevant. He has properly set the table for further analytical studies to be conducted in the future regarding this currently undeveloped area of law. I have taken up his proposal to further examine the issue. The aim of this book is indeed to offer a comprehensive guide to problems of State succession arising in the context of investment arbitration. The goal is that arbitrators and decision-makers facing complex questions of succession to BITs and State contracts will no longer need to venture into the other side of the library only to find old and (literally) dusty books on the matter. The hope is that they will be able to find some answers to their questions in this book.

This book examines two fundamental questions: **1.07**

- Is a successor State bound by investment treaties (including BITs) entered into by the predecessor State with other States?;
- Is a successor State bound by the obligations contained in State contracts (including arbitration clauses) which had been signed by the predecessor State with foreign companies before the date of succession?

I have decided to examine the question of succession to treaties and contracts **1.08** because they represent the two main ways by which States can decide to give their consent to international arbitration. It should be recalled that international arbitration is founded on the principle of consent. A tribunal's jurisdiction over a dispute is based on the consent to arbitration given by both the claimant (almost always an investor) and the respondent (almost always the host State). The host State's consent can be found in three different ways. First, consent can be found in a direct agreement between the investor and the host State (a so-called 'State contract'). Second, consent may be found in a

17 Tams (n 4) 314–43.
18 Ibid., 316.
19 Ibid.

provision of the host State's domestic legislation.[20] While in the former situation, the host State consents to arbitration with one *specific* investor, in the latter case, consent is given more broadly to any foreign investor (of any nationality) admitted into the country. Third, a host State's consent to arbitration can be found in a provision contained in a treaty entered into by that State and the 'home' State of the investor. Treaties for the promotion and protection of investments typically contain a dispute settlement clause whereby *each State* consents *in advance* to arbitration for claims submitted by *any* national of the other State party that fulfil certain requirements under the treaty.

2. THE STRUCTURE OF THIS BOOK

1.09 The rest of Part A examines the important distinction between situations of State succession and those of State 'identity' where the international legal personality of a State is unaffected by an event of succession. I will also differentiate the different types of State succession (unification of State; dissolution of State; incorporation of State; secession; Newly Independent States; and cession/transfer of territory).

1.10 Part B investigates the question of whether or not a successor State is bound by the BITs entered into by the predecessor State with other States. While State succession scholars have in the last 30 years comprehensively addressed the fate of *multilateral* treaties, they have surprisingly had very little interest regarding *bilateral* instruments (in general).

1.11 Chapter 3 begins by analysing the practice of States (both successor States and other States parties to BITs) regarding the continuation of the predecessor State's BITs after the date of succession. This chapter will demonstrate that it is not uncommon for States to reach an agreement as to whether or not a BIT, which was entered into by the predecessor State, should continue to apply after the date of succession. In this situation, the controversial question as to whether a new State *automatically* succeeds to prior BITs does not arise since the States have themselves decided the fate of these treaties. Also, there are many situations where there is a *tacit agreement* between the States for the

20 I have decided not to address in this book issues arising from the host State's domestic legislation. This is because a State's decision to offer an arbitration mechanism under its own investment law is essentially a domestic law matter over which it is entirely sovereign. This is not a matter involving any questions of State succession. The only scenario under which a succession issue could potentially arise is in the event that the claimant investor starts arbitration proceedings against a State which ceases to exist *during* the proceedings. The issue is examined in Chapter 15.

continuation of a specific BIT. Some of the questions examined in Chapter 4 include the form of a unilateral declaration and its effect on the new State making it. It is then necessary to analyse the response given by the 'other State party' to any such declaration and the relevant criteria to determine whether consent can be inferred from the silence and passivity of that State.

Chapter 5 examines the question of what happens to a BIT of the predecessor **1.12** State when the States concerned have *not* agreed (expressly or tacitly) on its continuation. In doing so, it is essential to analyse the different solutions that were adopted under the 1978 Vienna Convention on Succession of States in Respect of Treaties for each specific type of State succession. Specifically, I will critically examine the solution adopted under the Convention for secession and dissolution of States. I will argue that it is incoherent for the ILC to apply, on one hand, the solution of automatic continuity for bilateral treaties in the context of secession and dissolution of States, while adopting, on the other hand, the solution of *tabula rasa* for Newly Independent States. I will further argue that, in any event, it is plainly unjustifiable to apply the principle of automatic continuity to bilateral treaties given the particular nature of these instruments. In my view, bilateral treaties do not automatically continue to be in force as of the date of succession unless *both* States concerned have explicitly (or tacitly) agreed to such a continuation. This basic solution should apply to *all new States* rather than exclusively to those emerging from the process of decolonization. In fact, this is the solution that new States have adopted to resolve issues of succession to bilateral treaties in the context of the break-up of several States after the end of the Cold War.

The last section of Chapter 6 provides a critical analysis of all existing **1.13** investment arbitration case law involving BITs in the context of State succession. In addition to the *Sanum* case mentioned above, I will examine all cases in the context of the dissolutions of Czechoslovakia and Yugoslavia as well as the break-up of the USSR. I will also examine a number of complex legal issues relevant to the field of international investment law arising from the annexation of Crimea by Russia and, specifically, a number of pending arbitration cases.

Part C examines the question of whether the successor State is automatically **1.14** bound by the *multilateral* treaties to which the predecessor State was a party at the date of succession. In doing so, it is necessary to analyse the situation of succession to the ICSID Convention, which is an example of a special category of treaties creating international organizations. In this section, it will be shown that there is no automatic succession to the membership of an international organization and that, accordingly, the practice of new States has been to adhere to the organization (and become party to the Convention) via a formal application.

1.15 Part D focuses on the question of succession to State contracts (i.e., contracts concluded between foreign investors and States). The question being addressed is whether a successor State is bound by the obligations contained in a contract (which includes an arbitration clause) that had been signed by the predecessor State with a foreign company before the date of succession.

1.16 In order to answer this question, it is important to address the more general question of whether the successor State must respect the 'acquired rights' of foreign investors existing before the date of succession. Based on my analysis of this question, I will argue that the successor State can modify a State contract after the date of succession, but that it must do so by respecting a number of principles of international law, including providing proper compensation to an investor. Yet, in my view, the matter is more complex than that. Based on two observations mentioned in passing by O'Connell in his book, I propose a new framework of analysis concerning the question of succession to State contracts. I will show, on the one hand, that the solution to this problem will depend on the type of succession that is involved. There is not one solution that will apply to all cases. The answer to the question simply cannot be the same considering that in some cases the predecessor ceases to exist (dissolution) and in others it does not (secession). Unquestionably, the fact that in some instances no new State emerges (cession, integration) also has an impact on the outcome of the survival of the contracts. Based on this first comprehensive analysis (in the last 50 years) of relevant State practice and decisions of international and domestic courts, I will determine in Chapter 13 whether the solution of succession or that of non-succession should prevail for each type of State succession. Chapter 14 will demonstrate, on the one hand, that the solution to the problem of succession to State contracts depends on a number of factors and circumstances, which should be taken into account by a tribunal. I will examine the following four different factors that may have an impact on whether or not a successor State should be bound by a State contract signed by the predecessor State before the date of succession:

- The position taken by the successor State (after the date of succession) regarding the issue of succession to contracts;
- The existence of a 'territorial nexus' between a contract and the successor State;

- Whether the contract was signed by an organ of a territorial unit of the predecessor State that has a structural continuity with the successor State;
- The need to avoid any unjust enrichment.

Finally, this book will explore (in Part E) a number of specific issues that may arise when the State succession occurs *during* the arbitration proceedings. Such changes may thus affect the identity of the respondent State in the proceedings. For example, in the context of the dissolution of a State, the respondent will cease to exist during the proceedings. An event of succession may also affect the home State of the claimant investor and result in changes of nationality during the proceedings. As such, the present author will examine the approach tribunals should undertake towards such dramatic changes. **1.17**

3. DISTINGUISHING BETWEEN SITUATIONS OF STATE SUCCESSION AND STATE IDENTITY

The present study deals with the subject of 'State succession'. It should be noted that the term 'State succession' is somewhat misleading.[21] In the context of the present book, the term makes reference to 'the replacement of one State by another in the responsibility for the international relations of territory'. This is the definition of 'succession of States' that was adopted in the past by the ILC in different instruments dealing with the issue.[22] The same definition was also adopted by the Institut in its Resolutions in 2001[23] and in 2015.[24] Importantly, the term 'State succession' should not be understood as meaning that the successor State 'becomes invested with all the juridical consequences **1.18**

21 Mohammed Bedjaoui, 'Problèmes récents de succession d'États dans les États nouveaux', (1970–II) 130 Rec des Cours 463.

22 Art. 2(1)b), Vienna Convention on Succession of States to Treaties (n 15) 1488; Art. 2(1)a) of the 1983 Vienna Convention on Succession of States in Respect of State Properties, Archives and Debts, in: (1983) 22 ILM 306. The same definition can also be found at Art. 2 of the Draft Articles on Nationality of Natural Persons in Relation to the Succession of States, adopted by the ILC on second reading in 1999, ILC Report, UN Doc. A/54/10, 1999, chp. IV, [44]–[45] in: (1997) II *Yearbook ILC* 13.

23 Institut de Droit international, *State Succession in Matters of Property and Debts*, Session of Vancouver, 2001, in (2000–2001) 69 *Annuaire IDI* 713ff.

24 Institut de Droit international, *State Succession in Matters of State Responsibility*, 14th Commission, (Rap. M.G. Kohen), Resolution, 28 August 2015, Art. 1 [hereinafter 'IDI, State Succession to Responsibility, Resolution, 2015'].

of its predecessor's acts'.[25] These two distinct concepts should not be confused.[26] Stern refers to the latter meaning as one of 'succession in fact' rather than one of 'succession in law' (which is the topic discussed in this book).[27]

1.19 Situations of State succession need to be clearly distinguished from other situations where there is a *continuity* of State.[28] Thus, a State may be affected by important changes, but its legal identity can nevertheless remain intact.[29] One example is a change of government, which is *not* to be considered as an example of succession.[30] The present study does *not* deal with cases where the State remains identical and where no question or debate arises as to the continuity of its rights and obligations.

1.20 This section will first establish some fundamental distinctions between the phenomenon of State identity and State succession (Section 3.1.). The following section will examine the criteria which have been put forward to determine whether a particular situation falls into the former or the latter category (Section 3.2.).

3.1 Basic differences between the two concepts

1.21 To assess any question related to State identity, one must examine the characteristics of an entity at two different moments in time: *before* and *after*

25 O'Connell (n 16) 3.

26 According to Hans Kelsen, 'Théorie générale du droit international public. Problèmes choisis', (1932–IV) 42 Rec des Cours 314–35: 'On entend donc par succession des États aussi bien cette succession juridique que constitue la modification territoriale elle-même que la succession juridique qui intervient à la suite de la dite modification. Mais il s'agit là de deux phénomènes distincts'. See also, J. Basdevant, *Dictionnaire de la terminologie du droit international* (Sirey 1960) 587; Manlio Udina, 'La succession des États quant aux obligations internationales autres que les dettes publiques', (1933–II) 44 Rec des Cours 679.

27 Stern (n 8) 90.

28 A. Zimmermann, 'Continuity of States', *Max Planck Encyclopedia of Public International Law* (OUP, online edn, 2006) [6]: 'As a matter of principle, State continuity and State succession are mutually exclusive concepts.'

29 On the concept of 'identity' of States, see: Krystyna Marek, *Identity and Continuity of States in Public International Law* (Droz 1968); G. Cansacchi, 'Identité et continuité des sujets de droit international', (1970-I) 130 Rec des Cours 1–94; Matthew C.R. Craven, 'The Problem of State Succession and the Identity of States under International Law', (1998) 9(1) EJIL 142–63. See also, Stern (n 8) 39–87; I. Ziemele, 'Is the Distinction between State Continuity and State Succession Reality or Fiction? The Russian Federation, the Federal Republic of Yugoslavia and Germany' (2001) 1 *Baltic YIL* 191, 215.

30 See, the different approach adopted by Tai-Heng Cheng, *State Succession and Commercial Obligations* (Transnational Publ. 2006) 50, for whom:

> '[S]tate Succession' includes any fundamental internal governance reorganization that causes, or may potentially cause, disruptions to international commercial arrangements and that requires an authoritative international response. Internal governance reorganizations are changes in power and authority over the people of the territory in succession.

the events taking place at a certain date.[31] In other words, it must be examined whether the State is to be considered the *same* State before and after the events that led to the territorial transformation.[32] When the two entities, examined at two different moments, are considered as being 'identical', this means that there is a 'continuing' international legal personality. In other words, because there is an 'identity' of State (i.e., that it is the same State), it follows that there is a 'continuity' of that State's international personality.[33] When this is the case, no issue of succession arises. In practical terms, State identity means that this entity continues having the same rights and obligations.[34]

Yet, it should be added that qualifying two entities as being 'identical' at two different points in time is, of course, a legal fiction.[35] The State that exists *after* the events is necessarily not perfectly 'identical' to the one that existed *prior* to the territorial changes. Thus, the very question of continuity arises *because* some doubt may exist as to whether two entities are in fact truly identical. In other words, no question of continuity arises when a State's borders have not been altered in the slightest. For example, no one is doubting or questioning whether there is State identity between France in 2010 and France in 2012: it is clearly the same State. The relevant question to be asked is therefore not whether two entities are 'identical' per se, but rather whether they can be considered as the 'same' State (having the same international legal personality) *despite* substantial changes to its territory, name, and government.[36] As explained by Stern, 'Cette situation évoque irrésistiblement deux amis d'enfance qui se revoient après cinquante ans de séparation et déclarent: "Tu n'as pas changé, tu es toujours le même!" Identité essentielle, au-delà des changements existentiels'.[37] In other words, a State may very well remain the same in its 'essence' while at the same time having also changed in terms of its secondary characteristics. This question is further examined in the next section. **1.22**

31 This section is a modified and updated version of one previously published article: P. Dumberry, 'Is Turkey the "Continuing" State of the Ottoman Empire under International Law?' (2012) 59(2) *Netherlands ILR* 235–62.

32 W. Czaplinski, 'La continuité, l'identité et la succession d'États: évaluation de cas récents', (1993) 26 RBDI 374; Craven (n 29) 160ff.

33 Marek (n 29) 6 ('there can obviously be no continuity without identity').

34 Zimmermann, 'Continuity of States' (n 28) [6].

35 Stern (n 8) 40; Czaplinski (n 32) 374; E. Oktem, 'Turkey: Successor or Continuing State of the Ottoman Empire?', (2011) 24 *Leiden JIL* 566. More generally, Eric Wyler, 'Le droit de la succession d'États à l'épreuve de la fiction juridique', in G. Distefano, G. Gaggioli and A. Hêche (eds), *La Convention de Vienne de 1978 sur la succession d'États en matière de traités : Commentaire article par article et études thématiques* (Bruylant 2015), 1631–5.

36 Oktem, ibid., 567.

37 Stern (n 8) 40.

3.2 Relevant criteria to determine State identity

1.23 There are no formal criteria under international law that help categorically distinguish cases of continuity from those of discontinuity.[38] This section examines the most important criteria that have been proposed in doctrine to determine whether there is State identity: territory (Section 3.2.1), government (Section 3.2.2), population and a country's name (Section 3.2.3), the concept of the essential portion of a State (Section 3.2.4), and recognition (Section 3.2.5).[39]

3.2.1 Territory

1.24 Different theories regarding the concept of 'territory' under international law have been put forward by various writers. According to the 'space theory' (*Raumtheorie*), the territory is considered as the very body of a State, as constituting its essence.[40] Under this theory, a State would simply disappear as a result of *any* loss of its territory.[41] This theory is not well adapted to explain cases where the State lost only *part* of its territory. In the words of Delbez, 'Si le territoire est un élément constitutif, une qualité substantielle de l'Etat, les cessions territoriales sont impossibles comme destructrice de l'Etat lui-même'.[42] The modern interpretation of the element of territory in international law is represented by the 'competence theory', according to which the

---

38 Ibid, 52; Czaplinski (n 32) 379; Marek (n 29) 7, 9; Andreas Zimmermann and James G. Devaney, 'Succession to Treaties and the Inherent Limits of International Law' in Christian J. Tams, Antonios Tzanakopoulos, and Andreas Zimmermann (eds), *Research Handbook on the Law of Treaties*, (Edward Elgar 2014) 513; A. Vahlas, 'A Propos de Trois Questions Récurrentes en Matière de Succession d'États: Application au Cas Yougoslave', in Pierre Michel Eisemann and Martti Koskenniemi (dir), *State Succession: Codification Tested Against the Facts* (Martinus Nijhoff Publ. 2000) 857:

> Le problème est qu'il n'existe pas de critère objectif pour statuer sur cette identité juridique. II est simplement possible de mentionner plusieurs indices de continuité entre deux Etats: l'identité de dirigeants, l'identité de langue officielle, l'identité de nom, l'identité de capitale, l'identité de drapeau, la proportion de territoire et de population de l'Etat prédécesseur retrouvée chez l'Etat successeur, la prépondérance dans l'administration du prédécesseur de fonctionnaires de la nationalité du successeur, la formation de l'Etat prédécesseur à partir de l'Etat successeur, la volonté de l'Etat successeur, l'accord des autres Etats successeurs, etc. Aucun indice ou aucune combinaison de ces indices ne permet cependant d'aboutir à un mécanisme objectif de jugement de continuité.

39 It should be added that the temporary belligerent occupation by a State over the territory of another does not have any impact on the latter's identity which remains intact: International Law Association (ILA), 'Rapport Préliminaire: succession d'États en matière de traités', Committee on Aspects of the Law of State Succession, 1996, 658 [hereinafter 'ILA, 'Rapport Préliminaire', 1996'].

40 C.V. Fricker, *Gebiet und Gebietshoheit* (Tübingen, 1901). H. Lauterpacht, 'Règles générales du droit de la paix', (1937-IV) 62 Rec des cours 318–19, describing this theory in the following terms: 'le territoire n'est pas la propriété de l'État, mais est l'État lui-même, de même que les individus, loin d'avoir la propriété de leur corps, forment avec ce dernier un tout inséparable et ne sont pas concevables sans lui.'

41 G. Jellinek, *L'État moderne et son droit*, Vol II (Panthéon-Assas 2004) 16ff.

42 L. Delbez, 'Du territoire dans ses rapports avec l'État', (1932) RGDIP 719; W. Schoenborn, 'La nature juridique du territoire', (1929-V) 30 Rec. des cours 116:

territory is where the State exercises its competence (its sovereign power), which in turn is where it draws its 'territorial sovereignty' (a title) over a given territory.[43]

All writers agree that a State does not necessarily lose its international legal personality as a result of a change to its territory.[44] It is clear that territorial losses, per se, do not affect a State's identity.[45] This principle has been (perhaps surprisingly) qualified by one writer as 'custom'.[46] The existence of the legal personality of a State can uniquely be affected where the loss of territory is *total*.[47] This is, for instance, what happened to Poland in 1775 when it ceased to exist due to its territorial division among Austria, Prussia, and Russia. On the other hand, a *limited* loss of territory does not affect a State's identity.[48] An illustration of this is that France did not cease to exist when the territory of Alsace-Lorraine was ceded to Germany in 1871. The same conclusion applies to the identity of Germany when the same territory was ceded back to France in 1918. **1.25**

> Si le territoire appartient vraiment à l'essence même de l'État, une modification du territoire de l'État, résultant par exemple de cessions territoriales, constitueraient également une modification de la nature de l'État lui-même. L'État perdrait, au fond, son identité par suite de tout changement du territoire. Si le territoire est réellement un élément important de l'essence de la personnalité étatique, on ne peut pas bien se représenter que l'État puisse se séparer en principe de parties de son territoire, c'est-à-dire de parties de son essentiel! A moins que l'on admette une 'mutation du corps de l'État' analogue à l'amputation d'un membre du corps humain;

Lauterpacht (n 40) 319: 'On remarquera qu'il est plus facile pour un État de se défaire d'une partie de son territoire sans péril, et parfois avec avantages, que pour un individu, de se défaire de son corps.'

43 H. Kelsen, *Principles of International Law*, 2nd edn (Holt, Rinehart and Winston 1966) 308.

44 Schoenborn (n 42) 119: 'une autorité ne subit aucun changement dans sa nature propre et particulière lorsque sa compétence locale est étendue ou restreinte'; Delbez (n 42) 718: 'La modification territoriale aura bien entendu pour effet de déplacer les bornes de la compétence étatique, le sol national se trouvant agrandi ou restreint. Mais l'autorité de l'État ne se trouvera pas, par cela même, atteint dans sa nature. Aucun changement ne sera apporté dans l'identité de l'État. Il est clair en effet qu'une autorité ne subit aucune modification dans sa nature lorsque sa compétence territoriale est étendue ou restreinte.'

45 E. Suy, 'Réflexions sur la distinction entre la souveraineté et la compétence territoriale', in R. Marcic, et al. (eds) *Internationale Festschrift für Alfred Verdross* (Wilhem Fink Verlag 1971) 494; J.L. Kunz, 'Identity of States under International Law', (1955) 49 AJIL 72; Z. Meriboute, *La codification de la succession d'États aux traités: décolonisation, sécession, unification* (PUF 1984) 168; J. Crawford, *The Creation of States in International Law*, 2nd edn (Clarendon Press 2006) 673; Stern (n 8) 68–9; Vladimir D. Degan, 'Création et disparition de l'État (à la lumière du démembrement de trois fédérations multiethniques en Europe)' (1999) 279 Rec. des Cours 300; Czaplinski (n 32) 377; W. Fiedler, 'Continuity', in R. Bernhardt (ed), *Encyclopaedia of Public International Law*, Vol 1 (North Holland 1984) 807; Marek (n 29) 15, 21.

46 Cansacchi (n 29) 25.

47 Marek (n 29) 23–4; Kunz (n 45) 72; Cansacchi (n 29) 25.

48 Some authors have argued that a *significant* or 'very considerable' loss of territory could lead to a conclusion of non-identity. See: Marek (n 29) 23–4: for a review of doctrine; E.J. Castren, 'Aspects récents de la succession d'Etats', (1951-I) 78 Rec des cours 393: speaking of 'perte de territoire assez importante'. The obvious objection to this theory is, of course, to determine exactly when a loss of territory is considerable enough to jeopardize identity.

1.26 The present author has specifically examined elsewhere the question of identity between the Ottoman Empire and Turkey.[49] By some accounts, between 1878 and 1918 the Ottoman Empire lost some 85 per cent of its territory,[50] which constitutes a significant loss of territory.[51] As explained by Judge Kreca in his dissenting opinion in the *Application of the Convention on the Prevention and Punishment of the Crime of Genocide* case, a diminution of territory, even a substantial one, does not in itself affect the legal personality of a State.[52] In fact, Judge Kreca, as well as other experts,[53] gave the example of Turkey as an illustration. In the *Ottoman Debt Arbitration* case, the tribunal recognized that 'in international law, the Turkish Republic was deemed to continue the international personality of the former Turkish Empire' despite having sustained significant territorial losses.[54] In sum, Turkey is the same State as the Ottoman Empire, only with a much smaller territory.[55]

3.2.2 Government, population and a country's name

1.27 One generally accepted principle of international law is that a change of government does not in itself amount to the creation of a new State.[56] This remains the case even when it arises as a result of a revolution or a *coup d'État*.[57] State succession issues simply do not arise in such situations: the new government is bound by all of international obligations of its predecessor.[58] A classic example is that of France, which had radically changed regimes many times over the course of the last three centuries.[59] Another illustration is that

49 Dumberry (n 31) 235–62.

50 T. Akcam, *A Shameful Act: The Armenian Genocide and the Question of Turkish Responsibility* (Metropolitan Books 2006) 11.

51 In fact, it is generally recognized that the identity of a State is not affected even when the territory lost is substantially *greater* than the remaining territory, such as in the case of Turkey: Crawford, *The Creation of States* (n 45) 673; K.G. Bühler, *State Succession and Membership in International Organizations: Legal Theories versus Political Pragmatism* (Kluwer 2001) 15; Ziemele (n 29) 216; Kunz (n 45) 72; Cansacchi (n 29) 25.

52 *Application of the Convention on the Prevention and Punishment of the Crime of Genocide* (*Bosnia and Herzegovina v. Serbia and Montenegro*), Preliminary Objections, Judgment of 11 July 1996, ICJ Reports 1996, 762–3, Judge Kreca, Dissenting Opinion [87]: 'this principle of international law is deeply rooted in international practice'.

53 See, for instance, Kunz (n 45) 72.

54 *Affaire de la dette publique ottomane*, 18 April 1925, in (1948) 1 UNRIAA 529 at 573.

55 Ziemele (n 29) 215; Marek (n 29) 40; Crawford, *The Creation of States* (n 45) 676; Czaplinski (n 32) 376.

56 Marek (n 29) 24ff; Czaplinski (n 32) 378; Stern (n 8) 71; Crawford, *The Creation of States* (n 45) 678; Kunz (n 45) 73; ILA, 'Rapport Préliminaire', 1996 (n 39) 658; J.B. Moore, *Digest of International Law*, Vol I (GPO 1906) 249; Fiedler (n 45) 807; Castren (n 48) 395; C. Rousseau, *Droit international public* (Sirey 1953) 264; Degan (n 45) 297; Tams (n 4) 319–20.

57 Kunz (n 45) 73; Czaplinski (n 32) 378; Marek (n 29) 25.

58 One question, which has been the object of some controversy in doctrine, is the issue of whether in some situations a new government should not be bound by so-called 'odious debts'.

59 Sir Robert Jenning and Sir Arthur Watts, *Oppenheim's International Law*, vol I 9th edn (Longman 1996) 204–5:

of the 1979 Revolution in Iran which, although radical its effect may have been on all levels of Iranian society, did *not* alter Iran's continuous international legal personality as a State.[60] Similarly, the 1917 Revolution in Russia was considered as a mere change in government rather than the creation of a new State.

It is also clear that changes in population, such as increases/decreases, emigration/immigration, do not affect the identity of a State.[61] Only the (rather hypothetical) situation of a *total* loss of population could lead to the extinction of a State.[62] As a matter of illustration, by some accounts, the Ottoman Empire lost some 75 per cent of its population between the years 1878 and 1918.[63] Again, this is no doubt a significant loss of population, but it does not, in itself, constitute proof of discontinuity.[64] **1.28**

> The continuity of a State as an international person notwithstanding changes of the kind mentioned may be illustrated by the history of France, which has over the centuries retained its identity although it acquired, lost and regained parts of its territory, changed its dynasty, was a kingdom, a republic, an empire, again a kingdom, again a republic, again an empire, and is now once more a republic. All its international rights and duties as an international person continued in spite of these important changes. Even such loss of territory as occasions the reduction of a major power to a lesser status does not affect the state as an international person.

60 *The United States of America v. The Islamic Republic of Iran*, Award, IUSCT Case No. B36 (574-B36-2), 3 December 1996 [53]–[54]:

> Iran does not assert that its situation is one of State succession. It does not deny that it is subject to rights and liable to obligations of the former regime, as shown by the fact that it has brought to this Tribunal numerous claims arising between the former regime and the United States (…). Iran argues, however, that the debt based on the 1948 Contract was a debt personal to the former regime that should be considered non-transferable by analogy and that this position is supported by the principle of non-transferability of odious debts, which it asserts also is recognized in the field of State succession. The Tribunal does not take any stance in the doctrinal debate on the concept of 'odious debts' in international law. In any event, the Tribunal will limit itself to stating that the said concept belongs to the realm of the law of State succession. That law does not find application to the events in Iran. The revolutionary changes in Iran fall under the heading of State continuity, not State succession. This statement does not exclude a realist approach that recognizes that in practice the border between the concepts of continuity and succession is not always rigid. However, without denying the legal complexities which characterize the revolutionary and post-revolutionary situation in Iran or, for that matter, in some other countries, it has to be emphasized that in this Case we do not deal with an instance of State succession. In spite of the change in head of State and the system of government in 1979, Iran remained the same subject of international law as before the Islamic Revolution. For when a Government is removed through a revolution, the State, as an international person, remains unchanged and the new government generally assumes all the previous international rights and obligations of the State.

61 Kunz (n 45) 71; ILA, 'Rapport Préliminaire', 1996 (n 39) 658; Crawford, *The Creation of States* (n 45) 678; Czaplinski (n 32) 378; Marek (n 29) 48, 128.

62 Kunz (n 45) 72.

63 Akcam (n 50) 11.

64 Dumberry (n 31) 235–62.

1.29 Finally, changes to the name of a State are clearly not decisive to determine questions of identity.[65] It is true, however, that the fact that a State keeps its name despite changes to its territory may be considered as an element of continuity insofar as it shows (to some extent) its willingness to maintain its original international legal personality.[66] But the reverse is not true. Based on the fact that a State adopts a new name, in the context of territorial transformation, it simply cannot be automatically deduced that this is indeed a *new* State.[67]

1.30 In sum, changes related to the territory of a State, its government, its population and even its name do *not* affect, per se, its identity under international law. The question then becomes: what *is* actually relevant to the determination of identity issues?[68] This question is addressed in the next subsection.

3.2.3 The concept of the 'essential portion' of a State

1.31 There is one crucial criterion that has been used by some writers to decide issues of identity in the context of considerable losses of territory.[69] Writers have looked at whether what is left of a State's territory following a significant reduction in its size is the *core*, or the *nucleus* of the State that existed prior to

---

65 Stern (n 8) 74; ILA, 'Rapport Préliminaire', 1996 (n 39) 658; Czaplinski (n 32) 377; Castren (n 48) 393; Marek (n 29) 127.

66 Stern (n 8) 75.

67 Ibid., indicating that 'Yugoslavia' changed names no less than five times from 1918 until 1992. On the specific question of Turkey's name, see: Dumberry (n 31).

68 In his article Craven (n 29) 160ff explains the importance of the issue in the following words:

> Once identity is separated as a conceptually distinct issue, concerned as it is with the substance rather than the form of the state, much of the unnecessary rigidity in traditional doctrine may be avoided entirely. The task for the future, therefore, is to map out some of the characteristics and determinants of state identity in a way that takes into account not merely the formal properties of statehood, but also the sense of 'self, 'singularity', and 'community', that justifies the attachment of international legal obligations to particular territories and social groups. Without such a concept of Identity, international law will remain unable to appreciate properly, apart from in a very abstract or formal way, the sense of legitimacy that underlies its claim to be the medium by which individual and cosmopolitan values and interests are pursued on the international plane.

69 More generally, Zimmermann, 'Continuity of States' (n 28) [15] refers to other relevant factors:

> The determination whether in a given case one is facing an instance of State continuity where territorial changes have taken place depends on a number of factors. In particular, one has to evaluate the territorial size of the State claiming identity, even if there is no fixed minimum requirement for a State to be able validly to claim to continue the international legal personality of such State. Further factors include historical ties to the predecessor State and its internal legal order, as well as the way the territorial changes are taking place (ie in the case of a dissolution of a State whether the dissolution takes place *uno acto* or rather as a chain of separations) and whether such changes are occurring in conformity with applicable rules of international law and, in particular, the principle of self-determination of peoples. Finally, the self-proclaimed will of a State to continue the international legal personality of a given State and the acceptance of such claim by third States (both within and outside international organizations) play a decisive role.

its disintegration. In other words, they assess whether what remains of a territory after a radical change can be considered as the 'essential portion' of the territory of the 'old' State.[70] Stern, for instance, refers to the 'noyau irréductible de l'État'.[71] She explains that, 'Cette analyse se fonde sur la distinction entre l'essence et l'existence, et considère que chaque État possède une sorte de matrice fondamentale qui le rend irréductible à tout autre' and that '[t]ant que ce noyau persiste à travers les différents avatars de l'État, celui-ci doit être considéré comme restant identique à lui-même'.[72]

The reference to this 'essential portion' of territory is central to any conclusion about State identity. It certainly helps to explain why other States have recognized Russia's claims to being the continuous State of the former USSR. Thus, for many reasons, Russia can be considered as the nucleus of its predecessor, the USSR.[73] Interestingly enough, the Federal Republic of Yugoslavia (FRY)'s claim of continuity, which ultimately failed, was also essentially based on the argument that it constituted the nucleus of ex-Yugoslavia.[74] It is true that in some instances, it is difficult to determine 1.32

70 W.E. Hall, *A Treatise on International Law*, 8th edn (Clarendon Press 1924) 21; O. Schachter, 'The Development of International Law through the Legal Opinions of the United Nations', (1948) 20 *British YIL* 105; Castren (n 48) 393 (for whom, one of the important indicia of continuity is the fact that 'sa partie centrale ou sa capitale avec les régions qui l'entourent ainsi que d'autres régions de valeur historique et constituant le véritable noyau de l'Etat demeurent intactes').

71 Stern (n 8) 80.

72 Ibid.

73 M. Koskenniemi and M. Lehto, 'La succession d'États dans l'ex-URSS, en ce qui concerne particulièrement les relations avec la Finlande', (1992) 38 AFDI 189–90, affirming that the 'essence' of the USSR survived in the Federation of Russia:

> Il est clair – comme l'ont déclaré à plusieurs reprises les hommes politiques soviétiques – que la Russie formait l'épine dorsale de l'URSS. La Russie compte 147,4 millions d'habitants (51,7%), elle couvre environ 17,1 millions de kilomètres carrés sur un total de 22,4 (soit 76,3%), son produit national représente 60% de celui de l'URSS (92% de la production de pétrole et 74% de la production de gaz) et la proportion des revenus à l'exportation des biens produits en Russie représente 80% du total des exportations de l'Union. En d'autres termes, le noyau de la communauté humaine qu'était l'URSS survit dans la Fédération de Russie.

See also, the analysis in: Rein Mullerson, 'Law and Politics in Succession of States: International Law on Succession of States', in Geneviève Burdeau and Brigitte Stern (eds), *Dissolution, continuation et succession en Europe de l'Est* (Cedin-Paris I 1994) 18–21.

74 Declaration by the Foreign Minister, Vladislav Jovanovic, 9 March 1992, quoted in M. Weller, 'The International Response to the Dissolution of the Socialist Federal Republic of Yugoslavia. Current Developments', (1992) 86 AJIL 595:

> The bases for the continuity and personality of a State are: significant portions of the territory which continues its existence; a major portion of the population; an independent government and organization of authority operating in accordance with the country's constitution. The nucleus of Yugoslavia ... was formed by Serbia and Montenegro, which invested their statehood into the State of Yugoslavia together with all their rights and obligations, international treaties and membership in international organisations ... Consequently, we have all the physical and material as well as legal conditions for Yugoslavia's uninterrupted identity and existence. This view of continuity and identity does not prejudice the possibility of the new States acquiring international recognition in accordance with international law.

which portion of a territory should be considered as its 'core',[75] but such qualification is often quite straightforward. I have shown elsewhere that the territory of modern post-1923 Turkey was in fact reduced to what had always been the 'historical homeland' of the Turkish State. After centuries of territorial expansion of the Empire, which was then followed by slow disintegration, modern Turkey was reduced in 1923 to its nucleus, its 'essential' part.[76]

3.2.4 *Recognition by other States*

1.33 As previously mentioned, a determinant factor in resolving issues of identity is to assess whether what is left of a State's territory following a significant reduction in its size constitutes the nucleus of the State that existed before its disintegration. Such an assessment will be made by States.[77] First, the State affected by territorial changes will proclaim its position on the central question of identity. In doing so, the State must indicate to others how it perceived itself.[78] Any such determination, however, cannot be left to a unilateral decision by the State concerned.[79] Other States will have to respond by recognizing or refusing to recognize any such claim of continuity or non-continuity.[80]

1.34 The starting point of the analysis is to mention that, as a matter of principle, a claim of identity by a reduced-size State does *not* need to be formally recognized by other States.[81] This is because these States have already given such recognition in the past. This is, after all, the 'same' State that simply continues its existence despite territorial changes.[82] Some authors have also

---

75 Marek (n 29) 22.

76 Dumberry (n 31). See also, Oktem (n 35) 575–76; Shavarsh Toriguian, *The Armenian Question and International Law* 2nd edn (La Verne Press 1988) 111.

77 Zimmermann and Devaney, 'Succession to Treaties' (n 38) 513, indicating that distinguishing between succession and continuity or identity is 'strongly influenced by political considerations' and adding that (at 515):

> State practice, as well as the jurisprudence of the International Court of Justice, seems to suggest that, in relation to the distinction between succession and identity, what often matters most is not objective facts, such as the size of territory or population, but rather to what extent the claim to continuation of identity was generally accepted by the international community as a whole, including international organizations.

78 Mullerson (n 73) 20.

79 Marek (n 29) 129. The reason is simple. If this determination was to be left to the State concerned, it could at any time claim to be a *new* State in order to simply escape any obligations or to claim not to be bound by a treaty.

80 Czaplinski (n 32) 379.

81 Eric Wyler, *Théorie et pratique de la reconnaissance d'État: Une approche épistémologique du droit international* (Bruylant 2013), 108.

82 Stern (n 8) 59; V. Milulka, 'Article 35' in G. Distefano, G. Gaggioli and A. Hêche (eds), *La Convention de Vienne de 1978 sur la succession d'États en matière de traités: Commentaire article par article et études thématiques* (Bruylant 2015) 1219.

maintained that, in any event, recognition should not be a decisive factor because it is ultimately based on *subjective* political factors rather than objective ones.[83] This is no doubt true. However, the problem is that international law lacks any undisputed *objective* criteria which can unequivocally determine questions of identity of State. This is why recognition remains of pivotal importance to decide issues of identity and continuity.[84] As noted by Tams, 'the proper legal assessment' of any issue of identity/continuity 'is the result of a lengthy process of claim and contestation, in which historical narratives, perceptions of legitimacy, and the views of key players play an important role'.[85]

Recognition remains essential because, as noted by one writer, it 'has the important function to overcome uncertainties as to whether or not, in the eyes of the international community, in a case of dissolution the predecessor State continues to exist'.[86] Thus, recognition will ultimately be the *decisive* factor to determine issues of identity in cases of ambiguities.[87] For instance, it will evidently play an important role in situations where substantial territorial changes occurred.[88] Recent State practice has shown that third-party States will assess any claim of continuity to determine whether to give it any effect.[89] This is especially the case where a claim of continuity is controversial or has been contested by other States.[90] The following paragraphs briefly examine two recent examples of State practice to illustrate this point. **1.35**

The first example is that of the FRY. As a result of the different declarations of independence by Croatia, Slovenia, Macedonia, and Bosnia and Herzegovina in 1991–92, what remained of the former Socialist Federal Republic of Yugoslavia (SFRY) were the two former Republics of Serbia and Montenegro. **1.36**

---

83 Marek (n 29) 149:

> To sum up: recognition, as a test of State identity and continuity must be rejected, since: a) it fails to provide a reliable test on account of its inherent relativity, b) it withdraws the question of the continued existence of a State from the realm of objective norms and makes it dependent upon the will of third States and c) for this reason may place the very continuity of a State in jeopardy. This rejection is equivalent to a rejection of the constitutive in favour of the declaratory theory or recognition.

84 Czaplinski (n 32) 379, 392.

85 Tams (n 4) 319.

86 Bühler (n 51) 16.

87 Ibid., 17. Marek (n 29) 160, who generally rejects recognition as a relevant criterion, nevertheless admits that in 'doubtful cases' recognition should be considered as *prima facie* evidence, provided that it was granted in accordance with principles of international law (rather than based on political factors).

88 Crawford, *The Creation of States* (n 45) 670 ('where there are substantial changes in the entity concerned, continuity may depend upon recognition'); I. Brownlie, *Principles of Public International Law*, 4th edn (Clarendon Press 1990) 674.

89 Stern (n 8) 60, 66–7; Czaplinski (n 32) 379; Tams (n 4) 319.

90 Vahlas (n 38) 854–5.

In April 1992, both Republics reorganized the old federation in the form of the smaller two-member federation now called the 'FRY'. The new Constitution proclaimed it to be the 'continuator' of the former SFRY.[91] Other former Republics strongly opposed such a claim by the FRY.[92] The majority of States,[93] the UN Security Council and the UN General Assembly,[94] as well as the Badinter Commission,[95] refused to recognize the FRY such a status.[96] It was ultimately the third-party States' firm policy of non-recognition that proved to be the decisive factor in blocking the FRY's claim of continuity to have any practical effectiveness.[97] In fact, the FRY ultimately changed its position after the political changes that occurred in 2000; wherein it no longer asserted to be the 'continuator' of the former SFRY.[98]

1.37 The second example is the agreement among the former Republics of the USSR (with the exception of the three Baltic States and Georgia), that Russia would be considered as the 'continuator' of the international legal personality of the USSR in international organizations and in particular at the UN Security Council.[99] This decision was largely accepted by other States in the international community.[100] Thus, although a claim of continuity by Russia should not logically have required any 'recognition' by third-party States, it

91 Declaration on the Formation of the Federal Republic of Yugoslavia, joint session of the Yugoslavia Assembly, the National Assembly of the Republic of Serbia and the Assembly of the Republic of Montenegro, 27 April 1992, annexed to UN Doc S/23877, 5 May 1992. See also: Letter of the interim Chargé d'Affaires at the Permanent Mission of Yugoslavia at the United Nations to the UN Secretary-General, 6 May 1993, UN Doc A/46/915, 7 May 1992.

92 *See*, inter alia, Letter of the Minister of Foreign Affairs of the Republic of Slovenia to the UN Secretary-General, 27 May 1992, UN Doc. A/47/234, S/24028, 28 May 1992.

93 This is, for instance, the case of the European Union: 'Déclaration du Conseil Européen concernant l'ancienne Yougoslavie', 28 May 1992, UN Doc. A/47/234, S/24028, in Bull CE 6.1992.

94 UN SC Res. 777 (1992), 19 September 1992; UN GA Res. 47/1 (1992), 19 September 1992.

95 Opinion no. 10, 4 July 1992, in (1993) 92 ILR 206.

96 For an analysis of the different arguments used by all sides on the question of the FRY's claim of continuity, see: Juan Miguel Ortega Terol, 'The Bursting of Yugoslavia: An Approach to Practice Regarding State Succession', in P-M. Eisemann and M. Koskennemi (eds), *State Succession: Codification Tested against the Facts* (Martinus Nijhoff, 2000) 892–900.

97 Vahlas (n 38) 854–5.

98 The FRY was officially admitted (as a new State) to the United Nations on 1 November 2000: UN GA Res. 55/12.

99 Declaration of Alma Ata, 21 December 1991, UN Doc. A/46/60, 30 December 1991, in (1992) 31 ILM 147. See also, the 'Decision by the Council of Heads of State of the Commonwealth of Independent States', 21 December 1991, in ibid., 151, and Letter of Russia's President Mr. Yeltsin to the UN Secretary General, 24 December 1991, in ibid., 138: 'the membership of the USSR in the United Nations, including the Security Council ... is being continued by the Russian Federation (RSFSR), with the support of the countries of the CIS'. On this question, see: Y.Z. Blum, 'Russia Takes over the Soviet Union's Seat at the United Nations', (1992) 3 EJIL 354–61.

100 State practice is analysed in: K.G. Bühler, 'State Succession, Identity/Continuity and Membership in the United Nations', in P-M. Eisemann and M. Koskennemi (eds), *State Succession: Codification Tested against the Facts* (Martinus Nijhoff, 2000) 258–63.

remains that many States have nevertheless felt the need to notify Russia of their positions on the matter.[101]

These two examples show the importance of third-party States' recognition when it comes to deciding the fate of controversial and contested claims of continuity.[102] Recognition also seems to have been the main factor considered by the ICJ when deciding contested issues of State identity.[103] **1.38**

These two examples also illustrate that politics play a significant role in these matters. Non-legal reasons are the primary explanation why other States accepted Russia's claim to continuity, while denying the FRY's claim.[104] As mentioned by Stern, it is common for States to justify their positions with respect to controversial issues of identity and State succession based on objective criteria, while the true motives may have been based on economical and political factors.[105] Generally, third-party States will favour continuity over discontinuity.[106] One reason is that they seek to preserve their legal relations (contracts, treaties, etc.) with the already existing State. Another motive is that they want the State's financial obligations to remain undisturbed despite any territorial modifications. **1.39**

---

101 These statements are discussed in Stern (n 8) 60–63.

102 Stern (n 8) 85: 'Sera un État continuateur, l'État reconnu comme tel par l'acceptation générale de la communauté internationale. C'est dire que l'opinio juris de la communauté internationale est l'élément déterminant.' See also: Tams (n 4) 319.

103 A. Zimmermann, 'The International Court of Justice and State Succession to Treaties: Avoiding Principled Answers to Questions of Principle', in: Christian J. Tams and James Sloan (eds), *The Development of International Law by the International Court of Justice*, (OUP 2013) 57.

104 Stern (n 8) 78–9:

> Si l'on compare ainsi l'éclatement de l'URSS et celui de la Yougoslavie, il n'y a guère de différences objectives dans le processus de dislocation de l'État préexistant. Simplement, les nécessités stratégiques et géopolitiques dans le cas de la Russie, et les prises de position éthiques et juridiques dans le cas de la RFY engagée dans une politique de 'nettoyage ethnique' en Bosnie-Herzégovine, ont conduit la communauté internationale à analyser différemment les deux processus: sécessions des différentes républiques de l'URSS ayant laissé subsister la Russie en tant qu'État continuateur; dissolution de la RSFY faisant théoriquement naître des États successeurs tous placés sur le même plan par rapport à l'ancien État.

105 Stern (n 8) 8–3:

> Tout se passe un peu 'à l'envers' des apparences: il semble bien que la qualification ne soit qu'une conséquence de la préférence des États pour telles ou telles conséquences juridiques. En d'autres termes, ce n'est pas parce qu'un État *est* continuateur ou successeur que l'on en tirera certaines conséquences juridiques; c'est parce que les États souhaitent certaines conséquences juridiques qu'ils *qualifient* une situation de succession ou de continuation. … Les facteurs objectifs, situés en amont peuvent cependant être – et sont souvent – invoqués comme arguments à l'appui d'une solution dont la raison d'être est située en aval, dans le résultat à atteindre. Autrement dit, les États peuvent se fonder sur la présence ou l'absence des facteurs objectifs précédemment mentionnés, mais en réalité ils obéiront le plus souvent à des considérations politiques (emphasis in the original).

106 Cansacchi (n 29) 34–5.

1.40 As examined by the present writer elsewhere,[107] post-1923 Turkey is a prime illustration of a situation involving a substantial modification of territory coupled with a controversial claim of discontinuity. Turkey claimed to be a new State in 1923. One of the many reasons explaining why it took this position had to do with the fate of the Ottoman Empire's financial obligations. In the context of the *Ottoman Public Debt* case (1925), Turkey argued that because it was a new State it should not be held responsible for the entire debt of the defunct Ottoman Empire. Rather, Turkey was willing to accept only a portion of it just like all the other new States that emerged from the collapse of the Empire.[108] Other States rejected Turkey's claim of discontinuity and did not recognize it as a 'new' State.[109] One (very practical) reason was to ensure that Turkey's responsibility for the Ottoman Empire's financial obligations would remain intact after its defeat in 1918.[110] In any event, the position that Turkey is the continuing State of the Ottoman Empire was reflected in several provisions of the Lausanne Treaty[111] and subsequently endorsed by arbitral tribunals.[112]

---

107 Dumberry (n 31).

108 This position was clearly taken during negotiations at the Lausanne Conference leading to the signing of the Treaty of Lausanne: 'Le gouvernement d'Angora prendra à sa charge une part équitable de la dette au même titre que les autres États détachés de l'ancien Empire ottoman, étant donné qu'il n'est que l'un des États successeurs de cet Empire.' : Declaration by Hassan Bey, *Recueil des Actes de la Conference de Lausanne*, Serie I, Vol 3 (Imprimerie nationale 1923) 130 (quoted in Enrico Zamuner, 'Le Rapport entre Empire ottoman et la République turque face au droit international', (2004) 6 *J. Hist. Int'l L.* 227). See also: *Documents diplomatiques, Conférence de Lausanne (Livre Jaune)*, Vol 1 (Ministère des Affaires étrangères, Paris 1923) 494–5.

109 Oktem (n 35) 577; Cansacchi (n 29) 32; Udina (n 26) 688.

110 Degan (n 45) 304; Cansacchi (n 29) 35; Zamuner (n 108) 225.

111 Treaty of Peace of Lausanne, signed on 24 July 1923, in: UKTS 1923, No. 16 (Cmd. 1929); 28 LNTS 11; (1924) 18 AJIL, Supp., 4, see Arts 1, 30, 46, 58, 60, 65, 99, 240, 241. See, analysis in: Zamuner (n 108) 224–7; Cansacchi (n 29) 32.

112 *Affaire de la dette publique ottomane* (n 54) 573: '[À] l'égard de la D.P.O., [Dette publique ottomane, Ottoman public debt] la situation juridique de la Turquie n'est nullement identique à celle des autres États intéressés. En droit international, la République turque doit être considérée comme continuant la personnalité de l'Empire Ottoman'. Another relevant case is *Sentence arbitrale en date des 24/27 juillet 1956 rendue par le Tribunal d'arbitrage constitué en vertu du Compromis signé à Paris le 15 juillet 1932 entre la France et la Grèce*, 12 UNRIAA 155, also in (1956) 23 ILR, 1956 [hereinafter '*Lighthouse Arbitration* case']. Under Claim no. 12-a, France was seeking damages against Greece (as successor State) for acts committed by the authorities of the Ottoman Empire on the Island of Crete. The arbitral tribunal ultimately ruled that the Ottoman authorities had not committed any wrongful act. It added that had the Ottoman Empire committed such an act, Greece could nevertheless not be held liable since Turkey would be liable for its 'own' acts committed before the loss of a substantial portion of its territory. The tribunal therefore explicitly recognized that Turkey was the continuing State of the Ottoman Empire. See also: *Roselius and Company of Bremen in Germany (plaintiff) v. (1) Dr. Ch. F. Karsten, Advocate of Huizen in Holland (defendant); (2) The Turkish Republic at Angora (intervener)*, District Court of Amsterdam, 1925, in (1925–1926) *Annual Digest* no. 26:

> Although Turkey was no longer an Empire but a Republic and its size had been considerably curtailed after the Great War by loss of territory, yet it could not be considered that the Republic was not the successor of the Empire. The remaining part, which was the main portion of the country, was the

Having examined the distinction between State succession and identity, the next section will analyse the different types of succession.

4. CLASSIFICATION OF THE DIFFERENT TYPES OF STATE SUCCESSION

It is essential to establish a classification of the different types of succession of States and to define them. Scholars have highlighted the importance of making such distinction.[113] The two Vienna Conventions on State succession distinguish four basic types of succession: (a) cession and transfer of part of the territory of one State to another State; (b) separation of a part of the State's territory; (c) unification of States; and (d) succession in the context of decolonization (Newly Independent States).[114] As noted by Rapporteur Kohen in his Final Report in the context of the Institut's work on *State Succession in Matters of State Responsibility*, the classification adopted by the Vienna Conventions 'does not fully or accurately depict the different hypotheses of State succession'.[115] For instance, the 1978 Vienna Convention does not distinguish between separation and dissolution, providing for the same rule in both cases.[116] **1.41**

The present author has adopted elsewhere a different typology comprised of six types of State succession.[117] As further explained in the next paragraphs, they can be grouped in two broad categories. **1.42**

The first essential distinction between different types of succession of States concerns the consequences that an event may have on the predecessor State(s). There are cases where the predecessor State will *continue to exist* following the event affecting its territorial integrity. On the contrary, in other cases the **1.43**

---

continuation of the state which, under another form of government and larger in size, had formed Turkey, and it had retained all its rights and duties except such as were attached to the lost territories.

See, Dumberry (n 31).

113 See, for instance: Malcolm N. Shaw, *International Law* 4th edn (CUP 1997) 676–7; Kay Hailbronner, 'Legal Aspects of the Unification of the Two German States', (1991) 2(1) EJIL 33; D.P. O'Connell, 'Recent Problems of State Succession in Relation to New States', (1970–II) 130 Rec. des Cours 164. *Contra*: Jenning and Watts (n 59) 209, for whom these different types of succession of States are not 'terms of art with them carrying clearly established legal consequences'.

114 Vienna Convention on Succession of States in Respect of Treaties (n 15); Vienna Convention on Succession of States in Respect of State Property, Archives and Debts (n 22).

115 Institut de Droit international, *State Succession in Matters of State Responsibility*, 'Final Report', Rapporteur Marcelo G. Kohen, 28 June 2015, 21 [hereinafter 'IDI, State Succession to Responsibility, Final Report, 2015'].

116 Art. 34, Vienna Convention on Succession of States in Respect of Treaties (n 15).

117 Patrick Dumberry, *State Succession to International Responsibility* (Martinus Nijhoff 2007). See also, a similar categorization used by Zimmermann and Devaney, 'Succession to Treaties' (n 38) 519.

predecessor State will *cease to exist*. This distinction is recognized in doctrine;[118] it can be referred to as 'partial' or 'total' State succession.[119] As further explained below, not all cases of succession lead to the creation of a new State(s).[120]

4.1 Situations where the predecessor State ceases to exist

1.44 In the event that the predecessor State *ceases to exist* following an event affecting its territorial integrity, there are *three* different scenarios that need to be differentiated (which will be analysed separately in this study).

1.45 First, the extinction of the predecessor State may result in the creation of *one* new State. This is the case of a *unification* of States, whereby at least *two* existing States will merge to form a new State. In such a case, the predecessor States will cease to exist to create an entirely new entity, the successor State. Older examples include the merger of Egypt and Syria to form the United Arab Republic (1958), and the merger of Tanganyika and Zanzibar to form Tanzania (1964). The most recent case of unification is that of Yemen in 1990. In 2002, Serbia and Montenegro decided to form a 'union of the States' (Montenegro later seceded in 2006).[121] This so-called 'union of States' differs from more classical unification cases.[122]

1.46 Secondly, the extinction of the predecessor State may result in the creation of *many* new States on its original territory. This is the case in the *dissolution* of a State. Recent examples of dissolution are those of Czechoslovakia and Yugoslavia. The specific case of the USSR is controversial and will be further discussed below.[123]

1.47 Thirdly, the extinction of the predecessor State sometimes results not in the creation of a new State but in the *enlargement* of the territory of an *existing*

118 Stern (n 8) 111–12; B. Stern, 'Responsabilité internationale et succession d'États', in Laurence Boisson de Chazournes and Vera Gowlland-Debbas (eds), *The International Legal System in Quest of Equity and Universality, Liber amicorum Georges Abi-Saab* (M. Nijhoff 2001) 335; Udina (n 26) 677–8; Michael John Volkovitsch, 'Righting Wrongs: Toward a New Theory of State Succession to Responsibility for International Delicts', (1992) 92(8) *Colum L Rev* 2164–5; Degan (n 45) 300–301.

119 Jenning and Watts (n 59) 209; Yilma Makonnen, 'State Succession in Africa: Selected Problems', (1986–V) 200 Rec des Cours 102–103; O'Connell (n 16) 4.

120 Stern (n 8) 111–12.

121 Agreement on Principles of Relations Between Serbia and Montenegro within the Framework of a Union of States, signed in Belgrade on 14 March 2002 (see in particular, Arts 1.2, 1.5 and 5.1).

122 A union of States is sometimes considered as a different type than 'unification' because in the former case each State keeps its international personality and therefore no new State emerges. In reality, it is often difficult to distinguish between the two types and much will depend on the circumstances of each case.

123 See, Chapter 3, Section 2.4.

State. This is the case of *incorporation* (or 'integration', 'absorption') of a State where the territory of a State (the successor State) is enlarged as a result of the integration of the *entirety* of the territory of the predecessor State. The most recent example of an incorporation of State is in 1990 when the German Democratic Republic ceased to exist as an independent State and its territory, comprising five *Länder*, was integrated into the already existing Federal Republic of Germany.

4.2 Situations where the predecessor State continues to exist

In cases where the predecessor State *continues to exist* following an event affecting its territorial integrity, there are three different scenarios that also need to be differentiated. **1.48**

First, the event affecting the territorial integrity of the predecessor State may result in the creation of a *new State*. This is the case of *secession*, where a new State emerges from the break-up of an already existing State that nevertheless continues its existence after the loss of part of its territory. The term 'continuing' State is often used by scholars when referring to the predecessor State in the situation just described.[124] It should be noted, however, that in the *Genocide Case* (*Bosnia-Herzegovina v. Serbia-Montenegro*), the ICJ has used the term 'continuator' State instead.[125] There is also some controversy as to the proper terminology that should be used to make reference to this phenomenon and whether the term 'separation' should be used instead of 'secession'.[126] For example, the work of the ILC used the term 'separation'.[127] For some writers, the term 'secession' should be reserved more specifically to describe instances where the removal of one part of the territory is made *without the consent* of the predecessor State.[128] However, as valid as such distinctions may be, the term **1.49**

---

124 Dumberry (n 117) 16–17.

125 *Application of the Convention on the Prevention and Punishment of the Crime of Genocide (Bosnia and Herzegovina v. Serbia and Montenegro)*, Judgment 26 February 2007, ICJ Reports 2007, [71, 75, 80, 81, 106, 130, 131].

126 Some writers use the term 'separation' in the context of a unitary State and 'secession' for federal States. For instance: Jacques Brossard and Daniel Turp, *L'accession à la souveraineté et le cas du Québec*, (2nd ed. PUM 1995) 94; Daniel Turp, *Le droit de choisir: Essais sur le droit du Québec à disposer de lui-même/ The Right to Choose: Essays on Québec's Right of Self-Determination*, (Thémis 2001) 22.

127 Both the Vienna Convention on Succession of States in Respect of Treaties (n 15) (at Art. 34) and the Vienna Convention on Succession of States in Respect of State Property, Archives and Debts (n 22) (Art. 17), use the term 'separation'. This is also the case of the *Draft Articles on Nationality of Natural Persons* (n 22).

128 See: Marcelo G. Kohen, 'Le problème des frontières en cas de dissolution et de séparation d'États: quelles alternatives?', in Olivier Corten, Barbara Delcourt, Pierre Klein and Nicolas Levrat (eds), *Démembrement d'États et délimitations territoriales: L'uti possidetis en question(s)* (Bruylant 1999) 368–9; Marcelo G. Kohen, 'Introduction', in Marcelo G. Kohen (ed), *Secession: International Law Perspectives* (CUP 2006) 2–3; Crawford, *The Creation of States* (n 45) 247; James Crawford, 'State Practice and International Law in

'secession' will be used in this book in its general sense to refer to cases where a new State is created while the predecessor State continues to exist. Recent cases of secession include those of Montenegro and South Sudan.

1.50 Secondly, there is another type of succession of States that is similar to cases of secession insofar as the events affecting the territorial integrity of the predecessor State result in the creation of a new State while the predecessor State continues to exist. This is the case with '*Newly Independent States*' in the context of decolonization. It is generally admitted that the territory of a colony should not be considered as part of the territory of the colonial State administrating it.[129] In that sense, a Newly Independent State is a new State that cannot be said to have 'seceded' from the colonial power to the extent that its territory was never formally a part of it.[130] There is some controversy in doctrine as to whether Newly Independent States should be at all be viewed as a distinct type of succession of States.[131] Supporters of the distinction rely on the specific circumstances of the decolonization and the fact that different rules of State succession apply to these States in order for them to freely exercise their right to self-determination and to break the vicious circle of economic domination.[132] The work of the ILC on State succession has recognized the specificity of this category of State succession.[133] Both Vienna Conventions on matters of State succession have thus adopted different rules

---

Relation to Secession', (1998) *British YIL* 85. Similarly, O'Connell (n 16, vol II) 88, speaks of 'revolutionary secession' and 'evolutionary secession'.

129 Declaration of Principles of International Law Concerning Friendly Relations and Co-operation Among States in Accordance with the Charter of the United Nations, adopted by GA Res. 2625 (XXV), 24 October 1970.

130 Meriboute (n 45) 174.

131 Some writers do not view them as a distinct category: Degan (n 45) 298–9. See also: *Restatement (Third), Foreign Relations Law of the United States*, Vol I (American Law Institute Publ. 1987) § 210, Reporters' notes no. 4 (at 113).

132 See, for instance, the position held by Makonnen (n 119) 130–31, for whom 'the guiding principles governing the consequences of State succession are the complete elimination of 'colonialism' in all form and manifestation and creating the conditions for the realization of the right to self-determination by the newly independent States'. Similarly, the position of Bedjaoui (n 21) 468–9:

> Un État nouveau, pour remplir sa mission interne et sa fonction internationale, doit s'affermir et s'affirmer en tant que tel, faute de quoi son indépendance serait pleine d'illusion et sa viabilité, d'artifice. L'objectif essentiel consiste à purger les rapports anciens de leur contenu inégalitaire. Cela, on le pressent, doit conférer une tonalité spécifique à la succession d'États par décolonisation, par rapport à la succession du type classique où ne décelait pas l'existence de liens de subordination.

See also, the same writer's comment (at 530):

> L'impératif catégorique pour l'État nouveau demeure l'élimination des causes réelles de la colonisation ou de la colonisabilité par la suppression du sous-développement. Le droit de la succession d'États peut y contribuer ou non selon qu'il intègre les principes nouveaux, notamment de la Charte des Nations unies, ou qu'il demeure l'expression des intérêts impériaux.

133 This is discussed in: Meriboute (n 45) 29–30, 49, 56, 63.

applicable to Newly Independent States to adequately manage this distinction.[134] However, the ILC Draft Articles on Nationality in relation to State Succession does not.[135] The recent work of the Institut on State succession also adopted a specific regime for Newly Independent States in the context of decolonization.[136] In his Final Report, Rapporteur Kohen explained three reasons why he considered it 'indispensable' to include Newly Independent States as a specific category of State succession of its own:

> *First*, as some cases mentioned at the beginning of this report show, there can still be cases of emergence of new States that could fall within the realm of the category of newly independent States, as defined in the 1978 and 1983 Conventions. *Second*, as a recent judicial decision in the United Kingdom demonstrates, problems relating to the commission of internationally wrongful acts during colonial times and the question of responsibility of the predecessor or the successor States may emerge even long after the acts have occurred. Hence, cases of State succession giving rise to the emergence of a newly independent State that occurred in the past may have still kept open situations concerning international responsibility. *Third*, as for treaties, archives, debts and property, the subject matter of the consequences of internationally wrongful acts committed before the date of State succession also appeals for a specific treatment of succession with regards to States having been dependent territories before coming into existence. Given the particular territorial status prior to independence, the cases of newly independent States cannot be assimilated to those of the separation of a State, whether by agreement or not.[137]

Thirdly, the event affecting the territorial integrity of the predecessor State may sometimes result not in the creation of a new State but in the *enlargement* of the territory of an *existing* State. This is the case of a *cession* or *transfer of territory* from one existing State to another existing State. Although the term 'cession' is occasionally used in doctrine to include the concept of a 'transfer',[138] in this study, the term 'cession' will be used only to refer to cases where the **1.51**

---

134 Thus, Art. 16 of the Vienna Convention on Succession of States in Respect of Treaties (n 15) indicates that treaties entered into by the predecessor State are not binding on a Newly Independent State, while other new States emerging from a dissolution of State or separation/secession are bound by such treaties (Art. 34). Art. 38 of the Vienna Convention on Succession of States in Respect of State Property, Archives and Debts (n 22) indicates that, in principle, and without any agreement to the contrary, debts of the predecessor State do not pass to the Newly Independent State. A different regime applies to cases of unification of States (where debts pass to the successor State, Art. 39) and cases of separation and dissolution of State (where an 'equitable share' of the predecessor State's debts pass to the new State(s), Arts 40 and 41).

135 Draft Articles on Nationality of Natural Persons (n 22) at 41, [1] and [3] (dealing with Art. 26). The Commentary to the Articles recognizes the theoretical distinction between Newly Independent States and 'separation of part or parts of the territory' (i.e., secession). However, it also indicates that the 'substantive rules' established for cases of secession (i.e., Arts 24–26) would be applicable *mutatis mutandis* to any remaining cases of decolonization in the future. Therefore, no separate section was included in the Draft Articles to deal specifically with Newly Independent States.

136 IDI, State Succession to Responsibility, Resolution, 2015 (n 24), Art. 16.

137 IDI, State Succession to Responsibility, Final Report, 2015 (n 115) 12.

138 Shaw (n 113) 688.

territorial change is made pursuant to a treaty to which the predecessor State is a party. On the contrary, a 'transfer' of territory will apply to situations where there is no agreement between the predecessor State and the successor State.[139] Despite this semantic distinction having been explained, both cases of cession and transfer of territory will be analysed in this study as *a single* type of succession of States. This type of territorial transformation is somewhat different compared to other mechanisms of State succession insofar as it results in neither the extinction of a State nor in the creation of a new State.[140] Nevertheless, it remains a distinct type of State succession.[141] This conclusion was reached by the ILC in its analysis on matters of State succession,[142] as well as in the recent work of the Institut.[143] A classic example of cession of territory is that of Alsace-Lorraine from Germany to France in 1919.[144] Two more recent examples that will be examined in detail below, are the transfers of Hong Kong from Great Britain to China (1997) and that of Macao from Portugal to China (1999).[145]

1.52 In sum, the relevant State practice and international case law will be examined separately for the following six different types of succession of States (corresponding to the same typology recently adopted by the Institut[146]):

- unification of State;
- dissolution of State;
- incorporation of State;
- secession;
- newly independent States; and
- cession and transfer of territory.

---

139 O. Dorr, 'Cession', in *Max Planck Encyclopedia of Public International Law* (OUP, online edn, 2006) [1, 8].

140 There is one main difference between cases of 'cession' of territory and cases of 'incorporation'. Cases of cession of territory only deal with *part of a territory* of a State which passes to another State, while cases of incorporation involve the *whole territory* of the State which is integrated into another State. Another difference is that in the context of cession of territory, the predecessor State is not extinguished as a result of the loss of part of its territory.

141 This is emphasized by Stern (n 8) 105; Dorr (n 139) [1].

142 Article 15 of the Vienna Convention on Succession of States in Respect of Treaties (n 15) does not use the concept of 'cession' but refers instead to the situation '[w]hen part of the territory of a State, or when any territory for the international relations of which a State is responsible, not being part of the territory of that State, becomes part of the territory of another State'. See also: Art. 14, Vienna Convention on Succession of States in Respect of State Property, Archives and Debts (n 22); Art. 20, Draft Articles on Nationality (n 22).

143 IDI, State Succession to Responsibility, Resolution, 2015 (n 24), Art. 11.

144 Another famous older example is that of the transfer of Alaska from Russia to the USA in 1867. See other examples in: Dorr (n 139) [6].

145 See, Chapter 3, Section 6.5.

146 IDI, State Succession to Responsibility, Resolution, 2015 (n 24). See also, the work of Stern (n 8) 113, providing a survey of different typologies used in doctrine. See also: Annie Gruber, *Le droit international de la succession d'États* (Bruylant 1986) 17–18.

Part B

STATE SUCCESSION TO BILATERAL INVESTMENT TREATIES

2

INTRODUCTION

1. THE CONTROVERSIAL ISSUE OF STATE SUCCESSION TO TREATIES

2.01 This chapter examines the issue of State succession to treaties, undoubtedly one of the most controversial matters in international law. It has long been the battleground for opposing schools of thought. Essentially, supporters of the theory of *tabula rasa* (clean slate) argue that a new State (the 'successor' State) is not bound by the treaties to which the predecessor State was a party. On the contrary, advocates of the theory of continuity claim that the successor State is bound by such treaties. While this dichotomy is still valid, it should be added, as noted by two writers, that 'the debate surrounding this binary distinction has long been regarded as being unhelpful and overly simplistic, with neither theory providing a satisfactory theoretical underpinning for the law of State succession in respect of treaties nor being fully reflected in State practice'.[1] Craven makes the same assessment:

> In reality, neither of these two positions is wholly tenable, nor do they provide ready solutions to the range of problems that arise in the context of state succession. (…) Even when considered within the restricted context of treaties, the universal succession thesis demands too much. It argues for the maintenance of legal continuity in circumstances in which some alteration of legal relations is both inevitable and necessary. It assumes that states may be burdened with obligations in a situation where specific consent is palpably absent, not because of any universal necessity but because of some inchoate systemic interest in legal continuity. The clean slate thesis, by contrast is not properly a thesis of succession at all. It denies the possibility of the

1 Andreas Zimmermann and James G. Devaney, 'Succession to Treaties and the Inherent Limits of International Law' in Christian J. Tams, Antonios Tzanakopoulos, and Andreas Zimmermann (eds), *Research Handbook on the Law of Treaties*, (Edward Elgar 2014) 517. They further note that with regard to the theory of universal succession: 'the justification for imposing obligations on successor sovereign States without their consent is somewhat unclear to say the least, being based on unclear notions such as a communitarian interest in continuity of obligations'. On the concept of *tabula rasa*, they state that 'surveys of contemporary practice indicate that the clean slate rule in its purest form was rarely applied and that the concept as a whole has fallen into relative *desuetudo*'.

> passing of rights and duties in virtue of an overarching requirement of consent. But in denying the possibility of succession, it also appears to deny the possibility of law. (…) It is also very clear that on an evidential level, state practice does little to substantiate either position. In very few cases have newly emergent states discarded, in their entirety, all rights and duties that were formerly incumbent upon the previous sovereign. (…) On the other hand, it is equally rare to find examples where no alteration in the legal position of a state or territory has occurred following a change in sovereignty.[2]

2.02 The actual practice of States is indeed much more diverse and complex than this simplistic *tabula rasa*/automatic continuity dichotomy would suggest. This means, in turn, that there is a great level of uncertainty regarding the rules that govern the question of succession to treaties. Two authors have recently given five factors contributing to such uncertainty:

> First, State succession is inherently highly political given that whether a State is bound by a conventional obligation upon succession largely depends on recognition of that position as a successor State by other States. Second, instances of State succession often occur in the wake of armed conflicts (such as was the case of the breakdown of the former Yugoslavia) which can separate successor States from legal counsel and from the archives in most cases located in the respective capital of its predecessor State (such as in the case of South Sudan). Successor States, which in many cases are uncertain of the law and the appropriate procedures to be followed, are then open to being manipulated by third States with vested interests in the approach to, and eventual outcome of, the incident of State succession. Third, due to the fact that the law on State succession (both in relation to treaties specifically and more generally) depends on instances of State succession, State practice is relatively sparse. Fourth, there are a large number of actors who have a say in shaping the law in any given instance of State succession such as, apart from States, inter alia, depositaries of treaties and human rights treaty bodies. Fifth, and perhaps the most significant contributing factor, is the, at least partially, ideology-driven attempt at codifying the law that resulted in the 1978 Vienna Convention on the Succession of States in Respect of Treaties. From the outset, the limitations of the Vienna Convention were clear to the ILC. For instance, the Convention itself would not be binding on a successor State until it took specific steps to become itself a party to that Convention in one form or another. Even then, however, 'the convention would not be binding upon it in respect of any act or fact which took place before the date on which it became a party'. In addition, no other State would be bound by the Convention vis-à-vis a successor State until said new State had taken steps to become a party. As such it was clear that the Convention itself was not (primarily) meant to regulate the law of State succession to treaties by way of binding treaty obligations, but rather

2 Matthew C.R. Craven, 'The Problem of State Succession and the Identity of States under International Law' (1998) 9(1) EJIL 149–50.

sought to clarify, codify and progressively develop the law as a whole through attracting the accession of a significant number of States – a task only partly achieved.[3]

One important factor that led to the general state of confusion regarding the rules governing the question of succession to treaties was the 'failed' attempt at codification[4] by the ILC, and the adoption of the Vienna Convention on Succession of States in Respect of Treaties in 1978 (the 'Convention').[5] The Convention has been widely criticized by many authors.[6] **2.03**

One common ground of complaint is the Convention's emphasis on developing rules applicable to the situation of Newly Independent States resulting from decolonization.[7] The adoption of these rules was not appropriate from a temporal standpoint, since the phenomenon of decolonization was drawing to its end.[8] As explained by Zimmerman, 'rather than providing the intended clarification of customary law, the Convention was undermined by ideological **2.04**

3 Zimmermann and Devaney, 'Succession to Treaties' (n 1) 507–8.

4 A. Sarvarian, 'Codifying the Law of State Succession: A Futile Endeavour?', (2016) 27(3) EJIL 789–812. See also A. Zimmermann, 'La Convention de Vienne sur la succession d'États en matière de traités: codification réussie ou échouée ?, in G. Distefano, G. Gaggioli and A. Hêche (eds), *La Convention de Vienne de 1978 sur la succession d'États en matière de traités: Commentaire article par article et études thématiques* (Bruylant 2015), 1547ff.

5 Vienna Convention on Succession of States in Respect of Treaties, signed on 23 August 1978 and entered into force on 6 November 1996, 1946 UNTS 3, in: 17 ILM, 1978, 1488 [hereinafter 'Vienna Convention on Succession to Treaties'].

6 V. Degan, 'La succession d'États en matière de traités et les États nouveaux (issus de l'ex-Yougoslavie)', (1996) 42 AFDI 221, for whom the Convention 'ressemble à une mauvaise épreuve écrite d'un étudiant en droit de troisième cycle'.

7 D.P. O'Connell, 'Recent Problems of State Succession in Relation to New States', (1970–II) 130 Rec des Cours 102–3:

> It is necessary, then, to recall that if international law is to contain principles respecting State Succession these principles must exhibit juristic characteristics, and in particular must be available to resolve the problem of State Succession as it manifests itself in different epochs, in different modes, and in different geographical and political circumstances. The phase of decolonization, as a historical phenomenon, is now virtually complete-though the legal consequences of decolonization will no doubt persist in the form of actual questions to be answered diplomatically or judicially-and the experience which international law has gained from this historical event will only be valuable if it leads to insights respecting legal principles that will help to solve problems in future instances of State Succession.

See also: D.P. O'Connell, 'Reflections on the State Succession Convention' (1979) 39 *ZaöRV* 726: 'this particular essay in refashioning the law was marred from its inception by a preoccupation with the special problem of decolonisation, around which myth and emotion have accumulated like mists in the marsh, so that the whole context became intellectually distorted'.

8 P. Cahier, 'Quelques aspects de la Convention de 1978 sur la succession d'États en matière de traités', in B. Dutoit and E. Grisel (eds), *Mélanges Georges Perrin* (1984) at 76; Degan (n 6) 213; O'Connell, 'Reflections on the State Succession Convention' (n 7) 726; A. Gruber, *Le droit international de la succession d'États* (Bruylant 1986) 89; I. Sinclair, 'Some Reflections on the Vienna Convention on Succession of States in Respect of Treaties', in *Essays in Honour of Erik Castren* (1978) 181; P. Caggiano, 'The ILC Draft on the Succession of States in Respect of Treaties: A Critical Appraisal', (1975) 1 *Italian YIL* 82–3; M. Craven, *The Decolonization of International Law: State Succession and the Law of Treaties* (OUP 2007) 16; O'Connell, 'Recent Problems of State Succession' (n 7) 102. For arguments defending the Convention, see: R. Szafarz, 'Succession of States in Respect of Treaties in Contemporary International Law', (1983) 12 *Polish YIL* 131–9.

pressures exerted by States that had gained independence during decolonization who then exerted great pressure on the ILC to ensure the inclusion of a special regime for 'Newly Independent States' in the Convention'.[9] Similarly, for d'Aspremont, while 'the agenda of international law is generally forward-looking, its codification backward-looking, and its application present looking', it remains that 'the international law of State succession in respect of treaties has been constructed to vindicate the past and has been designed according to past experiences without much consideration for its applicability beyond those experiences'.[10] As a result, the provisions in the Convention that were developed to address issues surrounding decolonization have had a very limited impact on the way States have conducted themselves during the break-ups of the USSR and former Yugoslavia in the 1990s.[11]

2.05 More generally, the question remains as to whether or not any codification regarding State succession is, on one hand, realistic and possible and, on the other hand, necessary and useful.[12] This question arises because the Convention stands as a *supplementary* mechanism, wherein it always allows States to conclude an agreement that derogates from its dispositions. The Convention contains a set of 'default' rules that only apply when States have not otherwise agreed to specific principles governing succession issues. In reality, as noted by Zimmerman, States 'prefer ad hoc political solutions rather than fixed and somewhat rigid rules' and this 'further increases the uncertain nature of the rules on treaty succession which, in turn, then lead to an even further increase in pragmatic political solutions'.[13]

2.06 In any event, the practical effect of any codification in the area of succession of States is also uncertain. Thus, the text of the Vienna Convention is only binding for the 22 States that have become parties to the Convention.[14] The Convention is therefore not binding on other States, unless, of course, it can be concluded that a given provision codifies customary law on the topic (which is

---

9 Zimmermann and Devaney, 'Succession to Treaties' (n 1) 508. See also: Jean d'Aspremont, 'Decolonization and the International Law of Succession: Between Regime Exhaustion and Paradigmatic Inconclusiveness' (2013) 12 *Chinese JIL* 321–37.

10 d'Aspremont, ibid., 322.

11 Zimmermann and Devaney, 'Succession to Treaties' (n 1) 509. See also: d'Aspremont, ibid., 321–37; Sarvarian (n 4) 805ff.

12 O'Connell, 'Reflections on the State Succession Convention' (n 7) 726: 'State succession is a subject altogether unsuited to the processes of codification'; Sarvarian (n 4) 789–812; Zimmermann, 'La Convention de Vienne' (n 4) 1570ff.

13 Zimmermann and Devaney, 'Succession to Treaties' (n 1) 539.

14 United Nations Treaty Collection, Chapter XXIII, Law of Treaties, available at: https://treaties.un.org/Pages/ViewDetails.aspx?src=TREATY&mtdsg_no=XXIII-2&chapter=23&clang=_en.

the case for only a few provisions contained in the Convention[15]). One reason so few States have ratified the Convention is because they typically do not see the benefit of endorsing rules regarding succession in advance, when they do not yet know how such rules would affect them and which future successor States it would involve.[16] Regardless, under Article 7(1), the Convention only applies to cases of succession which took place after the entry into force of the instrument (i.e., November 1996).[17]

The ensuing practical implications are that upon its independence, a new State is simply *not* bound by the Convention.[18] In order for the Convention to have a binding force, a new State must ratify the Convention. Moreover, as mentioned by the ILC, 'the convention would not be binding upon [that new State] in respect of any act or fact which took place before the date on which it became a party'.[19] This principle is set out at Article 7 of the Convention.[20] In other words, even when a new State does ratify the Convention, it remains that legal issues arising from *its own* succession are still *not* covered by the instrument. This is in fact what happened with the successor States of former Yugoslavia (Bosnia, Croatia, Macedonia, Serbia, Slovenia and eventually also Montenegro), who ratified the Convention after becoming independent States. The same is true for Ukraine and Moldova in the context of the break-up of the USSR. However, there exists an exception to this general principle under Article 7(2) of the Convention.[21] This exception provides that a new State may, when ratifying the Convention, declare that its provisions are applicable with regards to *its own* succession that took place prior to the entry into force of the Convention itself. This is indeed the declaration that the Czech Republic and Slovakia made when ratifying the Convention.[22] Brigitte Stern has rightly referred to the fact that new States are almost always not bound by the Convention as the 'hidden defect' inherent to any convention **2.07**

15 Zimmermann and Devaney, 'Succession to Treaties' (n 1) 520, 531–3 indicating that this is the case for Arts 11 (border treaties), 12 (localized treaties) 15 (transfer of territory), 16, 17 and 27 (Newly Independent States).

16 A Zimmermann, 'La Convention de Vienne' (n 4) 1572–3.

17 A.P. Kaboré, 'Article 7' in Distefano, Gaggioli and Hêche (n 4), 238–9.

18 R. Mullerson, 'Law and Politics in Succession of States: International Law on Succession of States', in G. Burdeau and B. Stern (eds), *Dissolution, continuation et succession en Europe de l'Est* (Cedin-Paris I 1994) 16–17; Caggiano (n 8) 71–2; Zimmermann, 'La Convention de Vienne' (n 4) 1573.

19 ILC, Draft Articles on Succession of States in Respect of State Property, Archives and Debts with Commentaries, in (1981) *Yearbook ILC* vol II, Part II, at 9.

20 For an analysis of this provision, see: Kaboré (n 17) 227ff.

21 See, ibid., 245ff.

22 See: United Nations Treaty Collection, Chapter XXIII, Law of Treaties, available at: https://treaties.un.org/Pages/ViewDetails.aspx?src=TREATY&mtdsg_no=XXIII-2&chapter=23&clang=_en#EndDec. See also: Kaboré (n 17) 256ff.

concerning matters of State succession.[23] The work of the ILC on State succession to treaties has acknowledged these shortcomings.[24]

2.08 Finally, while the Convention may be considered as a codification of international law regarding certain issues, it is clearly a 'progressive development' of the law with respect to many others.[25] Ultimately, the Convention should be considered merely as a useful guide to resolve issues of State succession to treaties.[26] The principles set out in the 1978 Convention were 'tested' for the first time in the wave of succession in the 1990s with the break-ups of the USSR, Yugoslavia and Czechoslovakia, and the German 'unification'. It should be noted that at the time of their dissolutions, both Yugoslavia and Czechoslovakia were parties to the Convention. However, as noted by Tams, 'States and other stakeholders have drawn inspiration from it; but perhaps not much more: pragmatism, rather than adherence to abstract legal propositions, has been the guiding principle'.[27] The practice of these States regarding bilateral treaties will be examined below.[28]

2. OVERVIEW OF QUESTIONS ADDRESSED IN THIS PART

2.09 This Part examines one specific type of treaty: bilateral investment treaties for the protection and promotion of investments ('BITs'). It is now estimated that over 2,900 BITs have been concluded worldwide.[29] In addition, more than 340 international agreements (such as free trade and multilateral agreements) include provisions on investment protection.[30] In total, more than 3,200 international investment agreements ('IIAs') provide investors with investment protection.[31] The treaties provide investors with substantive as well significant procedural rights. They typically allow an investor of one treaty party to bring a direct claim before an international arbitral tribunal alleging the breach of investment protection contained in an IIA against another treaty party, known as the host State with regard to the investment. Such clauses are

23 B. Stern, 'Rapport de synthèse', in Geneviève Burdeau and Brigitte Stern (eds), *Dissolution, continuation et succession en Europe de l'Est* (Cedin-Paris I 1994) 385.

24 ILC, Report of the International Law Commission on the Work of its 26th Session, 6 May to 26 July 1974, A/9610/Rev.1, in: *YILC*, 1974, vol. II (Part One) [hereinafter 'ILC Report, 26th Session, 1974'] at 169–70.

25 Szafarz (n 8) 107–8; M. Lehto, 'Succession of States in the Former Soviet Union: Arrangements Concerning the Bilateral Treaties of Finland and the USSR' (1993) 4 *Finnish YIL* 194, 205; Mullerson (18) 474.

26 Szafarz (n 8) 108; Caggiano (n 8) 71.

27 C.J. Tams, 'State Succession to Investment Treaties: Mapping the Issues', (2016) 31(2) *ICSID Rev* 314–43, 318.

28 See, Chapter 3.

29 UNCTAD, *Recent Trends, in IIAs and ISDS*, IIA Issues Note, no. 1, Feb. 2015, 2.

30 Ibid.

31 Ibid., 2. See also: World Bank, *World Investment Report*, 2014, xxiii.

found in the overwhelming majority of IIAs.[32] With the increasing popularity of investment protection clauses in IIAs, the number of arbitration cases between investors and States have equally increased dramatically. The most recent UNCTAD report mentions a total of 767 known cases.[33] The majority of these cases were filed under an IIA.[34]

Specifically, this Part investigates the question of whether or not a successor State is bound by the BITs entered into by the predecessor State with other States (hereinafter referred to as the 'other State party').[35] It should be added that the analysis which follows could also apply to other investment treaties of a *bilateral* nature, such as free trade agreements. The question of succession to multilateral treaties will be examined in Part C. **2.10**

To the best of the present author's knowledge, apart from my article published in 2015,[36] and a general survey conducted by Tams in 2016[37] no comprehensive study on the question of State succession to bilateral treaties (in general) has been conducted in recent years.[38] The specific question of succession to BITs has also not been examined by writers.[39] The present author has **2.11**

32 OECD, *Dispute Settlement Provisions in International Investment Agreements: A Large Sample Survey*, (2012) OECD Working Papers on International Investment, 10, examining 1,660 BITs and concluding that only 4 per cent of them (mostly old BITs) did not provide any such provisions.

33 UNCTAD, *Investor–State Dispute Settlement: Review of Developments in 2016*, ILA Issue Notes No. 1, 2017, 1.

34 *ICSID Caseload, Statistics*, Issue 2015–1, 10, indicating that 61.8 per cent of all cases conducted under the ICSID Convention (and the ICSID Additional Facility Rules) were filed under BITs (10 per cent were filed under plurilateral treaties, 18.3 per cent under State contracts and 9.4 per cent under the investment law of the host State).

35 Under Art. 2 of the Vienna Convention on Succession to Treaties (n 5) the term 'other State party' 'means in relation to a successor State any party, other than the predecessor State, to a treaty in force at the date of a succession of States in respect of the territory to which that succession of States relates'. See: L. Gradoni, 'Article 2', in Distefano, Gaggioli and Hêche (n 4), 123ff.

36 P. Dumberry, 'State Succession to Bilateral Treaties: A Few Observations on the Incoherent and Unjustifiable Solution Adopted for Secession and Dissolution of States under the 1978 Vienna Convention' (2015) 28 *Leiden JIL* 13–30.

37 Tams (n 27) 314–43.

38 Regarding *specific* aspects in relation to succession to bilateral treaties: Qerim Qerimi and Suzana Krasniqi, 'Theories and Practice of State Succession to Bilateral Treaties: The Recent Experience of Kosovo' (2013) 14(9) *German LJ* 1359. Much older studies on succession to bilateral treaties include, K.J. Keith, 'Succession to Bilateral Treaties by Seceding States', (1967) 61(2) AJIL 521: A.P. Lester, 'State Succession to Treaties in the Commonwealth', (1963) ICLQ 475–507. It should be noted that a number of articles have examined the question of bilateral treaties between two specific States: M. Koskenniemi and M. Lehto, 'La succession d'États dans l'ex-URSS, en ce qui concerne particulièrement les relations avec la Finlande', (1992) 38 AFDI 179–219; G. Hafner and E. Kornfeind, 'The Recent Austrian Practice of State Succession: Does the Clean Slate Still Exist?', (1996) *Austrian RIEL* 1–49.

39 One rare exception is A. Genest, 'Sudan Bilateral Investment Treaties and South Sudan: Musings on State Succession to Bilateral Treaties in the Wake of Yugoslavia's Breakup' (2014) 3 TDM. See also: Raúl Pereira Fleury, 'State Succession and BITs: Challenges for Investment Arbitration', (2016) 27 *Am Rev Int'l Arb* 451.

published one article on the topic in 2015.[40] This gap in the literature is surprising considering the emergence of some 30 new States since the end of the Cold War. Some of the predecessor States involved in these cases of succession were parties to a number of BITs at the time of their break-ups. Recent events have also shown the importance of the question today in the context of the secessions of Montenegro, Kosovo and South Sudan, where the predecessor States were also parties to a number of BITs before independence.[41] For instance, at the time of Kosovo's declaration of independence, Serbia was a party to 41 BITs.[42] It should be added that potential candidates for secession (Scotland, Catalonia, Quebec, etc.) involve some of the world's largest economies that are currently parties to a significant number of BITs.[43]

2.12 The absence of any research on the issue of State succession to BITs is all the more peculiar given the fact that the issue arose in 46 investor-State arbitration cases in recent years.[44] These cases and many others are examined in this part.[45] The present book is therefore the first comprehensive study of the question of succession to BITs. It is also the first study to assess theoretical aspects of the question and to investigate thoroughly the work of the ILC on the specific issue of State succession to *bilateral* treaties.[46]

2.13 The first section (Chapter 3) will analyse the practice of States (both successor States and other States parties to BITs) regarding the continuation of the predecessor State's BITs after the date of succession. In his ground-breaking paper, Tams accurately observed that writers (including myself) have 'remain[ed] focused on the grand normative debate – do new States automatically succeed to prior BITs?'[47] While admitting that 'this question is no doubt relevant', he rightly points out that the question 'need[s] not always arise' and can often be avoided altogether.[48] This is indeed true. In many instances, the parties have mutually and *expressly* agreed upon a solution regarding succession to treaties. As further explained below, it is not uncommon for States to reach an agreement as to whether or not a BIT, which was

40 P. Dumberry, 'An Uncharted Question of State Succession: Are New States Automatically Bound by the BITs Concluded by Predecessor States Before Independence?', (2015) 6(1) *J Int Disp Settl* 74–96.

41 On the question of South Sudan, see: Genest (n 39).

42 Pierre-Emmanuel Dupont, 'Foreign Investment and the Status of Kosovo in International Law', (2009) 10 *J World Invest & Trade* 937. The practice of Kosovo is examined later in Chapter 3, Section 2.3.

43 The number of BITs in force at the time of writing (May 2017) was respectively: United Kingdom: 96; Canada: 32 and Spain: 72.

44 Dumberry, 'An Uncharted Question of State Succession' (n 40) 74–96.

45 See, Chapter 6, Section 6.

46 For a recent study regarding the work of the ILC more generally (and on State succession to multilateral treaties), see: Craven, *The Decolonization of International Law* (n 8).

47 Tams (n 27) 328.

48 Ibid.

entered into by the predecessor State, should continue to apply after the date of succession.[49] In this situation, the controversial question as to whether a new State automatically succeeds to prior BITs does not arise since the States have themselves decided the fate of these treaties. Also, there are many situations where there is a *tacit agreement* between the States for the continuation of a specific BIT. Tams favours the 'flexibility' of such an approach.[50] As further examined in Chapter 4, the existence of any *tacit agreement* is a complicated and multifaceted question. For these reasons, the actual practice of successor States and other States parties regarding succession to BITs should be the starting point of this analysis.

Chapter 5 then examines the question of what happens to a BIT of the predecessor State when the States concerned have *not* agreed on its continuation. In doing so, it is essential to analyse the framework of the ILC in regard to State succession to treaties undertaken in the 1970s and the different solutions that were adopted under the 1978 Convention for specific types of State succession. Specifically, I will critically examine the solution adopted under the Convention for unification of States. The emphasis of this section will, however, be put on the solution adopted for secession and dissolution of States. Apart from one article written by myself,[51] no investigation into the work of the ILC on this point has been conducted in order to discover how its adoption of the principle of automatic continuity in the context of secession and dissolution of States came about. I will argue that it is incoherent for the ILC to apply, on one hand, the solution of automatic continuity for bilateral treaties in the context of secession and dissolution of States, while adopting, on the other hand, the solution of *tabula rasa* for Newly Independent States. I will further argue that, in any event, it is plainly unjustifiable to apply the principle of automatic continuity to bilateral treaties (in the context of secession and dissolution of States) given the particular nature of these instruments. This conclusion is based on the work conducted by the ILC itself. In my view, bilateral treaties do not automatically continue to be in force as of the date of succession unless *both* States concerned have explicitly (or tacitly) agreed to such a continuation. This basic solution should apply to *all new States* rather than exclusively to those emerging from the process of decolonization. In fact, this is the solution that new States have adopted to resolve issues of succession **2.14**

49 Ibid.

50 Ibid.:

> given the uncertainty of the applicable legal standards, the attraction of 'pragmatic arguments from tacit consent' is obvious. And overall, it may perhaps be said that the more flexible approaches just outlined facilitate the search for equitable solutions reflecting the intentions of the parties, and at least offer guidelines for the application of a fairly unsettled legal framework.

51 Dumberry, 'State Succession to Bilateral Treaties' (n 36) 13–30.

to bilateral treaties in the context of the break-up of several States after the end of the Cold War.[52]

2.15 The last section (Chapter 6) provides a critical analysis of investment arbitration case law involving BITs in the context of State succession. I will examine all existing cases in the context of the dissolutions of Czechoslovakia and Yugoslavia and the break-up of the USSR. The main part of the analysis will focus on the *Sanum v. Laos* case in the context of the cession of the territory of Macao to China in 1999. The award rendered by the arbitral tribunal and the judgments of the Singapore High Court and the Singapore Court of Appeal have for the first time comprehensively addressed a number of important issues in relation to succession to BITs. Finally, I will examine a number of problems in the field of international investment law arising from the annexation of Crimea by Russia and, specifically, pending arbitration cases. It should be added that the *WWM v. Kazakhstan* award dealing with the issue of Kazakhstan's succession to the Canada-USSR BIT is still confidential and will therefore only be briefly examined in this section.[53]

52 International Law Association, *Conclusions of the Committee on Aspects of the Law on State Succession*, Resolution no. 3/2008, adopted at the 73rd Conference of the International Law Association, held in Rio de Janeiro, Brazil, 17–21 August, 2008 [hereinafter, 'ILA, Resolution no. 3/2008'] at point no. 6.

53 *World Wide Minerals Ltd. and Mr. Paul A. Carroll, QC v. Kazakhstan*, UNCITRAL, Award, 19 October 2015 [hereinafter '*WWM v. Kazakhstan*'].

3

STATE PRACTICE REGARDING THE CONTINUATION OF PREDECESSOR STATES' BITS

This chapter examines the practice of successor States and other States regarding the fate of BITs which had been concluded by predecessor States before the date of succession. As noted above, this is an important issue and it must logically be the starting point of any investigation on the question of State succession to BITs. This section will show that Tams is correct when stating that 'successor States and their treaty partners regularly provide explicit answers to questions of State succession'.[54] They generally do so by exchanges of letters providing for the continuation of old BITs and by signing new treaties. When the question of succession to BITs is expressly (or sometimes implicitly) decided by the parties, the controversial question regarding any automatic succession to treaties simply does *not* arise (this other question is examined in Chapter 5, below). 3.01

54 Tams (n 27) 328.

1. INTRODUCTORY REMARKS

3.02 It should be emphasized at the outset that the aim of this section is *not* to provide a comprehensive assessment of the fate of *all* BITs which existed at the time of the break-up of Czechoslovakia, Yugoslavia, USSR and all other States which have been involved in succession episodes in the last 30 years. Such an exercise would certainly require extensive empirical research.

3.03 The first difficulty arising from conducting such an empirical analysis is the basic problem of finding the relevant information. Thus, in many instances there is no publicly available documentation about the actual status of an old BIT between one successor State and the other State party to that treaty. Very few government websites provide comprehensive information about which old BITs are in force and, most importantly, how and when they have become binding on both the new State and the other State party to that treaty. Most websites contain almost no information at all. Others simply indicate that one old BIT is in force without explaining whether this is because of any automatic succession principle or as a result of negotiation and exchange of letters between the States concerned. In other words, not only is it rare to find information regarding the fate of old BITs, but even when the information is available, it is often not descriptive enough and is therefore not very useful.[55] One example is in the context of the independence of South Sudan and the question of its continuation of the 27 BITs to which Sudan was a party before the date of succession. South Sudan has apparently not signed any BIT of its own, nor expressed its willingness to continue the BITs to which Sudan was a party.[56] The German Government website indicates that the 1963 Sudan-Germany BIT applies to South Sudan, without however, providing any information as to how this is the case.[57] In an EU document, Germany listed the BIT as being applicable to South Sudan.[58] What matters in the context of this book is not so much the fact that this particular treaty is considered

---

55 It should be recalled here the critical comments made by O'Connell, 'Recent Problems of State Succession' (n 7) 117, regarding 'State practice':

> The truth of the matter is that this 'practice' is likely to consist of decisions taken by public officials who have not achieved the necessary intellectual penetration of the problem to perceive the true issues, who may be more influenced by political or other ephemeral considerations than by juristic logic, who may even be ignorant of the nature of the problem, or of its ramifications, or who may be equipped with obsolescent literature, or even no literature whatever. Some of the processes of decision-making respecting matters of State succession that have occurred in recent years can hardly be dignified as significant contributions to the elaboration of the law.

56 See, the analysis of Genest (n 39) 6.

57 Tams (n 27) 332, referring to:http://www.bmwi.de/DE/Themen/Aussenwirtschaft/Investitionsschutz/investitionsschutzvertraege.html.

58 EU, see at fn 137 below: http://eur-lex.europa.eu/legal-content/FR/TXT/?uri=CELEX%3A52014XC0605(01).

binding between these two States, but rather the way such continuation took place between them. Another valuable source of information is UNCTAD's 'Investment Policy Hub' website. Yet, it does not exlain why and how certain treaties of the predecessor State are considered binding by the other States.

In any event, a number of writers have recently conducted empirical investigations regarding specific countries. I will partially rely on their works. In my view, this is appropriate for the simple reason that my goal is not to have a full and complete picture of what happened to every single BIT which had been signed by a predecessor State. My intention is simply to show that it is common for States to expressly determine that an old BIT continues to be in force after the date of succession. Yet, since no work had been undertaken in the context of the break-up of the USSR, I have conducted a comprehensive analysis of all 14 BITs to which the USSR was a party before its break-up and determine their fate for each of the former Republics. The ultimate aim of such an exercise is to identify which mechanism States have used to be bound by a specific treaty. In other words, it needs to be determined whether the continuation of a BIT is the result of a negotiation and exchange of letters between the States concerned, or whether it is based on the existence of some general principle of 'automatic' succession. This is the most important question for the purpose of this book. In my view, this question can be examined in part with the help of the publicly available information compiled by other scholars with regards to the practice of specific States. Whenever this was not the case, I have conducted my own investigation. **3.04**

2. ANALYSIS OF THE PRACTICE OF SUCCESSOR STATES

2.1 The practice of the FRY and Serbia-Montenegro regarding SFRY's BITs

As explained by Tams, at the time of the break-up of the SFRY in 1991, the country had entered into seven BITs (with Canada, the Netherlands, France, Egypt, Sweden, Germany and Austria).[59] What happened to these treaties with respect to the Federal Republic of Yugoslavia (FRY) and subsequently, Serbia-Montenegro (both successor States of the SFRY) can be divided into three distinct categories. **3.05**

The first category of treaties concerns three BITs where Serbia-Montenegro and its respective partners have agreed on the continuation of the instrument **3.06**

59 Tams (n 27) 329.

to which the SFRY was a party (France, the Netherlands and Germany).[60] The agreement between Serbia-Montenegro and France is found in a treaty signed in 2003. The agreement provides that the treaties between France and SFRY, which are annexed and includes the 1974 France-SFRY BIT, 'continuent de lier les parties'.[61] Even more specific language is found in an exchange of letters of 2002 between the Netherlands and the FRY. The letter contains a 'proposal' by the FRY indicating that a number of treaties concluded between the SFRY and the Netherlands 'referred to in Attachment A are in force between and represent treaties concluded between' the two States and that other treaties 'referred to in Attachment B will not be considered in force between' them.[62] These two examples show that the continuation of BITs was the object of negotiation. In other words, these States did not simply presume that the old BITs would automatically continue to apply. They were of the view that they had to take formal steps for the instruments to continue to have legal effect between them after the date of succession.

3.07 The second category of treaties are the *new* BITs signed by Serbia-Montenegro with two treaty partners of the former SFRY (Egypt and Austria) as well as with the Netherlands (replacing the old BIT which they had initially agreed would continue to apply).[63] All three new BITs terminated and replaced the old BITs that were signed between the SFRY and these States.[64] The fact that Serbia-Montenegro entered into a new BIT with each of these three States, mentioning that these instruments were terminating and replacing the old BITs, suggests that these States considered that these old BITs had continued to exist until the date of the entry into force of the new BITs. Thus, as noted by Tams, 'while such a termination provision may have been included to clarify the situation, its existence suggests that the new treaty parties did not consider to have started from a clean slate'.[65] Yet, it may be that these States took that position simply to avoid any legal vacuum during the 'twilight

60 Ibid.

61 Accord entre le gouvernement de la République française et le Conseil des ministres de Serbie-et-Monténégro relatif à la succession en matière de traités bilatéraux conclus entre la France et la république socialiste fédérative de Yougoslavie, 26 March 2003, available at: http://basedoc.diplomatie.gouv.fr/exl-php/util/documents/accede_document.php.

62 Overeenkomst tussen het Koninkrijk der Nederlanden en de Socialistische Federatieve Republiek Joegoslavië inzake de bevordering en de wederzijdse bescherming van investeringen, met brieven, 16 February 1976, available at: https://zoek.officielebekendmakingen.nl/trb-2002–181.HTML.

63 Tams (n 27) 329.

64 Ibid., referring to Art. 12(4) of the Austria-Serbia/Montenegro BIT (2001):

> [t]he entry into force of this Agreement between the Government of the Republic of Austria and the Federal Government of the Federal Republic of Yugoslavia shall terminate the provisions of the Agreement on the Promotion and Protection of Investments between the Republic of Austria and the Socialist Federative Republic of Yugoslavia, signed in Belgrade on 25 October 1989.

65 Tams (n 27) 329.

period' (i.e., between the date of succession and the signature of the new BIT). In any event, it may be that this is the position they took at the time when the new BITs were signed. But it does not provide much of an idea as to what they really 'believed' was the fate of those BITs following the date of succession. In other words, even though Serbia-Montenegro and Austria considered, in 2001, that the old 1989 BIT had continued to be in force in the interim period, this does not say much on what their view was *right after* the break-up of the SFRY ten years earlier.[66] It may be that they only agreed on the continuation of the old BIT once negotiations for the new BIT started. The information available simply does not provide any clear answer to this important question.

The third category of treaties concerns those about which limited information **3.08**
is available. Thus, no express agreement was reached between Serbia-Montenegro and Sweden for the continuation of the old SFRY-Sweden BIT nor did they conclude a new BIT.[67] Tams is right to point out that the 'old BIT was clearly treated as applicable in proceedings between the European Commission and Sweden before the European Court of Justice'.[68] Thus, in that case rendered in 2009, the European Court of Justice:

> Declare[d] that, by not having taken appropriate steps to eliminate incompatibilities concerning the provisions on transfer of capital contained in the investment agreements concluded with (…) the former Socialist Federal Republic of Yugoslavia, the Kingdom of Sweden has failed to fulfill its obligations under the second paragraph of Article 307 EC.[69]

It is true that this passage of the decision suggests that the court considered the old BIT to be in force and binding on Sweden. However, the fact of the matter remains that the 'former Socialist Federal Republic of Yugoslavia' no longer existed as a sovereign State in 2009. The court does not identify the entity with which this old BIT was now in force. The UNCTAD website indicates that the BIT in force between Sweden and Serbia is the SFRY-Sweden BIT.[70] Since Serbia is the continuing State of Serbia-Montenegro, it can be logically presumed that the BIT was also in force with that State (and before that with the FRY). Yet, that does not explain *how* this BIT was continued between these States.

66 UNCTAD, available at: http://investmentpolicyhub.unctad.org/Download/TreatyFile/216.
67 Tams (n 27) 329.
68 Ibid., referring to European Court of Justice, *Commission of the European Communities v. Kingdom of Sweden*, Case C-249/06, 3 March 2009, available at: http://www.italaw.com/sites/default/files/case-documents/ita1010.pdf.
69 Ibid.
70 UNCTAD, available at: http://investmentpolicyhub.unctad.org/IIA/country/202/treaty/2894.

3.09 Canada entered into a new BIT with Serbia in 2014 (Serbia is the continuator of Serbia-Montenegro after the secession of Montenegro in 2006). This treaty remained silent on the fate of the SFRY-Canada BIT until then.[71] It can logically be presumed from such silence that the parties did *not* consider that the old SFRY-Canada BIT continued to apply after the date of succession. Yet, whether or not this is the case is unclear.

2.2 The practice of the Czech Republic regarding Czechoslovakia's BITs

3.10 As a result of the dissolution of Czechoslovakia (or CSFR) on January 1, 1993, two new States emerged as successor States: the Czech Republic and the Republic of Slovakia.[72] On the date of succession, Czechoslovakia was bound by some 2,000 bilateral treaties.[73] It should also be noted that both States became parties to the 1978 Vienna Convention in 1993 and explicitly declared, pursuant to Article 7(2)(3), that they would apply the Convention *retroactively* to their own succession (which occurred before the entry into force of the Convention).[74]

3.11 In accordance with Article 34 of the Convention, both new States adopted the general position of continuity regarding the bilateral treaties to which Czechoslovakia was a party before the date of succession.[75] The Czech Republic officially declared (in its Constitutional Law,[76] its 'Proclamation to all Parliaments and Nations of the World',[77] and in a letter sent to the UN Secretary-General[78]) that it would respect all obligations arising from Czechoslovakia's multilateral and bilateral treaties. The same types of declarations were made by

71 Tams (n 27) 329.

72 On 25 November 1992, the Czechoslovak Federal Assembly voted the Constitutional Act no. 542/1992 (which came into force on 8 December 1992) indicating that the Federation would cease to exist on 31 December 1992.

73 International Law Association, *Rapport Final sur la Succession en Matière de traités*, New Delhi Conference 2002, Committee on Aspects of the Law of State Succession, 9 [hereinafter 'ILA, Rapport Final, 2002'].

74 See: United Nations Treaty Collection, Chapter XXIII, Law of Treaties, available at: https://treaties.un.org/Pages/ViewDetails.aspx?src=TREATY&mtdsg_no=XXIII-2&chapter=23&clang=_en#EndDec.

75 Brigitte Stern, 'La succession d'États' (1996) 262 Rec des Cours 315; 316; J. Klabbers, M. Koskenniemi and A. Zimmermann (dirs), *Pilot Project on Documentation concerning State Practice relating to State Succession and Recognition*, (Council of Europe 1999) 110; V. Mikulka, 'Article 34', in Distefano, Gaggioli and Hêche (n 4), [122]–[124].

76 Constitutional Law No. 4/1993, proclaimed by the Czech Republic's National Council, 15 December 1992, see Art. 5.

77 Proclamation of the National Council of the Czech Republic to all Parliaments and Nations of the World, 17 December 1992, in: Klabbers et al (n 75).

78 Letter dated 16 February 1993, received by the Secretary-General on 22 February 1993, in: ILA, Rapport Final, 2002 (n 73) (dealing only with multilateral treaties).

Slovakia.[79] The Czech Republic notified all contracting parties and depositories of its automatic succession to these agreements.[80] The position of *other States* in response to the Czech and Slovak Republic's claims has varied. Some States seem to have accepted, as matter of principle, the position of automatic succession adopted by both new States.[81] This is, for instance, the position adopted by Germany regarding the Czech Republic.[82]

Tams explains that the Czech Republic agreed with other States for the continuation of all 16 BITs to which Czechoslovakia had been a party before the date of succession: **3.12**

> At the time of its dissolution, 16 BITs were in force for the CSFR. (…) Following independence, the Czech Republic and its treaty partners clarified the future application of bilateral treaties concluded with the CSFR. In 14 of the 16 cases, the Czech Republic and its respective treaty partner explicitly agreed that the prior CSFR BIT would continue to apply, typically by including the prior treaty on a list of treaties that would 'remain in force': agreements along the lines were reached with the Netherlands, Austria, Switzerland, Germany, France, the United Kingdom, the United States, as well as Denmark, Finland, Spain, Sweden, Greece, Norway, the United States and the Belgium-Luxembourg Economic Union.[83]

For Tams, 'when addressing the fate of prior BITs, the Czech Republic and its treaty partners opted for a near-absolute continuity'.[84] It is true that such agreements show a general desire by the States involved for the *continuity* of BITs.[85] This is certainly because the Czech Republic is formally a party to the

79 Declaration on the Sovereignty of the Slovak Republic, adopted by the Slovak National Council, 17 July 1992; Constitution of the Slovak Republic, adopted on 3 September 1992, Art. 153; Proclamation of the National Council of the Slovak Republic to Parliaments and Peoples of the World, 3 December 1992; Letter of 19 May 1993 to the UN Secretary-General, in: ILA, Resolution no. 3/2008 (n 52) at point no. 9.

80 The procedure was adopted under a resolution dated 24 February 1993. I am very grateful to Mr. Tomáš Fecák (Konečná & Zacha, Attorneys at Law) for having provided me with valuable information on this topic. See also, the same position adopted by Slovakia: ILA, Resolution no. 3/2008 (n 52) point no. 12.

81 Klabbers et al (n 75) 112, 116. See also: Report of the Czech Republic in: Klabbers (n 75), 440, 462–3 (providing a number of examples).

82 Report of the Czech Republic in: Klabbers et al (n 75) 462.

83 Tams (n 27) 330.

84 Ibid., see also, 331: 'when discussing the fate of a prior treaty, the Czech Republic, Serbia and Montenegro and their respective treaty partners have almost inevitably opted for some form of continuity – typically by agreeing that an old BIT should continue to apply, alternatively by replacing it with a new one'. See also: ILA, Rapport Final, 2002 (n 73) 11.

85 Mikulka (n 75) [124]:

> La pratique concernant les traités bilatéraux de l'ancienne Tchécoslovaquie montre, dans sa quasi-totalité, le maintien en vigueur des traités dans les relations entre la République tchèque ou la Slovaquie d'une part, et les autres Etats parties d'autre part. Les documents reflétant les résultats des consultations que chaque Etat successeur a menées avec les autres Etats parties auxdits traités, ainsi que d'autres échanges effectués par

1978 Vienna Convention which provides under Article 34 (as further discussed below[86]) for the automatic continuation of treaties in the context of a dissolution of State. Moreover, the Czech Republic has expressly decided to give a *retroactive* application to the Convention, thereby applying Article 34 with regards to *its own* succession. Importantly, all examples referred to in the Report of the Czech Republic submitted to the Council of Europe for its Pilot Project mention the existence of exchange of letters, diplomatic correspondence and/or consultation between the parties to decide the fate of these treaties.[87] Thus, the Czech Republic specifically informed each State about its intention to 'automatically' succeed to these treaties. These States have, in turn, deemed it necessary to respond to such claims[88] and to *confirm* their position as to the continuation of these treaties.[89] This exchange of letters can be explained by obvious reasons of legal certainty. The very fact that such exchanges of letters and negotiations took place between the Czech Republic and these 14 States suggests that they have worked under the presumption that old Czechoslovakia BITs would *not* have continued to apply *automatically* without their explicit consent.[90] This feature does not support the position of automatic succession set out at Article 34 of the Convention.

3.13 Tams further explains that in the two remaining instances (the CSFR-China and CSFR-Canada BITs), new BITs were concluded and that 'both of these new BITs expressly terminated (and thus replaced) the treaties agreed with the CSFR'.[91] He concludes that this 'suggest[s] that the old BITs had not simply ceased to apply' at the date of succession.[92] In January 2012, Canada entered

---

diverses voies diplomatiques, confirment que les traités bilatéraux sont restés en vigueur après la date de la dissolution et que le principe du maintien en vigueur des traités a été accepté comme étant le point de départ.

86 See, Chapter 5, Section 1.5.

87 Report of the Czech Republic in: Klabbers et al (n 75) 440ff, see also at 470; M. Koskenniemi, 'Report of the Director of Studies', in Pierre Michel Eisemann and Martti Koskenniemi (dir), *State Succession: Codification Tested Against the Facts* (Martinus Nijhoff Publ. 2000) 81; Mikulka (n 75) [124].

88 Report of the Czech Republic, providing, inter alia, the examples of Germany (at 462), Israel, (at 447), Japan (at 447) and South Korea (at 449). See also, many examples referred to in the Report of Slovakia, in: Klabbers et al (n 75) 508ff.

89 Klabbers et al (n 75) 112, 116; ILA, Rapport Final, 2002 (n 73) 11.

90 See also: Odysseas G. Repousis and James Fry, 'Armed Conflict and State Succession in Investor-State Arbitration' (2016) 23(3) *Columbia JEL* 440–41:

> Meanwhile, the Czech Republic and Slovakia have either continued to apply BITs concluded by Czechoslovakia or have entered into new BITs thus replacing older ones concluded by Czechoslovakia. All of the above indicate that for those treaties concluded by Czechoslovakia, a smooth transition took place that nevertheless departs from the default 'automatic' approach of Article 34 VCST.

91 Tams (n 27) 330.

92 Ibid.

into in a BIT with the Czech Republic.[93] Article 15(7) of the BIT makes it clear that the States agreed for the continuation of the Czechoslovakia-Canada BIT. Thus, the new BIT indicates that:

> Upon the entry into force of this Agreement [i.e., the *new* BIT], the Agreement between the Government of Canada and the Government of the Czech and Slovak Federal Republic for the Promotion and Protection of Investments, done at Prague on 15 November 1990 [i.e., the *old* BIT], *insofar as it is now an Agreement between Canada and the Czech Republic*, shall be terminated except that its provisions shall continue to apply to any dispute between either Contracting Party and an investor of the other Contracting Party that has been submitted to arbitration pursuant to that Agreement by the investor prior to the date that this Agreement enters into force. Apart from any such dispute, this Agreement shall apply retroactively, in particular the procedures outlined in Article X (Settlement of Disputes between an Investor and the Host Contracting Party).[94]

The phrase 'insofar as it is now an Agreement between Canada and the Czech Republic' contained in that clause clearly indicates that the parties considered that between the date of succession and the entry into force of the *new* BIT (2012), the *old* BIT had *continued* to apply between the parties for almost ten years.[95] This is a clear example when the parties have endorsed the continuity approach.

2.3 The practice of Kosovo regarding Serbia's BITs

At the time of Kosovo's declaration of independence (2008), Serbia was a **3.14**
party to 41 BITs.[96] Since its declaration of independence, Kosovo has signed ten BITs (or other investment protection instruments) of its own with Albania, Turkey, Austria, the Belgium-Luxembourg Economic Union, Switzerland, United States, Macedonia, Croatia, Montenegro, Kuwait and Qatar.[97] Six of these States were parties to BITs with Serbia in 2008. In addition, Kosovo made a general unilateral declaration of succession to the treaties to which Yugoslavia and the FRY had been parties.[98] However, in practice,

93 Agreement Between Canada and the Czech Republic for the Promotion and Protection of Investments, signed on 6 May 2009, into force on 22 January 2012.

94 Ibid., Art. 15(7) (emphasis added).

95 See, Tams (n 27) 330–31.

96 Dupont (n 42) 937.

97 Kosovo, 'Agreements on promotion and protection of investments', Investment Promotion Agency of Kosovo, available at: http://www.invest-ks.org/en/Legislation-and-Agreements.

98 Kosovo's Declaration of Independence, 17 February 2008, available at: http://www.assembly-kosova.org/?cid=2,128,1635. See, para. 9 indicating that the democratically-elected representatives of the people of Kosovo have: [U]ndertake[n] the international obligations of Kosovo, including (…) treaty and other obligations of the former Socialist Federal Republic of Yugoslavia to which we are bound as a former constituent part, including the Vienna conventions on diplomatic and consular relations'. See also: Qerimi and Krasniqi (n 38)

Kosovo contacted and negotiated with each State individually regarding the continuation of these treaties.[99] Kosovo has thus made a number of exchanges of notes with States who had entered into BITs with the SFRY (or the FRY and Serbia-Montenegro) before its dissolution. For instance, the exchange of notes between Kosovo and the Czech Republic indicates that the two States had negotiated the fate of the treaties that the Czech Republic and the FRY or Serbia-Montenegro were a party to.[100] Based on these negotiations, Kosovo proposed that a number of treaties (including the BIT) contained in an annex to the letter 'remain in force' between Kosovo and the Czech Republic. Kosovo also 'proposed that this note and the answering note constitute the agreement on the state of bilateral treaties' between the two States. In a subsequent letter, the Czech Republic agreed. The same type of exchanges of letters with Germany refers to the 1989 BIT with the former SFRY which 'shall continue in force in relation between Kosovo and Germany'.[101] The same solution of continuity was also applied by France regarding the France-SFRY BIT.[102] Interestingly, the same type of exchange of letters was done with the United Kingdom, but the list of treaties does not include the 2002 UK-FRY BIT.[103] This is a rather unique case where the parties have expressly agreed on the *non-continuation* of a BIT.

1652 ('the Paragraph in the Declaration of Independence concerning succession should be most properly conceived as a unilateral declaration providing for the continuance in force of the treaties in respect of its territory in the meaning of Article 9 of the 1978 Vienna Convention on Succession to Treaties'). On this question, see more generally: V. Osmani-Sadriu, *Treaty Application in Kosovo Through Rules of Succession and as Domestic Law: The Example of the CISG* (University of Pittsburgh, Ph.D. Thesis 2015), available at: http://d-scholarship.pitt.edu/25029; Tai-Heng Cheng, 'State Succession and Commercial Obligations: Lessons from Kosovo', in Mahnoush Arsanjani et al (eds), *Looking to the Future: Essays on International Law in Honor of W. Michael Reisman* (Nijhoff 2010), 675–703.

99 See: Qerimi and Krasniqi (n 38) 1639:

> The Ministry of Foreign Affairs of Kosovo addressed a Note Verbal to all Embassies, Liaison and Diplomatic Offices accredited in Kosovo, and to the Foreign Ministries of all States that recognize Kosovo but do not have a representation within the State, asking for a list and the texts of concerned treaties. The Ministry has received lists from a number of States, and most include the texts of the treaties. After studying the replies, the Ministry proposed several *Exchange of Notes* on treaty succession. To date, the treaty succession agreements with Austria, Belgium, Czech Republic, Finland, Germany, and the United Kingdom have been concluded.

See also: I. Panoussis, 'La succession d'États aux traités à l'épreuve du cas kosovar', in Distefano, Gaggioli and Hêche (n 4), 1879–80.

100 Decree for Ratification of the Agreements, Exchange of Notes, Republic of Kosovo-Czech Republic, Mar. 30, 2011, available at: http://www.mfa-ks.net/repository/docs/Marreveshja_Ks-Ceki_(anglisht).pdf.

101 Decree for Ratification of the Agreements, Exchange of Notes, Kosovo-Federal Republic of Germany, Sept. 2, 2011, available at: http://www.mfa-ks.net/repository/docs/Marr._Ks-Gjermani_(shkembimi_i_notave)_DMN-18_(anglisht).pdf. See also in: *Federal Gazette* (Bundesgesetzblatt) 2011, vol. II, 748.

102 See: Decree no. 2103–349, 24 April 2013, available at: http://basedoc.diplomatie.gouv.fr/exl-php/cadcgp.php?CMD=CHERCHE&QUERY=1&MODELE=vues/mae_internet___traites/home.html&VUE=mae_internet___traites&NOM=cadic__anonyme&FROM_LOGIN=1.

103 Decree for Ratification of the Agreements, Exchange of Notes, Kosovo-United Kingdom, Decree DMN-028–2010, available at: http://www.mfa-ks.net/repository/docs/Marrveshja_Ks-Mbretrine_e_Bashkuar_(028)_(anglisht).pdf.

In sum, Kosovo's practice with other States does not support any proposition in favor of the *automatic* continuation of treaties.[104] Out of the 41 States which had signed a BIT with Serbia when Kosovo declared its independence, only a few have decided to continue the instrument afterward. They have done so by exchanging letters confirming treaty continuation. One reason why States may have been less keen on following the continuation pattern is the remaining controversial status of Kosovo as an independent State. Those States which have recognized the new State were unsurprisingly less reticent towards continuation. It is interesting in that context to note that in an exchange of letters Belgium considered Kosovo 'as one of the successor States to the Republic of Yugoslavia, and as such all bilateral agreements made prior to UNSCC 1244 (1999) remain active' (which included no BITs).[105] **3.15**

2.4 The practice of new States in the context of the break-up of the USSR

The present section will first briefly examine the general question of succession to treaties in the context of the break-up of the USSR. I will then analyse specifically the fate of BITs to which the USSR was a party. **3.16**

The break-up was officially completed at the end of 1991 with the establishment of the 'Commonwealth of Independent States' (CIS).[106] It was agreed among the former Republics (with the exception of the three Baltic States) that Russia would be considered as the 'continuator' of the international legal personality of the USSR in international organizations, including the United Nations.[107] **3.17**

104 Panoussis (n 99) 1889.

105 See, letter of 9 Sept 2009 of Belgium's Head of Mission in Kosovo, available at: http://www.mfa-ks.net/repository/docs/5-french.pdf.

106 The CIS was first formed by Russia, Belarus and Ukraine on the basis of the Minsk Agreement of 8 December 1991: The Agreement Establishing the Commonwealth of Independent States, 13 December 1991, UN Doc. A/46/771, in (1992) 31 ILM 138. As a result of the Declaration of Alma Ata, 21 December 1991, UN Doc. A/46/60, in (1992) 31 ILM 147, the CIS was expanded to other former Republics (except for Baltic States), with Georgia joining in October 1993.

107 Declaration of Alma Ata, ibid. See also: Decision by the Council of Heads of State of the Commonwealth of Independent States, 21 December 1991, in (1992) 31 ILM 151: '[t]he States of the Commonwealth support Russia's continuance of the membership of the Union of Soviet Socialist Republics in the United Nations, including permanent membership of the Security Council and other international organizations'; Letter of Russia's President Yeltsin to the UN Secretary-General, 24 December 1991, UN Doc 1991/RUSSIA (24 December 1991), Appendix in: (1992) 31 ILM 138.

3.18 The legal qualification of the dismemberment of the USSR in 1991 is controversial.[108] It has been suggested by many writers that because Russia is the continuing State of the USSR, all other former Republics (with the exception of the Baltic States) seceded from the Union.[109] The affirmation that Russia is the continuing State of the USSR is clearly based on a legal fiction.[110] Thus, the USSR did, in fact, cease to exist in 1991 as a result of both the Declaration of Alma Ata and the Minsk Agreement.[111] Logically, Russia could not continue the existence of a State which had ceased to exist;[112] there is no 'resurrection' of States in international law.[113] It should therefore be understood that the break-up of the USSR is a case of State dissolution.[114] Yet, it may be that these statements were merely *political* and not meant to result in the actual dissolution of the USSR.[115] In any event, the fact remains that all States concerned (including Russia itself) have viewed Russia as the *continuing State* of the USSR. Thus, in their *actual practice*, States have considered the break-up of the USSR as a series of 'secessions' by the former Soviet Republics (except for the three Baltic States[116]).[117]

3.19 In spite of the general statement of continuity contained in the Alma Ata Declaration,[118] the practice of secessionist States with respect to *multilateral* treaties has been anything but uniform.[119] While some new States have

---

108 This question is examined in detail in: I. Ziemele, 'Is the Distinction between State Continuity and State Succession Reality or Fiction? The Russian Federation, the Federal Republic of Yugoslavia and Germany', (2001) 1 *Baltic YIL* 194.

109 W. Czaplinski, 'La continuité, l'identité et la succession d'États-évaluation de cas récents', (1993) 26 RBDI 388; Photini Pazartzis, *La succession d'Etats aux traités multilatéraux à la lumière des mutations territoriales récentes*, (Pedone 2002) 55–6; Mullerson (n 18) 19.

110 Pierre Michel Eisemann, 'Rapport du Directeur de la section de langue française du Centre', in Pierre Michel Eisemann and Martti Koskenniemi (n 87), 40; Eric Wyler, 'Le droit de la succession d'États à l'épreuve de la fiction juridique', in Distefano, Gaggioli and Hêche (n 4), 1632; V. Bilkova, 'La succession aux traités internationaux suite à la dissolution des fédérations ex-socialistes après 1990', ibid., 1820–21.

111 The preamble to the Minsk Agreement (n 106) clearly states that the USSR 'as a subject of international law and geopolitical reality no longer exists'. The Declaration of Alma Ata (n 106) also mentions that 'with the establishment of the C.I.S., the U.S.S.R. ceases to exist'.

112 For this reason, a number of writers have argued that Russia is *not* the 'continuator' of the USSR but a new State: R. Rich, 'Recognition of States: The Collapse of Yugoslavia and the Soviet Union', (1993) 4(1) EJIL 45; Y.Z. Blum, 'Russia Takes over the Soviet Union's Seat at the United Nations', (1993) 3(2) EJIL 357–9.

113 K. Marek, *Identity and Continuity of States in Public International Law* (Droz 1968), 6.

114 Stern, 'La succession d'États' (n 75) 220–22.

115 M. Shaw, 'State Succession Revisited', (1994) 5 *Finnish YIL* 49–50; J. Crawford, *The Creation of States in International Law* 2nd edn (OUP 2006) 677–8.

116 L. Mälksoo, *Illegal Annexation and State Continuity: The Case of the Incorporation of the Baltic States by the USSR (A Study of the Tension between Normativity and Power in International Law)* (Martinus Nijhoff 2003), 255–6.

117 Ziemele (n 108) 194.

118 This question is further discussed below at Chapter 4, Section 2.1.2.2.

119 Pazartzis (n 109) 78; Y. Gammara, 'Current Questions of State Succession Relating to Multilateral Treaties', in Eisemann and Koskennemi (n 87), 387, 414–19; Mikulka (n 75) [114].

become parties to the multilateral treaties of the USSR by way of accession,[120] others have declared themselves to be automatically bound by these treaties.[121] Overall, this confusing practice does not support the principle of 'automatic' succession to multilateral treaties.[122] The same conclusion can be reached regarding *bilateral* treaties.[123] The practice of the former Republics has been anything but uniform.[124]

The response by the *other States parties* to the treaties with the USSR has also varied.[125] Some States have applied the clean slate position.[126] This is, for instance, the position adopted by France[127] and Austria.[128] Others took the view that the former Republics were 'automatically' bound by these treaties.[129] This is, for instance, the position adopted by Germany. But, even in this case, the 'continuation' of treaties was often subject to *negotiations* between the **3.20**

120 A. Zimmermann, 'Secession and the Law of State Succession', in M.G. Kohen (ed), *Secession: International Law Perspectives* (CUP 2006) 215.

121 Pazartzis (n 109) 78–80.

122 Ibid.; T. Langstrom, 'The Dissolution of The Soviet Union in the Light of the 1978 Vienna Convention on Succession of States in Respect of Treaties', in Eisemann and Koskenniemi (n 87), 775:

> The practice analyzed does not support the view that in the case of dissolution of a State an *ipso jure* continuity rule would regulate the fate of the predecessor's treaties with regard to each successor State. Succession by the former Soviet republics to the treaties of their predecessor did not occur without an expression of will by the successor State concerned. Even when all plausible cases of exceptions to the main rule of Article 34 are eliminated, we are left with the chronology of depositary statistics. Not all successors have become parties to all treaties of the former USSR. Some States have become parties earlier, some later, succeeding to one treaty but acceding to another. The conclusion remains that the succession to the treaties of the former USSR, when it did occur, took place pursuant to a successor State's will to be bound.

123 ILA, Rapport Final, 2002 (n 73) 15; Mikulka (n 75) [116].

124 Pazartzis (n 109) 78–80; Mikulka (n 75) [114]; Koskenniemi (n 87) 75–6:

> Treaty succession proper concerns only the remaining 11 former Soviet Republics. In the Alma Ata Declaration of 21 December 1991, they declared that they would (...). However, this has not been fully followed in practice. Much has been obscured by the divergencies in the notifications of succession filed by these States. Often the new republics deposited notifications of succession indicating that they regarded themselves automatically bound by obligations of the former USSR. Sometimes they have limited succession to treaties that do not contradict their domestic laws.

125 ILA, Rapport Final, 2002 (n 73) 15; Mikulka (n 75) [116]; Langstrom (n 122) 775; Klabbers et al (n 75) 100.

126 See, the analysis in: Klabbers et al (n 75) 100–102, 114. See also: Koskenniemi and Letho (n 38), 208, 212, 217–18, explaining that the practice of Finland has been to enter into negotiations with the former Republics regarding the fate of the treaties which had been signed by the USSR.

127 H. Hamant, *Démembrement de l'URSS et problèmes de succession d'États* (Bruylant 2007), 240; ILA, Rapport Final, 2002 (n 73) 20:

> La France examine au cas pas cas les différents traités bilatéraux: dans la mesure où cet examen attentif peut prendre un certain temps, il est arrivé que, en cas d'urgence, soit confirmé par échange de lettres que telle ou telle convention reste en vigueur, c'est le cas d'un échange de lettres entre la France et le Turkménistan, concernant un accord bilatéral en matière fiscale.

128 ILA, Rapport Final, 2002 (n 73) 19.

129 See, the analysis of the position of several States in: Hamant (n 127) 237ff; J Klabbers et al (n 75) 100.

parties.[130] Thus, in the context of Germany, the 'automatic' continuity of treaties was nevertheless *confirmed* by *both parties* in common declarations or in exchanges of diplomatic notes.[131] The United Kingdom, Belgium and Poland have also adopted a position in favour of a presumption of continuity of bilateral treaties.[132] But again, all three States expressly *confirmed* such intention with the new States.[133] Similarly, while the United States adopted a general position in favour of the application of a presumption of continuity of treaties,[134] it has nevertheless entered into negotiation with each new States to determine which bilateral treaties should continue in force.[135] Such diverse practice by other parties does not support the principle of 'automatic' succession to bilateral treaties.[136]

3.21 The present writer has examined the fate of BITs specifically. At the time of its break-up, the USSR was a party to 14 BITs with the following States: United Kingdom, Switzerland, Belgium-Luxembourg, Spain, Netherlands, South Korea, Germany, France, Finland, Canada, Austria, Turkey, Denmark and China. Since Russia is the continuing State of the USSR all States have

130 Hamant (n 127) 239; Koskenniemi (n 87) 83–4; Mikulka (n 75) [116]: 'concernant les traités bilatéraux, plusieurs Etats européens, partant du principe que ces traités restaient automatiquement en vigueur entre eux et les Etats successeurs de l'URSS, *se sont mutuellement assurés de ce fait* avec les Etats successeurs concernés' (emphasis added).

131 Koskenniemi (n 87) 84.

132 Hamant (n 127) 238.

133 Ibid.; ILA, Rapport Final, 2002 (n 73) 20.

134 E.D. Williamson, 'State Succession and Relations with Federal States', (1992) 86 *ASIL Proc.* 12–13:

> [W]e have decided that the better legal position is to presume continuity in treaty relations between the United States and the former Soviet republics ... . [C]ontinuity of treaty relations is supported by our reading of state practice and by the policy considerations underlying the rule. Perhaps more importantly, continuity has been supported by the republics themselves. They affirmed this approach in the Alma Ata Declaration in December ... That the former republics themselves agreed to the result we have been seeking through principles of international law is the most important factor.

See also: E.D. Williamson and J.E. Osborn, 'A U.S. Perspective on Treaty Succession and Related Issues in the Wake of the Break-up of the U.S.S.R. and Yugoslavia', (1992) 33 *Virginia JIL* 264.

135 Williamson, ibid., 13; Williamson and Osborn, ibid., 267:

> As a practical matter, given the unsettled nature of the governing legal rules and the diversity of agreements in question, we concluded that the only way to establish clearly what agreements would remain in force for the former Soviet Union would be an explicit, case-by-case review of outstanding agreements with each of the former republics. Beginning in mid-1992, the Bush Administration engaged in just such a process with the republics in order to confirm which of the bilateral agreements would continue in force, and to determine which should be modified or terminated. In the interim, the United States regards the various agreements as continuing in force with all the republics, unless and until it makes a clear determination to the contrary.

See also: P.R Williams, 'The Treaty Obligations of the Successor States of the Former Soviet Union, Yugoslavia and Czechoslovakia: Do They Remain in Force' (1994–1995) 23 *Denver JILP* 24–5.

136 Langstrom (n 122) 775: 'As far as bilateral relations are concerned, adjustments and negotiations were needed, even in cases where both States proceeded from the presumption of continuity.' See also: Tai-Heng Cheng, *State Succession and Commercial Obligations* (Transnational Publ. 2006) 356.

considered that the old BITs signed with the USSR were now binding on Russia (and in some cases, the parties have subsequently signed new BITs). The practice of the 11 former Republics as successor States and that of the other States parties to the old BITs of the USSR is more diverse. Yet (as further discussed at the end of this section), some clear patterns can be distinguished. Based on the publicly available information found at the UNCTAD website and in the Official Journal of the European Union (based on notifications submitted by the Member States to the Commission),[137] the practice of each former Republic can be summarized as follows:[138]

- Ukraine signed new BITs with all 14 States;
- Armenia signed new BITs with ten States; Armenia and Spain have considered the Spain-USSR BIT to be still in force between them;[139]
- Belarus signed new BITs with all States (except one[140]); Belarus and Spain have considered the Spain-USSR BIT to be still in force between them;[141] Belarus and Belgium-Luxembourg took the same position regarding the Belgium-Luxembourg-USSR BIT[142] (a new treaty was signed between them, but has not yet entered into force[143]);
- Azerbaijan signed new BITs with all States (except for three[144]); Azerbaijan and Spain have considered the Spain-USSR BIT to be still in force between them;[145]
- Turkmenistan signed new BITs with six States and none with six other States (for which I have found no indicia of continuity of the old USSR

137 UNCTAD, available at: http://investmentpolicyhub.unctad.org. See also: EU, 'List of the bilateral investment agreements referred to in Article 4(1) of Regulation (EU) No 1219/2012 of the European Parliament and of the Council of 12 December 2012 establishing transitional arrangements for bilateral investment agreements between Member States and third countries (2014/C 169/01)', 5 June 2014, Official Journal of the European Union, C 169/1, available at: http://eur-lex.europa.eu/legal-content/FR/TXT/?uri=CELEX%3A52014XC0605(01) [hereinafter 'EU, 'List of BITs']. Under Art. 2 of Regulation (EU) No 1219/2012 adopted by the European Parliament and the Council on 12 December 2012, the Member States had the obligations to notify the Commission 'of all bilateral investment agreements with third countries (…) that they either wish to maintain in force or permit to enter into force under this Chapter'.

138 One Ph.D. thesis has recently examined the question of the former Republics' succession to the BITs signed by the USSR: Aima Samatova, *Die Auswirkungen der Staatensukzession auf bilaterale Investitionsschutzabkommen* (The impact of State succession on bilateral investment agreements), Vienna University, 2017.

139 See: EU, 'List of BITs' (n 137); UNCTAD, http://investmentpolicyhub.unctad.org/Download/TreatyFile/5118.

140 The only exception is Canada which does not have a BIT with Belarus. The Belarus-France BIT (signed in 1993) is not in force.

141 See: EU, 'List of BITs' (n 137); UNCTAD, http://investmentpolicyhub.unctad.org/IIA/country/18/treaty/3758.

142 See: EU, 'List of BITs' (n 137); UNCTAD, http://investmentpolicyhub.unctad.org/IIA/country/18/treaty/3637.

143 http://investmentpolicyhub.unctad.org/IIA/country/19/treaty/404.

144 Canada, Netherlands and Denmark.

145 See: EU, 'List of BITs' (n 137); UNCTAD, http://investmentpolicyhub.unctad.org/IIA/country/197/treaty/3757.

BIT); Turkmenistan and Spain have considered the Spain-USSR BIT to be still in force between them;[146] Turkmenistan and Belgium-Luxembourg took the same position regarding the Belgium-Luxembourg-USSR BIT;[147]

- Georgia signed new BITs with all States (except for three[148]); Georgia and Spain have considered the Spain-USSR BIT to be still in force between them;[149]
- Moldova signed new BITs with all States (except for three[150]);
- Uzbekistan signed new BITs with all States (except for two[151]);
- Kazakhstan signed new BITs with all States, except for Canada.[152] Yet, in *WWM v. Kazakhstan*, the Tribunal concluded that Kazakhstan was bound by the BIT which had been signed by the USSR based on existing elements of tacit consent by both States;
- Kyrgyzstan signed new BITs with all States (except for two[153]); Kyrgyzstan and Spain have considered the Spain-USSR BIT to be still in force between them;[154] Kyrgyzstan and Belgium-Luxembourg took the same position regarding the Belgium-Luxembourg-USSR BIT.[155]
- Tajikistan signed new BITs with all States (except for four[156]); Tajikistan and Spain have considered the Spain-USSR BIT to be still in force between them;[157] Tajikistan and Belgium-Luxembourg took the same position regarding the Belgium-Luxembourg-USSR BIT[158] (a new treaty was signed between them, but has not yet entered into force[159]); Tajikistan and Austria have signed a new BIT in 2012;[160] The treaty

---

146 See: EU, 'List of BITs' (n 137); UNCTAD, http://investmentpolicyhub.unctad.org/IIA/country/197/treaty/2954.

147 See: EU, 'List of BITs' (n 137); UNCTAD, http://investmentpolicyhub.unctad.org/IIA/country/215/treaty/3643.

148 Canada, South Korea and Denmark.

149 See: EU, 'List of BITs' (n 137); UNCTAD, http://investmentpolicyhub.unctad.org/IIA/country/77/treaty/1670.

150 Canada, South Korea and Denmark.

151 Canada and Denmark.

152 Canada and Kazakhstan have apparently since 2001 been negotiating a new BIT: http://international.gc.ca/trade-commerce/trade-agreements-accords-commerciaux/agr-acc/kazakhstan/fipa-apie/background-contexte.aspx?lang=eng.

153 Canada, Netherlands. The BIT signed with Austria is not in force yet, neither is the one with Denmark.

154 See: EU, 'List of BITs' (n 137); UNCTAD, http://investmentpolicyhub.unctad.org/IIA/country/197/treaty/3756.

155 See: EU, 'List of BITs' (n 137); UNCTAD, http://investmentpolicyhub.unctad.org/IIA/country/113/treaty/3639.

156 Canada, Finland, Denmark and the United Kingdom.

157 See: EU, 'List of BITs' (n 137); UNCTAD, http://investmentpolicyhub.unctad.org/IIA/country/197/treaty/2950.

158 See: EU, 'List of BITs' (n 137); UNCTAD, http://investmentpolicyhub.unctad.org/IIA/country/206/treaty/3641.

159 UNCTAD, http://investmentpolicyhub.unctad.org/IIA/country/19/treaty/540.

160 UNCTAD, http://investmentpolicyhub.unctad.org/Download/TreatyFile/3308.

does not refer to the Austria-USSR BIT. The UNCTAD website refers to the Austria-USSR BIT with the mention 'terminated' and 'Replaced by new treaty' at the same date as the entry into force of the new BIT.[161] Such a reference suggests that the parties considered the old BIT to have continued to be in force until the new BIT was signed in 2012.

Several aspects of State practice just examined are noteworthy. **3.22**

First, the overall practice of States shows that they have clearly favoured the solution of continuity of investment protection found in BITs. Thus, only in a small minority of cases have new States and the other States parties been inactive regarding the BIT protections which existed under old BITs signed by the USSR. This is the case for only 40 out of 154 possible treaty relationships. What is noticeable is that Canada has only signed two BITs with the former republics. Similarly, Denmark has only signed three BITs with them (one of which is not in force). This position contrasts with the approach adopted by all other States parties to BITs to which the USSR was a party which have signed new BITs with almost all former Republics. Thus, the States concerned have signed new treaties 74 per cent of the time (114 treaties out of a total of 154 possible treaty relationships). **3.23**

Secondly, while the States concerned have favoured the solution of continuity of BIT protection overwhelmingly, what is interesting is the way this goal was achieved. In the vast majority of instances, the old treaty relationship involving the USSR was simply replaced by new BITs signed with the former republics. These new instruments contain no indications that the parties have considered that the old BITs with the USSR were binding on them in the period between the independence of new States and the signature of the new treaties. In fact, these instruments do not contain any reference at all to the USSR's BITs. The websites of the States concerned (and the UNCTAD website) also contain no indication of any continuation of old BITs. In sum, in general (apart from two examples mentioned in the next paragraphs), there is no information available suggesting that the States concerned considered that the old BITs to which the USSR was a party *automatically* survived the break-up of the Federation. **3.24**

Thirdly, I have found a number of instances where, on the contrary, the States concerned have considered that the old BITs to which the USSR was a party were continuing to be binding on them after the break-up. These cases **3.25**

161 UNCTAD, http://investmentpolicyhub.unctad.org/IIA/country/206/treaty/278. The page indicates that the old BIT was terminated on 21 Dec. 2012 and was 'replaced by new treaty'. That date is indeed the date of the entry into force of the new BIT.

represent less than 10 per cent of the examples reviewed. Interestingly, this practice of BITs continuation has been adopted by two States.[162] Spain has thus considered the 1990 BIT signed with the USSR[163] to be continuing and binding on seven former Republics (Armenia, Azerbaijan, Belarus, Georgia, Kirghizstan, Tajikistan, and Turkmenistan).[164] Belgium-Luxembourg has considered the 1989 BIT with the USSR[165] as still in force with four former Republics (Belarus, Kyrgyzstan, Tajikistan, Turkmenistan).[166] It should be added, that Belgium-Luxembourg has signed new BITs with two of these States (Belarus and Tajikistan), but that they are not yet in force. Another important point is that these two States have not systematically adopted such a continuation approach. Thus, Spain signed new BITs with four other former Republics and Belgium-Luxembourg did the same with seven States. Overall, Spain and Belgium-Luxembourg have thus adopted this continuation approach for about half of their treaty partners.

3.26 It is not entirely clear why Spain and Belgium-Luxembourg have decided to adopt this position of continuation of BITs with some States and not with others. It should be recalled that EU Member States were under the obligation pursuant to Regulation No 1219/2012 to notify the Commission about the existence of their BITs with third countries entered into before 1 December 2009.[167] At that time, Spain was party to four new BITs with former Republics. One possibility is that in its notification to the Commission, Spain simply list the names of all the other former Republics with which it had *not* entered into BITs in 2009 as being bound by the Spain-USSR BIT. It may be that Belgium-Luxembourg followed the same approach regarding the Belgium-Luxembourg-USSR BIT.

3.27 If it were to be the case, such listing of the name of States next to a treaty should be considered as 'unilateral declarations' by these two countries on the matter (the question of the nature and effect of such declarations is examined below[168]). In other words, this would only show the position of these two States on the question of the continuation of BITs signed by the USSR. For

---

162 Reference should also be made to the USSR-Austria BIT which was also considered to be in force between Austria and Tajikistan until a new BIT entered into force between them.

163 Convenio de Fomento y Protección Recíproca de Inversiones entre España y la Unión de Repúblicas Socialistas Soviéticas, 26 October 1990.

164 See, EU, 'List of BITs' (n 137).

165 Accord entre les Gouvernements du Royaume de Belgique et du Grand-duché de Luxembourg et le Gouvernement de l'Union des républiques socialistes soviétiques, concernant l'encouragement et la protection réciproques des investissements, 9 February 1989.

166 See, EU, 'List of BITs' (n 137).

167 EU Regulation No 1219/2012.

168 See, Chapter 4, Section 2.1.1.

instance, Spain indicates on its website that it has BITs relationship with the seven former Republics mentioned above and refers expressly to the Spain-USSR BIT.[169] Interestingly, the webpage explains that such BIT continuation is actually based on the position initially taken by the former Republics themselves in the Declaration of Alma-Ata of December 1991[170] in favour of the continuity of all treaties to which the USSR was a party.[171] Yet, as further examined below,[172] *both* States (the new State and the other State party) must consent to the continuation of a treaty. Thus, it would have to be demonstrated that these seven former Republics have (expressly or tacitly) agreed to any such continuation. The position of Spain is that they have already done so under the Declaration of Alma-Ata of December 1991. Yet, as further discussed below,[173] the question as to whether any consent to be bound by a *specific* treaty can be deducted from such a general declaration regarding *all* treaties of the USSR is controversial. The issue is all the more confusing considering that very limited information is available on the actual position taken by the seven former Republics regarding the continuation of the Spain-USSR BIT. In any event, the websites of Armenia, Azerbaijan and Tajikistan do not list this BIT as being in force between the two States.[174]

---

169 Spain, Ministerio de Economía, Industria y Competitividad, Secretaría De Estado De Comercio, 'Acuerdos De Promocion Y Proteccion Reciproca De Inversiones', available at: http://www.comercio.es/es-ES/inversiones-exteriores/acuerdos-internacionales/acuerdos-promocion-proteccion-reciproca-inversiones-appris/Paginas/lista-appri-vigor.aspx.

170 Declaration of Alma Ata (n 106).

171 Spain, Ministerio de Economía (n 169), the footnote attached to each of the seven BITs reads as follows:

> De acuerdo con la Declaración de Alma-Ata de diciembre de 1991, los Estados sucesores de la URSS, que tras la extinción de la URSS se integraron en la Comunidad de Estados Independientes (CEI), han asumido el cumplimiento de las obligaciones internacionales derivadas de los tratados y acuerdos concluidos por la antigua Unión Soviética. En consecuencia, a excepción de Kazajstán, Ucrania, Uzbekistán y Moldavia, con los que después de 1991 España ha firmado nuevos APPRI, el APPRI con la URSS, en vigor desde el 28–11–1991, continua siendo de aplicación en Armenia, Azerbaiján, Bielorrusia, Georgia, Kirguizistán, Rusia, Tayikistán y Turkmenistán. (translation by the present author: 'According to the Declaration of Alma-Ata in December 1991, the successor States of the USSR, which after the Soviet Union had been dissolved into the Commonwealth of Independent States (CIS), have assumed compliance with international obligations arising from Treaties and agreements concluded by the former Soviet Union. As a result, with the exception of Kazakhstan, Ukraine, Uzbekistan and Moldova, with which, after 1991, Spain has signed new [BITs], [BITs] with the USSR, in force since 28–11–1991, continues to apply in Armenia, Azerbaijan, Belarus, Georgia, Kyrgyzstan, Russia, Tajikistan and Turkmenistan).

172 See, Chapter 5, Section 2.

173 See, Chapter 4, Section 2.1.2.2.

174 The webpage of the Ministry of Foreign Affairs of the Republic of Armenia concerning the bilateral relations between Spain and Armenia refers to seven treaties binding between the two States, but not to any agreement dealing with investment. See, document available at: http://www.mfa.am/en/country-by-country/es/. The webpage of the Ministry of Foreign Affairs of the Republic of Azerbaijan concerning the bilateral relations between Spain and Azerbaijan (available at: http://www.mfa.gov.az/files/file/Azerbaijan%20-%20Spain.pdf) refers to 'two documents' being signed by the two States, without indicating what these documents are. A similar webpage from the Ministry of Foreign Affairs of the Republic of Tajikistan

3.28 In sum, the practice of the former Republics and that of the other States parties to BITs to which the USSR was a party shows that they have overwhelmingly favoured the solution of continuity. In the vast majority of cases, the States concerned have signed new BITs. At first, the principle of 'automatic' continuity of treaties seems to have been adopted by both Belgium-Luxembourg and Spain regarding 11 treaty partners. Yet, Spain's position in favor of continuity seems to be based on the Republics' general consent to such treaty continuation. In other words, Spain's position does not support the principle of automatic continuation of BITs, but rather the idea that continuation is possible even without express consent.

2.5 The practice of Montenegro regarding Serbia-Montenegro's BITs

3.29 This author has examined the fate of BITs after Montenegro seceded from Serbia in 2006. As mentioned above,[175] at the time of the break-up of the SFRY in 1991, the country had entered into seven BITs.[176] I have already examined above what happened to these treaties with respect to the FRY (one of the successor States of the SFRY) which later changed its name to become the 'State Union of Serbia-Montenegro'. Since the break-up of the SFRY, the FRY (and later Serbia-Montenegro) has been very active in signing BITs. At the date of succession (June 2006), Serbia-Montenegro was a party to 36 BITs.[177] Serbia, as the continuing State after the separation of Montenegro, continued all of these treaties pursuant to Article 60(5) of the Serbia-Montenegro Constitution.[178] The question addressed in this section is what happened to these BITs regarding the new State of Montenegro.

3.30 Montenegro adopted a clear position in favour of succession to the treaties to which Serbia-Montenegro had been a party before the date of succession.[179]

(available at: http://mfa.tj/?l=en&cat=92&art=189) also refers to a Memorandum of Understanding signed between the two States, but is silent regarding any investment agreement.

175 See, Chapter 3, Section 2.1.

176 Tams (n 27) 329.

177 See, UNCTAD: http://investmentpolicyhub.unctad.org/IIA/CountryBits/187#iiaInnerMenu. Serbia-Montenegro had also signed six BITs which were however not in force at the date of succession.

178 Article 60(5) of the Serbia-Montenegro Constitution reads as follows: 'The member-state which resorts to the right to secession shall not inherit the right to personality under international law, while all disputes shall be separately regulated by the state-successor and the seceded state.' See also, letter of 16 June 2006 sent to the UN Secretary-General in which Serbia explained that it 'continue[d] to exercise its rights and honour its commitments deriving from international treaties concluded by Serbia and Montenegro' and requested that 'the Republic of Serbia be considered a party to all international agreements in force, instead of Serbia and Montenegro'.

179 Article 3 of the Declaration of Independence states that Montenegro 'shall establish and develop bilateral relations with the third states on the basic principles of the international law, accepting the rights and obligations stemming from existing arrangements and shall continue with active policy of good-neighbourly relations and regional cooperation'. See also, Article 3 of the Decision on Proclamation of Independence of

Montenegro's general statement was soon followed by concrete actions. It undertook the exercise of examining international treaties to decide which ones it wished to be bound by.[180] In October 2006, Montenegro sent a letter to the UN Secretary-General stating that it had 'decided to succeed to the treaties to which the State Union of Serbia and Montenegro was a party or signatory'.[181] Yet, there exists limited public information available about the position of Montenegro and that of the other States parties regarding the BITs. Based on the available information on the UNCTAD and EU websites, and that of a few other countries, three clear patterns have emerged.

The first pattern is what appears to be the non-continuation of BITs.[182] Thus, the UNCTAD's list of Montenegro BITs does not refer to any instrument being signed or in force between the new State and 17 States.[183] I have found no other information indicating the existence of any BIT relationship between Montenegro and these States. Given such a lack of information it is difficult to determine whether these States actually consider these BITs to be in force between them. **3.31**

The second pattern concerns signing new BITs. Belgium-Luxembourg, Finland, Turkey, and Macedonia (FYROM) have signed new BITs with Montenegro.[184] These new BITs do not mention the old BITs to which the predecessor State was a party. They do not offer any clue on the position of the parties regarding the application of these instruments in the 'interim period', i.e., between the date of succession and the date of the signature of the new BIT. **3.32**

The third pattern is that of BITs continuation. A number of States (14) have considered that the BIT that they had signed with Serbia-Montenegro would **3.33**

the Republic of Montenegro passed by the National Assembly on 3 June 2006: '[t]he Republic of Montenegro shall apply and adhere to international treaties and agreements that the state union of Serbia and Montenegro was party to and that relate to the Republic of Montenegro and are in conformity with its legal order'.

180 The website of the Ministry of Foreign Affairs explains the process, in some detail, in a document entitled 'Information on international multilateral conventions that Montenegro accessed or is in process of accessing', available at: http://www.mvpei.gov.me/en/sections/Multilateral-relations/UN-links/Montenegro-and-international-multilateral-conventi/.

181 Letter dated 10 October 2006, received by the UN Secretary-General on 23 October 2006. The letter also explains that Montenegro 'succeeds to the treaties listed in the attached Annex and undertakes faithfully to perform and carry out the stipulations therein contained as from June 3 2006, which is the date the Republic of Montenegro assumed responsibility for its international relations and the Parliament of Montenegro'.

182 Albania, Belarus, Bosnia-Herzegovina, Bulgaria, China, Croatia, South Korea, Egypt, Ghana, Guinea, Hungary, Kuwait, Libya, Nigeria, Russia, Slovenia, Sweden, Ukraine, and Zimbabwe.

183 UNCTAD: http://investmentpolicyhub.unctad.org/IIA/CountryBits/140#iiaInnerMenu.

184 The BITs with Belgium-Luxembourg, Macedonia and Turkey are not in force yet. Only the BIT with Finland is in force.

continue to be in force with the new State of Montenegro after its secession.[185] The important question is *how* any such continuation came about. Unfortunately, limited information exists on this essential question. In most instances, the only information available is that found on the UNCTAD website. The website simply indicates the existence of a BIT currently in force between Montenegro and each of these States and refers to a BIT which had been originally signed with Serbia-Montenegro, the FRY, or even the SFRY before its break-up. I have found only a limited number of instances where the two countries have expressly affirmed their willingness to continue the old BIT between themselves. Thus, such intent is clear in the context of an exchange of letters between Montenegro and the following States: Greece,[186] Cyprus,[187] the Netherlands,[188] France,[189] Germany,[190] Switzerland,[191] and

185 Germany, Austria, Cyprus, Spain, France, Greece, Israel, Lithuania, Netherlands, Poland, Czech Republic, Romania, Slovakia, and Switzerland. It should be added that the BIT signed with India in 2003 is not in force with Montenegro (but it is in force with Serbia since 2009). UNCTAD nevertheless lists this instrument amongst Montenegro's BITs.

186 Exchange of Notes, letter from the Greek Ministry of Foreign Affairs to the Embassy of Montenegro, 4 October 2011, no. 45374, and reply of 10 October 2011, in: Greece's official gazette, No. 275 A, 31 December 2011.

187 Exchange of Notes between the Government of the Republic of Cyprus and the Government of the Republic of Montenegro on the application of the Agreement between the Republic of Cyprus and Serbia and Montenegro on the Reciprocal Promotion and Protection of Investments, done at Nicosia on 21 July 2005 (Oct. 3 and 15, 2008, entered into force on Nov. 5, 2008), COG S.VII 4036, Nov. 30, 2005, at 573. See also: EU: http://eur-lex.europa.eu/legal-content/FR/TXT/?uri=CELEX%3A52014XC0605(01).

188 Exchange of Notes between the Kingdom of the Netherlands and the Republic of Montenegro regarding the continuation of bilateral treaties (Nov. 15, 2006 and Jan. 18, 2007), 51 Tractatenblad Van Het Koninkrij Der Nederlanden (2007), no. I, at 8. See also: EU, 'List of BITs' (n 137).

189 Accord sous forme d'échange de lettres entre le gouvernement de la République Française et le gouvernement de la République du Monténégro relatif à la succession en matière d'accords bilatéraux entre la France et l'Union de Serbie et Monténégro, 30 Sept. 2010, TRA00000468, Décret no. 2012–621 2 May 2012, available at: http://basedoc.diplomatie.gouv.fr/exl-php/cadcgp.php?CMD=CHERCHE&QUERY=1&MODELE=vues/mae_internet___traites/home.html&VUE=mae_internet___traites&NOM=cadic__anonyme&FROM_LOGIN=1. See also: EU, 'List of BITs' (n 137).

190 Bekanntmachung über die Fortgeltung von Verträgen im Verhältnis zwischen der Bundesrepublik Deutschland und Montenegro, 29. June 2011, Bundesgesetzblatt Jahrgang 2011 Teil II Nr. 21, ausgegeben zu Bonn am 9. August 2011, available at: http://www.bundesfinanzministerium.de/Content/DE/Standardartikel/Themen/Steuern/Internationales_Steuerrecht/Staatenbezogene_Informationen/Laender_A_Z/Montenegro/2011-08-09-Montenegro-Abkommen-DBA-Bekanntmachung.pdf?__blob=publicationFile&v=3. See also: EU, 'List of BITs' (n 137).

191 The website of the Swiss Ministry of Foreign Affairs refers to the 'Accord entre la Confédération suisse et la Serbie-et-Monténégro concernant la promotion et la protection réciproque des investissements', RS 0.975.257.3 and indicates that 'En raison de l'indépendance du Monténégro dès le 3 juin 2006, cet Accord est applicable séparément à la République de Serbie et à la République du Monténégro' and that 'Il a été ratifié de manière indépendante par les deux États et est entré en vigueur, selon son art. 14, séparément pour les deux Etats'. See: http://investmentpolicyhub.unctad.org/Download/TreatyFile/3050. Reference is also made to an exchange of letters between Switzerland and Montenegro dated 11 July 2007 for the continuation of this BIT.

Spain.[192] The Czech Republic also seems to be a clear example, as it has passed an amendment specific to Montenegro for the previous BIT.[193] Another reliable source of information is the EU website mentioned above[194] where EU Member States have listed the names of the countries with which they consider having a treaty relationship regarding investment protection. The list indicates that the following States consider the old BITs signed with the predecessor State (SFRY, FRY, or Serbia-Montenegro) as binding on Montenegro: Austria, Poland, Romania, Slovakia, Greece, and Lithuania.[195] While the list also refers to Croatia[196] and Hungary,[197] the fate of the old BIT for these two States is unclear. The same can be said regarding Israel.[198] Interestingly, the list also indicates that other EU Member States (Bulgaria, Slovenia, and Sweden), which were parties to BITs with the predecessor State, do *not* consider that the instrument continued with Montenegro.

In sum, Montenegro's practice is quite diverse. While a large number of States **3.34** do not seem to have considered the old BITs to continue with the new State, many others have adopted the opposite position of continuation. While in some instances, such a continuation was subject to an exchange of letters between the States concerned, it remains unclear how any such a continuation occurred regarding many other BITs.

192 Exchange of Notes between Spain and Montenegro on the continuation of the previous BIT, 19 May and 11 June 2010, available at: Spain, Ministerio de Economía (n 169); Boletin Official del Estado, n. 188, 4 August 2010.

193 See, 'Report on the state of the Czech Republic's bilateral relations', 2007, at 249, available at: http://www.mzv.cz/file/414987/Report_2007.pdf.

194 EU, 'List of BITs' (n 137).

195 The webpage of Lithuania's Ministry of Foreign Affairs refers to the old BIT as being in force with Montenegro, available at: https://www.urm.lt/default/en/montenegro. The webpage of Poland's Ministry of Foreign Affairs refers to the old BIT as being in force with Montenegro, available at: https://traktaty.msz.gov.pl/bape.php.

196 The webpage of Croatia's Ministry of Foreign and European Affairs contains a 'List of international treaties and international acts concluded between the Republic of Croatia and Montenegro', available at: http://www.mvep.hr/en/foreign-politics/bilateral-relations/overview-by-country/montenegro,236.html. The page does *not* list the 1998 FRY-Croatia BIT as being in force between Croatia and Montenegro. The list does however refer to a 'Trade treaty between the Government of the Republic of Croatia and the Federal Government of the Federal Republic of Yugoslavia' which was signed the same day as the BIT and which was terminated in 2013. It is not clear whether the 'Trade Treaty' is a reference to the BIT.

197 It should be added that the UNCTAD website does not refer to any BIT being in force between Montenegro and Hungary.

198 The website of Israel's Ministry of Foreign Affairs (available at: thttp://mfa.gov.il/MFA/AboutTheMinistry/LegalTreaties/Pages/Bilateral-Treaties.aspx) does not refer to any BIT in force with Montenegro.

3. ANALYSIS OF THE PRACTICE OF OTHER STATES PARTIES TO BITS

3.1 The practice of France regarding the France-SFRY BIT

3.35 Genest examined in detail the position adopted by France with respect to the different successor States of the SFRY regarding the fate of the BIT that was entered into with that State in 1974. France proceeded by exchanges of letters with respect to the continuation of the BIT with Slovenia, Serbia/ Montenegro, Croatia, Macedonia, Bosnia and Herzegovina and Montenegro.[199] The different letters identify lists of bilateral treaties that 'continue to bind' France and the different successor States. At first, the language contained in these letters suggests that these States considered that the old BIT simply continued to apply uninterruptedly from the date of succession to the date when the letters were exchanged. Thus, these exchanges of letters were aimed at simply confirming the continuous application of the 1974 BIT. Yet, the fact that such exchanges of letters took place between France and the different successor States after the date of succession could equally be interpreted as suggesting that these States presumed that the treaty would *not* have continued to apply automatically without the need to do something. Thus, had France and the different successor States truly believed in the existence of a general principle of automatic succession to BITs, they would have not considered it necessary to exchange letters confirming the continuation of such treaties.

3.36 France subsequently signed new BITs with Slovenia, Croatia, Macedonia and Bosnia and Herzegovina. With the exception of the France-Croatia BIT, these new BITs indicated that they cancelled and replaced the 1974 France-SFRY BIT.[200] Genest noted that the new France-Croatia BIT does not refer to the previous exchange of letters nor to the 1974 France-SFRY BIT. For him, 'it would appear as though upon entering into force the 1998 France-Croatia BIT did not cancel and replace the France-former SFRY BIT and it would appear as though both BITs would remain applicable between France and Croatia alongside one another'.[201] One can only agree with the general conclusion reached by Genest regarding the practice of France and its continuation of BITs:

> France appears to have adopted the clean slate (or *tabula rasa*) approach regarding its BITs with ex-Yugoslav Republics and appears to have rejected automatic continuity of

---

199 Genest (n 39) 15.
200 Ibid., 16.
201 Ibid.

bilateral treaties, in line with its overall treaty approach. France and the various Balkan States negotiated and expressed their consent (through exchanges of letters or agreements) to continue a specific and limited number of bilateral treaties while terminating others by the same token. However, it is unclear whether France and the Balkan States left periods of inapplicability behind when continuing the 1974 France-former SFRY BIT: it is unclear whether the 1974 France-former SFRY BIT would have applied during the 'twilight period,' i.e., the period between the date on which the independence of the various Balkan States was recognized and the date of entry into force of their respective exchanges of letters with France.[202]

3.2 The practice of the Netherlands regarding the Netherlands-SFRY BIT

Genest also examined the position of the Netherlands regarding the continuation of the 1976 Netherlands-SFRY BIT with the new successor States. The Netherlands continued the BIT (and other bilateral treaties) by exchanging notes with Macedonia, Bosnia, Croatia, the FRY, and Montenegro.[203] The Netherlands and Slovenia signed a 'Joint Declaration on Bilateral Treaty Relations' stating that the 1976 BIT had 'remained in force' between the two States. **3.37**

As noted by Genest, the language contained in these documents suggests that these States considered that the old BIT continued to apply uninterruptedly as of the date of succession.[204] Yet, as noted above, the very fact that they felt it was necessary to clarify the situation can be equally interpreted as suggesting that they did not consider that BITs automatically continue to be in force after the date of succession. In fact, this assumption seems to be supported by the fact that in all instances mentioned above (the exchanges of notes or the Joint Declaration), the States agreed that *some* of the former SFRY's treaties (including the 1976 BIT) would continue to be in force while *others would not*. A good example of such situation is this first letter sent by Macedonia to the Netherlands: **3.38**

> The Ministry of Foreign Relations of the Republic of Macedonia presents its compliments to the Ministry of Foreign Affairs of the Kingdom of the Netherlands and, with reference to its Note of 1 November 1993 notifying that the Republic of

---

202 Ibid. See, at 14–17.

203 Ibid., 16–17.

204 Ibid., 18:

> The language used within the exchanges of notes with Croatia, Macedonia, the Federal Republic of Yugoslavia/State Union of Serbia and Montenegro and then Montenegro, language such as 'bilateral agreements between the Netherlands and the former SFRY should continue to apply' and 'bilateral agreements between the Netherlands and the former SFRY constitute or 'represent' agreements between or 'are in force between' the Netherlands and the Balkan State' suggest that the 1976 Netherlands-former SFRY BIT would have continued uninterruptedly throughout the 'twilight period'.

Macedonia accepts as its own all valid international agreements of the former Socialist Federal Republic of Yugoslavia, and all bilateral and multilateral conventions with the Kingdom of the Netherlands.

Wishing to promote the relations between the Republic of Macedonia and the Kingdom of the Netherlands and reaffirming the attitude that the bilateral agreements that have been into force between the former SFRY and the Kingdom of the Netherlands should continue to be applied in the relations between the two countries, except if in any of these agreements or if stipulated elsewhere that the implementation of any agreement shall radically change the terms of their implementation, or if the two countries agree otherwise, the Ministry of Foreign Relations has the honour to propose that the following agreements concluded between the former Socialist Federal Republic of Yugoslavia and the Kingdom of the Netherlands represent agreements concluded between the Republic of Macedonia and the Kingdom of the Netherlands in the future: (…)

The Ministry of Foreign Relations has the honour to propose that the Agreement between the former SFRY and the Kingdom of the Netherlands concerning Regular Air Services, of 13 March 1957, and the Agreement between the former SFRY and the Kingdom of the Netherlands on Technical Cooperation Aiming at the Creation of Conditions for the Promotion of Employment in Economically Underdeveloped Areas of Yugoslavia, of 20 January 1977, be canceled between the Republic of Macedonia and the Kingdom of the Netherlands in the future, due to the changed circumstances in the relations between the two countries.

In case the Ministry of Foreign Affairs of the Kingdom of the Netherlands accepts the proposal contained herein, the Ministry of Foreign Relations of the Republic of Macedonia will consider the receipt of the Note of the Ministry of Foreign Affairs of the Kingdom of the Netherlands confirming the acceptance of the proposal as an agreement that the conventions between the former SFRY and the Kingdom of the Netherlands mentioned in this Note, constitute agreements between the Republic of Macedonia and the Kingdom of the Netherlands.

The Ministry of Foreign Relations of the Republic of Macedonia avails itself of this opportunity to renew to the Ministry of Foreign Affairs of the Kingdom of the Netherlands the assurances of its highest consideration.[205]

3.39 The response by the Netherlands was as follows:

The Ministry accepts the proposal of the Ministry of Foreign Relations of The Former Yugoslav Republic of Macedonia and confirms that its Note and this reply confirm that the agreements between the Socialist Federal Republic of Yugoslavia and the Kingdom of the Netherlands mentioned above under numbers 1 to 15, continue to be in force between The Former Yugoslav Republic of Macedonia and the Kingdom of

205 Exchange of Notes between the Government of the Kingdom of the Netherlands and the Government of the Former Yugoslav Republic of Macedonia on bilateral treaty relations (signed 27 June and 11 July 1994, entered into force on 11 July 1994), available at: https://verdragenbank.overheid.nl/en/Verdrag/Details/011806.

> the Netherlands and further that the Agreement concerning Regular Air Services of 13 March 1957 and the Agreement on Technical Cooperation Aiming at the Creation of Conditions for the Promotion of Employment in Economically Underdeveloped Areas of Yugoslavia of 20 January 1977 are no longer in force.
>
> The Ministry avails itself of this opportunity to renew to the Ministry of Foreign Relations of The Former Yugoslav Republic of Macedonia the assurances of its highest consideration.[206]

As noted by Genest, 'this approach suggests that the Netherlands did not consider itself automatically bound to continue bilateral treaties with each Balkan State'.[207] Thus, the very fact that one State (Macedonia) makes a 'proposal' about the continuation of some treaties and that the other State (the Netherlands) 'accepts the proposal' shows that the continuation of the old BIT (and other treaties) was *negotiated* between them. The existence of any such negotiation strongly suggests that they did not act based on the existence of any principle of automatic succession. **3.40**

Another illustration of this phenomenon is the exchange of notes between Bosnia and Herzegovina and the Netherlands. In a first letter, Bosnia stated that 'in conformity with general rules of international law on succession of States and the provisions of the Vienna Convention, [it] considers itself, as a legal successor State of the [SFRY], bound by the following bilateral treaties' concluded between the SFRY and the Netherlands 'which were in force on the date of succession of States in respect to the territory' of Bosnia.'[208] While the letter mentions that the treaties 'should remain in force between' the two States 'until the two parties agree otherwise', it nevertheless indicates that Bosnia 'would appreciate the notification of the Ministry of Foreign Affairs of the Kingdom of the Netherlands on the acceptance of this notification'. In response, the Netherlands first mentioned subscribing to 'the continued application of all treaties in force on the date of succession of States'. The letter then noted that the Netherlands 'concludes that with the abovementioned Note and the present Note it is established that' 11 out of the 12 treaties (so not all of them) proposed by Bosnia 'have continued to apply' between the two States. In the same letter, the Netherlands asked that two additional bilateral treaties be continued. Bosnia agreed to that in a subsequent note. This is an interesting example. Both States have clearly adopted a position in favour of **3.41**

---

206 Ibid.

207 Genest (n 39) 19.

208 Exchange of Notes between the Government of the Kingdom of the Netherlands and the Government of the Republic of Bosnia and Herzegovina on bilateral treaty relations (signed 21 September 1995 and 29 February 1996, entered into force on 29 February 1996), available at: https://verdragenbank.overheid.nl/en/Verdrag/Details/011803.

the continuation of treaties. Yet, they have concretely *not* acted based on the belief in the existence of any presumption of *automatic* continuation. The fate of these treaties was subject to negotiation between the parties.

3.42 Finally, it should be added that the Netherlands subsequently signed new BITs with Slovenia, Macedonia, Bosnia, Croatia and with the FRY.[209] They all indicate that upon entering into force the new BITs terminated and/or replaced the 1976 Netherlands-SFRY BIT.[210] These examples support the view that the States believed in the continuity of these BITs. Yet, as noted by Genest, while 'doubts remain as to the uninterrupted continuity of BITs with the former SFRY during the "twilight period", this ambiguity arises only in respect of the potential retrospective effect of the exchanges of notes/letters and does not alter the fact that in all instances explicit consent to continue BITs with the former SFRY intervened'.[211] Overall, the practice of the Netherlands does not support the principle of automatic continuity of treaties.

4. CONCLUSION

3.43 The practice examined in the previous sections suggests that both successor States and other States parties have generally agreed for the continuation of old BITs to which the predecessor State had been a party before the date of succession. However, while they have certainly adopted this pro-continuity position, it cannot be concluded that they have done so based on the existence of any principle of *automatic* succession to BITs. If any such principle of automatic succession to BITs existed, there would simply be no need for exchange of letters between these States. Tams agreed with this argument: 'the fondness of States for negotiated outcomes can equally be said to undermine the case for automatic succession'.[212]

3.44 In sum, this section illustrated that the States concerned have often *expressly* agreed to the continuation of BITs. As further examined in the next section, there are also situations where it can be concluded that both States have *tacitly* agreed for the continuation of an old BIT to which the predecessor State was a party. This question was at the heart of the *WWM v. Kazakhstan* case.[213] The

209 Genest (n 39) 20.

210 Ibid., referring to some exceptions in some BITs.

211 Ibid., 20–21.

212 Tams (n 27) 335, citing Dumberry (Dumberry, 'An Uncharted Question of State Succession' (n 40) 82): 'the very fact that such negotiation took place in most cases suggests that third States have generally not accepted the principle of automatic succession'.

213 *WWM v. Kazakhstan* (n 53).

question as to whether or not both States have tacitly agreed on the continuation of a BIT is a multifactorial question that depends largely on the circumstances of each case. Whenever there is *no indicia* of any express or tacit consent by both the successor State and the other State party, another question arises. The question is whether or not there exists any principle of international law by which the successor State is bound by the bilateral treaties to which the predecessor State had been a party before the date of succession. In other words, the question is whether or not there exists a principle in favor of the *automatic* continuation of BITs. This question is examined in Chapter 5.

4

DIFFERENT FORMS OF CONSENT BY STATES FOR THE CONTINUATION OF BITS

4.01 This chapter will show that a new State (such as in the context of secession and dissolution) is not automatically bound by the bilateral treaties which had been entered into by the predecessor State with other States. Thus, the continuation of BITs is based on the consent of *both* States concerned. The previous section demonstrated that States have in fact often consented to the continuation of BITs. There are essentially two forms of consent which can be given by both the new State and the 'other State Party': express consent (Section 1) and inferred or tacit consent (Section 2). This chapter examines these different forms of consent.

1. EXPRESS CONSENT

The most obvious form of consent to the continuation of a BIT is an *express* statement by the parties.[214] As explained by one writer, such express consent can take different forms: **4.02**

> Le consentement exprès des parties, au sens de l'alinéa *a* [of Article 24] se manifeste typiquement par voie d'accords écrits, des notes diplomatiques ou échanges de correspondance, des procès-verbaux approuvés des réunions, des accords verbaux enregistrés au su des deux parties et conformément à leur volonté, des déclarations conjointes des Etats intéressés, etc.[215]

Chapter 3 provided a number of examples where the new State and the other State party to a BIT have expressly agreed for the continuation of the treaty which had been entered into by the predecessor State. Several of these agreements are also mentioned in Tams' paper.[216] The analysis confirms Waldock's remarks that express statements of consent by States are 'very common',[217] which led him to conclude that this is 'a fact which in itself indicates that, in general, the continuance of bilateral treaties is a matter not of right but of agreement'.[218] It is, however, crucial to understand that consent to the continuation of a treaty can also exist in a situation where there is *no* express agreement by the parties. The next section examines the phenomenon of tacit consent. The question of tacit consent was central to the *WWM* award (which is confidential).[219] **4.03**

2. INFERRED OR TACIT CONSENT

From the fact that there is *no* express agreement by the States concerned regarding the continuation of a BIT, should it necessarily be concluded that the parties have not consented to such continuation and that, consequently, the *tabula rasa* principle should apply? In the words of Tams, 'the absence of an explicit party agreement on (dis-)continuity does not conclude matters; it **4.04**

214 See, J. Barale, 'L'acquiescement dans la jurisprudence internationale' (1965) 11 AFDI 394ff providing many examples.

215 Adriana Di Stefano, 'Article 24' in Distefano, Gaggioli and Hêche (n 4), 864–5.

216 Tams (n 27) 328ff.

217 ILC, Fourth Report on Succession in Respect of Treaties, prepared by the Special Rapporteur, Sir Humphrey Waldock, A/CN.4/249, 24 June 1971, A/8410/Rev.1, in: *YILC*, 1971, vol. II (Part One) [hereinafter ILC Report, Fourth Report, 1971] 148 [11]: 'The technique of an exchange of Notes or Letters regarding the continuance of a bilateral treaty, accompanied by an express statement that it is to be regarded as constituting an agreement, has indeed become very common (…)'.

218 Ibid.

219 *WWM v. Kazakhstan* (n 53).

means that the matter needs to be studied more fully'.[220] Tams further explains that 'where no explicit agreement has been reached, there is room to engage with arguments based on implied, or tacit, consent: such arguments no doubt need to be made carefully, but in principle are available'.[221] As such, the position of recent scholars is in contrast to that of others who have in the past rejected the possibility of tacit consent.[222] Any investigation on the possibility of tacit consent requires one to identify the *intention* of the States concerned, that is, 'whether the new State and the other party to the prior treaty intended to apply the treaty post-independence.'[223] Waldock in his Fourth Report also stated that determining whether or not a State has consented to the continuation of a treaty will depend on the '*general attitude* of the States concerned'.[224] Elsewhere, he reiterates that the continuity of a treaty 'is a matter of the *attitudes and intentions* of the interested States'.[225]

4.05 The next section examines different forms of tacit consent. As noted by Tams, the intention of the States concerned 'does not have to be expressed in a particular form' and 'can be deduced from other statements, or inferred from conduct'.[226] Thus, 'States can agree, even in the most informal fashion, to keep treaties in force.'[227] Yet, as rightly noted by Waldock, 'the great variety of ways in which a State may manifest its agreement to consider itself bound by a treaty' can lead to 'difficulties'.[228] This is clearly the case when 'neither State has given any clear indication of its intentions in regard to the continuance of bilateral treaties'.[229] The following section will examine the more common situation where (at least) *one* of the parties concerned has indicated its intention of continuing the treaties to which the predecessor State was a party.

4.06 The first section will examine the question of tacit consent in the context of statements made by States (Section 2.1) which will then be followed by an analysis of consent which can be inferred from the conduct of the parties (Section 2.2).

---

220 Tams (n 27) 334.

221 Ibid., 342.

222 See, for instance, A. Goncalves Pereira, *La succession d'États en matière de traités* (Pedone 1969), 158ff.

223 Tams (n 27) 332.

224 ILC, Fourth Report, 1971 (n 217) 146 [13]: '[i]ndividual instances of continuity have necessarily to be understood in the light of the *general attitude of the States concerned* in regard to succession in respect of bilateral treaties' (emphasis added).

225 Ibid., 148 [12] (emphasis added).

226 Tams (n 27) 334.

227 O'Connell, 'Reflections on the State Succession Convention' (n 7) 733.

228 ILC Report, 26th Session, 1974 (n 24) 240 [16] (emphasis added).

229 ILC, Fourth Report, 1971 (n 217) 150 [16].

2.1 Statements

The intentions of both the new successor State and the 'other State Party' to be bound by the bilateral treaty to which the predecessor State was a party before the date of succession can be deduced from a number of different statements. The present section examines unilateral declarations (Section 2.1.1) and devolution agreements (Section 2.1.2). **4.07**

2.1.1 Unilateral declarations

2.1.1.1 Introduction

A unilateral declaration is a method often used by new States to express their willingness to continue to be bound by treaties entered into by the predecessor State.[230] While such unilateral declarations can be made by the 'other State Party',[231] this section will focus on those made by new States. The most famous example of such a declaration is that of Prime Minister Nyerere of the new State of Tanganyika in a letter sent to the UN Secretary-General in December 1961.[232] As further discussed below, a number of new States have made a unilateral declaration in the context of the dissolution of Yugoslavia and Czechoslovakia as well as the break-up of the USSR. One concrete example is the declaration made by the Czech Republic, which reads as follows: 'In accordance with the applicable principles of the international law and to the extent set thereby, as of 1 January 1993, the Czech Republic will consider itself being bound by multilateral and bilateral agreements and treaties, to which the Czech and Slovak Federal Republic was a party on the same date.'[233] **4.08**

---

230 Di Stefano (n 215) 865–6:

> Mais le plus souvent la pratique diplomatique montre le recours aux déclarations unilatérales – exprimées dans des actes d'ordre interne ou dans le cadre des relations internationales – relatives à la manifestation ouverte des intentions étatiques en cas de succession aux traités bilatéraux. Comme reconnu par le commentaire au projet d'articles en matière de succession d'Etats aux traités, plusieurs Etats nouvellement indépendants ont fait des déclarations unilatérales de caractère général par lesquelles ils ont indiqué une certaine position à l'égard des traités qui s'appliquaient à leurs territoires respectifs avant la date de la succession.

See numerous examples in: M.G. Marcoff, *Accession à l'indépendance et succession d'États aux traités internationaux* (Fribourg 1969) 144ff. See also: Ian Brownlie, *Principles of Public International Law* 6th edn (OUP 2003) 635–6.

231 Tams (n 27) 28 referring to this example: 'Williams [(n 135, 30, 32] refers to letters sent by US President Bush to the Prime Ministers of the Czech and Slovak Republics on 1 December, proposing "that the United States and the respective states 'conduct full diplomatic relations' based on the affirmation of the Republics to fulfill a number of commitments, including the 'commitment to fulfill the treaty and other obligations of the former Czechoslovakia'".'

232 ILC Report, 26th Session, 1974 (n 24) 188.

233 Proclamation of the National Council of the Czech Republic to all Parliaments and Nations of the World, 17 December 1992 (n 77).

4.09 The next sections will examine the following questions regarding the nature and the effect of unilateral declarations:

- The required form of a unilateral declaration (Section 2.1.1.2);
- The effect on the new State making the declaration (Section 2.1.1.2);
- The response given by the 'other State party' following a unilateral declaration and the question of tacit consent (Section 2.1.1.3); and
- The relevant criteria to determine whether consent can be inferred from the silence and passivity of the 'other State party' (Section 2.1.1.4).

2.1.1.2 The required form of a declaration and its effect on the State making it

4.10 In the *Nuclear Tests* cases, the ICJ affirmed that:

> when it is the intention of the State making [a unilateral] declaration that it should become bound according to its terms, that intention confers on the declaration the character of a legal undertaking, the State being thenceforth legally required to follow a course of conduct consistent with the declaration.[234]

In other words, such a declaration may, depending on the circumstances,[235] have 'the effect of creating legal obligations' and be binding on the new State making it.[236] In the context of State succession, the question of the intention of a new State is not problematic when a declaration refers to a *specific* treaty. It becomes all the more problematic to determine a State's intention regarding its willingness to succeed to *all* treaties of the predecessor when the unilateral declaration is written in *general terms*.

4.11 In the *Genocide* case (*Croatia v. Serbia*), the ICJ dealt with the question of the form which a declaration must have to result in having any effect on the State making it. Interestingly, the ICJ analysed the issue in the specific context of State succession. As the court noted, the SFRY was a party to the Genocide Convention in the 1990s 'when it began to disintegrate into separate and

---

234 *Nuclear Tests (New Zealand v. France)*, Judgment, ICJ Reports 1974, 457 [46].

235 International Law Commission, 'Guiding Principles Applicable to Unilateral Declarations of States Capable of Creating Legal Obligations With Commentaries Thereto', in: ILC Ybk 2006/II(2), Principle no. 3: '[t]o determine the legal effects of such declarations, it is necessary to take account of their content, of all the factual circumstances in which they were made, and of the reactions to which they gave rise'. See also, Principle no. 7:

> A unilateral declaration entails obligations for the formulating State only if it is stated in clear and specific terms. In the case of doubt as to the scope of the obligations resulting from such a declaration, such obligations must be interpreted in a restrictive manner. In interpreting the content of such obligations, weight shall be given first and foremost to the text of the declaration, together with the context and the circumstances in which it was formulated.

236 *Nuclear Tests* (n 234).

independent States'.[237] Importantly, at that time, the FRY claimed to be the *same* State as the SFRY.[238]

4.12 Croatia took the position that 'the FRY was a party by succession to the Genocide Convention from the beginning of its existence as a State, since succession, unlike other modes of becoming bound by a treaty, is retrospective to the commencement of the successor State'.[239] Croatia relied in support of its claim on a formal declaration adopted on behalf of the FRY on 27 April 1992, indicating that the FRY was 'continuing the State['s] international legal and political personality of the [SFRY]' and 'shall strictly abide by all the commitments that the [SFRY] assumed internationally'.[240] Serbia argued that this declaration was not capable of constituting a notification of succession to the Genocide Convention. One reason was that 'specific notifications are necessary in order to bring about succession, in other words a notification of succession must specify precisely which treaty it is directed to; and the 1992 declaration was entirely general in its terms ("all the commitments that the SFR of Yugoslavia assumed internationally")'.[241]

4.13 The court first noted that '[w]hile the treaties contemplated [in the Declaration] were not specified by name, [it] referred to a class of instruments which was perfectly ascertainable at the moment of making of the declaration: the treaty "commitments" binding on the SFRY at the moment of its dissolution'.[242] For the court, there was 'no doubt that the Genocide Convention was one of these "commitments"'.[243] The court then made the following important statement about the nature and the form required for a unilateral declaration to be considered as having any legal effect on the State making it:

> While the practice of making declarations of succession to a treaty or treaties with an indication of the treaty or treaties to which they are intended to relate is of undoubted practical usefulness, the Court is unable to hold that international law regards as wholly ineffective an instrument that identifies by general reference the treaty to which it is addressed, rather than by designating it by its particular name.[244]

---

237 *Case Concerning Application of the Convention on the Prevention and Punishment of the Crime of Genocide* (*Croatia v. Serbia*), Preliminary Objections, Judgment, 18 Nov. 2008, ICJ Reports 2008 [97] [hereinafter '*Genocide* case (*Croatia v. Serbia*), 2008'].

238 Ibid., [100].

239 Ibid., [97].

240 Ibid., [97] (UN Doc. A/46/915, Ann. II.). See also: Note of 27 April 1992 from the Permanent Mission of Yugoslavia to the Secretary-General of the United Nations, UN Doc. A/46/915, Ann. I.

241 Ibid., [106].

242 Ibid.

243 Ibid.

244 Ibid., [108].

> In the view of the Court, there is a distinction between the legal nature of ratification of, or accession to a treaty, on the one hand, and on the other, the process by which a State becomes bound by a treaty as a successor State or remains bound as a continuing State. Accession or ratification is a simple act of will on the part of the State manifesting an intention to undertake new obligations and to acquire new rights in terms of the treaty, effected in writing in the formal manner set out in the Treaty (cf. Articles 15 and 16 of the Vienna Convention on the Law of Treaties). In the case of succession or continuation on the other hand, the act of will of the State relates to an already existing set of circumstances, and amounts to a recognition by that State of certain legal consequences flowing from those circumstances, so that any document issued by the State concerned, being essentially confirmatory, may be subject to less rigid requirements of form. Article 2 (g) of the 1978 Vienna Convention on Succession of States in respect of Treaties reflects this idea, defining a 'notification of succession' as meaning 'in relation to a multilateral treaty, any notification, however framed or named, made by a successor State expressing its consent to be considered as bound by the treaty'. Nor does international law prescribe any specific form for a State to express a claim of continuity.[245]

4.14 The court concluded that in the instant case, the declaration should be 'considered as having had the effects of a notification of succession to treaties' by the FRY to the SFRY in relation to the Genocide Convention.[246]

4.15 In sum, for the court, international law does not prescribe any specific form or a specific degree of specificity for a new State to express a general claim of succession to a group of treaties. What suffices is that the treaties to which a State wishes to succeed are 'perfectly ascertainable at the moment of making of the declaration'.[247] It is important to note that when the FRY made the above-mentioned statement, it considered itself to be the *continuator* of the SFRY and not a *new* successor State. It was therefore logical for the FRY to be considered bound by the treaties of the SFRY. It may be that the finding of the court on this point cannot automatically apply to succession cases more generally.[248] In any event, the conclusion reached by the court has been criticized by scholars. Thus, according to Zimmerman, this approach 'marks a shift away from the restrictive approach adopted in the 1978 Vienna Convention and increases uncertainty'; it is also contrary to the 'long-standing practice of [treaty] depositaries' whereby 'general declarations of succession are

245 Ibid., [109].

246 Ibid., [111], [117].

247 Ibid., [106].

248 Alexandro Kolliopoulos, 'Article 9' in Distefano, Gaggioli and Hêche (n 4), 336–7.

not understood to bring about treaty succession, much less devolution agreements'.[249]

4.16 The question as to whether or not a general declaration can be considered as an offer to succeed to all treaties will depend heavily on the circumstances of each case. There are situations where a successor State will make such a declaration with the clear intent to be legally bound by such a statement and to assume obligations arising from the treaties.[250] However, this will often not be the case.[251] In this context, two scholars have discussed Kosovo's intention from the general statement of succession contained in its Declaration of Independence.[252] They have concluded that it was indeed Kosovo's intention to be bound by all treaties of the SFRY given the specific terms found in the declaration,[253] its subsequent practice,[254] and how other States had interpreted such a declaration.[255]

4.17 Another closely related question is the legal *effect* that a unilateral declaration should have on the State making it. In practical terms, according to the ILC, the 'primary role' of these unilateral declarations in the specific context of State succession is 'to facilitate the provisional application of treaties previously applied to the territory in question'.[256] However, the ILC also rightly noted that a new State does not have any 'right' under international law for 'the provisional application of the treaties of its predecessor for a certain period after independence'.[257] In any event, as further discussed in the next section,

---

249 A. Zimmermann, 'The International Court of Justice and State Succession to Treaties: Avoiding Principled Answers to Questions of Principle', in: Christian J. Tams and James Sloan (eds), *The Development of International Law by the International Court of Justice* (OUP 2013) 67.

250 Kolliopoulos (n 248) 334ff.

251 Ibid., 337–8.

252 Kosovo's Declaration of Independence (n 98) [9]: 'We hereby undertake the international obligations of Kosovo, including (…) treaty and other obligations of the former Socialist Federal Republic of Yugoslavia to which we are bound as a former constituent part, including the Vienna Conventions on diplomatic and consular relations.' See also: Art. 145 of the Constitution of the Republic of Kosovo, which entered into force on 15 June 2008 (available in the online version of the Official Gazette of the Republic of Kosovo at http://gazetazyrtare.rks-gov.net/KK.aspx).

253 Such intent is clear in this provision: Ibid., [12]: 'We hereby affirm, clearly, specifically, and irrevocably, that Kosovo shall be legally bound to comply with the provisions contained in this Declaration (…). We declare publicly that all states are entitled to rely upon this declaration, and appeal to them to extend to us their support and friendship.'

254 Qerimi and Krasniqi (n 38) 1654.

255 Ibid., quoting from Letter from the President of the United States to the President of Kosovo (Feb. 18, 2008), available at http://georgewbush-whitehouse.archives.gov/news/releases/2008/02/20080218-3.html: 'The United States relies upon Kosovo's assurances that it considers itself legally bound to comply with the provisions in Kosovo's Declaration of Independence'. The same conclusion is reached by: Panoussis (n 99) 1878.

256 ILC Report, 26th Session, 1974 (n 24) 193, see also at 192. See also: Kolliopoulos (n 248) 327–9.

257 Ibid. at 192.

what matters in the context of *bilateral* treaties is the response given by the 'other State party' following such a declaration by the new State.

2.1.1.3 The response given by the 'other State party' following a declaration

4.18 It is uncontested that, *in and by itself*, a unilateral statement made by a new State *cannot* create rights and obligations for other States.[258] Such statements are not binding per se on the other State party to an agreement with the predecessor State.[259] This is indeed the solution adopted under Article 9 of the Vienna Convention (which has been considered as a customary rule[260]):

> Obligations or rights under treaties in force in respect of a territory at the date of a succession of States do not become the obligations or rights of the successor State or of other States Parties to those treaties by reason only of the fact that the successor State has made a unilateral declaration providing for the continuance in force of the treaties in respect of its territory.

4.19 Ultimately, a unilateral statement only represents the view expressed by *one* concerned party about the fate of bilateral treaties. What matters is not uniquely the unilateral statement on its own but the *response* to this offer by the 'other State party'.[261] This is because there is no unilateral right for a State to 'consider a bilateral treaty as continuing in force with respect to its territory after independence *regardless of the wishes of the other party to the treaty*'.[262] The ILC Report further adds that unilateral declarations which had been made by States 'have unmistakably been based on the assumption that, as a general rule, the continuance in force of their predecessor's bilateral treaties is a matter on which it would be necessary to reach an accord with the other party to each treaty'.[263] So, even in the context of a unilateral declaration, 'the express or tacit concurrence of the other contracting party has still been regarded as necessary to make a bilateral treaty enforceable as between it and the newly independent State'.[264]

4.20 As explained by the ILC, when there is a positive response by the other State party 'no problem arises'.[265] In such a case, there is in fact an express

258 Tams (n 27) 332–3; Zimmermann and Devaney, 'Succession to Treaties' (n 1) 536: 'unless the other State explicitly consents, can be said to have acquiesced, or otherwise implied its consent, neither a devolution agreement nor a unilateral declaration can have, in line with the *pacta tertiis* principle, any legal effect on any other State as such'; Kolliopoulos (n 248) 329.

259 See, the analysis in Kolliopoulos, ibid., 329ff.

260 Ibid., 307ff., 310, 313.

261 Di Stefano (n 215) 865–6.

262 ILC Report, 26th Session, 1974 (n 24) 238 (emphasis in the original).

263 Ibid., 238.

264 Ibid.

265 Ibid., 239.

agreement between the parties for the continuation of a treaty.[266] One example of such response is the one given by the United Kingdom in the context of the unilateral declaration made by Kosovo.[267] In this context, the unilateral declaration is part of the agreement between these States.[268] It consists of an 'offer' by one State which is followed and completed by an acceptance of that offer by the other State.

The situation is more problematic when the 'other State party' does *not explicitly* respond to the declaration made by the new State.[269] Yet, as put by one writer, the absence of any such explicit or formal response does *not* necessarily mean that there exists no agreement between the parties regarding the continuation of a bilateral treaty: **4.21**

> Des doutes surgissent toutefois lorsqu'il s'agit d'établir l'intention des deux parties concernées (au regard de la vigueur des relations bilatérales préexistantes à l'indépendance) en défaut de réactions explicites, ou bien dans les cas, quantitativement significatifs, de *comportements passifs* ou d'*inaction prolongée* de la part *d'un des Etats* contractants. La pratique montre en effet une pluralité des situations caractérisées par des mesures explicites (actes ou faits) relevant des intentions d'un Etat et par l'absence de réactions de l'autre Etat partie. On considérait ici la situation d'un acte (par exemple une déclaration) en apparence unilatéral, qui peut en réalité constituer un accord en raison de son contexte et de tout autre indice: son contenu, les circonstances dans lesquelles il a été réalisé, les comportements des parties. Il arrive alors qu'un accord puisse se manifester par voie d'autres conduites étatiques suffisamment univoques dont on peut déduire une intention manifeste d'être lié.[270]

---

266 Ibid.:

> Where there is an express agreement, as in the Exchange of Notes (…) no problem arises. Whether the agreement is phrased as a confirmation that the treaty is considered as in force or as a consent to its being so considered, the agreement operates to continue the treaty in force and determines the position of the States concerned in relation to the treaty.

267 Note Verbale No. 02/2008 of the British Embassy in Kosovo to the Ministry of Foreign Affairs (Succession to Treaties with the UK , *See* Decree for Ratification of the Agreements listed in the Exchange of Notes between the Republic of Kosovo and the United Kingdom, available at http://gazetazyrtare.rks-gov.net/Documents/Marrveshja%20Ks-Mbretrine%20e%20Bashkuar%20(028)%20(anglisht).pdf):

> The British Government … has the honour to note that, in that Declaration, Kosovo expressly undertook its international obligations, including those concluded on its behalf by the United Nations Interim Administration Mission in Kosovo and those to which Kosovo was bound as a former constituent part of the Socialist Federal Republic of Yugoslavia, and the British Government hereby confirms that the British Government regards treaties and agreements in force to which the United Kingdom and UNMIK, and the UK and the SFRY, and as appropriate the UK and the Federal Republic of Yugoslavia, were parties as remaining in force between the United Kingdom and the Republic of Kosovo.

268 Kolliopoulos (n 248) 330–31.

269 ILC Report, 26th Session, 1974 (n 24) 239.

270 Di Stefano (n 215) 867–8 (emphasis in the original).

4.22 In the absence of an explicit response by the 'other State party', the intention of both parties regarding the continuation of a treaty must be determined.[271] As mentioned above, treaty continuity 'is a matter of the attitudes and intention of the interested States'.[272] In fact, as noted by Tams, whenever a unilateral statement by the new State is *not* explicitly and expressly *opposed* by the 'other State party', this 'can provide the basis for an argument based on tacit party consent'.[273] As further explained below,[274] a number of tribunals in the context of the dissolution of Czechoslovakia seem to have adopted that position.[275] Yet, and importantly, from the mere fact that the 'other State party' does not explicitly *oppose* a unilateral declaration, it cannot be automatically deduced that it has implicitly consented to the continuation of a treaty. Whether any such consent can be inferred from the silence and passivity of the 'other State party' will have to be assessed by taking into account different factors and circumstances. The next section examines such criteria.

2.1.1.4 Relevant criteria to determine whether consent can be inferred from the silence and passivity of the 'other State party'

4.23 Whether or not any consent to the continuation of a treaty can be inferred from the silence of one State following a unilateral declaration made by another State in favour of continuity will depend on the circumstances of each situation and the relevant background.[276] This is because not all 'silence'

---

271 Tams (n 27) 27.

272 ILC Report, 26th Session, 1974 (n 24) 238.

273 Tams (n 27) 332.

274 See, Chapter 6, Section 2.

275 One example is *Saluka Investments BV v. Czech Republic*, UNCITRAL, Jurisdiction over the Counterclaim, 7 May 2004 [2], where the tribunal indicated that 'The Czech Republic confirmed to the Kingdom of The Netherlands that, upon the separation of the Czech and Slovak Federal Republic into two separate republics, the Treaty remained in force between the Czech Republic and the Kingdom of The Netherlands'. The tribunal does not refer to the actual response given by the Netherlands to such a unilateral declaration even though both States had actually expressly agreed to the continuation of the BIT.

276 Di Stefano (n 215) 871:

> D'une manière assez générale, l'acquiescement 'passif' peut aussi résulter de l'inaction prolongée, du silence, de l'absence de protestations ou de réactions d'un Etat vis-à-vis des positions ou prétentions manifestées par l'autre Etat. Cette attitude de passivité s'ajoute souvent à des indices autres d'acquiescement déduits des comportements actifs. C'est ainsi dans ces dernières situations, lorsque l'acquiescement résulte totalement ou en partie d'une attitude étatique de passivité, que se pose véritablement le problème de la vérification ou de la preuve de la connaissance de l'Etat qui acquiesce comme condition fondamentale de la fiction de la volonté tacite. (...) Aux fins de la réalisation du phénomène complexe de l'acquiescement, l'écoulement du temps, jouant un rôle dans l'information de l'Etat et dans la qualification des ses comportements (actifs et passifs), parait souvent tout aussi nécessaire, avec bien évidemment la condition de la connaissance. A la recherche des indices significatifs pour apprécier la connaissance (et donc l'acquiescement) on tient compte généralement de la notoriété de la situation, de l'existence d'accords de dévolution, ou d'autres circonstances de connaissance nécessaire ou d'ignorance fautive, élaborées par la jurisprudence internationale.

See also: Nuno Sérgio Marques Antunes, 'Acquiescence', in *Max Planck Encyclopedia of Public International Law* (OUP, online edn, 2006) [19]: 'the juridical value and meaning of silence or inaction depends on the

should be given a particular meaning and be susceptible to produce legal consequences. Indeed, it is important to distinguish the scenario of a State that simply does not react for no particular reason (for instance, a simple lack of interest for the issue), from an abstention, which produces legal consequences and implies a tacit agreement.[277] As explained by ILC Special Rapporteur Wood on the Identification of Customary International Law in his Third Report:

> [a]s there could be various reasons for a refusal or failure to act, including a lack of capacity to do so or a lack of direct interest, not every instance of inaction will amount to concurrence: only 'qualified silence' (…) may be construed as concurrence in the relevant practice. (…).[278]

For MacGibbon, the 'function of acquiescence may be equated with that of consent'.[279] One writer defined the concept of 'acquiescence' as the consent 'tacitly conveyed by a State, unilaterally, through silence or inaction, in circumstances such that a response expressing disagreement or objection in relation to the conduct of another State would be called for'.[280] Thus, a State's consent through acquiescence requires that the following conditions be met: **4.24**

> Acquiescence only emerges where it refers to facts that are (or ought to be) known by the acquiescing State (*notoriety*), where such facts are of direct interest for the acquiescing State (*interest*), when these facts have existed for a significant period (*lapse of time*) without significant change of context and the meaning conveyed (*consistency*), and in cases in which the conduct is attributable to a relevant representative of the State (*provenance*).[281]

Similarly, for Crawford 'the requirements for acquiescence include: the notoriety of the facts and the claims, their prolonged tolerance by the state(s) **4.25**

---

circumstances *in casu*'; C. MacGibbon, 'The Scope Of Acquiescence In International Law', (1954) 31 *Brit YIL* 170: 'Whether silence is to be interpreted as amounting to acquiescence depends primarily on the circumstances in which the silence is observed.'

277 J. Kammerhofer, 'Uncertainty in the Formal Sources of International Law: Customary International Law and Some of Its Problems', (2004) 15(3) EJIL 529. See, on the contrary the position adopted by Pereira (n 222) 163 for whom 'le silence n'est pas autre chose que l'inaction' and 'la motivation du silence est parfaitement indifférente'.

278 International Law Commission, 'Third Report on Identification of Customary International Law', by Michael Wood, Special Rapporteur, 67th session, Geneva, 4 May–5 June and 6 July–7 August 2014, A/CN.4/682, 11–14 [hereinafter ILC, Third Report Wood].

279 MacGibbon (n 276) 145.

280 Marques Antunes (n 276) [2].

281 Ibid., [21] (emphasis in the original).

whose interests are specially affected, and general toleration by the international community'.[282] I will examine these relevant factors in the following paragraphs.

4.26 The first point that should be mentioned is that a State can only tacitly 'consent' to a treaty's continuation if it *knows* the position of continuity adopted by the new State.[283] Nothing can be deduced from the silence of a State when it is simply *not aware* of the position adopted by another. Acquiescence necessarily requires the notoriety of the facts and a claim.[284] Thus, the new State must have made its position on treaty continuity known to other States (or, at the very least, to the other State party to the treaty). This being said, there is no requirement for the State making a claim to formally notify other State parties.[285] Here, an interesting analogy can be drawn from the publicity requirement which exists in the *different* context of the creation of rules of customary international law.[286] According to many writers, the only types of evidence of State practice that plays a role in the formation of customary rules are those which are communicated to another State, or made public to a certain extent.[287] Principle no. 5 of the ILA Report is to the effect that 'Acts do not count as practice if they are not public'.[288] As noted by ILC

---

282 J. Crawford, *Brownlie's Principles of Public International Law* 8th edn (OUP 2012) 419; Marques Antunes (n 276) [21].

283 Di Stefano (n 215) 871; MacGibbon (n 276) 173, citing many examples of State practice and judicial decisons. See also: Barale (n 214) 400, 401:

> il est bien certain qu'un Etat ne saurait être considéré comme ayant acquiescé à une situation qu'il ignorait. Seule une connaissance certaine des ambitions ou des agissements d'un autre Etat permet à un Etat d'élever une protestation, d'opposer une réaction, d'avoir un comportement qui ne puisse être considéré comme un acquiescement'.

284 Crawford, *Brownlie's Principles* (n 282) 419; Marques Antunes (n 276) [21].

285 MacGibbon (n 276) 176; Barale (n 214) 402.

286 On this question, see P. Dumberry, *The Formation and Identification of Rules of Customary International Law in International Investment Law* (CUP 2016) 152.

287 Maurice H. Mendelson, 'The Formation of Customary International Law', (1985) 192 Rec des Cours 204; Jean-Marie Henckaerts and Louise Doswald-Beck (eds), *Customary International Humanitarian Law*, vol. I (CUP 2005), Xxxviii; Y. Dinstein, 'The Interaction between Customary International Law and Treaties' (2006) 322 Rec. des cours 278, 275; L. Ferrari-Bravo, 'Méthodes de recherche de la coutume internationale dans la pratique des États', (1985) 192 Rec des cours 269.

288 International Law Association, 'Statement of Principles Applicable to the Formation of General Customary International Law', Final Report of the Committee on the Formation of Customary Law, Conference Report London (2000) 15. The Commentary to this principle reads as follows:

> For a verbal act to count as State practice, it must be public – not in the sense that it need necessarily be communicated to all of the world, but that, if it is not publicized generally (e.g., by legislation, press statements, etc.), it must be communicated to at least one other State. (For example, protests are not always generally publicized, but they are at least communicated to one other State.) Internal memoranda are therefore not, as such, forms of State practice, and the confidential opinions of Government legal advisers, for instance, are not examples of the objective element in custom. If the customary process is seen as one of claim and response, the reason is clear: an internal memorandum which is not communicated to others is not a claim or a response. (It is otherwise if the State publicizes the legal analysis in support of its

Special Rapporteur Wood, 'a State whose inaction is sought to be relied upon in identifying whether a rule of customary international law has emerged must have had actual knowledge of the practice in question or the circumstances must have been such that the State concerned is deemed to have had such knowledge'.[289]

Another important element is the degree of specificity of the *content* of a unilateral declaration and the *audience* to whom the statement is addressed. Thus, one needs to distinguish, on the one hand, a *general* statement by a new State addressed to all States, and, on the other hand, a *specific* declaration made directly to one State in particular. **4.27**

To illustrate the first point, let us take the example mentioned above of the unilateral proclamation by the Czech Republic upon its independence that it 'will consider itself being bound by multilateral and bilateral agreements and treaties, to which the Czech and Slovak Federal Republic was a party on the same date'.[290] This is a very general statement made potentially to *all States* regarding *all treaties* to which the predecessor State was a party. In my view, not much can be inferred from the silence or the passivity of one particular State following such a general declaration by the Czech Republic. This is, in fact, one of three 'situations' referred to by Waldock where he believes that there is a 'real difficulty' in determining whether or not tacit consent exists between the parties for the continuation of a bilateral treaty.[291] In this specific context, something more than mere silence would be necessary to recognize the consent of a State with regards to the continuation of bilateral treaties to which Czechoslovakia was a party. The Supreme Court of Austria has, however, held that one 1954 treaty signed by Yugoslavia and Austria was binding on Austria by the mere fact that Croatia had made a general declaration of succession in its declaration of independence.[292] In general, it is **4.28**

position: it then becomes part of its claim.) If the memorandum is only afterwards made public (e.g., through the operation of laws opening national archives to the public after a certain period of time), it may be evidence of the State's subjective attitude to the issue, but is not an instance of the 'objective element'.

289 ILC, Third Report Wood (n 278) 11–14.

290 Proclamation of the National Council of the Czech Republic to all Parliaments and Nations of the World (n 77).

291 ILC, Fourth Report, 1971 (n 217) 150 [16] defining the situation as one 'where the new State has evidenced a general intention in favour of the continuance of its predecessor's treaties but has not manifested any specific intention with reference to the particular treaty'.

292 Case no. 20b69/92, 16 Dec. 1992. See also other cases referred to in: Kolliopoulos (n 248) 333.

important to analyse how other States react to such a general declaration by a new State.[293] The question of State conduct is specifically examined below.[294] One example of a positive reaction to a general declaration would be for a State to list these treaties next to the name of a successor State in some official governmental publication.[295] For instance, if following the Czech Republic's declaration Canada was to list on its website a number of treaties to which Czechoslovakia was a party and indicate that the said treaties have a binding force on the Czech Republic, this would provide a strong presumption of Canada's consent for the continuation of these treaties.[296]

4.29 The situation is clearly different when a declaration of continuation is made specifically to a State. I have examined several examples above (at Chapter 3) where the successor State and the other State party have exchanged notes and diplomatic correspondence whereby they have specifically addressed the fate of one or several treaties. One example mentioned above is the exchange of notes between Bosnia and the Netherlands. In a first letter, Bosnia stated that it was 'bound' by a number of specifically listed bilateral treaties concluded between the SFRY and the Netherlands.[297] While the letter affirmed that 'these treaties should remain in force' between the two States until they 'agree otherwise', it also indicated that Bosnia 'would appreciate the notification' of the Netherlands 'on the acceptance of this notification'. In such a case, it would be *expected* that the Netherlands respond (as it did) to that letter by accepting or refusing the offer to continue each treaty. What would happen in the event that the Netherlands would not respond? In my view, from this silence, it could logically be inferred that the Netherlands did not oppose the continuation of these treaties.[298] This should indeed be the case after a certain reasonable period of time has elapsed after the offer was made.[299]

---

293 Kolliopoulos (n 248) 332.

294 See, Chapter 4, Section 2.2.

295 ILC, Fourth Report, 1971(n 217) 146 [13] giving the example of the United States.

296 Kolliopoulos (n 248) 333.

297 Exchange of Notes between the Government of the Kingdom of the Netherlands of the Government of the Republic of Bosnia and Herzegovina on bilateral treaty relations, signed on 21 September 1995 and 29 February 1996, entered into force on 29 February 1996, available at: https://verdragenbank.overheid.nl/en/Verdrag/Details/011803.

298 Di Stefano (n 215) 871, indicating that 'l'acquiescement "passif" peut aussi résulter de l'inaction prolongée, du silence, de l'absence de protestations ou de réactions d'un Etat vis-à-vis des positions ou prétentions manifestées par l'autre Etat'. See also: Kolliopoulos (n 248) 331–2.

299 On the time factor, see: MacGibbon (n 276), 143: 'The presumption of consent which may be raised by silence is strengthened in proportion to the length of the period during which the silence is maintained'; Barale (n 214) 404:

> L'écoulement du temps joue certainement un rôle dans l'information des Etats. La connaissance, en dehors de tout procédé de publicité formel, n'est pas toujours immédiate et instantanée; elle est déduite alors, selon l'opinion des juges et des arbitres, de manière quasi-nécessaire, de la notoriété prolongée de la

Thus, had the Netherlands been against such continuation of treaties, Bosnia would have been informed in a timely manner. This is because the Netherlands' interests are *specifically affected* by the declaration made by Bosnia. According to Crawford, the requirements for acquiescence include the 'prolonged tolerance' by a State 'whose interests are specially affected'.[300] Moreover, acquiescence can result from silence or inaction 'in circumstances such that a response expressing disagreement or objection in relation to the conduct of another State would be called for'.[301] A response by a State is indeed called for when a declaration or a claim made by another State affects its interests or *rights*.[302] This is a situation where a State that does not recognize a claim made by another should 'protest'.[303] Given the fact that the Netherlands' 'interests are specially affected' by the claim of treaty continuation made by Bosnia, it would be reasonable to expect an objection from its side. For that reason, this is a situation where silence or passivity could (depending on the circumstances) be considered as a form of tacit consent. Yet, as noted by one writer, this is just a presumption and can therefore be refuted.[304] **4.30**

2.1.2 Devolution agreements

Statements indicating the willingness of one State for the continuation of a treaty can take other forms than a unilateral declaration. Such statements can sometimes be found in so-called 'devolution agreements'.[305] This section will first examine the nature and effect of such agreements, which will then be followed by an analysis of the different instruments adopted in the context of the break-up of the USSR. **4.31**

---

situation. En de pareilles hypothèses, l'écoulement du temps est tout aussi nécessaire à la réalisation de l'acquiescement.

300 Crawford, *Brownlie's Principles* (n 282) 419. See also: ILC, Third Report Wood (n 278) 11–14, in the different context of whether an omission can be considered as relevant State practice for the elaboration of custom: 'the relevant practice ought to be one that affects the interests or rights of the State failing or refusing to act'.

301 Marques Antunes (n 276) [2, 22]. See also: MacGibbon (n 276) 143: 'Acquiescence thus takes the form of silence or absence of protest in circumstances which generally call for a positive reaction signifying an objection.' See further: ILC, Third Report Wood (n 278) 11–14, in the different context of whether an omission can be considered as relevant State practice for the elaboration of custom: 'inaction could be relevant only to establishing concurrence where reaction to the relevant practice is called for (…)'.

302 MacGibbon (n 276) 182: 'Acquiescence is equivalent to tacit-or implied consent. It takes the form of silence or absence of protest in circumstances which, according to the practice of States and the weight of authority, demand a positive reaction in order to preserve a right.'

303 See, Christopher Eick, 'Protest', *Max Planck Encyclopedia of Public International Law* (OUP, online edn, 2006).

304 MacGibbon (n 276) 183: 'The presumption of consent which may be derived from acquiescence may, of course, be rebutted by a clear indication of a contrary intention.'

305 Tams (n 27) 28.

2.1.2.1 The nature and effect of devolution agreements

4.32 The resolution adopted by the Institut de Droit international in 2015 on the question of State succession to State responsibility contains the following definition of the term 'devolution agreement':

> 'Devolution agreement' means an agreement, concluded by the predecessor State and the successor State or a national liberation, insurrectional or other movement, or an entity or organ that later becomes the organ of the successor State, providing that rights and/or obligations of the predecessor State shall devolve upon the successor State.[306]

4.33 These agreements are generally signed *before* independence between the predecessor State and the soon-to-be new State regarding the transfer of obligations or rights under bilateral treaties from the former to the latter.[307] It should be noted that the existence of any such agreement does *not* result in the new State succeeding *de facto* to all bilateral treaties of the predecessor State after its independence.[308] A devolution agreement is merely an *offer* made (*after* independence) by the new State to other States parties for the continuation of bilateral treaties. As noted by Zemanek, for these States a devolution agreement 'create[s] only a presumption that the State concerned intends to succeed to such treaties of its predecessor as it will determine.'[309] It is at the discretion of the other States to accept or refuse the offer made by the new State. In other words, just like unilateral declarations, devolution agreements are not binding on third parties.[310] This is specifically stated in Article 8 of the 1978 Vienna Convention:

> The obligations or rights of a predecessor State under treaties in force in respect of a territory at the date of a succession of States do not become the obligations or rights of the successor State towards other States Parties to those treaties by reason only of the fact that the predecessor State and the successor State have concluded an agreement providing that such obligations or rights shall devolve upon the successor State.[311]

---

306 Institut de Droit international, *State Succession in Matters of State Responsibility*, 14th Commission, (Rap. M.G. Kohen), Resolution, 28 August 2015, Art. 1 [hereinafter 'IDI, State Succession to Responsibility, Resolution, 2015'].

307 ILC Report, 26th Session, 1974 (n 24) 187, 183. For an analysis, see: Asier Garrido-Munoz, 'Article 8' in Distefano, Gaggioli and Hêche (n 4), 266ff.

308 Ibid., 274ff.

309 Karl Zemanek, 'State Succession after Decolonization', (1965–III) 116 Rec des cours 221, see also at 235 dealing specifically with bilateral treaties.

310 Tams (n 27) 333; Zimmermann and Devaney, 'Succession to Treaties' (n 1) 536; Evelyne Lagrange, 'Les successions d'États: pratiques françaises', (2003) 63 *La L Rev* 1224ff; C. Binder, '*Sanum Investments Limited v. The Government of the Lao People's Democratic Republic*' (2016) 17 *J World Invest & Trade* 292; Odysseas G. Repousis, 'On Territoriality and International Investment Law: Applying China's Investment Treaties To Hong Kong And Macao' (2015) 37(1) *Michigan JIL* 186; Pereira (n 222) 153ff.

311 Vienna Convention on Succession to Treaties (n 5).

One concrete example of such an agreement will be examined in the next section in the context of the break-up of the USSR. **4.34**

2.1.2.2 One illustration: different instruments adopted in the context of the break-up of the USSR

On 8 December 1991, Russia, Belarus and Ukraine signed an agreement (the 'Minsk Agreement') establishing a Commonwealth of Independent States ('CIS') in which they decided to 'undertake to discharge the international obligations incumbent on them under treaties and agreements entered into by the former Union of Soviet Socialist Republics'.[312] Two weeks later, eight of the remaining nine Soviet Republics joined the CIS by way of the 'Alma Ata Declaration' and a 'Protocol to the CIS Agreement'.[313] The Declaration provided that '[t]he States participating in the Commonwealth guarantee in accordance with their constitutional procedures the discharge of the international obligations deriving from treaties and agreements concluded by the former Union of Soviet Socialist Republics'.[314] Whether or not the Minsk Agreement and the Alma Ata Declaration should be considered as devolution agreements is the object of some controversy.[315] In fact, one writer noted that despite the collegial character of the Alma Ata Declaration, the declarations of succession made by the former Republics remain essentially *unilateral* in nature given the fact that each State would have to deal individually with the question of succession to specific treaties.[316] This unilateral dimension is further evidenced by the Moscow Memorandum (discussed below). **4.35**

One controversial question is the effect of such statements on the successor States themselves. Thus, for Tams, 'broad statements such as those made by the CIS member States may [be] too general to provide evidence of a willingness to continue specific treaties'.[317] Many scholars have indeed doubted whether this is the case. They have thus highlighted the fact that continuity of treaties under the Alma Ata Declaration is, in any event, dependent on the compatibility with the 'constitutional procedures' of each [of the] former Republics,[318] which would exclude any *automatic* succession.[319] In **4.36**

---

312 Minsk Agreement (n 106).

313 Declaration of Alma Ata (n 106), signed by ten former Republics and Russia.

314 Ibid.

315 Stern, 'La succession d'États' (n 75) 237 refers to them as such. Garrido-Munoz (n 307) 266–9, seems to be refuting this qualification on the ground that the agreements were signed by the successor States and the continuator State (Russia) *after* the date of succession, and did not involve the predecessor State (USSR).

316 Kolliopoulos (n 248) 317.

317 Tams (n 27) 334.

318 Pazartzis (n 109) 161; Hafner and Kornfeind (n 38) 13; Williams (n 135) 22–3.

319 Eisemann (n 110) 45:

any event, the Declaration represents (at best) an agreement *amongst* the CIS member States only and does *not* bind other States parties.[320] It is therefore important to analyse how other States have reacted to such a declaration. As mentioned above,[321] Spain indicates on its website that it has BITs relationship with seven former Republics (referring expressly to the Spain-USSR BIT[322]) based on their general declaration of treaty continuity contained in the *Alma Ata Declaration*.[323] Spain therefore accepted the offer made by the new States. Yet, as mentioned above, some of these States do not seem to consider themselves bound by the Spain-USSR BIT.

4.37 It should be added that CIS member States concluded on 6 July 1992 the 'Memorandum of Understanding Concerning the Issues of Succession to Treaties of the [F]ormer Union of SSR which Represent Mutual Interest' (Moscow Memorandum).[324] It provides that bilateral treaties of the former Soviet Union concerning 'two or more CIS States' 'require[s] the adoption of decisions or actions by those Commonwealth member states to which such treaties apply'.[325] It is not entirely clear whether the Memorandum covers the

---

> Comme il l'a été déjà mentionné, les États de la CEI ont, certes, garanti le respect des engagements internationaux découlant d'accords signés par l'ex-URSS mais en assortissant cette 'garantie' d'une réserve se référant à une 'conformité avec leurs propres procédures législatives' ce qui semble exclure toute succession *ipso jure* et, par suite, ouvrir la voie à une sélection unilatérale ou, à tout le moins, à une négociation avec les États intéressés.

See also: Hamant (n 127) 220, referring to the following position adopted by Mr. Verechtchatine, a member of the ILC, in an interview in Izvestia:

> les formules contenues dans l'accord de Minsk et la déclaration d'Alta Ata exprimaient seulement une position de principe des nouveau États (...). Toutefois, il ne ressortait pas de ces documents que les membres de la CEI devenaient automatiquement parties à tous les traités conclus en leur temps par l'URSS.

See also: Langstrom (n 122) 777

> this 'promise' of the CIS States did not mean that all treaties would be automatically in force in respect of their territories. What they must have committed themselves to was to consider the obligations in good faith and perhaps to negotiate on them with other States parties. However it is clear that the participation in a particular treaty was left subject to the sovereign decision of each State. This position was later confirmed, *inter alia*, in the Moscow Memorandum of Understanding of 6 July 1992.

320 Williams (n 135) 22–3, indicating that it remains 'unclear' whether it 'would be useful, aside from political persuasion, in attempting to bind a successor state to the treaty obligations of the former Soviet Union'.

321 See, Chapter 3, Section 2.4.

322 Spain, Ministerio de Economía (n 169).

323 Declaration of Alma Ata (n 106).

324 A French translation of the memorandum may be found in (1993) 26 RBDI 627–8. It should be added that on March 1992, the Council of the Heads of the State Members of the CIS stated, inter alia, that 'all state members of the Commonwealth of Independent States are the successors to the rights and obligations of the former Union of SSR'. (Resolution of the Heads of the Commonwealth of Independent States on Succession to Treaties of Mutual Interest, State Property, Archives, Debts and Assets of the former Soviet Union, 20 March 1992).

325 It should be added that the Memorandum stated the following regarding *multilateral* treaties:

specific case of BITs that had been entered into by the USSR with other States at the time of the date of succession. It has been argued that the Alma Ata Declaration must be read together with the Moscow Memorandum,[326] suggesting that succession to bilateral treaties would be subject to case-by-case negotiations to be undertaken *by each CIS member separately* with other States.[327]

2.2 Conduct of the parties

4.38 Statements and devolution agreements are not the only way for States to express their views on treaty continuation. As noted by Tams, 'while the applicability of a BIT is a matter for objective determination by the tribunal, the respondent State's views in the proceedings may be indicative'.[328] Tams rightly points out that 'in some of the proceedings brought against the Czech Republic and Slovakia, arbitral tribunals for example, seemed willing to treat questions of succession en passant because the Claimant and Respondent had agreed on the matter'.[329] Chapter 6 will examine a number of cases involving the Czech and Slovak Republics where tribunals stated that the issue of succession to the BIT was not disputed between the parties during the proceedings.[330] I have found another relevant example where the conduct of the *home* State of an investor during arbitration proceedings shows its intention to be considered bound by a BIT with a new State. As further discussed below, in the *WWM* case, a Canadian investor filed a claim against Kazakhstan invoking

---

> [I]n practice all multilateral treaties of the former Soviet Union have general interest for the member States of the Commonwealth. At the same time, these treaties do not require any joint decisions of or action by the member States. Participation in these treaties will be decided in accordance with the principles and norms of international law individually by every member State depending on specificity of every concrete case, and on the character and content of every treaty.

326 Hamant (n 127) 220, indicating regarding the Moscow Memorandum that 'les membres de la CEI sont convenue des démarches communes qu'ils auraient éventuellement à entreprendre en vue de la succession aux traités de l'URSS' À cette fin, ils sont adopté, le 6 juillet 1992, le Mémorandum (…)'. See also: Langstrom (n 122) 777.

327 Craven, *The Decolonization of International Law* (n 8) 240:

> In the case of the Republics of the former USSR, the general position as regards bilateral treaties was spelt out in the joint Memorandum of Understanding of 6 July 1992, by which the Member States of the CIS agreed that the fate of some bilateral treaties which concerned two or more of the Republics would be determined by them in negotiations with the respective third parties, and that other bilateral treaties (in particular border treaties) would remain in force for those Member States of the CIS who have a common border with a third State.

See also: Langstrom (n 122) 777; Kolliopoulos (n 248) 323.

328 Tams (n 27) 334.

329 Ibid., 29.

330 See, Chapter 6, Section 2. One example is the case of *HICEE BV v. Slovak Republic*, UNCITRAL, PCA Case No 2009–11, Partial Award, 23 May 2011, at [3 fn. 2], where the Tribunal affirmed that 'It is not in dispute that, after the dissolution of the Czech and Slovak Federal Republic on 31 December 1992, the Slovak Republic succeeded to the [CSFR-Netherlands BIT]'.

a breach of the 1991 Canada-USSR BIT. The question at the heart of this case was whether or not Kazakhstan is bound by this BIT as one of the successor States to the USSR.[331] Importantly, Canada and Kazakhstan did not formally continue the BIT. Canada submitted a 'Non-disputing party submission' in the context of the proceedings whereby it affirmed that it considered the BIT to be binding on Kazakhstan. The tribunal rendered an award that remains confidential, where it held that it had jurisdiction over the dispute under the Canada-USSR BIT.[332] The tribunal therefore considered the BIT to be binding on Kazakhstan based on the conduct of both Canada and the new State and their tacit consent for the continuation of the treaty.

4.39 The work of the ILC refers to the importance of State conduct *more generally*, that is, outside the specific context of court or arbitral proceedings. It should be recalled that Article 24 of the Convention indicates that a bilateral treaty can continue to be in force between a new State and the 'other State Party' if 'by reason of their conduct' they are considered to have agreed to such continuation.[333] In his Report, Waldock refers to a few examples of State conduct, which can be interpreted as showing an intention to be considered bound by a treaty:

> It then becomes a question whether the rule should seek to indicate particular acts or conduct which give rise to the inference that the State concerned has consented to the continuance of a bilateral treaty or whether it should merely be formulated in general terms. Among points which suggest themselves are whether any particular provisions should be inserted concerning the inferences to be drawn from a new State's conclusion of a devolution agreement, or from a unilateral declaration inviting continuance of treaties (provisionally or otherwise) or from a unilateral listing of a predecessor State's treaty as in force in relation to a new State, or from the continuance in force of a treaty in the internal law of a State, or from reliance on the provisions of the treaty by a new State or by the other State party to it in their mutual relations.[334]

4.40 Waldock believed that there were good reasons for Article 24 *not* to contain a detailed list of particular acts or conduct that could be considered as an inferred consent.[335] Di Stefano makes reference to the following positive actions taken by a State from which inferences could be drawn:

---

331 *WWM v. Kazakhstan* (n 53).

332 Disclaimer: The present author acted as counsel for Kazakhstan in these proceedings.

333 ILC Report, 26th Session, 1974 (n 24) 240 [16]: 'the Commission concludes that *the conduct of the particular States* in relation to the particular treaty should be the basis of the general rule for bilateral treaties' (emphasis added).

334 ILC, Fourth Report, 1971 (n 217) 150 [20].

335 Ibid.:

> It may, however, be doubted whether the insertion of any such provisions prescribing the inferences to be drawn from particular kinds of acts would be justified. In the case of devolution agreements and unilateral

> Parmi les *comportements actifs* des Etats retenus comme des indices d'acquiescement, à côté des *déclarations* contenues dans des instruments internationaux ou internes, d'autres *actes concrets* accomplis aussi dans le cadre des relations internationales ou de l'ordre interne peuvent bien constituer des manifestations de volonté: tel est le cas des échanges diplomatiques, de la conclusion d'autres traités internationaux, de l'invocation d'une norme conventionnelle relevant au cours d'une affaire contentieuse ou encore de la publication officielle du texte d'un accord bilatéral, etc. D'ailleurs, le plus simple et immédiat signe extérieur d'un accord tacite sur le régime juridique des conventions bilatérales objets de la succession est évidemment l'application même du traité en question.[336]

One interesting example of State conduct mentioned by Waldock (and Di Stefano) is the 'listing of treaties against the name of a successor State' in an official governmental publication.[337] This is indeed one the arguments which was raised by the respondent in the *WWM* case to convince the tribunal that Canada did not consider the Canada-USSR BIT to be in force with Kazakhstan.[338] Although the award is confidential, the publicly available information shows (still to this day) that the website of Canada's Ministry of Foreign Affairs (now known as 'Global Affairs') did not list the Canada-USSR BIT as one of the bilateral treaties in force with Kazakhstan.[339] Also, the Ministry's separate list of 'Foreign Investment Protection Agreements' to which Canada **4.41**

> declarations, much depends both on their particular terms and on the intentions of those who made them. As appears from the commentaries to articles 3 and 4, even where States may appear in such instruments to express a general intention to continue their predecessors' treaties, they frequently make the continuance of a particular treaty a matter of discussion and agreement with the other interested State. Moreover, in all cases it is not simply a question of the intention of one State but of both: of the inferences to be drawn from the act of one and the reaction – or absence of reaction – of the other. Inevitably the circumstances of any one case differ from those of another and it would hardly seem possible to lay down general presumptions without taking the risk of defeating the real intention of one or other State. Of course, one of the two States concerned may so act as to lead the other reasonably to suppose that it had agreed to the continuance in force of a particular treaty, in which event account has to be taken of the principle of good faith applied in article 45 of the Vienna Convention on the Law of Treaties (often referred to as estoppel or *preclusion)*. But subject to the application of that principle, the problem is always one of establishing the consent of each State to consider the treaty as in force in their mutual relations either by express evidence or by inference from the circumstances.

See also: P.K. Menon, 'The Newly Independent States and Succession in Respect of Treaties', (1990) 18 *Korean JCL* 158:

> If there is no express agreement, difficulties may arise as to determine what particular acts or conduct will constitute an agreement by implication. In an attempt to formulate a general rule, the Commission found it extremely difficult to enumerate the situations which gave rise to the inference that the State concerned had consented to the continuance of a treaty. What it concluded was that the conduct of the particular States in relation to the particular treaty should be the basis of the general rule for bilateral treaties.

336 Di Stefano (n 215) 870 (emphasis added).

337 ILC, Fourth Report, 1971 (n 217) 146 [13] giving the example of the United States.

338 *WWM v. Kazakhstan* (n 53).

339 See, Canada, Global Affairs, http://www.treaty-accord.gc.ca/search-recherche.aspx?type=1&page=TLB&lang=eng. The website lists a number of treaties as being in force between Canada and Kazakhstan, but not the Canada-USSR BIT.

is a party refers only to one BIT in force with Russia (which is in fact the 1989 Canada-USSR BIT) and one BIT with Kazakhstan which is under 'negotiation' and not in force yet.[340] In other words, to this day (i.e., after the award has been rendered) there is still no mention on Canada's official governmental websites that the Canada-USSR BIT is in force between Canada and Kazakhstan.

4.42 In my view, the listing of a specific BIT in a list of treaties in force naturally suggests that that State considered itself to be bound by that instrument.[341] The more complicated question is what to infer from the *absence* of listing an old BIT as one of the treaties in force with a successor State. At the heart of the issue is the question of the weight which should be given to any such information found on a governmental website. Thus, should one consider this information as representing the official position of a State with respect to treaties it considers to be in force? Suffice it to say, for the purpose of this book, that many governmental websites contain disclaimers expressly stating that this should not be the case.[342] In sum, while the absence of listings of a BIT on a State's official website is not insignificant, it remains that this fact alone should not be considered as the determinant factor when assessing that State's intention regarding the continuation of a treaty with a successor State.

---

340 See, Canada, Global Affairs, Trade and investment agreements, https://www.international.gc.ca/trade-commerce/trade-agreements-accords-commerciaux/agr-acc/index.aspx?lang=eng. The link to the document indicates that 'Canada and Kazakhstan have agreed to begin negotiations towards a Foreign Investment Promotion and Protection Agreement (FIPA)' and that 'The first round of negotiations took place in June 2011 in Astana': http://international.gc.ca/trade-commerce/trade-agreements-accords-commerciaux/agr-acc/kazakhstan/fipa-apie/background-contexte.aspx?lang=eng.

341 Kolliopoulos (n 248) 333.

342 See, for instance: UK Treaties Online, available at: http://treaties.fco.gov.uk/treaties/treaty.htm, which contains the following reference:

> Disclaimer: The information provided on this database is for guidance only. Whilst the FCO Treaty Section takes care to obtain its information from reliable sources, the accuracy of database records cannot be guaranteed. The FCO will not be liable for any loss or damage resulting from any reliance placed on this information.

United States Department of State, Treaties in Force. A List of Treaties and Other International Agreements of the United States in Force on January 1, 2016, available at: https://www.state.gov/documents/organization/267489.pdf: which contains the following reference: 'While all efforts are made to ensure the accuracy of this publication, the presence or absence of a particular agreement, as well as the details cited regarding a listed agreement, should not be regarded as determinative of the status of the agreement.' The website the Swiss Government also contains the same remark: 'Remarque: les informations sont régulièrement complétées et contrôlées. Il n'y a cependant de garantie ni d'exhaustivité ni d'exactitude absolue. Seules les informations publiées dans le Recueil officiel du droit fédéral (RO) ont une portée juridique contraignante', available at: https://www.eda.admin.ch/content/eda/fr/home/aussenpolitik/voelkerrecht/internationale_vertraege/datenbank_staatsvertraege.filterResults.term.country767.organization-1.topic0_975.html?_charset_=UTF-8.

In his Report, Waldock identified the following 'situation' as one involving a 'real difficulty' to determine whether or not any tacit consent exists between the parties as to the continuation of a treaty: 'one State may have evidenced in some manner an apparent intention to consider a treaty as continuing in force—for example by listing the treaty amongst its treaties in force – but the other State has done nothing in the matter'.[343] As mentioned above,[344] Spain indicates on its website that it has BITs relationship with seven former Republics (referring expressly to the Spain-USSR BIT[345]) based on their general declaration of treaty continuity contained in the Alma Ata Declaration.[346] Apart from the question (mentioned above) of the weight that should be given to information found on such a governmental website, the issue is whether anything can be inferred from the other State's passivity in this respect. There is no doubt that any reference to a BIT on a website remains of a very general character and is publicly available for everyone. In other words, it cannot be compared to an exchange of letters between States referring to the continuation of specific treaties. On the other hand, one would normally expect that State to react at some point in time to the assertion made by the other State on its website. This is because its interests are specifically affected by the other State's claim of continuity. Yet, overall the better position is probably that not much should be inferred from one State's silence. Thus, such inaction should not be considered as the determinant factor establishing that State's intention to be bound by that treaty. 4.43

There are a number of other situations where the common intention of States for the continuation of a treaty is easily assessable. For instance, Waldock refers to the situation where the parties have concretely *applied* the terms of a treaty in their actual practice which 'necessarily implies an agreement [between them] to consider it as being in force'.[347] He also refers to air-transport agreements where 'continuity has quite often simply occurred', and 'might be interpreted as indicating recognition of a right or obligation to maintain them in force' by 'tacit manifestation of the will of the interested States'.[348] 4.44

Waldock also refers to the situation where 'reliance on the provisions of the treaty by a new State or by the other State party to it in their mutual 4.45

343 ILC, Fourth Report, 1971 (n 217) 150 [16].
344 See, Chapter 3, Section 2.4.
345 Spain, Ministerio de Economía (n 169).
346 Declaration of Alma Ata (n 106).
347 ILC, Fourth Report, 1971 (n 217) 150 [16] referring to International Law Association, Report of the 53rd Conference, Buenos Aires, 1968 (1969) 597.
348 Ibid., 148 [12] (emphasis added).

relations'.[349] Thus, what should be inferred from the fact that the preamble of a treaty entered into by both the new State and the other State party refers explicitly to another treaty between them? Any explicit reference contained in a treaty to another treaty strongly suggests that both countries consider the latter instrument as being in force between them. The matter was dealt with in the *WWM* award. But what about the reverse situation where the preamble to a treaty refers explicitly to a number of instruments entered into by the two States, but not to one specific treaty. What should be inferred from such an omission? Should it be considered as an indication that they do not consider this specific treaty to be in force between them? One cannot answer this question in the abstract since it depends largely on the circumstances of each case, including the history of the drafting of the treaty and the reasons which led to this omission. Another relevant factor is the category of treaties and whether one would have normally (and logically) expected the parties to refer to this specific treaty in the preamble. For instance, it would seem odd for the preamble of a trade agreement that refers to all other treaties concerning investment and economic cooperation that are in force between the two States to omit to mention a BIT. From this oversight it could be inferred (yet, much will depend on the circumstances of each case) that the parties do not consider this BIT to be in force between them.

349 Ibid., 150 [20].

5

CRITICAL ANALYSIS OF THE SOLUTIONS ADOPTED BY THE VIENNA CONVENTION

INTRODUCTION

5.01 Having examined the practice of States regarding the fate of BITs that had been concluded by the predecessor State before the date of succession in Chapter 3, I will now analyse the solution that should prevail in the event where the States concerned have not agreed on that point. Thus, what happens when the successor State and the other State party to the BIT of the predecessor State have not expressly (or implicitly) agreed on the continuation (or non-continuation) of this instrument? The question then becomes whether there exists any principle of automatic continuation to BITs whereby the successor State is *de facto* bound by such instruments.[350]

5.02 The present section first examines the different solutions which have been adopted under the Vienna Convention for specific types of State succession (Section 1). The following section will specifically assess the soundness of the application in the principle of continuity, which has been adopted under the Vienna Convention for cases of secession and dissolution of States (Section 2). I will then argue that contrary to the position taken by the Vienna Convention, the *tabula rasa* principle should apply to these cases.

5.03 Before getting to the heart of the issue, it is important to understand the history of the Vienna Convention as well as its basic features. The Convention was adopted in 1978 and entered into force on 6 November 1996. The history of the work of the ILC on State succession to treaties can be roughly summarized as follows (as further explained,[351] this sequence of events is quite significant in the context of the drafting of Article 34 applying for secession and dissolution of State):

- The ILC Special Rapporteur, Sir Humphrey Waldock, submitted five reports: in 1968,[352] 1969,[353] 1970,[354] 1971,[355] and 1972.[356]

---

350 This question is examined in: Dumberry, 'An Uncharted Question of State Succession' (n 40) 74–96.

351 See, Chapter 5, Sections 1.5 and 2.3.

352 ILC, First Report on Succession of States and Governments in Respect of Treaties, prepared by the Special Rapporteur, Sir Humphrey Waldock, A/CN.4/202, 15 March 1968, A/7209/Rev.1, in: *YILC*, 1968, vol. II.

353 ILC, Second Report on Succession in Respect of Treaties, prepared by the Special Rapporteur, Sir Humphrey Waldock, A/CN.4/214 and Adds.1 and 2, 18 April, 9 June and 22 July 1969, A/8010/Rev.1, in: *YILC*, 1969, vol. II [hereinafter 'ILC Report, Second Report, 1969'].

354 ILC, Third Report on Succession in Respect of Treaties, prepared by the Special Rapporteur, Sir Humphrey Waldock, A/CN.4/224 and Add.1, 22 April and 27 May 1970, A/8010/Rev.1, in: *YILC*, 1970, vol. II [hereinafter 'ILC Report, Third Report, 1970'].

355 ILC, Fourth Report, 1971 (n 217).

356 ILC, Fifth Report on Succession in Respect of Treaties, prepared by the Special Rapporteur, Sir Humphrey Waldock, A/CN.4/256 and Adds.1–4, 10 April, 29 May and 8, 16 and 28 June 1972, A/8710/Rev.1, in: *YILC*, 1972, vol. II [hereinafter 'ILC Report, Fifth Report, 1972'].

- At its 24th session, in 1972, the ILC adopted a provisional draft during its first reading,[357] along with commentaries for each provision.[358] The draft articles were transmitted to Member States for their observations;
- In 1973, the ILC appointed a new Special Rapporteur, Sir Francis Vallat, who submitted a first report in 1974 summarizing the comments received from the various States;[359]
- At its 26th session, in 1974, the Commission adopted the final text of the draft articles on succession of States in respect to treaties, together with commentaries for each provision;[360] Member States were invited to submit their written comments and observations with regards to the draft articles;
- The United Nations Conference on Succession of States in Respect of Treaties, a conference of plenipotentiaries, was held in Vienna in May 1977 and August 1978;
- On 22 August 1978, the Conference adopted the Vienna Convention on Succession of States in Respect of Treaties and the Final Act of the Conference was signed the following day;
- The Convention entered into force on 6 November 1996.

Article 2 of the Convention defines the term 'treaty' as including both bilateral and multilateral treaties. The Convention gives effect to a fundamental distinction between 'Newly Independent States' emerging from decolonization (Arts 16–30) and other new States not emerging from decolonization (Arts 31 *et seq.*). As further discussed below, this basic distinction was, however, not apparent in the first four reports filed by ILC Special Rapporteur Waldock. It only transpired later, in 1972, when the ILC adopted its first provisional draft.[361] The next section provides a brief overview of the different solutions that have been codified through the Convention for the different types of successions. **5.04**

357 ILC, Draft Articles on Succession in Respect of Treaties: General Article submitted by the Special Rapporteur as a possible means of covering the question of lawfulness (A/CN.4/L.184, 12 June 1972, in: *YILC*, 1972, vol. II.

358 ILC, Report of the International Law Commission on the work of its 24th session, 2 May to 7 July 1972, A/8710/Rev.1, in: *YILC*, 1972, vol. II [hereinafter 'ILC Report, 24th Session, 1972'].

359 ILC, First Report on Succession of States in Respect of Treaties, Prepared by the Special Rapporteur, Sir Francis Vallat, A/CN.4/278 and Adds.1–6, 19 and 22 April, 8, 24 and 31 May and 10 and 21 June 1974, reproduced in A/9610/Rev.1, in: *YILC*, 1974, vol. II (Part One).

360 ILC Report, 26th Session, 1974 (n 24).

361 On the evolution of the work of the ILC, see Craven, *The Decolonization of International Law* (n 8) 131–2, 159–71.

1. OVERVIEW OF THE SOLUTIONS ADOPTED FOR DIFFERENT TYPES OF SUCCESSION

1.1 Transfer of territory

5.05 As mentioned above, events affecting the territorial integrity of the predecessor State do not always result in the creation of a new State, but may, in contrast, lead to the *enlargement* of the territory of an already *existing* State. This is the case in situations of a cession or transfer of territory from one existing State to another State. Article 15 of the Convention, which applies to both bilateral and multilateral treaties, provides as follows:

> When part of the territory of a State, or when any territory for the international relations of which a State is responsible, not being part of the territory of that State, becomes part of the territory of another State:
>
> (*a*) treaties of the predecessor State cease to be in force in respect of the territory to which the succession of States relates from the date of the succession of States; and
>
> (*b*) treaties of the successor State are in force in respect of the territory to which the succession of States relates from the date of the succession of States, unless it appears from the treaty or is otherwise established that the application of the treaty to that territory would be incompatible with the object and purpose of the treaty or would radically change the conditions for its operation.

5.06 The following subsections provide a detailed analysis of the principles and the exceptions contained in this clause.

1.1.1 The 'moving treaty frontier' rule

5.07 The basic principle set out at Article 15 is the 'moving treaty frontier' ('MTF') rule. Under that rule, when a territory of a State (State A) becomes (after the date of succession) part of the territory of another one (State B), the change of sovereignty over that territory has two effects: (i) the treaties of State B become applicable to the territory; and (ii) the treaties of State A cease to be applicable to that territory. In the words of Zimmermann, 'treaties of the predecessor [State] cease to be in force in respect of the ceded territory while treaties of the successor generally extend *ipso facto* to this territory'.[362] The

362 A. Zimmermann, 'State Succession in Treaties, in *Max Planck Encyclopedia of Public International Law* (OUP, online edn, 2006) [8]. See also, Tams (n 27) 337 referring to 'Waldock's more complicated formulation' distinguishing between a 'positive aspect' (i.e., 'the treaties of the successor State begin automatically to apply in respect of the [ceded] territory as from the date of the succession') and a 'negative aspect' ('the treaties of the predecessor State … cease automatically to apply in respect of the territory'), and adding that for Waldock 'in essence, the rule remains one of "a simple substitution of one treaty regime for another".' (referring to: ILC Report, Second Report, 1969 (n 353) 52).

'border' of the territorial application of a treaty is thus 'moved' on the map to take into account the cession of territory from one State to another. Tams further adds that the 'treaty status of the two States' is 'untouched' since the rule 'merely extends the geographical scope of treaties by moving their 'frontiers'.'[363] The following explanation about the rule is given by the Court of Appeal of Singapore in its 2016 judgment (further examined below[364]):

> Simply put, because a treaty is binding in respect of the *entire* territory of a State, the MTF Rule presumptively provides for the automatic extension of a treaty to a new territory as and when it becomes a part of that State. The MTF Rule further provides that as a territory undergoes a change in sovereignty, it passes automatically *out* of the treaty regime of the predecessor sovereign *into* the treaty regime of the successor sovereign.[365]

In the context of BITs, the application of this rule would have the following effect. After the cession of territory, a BIT entered into by State A with State Z would continue to be in force between them. The only difference would be with regards to its territorial application. Indeed, this BIT would solely bind the smaller territory of State A after the date of succession (i.e., without the territory that had been ceded to State B). The 'other State party' to the treaty (State Z) does not need to 'consent' to the continuation of the exact same treaty with the same State. This is because the international legal personality and identity of State A remains unaffected (it only has a smaller territory). The same is true with respect to BITs signed by State B (whose territory was *enlarged* as a result of the cession of territory) with other States. These BITs will continue to apply without any requirement to seek the consent of the parties concerned. **5.08**

A number of writers have affirmed that 'State practice, both before the adoption of the VCSST and ever since, was consistent in relation to this [MTF] rule'.[366] One recent example is the transfer of Walvis Bay from South Africa to Namibia in 1994.[367] Some writers now consider the MTF rule as **5.09**

363 Tams (n 27) 337.

364 See, Chapter 6, Section 5.2.

365 *Sanum Investments Ltd v. Government of the Lao People's Democratic Republic*, Judgment, 29 September 2016, Court of Appeal, [2016] SGCA 57 [49] (emphasis in the original) [hereinafter '*Sanum*, Judgment, Singapore of Court of Appeal, 2016'].

366 Zimmermann and Devaney, 'Succession to Treaties' (n 1) 520–21; A. Tanzi and L. Iapichino, 'Article 15' in Distefano, Gaggioli and Hêche (n 4), 547–9.

367 Tams (n 27) 339, referring to the Treaty between the Government of the Republic of South Africa and the Government of the Republic of Namibia with Respect to Walvis Bay and the Off-Shore Islands, (1994) 33 ILM 1526.

reflecting customary international law.[368] In the *Sanum* case (further examined in detail below[369]), the tribunal noted that there was 'unanimity or quasi-unanimity' among writers on the customary status of this provision.[370] The respondent in this case (Laos) accepted that the rule was an expression of custom,[371] but insisted that the specific case of the extension of the China-Laos BIT to the territory of Macao fell within the exceptions mentioned at Article 15.[372] In the *Sanum* case, both the Singapore High Court and the Court of Appeal noted that it was common ground between the parties that Article 15 reflects custom.[373]

1.1.2 The interaction between Article 15 and Article 29 VCLT

5.10 The MTF principle is also found in the 1969 Vienna Convention on the Law of Treaties ('VCLT') regarding the territorial scope of treaties. Thus, Article 29 states that '[u]nless a different intention appears from the treaty or is otherwise established, a treaty is binding upon each party in respect of its entire territory'.[374] The application of this provision has been at the heart of a number of arbitration cases (not involving succession issues per se) in recent years.[375] While Article 29 does not explicitly deal with matters of State succession,[376] the MTF principle is 'implicitly embodied' in this provision and finds application.[377] The Court of Appeal of Singapore came to the same

368 Tanzi and Iapichino (n 366) 547–9; Gerhard Hafner and Gregor Novak, 'State Succession in Respect of Treaties' in: Duncan B. Hollis (ed), *The Oxford Guide to Treaties* (OUP 2012) 411; Zimmermann and Devaney, 'Succession to Treaties' (n 1) 520, adding at 521:

> On the whole, it might be said that the respective parties involved in a transfer of territory have either followed the moving boundary rule, or where they have purported to deviate from this rule, have received the required (explicit or implicit) approval by third States. The moving boundary rule thus constitutes perhaps one of the most settled and clear-cut aspects of the law of State succession with regard to treaties.

See also: Tams (n 27) 337: 'This provision is widely held to reflect general international law'; K. Odendahl, 'Commentary to Article 29', in O. Dorr and K. Schmalenbach (eds), *The Vienna Convention on the Law of Treaties* (Springer 2012) 498–500; Daniel Costelloe, 'Treaty Succession in Annexed Territory' (2016) 65 ICLQ 351.

369 See, Chapter 6, Section 5.2.

370 *Sanum Investments Ltd. v. Laos*, UNCITRAL, PCA Case No 2013–13, Award on Jurisdiction, 13 December 2013 [221] see also [222]–[224] [hereinafter '*Sanum*, Award, 2013'].

371 Ibid., [53].

372 Ibid., [56].

373 *Sanum*, Judgment, Singapore of Court of Appeal, 2016 (n 365) [47].

374 On this provision, see: Marko Milanovic, 'The Spatial Dimension: Treaties and Territory', in C.J. Tams, A. Tzanakopoulos and A. Zimmermann (eds) *Research Handbook on the Law of Treaties' (*Cheltenham 2014); S. Karagiannis, 'Article 29,' in O. Corten and P. Klein (eds), *Les Conventions de Vienne sur le Droit des Traités. Commentaire Article par Article* (Bruylant 2006) 1189; Odendahl (n 368) 489; M. Villiger, *Commentary on the 1969 Vienna Convention on the Law of Treaties* (Nijhoff 2009) 387.

375 Odysseas G. Repousis, 'The Application of Investment Treaties to Overseas Territories and the Uncertain Provisional Application of the Energy Charter Treaty to Gibraltar', (2016) 32(1) *ICSID Rev* 170–92.

376 See, *YILC*, 1966, vol. II, p 214 [6].

377 Odendahl (n 368) 489, discussing the principle in the context of State succession at 498ff.

conclusion in its judgment.[378] It should be added that Article 29 VCLT is also considered to represent a rule of custom by writers,[379] by the *Sanum* Tribunal,[380] and by both the Singapore High Court and the Court of Appeal.[381]

The *Sanum* Tribunal explained that Articles 15 VCST and 29 VCLT were not incompatible but rather complementary as they referred to 'different moments in the evolution of a situation'.[382] Thus, while Article 15 deals with the situation at the moment of the date of succession, Article 29 has a wider application outside of a transitional period: 5.11

> Article 15 explains and regulates what happens at the moment of transition from one sovereign to another whereas Article 29 prescribes what the general situation is outside of a transitional period, whether a territory has undergone a transition or not. In other words, the rule of Article 15 can correctly be described as the 'moving treaty frontiers' rule. The rule of Article 29 does not deal with a situation of change, but only states the general principle of international law related to the territorial extension of a State's sovereignty, which can be described as the principle of the territorial application of a State's legal order.
>
> Of course, this does not mean that the two rules do not have an extremely close relationship, which explains why they were not always clearly distinguished by the Parties. The situation described in Article 29 can be the result of the application of Article 15, or, it can also be seen the other way around, i.e., that Article 15 regulates the transition in the way it does, because this is the normal result of the territorial application of the law.
>
> In other words, the two rules exist side-by-side, Article 15 being the corollary of Article 29 and Article 29 being a consequence of Article 15.[383]

1.1.3 Exceptions to the application of the MTF rule

Article 15 provides specific exceptions to the application of the MTF principle. Thus, the principle does not apply if it 'would be incompatible with the object and purpose of the treaty or would radically change the conditions for its operation'. The *Sanum* Tribunal explained the nature of the exceptions found at Articles 15 and 29: 5.12

378 *Sanum*, Judgment, Singapore of Court of Appeal, 2016 (n 365) [48]: 'Although Art 29 does not directly concern state succession, where state succession leads to territorial changes, such as in the present case, it is thought that the MTF Rule is *implicitly embedded* in Art 29 and would apply' (emphasis in the original).

379 Odendahl (n 368) 490; Villiger (n 374) 393.

380 *Sanum*, Award, 2013 (n 370) [220].

381 *Sanum*, Judgment, Singapore of Court of Appeal, 2016 (n 365) [47].

382 *Sanum*, Award, 2013 (n 370) [225].

383 Ibid., [225]–[228ff].

> In both Articles [15 VCST and 29 VCLT], the non-application of a treaty to the whole territory can only result from the treaty itself or if it is otherwise established. The reasons for the non-application of a treaty to an expanded territory at the moment of a succession are more limited than the reasons for the non-application of a treaty to the entire territory, but are included in them. Indeed, automatic succession applies unless it appears from the treaty itself or is otherwise established that such a result would not be appropriate *for one of two reasons*: either because such succession would be incompatible with the object and the purpose of the treaty or because it would radically change the conditions of its operation. As far as the non-application of a treaty to the whole territory is concerned, it is sufficient that such non-application results from the treaty or, for whatever reason, the State sees fit to decide such non-application: for example (China) and the Russian Federation decided that the (China)-Russia BIT would not apply to the Macao SAR, for no stated reason.[384]

5.13 The following paragraphs will examine how these three exceptions could apply in the context of succession to a BIT.

5.14 The question as to whether the extension of a BIT to a ceded territory can be considered as 'incompatible' with a treaty's object and purpose arose in the *Sanum* case. The tribunal examined the preamble to the BIT, which refers to both parties 'desiring to encourage, protect, and create favorable conditions for investment by investors [...] based on the principles of mutual respect for sovereignty, equality, and mutual benefit and for the purpose of the development of economic cooperation between both States (...)'.[385] The tribunal concluded that the extension of the China-Laos BIT to Macao (which Portugal ceded to China in 1999) was not incompatible with its object and purpose for the following reasons:

> The purpose is twofold: to protect the investor and develop economic cooperation. The Tribunal does not find—and no element has been provided by the Respondent to that effect— that the extension of the PRC/Laos BIT could be contrary to such a dual purpose. In fact, the larger scope the Treaty has, the better fulfilled the purposes of the Treaty are in this case: more investors—who would not otherwise be protected—are internationally protected, and the economic cooperation benefits a larger territory that would otherwise not receive such benefit.[386]

5.15 The same conclusion was reached by the Singapore Court of Appeal.[387] Almost all BITs contain the same type of language in their preambles providing for the enhancement of the protection of investors and investments.

384 Ibid., [230] (emphasis in the original).

385 Ibid., [239].

386 Ibid., [240]–[241].

387 *Sanum*, Judgment, Singapore of Court of Appeal, 2016 (n 365) [51]:

The reasoning of the tribunal and the court suggests that it is unlikely that the extension of a BIT to a ceded territory could be considered as incompatible with its object and purpose.

The second exception mentioned at Article 15 deals with whether the extension of a BIT to a ceded territory could be considered as radically changing the conditions of application of a treaty. In its award, the *Sanum* Tribunal referred to one specific case where it could be argued that this exception finds application: 'when a treaty is concluded between two States with planned economies, the extension of such [a] treaty to a capitalist economy would fundamentally change the conditions for its application if the treaty was based on features specific to a planned economy and irreconcilable with the liberal principles of a capitalist economy'.[388] But in the context of the Laos-China BIT, the tribunal concluded that its application to Macao would not 'endanger the capitalist system and the liberal way of life' in that territory.[389] Thus, the BITs entered into by China with other States 'do not need to be rejected for incompatibility with the capitalist economic system' existing in Macao.[390] The same reasoning was also adopted by the Singapore Court of Appeal.[391] The reasoning of these judicial bodies suggests that the extension of a BIT to a ceded territory will not, in most instances, be considered as radically changing the conditions of application of that treaty. **5.16**

Finally, the third exception under Article 15 is that the parties remain free to adopt a different solution than the MTF principle.[392] The same exception exists under Article 29 VCLT.[393] Tams speaks about the 'flexibility of the general framework, which does not preclude States from agreeing on special solutions for particular problems'.[394] In fact, as further examined below,[395] the *Sanum* case involved a situation where the parties seems to have decided to apply a different regime in the context of the territorial transfers of Hong Kong and Macao to China. The central question in the *Sanum* case was indeed **5.17**

We do not see how an extension of the application of the BIT to Macau could be said to be incompatible with such a purpose. On the contrary, such an extension of the BIT would enlarge the scope of protection to capture a larger pool of investors and further economic cooperation between both States over a larger territory.

388 *Sanum*, Award, 2013 (n 370) [248].

389 Ibid., [251].

390 Ibid., [252].

391 *Sanum*, Judgment, Singapore of Court of Appeal, 2016 (n 365) [52].

392 See, Odendahl (n 368) 491ff; Villiger (n 374) 391–3.

393 Thus, for the *Sanum* Tribunal '[t]he exceptions to Article 15 of the VCST are encompassed in the exceptions to Article 29 of the VCLT': *Sanum*, Award, 2013 (n 370) [228]–[229].

394 Tams (n 27) 339. See also: O. Dorr, 'Cession', in *Max Planck Encyclopedia of Public International Law* (n 276) [21].

395 See, Chapter 6, Section 5.2.

whether it was the general MTF rule or this exception that should find application.

1.2 Incorporation of State

5.18 As mentioned above, incorporation involves a situation where the territory of a State (the successor State) is enlarged as a result of the integration of the *entire* territory of the predecessor State. This is a type of State succession that was *not* specifically addressed by the Convention.[396]

5.19 The most recent example of an integration of State is that of Germany. On 3 October 1990, the Democratic Republic of Germany (GDR) ceased to exist as an independent State and its territory comprising five *Länder* was *integrated* into the already existing Federal Republic of Germany (FRG).[397] The practice of Germany was shaped by the MTF rule, applicable under Article 15 of the Vienna Convention, in the *different* context of a cession of territory.[398] Thus, under Article 11 of the 1990 Treaty of Unification,[399] all treaties of the FRG were extended to the territory of the former GDR. The same solution applied to BITs.[400] The BITs entered into by Germany should continue to apply without the consent by the other parties concerned being required. This is because the identity of Germany was not affected by the changes to its territory.

5.20 What happens to the treaties that were signed by the GDR before the date of succession? While the MTF rule would cause the treaties in force in the GDR to cease to apply to the territory of the FRG at the date of succession, a more pragmatic approach was adopted. Article 12 of the Treaty of Unification provides that treaties of the GDR would be subject to individual negotiations between unified Germany and each State parties to these treaties. As noted by

---

396 Zimmermann and Devaney, 'Succession to Treaties' (n 1) 521–2, explaining that: 'The reason for this is most likely that, at the time the VCSST was being drafted, it was hardly conceivable that a given population, in exercising its right of self-determination, would freely give up its own independent statehood. Yet, German reunification has proven this assumption to be wrong.'

397 Treaty on the Establishment of German Unity, 31 August 1990, in (1990) 30 ILM 457. One cannot speak of Germany as an example of a merger of States since no *new State* was created in the process. The term 'unification', which has been widely used to describe the process, should not be regarded as the proper legal definition. Thus, Article 1 of the Treaty speaks of the 'accession' of the GDR 'to' the FRG and the fact that the *Länder* of the GDR 'become *Länder* of the FRG'.

398 Tams (n 27) 338; Zimmermann and Devaney, 'Succession to Treaties' (n 1) 522; Odendahl (n 368) 501; A Zimmermann, *Staatennachfolge in völkerrechtliche Verträge—zugleich ein Beitrag zu den Möglichkeiten und Grenzen völkerrechtlicher Kodifikation* (Springer 2000), 245–82; Stern, 'La succession d'États' (n 75) 238–42; Graf-Brugère, 'Article 31', in Distefano, Gaggioli and Hêche (n 4), 1097–8.

399 Treaty on the Unification of Germany (n 397).

400 Binder (n 310) 280–94, at 291, referring to BITs entered into by the FRG with Nepal and the USSR.

one writer, 'almost all treaty partners of Germany subsequently accepted this position' and 'the vast majority of those treaties entered into by the then GDR – with the notable exception of localized treaties – were considered by their respective treaty partners to have lapsed *ipso facto* with the extinction of the GDR and its absorption into the FRG'.[401] The same general solution of extinction has also prevailed for *bilateral* treaties.[402] In my view, this is the appropriate solution that should apply more generally for all BITs. Given the fact that one of the original parties to the treaty disappeared, it seems logical that any continuation of the instrument should be based on the consent by *both* the successor State and the other State party. This is all the more appropriate when the successor State is a significantly different entity than the predecessor State in terms of global political weight, economic strength, and geopolitical influence. To take a simple example, negotiating a BIT with the GDR is not quite the same thing as with unified Germany. Hence, the other State party to a treaty signed with the GDR should consent to its continuation.

1.3 Unification of States

The unification of two (or more) States to form a new entity was envisaged by the Vienna Convention at Article 31, which reads as follows: **5.21**

> 1. When two or more States unite and so form one successor State, any treaty in force at the date of the succession of States in respect of any of them continues in force in respect of the successor State unless:
>
> (a) the successor State and the other State party or States Parties otherwise agree; or
>
> (b) it appears from the treaty or is otherwise established that the application of the treaty in respect of the successor State would be incompatible with the object and purpose of the treaty or would radically change the conditions for its operation.
>
> 2. Any treaty continuing in force in conformity with paragraph 1 shall apply only in respect of the part of the territory of the successor State in respect of which the treaty was in force at the date of the succession of States unless:

401 Zimmermann and Devaney, 'Succession to Treaties' (n 1) 522. See also for the same conclusion: ILA, Rapport Final, 2002 (n 73) 8.

402 ILA, Rapport Final, 2002 (n 73) 8:

> Conformément à l'article 12(1)3 du Traité d'unification, la RFA a consulté ses partenaires pour régler le sort des accords bilatéraux de la RDA. Les résultats des consultations ont été publiés au journal officiel (Bundesgestzblatt) sous forme d'une déclaration unilatérale ou d'un communiqué des négociations. Les annexes énuméraient les accords devenus caducs. Il ressortait que 130 pays avaient été consultés et qu'à la date de l'unification, le 3 octobre 1990, 2044 accords avaient expiré'.

(a) in the case of a multilateral treaty not falling within the category mentioned in article 17, paragraph 3, the successor State makes a notification that the treaty shall apply in respect of its entire territory;

(b) in the case of a multilateral treaty falling within the category mentioned in article 17, paragraph 3, the successor State and the other States Parties otherwise agree; or

(c) in the case of a bilateral treaty, the successor State and the other State party otherwise agree.

3. Paragraph 2 (a) does not apply if it appears from the treaty or is otherwise established that the application of the treaty in respect of the entire territory of the successor State would be incompatible with the object and purpose of the treaty or would radically change the conditions for its operation.

5.22 The first paragraph of Article 31 establishes the principle of continuity (for *both* bilateral and multilateral treaties), whereby the new State is generally bound by the treaties of both predecessor States. This solution of continuity is rather peculiar in the context of unification. Thus, the other parties to BITs signed by the predecessor States are in the presence of an entirely new State after the date of succession. As such, these States should be able to determine whether or not they wish to continue their treaty relationship with that new entity. In fact, the ILC extensively debated whether it should adopt the principle of continuity or that of the required consent of the new State.[403] The ILC ultimately adopted the continuity rule essentially to preserve the stability of conventional relations acknowledging that this exercise was not a codification of existing State practice but rather a progressive development of the law.[404]

5.23 In the context of bilateral treaties, Article 31 excludes the application of the principle of continuity when both the successor State and the other State party agree for the extinction of a specific treaty.[405] What happens when there is a disagreement between these States on the question of continuity? Article 31 is silent on this point. The provision suggests that the solution of continuity should prevail unless *both* the successor State and the other State party agree otherwise.[406] Yet, in my view (for reasons further explained below[407]) the consent of the other State party is fundamental for the continuation of any BIT.

403 See, analysis in: Graf-Brugère (n 398) 1082–8.

404 Ibid., 1099–100.

405 Another exception is mentioned at Art. 31(1)b).

406 Graf-Brugère (n 398) 1088–9.

407 See, Chapter 5, Section 2.2.

Article 31(2) adds another relevant element regarding the application of the general solution of continuity. Thus, the treaties of the predecessor States will continue to apply to the new State, but *only* 'in respect of the part of the territory of the successor State in respect of which the treaty was in force at the date of the succession of States'. This means that the BIT between State A (one of the predecessor States) and State Z (the other State party) would *not* apply to the entirety of State C (the new State), but *only* to the territory which used to be that of State A. The practical implication is that *two different BITs* may apply to *different parts* of the territory of the new State. As noted by one writer, the principle set out at Article 31(2) 'creates a hardly manageable split treaty regime whereby existing treaty obligations potentially apply only to part of the successor territory, creating disparity of obligations and potentially divergent rights for individuals, should the obligations so provide'.[408] The same writers are of the view that not only is it 'unclear why this system was adopted in the first place',[409] but also that 'the split treaty regime underlying Article 31 VCSST has proved problematic in both theory and practice'.[410] It is therefore clear that this split solution could cause confusion among investors. **5.24**

While it is true that this solution may be practical in the short term after the merger of two States since it prevents any legal vacuum, it remains that this 'split treaty regime' is unsustainable in the long run. It would seem more logical, after a short period of transition, for the new State and the other State party to a BIT to reconsider the situation. This is why Article 31(2)c) provides for an exception to the 'split treaty regime' rule when the States concerned agree otherwise. In my view, they should first determine whether the BIT will continue to apply at all. If so, logically, they should agree on the application of the treaty to the *entire territory* of the new State (rather than just one part of it). **5.25**

While the 1978 Convention provides for the application of the continuity principle, the question remains whether this solution is in fact supported by **5.26**

---

408 Zimmermann and Devaney, 'Succession to Treaties' (n 1) 523.

409 Ibid.:

> In fact, it is unclear why this system was adopted in the first place with the most likely answer being that most States participating in the codification effort considered the type of situation envisaged in Article 31 VCSST as largely unimportant and unlikely to occur sufficiently often in practice. Indeed, this has proven to be not so far away from reality with only one instance of this form of succession occurring ever since the adoption of the VCSST in 1978.

The question is examined in: Graf-Brugère (n 398) 1093–4.

410 Zimmermann and Devaney, 'Succession to Treaties' (n 1) 523. Craven, 'The Problem of State Succession' (n 2) 158 (indicating that the fact that treaties of the predecessor State should be maintained but only in relation to its former territory 'appears to deny the realities of absorption, where the objective is arguably to create and maintain a single constitutional and administrative structure').

State practice.[411] The most recent example of unification of States is that of North and South Yemen in 1990 forming the Republic of Yemen.[412] One writer noted that while the new State largely followed the model provided for in Article 31, 'the value of this practice as precedent is limited since the rationale behind the merger of these two States is unclear and the process of integration and succession is largely incoherent'.[413] For Zimmerman, the status of the solution adopted under Article 31 remains unsettled: 'it is hard to discern whether a customary rule of international law in this respect exists or whether the law is still developing, any such development then, in any event, running counter to the fundamental principle underlying Article [31] VCLT'.[414] Most writers reject the customary status of Article 31.[415]

1.4 Newly Independent States

5.27 Article 2 of the Convention defines a Newly Independent State as 'a successor State the territory of which immediately before the date of the succession of States was a dependent territory for the international relations of which the predecessor State was responsible'.[416] Article 16 provides for the general rule applying to both bilateral and multilateral treaties.[417] Under this provision, the principle of *tabula rasa* applies to Newly Independent States. They are therefore not automatically bound by the treaties entered into by the predecessor (colonial) State.[418] The new State thus 'begins its international life free of any general obligation to take over the treaties of its predecessor'.[419] According to the ILC, the general *tabula rasa* principle (applicable to both bilateral and

411 Zimmermann and Devaney, ibid., 523–4: 'Furthermore, practice regarding the type of merger envisaged in Article 31 VCSST is scarce (…). Indeed, this incoherent approach has curtailed the relevance of this instance of succession for the further development of customary international law.'

412 The Yemen Arab Republic (North Yemen) and the People's Democratic Republic of Yemen (South Yemen) merged on 22 May 1990 to form a unified Republic of Yemen. Art. 1 of the Agreement on the Establishment of the Republic of Yemen and the Organisation of the Thirty-Month Interim Period, 22 April 1990, entered into force on 21 May 1990, in: (1990) 30 ILM 820, indicates that: 'There shall be established between [the two Yemen] … a full and complete union, based on a merger, in which the international personality of each of them shall be integrated in a single international person called "the Republic of Yemen".'

413 Zimmermann and Devaney, 'Succession to Treaties' (n 1) 523.

414 Ibid., 524. See also: Zimmermann, 'La Convention de Vienne' (n 4) 1557, 1558, 1563.

415 Graf-Brugère (n 398) 1099–1100; Stern, 'La succession d'États' (n 75) 236; Stefan Oeter, 'German Unification and State Succession', (1991) 51(2) *ZaöRV* 358–9. See, however; Hafner and Novak (n 368) 412 (speaking of an 'emerging' customary rule).

416 For an historical overview of the development of this expression in the work of the ILC, see: Gradoni (n 35) 112ff.

417 ILC Report, 26th Session, 1974 (n 24) 236.

418 See, E. Henry, 'Article 16' in Distefano, Gaggioli and Hêche (n 4), 561ff.

419 ILC Report, 26th Session, 1974 (n 24) 236.

multilateral treaties) was based on State practice.[420] It has been noted that Newly Independent States have largely followed the regime set out under Articles 16 through 30 since the adoption of the Convention.[421]

The Convention also provides different specific rules for Newly Independent States regarding multilateral treaties (Arts 17–23) and bilateral treaties (Arts 24–26). **5.28**

The regime prevailing for *multilateral* treaties is clearly favourable to Newly Independent States.[422] Thus, on the one hand, a Newly Independent State has no obligation to succeed to the treaties of the predecessor State. Yet, on the other hand, a Newly Independent State has the right and option to become party to any multilateral treaty entered into by the predecessor State.[423] Under the Convention, the other States party to the treaty can only reject a Newly Independent State from being a party to the treaty when the 'application of the treaty in respect of the Newly Independent State would be incompatible with the object and purpose of the treaty or would radically change the conditions for its operation'.[424] **5.29**

The Convention, on the contrary, provides a less favourable regime for Newly Independent States regarding *bilateral* treaties.[425] Under Article 24, Newly Independent States are *not* automatically bound by bilateral treaties that have been entered into by the predecessor State with the 'other State party'.[426] The provision further indicates that there are two circumstances under which the principle of continuity will apply: when both the Newly Independent State and the 'other State party' have expressly agreed that the 'original treaty' continues to be force after the independence; or when both States 'by reason of **5.30**

---

420 Ibid. at 212. See also: M.K. Yasseen, 'La Convention de Vienne sur la Succession d'Etats en matière de Traités', (1978) 24 AFDI 105; Szafarz (n 8) 88; Menon (n 335) 145.

421 Zimmermann, 'La Convention de Vienne' (n 4) 1557, 1562–3; Hafner and Novak (n 368) 409; Zimmermann and Devaney, 'Succession to Treaties' (n 1) 531: 'the customary status of these provisions could be said to have already crystallized at least since 1978'.

422 Szafarz (n 8) 88–9; Menon (n 335) 145.

423 Art. 17, Vienna Convention on Succession to Treaties (n 5). See also: ILC Report, 26th Session, 1974 (n 24) 236.

424 Art. 17(2), ibid., [3] also provides for an exception to this principle.

425 On this question, see the analysis of Di Stefano (n 215) 833ff.

426 The full text of Art. 24(1) reads as follows:

> A bilateral treaty which at the date of a succession of States was in force in respect of the territory to which the succession of States relates is considered as being in force between a newly independent State and the other State party when:
>
> (a) they expressly so agree; or
>
> (b) by reason of their conduct they are to be considered as having so agreed.

their conduct (...) are to be considered' as having agreed to such a continuation (the scope of these two exceptions were examined above[427]).[428] In other words, the Convention does not support the continuity of bilateral treaties simply based on the unilateral will of either the 'other State party' or the Newly Independent State.[429] This basic principle of non-automatic continuity is further illustrated by Articles 8 ('devolution agreements') and 9 (unilateral declarations) of the Vienna Convention (both provisions were examined above[430]).[431] The reasons why the ILC adopted the solution of *tabula rasa* for Newly Independent States in the context of bilateral treaties is further examined in the next sections.[432]

1.5 Secession and dissolution of States

5.31 Article 34 of the Convention outlines the regime applicable to cases of 'separation' of States. While this provision uses the term 'separation', it is important to note that it applies to two different cases of State succession: 'secession' and 'dissolution' of States.[433] Another important point to mention is that this provision applies to *both* bilateral and multilateral treaties.[434]

5.32 Article 34 provides for the application of the principle of *automatic* continuity whereby the successor State is *ipso facto* bound by the bilateral treaties entered into by the predecessor State (the question of succession to multilateral treaties will be examined in Part C). This rule of continuity bears two exceptions. First, when the implicated parties have specifically agreed upon the application of the *tabula rasa* rule. In other words, the rule of automatic succession applies by default, unless the States concerned have agreed otherwise.[435] This exception was examined further above when discussing the concept of express and implicit consent to the continuation of BITs.[436] The second exception is when the automatic application of the treaty to the successor State would be 'incompatible with the object and purpose of the treaty or would radically

427 See, Chapter 4.

428 See analysis in: Di Stefano (n 215) 862ff.

429 Z. Meriboute, *La codification de la succession d'États aux traités: décolonisation, sécession, unification* (PUF 1984) 73–8; Di Stefano (n 215) 847–8.

430 See, Chapter 4, Sections 2.1.1. and 2.1.2.

431 See, ILC Report, 26th Session, 1974 (n 24) at 183, 187, 188, 192–219, 240, 246.

432 See, Chapter 5, Section 2.2.

433 Mikulka (n 75) 1176.

434 Ibid., 1179.

435 Vienna Convention on Succession to Treaties (n 5), Art. 34(2)(a).

436 See, Chapter 4.

change the conditions for its operation' (this exception will be further discussed below[437]).[438] Article 35 of the Convention provides that a treaty in force will continue to be binding on the continuator State on what remains of its territory after a secession.[439]

5.33 It is striking to note that the solution adopted by the Convention with respect to secession and dissolution regarding bilateral treaties is completely opposite to the one prevailing in the context of Newly Independent States. The present section examines the circumstances surrounding the ILC's espousal of such a controversial position.[440] The final wording of Article 34, in terms of the applicable regime in the case of secession, is the result of several developments, which can be succinctly summarized in the following three phases:

- First phase: a clear distinction is drawn between cases of secession and dissolution of States; secession cases are assimilated to Newly Independent States; the rule of *tabula rasa* applies to all secession cases (Section 1.5.1);
- Second phase: cases of secession and dissolution of States are now examined together; the principle of continuity generally applies for secession, except for those situations where a secession can be assimilated to that of a Newly Independent State, in which case, the *tabula rasa* rule applies (Section 1.5.2);
- Third phase: The above-mentioned exception is dropped, and, consequently, the principle of continuity of treaties applies now to *all* secession cases (Section 1.5.3).

1.5.1 First phase of the ILC work

5.34 In the initial phase of its work, the ILC's Draft Articles of 1972 clearly distinguished between cases of dissolution of States (Art. 27) and those of 'separation of one part of a State' (Art. 28). Article 28 provides as follows:

437 See, Chapter 5, Section 2.4.

438 Vienna Convention on Succession to Treaties (n 5), Art. 34(2).

439 Ibid., Art. 35 further adds two exceptions where the principle of non-continuity would apply: when the 'States concerned otherwise agree' as well as for treaties 'related only to the territory which has separated from the predecessor State'. For an analysis of this provision, see: V. Milulka, 'Article 35' in Distefano, Gaggioli and Hêche (n 4), 1210ff.

440 See, the discussion in: P. Dumberry and D. Turp, 'State Succession With Respect to Multilateral Treaties in the Context of Secession: From the Principle of Tabula Rasa to the Emergence of a Presumption of Continuity of Treaties', (2013) 13 *Baltic YIL* 27–65; Mikulka (n 75) [1158ff]; R.J. Zedalis, 'An Independent Quebec: State Succession to NAFTA', (1996) 2(4) *NAFTA: Law & Bus Rev Am* 8ff.

> 1. If part of the territory of a State separates from it and becomes an individual State, any treaty which at the date of the separation was in force in respect of that State continues to bind it in relation to its remaining territory, unless:
>
> (a) It is otherwise agreed; or
>
> (b) It appears from the treaty or from its object and purpose that the treaty was intended to relate only to the territory which has separated from that State or the effect of the separation is radically to transform the obligations and rights provided for in the treaty.
>
> 2. In such a case, the individual State emerging from the separation is to be considered as being in the same position as a newly independent State in relation to any treaty which at the date of separation was in force in respect of the territory now under its sovereignty.

5.35 The first paragraph of this provision indicates that in the event of secession, the continuator State remains bound by the treaties it had entered into at the date of secession. The second paragraph states that the secessionist State must be considered as having the same position as a Newly Independent State with regards to all treaties.[441] This is because the ILC concluded that:

> The available evidence of practice does not therefore support the thesis that in the case of a separation of part of a State, as distinct from the dissolution of a State, treaties continue in force *ipso jure* in respect of the territory of the separated State. On the contrary, evidence strongly indicates that the separated territory which becomes a sovereign State is to be regarded as a newly independent State to which in principle the rules of the present draft articles concerning newly independent States should apply.[442]

5.36 In other words, the rule of *tabula rasa* should apply not only to cases of Newly Independent States, but also to situations of secession. At the time, the Commission had decided that cases of secession should not be treated any differently than the special case of Newly Independent States since in both situations the detachment of a territory often occurred in the context of intense political tensions, accompanied by violence.[443] There was indeed a presumption that in both cases the new State had not participated in the elaboration of the treaties concluded by the predecessor State and that consequently it would be unjust for it to be bound by such treaties. It was therefore decided that the application of the rule of *tabula rasa* was preferable in *all instances* of secession. Moreover, some ILC members found support in State practice for the application of the rule of *tabula rasa* in situations of

441 ILC Report, 24th Session, 1972 (n 358) 297.

442 Ibid.

443 Meriboute (n 429) 216–17.

secession.[444] In sum, in the early 1970s, the application of the rule of *tabula rasa* to cases of secession was generally admitted by members of the Commission.[445]

1.5.2 Second phase of the ILC work

At its 26th session (in 1974), the ILC decided to re-examine the relevance of treating cases of dissolution and secession distinctly. It determined that examples of State dissolution had been exclusively examined from the perspective of 'union of States', where 'the component parts of the union retained a measure of individual identity during the existence of the union'.[446] The ILC admitted that 'from a purely theoretical point of view, there may be a distinction between dissolution and separation of part of a State'.[447] But it added that 'it does not necessarily follow that the effects of the succession of States in the two categories of cases must be different for the parts which become new States'.[448] The ILC therefore decided to analyse cases of dissolution and secession together.[449] As such, the Commission opined that both cases should be governed by a single provision (Art. 33). Article 33 provides as follows: **5.37**

> 1. When a part or parts of the territory of a State separate to form one or more States, whether or not the predecessor State continues to exist:
>
> (a) any treaty in force at the date of the succession of States in respect of the entire territory of the predecessor State continues in force in respect of each successor State so formed;
>
> (b) any treaty in force at the date of the succession of States in respect only of that part of the territory of the predecessor State which has become a successor State continues in force in respect of that successor State alone.
>
> 2. Paragraph 1 does not apply if:
>
> (a) the States concerned otherwise agree; or
>
> (b) it appears from the treaty or is otherwise established that the application of the treaty in respect of the successor State would be incompatible with its object and purpose or would radically change the conditions for the operation of the treaty.
>
> 3. Notwithstanding paragraph 1, if a part of the territory of a State separates from it and becomes a State in circumstances which are essentially of the same character as

444 ILC Report, 26th Session, 1974 (n 24) 263, 266.
445 Meriboute (n 429) 156–7.
446 ILC Report, 26th Session, 1974 (n 24) 265.
447 Ibid.
448 Ibid.
449 R.D. Kearney, 'The Twenty-Sixth Session of the International Law Commission', (1975) 69(3) AJIL at 600.

> those existing in the case of the formation of a newly independent State, the successor State shall be regarded for the purposes of the present articles in all respects as a newly independent State.

5.38 The first paragraph of this provision postulates for the same regime of *ipso facto* continuity of treaties to apply in both cases of secession and dissolution. It should be noted that this solution was adopted based on an analysis of State practice in the specific context of *dissolution only*.[450] The third paragraph of Article 33 stipulates for an exception to this rule of continuity in the context of secession. This third paragraph was added in light of the ILC's recognition that:

> the available evidence of practice during the United Nations period appears to indicate that, at least in some circumstances, the separated territory which becomes a sovereign State may be regarded as a Newly Independent State to which in principle the rules of the present draft articles concerning Newly Independent States should apply.[451]

The new paragraph therefore stipulates that the principle of *tabula rasa* would apply to those special cases of secession 'where the separation occurred in circumstances which were essentially of the same character as those existing in the case of the formation of a Newly Independent State'.[452]

5.39 It is at this juncture that the ILC's analytical shift occurred.[453] In order to determine the regime applicable to treaties concluded by the predecessor State, the Commission was now essentially focusing on the question of whether or not a new secessionist State could be assimilated to a Newly Independent State. This analysis was done by examining whether or not the new secessionist State had effectively participated in the elaboration of treaties concluded by the predecessor State. The evaluation of this degree of participation therefore became the focal point in deciding if a secessionist State should be bound by the predecessor State's treaties.[454] As a result of this analytical shift, the rule of *tabula rasa* would no longer apply to secessionist States based on the codification of past State practice, which, as the ILC expressly acknowledged, supported that principle.[455]

450 ILC Report, 26th Session, 1974, at 265.
451 Ibid., at 266.
452 Ibid.
453 See, Zedalis (n 440) 9.
454 Ibid.
455 ILC Report, 24th Session, 1972 (n 358) 296–297; ILC Report, 26th Session, 1974 (n 24) 265.

1.5.3 Third phase of the ILC work

The content of this third paragraph was, however, openly criticized by representatives of developing States because it (apparently) favoured secessionist movements (outside the context of decolonization).[456] In reality, it is not at all clear how the application of the rule of continuity can, in any way, diminish the willingness of a group of people in becoming an independent State by way of secession. What is clear is that political reasons led to the removal of the third paragraph of Article 33 from the final version of the text in 1978 (which later became Art. 34).[457] This removal resulted in the integral application of the principle of *continuity* of treaties for *all cases* of secession, even those instances that could be assimilated to Newly Independent States.[458] **5.40**

It also meant that the principle of continuity would now apply to *bilateral* treaties. This is a very strange outcome given that the ILC specifically adopted the exact opposite solution of *tabula rasa* for Newly Independent States. Intriguingly enough, the ILC's work on Article 34 barely mentions the specific situation of bilateral treaties. The reading of these reports clearly suggests that the ILC seemed to have solely the fate of *multilateral* treaties in mind. In fact, the ILC never discussed why the continuity principle should apply to bilateral treaties under Article 34. Interestingly, during the *Travaux* of the Diplomatic Conference adopting the Convention (in 1978) the FRG submitted an amendment whereby the principle of *tabula rasa* would apply to bilateral treaties in the context of both secession and dissolution.[459] The FRG's representative specifically mentioned that the principle of *tabula rasa* applicable at Article 23 for Newly Independent States (which later became Art. 24) should also apply in cases of secession mentioned at Article 33's third paragraph. The reason invoked by the FRG was that any continuation of bilateral treaties should be based on the consent of *both* States concerned. The FRG insisted that this basic requirement of consent should apply to cases *other* than Newly Independent States.[460] The amendment was however rejected **5.41**

456 See: Nations Unies, Conférence des Nations Unies sur la succession d'États en matière de traités, comptes rendus analytiques des séances plénières et des séances de la Commission plénière, deuxième session, vol. II (1979) at 53–73, 107–14; Szafarz (n 8) 103; Zedalis (n 440) 12–14; Meriboute (n 429) 159–61, 163; Cahier (n 8) 76.

457 Conférence des Nations Unies, ibid., at 114 (see also, at 53 *et seq.*). The context for the removal of the third paragraph is examined in detail in: Zedalis (n 440) 11–13; Mikulka (n 75) 1172ff; G. Hafner and I. Buffard, 'Les principales différences entre les propositions de la Commission du droit international et le résultat de la Conférence des Nations Unies à Vienne sur la succession d'États en matière de traités', in Distefano, Gaggioli and Hêche (n 4), 1538–42.

458 Yasseen (n 420) 103.

459 Conférence des Nations Unies (n 456) vol. II, 56 (amendement no. A/CONF.80/C.1/L.52).

460 Mikulka (n 75) 1172:

without much discussion.[461] As a result, under the final text of Article 34, the principle of continuity applies to bilateral treaties in the context of secession and dissolution of States.

5.42 The next section discusses why, in my view, the solution adopted by the ILC for bilateral treaties for cases of secession and dissolution of States is both incoherent and unjustifiable.

2. THE APPLICATION OF THE PRINCIPLE OF CONTINUITY TO CASES OF SECESSION AND DISSOLUTION OF STATES IS INCOHERENT AND UNJUSTIFIABLE

5.43 Under Article 34 of the Vienna Convention, a new State is *ipso facto* bound by all bilateral treaties entered into by the predecessor State before its independence. This solution of automatic continuity is simply incoherent with the ILC's position of *tabula rasa* adopted for Newly Independent States. In any event, it is plainly unjustifiable to adopt the principle of automatic continuity to bilateral treaties given the very particular nature of these instruments. The present section explains why this is so by using the four following steps:

- First, I will examine the reasons why the principle of *tabula rasa* was adopted for Newly Independent States in the different context of *multilateral* treaties. This section will show that the ILC adopted specific rules for these States in order to protect their right to self-determination (Section 2.1);
- Secondly, I will demonstrate that the ILC adopted the rule of *tabula rasa* in the context of *bilateral* treaties for reasons entirely extraneous to protecting Newly Independent States' right to self-determination. The rule was adopted because of the particular nature of these treaties and the basic requirement that the other party to an original bilateral treaty must

---

L'amendement soumis par la République fédérale d'Allemagne visait à limiter la portée du principe de continuité des traités, énoncé à l'alinéa a), aux seuls traités multilatéraux et à assimiler le régime applicable aux traités bilatéraux à celui prévu pour les traités bilatéraux dans la Troisième partie concernant les Etats nouvellement indépendants. Les traités bilatéraux allaient rester en vigueur entre l'Etat successeur et un autre Etat partie seulement si ces Etats en étaient expressément convenus ou si, à raison de leur comportement, ils devaient être considérés comme en étant ainsi convenus.

461 Conférence des Nations Unies (n 456) vol. II, 113. The amendment was rejected by 57 votes against, five in favour and 20 abstentions. The amendment proposed by the FRG was not discussed at great length by States. The main focus of discussion was another amendment proposed by Switzerland and France to the effect of applying the principle of *tabula rasa* to all secession cases, not just those similar to Newly Independent States. The amendment was rejected by a large majority of States. After that vote, the amendment proposed by the FRG was also rejected.

consent to the continuation of that treaty with a Newly Independent State (Section 2.2);

- Thirdly, I will demonstrate that there are no logical reasons as to why the *tabula rasa* principle adopted for Newly Independent States should not also find application for all new States (Section 2.3).
- Finally, I will examine the extent to which one of the two exceptions mentioned in Article 34(2) can be used by a State to reject the continuous application of a bilateral treaty (Section 2.4).

2.1 The principle of *tabula rasa* was adopted in the case of multilateral treaties to protect Newly Independent States' right to self-determination

It should be first recalled that under Article 16 of the Vienna Convention, the principle of *tabula rasa* applies to Newly Independent States which are therefore not automatically bound by treaties entered into by the predecessor (colonial) State. It is true that the ILC did refer to some State practice in favour of the application of this principle.[462] Yet, this is clearly not the reason why it was ultimately decided to apply the rule of *tabula rasa* to Newly Independent States regarding *multilateral* treaties. This rule was chosen because of the specific characteristics of these new States. The 1960s and 1970s were fundamentally marked by the arrival of a growing number of emerging States in Asia and Africa that openly contested the legitimacy of the existing rules of international law. These States demanded a revision of these 'outdated' rules that did not respond to the pivotal changes that had prevailed in the international community since the end of the colonization period.[463] According to one prominent scholar, these States '[did] not easily forget that the same body of international law that they [were] now asked to abide by, sanctioned their previous subjugation and exploitation and stood as a bar to their emancipation'.[464] **5.44**

The rule of *tabula rasa* was therefore adopted based on the simple notion that 'State succession in the event of decolonization [was] a new phenomenon which [was] different in many ways from the traditional theories and practices **5.45**

462 ILC Report, 26th Session, 1974 (n 24) 6, 211.

463 Georges Abi-Saab, 'The Newly Independent States and the Rules of International Law: An Outline', (1962) 8 *Howard LJ* 97, 118.

464 Ibid., 100.

of State succession.'[465] As explained by Makonnen, the process of decolonization is an entirely different type of succession of States because it is not aimed 'merely at the change of sovereignty in a territory', but rather at the 'creation of new sovereignty over a territory by totally displacing the old sovereignty over that territory'.[466] The same explanation is given by Bedjaoui, who contends that the aim of decolonization is to 'purger les rapports anciens de leur contenu inégalitaire'.[467] Accordingly, 'the rules governing the conduct of succession are to be derived from the purposes and goals of decolonization'[468] which is to 'undo what has been done through colonization'[469] and to protect new States' right to self-determination.[470]

5.46 As explained by one writer, while the principle of automatic continuity of multilateral treaties was adopted under Article 34 (in general) because the 'overriding factor must be that of the interests of third [party] States which are entitled to stable treaties',[471] the situation is entirely different for Newly Independent States where it is *their interests* which must be overriding.[472] A Newly Independent State is thus free to decide which treaties it wishes to be bound by and free to reject those that are inconsistent with its own interests.[473] As explained by Yasseen, '[l]e principe de l'autodétermination exige qu'un État nouvellement indépendant puisse exercer sa pleine souveraineté, et cela nécessite qu'il jouisse d'une liberté totale quant à ses relations conventionnelles avec les autres États'.[474]

5.47 In sum, the ILC adopted the rule of *tabula rasa* for *multilateral* treaties because it was more congruous with Newly Independent States' right to self-determination.[475] The next section examines the different reasons which led the ILC to adopt the rule of *tabula rasa* for *bilateral* treaties.

---

465 Yilma Makonnen, 'State Succession in Africa: Selected Problems', (1986–V) 200 Rec des Cours 102–3, 129. See also: Mohammed Bedjaoui, 'Problèmes récents de succession d'Etats dans les Etats nouveaux', (1970–II) 130 Rec des Cours 490.

466 Makonnen (n 465) 129.

467 Bedjaoui (n 465) 469, 530.

468 Makonnen (n 465) 129–30.

469 Ibid., 131.

470 Bedjaoui (n 465) 493.

471 Szafarz (n 8) 110.

472 Ibid.

473 Bedjaoui (n 465) 526.

474 Yasseen (n 420) 105, see also at 106.

475 ILC Report, 26th Session, 1974 (n 24) 169; Menon (n 335) 145, 172.

2.2 The principle of *tabula rasa* was adopted for bilateral treaties of Newly Independent States based on the requirement that both states must consent to the continuation of a treaty

According to the ILC, the rule of *tabula rasa* set out at Article 24 of the Vienna Convention for *bilateral* treaties reflected the practice of Newly Independent States.[476] This conclusion is supported by some writers[477] who have in fact highlighted the customary nature of this rule in the context of bilateral treaties.[478] For them, the customary status extends to all States, not only Newly Independent States.[479] At the opposite end of the spectrum of views on this matter, one author went as far as to argue that new States are in fact bound by certain categories of bilateral treaties under an international law obligation.[480] The ILA also adopted a presumption in favour of the continuity of treaties in 1965.[481] In any event, this debate surrounding the customary nature of Article 24 is of limited relevance. This is because the ILC's decision to ultimately adopt the rule of *tabula rasa* was not at all based on State practice. It was also unrelated to the protection of Newly Independent States' right to self-determination. The specific reasons for adopting the *tabula rasa* principle are explained in the following sections. 5.48

2.2.1 No right to become party to a treaty in the absence of a legal nexus with the territory

The ILC rightly explained that an important distinction must be made between bilateral and multilateral treaties regarding the question as to whether or not a Newly Independent State has the *right* to be party to the treaties concluded by the predecessor State. Special Rapporteur Waldock stated that a Newly Independent State enjoys a right to become party to an existing *multilateral* treaty 'independently of the consent of the other parties to the treaty'.[482] This right hinges upon the existence of a 'legal nexus of a certain 5.49

---

476 ILC Report, ibid., 211. It also mentioned that in 'some categories of treaties, it is true, continuity in one form or another occurs with impressive regularity' (at 237). See: Succession of States in Respect of Bilateral Treaties: Second and Third Studies Prepared by the Secretariat, in: *YILC*, 1971, vol. II, part two, UN A/CN.4/243 and Add.l, at 111ff.

477 Di Stefano (n 215) 844–5; Meriboute (n 429) 78; Menon (n 335) 145; Szafarz (n 8) 97. For an earlier study supporting the principle of *tabula rasa*, see: Lester (n 38) 476–7, 506–7.

478 Di Stefano (n 215) 844–5; 884, 907; Szafarz (n 8) 130.

479 Di Stefano, ibid.

480 Keith (n 38) 545.

481 ILA, State Succession, Report of the Helsinki Conference, 1966, 557–96; ILA, State Succession, Report of the Buenos Aires Conference, 1969, 589–633.

482 ILC Report, Third Report, 1970 (n 354), 37. See also: Craven, *The Decolonization of International Law* (n 8) 142ff.

degree between the treaty and the territory'.[483] The ILC further explained the nature of this 'legal nexus' as follows:

> the fact that prior to independence, the predecessor State had established its consent to be bound by a multilateral treaty and its act of consent related to the territory now under the sovereignty of the Newly Independent State creates a legal nexus between that territory and the treaty in virtue of which the Newly Independent State has the right, if it wishes, to participate in the treaty on its own behalf as a separate party or contracting State.[484]

5.50 What about *bilateral* treaties? In his Fourth Report, ILC Special Rapporteur Waldock explained that a 'new State' does *not* enjoy a right to become party to a bilateral treaty because there is no 'legal nexus' between the treaty and the territory of the predecessor State:

> The evidence is plain that a treaty in force with respect to a territory at the date of a succession is frequently applied afterwards as between the successor State and the other party or parties to the treaty; and this indicates that the former legal nexus between the territory and the treaties of the predecessor State has at any rate some legal implications for the subsequent relations between the successor State and the other parties to the treaties. If in the case of many multilateral treaties that legal nexus appears to generate an actual right for the successor State to establish itself as a party, this does not appear to be so in the case of bilateral treaties.[485]

5.51 The ILC put forward that 'a difference does exist and should be made between bilateral treaties and certain multilateral treaties in regard to a Newly Independent State's *right* to be a party to a treaty concluded by its predecessor'.[486] A new State does not have the right to become party to a bilateral treaty without the consent of the other party to the treaty.[487] There exists no automatic continuity because 'succession in respect of bilateral treaties has an essentially *voluntary character*, that is, on the part not only of the Newly Independent State but also of the other interested State'.[488] The issue is further examined in the next section.

---

483 Ibid., 39. See also: ILC Report, 26th Session, 1974 (n 24) 237.

484 ILC Report, 26th Session, 1974 (n 24) 237 (see also at 169). On this question, see: Szafarz (n 8) 119–20.

485 ILC, Fourth Report, 1971 (n 217) 146 [2].

486 ILC Report, 26th Session, 1974 (n 24) 212 (emphasis in the original). See also, at 237.

487 This principle is reflected in Art. 24 of the Convention stating that the principle of *tabula rasa* applies to bilateral treaties unless the other State party to the original treaty has expressly (or tacitly) agreed to the continuation of that treaty.

488 ILC Report, 26th Session, 1974 (n 24) 239 (emphasis added). See also: Gruber (8) 182; Genest (n 39) 9–11.

2.2.2 *The importance of the 'personal equation'*

The ILC explained that the 'personal equation' (i.e., 'the identity of the other contracting party') necessarily plays a more dominant role in bilateral treaty relations.[489] Thus, 'the very object of most bilateral treaties is to regulate the mutual rights and obligations of the parties by reference essentially to their own particular relations and interests'.[490] While multilateral treaties are entered into by States to safeguard the *general* interests of the international community (i.e., all States), the same cannot be said about bilateral treaties. These treaties are signed to preserve the *specific* interests of the two parties involved.[491] As a result of this 'personal equation' of the two parties involved in a bilateral relationship, 'it is not possible automatically to infer from a State's previous acceptance of a bilateral treaty as applicable in respect of a territory [as] its willingness to do so after a succession in relation to a wholly new sovereign of the territory'.[492] 5.52

In other words, from the mere fact that the 'other State party' (State A) has entered into a treaty (the original treaty) with the predecessor State (State B) at some point in time, it cannot be inferred in any way that State A would be willing to later sign and ratify the exact same treaty with another State (State C, the new State). This is because treaty negotiations between different entities necessarily leads to different outcomes. The object and the goal of a bilateral treaty is to allocate specific rights and obligations between two parties. Such an allocation will depend on the comparative strength and weakness of each State, including their political and economical powers, their geopolitical influence, their different sizes and population, etc. The outcome of negotiation will also depend on the unique and special relationship between these two States as well as their particular interests at the time the treaty is concluded. In the example aforementioned, one should assume that State A would want to negotiate a set of rights and obligations with the new State (State C) different from those entered into previously with the predecessor State (State B). This is simply because States B and C are not the same entity. They not only have different sizes and population, but also different political and economical powers as well as different interests. 5.53

In sum, a Newly Independent State does not have a *right* to become a party to a bilateral treaty.[493] The consent and approbation by the other State party is essential in order for the treaty in question to apply to this new and different 5.54

489 ILC Report, ibid., 237. See also: Di Stefano (n 215) 851–2.
490 Ibid.
491 Meriboute (n 429) 79.
492 ILC Report, 26th Session, 1974 (n 24) 1974, 237.
493 Ibid.

treaty partner.[494] In the ILC's opinion's, 'practice does not seem to support the existence of a unilateral right in a Newly Independent State to consider a bilateral treaty as continuing in force with respect to its territory after independence *regardless of the wishes of the other party to the treaty*'.[495] Scholars generally support this position.[496]

2.2.3 Treaty relationship between the parties concerned is not triangular

5.55 One important point to mention is that the original treaty between the predecessor State (State B) and the 'other State party' (State A) will remain in force despite its reduced scope of geographical application.[497] This principle is specifically set out at Article 35 of the Convention (which applies to cases of secession, but also to other new States[498]). But if State A and State C (the new State) agree on the continuity of the original treaty, this will be based on a new and *entirely different* treaty relationship.[499] In fact, some have even suggested that this should be considered as a *new* treaty.[500] The point is explained as follows in the Fourth Report:

> Secondly, in the case of a bilateral treaty there is no question of the treaty's being brought into force *between the successor State and its predecessor*, as happens in the case of a multilateral treaty. True, in respect of the predecessor State's remaining territory the treaty will continue in force bilaterally as between it and the other party to the treaty. But should the treaty become applicable as between that other party and the successor State, it will do so as *a new and purely bilateral relation between them which is independent of the predecessor State*. Nor will the treaty come into force at all as between the successor and predecessor States. No doubt, the successor and predecessor States may decide to regulate the matter in question—e.g. extradition or tariffs—on a similar

494 Yasseen (n 420) 108.

495 ILC Report, 26th Session, 1974 (n 24) 238 (emphasis in the original).

496 Cahier (n 8) 72; Meriboute (n 429) 74, 78; Yasseen (n 420) 108; Menon (n 335) 156; Szafarz (n 8) 97.

497 Gruber (8) 181.

498 It is surprising that the Convention's section dealing specifically with Newly Independent States (Arts 24–26) does not contain a provision equivalent to Art. 35. Yet, as noted by Milulka, 'Article 35' (n 439) this principle is well-established by State practice and doctrine (at 1221) and should be considered as rule of custom (at 1223–4) applicable to *all new States*, not just in the context of secession. For the same conclusion about the customary status of Art. 35, see: Zimmermann, 'La Convention de Vienne' (n 4) 1559.

499 ILC Report, 26th Session, 1974 (n 24) 241. See also: Di Stefano (n 215) 851–2.

500 ILA, Rapport Final, 2002 (n 73) 5:

> L'État nouvellement indépendant n'est pas obligé de les maintenir en vigueur, conformément à l'article 16 de la Convention. Cependant, il est possible que l'État nouvellement indépendant décide de les maintenir en vigueur. Dans ce cas, il est évident que l'État nouvellement indépendant ne peut décider leur maintien en vigueur unilatéralement. Il faut son accord mais aussi celui de l'État intéressé pour qu'un traité bilatéral puisse être maintenu en vigueur (ce qui équivaut en réalité à la *conclusion d'un nouveau traité*), cet accord pouvant être exprès ou tacite selon l'article 24. (emphasis added).

See also: Gruber (8) 181–2.

basis. But if so, it will be through a new treaty which is exclusive to themselves and legally unrelated to any treaty in force prior to independence.[501]

Article 25 of the Convention further explains that the fact that States A and C have agreed to the continuity of the original treaty does not result in that treaty being 'considered as being in force also in the relations between the predecessor State and the Newly Independent State'.[502] In other words, it is entirely up to the predecessor State (State B) and the new State (State C) to decide whether or not they want their relationship to continue to be governed by the original treaty. If they do, this instrument should be considered as an entirely *new* treaty that is distinct from the original treaty.[503] In sum, the relationship between the different actors is not triangular. It is rather the juxtaposition of three separate and distinct bilateral relationships involving the new State, the other State party, and the continuing State. **5.56**

2.2.4 Distinguishing State practice favouring continuity

Craven explains that Waldock adopted the position of *tabula rasa* even if some evidence of State practice suggested that States had actually followed the principle of continuity regarding certain categories of bilateral treaties: **5.57**

> Waldock was very aware that, in proposing this solution, he was to depart once again from the position emerging in contemporary scholarship. The ILA Committee had undertaken quite a detailed survey of different kinds of agreements and had observed that a considerable degree of continuity was evident in relation to a range of bilateral treaties including air transport agreements, extradition treaties, technical assistance agreements, commercial agreements, boundary or territorial agreements, and to a lesser extent with double taxation agreements. Similar findings were evident in the Secretariat reports on succession in respect of extradition agreements, air transport and trade agreements, and in its *Materials on Succession of States*.[504]

In fact, in one study conducted in 1967, Keith argued that '[t]he majority of States which have become independent since 1945 have indicated that they remain bound by many bilateral treaties'.[505] He also added that the 'consistent pattern of continued compliance' has been especially apparent with regard to certain categories of treaties, including 'trade, air transport, tax, postal matters, **5.58**

501 ILC, Fourth Report, 1971 (n 217) 146 [3] (emphasis added).

502 Article 25, Vienna Convention on Succession to Treaties (n 5). See also, Menon (n 335) 161; Gruber (8) 181; Meriboute (n 429) 74; G. Bartolini, 'Article 25' in Distefano, Gaggioli and Hêche (n 4), 912ff.

503 Ibid.

504 Craven, *The Decolonization of International Law* (n 8) 144.

505 Keith (n 38) 545.

technical and economic assistance, investment guarantee, [and] visa abolition'.[506] Keith argued that under customary international law, new States were bound by these treaties.[507] In fact, in his Report, Waldock acknowledged the existence of these studies in favour of the application of the principle of continuity to bilateral treaties:

> The International Law Association derives from the considerable measure of continuity found in practice a general presumption that bilateral treaties in force with respect to a territory and known to the successor State continue in force unless the contrary is declared within a reasonable time after the new State's attainment of independence. Some writers even see in it a general principle of continuity implying legal rights and obligations with respect to the maintenance in force of a predecessor State's bilateral treaties. In some categories of treaties, it is true, continuity in one form or another occurs with impressive regularity. This is, for example, the case with the air transport and trade agreements examined in the second and third Secretariat studies on 'Succession of States in Respect of Bilateral Treaties'.[508]

5.59 However, Waldock observed that States adopted the principle of continuity regarding these treaties for essentially *practical* reasons:[509]

> The prime cause of the frequency with which some measure of continuity is given to such treaties as air transport and trade agreements in the event of a succession seems to be the practical advantage of continuity to the interested States in present conditions. Air transport is as normal a part of international communications today as railway and sea transport; and as a practical matter it is extremely likely that both the successor State and the other interested State will wish any existing air services to continue at least provisionally until new arrangements are made.[510]
>
> Again, international trade is an integral part of modern international relations; and as a practical matter both the successor State and the other interested States will find it convenient in many instances to allow existing trade arrangements to run on provisionally until new ones are negotiated.[511]

---

506 Ibid.

507 Ibid.

508 ILC, Fourth Report, 1971 (n 217) 146 [4].

509 Ibid., [5].

510 Ibid.

511 Ibid., [6]. The Report refers to the work of the UN Secretariat indicating:

> In the light of the relevant materials collected in the present study, about 40 new States and 34 original parties, other than predecessor States, have taken a position concerning the continued force of bilateral trade agreements which were applicable to former non-metropolitan territories before independence. In most of the recorded cases continuity has been achieved or recognized at least during a certain period of time after independence' (in: *Yearbook ILC* 1971, vol. II, Part Two, UN doc. A/CN.4/243/Add.l, [169, 172]).

In any event, Waldock arrived at the conclusion that such practice of continuity of bilateral treaties was derived only from 'the will of the States concerned' and not from the application of any rule of law: 5.60

> If, therefore, State practice shows a tendency towards continuity in the case of certain categories of treaties, it may be doubted whether the practice justifies the conclusion that the continuity derives from a customary legal rule rather than the will of the States concerned (the successor State and the other party to its predecessor's treaty). At any rate, it does not seem to support the existence of a unilateral right in a new State to consider a bilateral treaty as continuing in force with respect to its territory after independence *regardless of the wishes of the other party to the treaty.*[512]

Waldock's final conclusion on this point clearly supports the proposition that succession to bilateral treaties for *all* 'new States' (including in the context of secession) is based on the agreement of both States, rather than on the unilateral will of one of them: 5.61

> Enough evidence has been adduced in the preceding paragraphs to establish the essentially voluntary character of succession in respect of bilateral treaties: voluntary, that is, on the part not only of the successor State but also of the other interested State. On this basis the fundamental rule to be laid down for bilateral treaties would seem to be that their continuance in force after independence is a matter of agreement, express or tacit, between the successor State and the other interested State (the other party to the predecessor State's treaty).[513]

In sum, the work of the ILC clearly shows that the *tabula rasa* principle was adopted for bilateral treaties of Newly Independent States based on the requirement that both States concerned consent to the continuation of such instruments. 5.62

2.3 Both logics and the history of the drafting of the Convention support the proposition that the *tabula rasa* principle should apply to cases of secession and dissolution

As explained above, the principle of *tabula rasa* was correctly adopted by the ILC for bilateral treaties, requiring that both States concerned consent to the continuation of a treaty after the date of independence. There is simply no reason why this sound solution should be reserved only for Newly Independent States. Thus, why should State A (the 'other State party') be automatically bound by a bilateral treaty in certain situations and not in others? If the ILC is 5.63

512 ILC Report, Fourth Report, 1971 (n 217) 148 [10] (emphasis in the original), providing ([11]) a number of examples of State practice supporting this conclusion.
513 Ibid.,149 [14].

right in specifying that 'succession in respect of bilateral treaties has an essentially voluntary character',[514] this basic proposition should presumably apply to *all types* of State succession, not only to Newly Independent States. It simply cannot be that the consent of the other States party to a BIT is considered *essential* when dealing with Newly Independent States, but becomes rather mysteriously *irrelevant* outside the context of decolonization. Protecting the interests of the 'other State party' to the original treaty in the context of Newly Independent States and not in situations of secession and dissolution is unjustifiable. Simple common sense dictates that the rule of *tabula rasa* should apply to both cases of secession and dissolution.

5.64 Moreover, this solution is in fact supported by the history of the drafting of the Convention. Thus, as further explained in the following two sections, throughout the work of the ILC, the rule of *tabula rasa* was clearly meant to apply to cases of secession and dissolution.[515] It was only when the first Draft Articles were adopted by the ILC in 1972 that a distinction between Newly Independent States and other cases outside the context of decolonization was made.[516] It is only at that point that a whole series of provisions were introduced to deal specifically with Newly Independent States.[517] It is at this stage that suddenly (and without any explanation) the *tabula rasa* principle began to apply only to Newly Independent States. As further explained below, this is at best a very peculiar outcome.

5.65 The following sections provide a detailed account of the evolution of the work of the ILC on the question. No one has ever conducted such an analysis.[518]

2.3.1 Waldock's first four reports (1969–71)

5.66 In his Second Report (1969), Waldock mentioned that 'during the discussion, members of the Commission commented upon the possible implications of "decolonization" in regard to its study of succession of States'.[519] He added that the ILC concluded that 'the problem of new States should be given special attention throughout the study of the topic without, however, neglecting other causes of succession on that account'.[520] While noting that the ILC 'cannot fail to give particular importance to the case of "new" States because it

---

514 ILC Report, 26th Session, 1974 (n 24) 239.

515 See, the discussion in: Craven, *The Decolonization of International Law* (n 8) 131–2.

516 ILC Report, 24th Session, 1972 (n 358) 227.

517 Ibid., 250.

518 A preliminary analysis of the question was conducted by the present author in Dumberry, 'State Succession to Bilateral Treaties' (n 36) 13–30. See, also: Genest (n 39) 9–12.

519 ILC Report, Second Report, 1969 (n 353) 46 [9].

520 Ibid., 218, [60]–[61].

is both the commonest and the most perplexing form in which the issue of succession arises', he also added that 'there [was] a risk that the perspective of the effort at codification might become distorted if succession in respect of treaties were to be approached too much from the viewpoint of the "new" State alone'[521] and, would be consequently, 'neglecting other causes of succession on that account'.[522]

The Report refers in detail to the discussions amongst ILC members about the significance of the phenomenon of 'decolonization' regarding the topic of State succession and its impact on codification.[523] Waldock concluded, at that time, that these States should *not* be recognized as a distinct category to which different rules would apply: **5.67**

> The principal new factor which has appeared in the practice regarding succession of States during the period of decolonization under the United Nations has been the use of the agreements commonly referred to as 'devolution' or inheritance agreements. Otherwise, the State practice which has so far been published—and this is now quite extensive—contains comparatively little evidence suggesting, so far as concerns the present topic, a need to treat decolonization as a specific category of succession. Equally, it contains little evidence to suggest that decolonization, as such, calls for recognition as a specific element in the legal rules applicable to the succession of new States. The points mentioned in the Commission or in the Sixth Committee as possibly calling for a special treatment of decolonization appear for the most part to be

---

521 Ibid., 90 [14].

522 Ibid., 218 [60]–[61].

523 Ibid., 90 [14]:

> Both in the International Law Commission and in the Sixth Committee of the United Nations General Assembly, varying views were expressed regarding the significance of the process of 'decolonization' as an element in the law of succession. Some members considered that succession resulting from decolonization should be the subject of a special study by the Commission, envisaging as a possibility the need to include a separate chapter on decolonization in the Commission's draft. These members urged that decolonization is one of the aims of the international community and is proceeding under its supervision; that succession resulting from decolonization, as a result, presents specific aspects peculiar to it; and that decolonization has given rise to rules which affect the rules of traditional succession. It was not, they said, a question of minimizing the other aspects of succession, but of emphasizing the aspects resulting from decolonization. Other members, however, stressed the need to avoid confusing succession with decolonization, which they considered as merely one of the processes of transferring sovereignty from one State to another that create succession problems. In the view of these other members elements of continuity and rupture appear both in decolonization and traditional succession; decolonization is approaching completion, and the adoption of rules governing it will not satisfy future needs; attention should therefore be devoted mainly to the cases of succession most likely to occur in the future, e.g., dissolution, merger, economic integration, and not only to the important but transitory problems of decolonization. Certain other members took the view that, since the Commission was to study the problems of succession affecting all new States, the question of studying decolonization was ultimately only a question of priorities.

> points which, if valid, will be valid also in the case of a new State arising from a dismemberment outside the process of decolonization.[524]

5.68 The same reasoning is found in Waldock's Third Report (1970). He explained that the expression 'new State' was 'used here and throughout the draft as a term of art',[525] and that it was clearly meant to *include both* cases of secession (*outside* decolonization) and Newly Independent States.[526] As noted by Craven, in making no differentiation between cases involving decolonization or not, Waldock understood 'the category purely in terms of the nature of the process rather than in terms of the putative effect of self-determination upon the rules of succession'.[527] Yet, at this stage he seems to have opened the door to the possibility of eventually making such differentiation.[528]

5.69 Finally, when examining Article 13 of the proposed Draft Articles dealing with bilateral treaties in his Fourth Report (1971), Waldock stated the above-mentioned reasons for concluding that a 'new State' does not have the right to become party to a bilateral treaty without the consent of the other party to the treaty.[529] What is clear is that at this stage of the work of the ILC, the rule of *tabula rasa* was still meant to apply also to secession cases *outside* the context of decolonization.

2.3.2 ILC's adoption of the Draft Articles (1972)

5.70 During the 'General debate', Waldock first commented that the expression 'new State' 'was provisional' and 'had been adopted purely for purposes of

---

524 ILC Report, Second Report, 1969 (n 353) 49 [21]. He nevertheless left open the more general question of the possible 'implications' of the principle of self-determination on 'the modern law concerning succession in respect of treaties' ([22]) and, specifically, regarding devolution agreements in the context of decolonization.

525 ILC, Third Report, 1970 (n 354) 27 [8]. See also: ILC, Fourth Report, 1971 (n 217) 144 [4 fn 9].

526 ILC, Third Report, 1970 (n 354) 27 [9] (emphasis added). See also, at 28 [2]:

> The term 'new State' as used in the present articles means a succession where a territory which previously formed part of an existing State has become an independent State. It thus covers a State formed either through the secession of part of the metropolitan territory of an existing State *or through the secession or emergence to independence of a colony*; but it excludes a State formed by a union of States, by a federation of a State with an existing State, by the termination of the protection of a protected State or by the emergence of a trusteeship or mandated territory to independence (emphasis added).

527 Craven, *The Decolonization of International Law* (n 8) 131–2.

528 ILC, Third Report, 1970 (n 354) at 27 [9], deciding to 'postpone until later the consideration of new States whose particular form of succession may *arguably* call for some differentiation in the rules applicable to them' (emphasis in the original). Waldock added:

> On close examination, the Commission may or may not conclude that States arising through other particular forms of succession are in any respect governed by different principles from those applicable to a new State in its purest form. But for purposes of study it seems convenient, and even essential, first to identify the basic principles applicable to 'new States' in their purest form before considering the possible effect of special factors in particular cases of succession.

529 The question is also discussed in: Craven, *The Decolonization of International Law* (n 8) 146–7.

study'.[530] Yet, a couple of days later he explained that 'on further consideration, it might perhaps be decided to refer only to the "successor State" and to eliminate the concept of a "new State" altogether'.[531] The 'Draft Articles Proposed by the Drafting Committee' in fact dropped the reference to 'new State' and introduced a definition of the expression 'Newly Independent State'.[532] Waldock agreed and the new text was approved at the ILC's 1196th Meeting.[533] At the next meeting, the ILC adopted on first reading the Draft Articles.[534]

In its Report on the work of its 24th session (1972), the ILC briefly explained that it would no longer group together under the same roof of 'New States' cases of secession outside decolonization and Newly Independent States.[535] Surprisingly, apart from the following two general comments, the ILC Report does not contain any other explanation as to why it decided to include an entirely new part dealing *exclusively* with Newly Independent States: **5.71**

> The Commission has therefore given special attention throughout the study of the topic to the practice of the Newly Independent States referred to in the above-mentioned resolutions of the General Assembly without, however, neglecting the relevant practice of older States.[536]
>
> It is in the nature of things that more recent practice must be accorded a certain priority as evidence of the *opinio juris* of today, especially when, as in the case of succession of States in respect of treaties, the very frequency and extensiveness of the modern practice tends to submerge the earlier precedents. No purpose would, however, be served by distinguishing sharply between the value of earlier and later precedents, since the basic elements of the situations giving rise to the questions of succession in respect of treaties in the earlier precedents were much the same as in modern cases. Moreover, if recent practice is extremely rich in matters relating to new States emerging from a dependent territory, the same cannot be said for other cases, such as, for instance, secession, dismemberment of an existing State, the formation of unions of States and the dissolution of a union of States. Nor can the Commission fail to recognize that the era of decolonization is nearing its completion and that it is in connection with these other cases that in future problems of succession are likely to arise. The Commission has therefore taken into account, as appropriate, earlier

530 ILC, 'Summary Records of the 24th Session', 2 May–7 July 1972, in: (1972) *Yearbook ILC*, vol. I, 1156th meeting (11 May 1972), 32 [10], see also [25]–[27].

531 Ibid., 1158th Meeting (15 May 1972), 42 [7]. See also: ibid., 1156th meeting (11 May 1972) 37 [68], 70.

532 Ibid., 1196th Meeting, (5 July 1972) 270 [28].

533 Ibid., [33].

534 ILC Report, 24th Session, 1972 (n 358) 224 [22].

535 ibid., 229 [45]: '[the ILC] concluded that for the purpose of codifying the modern law of succession of States in respect of treaties it would be sufficient to arrange the cases of succession of States under three broad categories: (a) transfers of territory; (b) newly independent States; (c) the uniting of States, the dissolution of a State and the separation of part of a State'.

536 Ibid., 225 [25].

> precedents that throw light on these cases. In considering the various precedents, the Commission has tried to discern with sufficient clearness how far the State practice was an expression simply of policy and how far and in what points an expression of legal rights or obligations.[537]

5.72 Article 2 of the Draft Articles (entitled 'the use of terms') no longer referred to the expression 'new State' but instead to 'Newly Independent States'.[538] Importantly, the new expression did *not* include secession cases outside the context of decolonization:

> The definition excludes cases concerning the emergence of a new State as a result of a separation of part of an existing State, of a uniting of two or more existing States or of a dissolution of an existing State. It is to differentiate clearly these cases from the case of the emergence to independence of a former dependent territory that the expression 'newly independent State' has been chosen instead of the shorter expression 'new State'.[539]

5.73 Part III of the Draft Articles adopted by the ILC contained a specific provision for bilateral treaties in the context of Newly Independent States (Art. 19), which was very similar to the original text of Article 13 (which applied to *all* new States, including those outside the context of decolonization). In fact, the commentary regarding Article 19 is to a *large extent identical* to the commentary dealing with Article 13[540] (which would later become Art. 24[541]). Thus, the reasons that were given by Waldock to explain why the consent of *both States* was necessary for the continuation of bilateral treaties in the context of 'new States'[542] were simply copied in the commentary dealing with Article 19 and the expression 'Newly Independent State' was now used. More importantly, the same reasons for applying the *tabula rasa* principle were, however, *not* copied in the commentary concerning secession and dissolution (Part IV, Arts 26–28).

5.74 Surprisingly, the ILC never explained why the fundamental importance of consent for any continuation of bilateral treaties was now suddenly *only relevant* in the specific context of Newly Independent States and not for cases of secession and dissolution. This is a rather strange outcome considering the obvious fact that these reasons were intrinsically linked to the *particular nature*

---

537 Ibid., [26].

538 Ibid., 230.

539 Ibid., 231 [6].

540 The only difference is that the commentary to Art. 19 contains fewer examples when compared to Art. 13.

541 At its 26th session, in 1974, the Commission adopted the final text, including Art. 23, which is virtually identical to Art. 19. The commentary to Art. 23 is also the same as for Art. 19. In the final text adopted at the Conference, Art. 23 became Art. 24.

542 ILC, Fourth Report, 1971 (n 217) 145–6.

of these treaties, including the existence of a 'personal equation'.[543] In other words, as explained above, the adoption of the *tabula rasa* principle to bilateral treaties has *nothing* do to with the special status of Newly Independent States, but was related to the very nature of these instruments. In all of Waldock's four reports, the principle of *tabula rasa* was clearly meant to apply to all 'new States', *including* cases of secession and dissolution outside of the context of decolonization. In fact, the work of the ILC is completely silent on why the principle of automatic continuity should apply specifically to *bilateral* treaties in the context of dissolution and secession. This omission is not only regrettable; it is unexplainable.

2.4 Can a State claim the benefit of the *rebus sic stantibus* exception mentioned at Article 34(2)(b) to prevent the continuous application of a treaty?

There is one possible explanation as to why the ILC may have decided to apply the rule of automatic continuity in the context of secession and dissolution despite the fact that this solution was contrary to its past statements with respect to the importance of consent in the specific context of bilateral treaties. It may be that the ILC arrived at the conclusion that, in any event, the solution of continuity could *never* be imposed on a reluctant State as a result of Article 34(2)(b). **5.75**

As mentioned above, the rule of continuity of treaties under Article 34 bears two exceptions. The second one reads as follows: **5.76**

> Paragraph 1 does not apply if: (...)
>
> (b) it appears from the treaty or is otherwise established that the application of the treaty in respect of the successor State would be incompatible with the object and purpose of the treaty or would radically change the conditions for its operation.

The question arises as to whether or not a State (either the 'other State party' or the new State) can argue that the replacement of one State (the predecessor State) by another one (the new State) as a party to the treaty is 'incompatible with the object and purpose of the treaty or would radically change the conditions for its operation'. In other words, can a State claim the benefit of the *rebus sic stantibus* exception mentioned at Article 34(2)(b) to prevent the continuous application of a treaty? **5.77**

543 Ibid., 146 [3].

5.78 The work of the ILC shows that the wording of this provision was adopted based on Article 62 of the Vienna Convention on the Law of Treaties.[544] The ILC did not specifically address the scope of the *rebus sic stantibus* exception in the context of bilateral treaties.[545] This omission is unfortunate. In fact, the only reference the present author could find in the work of the ILC on this point is the following brief explanation: 'in most, if not all, cases of succession of States the territorial changes might result in "incompatibility with the object and purpose of the treaty" or a "radical change in the conditions for the operation of the treaty"'.[546] This comment seems to suggest that the exception set out at Article 34(2)(b) could be used in certain circumstances by a State in order to prevent the continuous application of a treaty. This is also the position supported by some writers.[547] A different view had been adopted by Zedalis, who is the only writer to have comprehensively examined the question.[548]

5.79 Recent State practice shows that 'other State parties' have actually *not* used this argument when undertaking negotiations with new States.[549] The same is true for successor States. For instance, *rebus sic stantibus* was not invoked during the

544 ILC Report, 26th Session, 1974 (n 24) 210. The following explanation is given by Zedalis (n 440) 23 and 25:

> there is absolutely no reason to believe the delegates to the Vienna Conference on Succession of States thought the language of what was to become article 34 (2)(b) of the 1978 Succession Convention meant something different from the like concepts in articles 61 and 62 of the 1969 Treaty on Treaties. The ILC in 1972, and again in 1974, expressed this understanding of the language, and nothing indicates the Vienna Conference delegates desired to move in an opposite direction.

See also: Yasseen (n 420) 82; Mikulka (n 75) 1182ff.

545 See, Zedalis (n 440) 21ff. at 24.

546 ILC Report, 26th Session, 1974 (n 24) 210.

547 Eisemann (n 110) 51, 53; Stern, 'La succession d'États' (n 75) 314.

548 Zedalis (n 440) 22, fn 102. He first explained the meaning of the words 'it appears from the treaty' contained in Art. 34 and asked the question whether the ground of 'incompatibility with the object and purpose of the treaty' could be raised against succession to a multilateral treaty by the mere fact the instrument does not (and, logically, could not) mention the name of a new State. He answers in the negative:

> Reliance on the fact that the NAFTA applies to 'Canada' and then defines that in a way which, necessarily, would exclude Quebec in the event of separation, begs the question of whether the treaty contains language incompatible with succession. After all, every treaty which indicates that it applies between named countries would be affected in the event territory separates from those countries or the countries themselves, by name, cease to exist (e.g., Czechoslovakia or Yugoslavia). Nor does it seem acceptable to infer that the presence of an accession provision in a treaty means succession is incompatible therewith. The presence of such a provision can be explained as allowing nations not controlling territory under the sovereign authority of extant states party to commit themselves to the treaty's terms. It need not be understood as having but a single meaning – succession is inoperative.

549 Eisemann (n 110) 53; G. Hafner, 'Austria and Slovenia: Succession to Bilateral Treaties and the State Treaty of 1955', in M. Mrak (ed), *State Succession* (Brill 1999) 136 (examining the position of Austria). *Contra*: ILA, Resolution no. 3/2008 (n 52) [8]:

> With regard to bilateral treaties concluded by the predecessor State, practice shows that the fate of these treaties is generally decided through negotiation between the successor State and the other party, no matter the category of State succession involved. The *rebus sic stantibus* rule is sometimes invoked as a way to obtain the renegotiation of the treaty.

negotiations that took place between the Czech Republic and other States concerning the fate of the bilateral treaties to which Czechoslovakia was a party.[550]

The question of the practical application of the exceptions set out at Article 34(2)(b) remains unsettled.[551] In my view, a State would likely have a limited chance of success in convincing a court that the continuous application of a treaty should be denied *merely* on the ground that State succession has occurred.[552] Thus, the object and purpose of BITs are always the same: the promotion and protection of investments. It is hard to see how replacing one State by another as a party to the treaty could in any way affect the object of the treaty or even change radically its conditions of operation. Other writers have reached the same conclusion.[553] For instance, Zedalis explained that the 'incompatibility' and 'radical change' exceptions would have a limited chance **5.80**

550 Report by the Czech Republic, in Klabbers et al (n 75) 469, ad. No. 3; Mikulka (n 75) 1184.

551 This is also the position of Mikulka (n 75) 1185. It should be added that according to one writer, Pereira Fleury (n 39) 470ff, one test which should be used to determine whether there is any succession to a BIT is to consider whether there has been a 'fundamental change of circumstances' since the agreement was concluded. The author suggests that the event of State succession *itself* could be considered as a 'fundamental change of circumstances'. Yet, under Art. 62 of the Vienna Convention on the Law of Treaties, the existence of such circumstances must have been 'unforeseen' by the parties when they signed the treaty. Moreover, such circumstances must have 'constituted an essential basis of the consent of the parties to be bound by the treaty'. It is hard to see how these concepts would actually apply in the context of succession to BITs. When two States signed a treaty it goes without saying that they believe (and hope) that they will continue to exist in the future. In other words, the disappearance or extinction of a State is necessarily always an 'unforeseen' event at the time when two States sign a BIT. Similarly, it would seem quite obvious that the very existence of these two States 'constituted an essential basis of the consent of the parties to be bound by the treaty'. A State would simply not sign a treaty with another one if it believed that that State did not exist! For all of these reasons, the 'fundamental change of circumstances' element is not relevant at all to determine the question of succession to BITs.

552 The present author is very grateful to Prof. Caroline Fournet (Groningen University, Netherlands) for her insightful comments and remarks on this question.

553 M.N. Shaw and C. Fournet, 'Article 62 – Changement Fondamental de Circonstances', in O. Corten and P. Klein (eds), *Les Conventions de Vienne sur le droit des traités – Commentaire article par article* (Bruylant 2006 vol. III) 2256, arguing that a succession of States should not be considered as a 'fundamental change of circumstances' in the context of the application of Art. 62 of the Vienna Convention on the Law of Treaties. As further discussed below (see, Part D), the Restatement of the Law Third, the Foreign Relations Law of the United States (American Law Institute Publ. 1987 vol. I) has adopted the rule of succession to *State contracts* in the context of secession and cession of territory when there is a nexus between the contract and the territory of the successor State (§ 209(2)) In its comment on this rule, the Restatement noted the possibility of applying the *rebus sic stantibus* rule to contracts, but added that 'succession does not itself constitute such a change of circumstances or frustration' (ibid., comment f). Yet, the Restatement also seems to suggest the application of the *rebus sic stantibus* rule in other circumstances involving succession to multilateral treaties (ibid., § 210, see comments b) and e)). On this point, see also the analysis of Zedalis (n 440) 21ff; Steven C. Young, 'Foreign Direct Investment Disputes with Unrecognized States: FDI Arbitration in Kosovo', (2016) 22(5) *J Int Arb* 504.

of success to prevent (hypothetically) the independent State of Quebec from becoming party to the NAFTA (a multilateral treaty).[554]

5.81 These two exceptions were specifically discussed by the *Sanum* Tribunal examining whether the China-Laos BIT should extend to the territory of Macao in the context of the transfer of this territory from Portugal to China in 1999. As mentioned above (and further discussed below[555]), the tribunal specifically examined the exceptions mentioned in Article 15 of the Vienna Convention (the content is similar to the exceptions provided by Art. 34). The tribunal made an important observation on whether expanding the protection of the BIT to Macao would radically change the conditions of application of the BIT:

---

554 Zedalis (n 440) 25–6:

> Article 34 (2)(b)'s reference in the 1978 Succession Convention to the notion of radical change, seem to mean complications exist in trying to show the rule of continuation would not operate upon an independent Quebec. Two complications spring readily to mind. The first is that the idea of a separate Quebec has been around since at least the 1970s and as early as May 1980, a decade before NAFTA negotiations commenced, a provincial referendum on the matter was sponsored by the ruling government. Given this, it would be difficult to persuade most that, at the time the NAFTA was negotiated, facts which could lead to separation were not foreseen. The second, but less acute, complication has to do with radical change (like fundamental change of circumstances) requiring a transformation of treaty obligations which renders performance different from what was originally agreed. Separate and independent trading status would require additional attention be devoted to Quebec by the other NAFTA countries, however since it already participates in trade under the NAFTA, the burden for those countries of succession is unlikely to render performance essentially different from what was originally undertaken. Far more vexing than these two complications is that change of circumstances is not an automatic, unilateral basis for suspending or terminating the application to some particular territory of a treaty or other international commitment. Therefore, the best the NAFTA countries could ever claim under radical change is the right to call for non-application to Quebec of NAFTA's liberal trading regime, triggering Quebec's right to insist on authoritative dispute settlement. With regard to article 34(2)(b)'s reference to incompatibility with the treaty's object or purpose, any understanding of it as requiring disappearance or destruction of an object indispensable for the execution of NAFTA is likely to preclude its use to avoid succession by Quebec. Such an understanding erects a tough condition that is not easily met in cases in which the only matter is the application of liberal international trade and investment policies. Reading the term incompatibility so it includes inconsistency or conflict increases the potential for use in preventing an independent Quebec from accessing NAFTA. Nonetheless, since the precise language of paragraph (2)(b) speaks of incompatibility with 'the' object or purpose, it would be essential to show succession as in conflict with the NAFTA's basic market opening goal. Proof that succession is inconsistent with one of the NAFTA's many constituent sector aims would be insufficient. Furthermore, and consonant with recourse to the notion of radical change, invocation of incompatibility would simply set in motion dispute settlement concerning treaty succession. Automatic or unilateral action would be impermissible.

See also at 27:

> in the context of Quebec and NAFTA, difficulties exist in relying upon incompatibility with the object or purpose of the treaty, or radical change in circumstances, as bases for denying that an independent Quebec has succeeded to what Canada negotiated with the United States and Mexico. It is not impossible to hypothesize a factual configuration that would allow denial. Even in such a case, however, automatic, unilateral action upon a denial would be forbidden.

For the same position, see: A. Berbner, 'Things Fall Apart? NAFTA After Quebec', (1997) 6 *Dalhousie J Legal Stud* 301–3.

555 See, Chapter 6, Sections 5.2.2.2., 5.2.3.2. and 5.2.4.1.

> Concerning the question of bilateral treaties and whether or not a succession to them radically changes the conditions for their operation, there are two schools of thought.
>
> For some States, the personal aspect of a bilateral treaty implies that the replacement of one State with another in a bilateral relationship radically changes the condition for its operation with the consequence that the general rule of continuity should not apply. For other States, the continuity rule applies generally to bilateral treaties as well as to multilateral treaties, unless there are specific elements that lead to the conclusion that a change in the Contracting Parties would radically change the conditions for their operation.
>
> The Tribunal notes first that Article 15 does not distinguish between multilateral and bilateral treaties. Second, the Tribunal considers that it would be excessive to say that all bilateral treaties are *so* personal, *so* related to *intuitu personae* questions that they cannot survive a State's succession. In other words, the Tribunal considers that it is necessary to consider the application of the general rule to bilateral treaties on a case-by-case basis.[556]

This passage makes it clear that, for the tribunal, the mere fact that a succession of States has taken place does not *in itself* radically change the conditions for the operation of a BIT. Yet, the tribunal also mentioned that the ground of 'incompatibility with the object and purpose of the treaty' could potentially be successfully invoked against the extension of a treaty in the context of a transfer of territory in one *very specific* case. This is the situation where the successor State and the ceded territory would be governed by drastically different economic systems at the time of the succession: **5.82**

> In the case at hand, a specific element is the fact that the States Parties to the PRC/Laos BIT were States with planned economies, and that the extension of this BIT was to include a capitalist region. This could give some credibility to the argument that there is a fundamental change of circumstances which would call for the non-extension of the Treaty. Some doctrinal approaches would seem to support to such an argument. [quoting the work of Stern] (...) It can indeed be the case that when a treaty is concluded between two States with planned economies, the extension of such treaty to a capitalist economy would fundamentally change the conditions for its application if the treaty was based on features specific to a planned economy and irreconcilable with the liberal principles of a capitalist economy.[557]

---

556 *Sanum*, Award, 2013 (n 370) [244]–[246] (emphasis in the original).

557 Ibid., [247–248]. The Award refers to Stern, 'La succession d'États' (n 75) 170:

> Les traités politiques constituent une catégorie spécifique de traités conclus *intuitu personae*, en fonction des caractéristiques d'un Etat précis, tels que des traités d'alliance, ou certains traités commerciaux conclus entre Etats à économie planifiée. Leur extinction en cas de succession apparaît, encore une fois, comme une mise en œuvre d'un principe général du droit international qui est le changement fondamental de circonstances.

5.83 In any event, as explained below,[558] the tribunal ultimately held that the extension of the China-Laos BIT to Macao would not constitute a fundamental change of circumstances.[559] Thus, the application of the BIT to the ceded territory would not 'endanger the capitalist system and the liberal way of life' prevailing in Macao.[560]

5.84 In sum, the reasoning of the *Sanum* Tribunal suggests that the *rebus sic stantibus* exception set out in Article 34 would rarely find application in the context of succession to BITs, which all basically have the same object and purpose.

2.5 Concluding remarks regarding secession and dissolution of States

5.85 My conclusion is that upon its independence, a new State is not automatically bound by the bilateral treaties which had been entered into by the predecessor State with other States. The continuation of treaties is ultimately dependent on the express or tacit agreement of both States concerned. This is indeed the solution favoured by scholars.[561] The ILC has clearly endorsed, *as a matter of*

---

558 See, Chapter 6, Section 5.5.2.2.

559 *Sanum*, Award, 2013 (n 370) [248]–[251].

560 Ibid., [251].

561 Di Stefano (n 215); Stern, 'La succession d'États' (n 75) 315–16: 'Les traités bilatéraux semblent ne jamais avoir été considérés comme continuant automatiquement à s'appliquer'; Hafner and Novak (n 368) 414; Kolliopoulos (n 248) 301–2, 307ff; Genest (n 39) 9–12; M.N. Shaw, *International Law* (6th ed. CUP 2008) 967: 'it would appear, the consent of the other parties to the treaties in question or an agreement with the predecessor State with regards to bilateral treaties is required'; Menon (n 335) 156: 'As a practical matter, no bilateral treaty can exist without the will of the parties. Stated otherwise, a new State can become a party to a multilateral treaty independently of the will of the other party whereas the latter's consent is necessary in the case of a bilateral'; Degan (n 6) 226:

> En matière de traités bilatéraux une pratique assez uniforme s'est stabilisée déjà à l'époque de la décolonisation. Les accords sur la dévolution et les déclarations unilatérales sur le même sujet ont été la base pour une application provisoire de nombreux traités bilatéraux jusqu'aux négociations sur leur sort, ou jusqu'à l'expiration d'un certain délai. Cette pratique a été poursuivie après 1990. Mais pour une telle application provisoire, l'accord ou le consentement tacite de tous les Etats intéressés est toujours nécessaire. Il ne s'agit donc pas d'une obligation juridique sur cette application provisoire des traités bilatéraux.

Pereira (n 222) 149:

> Dans les cas de traites bilatéraux ou multilatéraux restreints, cependant, il est inconcevable que la novation puisse s'effectuer par acte seul du successeur: c'est la un fait déjà reconnu par Strupp qui, bien qu'il partît de la négation absolue de la succession, admettait la nécessité du consentement des États cocontractants aux fins d'opérer la novation et, par conséquent, de conserver au traité ses effets.

O. Udokang, *Succession of the New States to International Treaties* (Oceana 1972) 501; Zemanek (n 96) 238:

> The only conclusion which this rather heterogenous practice seems to permit is that with the exception of dispositive treaties succession to bilateral treaties does not occur without an express declaration to this effect by the succeeding state, which is at least tacitly accepted by the other contracting party.

Cahier (n 8) 72; '[L]e maintien en vigueur des traités bilatéraux exige le consentement de l'État nouvelle indépendant et de l'autre partie'; Meriboute (n 429) 74; Yasseen (n 420) 105; 108; Dupont (n 42) 23.

principle, the *tabula rasa* principle for bilateral treaties because of the specific *nature* and *characteristics* of these instruments: 'succession in respect of bilateral treaties has an essentially voluntary character', and consequently, 'their continuance in force after independence is a matter of agreement, express or tacit, between the Newly Independent State and the other State party to the predecessor State's treaty'.[562] It is true that the *Sanum* Tribunal stated in its award that it 'would be excessive to say that all bilateral treaties are *so* personal, *so* related to *intuitu personae* questions that they cannot survive a State's succession'.[563] Yet, this passage should not be interpreted as a rejection of the 'personal equation' argument invoked by the ILC for applying the *tabula rasa* principle to Newly Independent States. The comment was made in the specific situation of a transfer of territory where the question of continuation of treaties simply *did not arise*.[564] In fact, the tribunal was only addressing the scope of the exceptions set out at Article 15 of the Convention. As mentioned above, the tribunal supports the proposition that a State would have a limited chance of success to convince a court to deny the continuous application of a treaty on the mere ground that a State succession has occurred.

In my view, the basic and logical *tabula rasa* solution should apply *not only* to Newly Independent States but also to cases of secession and dissolution. For one scholar, the reason for extending the *tabula rasa* principle to all new States is because Article 24 (which applies to Newly Independent States) should be considered as a rule of customary law.[565] **5.86**

Moreover, as already mentioned above[566] and further explained in the following paragraphs, the principle of *automatic* succession is also *not* the general position that has been adopted by States in recent years in the context of secessions and dissolution of States.[567] In 1996, Professor Stern noted in her **5.87**

562 ILC Report, 26th Session, 1974 (n 24) 239.

563 *Sanum*, Award, 2013 (n 370) [244]–[246] (emphasis in the original).

564 Thus, in this specific context (and contrary to all other types of succession) the question is not whether the successor State should be bound by the treaties to which the predecessor State was a party. The question which arises is different: whether the treaties entered into by successor State should apply to the ceded territory after the date of succession. The answer is unambiguously positive under the well-established MTF rule set out at Art. 15 of the Convention.

565 Di Stefano (n 215) 845–5: 'la règle établie à l'article 24, 1er paragraphe, constitue le reflet du droit international coutumier à la fois pour les Etats nouvellement indépendants et les autres Etats, au delà du champ d'application *ratione personae* de la disposition conventionnelle'.

566 See, Chapter 2, Section 2.

567 ILA, Resolution no. 3/2008 (n 52). See also: Tams (n 27) 326:

> Article 34 has had a limited impact on international practice. In fact, there is widespread agreement that international practice since 1978 does not bear out a general rule of automatic succession for *all treaties*. Rather than relying on the operation of one overarching principle, States have sought actively to shape the fate of 'their' treaty rights and obligations post independence. The various State successions of the 1990s in particular resulted in rich body of treaty practice, including unilateral declarations by successor States,

(now) classic course at the Hague Academy of International Law that the practice of States has varied with respect to bilateral treaties and that while some have adopted the position of *tabula rasa*, others have favoured continuity.[568] Thus, a number of new successor States (for instance, in the context of the dissolutions of Czechoslovakia and Yugoslavia) seem to have adopted a *general position* in favour of *continuity* regarding bilateral treaties.[569] Yet, as mentioned above,[570] these States have in practice all started negotiations with other States to determine the actual status of these bilateral treaties.[571] The practice of *other States* in response to these claims of continuity by new States has been anything but coherent.

5.88 Overall, the general conclusion reached by the ILA in 2008 about State practice is that 'the fate of these [bilateral] treaties is generally decided through negotiation between the successor State and the other party, no matter the category of State succession involved'.[572] The same conclusion was reached in the ILA's 1996 'Rapport préliminaire sur la succession d'États en matière de

---

agreements with their treaty partners, and depositary statements, which provide guidance on the fate of specific treaties. This practice has usually accommodated a general desire to avoid ruptures; as a consequence, in the majority of instances, the States involved in negotiations have sought to ensure the stability of treaty relations. But this overarching goal has been reached in different ways, and pursued with different degrees of vigour.

568 Stern, 'La succession d'États' (n 75) 314:

> Deux approches opposées se rencontrent pour ce qui est des traités bilatéraux, selon le rôle accordé au caractère personnel inhérent ou non à cette catégorie de traités. Pour certains États, le caractère personnel du traité bilatéral entraîne automatiquement que le remplacement d'un État par un autre dans la relation bilatérale change radicalement les conditions d'exécution du traité: en conséquence, la règle de continuité doit être écartée en principe, sauf accord contraire. Pour d'autres États, la règle de la continuité s'applique aux traités bilatéraux comme aux autres, conformément à ce qui est prévu par l'article 34, sauf s'il est démontré dans le cas particulier que le maintien en vigueur du traité bilatéral à l'égard de l'État successeur change radicalement les conditions d'exécution du traité. Dans le premier cas, il y a présomption de discontinuité, qui peut donc être écartée par accord contraire. Dans le second cas, il y a au contraire une présomption de continuité, qui peut également être écartée par accord contraire, cette fois sur le caractère personnel du traité.

See also, for the same conclusion: ILA, Resolution no. 3/2008 (n 52) point no. 6.

569 Mikulka (n 75) 1204, 1206.

570 See, Chapter 3, Section 2.

571 ILA, Resolution no. 3/2008 (n 52) point no. 6; ILA, Rapport Final, 2002 (n 73). See, however, the different assessment made by Degan (n 6) 222:

> Tous les États issus de la dissolution des trois fédérations communistes ont adopté le principe de la succession automatique de tous les traités de l'État prédécesseur, ne faisant même aucune réserve quant aux traités bilatéraux ni aux traités multilatéraux de caractère restreint. Aucun de ces pays n'a prétendu être un État nouvellement indépendant. Donc, l'article 34 de la Convention de 1978 les a conduits à assumer cette obligation, en estimant qu'il s'agissait déjà d'une règle du droit international positif.

572 ILA, Resolution no. 3/2008 (n 52) point no. 6. See also: ILA, *Conclusions of the Committee on Aspects of the Law on State Succession*; ILA, 'Rapport préliminaire sur la succession d'États en matière de traités', 1996, Helsinki Conference, 690–91.

traités'.[573] The ILA also noted that such negotiations about the fate of bilateral treaties often took place based on the existence of some kind of 'presumption' of continuity.[574] Yet, the very fact that such negotiations took place in most situations suggests that States have generally not accepted the principle of *automatic* succession.[575] In sum, there seems to be limited practice supporting the principle of *automatic* continuity set out at Article 34.[576] Clearly, no rule of customary international law has emerged on succession to bilateral treaties.[577]

Finally, State practice further demonstrates that the 1978 Convention experiment regarding the issue of State succession to *bilateral* treaties has been a failure. On the one hand, while the solution of *tabula rasa*, which the ILC **5.89**

---

573 ILA, 'Rapport préliminaire', ibid:

> La pratique en matière de traités bilatéraux ne semble pas différente selon qu'il s'agit d'un État continuateur ou d'un État successeur. Cette pratique générale semble être très caractérisée et peut être décrite ainsi: l'État successeur et l'État partenaire de l'État prédécesseur dans un traité bilatéral engagent des consultations et procèdent à un bilan des relations bilatérales. Le plus souvent l'initiative vient de l'État successeur, parfois elle vient de son partenaire. Avant l'achèvement de ce bilan, il est très fréquent qu'un échange de volonté précise de façon expresse le *maintien en vigueur* des traités de l'État prédécesseur (avec peut-être une position différente de la France à ce sujet). Au terme du bilan, plusieurs catégories de traités émergent. La procédure utilisée est celle de *différentes listes de traités:* – ceux qui sont maintenus en vigueur par application du principe de continuité; – ceux qui sont maintenus en vigueur par application du principe de continuité, mais que les deux États décident d'un commun accord de terminer ou de modifier pour l'avenir, c'est-à-dire à partir de la date du protocole ou de l'accord formalisant l'achèvement des consultations; – ceux qui sont terminés en application des règles de la succession d'États, c'est-à-dire à partir de la date de la succession d'États. On peut ajouter que parfois, à l'occasion d'une succession d'États, on constate que certains traités ne sont plus en vigueur, car ils sont obsolètes. Ce bilan s'effectue tantôt et le plus souvent à la suite de *simples consultations* au niveau des experts – rarement à la suite de *véritables négociations* – tantôt à la suite d'un *simple échange de lettres* ou de notes diplomatiques (emphasis in the original).

574 ILA, Rapport Final, 2002 (n 73) 18:

> En ce qui concerne les traités bilatéraux, la pratique générale est celle de discussions bilatérales plus ou moins formelles destinées à clarifier la situation. Un examen attentif de la pratique semble cependant démontrer que ces discussions sont fondées sur l'idée qu'il existe une règle de continuité des traités bilatéraux.

See also, ibid 22:

> Mais l'analyse des politiques menées par des États tiers vis-à-vis des États successeurs, montre que *la pratique de la négociation prévaut* concernant la succession en matière de traités. Même si la présomption de la continuité est la prémisse fondamentale en matière de succession d'États – afin de sauvegarder la stabilité des relations internationales -, chaque traité mérite une attention toute particulière puisque, dans chaque cas, des considérations politiques, idéologiques, militaires, religieuses, éthiques, sociales, économiques, historiques spécifiques rentrent en jeu et les États ne sauraient donc spolier une partie de leur souveraineté au nom d'un principe de succession automatique universelle aux traités: *la règle générale est donc la négociation des traités au cas par cas, sur le fondement du principe de continuité, modulé par ses exceptions.*' (emphasis added).

575 Eisemann (n 110) 53.

576 Ibid., 54–5; Tams (n 27) 334: 'the better view is that Article 34 does not reflect customary international law – and that it certainly does not reflect customary international law as far as bilateral treaties are concerned'; Pereira Fleury (n 39) 456.

577 Klabbers et al (n 75) 116; Pereira Fleury (n 39) 457.

adopted for Newly Independent States, was both legally sound and logical, it remains that it has been of very limited practical use for States. This is because the phenomenon of decolonization was near its end when the Convention was adopted in 1978. On the other hand, the solution of automatic continuity, which was adopted by the ILC for bilateral treaties in the context of secession and dissolution of States, is not only incoherent with the solution of *tabula rasa* being applicable to Newly Independent States, it is also plainly unjustifiable given the particular nature of these instruments. Unsurprisingly, this solution has not been observed by States in their actual practice in the context of secession and dissolution of States in the last 25 years. In fact, they have adopted an opposing principle which was designed for an entirely different category of States (Newly Independent States). Tribunals have also very rarely mentioned the Convention in their awards when examining cases involving dissolution and secession (the *Sanum* award dealing with a matter of cession of territory is an exception). New States' rejection of the solution of automatic continuity specifically designed for them by the ILC is the ultimate evidence of the Convention's important shortcomings regarding bilateral treaties.

6

BIT ARBITRATION CASES INVOLVING STATE SUCCESSION ISSUES

1. INTRODUCTION

6.01 Chapter 3 examined the practice of States regarding the fate of BITs that were concluded by predecessor States. Another aspect that was previously examined is the outcome of the situation where the States concerned have *not* expressly (or implicitly) agreed upon the continuation of this instrument (Chapter 5). The present author's position is that whenever this is the case, there exists no principle of automatic succession to BITs. If there no evidence of any express or tacit consent by both the successor State and 'other State Party' to the BIT, the instrument should not be considered as binding on the successor State. A tribunal faced with such a situation should decline its jurisdiction over the dispute.

6.02 The present chapter contains a critical analysis of publicly-available BIT arbitration cases involving State succession issues. In my previous article published in 2015, I examined 28 investor-State arbitration cases where questions of State succession arose.[578] This chapter will examine a number of other significant cases, including one important award in the context of the

578 Dumberry, 'An Uncharted Question of State Succession' (n 40) 74–96.

cession of Macao to China (*Sanum*) and several controversial new cases arising from the annexation of Crimea by Russia. Overall, at the time of writing (May 2017), the issue of State succession had arisen in no less than 46 publicly-known cases.

These cases typically involve the following factual pattern: **6.03**

- A foreign investor filed a claim before an arbitral tribunal against a *new* State *after* its independence (i.e. after the date of succession);[579]
- The foreign investor alleged that certain actions/omission were committed by the new State *after* it became an independent State;
- Yet, the foreign investor alleged that these actions/omissions were in breach of a BIT that had been entered *by the predecessor State* with another State (the 'other State party') *before* the date of succession;
- In other words, the question is whether or not *one State* (the new State) is bound by a treaty which was originally concluded by *another State* (the predecessor State).

The following sections will separately examine the case law involving three break-up situations: Czechoslovakia (22 cases, Section 2), USSR (seven cases, Section 3) and Yugoslavia (eight cases, Section 4) as well as the cession of the territory of Macao to China (one case, Section 5) and the annexation of Crimea by Russia (eight cases, Section 6). **6.04**

2. THE DISSOLUTION OF CZECHOSLOVAKIA

As a result of the dissolution of Czechoslovakia on 1 January 1993, two new States emerged as successor States: the Czech Republic and the Republic of Slovakia.[580] As mentioned above,[581] both new States adopted the general position of continuity regarding the bilateral treaties to which Czechoslovakia was a party before the date of succession. All BITs have remained in force following consultation and negotiation between the new States and the other States parties.[582] **6.05**

---

579 As further explained below, the situation is different for cases involving the Russian Federation because it is *not* a 'new' State, but rather the 'continuing State' of the USSR. The situation is also different in the context of the cession of Macao to China, since it does not involve the creation of a new State. The annexation of Crimea also deserves special treatment for reasons explained below (see, Chapter 6, Section 6).

580 On 25 November 1992, the Czechoslovak Federal Assembly voted the Constitutional Act no. 542/1992 (which came into force on 8 December 1992) indicating that the Federation would cease to exist on 31 December 1992.

581 See, Chapter 3, Section 2.2.

582 Tams (n 27) 330.

6.06 In the following paragraphs, I will examine 17 cases involving claims against either the Slovak Republic or the Czech Republic concerning allegations of breach of BITs that had been entered by Czechoslovakia with other States.[583] It should be added that I have identified five other cases involving the issue of State succession with regards to Czechoslovakia's BITs, but the available information pertaining to them is very limited.[584]

6.07 The Czech Republic and Slovakia have never challenged the jurisdiction of arbitral tribunals over disputes arising from these BITs on the grounds that they were not bound by these instruments. This important fact certainly explains the reason why tribunals have not been overly attentive to State succession issues.[585] Similarly, the ICJ does not typically address questions pertaining to State succession and identity of States when the issue is non-contentious and has not been challenged by the parties.[586] Yet, as further explained in the following paragraphs, tribunals' general lack of reasoning on important State succession issues is regrettable. These awards can be divided into three categories:

- Some tribunals have simply refrained from explaining why a new State should be considered to be bound by obligations arising from a treaty entered into by another State (Section 2.1);
- Other tribunals have only offered the beginning of an explanation on the issue (Section 2.1);
- A number of tribunals have correctly addressed the State succession issue in their awards (Section 2.2).

2.1 The silence of some tribunals and the limited analysis of others

6.08 Some tribunals have failed to address the fundamental question of how the Czech Republic could be bound by obligations arising from a BIT concluded by Czechoslovakia before independence. A good example is the case of *Ronald S. Lauder v. Czech Republic* involving a claim filed in 1999 by a US investor,

583 See, more generally, Tomáš Fecák, 'Czech Experience with Bilateral Investment Treaties: Somewhat Bitter Taste of Investment Protection', (2011) 2 *Czech YPPIL* 23.

584 A number of awards were not publicly available at the time of writing (May 2017) for the following cases: *Georg Nepolsky v. Czech Republic*, UNCITRAL (filed under the Germany-Czechoslovakia BIT); *Voltaic Network GmbH v. Czech Republic*, UNCITRAL (filed under the Germany-Czechoslovakia BIT). At the time of writing, a number of other relevant cases were pending, including: *EuroGas GmbH v. Slovak Republic*, UNCITRAL (filed under the Austria-Czechoslovakia BIT). The proceedings of another case *Konsortium Oeconomismus v. Czech Republic* (filed under the Switzerland-Czechoslovakia BIT) was terminated by the parties. In the case of *US Steel Global Holdings I. BV v. Slovak Republic*, UNCITRAL, PCA Case No. 2013–6 (filed under the Netherlands-Czechoslovakia BIT) the claimant withdrew its claim.

585 See, Tams (n 27) 25. On this point, see also: Pereira Fleury (n 39) 459.

586 See, Zimmermann, 'The International Court of Justice' (n 249) 55.

Mr. Lauder, against the Czech Republic for allegedly violating the 1991 US-Czechoslovakia BIT.[587] The award contains no reasoning whatsoever as to the Czech Republic's succession to this BIT. The tribunal simply *assumed* that the BIT was binding on the Czech Republic upon its independence. One reason that may explain the tribunal's silence on this question is the fact that the respondent did not raise any jurisdictional challenge on this point.[588] In any event, the tribunal also failed to explain that the United States had actually agreed upon the continuation of this BIT with the Czech Republic after the date of succession. This is regrettable given the fact that such information regarding the succession to the US-Czechoslovakia BIT was readily available and had, in fact, been previously discussed in doctrine.[589]

Another example of a tribunal's silence on relevant State succession issues is the *Frontier Petroleum Services Ltd. v. Czech Republic* case,[590] which involved a claim by a Canadian company alleging a breach by the Czech Republic of the 1990 Canada-Czechoslovakia BIT.[591] It should be added that since then, in January 2012, Canada entered into a BIT with the Czech Republic.[592] Article 15 of the 2012 BIT makes it clear that both States have agreed on the continuation of the old BIT.[593] The new agreement was signed by the parties in 2009. It is therefore surprising that the award rendered in 2010 does not mention that important fact. Similarly, in the case of *InterTrade Holding GmbH v. Czech Republic*,[594] the tribunal simply referred to the Germany-Czechoslovakia BIT as the 'German-Czech BIT' without mentioning the important fact that both States had agreed upon the continuation of the old **6.09**

587 *Ronald S. Lauder v. Czech Republic*, UNCITRAL, Final Award, 3 September 2001 [2], [10].

588 See, discussion in Cheng (n 136) 248–51.

589 Williams (n 135) 30, explaining that the US conditioned the establishment of diplomatic relations with the Czech Republic upon commitments to fulfil the treaty and other obligations of the former Czechoslovakia. The Czech Republic agreed to these terms. See, exchange of letters between US President G.W. Bush and the Czech Republic Prime Minister V. Klaus, 1 January 1993. Williams also explains (ibid. at 40) that in June 1993, the Czech Ministry of Foreign Affairs notified the US Department of State that a number of US-Czechoslovakia treaties (including the US-Czechoslovakia BIT) would continue to be in force between the two States. Williams does not refer to the response of the US to this letter. The website of the Office of the United States Trade Representative simply indicates that 'After the breakup of Czechoslovakia in 1993, this treaty [i.e., the US-Czechoslovakia BIT] continued in effect for the successor states, the Czech Republic and Slovakia'.

590 *Frontier Petroleum Services Ltd. V. Czech Republic*, UNCITRAL, Final Award, 12 November 2010.

591 Ibid., [3].

592 Agreement between Canada and the Czech Republic for the Promotion and Protection of Investments, signed on 6 May 2009, and brought into force on 22 January 2012.

593 This question was examined above, see Chapter 3, Section 2.2.

594 *InterTrade Holding GmbH v. Czech Republic*, UNCITRAL, PCA Case No. 2009–12, Final Award, 29 May 2012 [5].

instrument.[595] The same lack of reasoning is also found in the case *Peter Franz Vocklinghaus v. Czech Republic* filed under the Germany-Czechoslovakia BIT.[596]

6.10 A number of tribunals have acknowledged the existence of a question surrounding State succession, but have nonetheless failed to provide any comprehensive analysis of the issue. A good illustration is the case of *CME Czech Republic BV v. Czech Republic* involving a Dutch company alleging that the Czech Republic committed a breach of the 1992 Netherlands-Czechoslovakia BIT.[597] The reasoning of the tribunal on the question of State succession is limited to one single sentence: 'after the Czech and Slovak Federal Republic ceased to exist on December 31, 1992, the Czech Republic succeeded to the rights and obligations of the Czech and Slovak Federal Republic under the Treaty'.[598]

6.11 A number of other tribunals (examined in the next paragraphs) have been slightly more explicit by briefly referring to the above-mentioned declaration of willingness made by both new States to succeed to Czechoslovakia's international obligations. They also (very briefly) explained that as a result of such a declaration, the new State was bound by obligations arising from Czechoslovakia's BITs. Yet, it is noteworthy that these tribunals have nevertheless failed to explain that any continuation of a BIT requires the agreement of the 'other State party' to the original treaty. An illustration of this trend is provided by the case *Eastern Sugar v. Czech Republic*, involving a claim by a Dutch company against the Czech Republic under the 1992 Netherlands-Czechoslovakia BIT.[599] The Czech Republic argued that as a result of its recent accession to the EU, the BIT with the Netherlands was no longer applicable and that the tribunal therefore lacked jurisdiction over the dispute.[600] The tribunal ultimately rejected this line of defence.[601] One of the reasons mentioned by the tribunal was that 'to this day, no notice of termination of the BIT was given by either the Czech Republic or the Kingdom of the Netherlands'.[602] This being said, the tribunal does not explain how the BIT could still be in force between them; it simply stated that 'the Czech

595 Germany's Federal Gazette (Bundesgesetzblatt) 1993, vol. II, 762 (referred to in: Tams (n 27) 24).

596 *Peter Franz Vocklinghaus v. Czech Republic*, UNCITRAL, Award, 26 June 2009 [6].

597 *CME Czech Republic BV v. Czech Republic*, UNCITRAL, Partial Award, 13 Sept. 2001.

598 Ibid., [3]. See also the same sentence in: ibid., Final Award, 14 March 2003 [3].

599 *Eastern Sugar BV (Netherlands) v. Czech Republic*, SCC Case No. 088/2004, Partial Award, 27 March 2007.

600 Ibid., [97].

601 Ibid., [142ff].

602 Ibid., [153].

Republic succeeded into [Czechoslovakia's] international obligations, including those arising from the BIT'.[603] This omission is surprising considering that evidence of both States' consent was readily available.[604]

The same reasoning is followed by the tribunal in the *Binder v. Czech Republic* award, involving a claim by a German investor filed under the Germany-Czechoslovakia BIT.[605] The tribunal referred to the Germany-Czechoslovakia BIT as the 'Czech-German BIT'.[606] The Czech Republic argued that as a result of its recent accession to the EU in 2004, the BIT with Germany was no longer applicable and that the tribunal lacked jurisdiction over the dispute.[607] The tribunal made the following observations on that point: **6.12**

> The Arbitral Tribunal notes that the Czech-German BIT was concluded on 2 October 1990 and that it entered into force on 2 August 1992. On 1 May 2004, the Czech Republic became a Member State of the EU in accordance with the Accession Treaty. The status of the Czech-German BIT was not regulated in connection with that Treaty, and there is no indication that it was discussed during the negotiations on the Czech Republic's accession to the EU.[608]
>
> The Czech-German BIT has not been terminated pursuant to the provision in Article 13(2) of the BIT. Nor would it seem that the Czech Republic and Germany have agreed in any other way that the BIT should be terminated or cease to be operative.[609]

While the tribunal clearly considered the BIT to still be in force, it does not explain the preliminary question as to why the treaty that was initially signed by Germany and Czechoslovakia was now binding upon Germany and the Czech Republic. **6.13**

The same argument was raised by Slovakia in the case of *Eureko BV v. Slovak Republic* involving a Dutch company alleging that Slovakia had committed a breach of the 1992 Netherlands-Czechoslovakia BIT.[610] It was also argued that the tribunal lacked jurisdiction to hear the dispute since the 1992 BIT **6.14**

603 Ibid., [5].

604 See, Exchange of Letters between the Netherlands and the Czech Republic regarding the continuation of bilateral treaties, 8 and 9 December 1994, in: *Tractatenblad Van Het Koninkrij der Nederlanden*, Jaargang 1995 Nr. 27 (available at: https://zoek.officielebekendmakingen.nl/trb-1995–27.html) (also mentioned in: ILA, Rapport Final, 2002 (n 73) 26). See the discussion in: Report of Slovakia, in: Klabbers et al (n 75) 515–16.

605 *Binder v. Czech Republic*, UNCITRAL, Award on Jurisdiction, 6 June 2007.

606 Ibid., [1].

607 Ibid., [11]–[12].

608 Ibid., [59].

609 Ibid., [60].

610 *Eureko BV v. Slovak Republic*, UNCITRAL, PCA Case No. 2008–13, Award on Jurisdiction, Arbitrability and Suspension, 26 October 2010. This name of the case was later changed to: *Achmea BV v. Slovak Republic*, UNCITRAL, PCA Case No. 2008–13.

had been terminated as a result of Slovakia's accession to the EU in May 2004.[611] The tribunal rejected the 'Intra-EU jurisdictional objection' advanced by the respondent. As in the award in *Eastern Sugar*, the tribunal limited its reasoning on the question of Slovakia's succession to the 1992 BIT to the following short and general passage: 'The Slovak Republic separated from the CSFR and became an independent State on January 1, 1993. It succeeded to the CSFR-Netherlands BIT, as well as to the ECHR, as of the day of its independence.'[612] It is noteworthy that the award mentions the Netherlands's position as to whether or not Slovakia's accession to the EU had terminated the BIT.[613] The other question as to when and how the Netherlands agreed to Slovakia's continuation of the BIT is not addressed by the tribunal. This is regrettable since the information was easily accessible.[614]

6.15 A number of other awards also contain the same typical failure by tribunals to concretely explain how the new State succeeded to a BIT upon its independence and, importantly, how the other State party to that treaty reacted to such an intent:

- *Alps Finance v. Slovakia* (1991 Switzerland-Czechoslovakia BIT).[615] Although the tribunal acknowledged that Slovakia was not a sovereign State when the 1991 BIT was concluded,[616] it merely mentioned that following its independence, Slovakia had 'succeeded to the BIT as a legal successor of the previous (united) Federal Republic',[617] without providing any further explanation. The tribunal did not mention the important fact that Slovakia and Switzerland had in fact agreed to the continuation of the treaty.[618]
- *HICEE v. Slovakia* (1992 Netherlands-Czechoslovakia BIT).[619] In the award, the tribunal only briefly mentioned that 'it is not in dispute that,

---

611 Ibid., [9].

612 Ibid., [48]. See also the same comment in the final award: *Achmea BV v. Slovak Republic*, UNCITRAL, PCA Case No. 2008–13, Final Award, 7 December 2012 [82].

613 See, at ibid., [154ff]. The Netherlands argued that 'the BIT was in force long before the Slovak Republic's accession to the European Union' and had continued to be in force thereafter ([156], see also at [161]).

614 Exchange of Letters between the Netherlands and the Slovak Republic regarding the continuation of bilateral treaties, 9 December 1994, in: *Tractatenblad Van Het Koninkrij der Nederlanden*, Jaargang 1995 Nr. 27 (available at: https://zoek.officielebekendmakingen.nl/trb-1995–27.html, in Slovak Republic's official Collection of Laws (zbierka zákonov), no. 493/2005, 4721 (also mentioned in: ILA, Rapport Final, 2002 (n 73) 26). See also in: Klabbers et al (n 75) 285ff.

615 *Alps Finance and Trade AG v. Slovak Republic*, UNCITRAL, Award, 5 March 2011.

616 Ibid., [1].

617 Ibid.

618 Exchanges of Notes of 13 October and 25 November 1994 (available at the website of the Swiss Ministry of Foreign Affairs: http://www.dfae.admin.ch/eda/fr/home/topics/intla/intrea/dbstv/data05/e_99991005.html). See the discussion in: Report of Slovakia, in: Klabbers et al (n 75) 520.

619 *HICEE BV v. Slovak Republic*, UNCITRAL, PCA Case No. 2009–11, Partial Award, 23 May 2011.

after the dissolution of the Czech and Slovak Federal Republic on 31 December 1992, the Slovak Republic succeeded to the [BIT]'.[620]

- *Oostergetel & Laurentius v. Slovakia* (1992 Netherlands-Czechoslovakia BIT).[621] The tribunal rejected Slovakia's argument that the BIT had been terminated upon its accession to the EU in 2004.[622] The tribunal's only reference to the State succession issue is this brief passage: 'On 1 January 1993 the Czech and Slovak Federal Republic separated into two separate sovereign states. The Slovak Republic succeeded the former State's international obligations, including those arising under the BIT.'[623]
- *Nagel v. Czech Republic* (1992 UK-Czechoslovakia BIT).[624] The tribunal's only comment regarding State succession is that the BIT 'is binding on the Czech Republic as one of the two successor States of Czechoslovakia'.[625] Yet, both the Czech Republic and the United Kingdom had agreed to the continuation of the 1992 UK-Czechoslovakia BIT.[626]
- *European Media Ventures SA v. Czech Republic* (1989 Belgium/Luxembourg-Czechoslovakia BIT).[627] The tribunal's only comment regarding succession is that 'the Respondent became a contracting party to the Treaty by virtue of succession to the rights and obligations of the Czechoslovak Socialist Republic on 1 January 1993'.[628] The tribunal does not mention that the Czech Republic and Belgium/Luxembourg had agreed to the continuation of the 1989 BIT.[629]

2.2 A number of tribunals have correctly addressed the issue

A more comprehensive approach to the issue of State succession was adopted by other tribunals. For instance, in the *Saluka v. Czech Republic* case, involving a claim by a Dutch company against the Czech Republic under the 1992 Netherlands-Czechoslovakia BIT,[630] the tribunal explained the relevant State succession question as follows: 6.16

620 Ibid., [3, fn 2].
621 *Jan Oostergetel and Theodora Laurentius v. Slovak Republic*, UNCITRAL, Decision on Jurisdiction, 30 April 2010.
622 Ibid., [41, 65ff., 98].
623 Ibid., [56].
624 *William Nagel v. Czech Republic*, SCC Case No. 049/2002, Award, 9 Sept. 2003.
625 Ibid., [266].
626 See, UK Treaty Series 1996, Third Supp. List, 96.
627 *European Media Ventures SA v. Czech Republic*, UNCITRAL, Award on Jurisdiction, 15 May 2007.
628 Ibid., [1].
629 See, Tams (n 27) 24.
630 *Saluka Investments BV v. Czech Republic*, UNCITRAL, Decision on Jurisdiction over the Czech Republic's Counterclaim, 7 May 2004.

> The Czech and Slovak Federal Republic was dissolved on 31 December 1992, and its two constituent parts became independent States, as the Czech Republic and the Slovak Republic. The Czech Republic confirmed to the Kingdom of The Netherlands that, upon the separation of the Czech and Slovak Federal Republic into two separate republics, the Treaty remained in force between the Czech Republic and the Kingdom of The Netherlands.[631]

6.17 In its partial award of 2006, the tribunal elaborated on the question of succession:

> The Treaty had been concluded with the former State, the Czech and Slovak Federal Republic. By letter of 8 December 1994, the Minister of Foreign Affairs of the Czech Republic confirmed to the Minister of Foreign Affairs of the Kingdom of The Netherlands that the Treaty remained in force between the two States. No question of State succession in relation to the Treaty has been raised by the parties in this arbitration. The Tribunal, and the parties, have therefore proceeded on the basis that the Treaty applies to the situation which has given rise to the present dispute.[632]

6.18 Similar statements were also made by the tribunals in the following two cases:

- *Achmea BV v. Slovak Republic* involving a claim by a Dutch company (formally known as Eureko BV) filed under the Netherland-Czechoslovakia BIT:[633]

  > After the dissolution of the Czech and Slovak Federal Republic into the Czech Republic and the Slovak Republic, the Slovak Republic confirmed in an exchange of letters dated 9 December 1994 that the BIT remained in force between the Slovak Republic and the Kingdom of the Netherlands.[634]

- *Invesmart v. Czech Republic* under the Netherlands-Czechoslovakia BIT:

  > This arbitration arises from alleged violations of the Agreement on Encouragement and Reciprocal Protections of Investments between The Kingdom of the Netherlands ('Netherlands') and the Czech and Slovak Federal Republic dated 29 April 1991 (the 'BIT' or the 'Treaty'). On 8 December 1994, the Czech Republic confirmed to the Netherlands that the Treaty remains in force for the Czech Republic as a successor state to the Czech and Slovak Republic.[635]

---

631 Ibid., [2].

632 Ibid., Partial Award, 17 March 2006, [30]–[31].

633 *Achmea BV v. Slovak Republic*, UNCITRAL, PCA Case No. 2008-13 (Number 2), Award on Jurisdiction and Admissibility, 20 May 2014 (this case should not be confused with the *Eureko BV* case mentioned above (n 610).

634 Ibid., [1, fn 1].

635 *Invesmart v. Czech Republic*, UNCITRAL, Award, 26 June 2009 [8].

In the *Austrian Airlines* case, involving a claim by an Austrian company against Slovakia under the 1991 Austria-Czechoslovakia BIT,[636] the tribunal recognized that Slovakia did not exist as a sovereign State at the date the BIT entered into force, but added that the BIT was now binding on *both* States as a result of their explicit consent: 'The applicability of the [BIT] by way of State succession was confirmed by an exchange of diplomatic notes on 4 August and 25 November 1994 (and entered into force on 1 January 1995).'[637] **6.19**

Another example of a comprehensive approach adopted by a tribunal is the one found in award in the *ECE Projektmanagement v. Czech Republic* case involving a claim started by a German investor under the Germany-Czechoslovakia BIT. The tribunal fully addressed the relevant issue of State succession in the following paragraph of the award: **6.20**

> The original parties to the BIT were, on the one hand, the Federal Republic of Germany, and on the other, the Czech and Slovak Federal Republic. Following the separation of the latter the two successor States (one of which is the Respondent in this Arbitration) regulated between them succession to bilateral treaties concluded by the predecessor State. On the first day of the hearing in London on jurisdiction and the merits, in response to a question from the Tribunal, the representatives of both Parties confirmed that there were no issues resulting from application of the rules of State succession. The Tribunal has accordingly treated the BIT in the same way as if it had been from the outset a treaty concluded between Germany and the Czech Republic.[638]

Finally, it is important to analyse the reasoning of the tribunal in the case *European American Investment Bank AG (EURAM) v. Slovak Republic*, involving a claim brought forward by an Austrian claimant under the Austria-Czechoslovakia BIT. The tribunal first made the following general comment regarding the relevant succession issue: **6.21**

> The BIT under which the present proceedings have been brought was concluded on 15 October 1990 between the Federal Republic of Austria and the Czech and Slovak Federal Republic. It entered into force on 1 October 1991. The Czech and Slovak Federal Republic was dissolved and Slovakia became an independent State on 1 January 1993. The Parties agree that the BIT became binding on the Slovak Republic by succession. The Respondent maintains that the BIT became binding on the Slovak Republic with effect from 1 January 1995.[639]

---

636 *Austrian Airlines v. Slovak Republic*, UNCITRAL, Final Award, 9 October 2009.

637 Ibid., [8]. On this award, see: Pereira Fleury (n 39) 460.

638 *ECE Projektmanagement v. Czech Republic*, UNCITRAL, PCA Case No. 2010-5, Award, 19 September 2013, [1.17].

639 *European American Investment Bank AG (EURAM) v. Slovak Republic*, UNCITRAL, Award on Jurisdiction, 22 October 2012, [40].

6.22 With regard to Slovakia's argument that the VCLT did not apply to the BIT, the tribunal referred to the pleadings of Slovakia concerning the question of the moment when the BIT became binding:

> The Treaty was concluded on October 15, 1990 and entered into force in the relations of Austria and Czechoslovakia on October 1, 1991. The Slovak Republic emerged as a successor sovereign State on January 1, 1993. The applicability of the Treaty by way of State succession was confirmed by an exchange of diplomatic notes on 4 August and 25 November 1994, entering into force on January 1, 1995.[640]

6.23 It is in this context that the tribunal made a number of very interesting remarks. First, it noted that the 'exchange of diplomatic notes in the framework of the process of State succession' (which took place in 1995 between Austria and Slovakia) 'can be considered as equivalent to a ratification by the successor State'.[641] Most importantly, it stated that:

> [O]nce Slovakia became an independent successor State, *it could not be bound by the BIT*, notwithstanding the fact that its predecessor State had signed and ratified the BIT, *until it had taken the steps necessary to succeed to the BIT*. Only once it had taken those steps could it be regarded as having concluded the BIT.[642]

6.24 The tribunal then referred to the position that Austria took in the proceedings on this question:

> This conclusion is confirmed by information given by Austria in its submission, which explains that, as regards the BIT an Exchange of Diplomatic Notes took place in 1994, and the BIT entered into force between Austria and the Slovak Republic in 1995, after the entry into force of the VCLT:[643]
>
> 'The Agreement between the Republic of Austria and the Czech and Slovak Federative Republic on the Promotion and Protection of Investments was signed on 15 October 1990 and entered into force on 1 October 1991 (…). Following the dissolution of the Czech and Slovak Federative Republic, Austria and the newly independent Slovakia jointly identified the BIT, among other treaties, to be in force and applicable between them by means of an Exchange of Diplomatic Notes (See Federal Law Gazette No. 1046/1994). Moreover, the Exchange of Diplomatic Notes also amended the BIT, so as to insert the designations "Slovak Republic" and "Slovak" into the text of the Agreement as appropriate.'[644]

6.25 The tribunal then made this important closing comment:

---

640 Ibid., [77].
641 Ibid., [79].
642 Ibid., [79] (emphasis added).
643 Ibid., [80].
644 Ibid.

> In other words, the BIT would not have become applicable between Austria and the Respondent had it not been for the Exchange of Notes. The Tribunal therefore concludes that the BIT cannot be considered to have been concluded by the Respondent until, at the earliest, the date of the Exchange of Notes in 1994.[645]

These passages are important insofar as they include a clear endorsement of the *tabula rasa* principle in the context of bilateral treaties. Thus, the tribunal unambiguously indicated that there is no automatic succession to the treaties to which the predecessor State was a party before the date of succession. Both the successor State and the other State party must take 'steps necessary to succeed to the BIT'.[646] **6.26**

In conclusion, this overview of awards rendered by tribunals in the context of the dissolution of Czechoslovakia illustrates that tribunals have not, in general, attempted to identify the consent of the parties involved regarding the continuation of BITs. In fact, this is the case for 13 out of the 17 cases examined. Many of them have thus failed to explain how (and when) the new State had succeeded to the BIT entered into by Czechoslovakia. They have not examined how the other State party to the treaty reacted to a claim of continuity by the new State. In my view, the reason so many tribunals have failed to conduct such an enquiry is simply because the respondent States did not challenge their jurisdiction on this point. For that reason, the tribunals did not deem it necessary to address the issue of State succession.[647] **6.27**

3. THE BREAK-UP OF THE USSR

As explained above,[648] the break-up of the USSR should be considered as a series of 'secessions' by the former Soviet Republics (except for the three Baltic States) with Russia being the continuing State. As the continuing State of the **6.28**

---

645 Ibid., [81].

646 Ibid., [79].

647 See, Tams (n 27) 331:

> And while brief statements like this one may indeed not do full justice to the intricacies of the law of State succession, the tribunals' telegraphic 'reasoning' no doubt gives effect to the intention of the treaty parties. In the various proceedings against the Czech Republic, it simply (as noted by another tribunal) was 'not in dispute that the Respondent succeeded to the rights and obligations under the BIT as originally entered into by the Czech and Slovak Federal Republic

(referring to: *ECE Projektmanagement & Kommanditgesellschaft PANTA Achtundsechzigste Grundstücksgesellschaft mbH & Co. v. Czech Republic*, UNCITRAL, PCA Case No. 2010–5, Award, 19 September 2013, [3.139]).

648 See, Chapter 3, Section 2.4.

USSR,[649] Russia naturally remained bound by the treaties to which the USSR had been a party.[650] This is in accordance with Article 35 of the Vienna Convention, which is considered to be reflecting a rule of custom.[651] It should be added that Russia (and other continuator States in other contexts) has nevertheless considered it necessary to confirm its continuation of treaties to other States, essentially for legal certainty purposes, since such notifications were unnecessary.[652] As examined above, the question of succession to treaties only arises in the context of the other former Soviet Republics (with the exception of the Baltic States).

6.29 The present author has found five cases involving the Russian Federation where a foreign investor based its claim under one of the 14 BITs to which the USSR was a party before 1992.[653] All awards have considered that Russia (as the continuing State) remains bound by the treaties that had been previously entered into by the USSR.[654]

6.30 The case of *Mr. Franz Sedelmayer v. Russian Federation* involved a German investor submitting a request for arbitration based on the 1991 Germany-USSR BIT.[655] The tribunal concluded that this treaty was binding on Russia based on the following grounds:

> The Treaty was signed by representatives of the Federal Republic of Germany and the Soviet Union. In a note issued in the fall of 1992 to the heads of diplomatic missions in Moscow, the Ministry of Foreign Affairs of the Russian Federation stated that the Russian Federation would continue to exercise the rights and honour the obligations

---

649 See: *Application of the International Convention on the Elimination of all Forms of Racial Discrimination (Georgia v. Russian Federation)*, Provisional Measures, Order of 15 October 2008, ICJ Reports 2008, 353, [105], where the Court noted that the Russian Federation is 'the State continuing the legal personality of the Union of Soviet Socialist Republics'.

650 Multilateral Treaties Deposited with the Secretary-General, available at: https://treaties.un.org/pages/HistoricalInfo.aspx?#%22Russian%20Federation%22:

> By a communication dated 24 December 1991, the President of the Russian Federation notified the Secretary-General that membership of the Union of Soviet Socialist Republics (USSR) in the United Nations is being continued by the Russian Federation. The Government of the Russian Federation subsequently informed the Secretary-General that as at 24 December 1991, the Russian Federation maintains full responsibility for all the rights and obligations of the USSR under the Charter of the United Nations and multilateral treaties deposited with the Secretary-General […].

651 See, Milulka, 'Article 35' (n 439) 1223–4; Zimmermann, 'La Convention de Vienne' (n 4) 1559.

652 See, ILA, Resolution no. 3/2008 (n 52) 273; Milulka, 'Article 35' (n 439) 1227–8.

653 One case was pending at the time of writing: *Sergei Viktorovich Pugachev v. Russian Federation*, UNCITRAL (filed under the France-USSR BIT).

654 It should be added that in another case the tribunal remained completely silent on the continuation issue: *Renta 4 S.V.S.A, Ahorro Corporación Emergentes F.I., Ahorro Corporación Eurofondo F.I., Rovime Inversiones SICAV S.A., Quasar de Valors SICAV SA, Orgor de Valores SICAV SA, GBI 9000 SICAV SA v. Russian Federation*, SCC No. 24/2007, Award on Preliminary Objections, 20 March 2009, [4].

655 *Mr. Franz Sedelmayer v. Russian Federation*, SCC, Award, 7 July 1998.

arising from international treaties signed by the Soviet Union. Thus, the Treaty is binding for the Russian Federation.[656]

The same finding was made by the tribunal in the case of *RosInvestCo UK Ltd. v. Russian Federation*, involving allegations of breach of the 1991 United Kingdom-USSR BIT.[657] In its award on jurisdiction the tribunal mentioned the claimant's position on matters of succession: 6.31

> It is common ground that the IPPA came into force on 3rd July 1991, pursuant to an exchange of notes between the United Kingdom and the USSR. It is also common ground that the Respondent was at all material times and remains a state party to the IPPA as the USSR's successor under international law, as confirmed by the letter dated 13th January 1992 from the Respondent's Ministry of Foreign Affairs to (inter alios) the United Kingdom's Ambassador in Moscow, and the joint declaration dated 30th January 1992 issued by the United Kingdom and the Respondent.[658]

Since the respondent did not refute this statement (even though Russia is described as the USSR's 'successor'), the tribunal did not specifically examine Russia's status: it just mentioned, in passing, that Russia was the 'legal continuation' of the USSR[659] and the fact that both parties regarded the BIT as binding between them.[660] 6.32

The issue of continuity also arose in the case of *Vladimir Berschader and Moïse Berschander v. Russian Federation* involving a claim initiated by Belgian nationals under the Belgium/Luxembourg-USSR.[661] Russia did not contest being bound by the BIT. Russia rejected, however, the investor's use of the MFN clause contained in the BIT to claim the benefit of more recent (post-Soviet) BITs entered into by the Russian Federation. The arbitration clause in the BIT limited the tribunal's jurisdiction to disputes concerning the amount (or mode) of compensation to be paid, and did not cover the other question of whether or not an act of expropriation had actually occurred in the first place.[662] The claimant wanted to use the MFN clause in the BIT to take advantage of more favourable arbitration clauses found in BITs signed by 6.33

656 Ibid., 17.

657 *RosInvestCo UK Ltd. v. Russian Federation*, SCC Case No. V079/2005, Award on Jurisdiction, 1 October 2007.

658 Ibid., [31] quoting from claimant's First Memorial on Jurisdictional Issues. See also, Award, 12 Sept. 2010, [1]: 'Respondent the Russian Federation is under international law the successor or "continuator" of the USSR.'

659 Ibid., [37].

660 Ibid., [42].

661 *Vladimir Berschader and Moïse Berschander v. Russian Federation*, SCC Case No. 080/2004, Award, 21 April 2006.

662 Ibid., [151ff].

Russia in the late 1990s, which cover disputes concerning the occurrence of an act of expropriation. One of the arguments put forward by Russia to reject this claim was that 'reference to "the territory of the Soviet Union" in the Protocol [to the Belgium/Luxembourg-USSR BIT] means that the MFN clause may only be applied in relation to BITs signed by the Soviet Union and not BITs signed by the Russian Federation'.[663] The tribunal rejected Russia's argument by simply mentioning that 'the official position consistently adopted by the Respondent in international affairs is that the Russian Federation is the legal successor to the Soviet Union'.[664] The tribunal did not further discuss Russia's status. While one can disagree with the use of the term 'legal successor' rather than the more appropriate expression 'continuing' State, it seems that these expressions were used interchangeably by the tribunal.

6.34 Finally, the present author has found two (currently pending) arbitration cases involving a former Soviet Republic as the respondent in circumstances involving allegations of breach of a BIT entered into by the USSR before its break-up. World Wide Minerals, a Canadian investor, filed a claim against Kazakhstan invoking a breach of the 1991 Canada-USSR BIT. The question at the heart of this case is whether or not Kazakhstan is bound by this BIT.[665] In its award of 19 October 2015, the tribunal held that the Canada-USSR BIT was binding on Kazakhstan.[666] The award is confidential.[667] Another claim was also recently submitted by a Canadian investor also claiming that Kazakhstan breached the Canada-USSR BIT.[668]

4. THE DISSOLUTION OF YUGOSLAVIA

6.35 This section first examines the *Mytilineos* case (Section 4.1.). I will then briefly refer to six other cases (Section 4.2).

---

663 Ibid., [161], see also at [66].

664 Ibid., [161].

665 *WWM v. Kazakhstan* (n 53). See, the story reported in: Iareporter, 'After failure of claim under Kazakh statute, Canadian miner hopes that USSR-Canada investment treaty permits arbitration with Kazakhstan', 18 December 2013, available at: http://www.iareporter.com/articles/20131218.

666 Ibid. See, the story reported in: Iareporter, 'In a Dramatic Holding, UNCITRAL Tribunal Finds That Kazakhstan is Bound by Terms of Former USSR BIT With Canada', 28 January 2016, available at: https://www-iareporter-com.proxy.bib.uottawa.ca/articles/in-a-dramatic-holding-uncitral-tribunal-finds-that-kazakhstan-is-bound-by-terms-of-former-ussr-bit-with-canada/.

667 Disclaimer: the present author acted as counsel for the respondent in this case.

668 *Gold Pool LP v. Republic of Kazakhstan*, UNCITRAL. The story is reported at IAReporter, 'Uncitral Tribunal Is Finalized To Hear Second Investor Claim Against Kazakhstan Under Long-Dormant USSR-Canada Investment Treaty', 7 August 2016, available at: https://www-iareporter-com.proxy.bib.uottawa.ca/jarticles/uncitral-tribunal-is-finalized-to-hear-second-investor-claim-against-kazakhstan-under-long-dormant-ussr-canada-investment-treaty/.

4.1 *Mytilineos v. The State Union of Serbia & Montenegro and Republic of Serbia*

The case of *Mytilineos Holdins SA v. The State Union of Serbia & Montenegro and Republic of Serbia* involved a Greek claimant starting arbitration proceedings in 2004 under the 1997 Greece-FRY BIT.[669] This case is interesting for two reasons. First, the claimant commenced proceedings against *two* respondents: The 'State Union of Serbia & Montenegro' and the 'Republic of Serbia'. Secondly, at the time when the award was rendered by the tribunal in 2006, Montenegro had seceded from Serbia-Montenegro. 6.36

During the proceedings, Serbia-Montenegro objected to the fact that 'Serbia' was listed as a second respondent by the claimant.[670] It should be recalled that at the time (2004) the 'State Union of Serbia and Montenegro' (as the name suggests) was a 'union of States' between two entities, Serbia and Montenegro, which was established in 2002. Serbia-Montenegro argued that the 'consent to arbitration contained in [the 1997 BIT] does not cover Serbia' and that it 'only binds the Federal Republic of Yugoslavia (Serbia and Montenegro)' and that, therefore, 'Serbia cannot be a party to the arbitration'.[671] The claimant explained that the 'Republic of Serbia' was added as a second respondent because Montenegro had become a new independent State during the proceedings. 6.37

In accordance with the Constitution, a referendum on independence was held in Montenegro on 21 May 2006. On 3 June 2006, the National Assembly of Montenegro made a formal declaration of independence.[672] The independence of the new State was soon recognized by several members of the international community. Serbia recognized the new State on 15 June 2006 and Montenegro was admitted to the United Nations on 28 June 2006.[673] Thus, in its post-hearing brief (dated 7 June 2006), the claimant noted that the 'Republic of Serbia' was 'due to become legal successor to First Respondent [Serbia-Montenegro] with full international legal personality following the public referendum under Article 60 of the Constitutional Charter of First Respondent that had then recently taken place'.[674] 6.38

669 *Mytilineos Holdings SA v. State Union of Serbia and Montenegro and Republic of Serbia*, UNCITRAL, Partial Award on Jurisdiction, 8 September 2006 [7].

670 Ibid., [170].

671 Ibid.

672 Decision on Proclamation of Independence of the Republic of Montenegro, Art. 1, declaring that Montenegro is 'an independent state with a full international legal personality'.

673 UN SC Res. 1691 (2006); GA Res. A/60/264 (2006).

674 *Mytilineos Holdings* (n 669) [85].

6.39 In its award rendered in September 2006, the tribunal noted that since the claim had been filed, 'Montenegro, a constituent unit of the State Union of Serbia and Montenegro, declared its independence.'[675] The tribunal added that this event was, however, not problematic in the present case: 'While the tribunal has not been requested to rule on any ensuing State succession issues, it takes note that it appears uncontroversial that the Republic of Serbia will continue the legal identity of the State Union of Serbia and Montenegro on the international level.'[676] The accession of Montenegro to independence is indeed a case of secession. Thus, Article 60(1) of Serbia-Montenegro's Constitution mentioned the right for each entity to 'secede from' the Union and paragraph 4 of the same provision expressly envisioned the 'secession of the state of Montenegro from the State Union of Serbia and Montenegro'.[677] Finally, Article 60(5) indicates that the member pursuing secession should be considered as a new State under international law, while the other member State would be continuing the international legal personality of Serbia-Montenegro. The position adopted by Serbia[678] as well as the analysis of the ICJ[679] also supports the fact that Montenegro is a case of secession.

6.40 Since there was no doubt that the Republic of Serbia was the continuing State to the 'State Union of Serbia and Montenegro'[680] at the time when the award was rendered in September 2006, the tribunal rightly concluded that it had become unnecessary to add Serbia as a second respondent. In any event, the tribunal decided to examine its jurisdiction *ratione personae* over the two respondents based on the 'established principle that jurisdiction is to be determined in light of the situation as it exists on the date the judicial proceedings are instituted'.[681] The tribunal concluded that Serbia, as a constituent part of the FRY was clearly not a 'Contracting Party' to the 1997 BIT and, as a result, could not act as a respondent in the instant arbitration proceedings.[682] In its final award rendered in September 2009, the tribunal

---

675 Ibid., [158].

676 Ibid.

677 Constitution of the State Union of Serbia and Montenegro, Art. 60.

678 Decision on Obligations of Public Authorities of the Republic of Serbia in Assuming Powers of the Republic of Serbia as Successor State to the State Union of Serbia and Montenegro, 12 June 2006.

679 *Application of the Convention on the Prevention and Punishment of the Crime of Genocide (Bosnia and Herzegovina v. Serbia and Montenegro)*, Judgment, ICJ Reports 2007 43, [71ff]; *Genocide* case (*Croatia v. Serbia*), 2008 (n 237) 412 [33].

680 See, Constitution of the State Union of Serbia and Montenegro, Art. 60(5); Letter of 3 June 2006 of the President of the Republic of Serbia to the UN Secretary-General; Declaration of the National Assembly of Serbia, 5 June 2006.

681 *Mytilineos Holdings* (n 669) [159].

682 Ibid., [172]–[173], [175], [226].

dismissed all claims against the respondent.[683] Interestingly, the respondent at this later phase of the proceedings was the 'Republic of Serbia' (i.e., the *continuing* State of the 'State Union of Serbia and Montenegro').[684]

4.2 Other cases

The case of *MNSS BV and Recupero Credito Acciaio NV v. Montenegro* involved a claim instituted by a Dutch investor under the Netherlands-Yugoslavia BIT and the Foreign Investment Law of Montenegro.[685] The award does not discuss the issue of Montenegro's succession to the BIT. This lack of analysis by the tribunal is unfortunate given the fact that the continuation of the BIT to Montenegro had been agreed upon through an Exchange of Notes between the two States.[686] The case of *CEAC Holding Lmt. v. Montenegro* involved a claim by a Cyprus company under the Cyprus-Serbia-Montenegro BIT.[687] The award refers to the treaty as the 'Cyprus-Montenegro BIT'[688] without explaining Montenegro's succession to that instrument and without mentioning that both States had agreed upon its continuation in an Exchange of Notes.[689] In both cases, the tribunals' silence on this point may be explained by the fact that this question was not contested by the parties during the proceedings. A parallel case was started in 2016 by the Russian owner of *CEAC* against Montenegro, but under the BIT entered into between Russia **6.41**

683 The award is not publicly available, but the story is reported in: Iareporter, 'In final UNCITRAL award, door left open for Greek company to bring another BIT claim against Serbia', 26 April 2013, available at: http://www.iareporter.com/articles/20130426_1.

684 Ibid. On this aspect of the reasoning of the tribunal, see the critical analysis of Pereira Fleury (n 39) 463. Mytilineos Holdings filed a new claim in 2013 against the 'Republic of Serbia' invoking violation of the same 1997 BIT. See, story in: Iareporter, 'Serbia disputes: Mytilineos files a new BIT claim in long-running fight, while solar park investor adds treaty claim to threat of contract arbitration', 10 December 2013, available at: http://www.iareporter.com/articles/20131210_4.

685 *MNSS BV and Recupero Credito Acciaio NV v. Montenegro*, ICSID Case No. ARB(AF)/12/8, Award, 4 May 2016.

686 Exchange of Notes between the Kingdom of the Netherlands and the Republic of Montenegro regarding the continuation of bilateral treaties (15 November 2006 and 18 January 2007), in: 51 Tractatenblad Van Het Koninkrij Der Nederlanden (2007), no. I, at 8.

687 *CEAC Holding Lmt. v. Montenegro*, ICSID Case No. ARB/14/8, Award, 26 July 2016. Another case was filed by CEAC *against* Montenegro under the UNCITRAL Arbitration Rules. It appears that the claim was filed under a contract. The tribunal dismissed all claims. See, story reported in Iareporter: http://www.iareporter.com/articles/ceac-sees-another-setback-this-time-in-uncitral-arbitration-in-its-fight-with-montenegro/.

688 Ibid., 16.

689 Exchange of Notes between the Government of the Republic of Cyprus and the Government of the Republic of Montenegro on the application of the Agreement between the Republic of Cyprus and Serbia and Montenegro on the Reciprocal Promotion and Protection of Investments, 21 July 2005, 3 and 15 October 2008, entered into force on 5 November 2008, COG S.VII 4036, Nov. 30, 2005, at 573.

and the FRY in 1995.[690] One question at the heart of this case will be that of Montenegro's continuation of a BIT which was signed by the predecessor State (the FRY).

6.42 Another noteworthy case is *Adria Beteiligungs GmbH v. Croatia* involving an investor from Austria which apparently filed a claim under both the Austria-Yugoslavia BIT (1989) and the 1997 BIT between Austria and Croatia.[691] The award is unpublished and very limited information was found about the case.

6.43 Finally, it should be added that a German investor has recently filed a claim against Kosovo under the 1989 Germany-Yugoslavia BIT.[692] One of the central arguments of this case will be whether Kosovo is a successor State to BITs entered into by Yugoslavia. The answer to the question is rather simple considering that there was an exchange of notes between Germany and Kosovo for the continuation of this BIT.[693] A claim was also recently filed by Mera Investment Fund Ltd, a Cyprus-based company, against Serbia under the 2005 Cyprus-Serbia/Montenegro BIT.[694] The succession issue in this case is not likely to be controversial given the fact that Serbia is the continuing State of the entity which signed the BIT.

5. THE CESSION OF HONG KONG AND MACAO TO CHINA

5.1 Overview of State practice

6.44 The legal framework for the 'hand over' of Hong Kong (1997) and Macao (1999) to China are found in the China-UK and China-Portugal Joint Declarations as well as the Hong Kong and Macao Basic Laws. These

690 *Mr. Oleg Vladimirovich Deripaska (Russian Federation) v. Montenegro*, PCA Case 2017–07. See the story reported in Iareporter: http://www.iareporter.com/articles/bit-claim-by-russian-oligarch-appears-to-be-latest-move-in-dispute-that-has-already-spawned-several-other-arbitrations-against-montenegro/.

691 *Adria Beteiligungs GmbH v. Croatia*, UNCITRAL, Award, 21 June 2010.

692 *ACP Axos Capital GmbH v. Kosovo*, ICSID Case No. ARB/15/22. The issue is examined in: Young (n 553).

693 Decree for Ratification of the Agreements, Exchange of Notes, Republic of Kosovo-Federal Republic of Germany, Sept. 2, 2011, available at: http://www.mfa-ks.net/repository/docs/Marr._Ks-Gjermani_(shkembimi_i_notave)_DMN-18_(anglisht).pdf. See also: *Federal Gazette* (Bundesgesetzblatt) 2011, vol. II, 748.

694 *Mera Investment Fund Ltd v. Serbia*, ICSID Case No. ARB/17/2. The story has been reported at IAReporter: https://www-iareporter-com.proxy.bib.uottawa.ca/articles/icsid-roundup-new-investor-state-arbitrations-registered-against-latvia-greece-and-serbia/.

documents established the 'one country, two systems principle'. For instance, the China-UK Joint Declaration for Hong Kong (signed in 1984) provides as follows:

> The Hong Kong Special Administrative Region may on its own, using the name 'Hong Kong, China', maintain and develop relations and conclude and implement agreements with states, regions and relevant international organisations in the appropriate fields, including the economic, trade, financial and monetary, shipping, communications, touristic, cultural and sporting fields.[695]

6.45 The same provision is also mentioned in the Hong Kong Basic Law along with the majority of provisions of the China-UK Joint Declaration.[696] The question of the application of treaties entered into force by China to Hong Kong is specifically dealt with in the Joint Declaration, and subsequently in the Hong Kong Basic Law;[697]

> The application to the Hong Kong Special Administrative Region of international agreements to which the People's Republic of China is or becomes a party shall be decided by the Central People's Government, in accordance with the circumstances and needs of the Hong Kong Special Administrative Region, and after seeking the views of the Hong Kong Special Administrative Region Government.[698]

6.46 The modalities of the handover of Macao have been regulated in the 1987 devolution treaty between China and Portugal (the Joint Declaration).[699] Specifically, the document explains how China's treaties can extend to Macao:

> subject to the principle that foreign affairs are the responsibility of [China's government], [Macao] may on its own ... maintain and develop relations and conclude and implement agreements with states, regions and relevant international or regional organizations in the appropriate fields ... The application to [Macao] of international agreements to which [China] is or becomes a party shall be decided by [China's

695 Joint Declaration of the Government of the United Kingdom of Great Britain and Northern Ireland and the Government of the People's Republic of China on the Question of Hong Kong with Annexes, China-UK, 19 December 1984, 26 UKTS (1985), Annex 1, Art. XI.

696 The Basic Law of the Hong Kong Special Administrative Region of the People's Republic of China, Art. 151, adopted at the Third Session of the Seventh National People's Congress on Apr. 4, 1990, promulgated by Order No. 26 of the President of the People's Republic of China on 4 April 1990, and effective as of 1 July 1997.

697 As noted by Repousis, 'On Territoriality and International Investment Law' (n 310) 152, this provision 'dictate that China's IIAs are not applicable to Hong Kong unless a relevant territorial extension has taken place' adding that 'the practice of the Sino-British Joint Liaison Group, set up by the 1984 Joint Declaration, could likewise support this interpretation'.

698 Joint Declaration regarding Hong Kong (n 695).

699 Joint Declaration of the Government of the People's Republic of China and The Government of the Republic of Portugal on the Question of Macao, China-Port., 13 April 1987, 1498 UNTS 229 Annex 1, Art. VIII.

> government], in accordance with the circumstances of each case and needs of [Macao] and after seeking the views of the [Macao government].[700]

6.47 The wording of the joint declaration suggests that the application of China's treaties to Macao is *not* automatic[701] insofar as it requires a decision from the Chinese Government 'after seeking the views' of the Macao Government. Whether or not this is indeed the interpretation which should be given to the joint declaration is a matter of great controversy. The question was the heart of the *Sanum* saga, which will be discussed in the next section.

5.2 Critical analysis of the *Sanum v. Laos* case

5.2.1 Introduction

6.48 The *Sanum* case is of great importance for many reasons. First, it is the first arbitration case to deal with the issue of the territorial scope of application of Chinese BITs regarding the Chinese Special Administrative Region (SAR) of Macao after its handover to China.[702] The findings of the tribunal and two Singapore courts are likely to have an important impact on the closely-related question of whether Chinese BITs apply to the territory of Hong Kong. This is due to the fact that the devolution agreements signed by China and the predecessor States provide the same type of regime for both cases. Secondly, the award and the two judgments are the first publicly available awards/decisions which provide a comprehensive analysis regarding questions of State succession in the specific context of investment arbitration. Thus, to this day, these decisions are the only ones that have thoroughly examined a number of issues that are at the heart of this book (it should be noted that the *WWM v. Kazakhstan* award is still confidential[703]). In the words of Binder, the *Sanum* case 'reads like a textbook example of the difficulties arising from the application of the general international law of State succession to a particular situation'.[704] Indeed, this is true as further illustrated by the reasoning of these judicial bodies examined in the next sections.

6.49 The case involved Sanum Investments Limited, a company incorporated in Macao. The claimant relied on the 1993 China-Laos BIT arguing that its investments in the gambling and hospitality sectors in Laos (through a joint

---

700 Section VIII of the Annex of the Joint Declaration. Art. 138 of the Basic Law of the Macau Special Administrative Region of the People's Republic of China, adopted 31 March 1993, Arts 136, 138 (effective Dec. 22, 1999) contains the same language.

701 Repousis, 'On Territoriality and International Investment Law' (n 310) 153.

702 Binder (n 310) 290.

703 *WWM v. Kazakhstan* (n 53).

704 Binder (n 310) 290.

venture with a Laotian company) were negatively affected by measures adopted by Laos and constituted a violation of the treaty.[705]

A UNCITRAL Arbitral Tribunal issued its Award on Jurisdiction on 13 December 2013 and found that it had jurisdiction over the dispute.[706] Thus, based on the moving treaty frontiers (MTF) principle,[707] the tribunal held that the BIT applied to Macao after its handover from Portugal to China in 1999. The Award was later set aside by a judgment of the High Court of Singapore on 20 January 2015.[708] Sanum brought an appeal against the judge's decision. In a judgment rendered in 2016, the Court of Appeal held that the BIT applied to Macao and thus the tribunal had jurisdiction over the claim brought by Sanum.[709] **6.50**

The award and the two decisions have been examined by a number of writers recently.[710] The following sections will examine the State succession issues that have been dealt by the award (Section 5.2.2), the decision of the High Court of Singapore (Section 5.2.3) and that of the Court of Appeal (Section 5.2.4). **6.51**

5.2.2 The UNCITRAL award

The central question in the case was whether the China-Laos BIT extended to Macao after 1999. One important point to highlight from the outset is the fact that the BIT did not contain a definition of 'territory'. Before the tribunal began its analysis, it set out a number of preliminary observations. **6.52**

5.2.2.1 Preliminary observations

The tribunal mentioned at the beginning of its analysis that the rules of State succession applied to the present situation of Macao. Thus, the tribunal noted **6.53**

705 Separately, the parent company of Sanum Investments, incorporated in the Netherlands Antilles, instituted arbitral proceedings against Laos under the Laos-Netherlands BIT: *Lao Holdings NV v. Lao People's Democratic Republic*, ICSID Case No ARB(AF)/12/6.

706 *Sanum*, Award, 2013 (n 370).

707 See, Chapter 5, Section 1.1.1.

708 *Lao People's Republic v. Sanum Investments Ltd.*, Singapore High Court, Judgment, [2015] SGHC 15 [hereinafter '*Sanum*, Judgment, Singapore High Court, 2015'].

709 *Sanum*, Judgment, Singapore of Court of Appeal, 2016 (n 365).

710 See, inter alia: N. Hart and S. Srikumar, 'Investor-State Arbitration before the High Court of Singapore: Territoriality, Nationality and Arbitrability', (2015) 4 *Cambridge JICL* 191; G. Wang, *International Investment Law: A Chinese Perspective* (Routledge 2014) 568–70; M. Hwang and A. Chang, 'Case Comment: Government of the Lao People's Democratic Republic v. Sanum Investments Ltd: A Tale of Two Letters', (2015) 30 *ICSID Rev* 506; D Lim, 'Case Comment: Government of the Lao People's Democratic Republic v. Sanum Investments Ltd [2015] SGHC 15', Singapore Law Blog, at http://www.singaporelawblog.sg/blog/article/95; D Lim, 'The Virtue of Judicial Restraint: Two Comments on Laos v. Sanum', (2015) 10(2) *Global Arbitration Rep*; Tams (n 27) 339ff; Binder (n 310) 280–94.

that the case of Macao was indeed one of succession despite China's 'contention that no transfer of sovereignty took place in December 1999, since it merely "resumed" its exercise of sovereignty over Macao, as it did over Hong Kong'. The question which the tribunal considered as the most crucial was whether the BIT should be considered to fall within the general MTF rule set out in both Articles 15 VCST and 29 VCLT or, on the contrary, it fell within the exceptions mentioned in these two provisions. The tribunal provided the following framework of analysis:

> Does the PRC/Laos BIT enter into the general rule or the exceptions to Article 15 and Article 29? If the general rule applies, the BIT will be applicable to the Macao SAR; if one of the exceptions applies, the BIT will not be applicable to the Macao SAR. The general rule—i.e., the extension of the treaty to the whole territory, at the moment of a transfer of sovereignty or at any time—applies if none of the exceptions are satisfied.[711]

6.54 Before examining Articles 15 VCST and 29 VCLT, the tribunal acknowledged 'the difficulty it faced in ascertaining the application or non-application of the PRC/Laos BIT to the Macao SAR due to the paucity of factual elements presented by the Parties', adding that 'there were no affidavits from the PRC, Laos or the Macao SAR, which could probably have been obtained from the respective authorities'.[712] In fact, the tribunal stated that 'being left with no actual information on the status of the PRC/Laos BIT [it] must analyze the situation by application of the relevant rules'.[713] This question of the 'paucity of factual elements' would later become significant in the proceedings before the Singapore courts when Laos put forward an exchange of letters between Laos and China (which took place *after* the Award was rendered) on the application of the BIT to Macao. In any event, because of the 'paucity of factual elements' which prevailed at the time the arbitration proceedings took place, the tribunal decided to 'verif[y] first whether any of the exceptions [contained in Articles 15 VCST and 29 VCLT] apply'.[714]

5.2.2.2 Analysis of the exceptions under Article 15 VCST

6.55 The tribunal examined the exceptions mentioned at Article 15 VCST (those examined in previous sections[715]). It held that extending the protection of the BIT to Macao would not be incompatible with its object and purpose, which

711 *Sanum*, Award, 2013 (n 370) [238].
712 Ibid., [232].
713 Ibid., [236].
714 Ibid., [238].
715 See, Chapter 5, Section 1.1.3.

is protecting investors and developing economic cooperation.[716] Such an extension would also not fundamentally change the conditions of application of the BIT.[717] The tribunal then made an interesting observation, as already mentioned above, that, as a matter of principle, a fundamental change in the conditions of application of a treaty could exist in the context of a treaty between two States with planned economies or to a State with a capitalist economy.[718] But, the tribunal considered that this was not the case at hand. Thus, the BITs entered into force by China were not different from those concluded by Macao directly with other States.[719]

The tribunal then examined the other possible exception under Article 15 VCST, namely whether the extension of the BIT to Macao was prevented since the Joint Declaration and the Basic Law of Macao established otherwise.[720] As mentioned above, these documents provide that the extension of treaties to Macao is subject to previous consultations between the Chinese and Macao Governments.[721] At the outset, the tribunal mentioned that: **6.56**

> this argument merits consideration as it could appear at first sight that [China] and Portugal have provided for a specific way to deal with the extension of international agreements of [China] to the Macao SAR, and have therefore superseded the automatic extension provided for as the general rule in Article 15 of the VCST.[722]

Ultimately, the tribunal rejected the argument on two grounds. First, the tribunal relied on the well-established treaty law rule whereby the internal law of a State (the Basic Law of Macao) could not 'be considered as legally capable of modifying the international rule set out in Article 15 VCST'.[723] Secondly, the tribunal held that the joint declaration should be considered a devolution treaty between Portugal and China in which they decided on the modalities of the process of succession.[724] A devolution treaty (as already examined above[725]) is not binding on a third State (Laos) without its consent.[726] In fact, according to the tribunal:

716 *Sanum*, Award, 2013 (n 370) [239]–[242]. For a critical analysis on this point, see: Q. Zhang, 'Are the PRC BITs Applicable to China's Special Administrative Regions? In Consideration of the Sanum v. Laos Case' (2016) 2(1) *China and WTO Review* 105–34.

717 *Sanum*, ibid., [248].

718 Ibid.

719 Ibid., [252].

720 Ibid., [253ff].

721 Ibid.

722 Ibid., [256].

723 Ibid., [257].

724 Ibid., [258ff].

725 See, Chapter 4, Section 2.1.2.

726 The tribunal also noted that the treaty could only be considered as binding on Laos if it was applying customary principles of international law.

> Laos, having not been informed that its treaty with the PRC [the China-Laos BIT] would only be extended after a procedure of consultation – which in fact never seems to have been enforced – cannot claim that such an agreement between the PRC and Laos could set aside the international rule applicable to a bilateral treaty between itself and the PRC.[727]

6.57 The tribunal concluded that the joint declaration and the Basic Law of Macao did not fall within the exceptions contained at Article 15 VCST and, consequently, did not set aside the applicable rules of general international law.[728] As a result, the tribunal applied the MTF rule and held that the China-Laos BIT should be 'deemed to have been extended' to Macao.[729]

5.2.2.3 Analysis of the exceptions under Article 29 VCLT

6.58 The tribunal then examined the concrete application of Article 29 VCLT to the present case. It noted that the BIT 'does not contain an express provision stating that *it applies to the Macao SAR*'.[730] For the tribunal, such an express statement 'is not necessary as the principle of territorial extension of the State's legal order embodied in Article 29 applies, unless otherwise indicated'.[731] The tribunal also noted that the BIT did '*not expressly exclude its application to the Macao SAR*', contrary, for instance, to the Protocol accompanying the China-Russia BIT.[732] Yet, the tribunal added that:

> this element should, however, not be overestimated as it might simply be explained by the fact that the PRC/Laos BIT was signed in 1993, and that at that time it would not have made sense to exclude the Macao SAR which was not then a part of the Chinese territory under PRC sovereignty.[733]

The tribunal mentioned, nonetheless, that 'at the moment of the conclusion of the PRC/Laos BIT, it was already common knowledge that in a few years' time, Macao would be under the PRC's sovereignty'.[734] Ultimately, the tribunal concluded on this point that 'no definite conclusion can be drawn either from the silence of the Treaty on its extension to the Macao SAR, or its silence on the non-extension of the Treaty to the Macao SAR'.[735]

727 *Sanum*, Award, 2013 (n 370) [268].
728 Ibid.
729 Ibid., [269].
730 Ibid., [270] (emphasis in the original).
731 Ibid.
732 Ibid., [271] (emphasis in the original).
733 Ibid., [274].
734 Ibid., [276].
735 Ibid., [277].

The tribunal then examined the 'meaning of the existence of two sets of BITs for Laos' and asked the question 'whether the possibility of co-existence' of a China-Laos BIT and a Macao-Laos BIT 'otherwise establishes' that the former cannot apply to Macao.[736] For the tribunal, the fact that China authorized Macao to enter into a BIT with Laos does not 'otherwise establish' its intention for the China-Laos BIT not to extend to Macao.[737] Moreover, for the tribunal 'the superposition of instruments of protection does not bring about chaos, but rather better protection to foreign investors'.[738] **6.59**

The tribunal therefore concluded that the BIT was applicable to Macao[739] and that it had jurisdiction over the dispute (but only for the expropriation claim of the claimant).[740] **6.60**

5.2.3 Judgment of the Singapore High Court

In January 2014, Laos started set aside proceedings before the Singapore High Court.[741] The court set aside the award of the tribunal and found that the BIT was *not* applicable to Macao.[742] The following section will focus only on the succession issues examined by the court.[743] **6.61**

5.2.3.1 The judgment's silence regarding the question of the investor's nationality

The judgment only focused on the question of the territorial application of the BIT to Macao. It did not address any other question regarding the nationality of the investor and whether Sanum was covered under the BIT. This aspect of the judgment has been criticized by writers.[744] The High Court described **6.62**

---

736 Ibid., [278].

737 Ibid., [292].

738 Ibid. See also: [295]: 'In the Tribunal's view, the existence of two treaties facilitates rather than hinders the fulfillment of the goals of the BITs, which are the protection of the foreign investors and the economic development of the host State.'

739 Ibid., [300].

740 The tribunal came to this conclusion based on the claimant being a protected investor and its claims an 'investment' under the BIT (see ibid., [301ff]).

741 *Sanum*, Judgment, Singapore High Court, 2015 (n 708).

742 It should be noted that both the High Court and the Court of Appeal of Singapore referred in their judgments to the territory of 'Macau' instead of 'Macao'. The latter term will be used in this section.

743 One preliminary question addressed by the court was whether the interpretation of a treaty concluded between two foreign States was justiciable before a Singaporean court. Another one was whether the standard of review for jurisdictional challenges under the IAA was lower for investor-State arbitration than for private arbitration agreements. For a discussion on these questions, see: Hart and Srikumar (n 710) 198–9; Hwang and Chang (n 710) 508–10, 514–16.

744 Hart and Srikumar, ibid., 195: 'The High Court's exclusive focus on the territorial application of the China-Laos BIT, as opposed to the nationality of the Macanese investor, is somewhat puzzling.'

Sanum Investments as 'a company incorporated in Macao'[745] without examining the issue as to whether this meant that the company qualified as a 'Chinese' investor under the BIT. The court's silence on the issue can probably be explained by the fact that in its award the tribunal concluded that an entity incorporated in Macao did satisfy the definition of an investor protected under the China-Laos BIT.[746] In any event, as noted by two writers, 'the assumption implicit in the High Court's approach in *Sanum Investments* is that an investor's entitlement to invoke a BIT's protection rests on both its nationality *and* whether the BIT extends to the territory in which it is incorporated'.[747] The 'assumption' adopted by the court on this point is, in my view, correct.[748]

6.63 On the contrary, in the case of *Tza Yap Shum v. Peru*, the tribunal only examined the question of whether a Chinese national making an investment in Peru could qualify as an investor. The claimant was a natural person born in China and a resident in Hong Kong. As noted by one writer, 'the nationality test for natural persons, unlike that for legal entities, is somewhat detached from the notion of territory'.[749] He noted[750] that the definition of natural persons found in the China-Peru BIT[751] 'does not contain the territorial element found in the definition of legal entities'.[752] The *Tza Yap Shum* Tribunal stated that it was *not necessary* to determine whether the scope of the China-Peru BIT applied to the territory of Hong Kong.[753] In my view, such a determination is in fact crucial.[754] It is simply illogical to assume that the same BIT could apply to Chinese nationals (living in Hong Kong) investing in Peru, but not to those Peruvian investors investing in Hong Kong. Yet, the lack of reasoning of the tribunal on this point may be explained by the fact that it was 'concerned with the nationality test of natural persons, which (…) does

745 *Sanum*, Judgment, Singapore High Court, 2015 (n 708) [2].

746 *Sanum*, Award, 2013 (n 370) [301]–[315].

747 Hart and Srikumar (n 710) 196 (emphasis in the original).

748 Ibid., 197.

749 Repousis, 'On Territoriality and International Investment Law' (n 310) 157–8.

750 Ibid.

751 The definition of a legal entity reads as follows: 'natural persons who have the nationality of the People's Republic of China in accordance with its laws'.

752 The definition reads as follows: 'economic entities established in accordance with the laws of the People's Republic of China and domiciled in the *territory* of the People's Republic of China'.

753 *Tza Yap Shum v. Peru*, ICSID Case No. ARB/07/6, Decision on Jurisdiction and Competence, 19 June 2009 [68].

754 The award has been examined by the following writers: Wei Shen, 'Conceptuality or Textuality? Understanding the Notion of Expropriation in the Context of Tza Yap Shum v. The Republic of Peru', (2014) 7 *J East Asia & Int'l L* 379–407; An Chen, 'Queries to the Recent ICSID Decision on Jurisdiction upon the Case of Tza Yap Shum v. Republic of Peru: Should China-Peru BIT 1994 Be Applied to Hong Kong SAR under the "One Country Two Systems",' (2009) 10 *J World Inv & Trade* 829–64; Hailang Wang, 'The (In)applicability of Sino-Foreign BITs to Hong Kong and Macao', (2011) 8 *Manchester J Int'l Econ L* 81–101; Wei Shen, 'The Good, the Bad or the Ugly? A Critique of the Decision on Jurisdiction and Competence in Tza Yap Shum v. The Republic of Peru' (2011) 9 *Chinese JIL* 55.

not include a territorial link similar to the one necessary in determining the nationality of legal entities'.[755]

5.2.3.2 The exceptions under Articles 29 VCLT and 15 VCST and the exchange of letters between Laos and China

6.64 The judge came to the conclusion that the BIT was *not* applicable to Macao by applying the exceptions mentioned at Articles 29 VCLT and 15 VCST.[756] He explained that the 'effect' of these exceptions was 'that a treaty is binding on the entire territory of each contracting State unless it (a) appears from the treaty; or (b) is otherwise established that the contracting States had intended otherwise'.[757] As noted by one writer, in doing so the judge may not have fully appreciated some of the textual differences between these two provisions.[758]

6.65 With respect to the first exception (i.e., that a contrary intention appears from the treaty), the judge affirmed that 'no definite conclusion' could be drawn since the BIT 'does not state positively that the treaty applies to Macao; nor does it exclude Macao from its scope of application'.[759] The judge then turned to analysing the second exception (i.e., whether it has been 'otherwise established' that the BIT does not apply to Macao). He examined a number of documents, including an exchange of letters between the Laotian Ministry of Foreign Affairs and the Chinese Embassy in Laos.[760] The first letter (dated 7 January 2014) stated Laos' view that the BIT was not to extend to Macao and sought the views of China's Government on the matter:

> (…) The Ministry of Foreign Affairs has the further honor to inform the Embassy that the Laos Government is of the view that the Agreement does not extend to [Macao] for the reasons based on the People's Republic of China's policy of one *country*, two systems, its constitutional and legal framework, the Basic Law of [Macao] as well as the fact that the Agreement itself is silent on its extension to [Macao], which returned to the sovereignty of the People's Republic of China in 1999, six years after the signing of the Agreement. It would be highly appreciated if the Embassy would communicate this request to the agencies concerned of the People's Republic of China and could provide a response in due course. (…).[761]

---

755 Repousis, 'On Territoriality and International Investment Law' (n 310) 158.

756 *Sanum*, Judgment, Singapore High Court, 2015 (n 708) [57ff].

757 Ibid., [61].

758 Repousis, 'On Territoriality and International Investment Law' (n 310) 164: 'Indeed, [Article 15 VCST] provides for a departure from the default rule of continuity if it appears from the treaty or is otherwise established that this would be incompatible with the object and purpose of the treaty or would radically change the conditions for the treaty's operation.'

759 *Sanum*, Judgment, Singapore High Court, 2015 (n 708) 63.

760 Ibid., [15]. See: Hwang and Chang (n 710) 516–17.

761 Ibid., [39].

6.66 The reply from China (letter dated 9 January 2014) concurred with the position adopted by Laos:

> (…) In accordance with the "Basic Law of [Macao]", the Government of [Macao] may, with the authorisation of the Central People's Government conclude and implement investment agreements on its own with foreign states and regions; in principle the bilateral investment agreements concluded by the Central People's Government are not applicable to [Macao], unless the opinion of the Special Administrative Region Government has been sought, and separate arrangements have been made after consultation with the contracting party.
>
> In view of the foregoing, [the PRC-Laos BIT] concluded in Vientiane on 31 January 1993 is not applicable to [Macao] unless both China and Laos make separate arrangements in the future (…).[762]

6.67 In sum, the letters expressly provided for the non-application of the BIT to Macao.[763] Importantly, the exchange of letters took place *after* the tribunal's award was rendered. The central controversial question of the admissibility of these letters into evidence is further discussed in the following section.

5.2.3.3 The admission of the letters as evidence, the critical date and the issue of retroactivity

6.68 One fundamental question discussed in the judgment was whether the letters could be admitted into evidence.[764] For the judge, this was ultimately a question to be decided under Singapore law.[765] He considered that the letters represented a subsequent agreement under Article 31(3)(a) VCLT between China and Laos to the effect that the BIT did not apply to Macao.[766] Yet, as noted by one writer, the judge 'did so without adequately explaining whether they constituted a subsequent amendment or interpretation'.[767] It has been argued that the letters should be considered as a subsequent treaty amendment.[768]

---

762 Ibid., [40].

763 Ibid., [67ff].

764 Ibid., [38]–[56].

765 The investor objected to the admission of these letters in the proceedings alleging that they did not fulfill the criteria of a test established in the English case of *Ladd v. Marshall* which had been subsequently adopted by Singaporean courts concerning the admissibility of fresh evidence in a case in which a judgment has already been delivered. The Court found that the letters satisfied that test.

766 *Sanum*, Judgment, Singapore High Court, 2015 (n 708) [78].

767 Repousis, 'On Territoriality and International Investment Law' (n 310) 141. See his analysis at 141ff.

768 Binder (n 310) 293 ('Rather than being a technique of treaty *interpretation* (Art. 31(3)(a) VCLT), the exchange of letters may be considered as a subsequent treaty *amendment* since it lacks any legal foundation in the treaty text'); Repousis, 'On Territoriality and International Investment Law' (n 310) 182.

The judge rejected the argument that the letters were irrelevant as a matter of international law because they were admitted after the date on which the arbitral proceedings commenced (i.e., the 'critical date'). For him, this would be contrary to Article 31(3)(a) VCLT, which expressly allows for subsequent agreements between the contracting States to be taken into account with regard to the interpretation of the treaty or the application of its provisions. Writers have criticized the judge's position on the question of the 'critical date'.[769] **6.69**

In another controversial statement, the judge also affirmed that the letters 'did not amount to a retroactive agreement that altered the positions and expectations of third parties such as the defendant'.[770] In fact, the letters were 'rather an affirmation of the common understanding between the States that the treaty from its inception did not apply to Macao'.[771] Scholars have been critical of the reasoning of the judge on this question of retroactivity.[772] The judge's conclusion regarding the two letters was that they 'strongly support the plaintiff's claim that the PRC-Laos BIT did not apply to Macao'.[773] **6.70**

5.2.3.4 Other evidence confirming that the BIT did not apply to Macao

The court also considered other elements which confirmed that the BIT did not apply to Macao.[774] The most important amongst them was the joint **6.71**

769 Hwang and Chang (n 710) 518–19:

> [I]t is an accepted principle of international adjudication that, in the absence of treaty provisions to the contrary, the relevant date for purposes of jurisdiction is the date of *the institution of proceedings*, with all measures and events taking place after that date being irrelevant to the question of jurisdiction. A tribunal's jurisdiction is therefore vested at the point that consent is perfected, even if the contracting States have amended or terminated the investment treaty retroactively. Further, in treaty interpretation, the general rule as a matter of international judicial practice is that the principle of contemporaneity applies, i.e., treaty terms are to be interpreted according to the meaning that they possessed, or which would have been attributed to them, and in the light of current linguistic usage, *at the time when the treaty was originally concluded*. (…) The Judge did not consider whether the Two Letters, in view of the principle of contemporaneity and the relevant date for determining jurisdiction, would have taken effect as a 'subsequent agreement' only from the date on which it was made, making them irrelevant for the purposes of determining whether the Tribunal had jurisdiction (emphasis in the original).

770 *Sanum*, Judgment, Singapore High Court, 2015 (n 708) [77].

771 Ibid.

772 Repousis, 'On Territoriality and International Investment Law' (n 310) 166. For him, 'if the [letters] is a subsequent modification rather than a subsequent interpretation, it will not have a retroactive effect, as there were no stipulations to the contrary' (182). In any event, 'even accepting that the Exchange of Letters was a subsequent interpretation, thus having *ipso facto* retroactive effect, it would not necessarily mean that this Exchange could affect pending and, as in the present case, concluded investor-state arbitrations' (ibid). He concludes on this point that 'a subsequent modification as well as interpretation should generally not affect pending cases or even cases that have already been concluded' (183).

773 *Sanum*, Judgment, Singapore High Court, 2015 (n 708) [78].

774 Ibid., [79ff]. The judge determined that the 2006 China-Russia BIT which specifically excludes Hong Kong and Macao from its application did 'not advance either party's case in any meaningful way' [82]. He also came to this conclusion regarding other BITs referred to by the parties. He was also 'unable to place any

declaration which conditions the application of China's agreements to a decision taken by the government after consultation with Macao.[775] The judge noted that there was 'no evidence before [him] to suggest that China had taken measures to extend the scope of the PRC-Laos BIT to Macao'. For him, 'all this pointed towards the conclusion that the PRC-Laos BIT does not extend to Macao'.[776] Yet, as noted by two writers, the judge never explained how and why the joint declaration between Portugal and China could be binding on Laos, a third State.[777] The court also relied upon the fact that the same general legal framework was implemented for the application of China's treaties to Hong Kong.[778]

6.72 Based on all the evidence mentioned in the previous paragraphs, the court concluded that 'the plaintiff ha[d] established, on a balance of probabilities, that the PRC-Laos BIT does not apply to Macao'.[779] The judge consequently set aside the award.[780] Importantly, the judge criticized the tribunal for having only applied the general MTF rule at Articles 15 VCST and 29 VCLT without having sufficiently considered the exceptions:

> The Tribunal reached the opposite conclusion by relying on the default application of the general rule found in Art 29 VCLT and Art 15 VCST that a treaty is binding on the entire territory of each contracting state. They found that a different intention had not been otherwise established by the evidence. In my view, there was sufficient evidence to rebut the general rule that the PRC-Laos BIT applies to Macao, even if one was restricted only to the evidence that was placed before the Tribunal. With the

---

weight' on a 1999 document entitled 'Multilateral Treaties deposited with the Secretary-General' making reference to the 1987 Joint Declaration and listing treaties applicable to Macao ([94–98]).

775 Ibid., [89]–[92].

776 Ibid., [92].

777 Hart and Srikumar (n 710) 197; see also: Repousis, 'On Territoriality and International Investment Law' (n 310) 153, 166, 185ff.

778 *Sanum*, Judgment, Singapore High Court, 2015 (n 708) [104]–[106]:

> I accept that nothing in the arrangements made by PRC and the UK concerning Hong Kong can be regarded as *conclusive* of the arrangements made by PRC and Portugal regarding Macao. However, the identical wording found in the two joint declarations and the approach taken by the Hong Kong Joint Liaison Group suggest that PRC is likely to have adopted the same approach towards Hong Kong and Macao. In other words, the approach and arrangements made with respect to Hong Kong was likely to have been used as a model for Macao. I would note in this regard that the Basic Law for both Hong Kong and Macao are similar in many aspects, and this also supports my view that the approach that was taken for Hong Kong was the same as that for Macao. Consequently, the PRC was likely to have been of the view that their treaties would not automatically apply to Macao after the 1997 handover and the Hong Kong experience is to that extent relevant to the determination of the central question in the present case (emphasis in the original).

Another piece of evidence mentioned by the judge ([107]–[109]) supporting the non-application of the BIT to Macao was the fact that a World Trade Organization Trade Policy Report affirmed that Macao had no other BITs apart from those mentioned in the Report.

779 Ibid., [110].

780 Ibid., [128]–[129].

introduction of the Two Letters and the 2001 report in the present proceedings, the conclusion that the PRC-Laos BIT does not apply to Macao becomes all the more clear and I decide accordingly.[781]

5.2.4 Judgment of the Singapore Court of Appeal

As mentioned above, after the arbitral award was rendered in December 2013, Laos commenced proceedings in January 2014 to set aside the award in front of the High Court. Some six months after Laos had commenced these proceedings, the case was settled along with a parallel claim under the Laos-Netherlands BIT filed by Lao Holdings, the parent company of Sanum.[782] Shortly after the settlement, Lao Holdings pursued a claim over the alleged breach of the settlement agreement. In June 2015, an ICSID Tribunal found that Laos had not breached the settlement agreement thus, rejecting the claim of Lao Holdings.[783] As noted by one writer, in practical terms 'this meant that the *Sanum* case remained the only avenue for the investor's ability to directly sue the Government of Laos'.[784] Soon after the High Court rendered its judgment, Sanum filed a petition for leave to appeal before the Singapore Court of Appeal.[785] The court rendered its judgment in 2016. **6.73**

5.2.4.1 Interaction between Articles 15 VCST and 29 VCLT and their exceptions

The main issue dealt by the court was whether the China-Laos BIT applied to Macao.[786] The court explained the content of both Articles 15 VCST and 29 VCLT as follows: **6.74**

> Simply put, because a treaty is binding in respect of the *entire* territory of a State, the MTF Rule presumptively provides for the automatic extension of a treaty to a new territory as and when it becomes a part of that State. The MTF Rule further provides that as a territory undergoes a change in sovereignty, it passes automatically *out* of the treaty regime of the predecessor sovereign *into* the treaty regime of the successor sovereign. At the same time, it is evident from the language of both Art 15 of the VCST and Art 29 of the VCLT that the MTF Rule is a presumptive rule that may be displaced by proof of certain specified matters. We return to this shortly, but what it means is that the PRC-Laos BIT will be presumed to automatically apply to the

781 Ibid., [111].

782 *Lao Holdings NV v. Lao People's Democratic Republic*, ICSID Case No. ARB(AF)/12/6, Settlement Agreement, 15 June 2014; *Sanum Investments Ltd. v. Lao People's Democratic Republic*, PCA Case No. 2013–13, Settlement Agreement, 15 June 2014.

783 *Lao Holdings NV v. Lao People's Democratic Republic*, ICSID Case No. ARB(AF)/12/6, Decision on the Merits, 10 June 2015.

784 Repousis, 'On Territoriality and International Investment Law' (n 310) 162.

785 *Sanum*, Judgment, Singapore of Court of Appeal, 2016 (n 365).

786 Prior to the hearing, Laos sought to admit into evidence two 'Note Verbale' of 2015. The first letter was from the Laos' Ministry of Foreign Affairs to China's Embassy in Vientiane, Laos, requesting confirmation that the 2014 letter received from China was authentic. China confirmed in a second letter. The court admitted the letters into evidence in the proceedings.

territory of Macao upon restoration of Chinese sovereignty with effect from 20 December 1999. On that date, the treaties of the predecessor sovereign, Portugal, will cease to apply in respect of Macao, while those of the PRC would apply instead unless the MTF Rule has been displaced. The experts who furnished opinions in this case are agreed that this is the approach to be taken when assessing the relevance and effect of the MTF Rule.[787]

6.75 The court then explained the scope of the exceptions contained in those provisions ('which overlap even though they are worded slightly differently'[788]) and how they would apply to the present case:

> [T]he PRC-Laos BIT will by operation of law apply to Macao unless one or more of the following exceptions can be shown:
>
> (a) It appears from the PRC-Laos BIT, or is *otherwise established*, that the application of the PRC-Laos BIT would be *incompatible with the object and purpose* of the BIT (see Art. 15(*b*) of the VCST).
>
> (b) It appears from the PRC-Laos BIT, or is *otherwise established*, that the application of the BIT to Macao would *radically change the conditions of its operation* (see Art. 15(*b*) of the VCST).
>
> (c) An intention appears from the PRC-Laos BIT, or is *otherwise established*, that the BIT does not apply in respect of the entire territory of the PRC (see Art. 29 of the VCLT).[789]

6.76 With respect to the first exception, the court stated that it could not apply to the present case since 'the purpose and object' of the BIT is 'to protect investments for the purpose of the development of economic cooperation between both States'.[790] The court could 'not see how an extension of the application of the BIT to Macao could be said to be incompatible with such a purpose' since, on the contrary, it 'would enlarge the scope of protection to capture a larger pool of investors and further economic cooperation between both States over a larger territory'.[791] The court also rejected the second exception on the ground that the extension of the BIT to Macao 'would have the effect of radically altering the conditions for the operation of the treaty'.[792] The third exception is examined in detail in the next section.

787 *Sanum*, Judgment, Singapore of Court of Appeal, 2016 (n 365) [49] (emphasis in the original).
788 Ibid., [50].
789 Ibid. (emphasis in the original).
790 Ibid., [51].
791 Ibid., [51].
792 Ibid., [52].

5.2.4.2 *Context, object and purpose of the BIT*

With respect to the third exception, the court first analysed 'whether an intention appears from the PRC-Laos BIT that it is not meant to apply to Macao'.[793] On that point, the court considered that it would be 'appropriate' to first 'consider the provisions of the PRC-Laos BIT and its context, objects and purposes *without recourse*' to the letters exchanged between Laos and China.[794] This is because the letters 'are not part of the BIT and if one is to ascertain the intention of the parties as it appears from the treaty, then it would not be correct *in this context* to also examine other evidence'.[795] For the court, there was 'nothing in the text, the objects and the purposes of the PRC-Laos BIT, or in the circumstances of its conclusion, that points to an intention to displace the MTF Rule such that it would lead to the conclusion that the BIT does not apply to Macao'.[796] The reasoning of the tribunal on this point is further explained in the next sections. **6.77**

5.2.4.2.1 *The meaning of the BIT's silence on its application to Macao and the analysis of other relevant factors*

The court first noted that the BIT was silent on its applicability to Macao: 'it contains neither an express provision stating that *it applies to Macao*, nor one *excluding* its application to Macao'.[797] Although it was 'perhaps unsurprising' that the BIT did not refer to Macao, considering the fact that it pre-dated the cession of territory in 1999, the court said that 'no definite conclusion can be drawn from the absence of any express provisions on this issue in the BIT'.[798] For the court, two 'factors present within the factual context of this case support the applicability of the PRC-Laos BIT to Macao'.[799] These factors will now be examined. **6.78**

With respect to the first factor, the court affirmed that the question of the extension of China's treaties to Macao 'cannot be said to have been an unforeseen event at the time the PRC-Laos BIT was concluded' in 1993.[800] In any event, a specific provision in the BIT dealing with the issue is *not* necessary under the MTF principle: **6.79**

> Although the PRC-Laos BIT does not contain an express provision stating that it *does apply* to Macao, this is not necessary, since the default position under the MTF Rule is

---

793 Ibid., [54].
794 Ibid. (emphasis in the original).
795 Ibid. (emphasis in the original).
796 Ibid., [55].
797 Ibid., [56] (emphasis in the original).
798 Ibid.
799 Ibid., [57].
800 Ibid.

that the PRC's treaties would *automatically* apply to Macao upon Macao's reversion to the PRC. In contrast, the fact that the PRC and Laos ('the Contracting States') did not exclude the applicability of the BIT to Macao despite the anticipated reversion of Macao seems to point, if anything, towards the applicability of the BIT to Macao.[801]

6.80 As highlighted by the court, when the BIT was concluded in 1993, the two States 'must be taken to have been aware that by virtue of the operation of the MTF Rule' the BIT 'would apply to Macao upon the handover unless the Contracting States did something to exclude its application'.[802] For the court, 'at the very least, the silence or inaction of the parties in this connection cannot displace the presumptive position that the PRC-Laos BIT would extend to Macao from 1999'.[803]

6.81 The court then referred to a second factor supporting the extension of the BIT to Macao: 'the structure and in particular the time period for implementation and review of the BIT was such that the Contracting States would have undertaken a review of the PRC-Laos BIT shortly *after the handover*'.[804] Thus, the BIT was initially drafted to apply for a ten-year period in which the parties could give notice to terminate it one year prior to its expiration. According to the court, any such termination 'would necessarily have entailed a review of the application of the BIT' whose timing would have 'coincided quite closely with the handover of Macao'.[805] The court noted that despite this, 'the parties chose not to include any specific provision expressly excluding the applicability of the treaty to Macao'.[806] For the court, 'it cannot be said that they (in particular [China]) were unaware of the significance of Macao falling under the sovereignty of China by this time' and, yet, 'the Contracting States did nothing to expressly displace the effects of the MTF Rule'.[807] The court concluded on this point that these considerations show that 'there is no force in the argument that an intention "appears" from the PRC-Laos BIT to exclude its application to Macao'.[808]

6.82 The court then turned to the other question (examined in the next section) of whether it had been 'otherwise established' that the BIT would not apply to Macao.

---

801 Ibid., [57] (emphasis in the original).
802 Ibid., [58].
803 Ibid.
804 Ibid., [59] (emphasis in the original).
805 Ibid.
806 Ibid.
807 Ibid.
808 Ibid., [60].

5.2.4.2.2 The nature and the effect of the joint declaration

The court examined the reasoning of the judge who had considered that the 1987 China-Portugal Joint Declaration 'reflected the intention' of China that the BIT 'would not apply to Macao unless some further steps were taken'.[809] Since no positive steps were taken, the Judge had concluded that the BIT did not extend to Macao. For the court, the 'real question' was whether China's position, as reflected in the joint declaration, 'could and in fact did displace the MTF Rule with respect to the PRC-Laos BIT'.[810] The court noted that the joint declaration is a treaty that is only binding on these two States and not on Laos. In fact, as a matter of principle, Laos could rely on the 'presumptive effect' of the MTF rule when contracting with China: **6.83**

> In our judgment, absent specific steps being taken by the PRC to displace such a rule in any given case, the terms of a specific declaration such as the Joint Declaration made in the context of discussions between two sovereigns in connection with the imminent handover of a territory by one to the other, cannot override it. In our judgment, the MTF Rule, being a rule of customary international law, would and did apply to and bind the PRC. As a result, treaties to which the PRC was party – in this context, the PRC-Laos BIT – would extend to Macao upon the PRC resuming sovereignty of that territory, unless steps had been taken to disapply the MTF Rule in relation to any such treaty.[811]

Thus, while noting that it 'is an accepted principle of international law that States may, by agreement, elect to derogate *inter se* from customary international law', the court added that a State cannot do so unilaterally.[812] Consequently, even if one were to consider that China 'had intimated a general intention in the 1987 PRC-Portugal Joint Declaration for its treaties not to extend by operation of the MTF Rule to Macao', for the court 'it remains necessary for the Lao Government to establish that this was an understanding it in fact shared with the PRC during the negotiation of the PRC-Laos BIT'.[813] The court stated that there was no evidence of the parties' intention for China's treaties not to apply to Macao which 'formed an agreed basis upon which the PRC-Laos BIT was concluded'.[814] In any event, for the court, the joint declaration was essentially a domestic law of China.[815] **6.84**

---

809 Ibid., [74].
810 Ibid., [75].
811 Ibid., [76].
812 Ibid., [77].
813 Ibid.
814 Ibid.
815 Ibid., [79]. The court noted that the joint declaration is 'primarily a statement of undertakings' given by China to Portugal 'as to how [it] would conduct certain *internal constitutional arrangements* in relation to Macao' (emphasis added). The court concluded on this point that the joint declaration 'could not constitute evidence that "otherwise establishes" that the PRC-Laos BIT is not intended to apply to Macao' [82].

6.85 For all of these reasons, the court concluded on this point that the joint declaration 'could not constitute evidence that "otherwise establishes" that the PRC-Laos BIT is not intended to apply to Macao'.[816]

5.2.4.3 The exchange of letters and the question of their admissibility after the critical date

6.86 Having concluded that there was 'insufficient evidence in the period leading up to the handover of Macao to find that it had been "otherwise established" that the MTF Rule would not apply in respect of the PRC-Laos BIT',[817] the court then examined the evidence which was presented *after* the 'critical date' (i.e., the date on which the arbitration proceedings were initiated in August 2012).[818] The court explained that the 'critical date doctrine' was acting as 'a time constraint in the context of determining the relevance or weight of evidence in cases concerning issues of public international law'.[819] The court affirmed that any evidence which surfaces after that date 'and is self-serving and intended by the party putting it forward to *improve* its position in the arbitration' is of 'little, if any, weight'.[820]

6.87 The court disagreed with Laos' position that the two letters simply 'confirmed' the pre-existing position. This is because, on the one hand, the pre-critical

---

816 Ibid., [82]. The court also reached the same conclusion [90] regarding the judge's reliance upon the experience of China and the UK in relation to Hong Kong as an analogy to the situation in Macao. After having examined the work of the Joint Liaison Group for Hong Kong and State practice regarding treaties, the court concluded that, in any event, 'the experience of the PRC in relation to its discussions with the UK over HK would only be relevant to the present discussion if there was sufficient evidence before the court to conclude that this was a true analogue for the situation with Macao' which it considered not to be the case.

817 Ibid., [91].

818 The court also examined the evidence which were presented between the handover of Macao and the 'Critical Date'. The court gave no weight to the 1999 UN document entitled 'Multilateral Treaties deposited with the Secretary-General' because it does not apply to bilateral treaties (ibid., [94]). The court also explained that the judge should not have placed any reliance on the 2001 WTO Report [98]. It concluded on this point that the evidence were not 'persuasive or sufficient to "otherwise establish" that contrary to the operation of the MTF Rule, the PRC-Laos BIT was not intended to apply to Macao' [99].

819 Ibid., [104].

820 Ibid. (emphasis added). The court explained that different situations can be envisaged regarding the application of the critical date doctrine:

> In our judgment, there is a spectrum of possible positions. At one end of that spectrum, it seems clear that post-critical date evidence should not be accorded any weight if it is adduced in order to contradict a position which has been *established* by the pre-critical date evidence. Since a party cannot rely on post-critical date doctrine to *improve* its position, such evidence would be rendered irrelevant. At the other end of the spectrum, if the post-critical date evidence merely confirms the position which has been established by the pre-critical date evidence, such evidence could be relevant and may be considered. The difficulty arises where the pre-critical date evidence is inconclusive. In our judgment, it is possible to admit post-critical date evidence in such a situation but we consider that special attention should then be given to the weight that should be attached to such evidence. Greater weight may be placed on such evidence, for example, if the content of such evidence demonstrates evidentiary continuity and consistency with pre-critical date evidence [108] (emphasis in the original).

date evidence 'does not establish that the MTF Rule had been displaced', and, on the other hand, in contrast, the letters 'advance the position that the PRC-Laos BIT does not extend to Macao and therefore that the MTF Rule has been displaced'.[821] In other words, the letters cannot 'confirm' something which has not been established before the critical date. For that reason, the court concluded that the letters 'should not bear any weight because they are post-Critical Date evidence adduced to *contradict* the pre-Critical Date position'.[822] Moreover, even if the letters were admissible, 'no material weight can be placed on them'.[823] Thus, the only justification in the letters to support China's view that the BIT is inapplicable to Macao is its own internal legislation in relation to Macao (namely the Basic Law). However, for the court, 'this is irrelevant and inadmissible as a consideration in international law given Art 27 of the VCLT, (…) which states that the internal laws of a State cannot be invoked to justify the non-performance of a treaty'.[824]

The court also rejected Laos' characterization of the letters as evidencing a 'subsequent agreement' or 'subsequent practice' (Art. 31(3)(a) and (b) of the VCLT). The court noted that any such subsequent agreement or practice cannot have a retroactive effect.[825] The court also rejected Laos' argument that the letters show what the parties' intention had always been. Thus, 'there is nothing by way of evidence, prior to the Critical Date, to demonstrate that there was ever any accord between the Contracting States for the PRC-Laos BIT not to apply to Macao'.[826] In fact, for the court the evidence 'suggests either that the parties were aware of the issue and did nothing that was effective, as a matter of international law, to exclude the operation of the MTF Rule in relation to the applicability of the PRC-Laos BIT to Macao, or they overlooked it'.[827] **6.88**

Finally, the court then made this statement: 'We recognize that this conclusion might appear counter-intuitive because the two States that are the parties to the treaty in question, namely the PRC and Laos, both take the position **6.89**

---

821 Ibid., [112].

822 Ibid. (emphasis in the original).

823 Ibid., [113].

824 Ibid., [114].

825 On this point, the court concluded (at [116]) that 'giving effect to the [letters] as a subsequent agreement in relation to the interpretation of the PRC-Laos BIT would amount to effecting a retroactive amendment of the BIT' which is not 'permissible'. The court also affirmed that even if both States were to enter into an express agreement today to modify the treaty and exclude Macao from its scope of application, this could *not* 'take retroactive effect and adversely affect a third party which has already brought proceedings'. The court then discussed and distinguished a number of arbitration cases where notes of interpretation were issued after the critical date (ibid., [117ff]).

826 Ibid., [116].

827 Ibid.

before us that the treaty does not extend to Macao.'[828] The court further detailed its position and observed that the MTF is a rule of customary international law, which can only be 'derogated from if the parties to such a treaty expressly agree or share an understanding that it will be excluded'.[829] Even if one were to consider that China 'had manifested an intention to exclude the MTF Rule in relation to Macao by way of the Joint Declaration in 1987', the court opined that 'there is nothing to suggest[s] that Laos had the same understanding in relation to the PRC-Laos BIT prior to the commencement of the arbitration'.[830] In any event, 'nothing' in the letters 'suggests that both the parties to the PRC-Laos BIT *shared* a common understanding to this effect either at the time the treaty was concluded or even at any subsequent time prior to the Critical Date'.[831] For the court, the 'conclusion that is expressed' in the letters about the non-extension of the BIT to Macao 'is based neither on any prior agreement or understanding nor even on an interpretation of the Treaty'.[832] The court concluded that the judge 'was wrong to place any evidentiary weight' on the letters.[833] It added that it was 'satisfied that there is insufficient evidence to prove that it has been otherwise established that the PRC-Laos BIT was not to apply to Macao'.[834]

6.90 The court therefore concluded that the BIT *did* apply to Macao and that the tribunal had jurisdiction over the claim brought by Sanum.[835]

5.2.5 Conclusion

6.91 The award and the two judgments have reached different conclusions as to whether or not the China-Laos BIT applies to the territory of Macao. They differed as to whether this situation fell within the MTF principle or whether it concerned the exceptions stated at Articles 15 VCST and 29 VCLT.[836] The complexity of this question of the articulations between the principle and the exceptions is compounded in the context of Macao by the existence of one very particular instrument, the 1987 Joint Declaration, which established a very unique situation, namely the 'one country two systems' principle under which Macao has a high degree of autonomy.[837] Moreover, the 1987 Joint Declaration expressly subjects the extension of China's BITs to a particular

828 Ibid.
829 Ibid., [116(a)].
830 Ibid., [116(b)].
831 Ibid., [116(c)] (emphasis in the original).
832 Ibid., [116(d)].
833 Ibid., [121].
834 Ibid., [121].
835 Ibid., [152].
836 Tams (n 27) 340.
837 Ibid., 339ff.

procedure, that is, a decision of the Chinese Government after seeking the views of the Macao Government.[838] The fact that no such decision was ever taken by China would suggest, at first, that the BIT simply does not cover the territory of Macao.[839] Yet, as rightly highlighted by Binder, the interplay between the general rule (the MTF principle) and the exceptions 'is not without ambiguities' in the specific context of Macao:

> The rule for situations of norm conflict, the *lex specialis* principle, would call for the application of the Joint Declaration rather than of Article 15 VCST as more special rule (as regards parties and scope). At the same time, the Joint Declaration, as a bilateral treaty between China and Portugal, does not create rights and obligations for third States such as Laos without their consent. (See Articles 34 and 35 VCLT; Article 8 VCST). No evidence is available on any involvement of Laos. In accordance with the *pacta tertiis nec nocent nec prosunt* rule, the Joint Declaration's applicability to the *Sanum* case is thus questionable.[840]

Ultimately, this is the reason why the tribunal declined to apply the joint declaration to the Laos-China BIT and concluded that the BIT extended to Macao. As noted by Binder, 'the tribunal's approach is more plausible from the perspective of the general law of treaties'.[841] Indeed, the tribunal was correct in concluding that the BIT applied to Macao based on that reason. The soundness of the approach adopted by the tribunal was confirmed by the detailed and convincing demonstration of the Singapore Court of Appeal. The Singapore Court of Appeal was also right in concluding that the exchange of letters between China and Laos, which occurred after the award was rendered, was inadmissible based on the critical-date doctrine and the principle of non-retroactivity. Binder has also identified another problem with the reasoning of the High Court on this point which concerns the special nature of investment treaties and the unique fact that they incorporate investors' substantive and procedural rights.[842] **6.92**

---

838 Binder (n 310) 292.

839 Ibid.

840 Ibid., 294.

841 Ibid., 293.

842 Ibid., 294:

> Would the exchange of letters have only altered the position of the concerned States, this still might have been fine. However, the letters deprive investors of their protection under the PRC-Laos BIT and thus change the position of right holders under the BIT (third-party beneficiaries at the least). This seems highly problematic in view of the nature of investors' rights and given the mechanism of perfected consent in investment treaty arbitration. It should not have had any relevance for the dispute at stake which arose prior to the exchange of letters. Questions of State succession may accordingly turn even more complex when applied to investment treaties.

6.93 In any event, as noted by Tams, the reliance placed by the High Court on the existence of these two letters 'limits the impact of the *Sanum* decision on future cases'.[843] This is true for three reasons.

6.94 First, it is difficult to see how these two letters could have any impact on other arbitration cases involving Chinese BITs.[844] Thus, the fact that Laos and China had concluded during the exchange of letters that the territorial scope of the Laos-China BIT does not apply to Macao is not indicative as to whether *other BITs* concluded by China with *other States* should extend to that territory.[845] Put differently, the view expressed by China and Laos on the territorial scope of this *specific* BIT is not relevant to determine *in general* whether *other BITs* concluded by China extend to Macao.

6.95 Second, in any event, the position adopted by China and Laos in these letters *after* the award was rendered is clearly opportunistic.[846] Accordingly, future tribunals having to deal with other BITs entered into by China will likely be reluctant to give any weight to the position taken by Laos and China in these letters.

6.96 Third, the general impact of the *Sanum* saga on future arbitration cases dealing with State succession issues is also ultimately limited by the very specific and unique characteristics of Macao. The reasoning of the tribunal in its award and of the two courts in their judgments will certainly have a long-lasting impact regarding the general discussion about the interaction between Article 15 VCSS and Article 29 VCLT. The same is true regarding the delimitation between the general MTF principle and the exceptions set out under these provisions. Apart from these important questions, it may be that the outcome of these decisions will be minimal for other 'more classical' situations involving issues of State succession in the context of cession of territories. This is because the reasoning of these judicial bodies is intrinsically linked to the very

---

843 Tams (n 27) 340.

844 Hart and Srikumar (n 710) 198: 'the letters exchanged in relation to the China-Laos BIT will have little salience for the interpretation of other BITs in future disputes'.

845 See, however, Repousis, 'On Territoriality and International Investment Law' (n 310) 167, for whom the exchange of letters 'is significant' and 'it still remains unclear whether it can be regarded as a position of general application for both Hong Kong and Macao'.

846 Hwang and Chang (n 710) 519, for whom the conclusion reached by the High Court was taken 'without considering whether a State, upon being sued, would admit to belatedly changing its mind about a treaty that created liability, or whether it would instead simply claim that it never intended the treaty to apply, in an attempt to invalidate an existing arbitral award on jurisdiction'. They added that: 'Although it may not have been prudent for the Judge to impugn the intentions of both the PRC and Laos, those considerations alone ought to have, at the very least, diminished the evidential value of the Two Letters.'

unique situation of Macao.[847] Thus, for Tams, 'the better view would be to accept that for the unusual cases of cessions such as Hong Kong and Macao (which purposefully avoid the full integration of the ceded territory), the MTF rule needs to be qualified'.[848] But, ultimately, as he notes, 'outside the particular arrangements obtaining in Macao and Hong Kong, cessions and incorporations raise few problems'.[849]

Binder (writing her article before the decision of the Court of Appeal was rendered in 2016) emphasized the fact that 'the diametrically opposed approaches of both decisions trigger legal insecurity'.[850] Any such legal uncertainty is, of course, considerably diminished as a result of the decision rendered by the Court of Appeal. Yet, the decision of the Court of Appeal only solves the question of the application of *one* BIT to Macao. The question of whether other BITs entered into by China apply to Macao (and Hong Kong) remains controversial.[851] According to one recent analysis, while many of the 130 BITs that China concluded in 2015 do not define the term 'territory', there 'exists a considerable number of Chinese BITs that define the notion of territory but do not explicitly refer to Hong Kong and Macao'.[852] In fact, the author indicates that there is only one Chinese BIT that makes an express reference to Hong Kong and Macao without explicitly carving out these territories from its application (the China-Mexico BIT) and only one BIT that explicitly carves out these two territories from its application (the China-Russia BIT).[853] He also notes that Hong Kong has entered into 17 BITs and Macao into two BITs with other States.[854] The silence of almost all Chinese BITs on their application to Hong Kong and Macao means that this question is likely to be the object of a great amount of controversy in future arbitration cases. 6.97

847 Tams (n 27) 340:

> Read properly, the decisions rendered in the *Sanum* litigation reflect different interpretations of the peculiar status of Macao under Chinese BITs entered into before Macao's return. These different interpretations might have implications for the status of Hong Kong (in relation to which similar questions might arise), but are unlikely to be of more general relevance.

848 Ibid.

849 Ibid.

850 Binder (n 310) 293. See also: Repousis, 'On Territoriality and International Investment Law' (n 310) 167: the two decisions makes 'it abundantly clear that the application of China's IIAs to Hong Kong and Macao is unsettled, even after the ruling of the SGHC'.

851 Tams (n 27) 340; Binder (n 310) 294. See also: Repousis, 'On Territoriality and International Investment Law' (n 310) 167: 'The reasoning of both the UNCITRAL Tribunal and the SGHC is inescapably trapped in the pervasive uncertainty over the territorial application of China's IIAs.' The general conclusion of the author (at 190) is that 'the application of China's IIAs to Hong Kong and Macao is an issue of great ambiguity and is therefore not susceptible of being expressed in terms of a fixed Procrustean rule'.

852 Repousis, 'On Territoriality and International Investment Law' (n 310) 123.

853 Ibid., 126–7.

854 Ibid., 136–9.

6.98 Future tribunals having to deal with this issue will certainly find guidance in the tribunal's award and the decision of the Court of Appeal regarding the scope of application of the 1987 Joint Declaration. The basic starting point of their analysis (in the very likely event that the BIT is silent on its application to Macao) should be the application of the MTF rule contained at Articles 15 VCSS and 29 VCLT. Under this principle, BITs entered into by China should apply to the territory of Macao. This should be the case unless it can be shown that *both* parties to the BIT intended otherwise. It may be argued that China has indeed manifested under the 1987 Joint Declaration its intention to exclude the MTF Rule in relation to Macao. Yet, other States (apart from Portugal) are simply not bound by such an 'intention'. Thus, the joint declaration is a devolution agreement between China and Portugal which does not create rights and obligations for third States without their consent. For the MTF rule to be excluded, it would have to be shown that the joint declaration was central to the negotiation between China and the other State party and that it formed part of their *common understanding* regarding the territorial application of the BIT to Macao. In other words, it would have to be demonstrated that the other State party signed the BIT based on the understanding that it would not apply to Macao. In the event that no such *common understanding* by the parties can be demonstrated, a tribunal would have to simply apply the MTF rule.[855] In this respect, the convincing reasoning of the award and the decision of the Court of Appeal will have some long-lasting consequences.

6. THE ANNEXATION OF CRIMEA BY RUSSIA

6.99 This section examines the legal issues arising from Russia's annexation of Crimea in the context of investment arbitration. It is first and foremost necessary to follow the sequence of events that led to the annexation of the territory and analyse the consequences that this had (Section 6.1). This analysis will be followed by an overview of relevant international law issues arising from the annexation of Crimea, including the absence of a right to self-determination and secession, the illegal use of force by Russia, and the

855 Tams (n 27) 340:

> Given the recent focus on the *Sanum* litigation with its contradictory outcomes, it is worth underlining that there is a large measure of agreement on the applicable regime, and on the presumptive relevance of the moving frontiers principle in particular. (…) In fact, in their approach to the status of Macao, the UNCITRAL arbitral tribunal and the Singapore High Court may not have been that far apart. Proceeding from the rule set out in Article 15 of the 1978 Vienna Convention, they both agreed that treaties presumptively applied to the entirety of a State's territory (and thus 'moved' with the treaty party's frontiers), but that this presumption could be rebutted.

obligation for other States not to recognize the annexation or to give any effect to Crimea's change of status (Section 6.2). One question dealt with in this section is whether the provisions of the Vienna Convention apply to cases of illegal annexation. The main focus of this section is the analysis of a number of legal issues arising from the annexation in the field of international investment law (Section 6.3). Two issues will be examined separately: the effect of the annexation on State contracts (Section 6.3.1) and its impact on investment treaties (Section 6.3.2). The most controversial issue is whether the BITs to which Ukraine was a party prior to the events should continue to apply to the territory of Crimea after the annexation or whether Russia's BITs should now find application. Another question examined below is the fate of the Ukraine-Russia BIT after the events. Finally, I will analyse a number of arbitration claims filed by Ukrainian investors against Russia under the Ukraine-Russia BIT, which arose due to the aftermath of the annexation.

6.1 The sequence of events

In 1783, Crimea was annexed by the Russian Empire. Following the Russian Revolution of 1917, Crimea became an autonomous republic within the Russian Soviet Federative Socialist Republic in the USSR (and was later given the status of an 'Oblast'). Crimea is populated by a Russian-speaking majority.[856] In 1954, the territory of Crimea was transferred to the Ukrainian Soviet Socialist Republic. When Ukraine became an independent State in 1991, Crimea was part of its territory. Ukraine's territorial integrity, including the territory of Crimea, was recognized by Russia after its independence.[857] **6.100**

The February 2014 revolution, which ousted Ukrainian President Viktor Yanukovych, sparked a political crisis in Crimea. By the end of the month, elements of Russian troops (although this point is contested by Russia) had seized official buildings and were occupying part of the territory.[858] In any event, it is indisputable that after the referendum Russian troops openly took **6.101**

856 See, Natalia Cwicinskaja, 'The Legality and Certain Legal Consequences of the "Accession" of Crimea to the Russian Federation' (2014) 34 *Polish YIL* 72, referring to the latest Ukrainian census in 2001 showing that Russians accounted for close to 60 per cent of the population in Crimea. Other groups include Ukrainians (25 per cent), Crimean Tatars (12 per cent), etc.

857 Under the Budapest Memorandum, signed on 5 December 1994, the US, the UK and Russia committed to 'respect the Independence and Sovereignty and the existing borders of Ukraine' and reaffirmed 'their obligation to refrain from the threat or use of force against the territorial integrity or political independence of Ukraine and that none of their weapons will ever be used against Ukraine except in self-defense or otherwise in accordance with the Charter of the United Nations' ([1]–[2]). The 1997 Treaty on Friendship, Cooperation, and Partnership (signed on 31 May 1997) between Ukraine and Russia also affirmed the inviolability of the borders between both States (Art. 3).

858 For a detailed analysis: Veronika Bílková, 'The Use of Force by the Russian Federation in Crimea', (2015) 745 *ZaöRV* 27.

control of Crimea, seized Ukrainian military equipment, and forced Ukrainian troops to surrender.[859]

6.102 On 6 March, the local legislative organ of Crimea, the Supreme Council, adopted a decree on the *All Crimean Referendum* presenting two options to the population, including the 'reunification' of Crimea with the Russian Federation.[860] In the meantime, a 'Declaration of independence of the Republic of Crimea' was adopted on 11 March 2014. The Ukrainian Ministry of Foreign Affairs issued a statement the same day stating that the declaration was 'unconstitutional, illegal and having no legal effect'[861] which was followed by an order by the Acting President of Ukraine to the same effect.

6.103 The referendum took place on 16 March. The overwhelming majority of participating voters (96.77 per cent) voted in favour of the 'reunification' with Russia. Many commentators have raised serious doubt about the legitimacy of the referendum and the accuracy of the result given the fact that it took place in a context of an armed emergency with Russian troops on the ground.[862] There is little doubt that the referendum and the declaration of independence were illegal acts under Ukrainian law which upholds the principle of territorial integrity and the inviolability of borders.[863] The referendum was deemed unconstitutional by the Constitutional Court of Ukraine.[864] The same position was adopted, inter alia, by the Venice Commission of the Council of Europe as well as by the Chairman of the OSCE,[865] the G-7,[866] and in a joint

---

859 C. Marxsen, 'The Crimea Crisis – An International Law Perspective' (2014) 74 ZaöRV 389.

860 The questions asked was as follows: '1. Are you in favour of the Autonomous Republic of Crimea reuniting with Russia as a constituent part of the Russian Federation?' *or* '2. Are you in favor of restoring the Constitution of the Republic of Crimea of 1992 and of Crimea's status as part of Ukraine?'.

861 Statement of the Ministry of Foreign Affairs of Ukraine, 11 March 2014.

862 Thomas D. Grant, 'Annexation of Crimea' (2015) 109(1) AJIL 85; Marxsen (n 859) 381; Cwicinskaja (n 856) 74–5; Thomas D. Grant, 'International Dispute Settlement in Response to an Unlawful Seizure of Territory: Three Mechanisms', (2015) 16(1) *Chicago JIL* 6; Thomas W. White, 'Referendum in Crimea: Developing International Law on "Territorial Realignment" Referendums' (2016) 38(3) *Houston JIL* 843–86; Anne Peters, 'Sense and Nonsense of Territorial Referendums in Ukraine, and Why the 16 March Referendum in Crimea Does Not Justify Crimea's Alteration of Territorial Status under International Law', 16 April 2014, EJIL Talk!, http://www.ejiltalk.org/sense-and-nonsense-of-territorial-referendums-in-ukraine-and-why-the-16-march-referendum-in-crimea-does-not-justify-crimeas-alteration-of-territorial-status-under-international-law/.

863 Grant, 'Annexation of Crimea' (n 862) 69–70; Marxsen (n 859) 380; Cwicinskaja (n 856) 66ff.

864 The Decision of Constitutional Court of Ukraine in relation to the case arising from the constitutional petition of the Acting President of Ukraine, Chairman of the Verkhovna Rada of Ukraine and the Ukrainian Parliament Commissioner for Human Rights on compliance with the Constitution of Ukraine (constitutionality) of the Resolution of the Supreme Council of the Autonomous Republic of Crimea 'On holding the Crimean referendum' (the case of local referendum in the Autonomous Republic of Crimea), Official Journal of Ukraine, 2014, No. 26, item 766.

865 See, Grant, 'Annexation of Crimea' (n 862) 69.

866 Statement of G-7 Leaders on Ukraine, 12 March 2014, available at: www.whitehouse.gov/the-press-office/2014/03/12/statement-g-7-leaders-ukraine.

statement issued by the President of the European Commission and the President of the European Council.[867] It should be added (as further examined below) that the UN General Assembly Resolution 68/262 also held that the referendum was invalid.[868]

On 17 March, the Supreme Council of Crimea declared the formal independence of the Republic of Crimea.[869] It should be noted that the actual wording of the resolution is quite illogical. While correctly stating that the referendum 'showed that the people of the Crimea want[ed] to join Russia, and consequently, separate from Ukraine', it also added that the people wanted to 'create an independent State' and decided 'to proclaim Crimea an independent sovereign State'. Yet, voters were not asked any question on independence per se, but only on 'reunification'.[870] In any event, the very same day, the Parliament of Crimea submitted a formal request to the Russian government for Crimea to be integrated into Russia.[871] **6.104**

The declaration of independence *in itself* was not illegal under international law.[872] The ICJ in the *Kosovo* opinion case stated that while there is no *right* to unilateral secession under international law, the practice of States 'does not point to the emergence in international law of a new rule prohibiting the making of a declaration of independence in such cases'.[873] The ICJ also mentioned that certain declarations have been considered to be illegal, but added that the: **6.105**

> illegality attached to the declarations of independence thus stemmed not from the unilateral character of these declarations as such, but from the fact that they were, or would have been, connected with the unlawful use of force or other egregious violations of norms of general international law, in particular those of a peremptory character (*ius cogens*).[874]

It has been rightly noted by one writer that since 'the referendum process was backed up by Russian troops in Crimea and relied on the use of force' by

867 Joint statement on Crimea by the President of the European Council, Herman Van Rompuy, and the President of the European Commission, José Manuel Barroso, 16 March 2014, available at: <http://ec.europa.eu/commission_2010–2014/president/news/archives/2014/03/20140317_1_en.htm>.

868 GA Resolution 68/262.

869 Resolution State Council Republic of Crimea no. 1745–6/14, 17 March 2014.

870 Cwicinskaja (n 856) 69.

871 *The Guardian*, 'Crimea applies to be part of Russian Federation after vote to leave Ukraine', 17 March 2014.

872 Théodore Christakis, 'Les conflits de sécession en Crimée et dans l'est de l'Ukraine et le droit International', (2014) JDI 7.

873 *Accordance with International Law of the Unilateral Declaration of Independence in Respect of Kosovo*, Advisory Opinion, ICJ Reports 2010 403 [79].

874 Ibid., 437.

Russia, the declaration of independence 'cannot be regarded in isolation of that illegality' and should therefore be considered as illegal under international law.[875]

6.106 On 17 March, Russia officially recognized the Republic of Crimea 'as a sovereign and independent State' by an executive order signed by the President.[876] The same day, President Putin also notified the Russian parliament[877] of the proposal made by Crimea to become part of Russia. Notably, such recognition took place merely *one day* after the referendum, which is rather premature given the circumstances on the ground at the time. On 18 March, Russia's President and Crimean authorities signed an 'Agreement' on the accession of Crimea to Russia.[878] The annexation was formalized under Russian law in the days following.[879]

6.107 In sum, the sequence of events can be summarized as follows:

- after a referendum, Crimea declared its independence and seceded from Ukraine;
- the day after, Russia recognized the Republic of Crimea as a 'sovereign and independent State' by decree;

875 Marxsen (n 859) 384. See also: Cwicinskaja (n 856) 74.

876 Order of the President of the Russian Federation of 17 March 2014, No. 147 'On recognition of the Republic of Crimea', The Collection of Legislation of the Russian Federation, 24 March 2014, No. 12, item 1259: 'Given the declaration of will by the Crimean people in a nationwide referendum held on March 16, 2014, the Russian Federation is to recognize the Republic of Crimea as a sovereign and independent state, whose city of Sevastopol has a special status.'

877 Specifically, the Federation Council of the Federal Assembly and the State Duma of the Federal Assembly.

878 The Agreement between the Russian Federation and the Republic of Crimea on the Accession of Republic of Crimea to the Russian Federation and on Forming New Federal Constituent Entities within the Russian Federation, signed in Moscow on 18 March 2014, The Collection of Legislation of the Russian Federation, 7 April 2014, No. 14, item 1570. Russia's Constitutional Court confirmed on 19 March the 'compliance' of the treaty between two 'subjects' of international law with the Constitution. The question remains whether Crimea was indeed an 'independent State' merely two days after the referendum and whether it had the legal capacity to enter into a treaty with another sovereign State. On this question, see: Grant, 'Annexation of Crimea' (n 862) 71; Marxsen (n 859) 390.

879 The State Duma and the Federation Council ratified the Agreement on 20 and 21 March, respectively, and a federal constitutional law was adopted on 21 March 2014: The Federal Constitutional Law of 21 March 2014, No. 6-FCL 'On the Accession to the Russian Federation the Republic of Crimea and Establishing within the Russian Federation new constituent entities of the Republic of Crimea and the City of Federal Importance Sevastopol', The Collection of Legislation of the Russian Federation, 24 March 2014, No. 12, item 1201. The law was then signed by President Putin: The Federal Law of 21 March 2014 No. 36-FL 'On Ratifying the Agreement between the Russian Federation and the Republic of Crimea on the Accession of the Republic of Crimea in the Russian Federation and on Forming New Constituent Entities within the Russian Federation', The Collection of Legislation of the Russian Federation, 24 March 2014, No. 12, item 1202. On this question, see: Cwicinskaja (n 856) 68ff, 69 (noting that 'It thus appears that during the Crimean accession process the sequence of events and the events themselves were artificially created in an attempt to ensure their compliance with the Russian legislation').

- one day later, the Republic of Crimea and Russia signed a Treaty on Accession of Crimea to the Russian Federation;
- three days later, the annexation of Crimea was formalized by a Russian law.

6.2 Overview of relevant international law issues arising from the annexation of Crimea

6.2.1 The importance of the legal qualification of the Crimean crisis as a type of succession

As mentioned above, the sequence of events seems to suggest that what took place in Crimea is a case of 'secession', whereby a new State was established. This seems to be the position adopted by some writers.[880] If it were to be the case, as rightly noted by one writer, 'les habitants de la Crimée resteront dans les annales comme ayant procédé à la sécession effective la plus rapide de l'histoire moderne'.[881] Not only would that secession be the *quickest* in history, but it would also be the *shortest*. This is because 'secession' was very rapidly followed by the integration of one 'State' (Crimea) into an already existing State (Russia). Yet, the fact that all these events took place *within only a couple of days* clearly suggests that this is not a case of secession where the newly independent State subsequently freely 'decided' to be integrated into another existing State. If one looks at the events with a rather limited measure of 'distance' (in fact, merely *one week* would suffice in that case …), the most realistic view is to consider the Crimean crisis as a 'transfer of territory'. Thus, part of the Ukraine territory was 'transferred' (without its consent) to Russia. **6.108**

Yet, as further explained below, the Crimean crisis *cannot* be considered as a 'normal' case of 'transfer of territory'. This is because the transfer was carried out contrary to basic principles of international law. The applicable rules for 'transfer of territory' under the Vienna Convention only come into play when a succession is in accordance with international law. As explained in greater detail below, the Crimean crisis is a case of illegal annexation of territory. This feature has important consequences regarding the fate of BITs to which both **6.109**

---

880 For instance, this seems to be the position adopted by Odysseas G. Repousis, 'Why Russian Investment Treaties Could Apply to Crimea and What Would This Mean For the Ongoing Russo–Ukrainian Territorial Conflict', (2016) *Arb Int* 7: 'However, a closer look at the factual background of the Crimean crisis reveals that Crimea's 'annexation' can also be treated as a case of secession and subsequent accession of an independent state rather than a succession in respect of territory.'

881 Christakis, 'Les conflits de sécession en Crimée' (n 872) 2.

Ukraine and Russia were parties with other States before the annexation as well as concerning the Ukraine-Russia BIT (a question further examined below[882]).

6.2.2 The absence of a right to self-determination

6.110 For many scholars, Crimea did not have the right to self-determination nor the right to declare independence because it was not in a colonial situation and had never been considered as a 'non self-governing territory' (under Chapter XI of the UN Charter).[883] Thus, outside the colonial context and situations which have been considered to be similar,[884] international law does not explicitly provide for a right to secession. Yet, international law does not specifically prohibit secession either.[885] As Crawford puts it, 'the position is that secession is neither legal nor illegal in international law, but a legally neutral act the consequences of which are regulated internationally'.[886] Other scholars have correctly added that 'la sécession est un fait politique et le droit international se contente d'en tirer les conséquences lorsqu'elle aboutit à la mise en place d'autorités étatiques effectives et stables'.[887] The Supreme Court of Canada rightly concluded that 'international law may well adapt to recognize a political and/or factual reality, regardless of the legality of the steps leading to its creation'[888] and that if a secession is 'successful in the streets, it might well lead to the creation of a new State'.[889] The effectivity of the new situation on the ground will be a key factor to determine the success of a contested secession.[890] Yet, effectivity, in itself, is not enough.[891]

6.111 As affirmed by the Supreme Court of Canada, the 'ultimate success' of a secession will be 'dependent on recognition by the international community'.[892] Importantly, any such recognition must not be 'premature', that is, given before real and incontestable effectivity could be shown. Clearly, no such

---

882 See, Chapter 6, Section 6.3.2.2.

883 Grant, 'Annexation of Crimea' (n 862) 72; Christakis, 'Les conflits de sécession en Crimée' (n 872) 3ff. See also: A. Gdalina, 'Crimea and the Right to Self-Determination: Questioning the Legality of Crimea's Secession from Ukraine', (2016) 24 *Cardozo JICL* 531–63; Majid Nikouei and Masoud Zamani, 'The Secession of Crimea: Where Does International Law Stand?' (2016) 85(1) *Nordic JIL* 37–64; Anna Stepanowa, 'International Law and Legality of Secession in Crimea', (2014) *Cambridge JICL*.

884 See, *Reference Re Secession of Quebec* [1998] 2 SCR 217 [154] referring to those peoples 'subject to alien subjugation, domination or exploitation'.

885 Cwicinskaja (n 856) 70.

886 Crawford, *The Creation of States* (n 115) 390. See also: Christakis, 'Les conflits de sécession en Crimée' (n 872) 6ff.

887 Nguyen Quoc Dinh, Patrick Daillier and A. Pellet, *Droit international public*, 6th edn (LGDJ 1999) 521.

888 *Reference re Secession of Quebec* (n 884) [141].

889 Ibid., [142].

890 Christakis, 'Les conflits de sécession en Crimée' (n 872) 7.

891 Ibid., 8–9.

892 *Reference re Secession of Quebec* (n 884) [155].

effectivity existed when Russia recognized Crimea nearly *one day* after its declaration of independence.[893] In any event, as further examined below, any such recognition is prohibited whenever secession is the result of a violation of a fundamental principle of international law, such as the prohibition of the use of force.[894]

6.2.3 *The controversial existence of a 'remedial' right to secession and its inapplicability to the situation of Crimea*

The question as to whether there exists a 'remedial' right to secession under international law is controversial.[895] The ICJ did not take a position on the matter in its advisory opinion on Kosovo. This being said, Russia denied the existence of such a 'right' before the ICJ in the Kosovo advisory opinion.[896] But in the context of the Crimean crisis, it took the position that the conditions under which the Russian ethnic population were said to be living in Crimea called for the exercise of a remedial right to secession.[897] The claim of human rights violations committed against Russians has not been supported by any convincing evidence.[898] This is the conclusion reached by the Office of the High Commissioner for Human Rights as well as by the OSCE.[899] Also, the incidents were clearly not of the magnitude which has been the legal basis for other entities to claim a remedial right to secession, such as in the case of Kosovo and Bangladesh.[900] **6.112**

In any event, any such remedial right to secession is generally considered to be only available as a 'last resort' solution when the right to self-determination of a people cannot be implemented within a given State. This is the case when there is a systemic pattern of discrimination and/or severe violations of human **6.113**

893 Cwicinskaja (n 856) 69. It has been suggested by R. Geiss, 'Russia's Annexation of Crimea: The Mills of International Law Grind Slowly but They Do Grind', (2015) 91 *Int'l L Stud* 448, that Russia's recognition of the independence of Crimea is a violation of international law.

894 See, Théodore Christakis, 'Self-Determination, Territorial Integrity and *Fait Accompli* in the Case of Crimea', (2015) 75 *ZaöRV* 75–100.

895 Jure Vidmar, 'Remedial Secession in International Law: Theory and (Lack of) Practice', (2010) 6 *St Antony's Int Rev* 37; Théodore Christakis, *Le droit à l'autodétermination en dehors des situations de décolonisation* (La documentation française 1999) 285–315.

896 Written Statement of the Russian Federation, *Accordance with International Law of the Unilateral Declaration of Independence in Respect of Kosovo, Advisory Opinion* (Apr. 16, 2009), available at: http://www.icj-cij.org/docket/files/141/15628.pdf. indicating that the so-called 'safeguard clause' 'may be construed as authorizing secession under certain conditions', adding that 'those conditions should be limited to truly extreme circumstances, such as an outright armed attack by the parent State, threatening the very existence of the people in question' [88].

897 Grant, 'Annexation of Crimea' (n 862) 72ff. 94. Marxsen (n 859) 374; Cwicinskaja (n 856) 72.

898 Grant, ibid., 72–5, 94; Marxsen (n 859) 374; Cwicinskaja (n 856) 72.

899 OSCE High Commissioner on National Minorities, 6 March 2014, available at: http://www.osce.org/hcnm/116180.

900 Grant, 'Annexation of Crimea' (n 862) 75, 94.

rights.[901] In the words of the Supreme Court of Canada, such a remedial right to secession 'possibly'[902] exists 'when a people is blocked from the meaningful exercise of its right to self-determination internally'.[903] In the context of Crimea, no efforts to end the crisis were made and no sort of negotiation took place.[904] All of this suggests that the strict substantive and procedural conditions generally recognized for a people to exercise any remedial right to secession were not present in the case of Crimea in 2014.[905]

6.2.4 The illegal use of force by Russia

6.114 The annexation of Crimea was preceded by an armed intervention by Russian forces in the territory of Crimea (and also in other parts of Eastern Ukraine). As a consequence of the general prohibition of the use of force in international relations following the adoption of the Charter of the United Nations (Art. 2(4)), the annexation of a territory is illegal. This has not always been the case. Conquest and territorial changes resulting from armed conflicts and the use of force have long been recognized as a legal way for the acquisition of territory under international law. This was the case as late as the 1920s[906] and 1930s.[907]

6.115 Under contemporary international law, as set out in the UN GA 'Friendly Relations Declaration', 'no territorial acquisition resulting from the threat or use of force shall be recognized as legal'.[908] The Security Council has repeatedly stated the 'inadmissibility of the acquisition of territory by war'.[909] Such proclamations were done, inter alia, in the context of Iraq's annexation of

---

901 Marxsen (n 859) 386; Cwicinskaja (n 856) 71–2; Geiss (n 893) 441.

902 *Re Secession of Quebec* (n 885) [134], [154].

903 Ibid., [133].

904 Grant, 'Annexation of Crimea' (n 862) 76–7, 93; Cwicinskaja (n 856) 73.

905 Grant, ibid., 77; Marxsen (n 859) 390; Cwicinskaja, ibid., 73; Geiss (n 893) 441.

906 *Island of Palmas* (*United States v. Netherlands*), PCA, Award, 4 April 1928, 2 RIAA 829, 839:

> Titles of acquisition of territorial sovereignty in present-day international law are either based on an act of effective apprehension, *such as occupation or conquest*, or, like cession, presuppose that the ceding and the cessionary Powers or at least one of them, have the faculty of effectively disposing of the ceded territory (emphasis added).

907 *Legal Status of Eastern Greenland* (*Norway v. Denmark*), PCIJ Series A/B, No. 53, 29 (1933): 'Conquest … operates as a cause of loss of sovereignty where there is war between two States and by reason of defeat of one of them sovereignty over territory passes from the loser to the victorious States.'

908 Declaration on Principles of International Law Concerning Friendly Relations and Co-operation among States in Accordance with the Charter of the United Nations, GA Res. 2625 (XXV), UN GAOR, 25th Sess., Supp. No. 28, UN Doc. A/RES/8082 (24 October 1970), principle I.

909 Geiss (n 893) 434, referring to SC Res. 242, UN Doc. S/RES/242 (22 November 22 1967). See also: SC Res. 859, UN Doc. S/RES/859 (24 August 1993); SC Res. 874, UN Doc. S/RES/874 (14 October 1993); SC Res. 896, UN Doc. S/RES/896 (31 January 1994).

Kuwait[910] and the annexation of the Golan Heights[911] and East Jerusalem[912] by Israel.[913] Annexation is therefore no longer recognized as a legal way for one State to acquire a title over a territory.[914] This is because the prohibition of the use of force is largely considered as a *jus cogens* norm.[915] Consequently, it is generally recognized that the acquisition of territory by the use of force is in violation of a *jus cogens* norm.[916]

The justifications which have been put forward by Russia to legitimize its intervention, including the protection of ethnic Russians and having been 'invited' by the former Ukrainian President, have largely been considered by scholars as having no base under international law.[917] The illegal use of force by Russia led to a violation of the territorial integrity of Ukraine, and ultimately resulted in the annexation by Russia of the territory of Crimea.[918] As noted by one writer, in this case the 'unlawful use of force is inseparably connected to the purported subsequent status alteration of Crimea'.[919] The annexation of Crimea is therefore illegal under international law.[920] **6.116**

910 SC Res. 662, UN Doc. S/RES/662 (9 August 1990).
911 SC Res. 497, UN Doc. S/RES/497 (17 December 1981).
912 SC Res. 478 (1980).
913 SC Res. 497, UN Doc. S/RES/497 (17 December 1981).
914 Rainer Hofmann, 'Annexation', in *Max Planck Encyclopedia of Public International Law* (OUP, online edn, 2006).
915 Crawford, *Brownlie's Principles* (n 282) 242–3, 595; Cwicinskaja (n 856) 71; Bílková (n 859) 27; C. Christakis, 'L'obligation de non-reconnaissance des situations créées par le recours illicite à la force ou d'autres actes enfreignant des règles fondamentales', in Ch. Tomuschat and J-M Thouvenin (eds), *The Fundamental Rules of the International Legal Order: Jus cogens and Obligations Erga Omnes* (Martinus Nijhoff 2005) 127.
916 See, J. Dugard, *Recognition and the United Nations* (Grotius Publ. 1987) 135–6; 152ff, 155–6.
917 Grant, 'Annexation of Crimea' (n 862) 77ff; 94; Marxsen (n 859) 372ff; Geiss (n 893) 431; Daniel Wisehart, 'The Crisis in Ukraine and the Prohibition of the Use of Force: A Legal Basis for Russia's Intervention?', EJIL Talk! (4 March 2014), http://www.ejiltalk.org/the-crisis-in-ukraine-andthe-prohibition-of-the-use-of-force-a-legal-basis-for-russias-intervention/; Christakis, 'Les conflits de sécession en Crimée' (n 872) 6, 10–11; Shane Reeves, 'To Russia with Love: How Moral Arguments for a Humanitarian Intervention in Syria Opened the Door for an Invasion of the Ukraine', (2014–15) 23 *Mich St Int'l L Rev* 226–7; Thomas D. Grant, 'The Yanukovych Letter: Intervention and Authority to Invite in International Law', (2015) 2 *Indon J Intl and Comp L 281*, 282–84; Oleksandr Zadorozhnii, 'To Justify against All Odds: the Annexation of Crimea in 2014 and the Russian Legal Scholarship', (2015) 35 *Polish YIL* 139–69; Bílková (n 859) 37ff; Antonello Tancredi, 'The Russian Annexation of the Crimea: Questions Relating to the Use of Force', (2014) 1 *Questions Int'l L* 10.
918 Marxsen (n 859) 389; Christakis, 'Les conflits de sécession en Crimée' (n 872) 6ff; A. Tancredi, 'Neither Authorized nor Prohibited?: Secession and International Law after Kosovo, South Ossetia and Abkhazia' (2008) 18 *Italian YIL* 37–62; Peter M. Olson, 'The Lawfulness of Russian Use of Force in Crimea', (2014) 53 *Mil L and LWar Rev* 17, 19 24; Bílková (n 859) 27; Tancredi, 'The Russian Annexation of the Crimea' (n 917) 5.
919 Geiss (n 893) 432.
920 Grant, 'Annexation of Crimea' (n 862); Marxsen (n 859) 379; Geiss (n 893) 431; Tancredi, 'Neither Authorized nor Prohibited' (n 918) 37–62; Christakis, 'Les conflits de sécession en Crimée' (n 872) 10–11.

6.2.5 *States have the obligation not to recognize the annexation or to give any effect to Crimea's change of status*

6.117 States have an obligation not to recognize new situations arising from an illegal act of annexation.[921] This obligation is found in the 1974 General Assembly Resolution 3314 (XXIX) on the definition of aggression,[922] and at Article 41 of the ILC Articles on State responsibility.[923] The Security Council has affirmed the existence of such an obligation not to recognize on many occasions.[924] It is now well-recognized that this non-recognition obligation in the context of violations of *jus cogens* norms is a rule of *customary international law*.[925] This is indeed the position taken by the ICJ in the *Wall* advisory opinion,[926] and that of the ILC.[927]

921 Christakis, ibid., 9–10, 12ff.

922 Art. 5(3) G.A. Res. 3314 (XXIX) declaring that '[n]o territorial acquisition or special advantage resulting from aggression is or shall be recognized as lawful'.

923 Titles and Texts of the Draft Articles on Responsibility of States for Internationally Wrongful Acts Adopted by the Drafting Committee on Second Reading, 26 July 2001, UN Doc. A/CN.4/L.602/Rev.1.

924 SC Res. 662, UN Doc. S/RES/662 (9 August 1990) (Iraq's annexation of Kuwait); SC Res. 497, UN Doc. S/RES/497 (annexation of the Golan Heights by Israel). See also: proclamation of the Republic of Northern Cyprus in 1983: SC Res. 541, UN Doc. S/RES/541 (18 November 1983); SC Res. 550, UN Doc. S/RES/550 (11 May 1984).

925 Crawford, *Brownlie's Principles* (n 282) 598, 600; Dugard, *Recognition and the United Nations* (n 916) 135–6; 152ff; M. Dawidowicz, 'The Obligation of Non-Recognition of an Unlawful Situation' in J. Crawford, A. Pellet and S. Olleson (eds), *The Law of International Responsibility* (OUP 2010) 683; Christakis, 'Les conflits de sécession en Crimée' (n 872) 11; Anne Lagerwall, 'L'agression et l'annexion de la Crimée par la Fédération de Russie: Quels enseignements au sujet du droit international? (2014) *Questions Int'l L., Zoom Out I*, 63–4; Mälksoo (n 116) 294; Christakis, 'L'obligation de non-reconnaissance' (n 915) 142–4; Crawford, *The Creation of States* (n 115) 160. See however, Stefan Talmon, 'The Duty Not to "Recognize as Lawful" a Situation Created by the Illegal Use of Force or Other Serious Breaches of a Jus Cogens Obligation: An Obligation without Real Substance?', in Tomuschat and Thouvenin (n 915) 125:

> Many problems still remain with regard to the obligation 'not to recognize as lawful' a situation created by the illegal threat or use of force or other serious breaches of *jus cogens* norms. There is more authority for the obligation as such (especially in cases of the illegal use of force, the denial of the right of self-determination of peoples, and the prohibition of racial discrimination) than for its particular content, and rules which readily correspond to the obligation have not yet fully developed in customary international law. In view of the content given to the obligation it is doubtful whether such rules will ever be developed with regard to serious breaches of some of the jus cogens norms identified by the ILC and others. The obligation of non-recognition of the legality of a specific situation amounts to a duty of active abstention.

926 *Legal Consequences of the Construction of a Wall in the Occupied Palestinian Territory*, Advisory Opinion, ICJ Reports 2004, 136 [87]: 'As the Court stated in its Judgment in the [Nicaragua] case (…) the principles as to the use of force incorporated in the Charter reflect customary international law (….); the same is true of its corollary entailing the illegality of territorial acquisition resulting from the threat or use of force.'

927 Commentaries to the Draft Articles on Responsibility of States for Internationally Wrongful Acts Adopted by the International Law Commission at its 53rd Session (2001), November 2001, Report of the ILC on the work of its 53rd Session, Official Records of the General Assembly, 56th Session, Supplement No. 10 (A/56/10), chp.IV.E.2), 114: 'the existence of an obligation of non-recognition in response to serious breaches of obligations arising under peremptory norms already finds support in international practice and in decisions of ICJ'.

How do these principles apply to the case of Crimea?[928] As put by one writer, 'the process in which Crimea was integrated into Russia relied on the use of force by Russian troops and therefore gives rise to an obligation not to recognize Crimea's accession to Russia'.[929] Many States have declared that the annexation of Crimea is an illegal act under international law. They have consequently refused to recognize the annexation.[930] For instance, this is the position adopted by the European Union.[931] The same position was also adopted by international organizations, such as NATO,[932] and the Parliamentary Assembly of the OSCE.[933] The Parliamentary Assembly of the Council of Europe adopted a resolution stating that the annexation of Crimea 'constitute[s], beyond any doubt, a grave violation of international law'.[934] A number of States have put in place sanctions against Russia.[935] Only a small number of States have recognized Crimea's accession to Russia.[936] **6.118**

The General Assembly's Resolution 68/262, adopted on 27 March 2014 (with 100 votes in favour, 11 against and 58 abstentions), affirmed the Assembly's commitment to the territorial integrity of Ukraine and directed States 'not to recognize any alteration of the status of [the] autonomous Republic of Crimea and the city of Sevastopol on the basis of referendum'.[937] The Resolution also called all States 'to refrain from any action or dealing that might be interpreted as recognizing any such altered status'. The Resolution has been considered as a 'collective application of the rule of non-recognition'.[938] A similar resolution **6.119**

928 See: E. Milano, 'The Non-Recognition of Russia's Annexation of Crimea: Three Different Legal Approaches and One Unanswered Question' (2014) 1 *Questions Int'l L* 37.

929 Marxsen (n 859) 391.

930 See, discussion in: Grant, 'Annexation of Crimea' (n 862) 87ff.

931 Joint statement on Crimea by the President of the European Council, Herman Van Rompuy, and the President of the European Commission, José Manuel Barroso, 18 March 2014, available at: http://europa.eu/rapid/press-release_STATEMENT-14-74_en.htm: 'The sovereignty, territorial integrity and independence of Ukraine must be respected. The European Union does neither recognize the illegal and illegitimate referendum in Crimea nor its outcome. The European Union does not and will not recognize the annexation of Crimea and Sevastopol to the Russian Federation.'

932 NATO, 'Crimea's annexation is illegal and illegitimate and NATO Allies will not recognize it', 18 March 2014, available at: www.nato.int/cps/en/natolive/news_108100.htm.

933 OSCE, 'Resolution on Clear, Gross and Uncorrected Violations of Helsinki Principles by the Russian Federation', Declaration and resolutions adopted by the OSCE Parliamentary Assembly at the 23rd annual secession, Baku, 28 June to 2 July 2014, 17–19.

934 Resolution 1990 (2014), 'Reconsideration on substantive grounds of the previously ratified credentials of the Russian delegation', Assembly debate on 10 April 2014 (16th Sitting).

935 See, on this point, Christakis, 'Les conflits de sécession en Crimée' (n 872) 13ff. For an overview of sanctions imposed by the European Union, see: 'Sanctions against Russia over Ukraine Crisis', EU Newsroom, available at: http://europa.eu/newsroom/highlights/special-coverage/eusanctions/index en.htm. For sanctions imposed by the US, see: US Department of State, 'Ukraine and Russia Sanctions', available at http://www.state.gov/e/eb/tfs/spi/ukrainerussia/.

936 Afghanistan, Cuba, Kyrgyzstan, Nicaragua, North Korea, Syria, Venezuela.

937 GA Res. 68/262, March 27 2014 [1,4,5].

938 Grant, 'Annexation of Crimea' (n 862) 91.

was blocked by a Russian veto at the Security Council.[939] In any event, it is important to note that any determination by the Security Council of the illegality of an annexation is not essential for the non-recognition obligation to arise.[940] The obligation not to recognize exists for all States *notwithstanding* any prior determination by the Security Council or any other UN body. The non-recognition obligation arises from the unlawful character of the annexation.

6.120 The illegality of the annexation of Crimea and the resulting obligation for other States not to recognize this new situation has some important consequences regarding issues of State succession. This question is examined in the next section.

6.2.6 The provisions of the Vienna Convention do not apply to the case of the annexation of Crimea

6.121 Article 6 of the Vienna Convention indicates that its provisions 'apply only to the effects of a succession of States occurring in conformity with international law and, in particular, the principles of international law embodied in the Charter of the United Nations'.[941] In other words, the Convention does not apply to cases of annexation that are considered to be illegal under international law. The goal of this provision is to prevent giving any *legal effect* to a factual situation which is considered to be illegal under international law.[942]

6.122 During the drafting of the Convention, members of the Commission examined the question as to whether or not the inclusion of such a clause was at all necessary.[943] The 1974 ILC Report indicates that 'the Commission in preparing draft articles for the codification of the rules of international law relating to normal situations naturally assumes that those articles are to apply to facts occurring and situations established in conformity with international law'.[944] The Report added that some members of the Commission 'considered that it would suffice to rely upon the same general presumption in drafting the

---

939 The draft resolution was presented by 41 countries at the meeting of 15 March but was vetoed by Russia (China abstained): UNSC Draft Res. UN Doc S/2014/189; UNSC Verbatim Record (15 March 2014) UN Doc S/PV.7138. The resolution reaffirmed in the preamble that 'no acquisition of territory resulting from the threat or use of force shall be recognised as legal'; it declared that the referendum could 'not have legal validity' and could 'not form the basis for any alteration of the status of Crimea'; and it 'call[ed] upon all States, international organizations and specialized agencies not to recognize any alteration of the status of Crimea on the basis of this referendum and to refrain from any action or dealing that might be interpreted as recognizing such altered status.' (see, Milano (n 928) 38).

940 Christakis, 'Les conflits de sécession en Crimée' (n 872) 13.

941 For an analysis of this provision, see G. Gaggioli, 'Article 6' in Distefano, Gaggioli and Hêche (n 4), 181ff.

942 Ibid., 193–5.

943 A detailed analysis is found in: ibid., 184ff.

944 ILC Report, 26th Session, 1974 (n 24) 181.

present articles' and that it 'was unnecessary to specify that the articles would apply only to the effects of a succession of States occurring in conformity with international law'.[945] Ultimately, the Commission decided to include Article 6. This decision had much to do with the specific situation of transfer of territory (although it is clear that Art. 6 applies to *all cases* of State succession[946]).[947]

The 1978 Vienna Convention does not explain what are those situations which are considered *not* to be 'occurring in conformity with international law'.[948] Reference should be made to the preamble of the Vienna Convention,[949] which refers to a number of 'principles of international law embodied in the Charter of the United Nations'.[950] In any event, when drafting Article 6, the illegal use of force prohibited under the UN Charter was undoubtedly one of the cases envisioned.[951] **6.123**

The same clause as Article 6 is also found in the Vienna Convention on Succession of States in Respect of State Property, Archives and Debts,[952] and in the Draft Articles on Nationality of Natural Persons in Relation to the Succession of States.[953] A recent resolution adopted by the Institut de Droit **6.124**

---

945 Ibid.

946 Christakis, *Le droit à l'autodétermination* (n 896) 168ff.

947 Tanzi and Iapichino (n 366) 554–5. Thus, some members of the Commission felt that 'it was desirable to underline that only transfers occurring in conformity with international law would fall within the concept of "succession of States" for the purpose of the present articles': ILC Report, 26th Session, 1974 (n 24) 181. The same comment is found regarding the application of Art. 15 (the 'MTF rule'): (1974) *Yearbook ILC*, vol II (Pt Two), 209 (draft Art. 14 commentary):

> This article [draft article 14, viz Article 15 VCST], like the draft articles as a whole, has to be read in conjunction with article 6 which limits the present articles to lawful situations (…). Article 14 is limited to normal changes in the sovereignty or in the responsibility for the international relations of a territory. … As to Article 6, although the limitation to lawful situations applies throughout the draft articles, some members of the Commission considered it to be of particular importance in the present connexion.

948 The question is examined in: Gagglioli (n 941) 197ff.

949 Ibid., 198–9.

950 The relevant part of the preamble reads as follows:

> *Having in mind* the principles of international law embodied in the Charter of the United Nations, such as the principles of the equal rights and self-determination of peoples, of the sovereign equality and independence of all States, of non-interference in the domestic affairs of States, of the prohibition of the threat or use of force, and of universal respect for, and observance of, human rights and fundamental freedoms for all
>
> *Recalling* that respect for the territorial integrity and political independence of any State is required by the Charter of the United Nations.'

951 Christakis, *Le droit à l'autodétermination* (n 896) 172–3; Gagglioli (n 941) 202–4.

952 Art. 3 of the 1983 Vienna Convention on Succession of States in Respect of State Property, Archives and Debts, in (1983) 22 ILM 306.

953 Art. 3 of the Draft Articles on Nationality of Natural Persons in Relation to the Succession of States, adopted by the ILC on second reading in 1999, ILC Report, UN Doc. A/54/10, 1999, Chapter. IV [44]–[45] in: (1997) *Yearbook ILC*, vol. II, 13.

international also took the same position.[954] It should be added that the 2001 Institut's resolution on State Succession in Matters of Property and Debts[955] does not contain such a clause, but rather refers to this legality requirement in its preamble.[956]

6.125 In sum, the Convention does not apply to situations of illegal occupation of territory[957] or to changes of borders resulting from the use of force.[958] It does not find application in the context of the annexation of Crimea.[959] Yet, this does *not* mean that there are no rules of State succession that apply to the situation of Crimea. The rules of succession which are considered as reflecting customary international law will continue to apply (whether or not such rules have been codified in the Convention).[960] These rules will apply to all situations regardless of whether they are considered to be legal under international law (the practical implication of this finding will be examined below[961]).

6.2.7 Crimea is still part of the territory of Ukraine and is under Russian occupation

6.126 Under international law, Crimea still belongs to Ukraine 'whatever the *de facto* situation may look like'.[962] Ukraine retains international responsibility for its entire territory, including Crimea.[963] Yet, it is undeniable that Ukraine's responsibility is affected and greatly limited by the presence of Russia in Crimea.[964] On the ground, there is no doubt that Crimea has been fully integrated within Russia. However, because the annexation is illegal, Russia

954 IDI, State Succession to Responsibility, Resolution, 2015 (n 306), Art. 2(2). As explained by Rapporteur Kohen in his Final Report, an entity claiming statehood which has employed illegal means under international law should be excluded from the scope of this Resolution simply because such an entity cannot claim to be a State (Institut de Droit international, State Succession in Matters of State Responsibility, 14th Commission, Rapporteur Marcelo G. Kohen, Final Report, 28 June 2015, 14).

955 Institut de Droit international, State Succession in Matters of Property and Debts, Session of Vancouver, 2001, in (2000–2001) 69 *Annuaire I.D.I.*, 713ff).

956 IDI, State Succession to Responsibility (n 306), Session de Tallinn – 2015, PVPL plénière n° 1, 1ère séance plénière, 26.

957 Tams (n 27) 320.

958 Gagglioli (n 941) 206–7.

959 Grant, 'Annexation of Crimea' (n 862) 92–3.

960 Gagglioli (n 941) 219, citing Rapporteur Special Vallat in (1974) *Yearbook ILC*, vol 2 (2nd part), 35.

961 See, Chapter 6, Section 6.3.2.2.2.

962 Marxsen (n 859) 390. See also: Cwicinskaja (n 856) 75; Geiss (n 893) 431.

963 Grant, 'Annexation of Crimea' (n 862) 93.

964 Ibid. See also: Cwicinskaja (n 856) 76ff. examining many questions which remain to this day unanswered in the context of specific international organizations, including which State is actually responsible for the safety of civil aircraft operating in the regions (International Civil Aviation Organization), which one can provide adequate level of navigational safety and compliance with international obligations in the region (International Maritime Organization), and the safeguards of two nuclear facilities (International Atomic Energy Agency).

cannot be considered as the beneficiary of any *rights* connected with the annexed territory of Crimea.[965] For instance, as noted above, Russia does not benefit from any of the rights contained in the two Vienna Conventions on State succession. Crimea is an 'occupied territory' under international law.[966] International law imposes important *obligations* and responsibilities on Russia, as the force occupying Crimea.[967] In sum, as noted by one writer, 'the annexation may be expected to impose some of the main obligations of territorial power on Russia without transferring the main rights, those remain where they had been – that is to say, with Ukraine'.[968]

Regardless, it is unlikely that Crimea will reintegrate the territory of Ukraine in the near future. The more time elapses between the moment of the annexation and the continuing occupation by Russia, the more the claim of Ukraine's title over Crimea will appear to be a 'fiction'. Over time, other States may begin to consider the transfer of territory to be a *fait accompli*.[969] This is indeed the position Australia took years after Indonesia's annexation of East Timor.[970] However, this position certainly goes against the *ex iniuria ius non oritur* principle that is well known to be a 'principe fondamental du droit constituant une sorte de clef de voûte de tout système juridique'.[971] For Christakis, 'l'obligation de non-reconnaissance n'est certainement pas une panacée, elle constitue néanmoins la sanction minimale de droit commun prévue par un ordre juridique qui ne pourrait, sans s'autodétruire, accepter sa capitulation devant le fait accompli'.[972] One can only agree with him when he affirms that while international law cannot be blind regarding effectivity on **6.127**

965 Grant, 'Annexation of Crimea' (n 862) 93.

966 Geiss (n 893) 443ff; Tancredi, 'The Russian Annexation of the Crimea' (n 917) 21ff.

967 See, discussion in: Philip Reznik, 'Survival of BITs and Investor Rights in Crimea – Russia's Trick or Treat(y) with Investors', (Ph.D. Thesis, Stockholm University, 2014) 29ff. See also: Tomer Broude, 'The Protection of Investments in Occupied Territories: Some Considerations', *International Investment Law & the Law of Armed Conflict*, 5–6 October 2017, Athens Colloquium; Martins Paparinskis, 'International Investment Law and Disputed Territories: A Generalist Perspective', ibid; Tobias Ackermann, 'Investments Under Occupation: Belligerent Occupation and the Application of Investment Treaties', ibid; Antal Berkes, 'The Responsibility of the Host State for the Violations of Investors' Rights in a Part of its Territory under Occupation', ibid.

968 Grant, 'Annexation of Crimea' (n 862) 93.

969 Costelloe (n 368) 347.

970 Comm Rec 1978, 25–26, reprinted in 'Recognition: Australian Practice in International Law' (1978–80) 8 *Australian YIL* 279: 'This is a reality with which we must come to terms. Accordingly, the Government has decided that although it remains critical of the means by which integration was brought about it would be unrealistic to continue to refuse to recognize de facto that *East Timor* is part of Indonesia.' See also, the position taken by Australia before the ICJ in the East Timor case to justified having signed a treaty with Indonesia concerning the exploitation of oil resources on the continental shelf of East Timor.

971 Christakis, 'Les conflits de sécession en Crimée' (n 872) 17.

972 Ibid.

the ground, it remains that 'l'effectivité ne peut pas, en principe, aller jusqu'à l'emporter sur la licéité'.[973]

6.128 The next section will examine a number of legal issues arising from the illegal annexation of Crimea in the context of investment arbitration.

6.3 Legal issues arising from the annexation of Crimea in the field of international investment law

6.129 This section will first examine legal issues arising from the annexation of Crimea in the context of State contracts (Section 6.3.1). This analysis will be followed by an examination of the problematic issues arising in the context of investment treaties signed by both Ukraine and Russia with other States as well as the controversial question of the application of the Ukraine-Russia BIT in the territory of Crimea (Section 6.3.2).

6.3.1 The effect of the annexation on State contracts

6.130 Before the annexation of Crimea, many oil companies had signed contracts with Ukraine regarding the exploitation of natural resources.[974] The present section only focuses on *State* contracts to which Ukraine was a party. The separatists from Crimea have apparently stated that contractual obligations will continue to be respected.[975] In other words, these contracts will continue their existence after the annexation with Russia by simply replacing Ukraine as the contracting party. It is generally recognized that State contacts are unaffected by belligerent occupation.[976] This is certainly the case when the occupation is temporary and does not involve any question related to State succession (a classic example of such a situation would be the US occupation of Iraq). Yet, the annexation of Crimea is not a 'simple' of case of occupation. Russia claims sovereignty over the territory of Crimea. This controversial question of State succession to State contracts will be fully examined later (Part D). I will show that while, in general, the successor State can modify a State contract after the date of succession, it must do so by respecting basic

973 Ibid.

974 V.W. Broad, 'In Taking Crimea Putin Gains a Sea of Fuel Reserves', *New York Times*, 17 May 2014.

975 Apparently, Russia's Federal Constitutional Law No. 6-FKZ, dated 21 March 2014, provides that most existing permits and licenses, which were issued by the Ukrainian authorities, would be deemed effective for the term of their validity: Jones Day, 'Crisis in Crimea: Is Your Foreign Investment There Protected By a Treaty?', April 2014, available at: http://m.jonesday.com/crisis-in-crimea-is-your-foreign-investment-there-protected-by-a-treaty-04-10-2014/.

976 On this question, see: Ofilio J. Mayorga, 'Arbitration of Disputes Under State Contracts in Times of Belligerent Occupation', *International Investment Law & the Law of Armed Conflict*, 5–6 October 2017, Athens Colloquium. See also: Mayorga, Ofilio, 'Occupants, Beware of BITs: Applicability of Investment Treaties to Occupied Territories', (2017) 19 *Palestine YIL*.

principles of international law (including compensation for expropriation). I will also explain that in the specific context of a transfer of territory, the successor State is generally bound by State contracts. This is based on a number of circumstances and factors (including the nexus between the contract and the territory transferred and the concept of unjust enrichment). Yet, the case of Crimea is not a simple case of transfer of territory because it involves the breach of a *jus cogens* norm. Thus, Russia cannot be considered to have simply 'replaced' Ukraine as the contracting party in the context of these State contracts.

This section will focus on the question as to whether the obligation to not give any legal effect to the illegal annexation of Crimea (which is binding on States) can be imposed directly on foreign *non*-State actors (such as companies and individuals) parties to these contracts. Before answering this question, it is necessary to examine the more general question of whether international law imposes any direct legal obligations on corporations. **6.131**

6.3.1.1 The status of corporations under international law and investment arbitration

As mentioned above, the obligation to not give any legal effect to the illegal annexation of Crimea is a rule of customary international law. As highlighted by the ICJ,[977] the work of the ILC and the ILA,[978] non-State actors do not *directly* participate in the creation of customary rules.[979] The question of whether or not rules of customary international law are binding on corporations is a controversial one.[980] It is generally assumed that this is not the case because rules of customary international law impose obligations only on *subjects* of international law.[981] Corporations are generally not considered as subjects of international law.[982] For this reason, it has often been assumed that they are not capable of having obligations under international law. The **6.132**

977 *Jurisdictional Immunities of the State* (*Germany v. Italy: Greece intervening*), Judgment, ICJ Reports 2012, 99, 143 [101].

978 International Law Commission, 'Second Report on Identification of Customary International Law', by Michael Wood, Special Rapporteur, ILC, 66th session, Geneva, 5 May–6 June and 7 July–8 August 2014, UN doc. A/CN.4/672, 30; ILA, 'Second Report of the Committee Non-State Actors in International Law: Lawmaking and Participation Rights', Committee on 'Non-state Actors' (2012), 5.

979 This question is examined in detail in: Dumberry, *Formation and Identification of Rules of Customary International Law* (n 286) 117.

980 Markos Karavias, *Corporate Obligations under International Law* (OUP 2013).

981 See, however, the position of Jose E. Alvarez, 'Are Corporations "Subjects" of International Law?', (2011) 9 *Santa Clara JIL* 23–4, arguing that this is not the question which should be asked.

982 See, the analysis of the question in: P. Dumberry, 'L'entreprise, sujet de droit international? Retour sur la question à la lumière des développements récents du droit international des investissements', (2004) 108(1) RGDIP, 103–22.

following paragraphs will examine whether the conclusion should be the same in the context of investment arbitration.

6.133 The starting point of the analysis is to ask what it means to have an 'international legal personality'? To say that corporations (who represent the great majority of foreign investors) possess an international legal personality is not to say that they are co-equal with States. As famously stated by the ICJ in the *Reparations* case, 'subjects of law in any legal system are not necessarily identical in their nature or in the extent of their rights, and their nature depends upon the needs of the community'.[983] In other words, not all international legal persons are created equal. States occupy a unique place in the international legal order, serving as both the source and the object of legal norms. It is, after all, appropriate that States should possess certain powers and privileges denied to other entities. However, it has long been recognized that as the primary subjects of international law, States have the power to create new, non-State legal persons through their mutual consent.[984] For the ICJ, the international personality of the United Nations means that it is 'a subject of international law' which is 'capable of possessing international rights and duties' and has 'the capacity to maintain its rights by bringing international claims'.[985] In other words, possession of a legal personality gives an entity the right to bring a claim against a State before an international tribunal. The analytical framework developed by the court in the *Reparations* case has since been endorsed in doctrine.[986] It has also been applied in other contexts in reverse order: the fact that an entity has been granted direct right of action has been used as evidence that it possesses international legal personality. For example, some authors have concluded that private individuals are subjects of international human rights law when, as in the case of the European Convention on Human Rights, they are given a direct right of action against a State before an international tribunal.[987]

---

983 *Reparations for Injuries Suffered in the Service of the United Nations*, Advisory Opinion, ICJ Reports 1947, 179.

984 W.C. Jenks, 'Multinational Entities in the Law of Nations', in *Transnational Law in a Changing Society: Essays in Honor of Philip C. Jessup* (Columbia UP 1972), 74–5; G. Schwarzenberger, *International Law as Applied by International Courts and Tribunals* (vol. I, Stevens and Sons 1957) 146.

985 *Reparations for Injuries Suffered* (n 983) 179.

986 C. Berezowski, 'Les problèmes de la subjectivité internationale', in V. Ibler (ed), *Mélanges offerts à Juraj Andrassy* (Martinus Nijhoff 1968), 33–5; J.A. Barberis, 'Nouvelles questions concernant la personnalité juridique internationale', (1983-I) 179 Rec. des cours 168–9.

987 Article 34, Convention for the Protection of Human Rights and Fundamental Freedoms, Protocol 11 of 1st November 1998. In doctrine, see: C. Dominicé, 'L'émergence de l'individu en droit international public' (1987–1988) 16 AEI 8; K.P. Menon, 'The Legal Personality of Individuals', (1994) 6 *Sri Lanka JIL* 127, 128; Alexander Orakhelashvili, 'The Position of the Individual in International Law', (2001) 31 *Cal W Int'l J* 264; Edwin W. Tucker, 'Has the Individual Become the Subject of International Law?', (1965) 34 *U Cin L Rev* 341, 345.

Corporations possess both substantive rights and the ability to bring claims on the basis of those rights before international tribunals under many 'State contracts'[988] and under most modern BITs (and multilateral investment treaties). Although this is controversial in doctrine,[989] many writers (including myself[990]) have argued that in both situations corporations should be considered as having an international legal personality.[991] Interestingly, the *Plama* Tribunal qualified the ECT (and specifically Art. 26) as 'a very significant treaty for investors, marking another step in their transition *from objects to subjects* of international law'.[992] The issue was recently addressed by the *Urbaser* Tribunal in the following terms: **6.134**

> A principle may be invoked in this regard according to which corporations are by nature *not able to be subjects of international law and therefore not capable of holding obligations* as if they would be participants in the State-to-State relations governed by international law. While such principle had its importance in the past, it has lost its impact and relevance in similar terms and conditions as this applies to individuals. A simple look at the MFN Clause of Article VII of the BIT shows that the Contracting States accepted at least one hypothesis where investors are entitled to invoke rights resulting from international law (in addition to the rights resulting from Article X). If the BIT therefore is not based on a corporation's incapacity of holding rights under

988 P. Dumberry, 'International Investment Contracts', in T. Gazzini and E. de Brabandere (eds), *International Investment Law. The Sources of Rights and Obligations* (Martinus Nijhoff Publ. 2012) 215–43.

989 For an overview of the controversy, see: Dumberry, 'L'entreprise, sujet de droit international?' (n 982). See also: Markos Karavias, 'Treaty law and Multinational Enterprises: More Than Internationalized Contracts'? in Christian J. Tams, Antonios Tzanakopoulos and Andreas Zimmermann (eds), *Research Handbook on the Law of Treaties* (Cheltenham 2014).

990 P. Dumberry and E. Labelle Eastaugh, 'Non-State Actors in International Investment Law: The Legal Personality of Corporations and NGOs in the Context of Investor-State Arbitration', in Jean d'Aspremont (ed), *Participants in the International Legal System: Multiples Perspectives on Non-State Actors in International Law* (Routledge-Cavendish 2011) 360–71. See also: Tillmann Rudolf Braun, 'Globalization-Driven Innovation: The Investor as a Partial Subject in Public International Law – An Inquiry into the Nature and Limits of Investor Rights' (New York University School of Law, Jean Monnet Working Paper Series, JMWP 04/13, 2013) 46ff; Dumberry, 'L'entreprise, sujet de droit international?' (n 982).

991 Shaw (n 561) 262. For the same conclusion regarding State contracts, see: D.A. Ijalaye, *The Extension of Corporate Personality in International Law, (Oceana Publ. 1978) 5, 226, 243; Charles Leben, 'Quelques réflexions théoriques à propos des contrats d'État'*, in *Souveraineté étatique et marchés internationaux à la fin du 20e siècle: Mélange en l'honneur de Philippe Kahn* (Litec 2000) 120, 134–5; C. Leben, 'La théorie du contrat d'État et l'évolution du droit international des investissements', (2003) 302 Rec des Cours 308–11; Cahier (n 8) 158; Stephen M. Schwebel, 'International Protection of Contractual Arrangements', (1959) ASIL Proc. 267; Nguyen (n 888) 690; Barberis (n 986) 206; G. Cohen-Jonathan, 'L'arbitrage Texaco-Calasiatic contre Gouvernement Libyen', 1977 23 AFDI 457–9; W. Friedmann, 'General Course in Public International Law', (1969-II) 127 Rec des Cours; I. Seidl-Hohenveldern, 'The Theory of Quasi-International and Partly International Agreements', (1975) 11 RBDI 570; Peter Muchlinski, Corporations in International Law, in *Max Planck Encyclopedia of Public International Law* (n 276) [7].

992 *Plama Consortium Ltd. v. Bulgaria*, ICSID Case No.ARB/03/24, Decision on Jurisdiction, 8 February 2005 [141] (emphasis added).

international law, it cannot be admitted that it would reject by necessity any idea that a foreign investor company could not be *subject to international law obligations*.[993]

6.135 The conclusion reached by the *Urbaser* Tribunal was that 'in light of this more recent development, it can no longer be admitted that companies operating internationally are immune from becoming subjects of international law'.[994]

6.136 The present author does *not* suggest that corporations should be considered *full* subjects of international law having an equal status with States. Corporations have a *qualified* legal personality for two reasons. First, it is a *limited* personality, in the sense that corporations under BITs or contracts do not possess the full range of capacity recognized by States under international law. A corporation may only exercise the limited powers and claim the rights that its 'constituent instrument' has granted it. In practice, the extent of an investor's legal personality is determined by the arbitration clause, which will indicate which substantive rights contained in the treaty can form the basis of a claim. Second, the legal personality is *derivative* in the sense that a corporation is a 'secondary' subject of international law. Its personality is not inherent, but rather it emanates from the express will of (at least) one State either in a BIT or in a State contract. In the context of BITs, corporations are also *passive* subjects in the sense that they are not direct participants in the negotiation and generation of the legal norms on which their personality rests. Indeed, this personality can be modified or withdrawn without their consent, as treaties may always be modified by the contracting States. However, the situation is somewhat different in the context of State contracts, where a corporation is a direct participant in the *creation* of legal norms (the contractual terms), which must be complied with by the contracting State. In these circumstances, a corporation is not a mere bystander, but it rather possesses a *law-making* power on the international plane.[995]

6.137 In sum, there are good reasons to believe that corporations can be considered as having an international legal personality *in the context of State contracts*.[996] What should be the consequences of these findings?[997] On the one hand, international law, as it now stands, *does not* impose any *direct* legal obligations

993 *Urbaser SA and Consorcio de Aguas Bilbao Bizkaia, Bilbao Biskaia Ur Partzuergoa v. Argentina*, ICSID Case No. ARB/07/26, Award, 8 December 2016 [1193] (emphasis added).

994 Ibid., [1194].

995 See discussion, Julian Arato, 'Corporations as Lawmakers', (2015) 56 *Harv ILJ* 244ff.

996 See also, more generally, the analysis in Andrew Clapham, *Human Rights Obligations of Non-State* (OUP 2006), 68–9, 79, 82.

997 Braun (n 990) 48ff. See also: Alvarez (n 981) 23–4, examining the *different question* of the consequences of recognizing a *full* international law personality to corporations under investor-State arbitration, including their entitlement to a wider panoply of protections under international human rights law.

on corporations.[998] This being said, there are no theoretical objections preventing the imposition of obligations on corporations under international law.[999] In fact, I have shown elsewhere how new BITs could be drafted (and existing ones be amended) in order to directly impose certain human rights, labour, and environmental obligations on corporations.[1000] On the other hand, it is generally recognized that corporations can be held directly accountable for their violations of *jus cogens* norms.[1001] In fact, several authors[1002] (including myself[1003]) as well as UNCTAD,[1004] have argued, just like the *Phoenix Action* Tribunal,[1005] that a tribunal should find a claim submitted by an investor having committed *jus cogens* violations to be inadmissible. Given that corporations can be considered as (partial) subjects of international law (at the very

998 David Kinley and Junko Tadaki, 'From Talk to Walk: The Emergence of Human Rights Responsibilities for Corporations at International Law' (2004) 44(4) *Virginia JIL* 931; Clara Reiner and Christoph Schreuer, 'Human Rights and International Investment Arbitration', in Pierre-Marie Dupuy, Ernst-Ulrich Petersmann, and Francesco Francioni (eds) *Human Rights in International Investment Law and Arbitration* (OUP 2009), 86–7; Howard Mann, 'International Investment Agreements, Business and Human Rights: Key Issues and Opportunities', IISD (2008), 9 available at http://www.iisd.org/pdf/2008/iia_business_human_rights.pdf; Adefolake Adeyeye, 'Corporate Responsibility in International Law: Which Way To Go?,' (2007) 11 *Singapore YBIL* 148; Luke Eric Peterson, 'Human Rights and Bilateral Investment Treaties. Mapping the Role of Human Rights Law within Investor-State Arbitration', Rights and Democracy Report (2009) 15, available at http://publications.gc.ca/collections/collection_2012/dd-rd/E84-36-2009-eng.pdf.

999 'Interim Report of the Special Representative of the Secretary-General of the United Nations on the Issue of Human Rights and Transnational Corporations and other Business Enterprises,' John Ruggie, UN Doc. E/CN.4/2006/97 22 February 2006 [65].

1000 P. Dumberry and G. Dumas-Aubin, 'When and How Allegations of Human Rights Violations can be Raised in Investor-State Arbitration', (2012) 13(3) *J World Invest & Trade* 349–72.

1001 'Interim Report of the Special Representative' (n 999) [61]:

> under customary international law, emerging practice and expert opinion increasingly do suggest that corporations may be held liable for committing, or for complicity in, the most heinous human rights violations amounting to international crimes, including genocide, slavery, human trafficking, forced labour, torture and some crimes against humanity.

See also: Carlos M. Vazquez, 'Direct vs. Indirect Obligations of Corporations Under International Law' (2005) 45 *Colum J Transnat'l L* 927; Lahra Liberti, 'Investissements et droits de l'homme', in P. Kahn and T. Wälde (eds), *New Aspects of International Investment Law* (Hague Academy of International Law, Nijhoff, 2007) 836.

1002 Luke E. Peterson and Kevin Gray, 'International Human Rights in Bilateral Investment Treaties and Investment Treaty Arbitration', Working Paper for the Swiss Ministry for Foreign Affairs (2003), 18 (referring to 'certain egregious human rights violations'); Liberti (n 1001) 830–31 (speaking of 'graves violations des droits de l'homme'), see also at 840.

1003 Dumberry and Dumas-Aubin (n 1000) 366. See also: P. Dumberry and G. Dumas-Aubin, 'The Doctrine of "Clean Hands" and the Inadmissibility of Claims by Investors Breaching International Human Rights Law', in Ursula Kriebaum (ed), *Aligning Human Rights and Investment Protection*, (10(1) *TDM Special Issue* 2013).

1004 UNCTAD, 'Selected Recent Developments in IIA Arbitration and Human Rights', *IIA Monitor* No. 2 (2009) 15.

1005 *Phoenix Action, Ltd. v. Czech Republic*, ICSID Case No. ARB/06/5, Award, 15 April 2009 [78]: 'To take an extreme example, nobody would suggest that ICSID protection should be granted to investments made in violation of the most fundamental rules of protection of human rights, like investments made in pursuance of torture or genocide or in support of slavery or trafficking of human organs.'

least in the context of State contracts), logically, this should mean that they can be subject to obligations under international law. It would seem rather logical to assume that they should respect the *most important* of such obligations, that is, those which have acquired the status of rules of customary international law. Viewed from this perspective, the proposition that corporations must respect the customary rule of non-recognition of situations arising from the violation of *jus cogens* norms seems less controversial. In any event, as mentioned above, since it is recognized that corporations can be held accountable for having *committed* a violation of a *jus cogens* norm, it would seem logical that they should also have the obligation to *respect* the customary non-recognition obligation in the context of the violation of a *jus cogens* norm. The scope of any such obligation is discussed in the following section.

6.3.1.2 The potential scope of the obligation for corporations not to recognize a situation resulting from an illegal annexation

6.138 The starting point is to recall the scope of the non-recognition obligation existing for *States*. While Judge Kooijmans noted in the *Wall in the Occupied Palestinian Territory* advisory opinion that 'the duty not to recognize amounts (...) to an obligation without real substance,'[1006] it remains that several scholars have defined the content of this obligation.[1007] In fact, in its 1971 *Namibia* Advisory Opinion, the ICJ explained in some detail what States (including those not members of the UN[1008]) were prohibited to do as a result of this obligation of non-recognition. According to the ICJ, 'member States are under [an] obligation to abstain from entering into treaty relations with South Africa in all cases in which the Government of South Africa purports to act on behalf of or concerning Namibia'.[1009] In my view, the same solution

---

1006 *Wall in the Occupied Palestinian Territory* (n 926) [43, 44] (sep. op. Kooijmans).

1007 Talmon (n 925) 103ff; Dawidowicz (n 925) 683. See also: Christakis, 'Les conflits de sécession en Crimée' (n 872) 15, noting that the following obligations are imposed on States:

- une obligation de ne pas établir des relations conventionnelles avec l'autorité illégale (...);
- une obligation de ne pas accréditer de missions diplomatiques ni d'en recevoir, ce qui concerne tant l'interdiction de nouer des relations diplomatiques avec les régimes illégalement créés, que l'interdiction d'établir des relations diplomatiques qui pourraient être perçues comme une reconnaissance de l'autorité exercée sur un territoire annexé;
- une obligation de refuser l'admission et la participation de l'autorité illégale à une organisation internationale ou à un procès devant un juge interne ou international (...);
- une obligation de refuser d'entretenir des relations économiques, commerciales ou autres avec l'autorité illégale;
- une obligation de refuser tout effet juridique à des actes constitutionnels, législatifs ou administratifs édictés par un régime illicite.

See also: Christakis, *Le droit à l'autodétermination* (n 896) 144ff; Christakis, 'L'obligation de non-reconnaissance' (n 915) 127–66.

1008 *Legal Consequences for States of the Continued Presence of South-Africa in Namibia (South-West Africa) notwithstanding Security Council Resolution 276 (1970)* (Advisory Opinion) ICJ Reports 1971 16, at 55.

1009 Ibid., [122].

should also apply to contracts. Thus, a corporation continuing a contract with Russia in the circumstances described above would certainly be considered to be in a situation where Russia 'purports to act on behalf of or concerning' Crimea (which is still part of Ukraine under international law). Regarding bilateral treaties, the Court affirmed that States 'must abstain from invoking or applying those treaties or provisions of treaties concluded by South Africa on behalf of or concerning Namibia which involve active intergovernmental cooperation'.[1010] In my view, the same obligations should apply to companies regarding contracts. Finally, and more generally, the Court refers to 'the obligation to abstain from entering into economic and other forms of relationship or dealings with South Africa on behalf of or concerning Namibia which may entrench its authority over the Territory'.[1011] A company that continues doing business in Crimea after the annexation under a State contract originally signed with Ukraine would certainly be acting in violation of the non-recognition obligation as described by the ICJ.

It should be noted that General Assembly Resolution 68/262 only calls upon 'States, international organizations and specialized agencies' (but not other non-State actors) to respect the non-recognition obligation. I have found two examples where organs of the United Nations have called upon *home States* to take action against corporations (that had been incorporated under their own laws) doing business in specific territories contrary to the principle of non-recognition of a situation arising from a violation of a *jus cogens* norm. **6.139**

The first example concerns *Decree No. 1 on the Natural Resources of Namibia* enacted on 27 September 1974 by the United Nations Council for Namibia.[1012] The United Nations Council for Namibia, which was established in 1967, was expressly authorized to 'promulgate laws, decrees and administrative regulations as are necessary for the administration of [Namibia]', which had been annexed by South Africa.[1013] *Decree No. 1* forbade the prospecting, mining, processing, selling, exporting, etc., of natural resources within the territorial limits of Namibia without permission of the Council.[1014] Most importantly for the present discussion, Paragraph 6 of the Decree stated that the *future government* of an independent Namibia could hold individuals and **6.140**

1010 Ibid.

1011 Ibid., [124].

1012 *Decree on the Natural Resources of Namibia*, Addendum to the Report of the United Nations Council for Namibia, 29 UN GAOR Supp. 24A, at 27–28, UN Doc.A/9624/add 1(1975). The Decree was endorsed by GA Res. 3295 (XXIX), 13 December 1974, in: 29 UN GAOR Supp. 31, at 106, UN Doc. A/9631 (1975).

1013 GA Res. 2248 (s-v), 19 May 1967. The Council was dissolved after the independence of Namibia by GA Res. 44/243, 11 September 1990.

1014 It also gave the UN Council the power to seize such materials as well as any vehicle, ship or container which transported these illegally-obtained resources.

corporations that had been contravening the Decree liable for damages. In fact, the right to claim reparation against individuals or companies was explicitly recognized in two General Assembly resolutions.[1015] The Council took legal action in Dutch courts against a corporation accused of having breached Decree No. 1.[1016] One UN Security Council resolution specifically '[c]all[ed] upon all States to discourage their nationals or companies of their nationality not under direct governmental control from investing or obtaining concessions in Namibia, and to this end to withhold protection of such investment against claims of a future lawful Government of Namibia'.[1017] Another General Assembly resolution went further and 'call[ed] upon all States to prohibit companies' from pursuing such activities.[1018]

6.141 The second example concerns the creation by South Africa, during the period of the Apartheid, of four 'Homelands' (Transkei, Ciskei, Bophuthatswana, and Venda) on its territory which were given 'independence'. Several General Assembly resolutions have condemned this policy as contrary to the principle of self-determination and called upon all States to deny any form of recognition to these 'Bantustans'.[1019] Importantly, the President of the Security Council made a statement on behalf of the Council condemning the 'independence' of Venda and 'urge[d] Member Governments to take effective measures to prohibit all individuals, corporations, and other institutions under

1015 GA Res. 40/52, 2 December 1985 [14]; GA Res. 38/36, 2 December 1983 [42]: 'Declares that all activities of foreign economic interests in Namibia are illegal under international law and that consequently South Africa and all the foreign economic interests operating in Namibia are liable to pay damages to the future lawful Government of an independent Namibia'.

1016 Writ of summons, *Nauta van Haersolte*, no. VM/1 w 3720817, in: United Nations, 'The URENCO Case', (1988) II(7) Namibia Bulletin, Special Issue. In this case, the Council summoned on 14 July 1987 the Dutch corporations Urenco Nederland v.o.f. and Ultra-Centrifruge Nederland N.V. (as well as the Netherlands) to appear in the District Court in The Hague. It was alleged that during the 1970s the companies based in the Netherlands were involved in the processing of uranium originating from Namibia in violation of the Decree prohibiting the processing and refining of natural resources of Namibia without the permission of the Council. The Council asked for a court order prohibiting Urenco from carrying out further enrichment of uranium originating from Namibia; it also sought a declaratory judgment. This case is analysed in: Nicolaas Jan Schrijver, 'The UN Council for Namibia *vs.* Urenco, UCN and the State of the Netherlands', (1988) 1 *Leiden JIL* 25–48; Caleb M. Pilgrim, 'Some Legal Aspects of Trade in the Natural Resources of Namibia', (1990) 61 *British YIL* 263ff; Andrew Lyall, 'Violations of the Decree no. 1 for the Protection of the Natural Resources of Namibia', in: *Proceedings of the Regional Symposium on International Efforts to Implement Decree No.1 for the Protection of the Natural Resources of Namibia* (United Nations, 1984, UN Doc. DPI-839–40047).

1017 SC Res. 283 (1970) [7]. See also: SC Res. 301 (1971), 20 October 1971, at [12], whereby the Security Council '*[d]eclares* that franchises, rights, titles or contracts relating to Namibia granted to individuals or companies by South Africa after the adoption of General Assembly Res. 2145 (XXI) are not subject to protection or espousal by their States against claims of a future lawful Government of Namibia'.

1018 GA Res. 36/121, 10 December 1981 [11].

1019 See, for instance, GA Res. 2775E(XXVI), 29 November 1971.

their jurisdiction from having any dealings with the so-called "independent" Bantustans'.[1020]

It is noteworthy that in both situations, the UN organs did not *directly* impose any obligation under international law for corporations not to recognize a situation resulting from an annexation in violation of a *jus cogens* norm. These resolutions left it to the discretion of the home States to enforce the non-recognition obligation under their own jurisdictions. These States can (but they have no obligation to) take any measure against a corporation doing business in Crimea after the annexation.[1021] In fact, the question of the legality of the continuation of State contracts by companies may be covered by the regime of economic sanctions which have been imposed by many States on Russia. An analysis of these sanctions is clearly beyond the scope of this book. Suffice it to say, that the EU has adopted sanctions that cover a wide range of activities by companies that are now prohibited in Crimea.[1022] Similar sanctions have also been adopted by the United States.[1023] Whether or not a home State decides to take measures against a company that continues doing business in Crimea under a State contract will depend on many factors, including that State's position on the recognition of Russia's annexation of Crimea.[1024] **6.142**

1020 SC Res. 2168th mtg., UN Doc. S/13549, 21 September 1979.

1021 Milano (n 928) 53: 'States may adopt guidelines for national companies on the legal implications of operating and/or investing in Crimea – including the legality of transactions with businesses that own or make use of assets expropriated by the Russian authorities or Crimean authorities.'

1022 The core of the regulations has been summarized by the EU as follows:

- A ban on imports of goods originating in Crimea or Sevastopol unless they have Ukrainian certificates;
- A prohibition to invest in Crimea. Europeans and EU-based companies can no longer buy real estate or entities in Crimea, finance Crimean companies or supply related services. In addition, they may not invest in infrastructure projects in six sectors;
- A ban on providing tourism services in Crimea or Sevastopol. European cruise ships may not call at ports in the Crimean peninsula, except in case of emergency. This applies to all ships owned or controlled by a European or flying the flag of an EU Member State;
- Goods and technology for the transport, telecommunications and energy sectors or the exploration of oil, gas and mineral resources may not be exported to Crimean companies or for use in Crimea;
- Technical assistance, brokering, construction or engineering services related to infrastructure in the same sectors must not be provided.

(See: https://europa.eu/newsroom/highlights/special-coverage/eu_sanctions_en, referring to: Council Regulation (EU) No 692/2014, 23 June 2014 concerning restrictive measures in response to the illegal annexation of Crimea and Sevastopol, http://eur-lex.europa.eu/legal-content/EN/TXT/PDF/?uri=CELEX:02014R0692-20141220&qid=1444987014323&from=EN).

1023 US Department of State, 'Ukraine and Russia Sanctions' (n 835).

1024 Christakis, 'Les conflits de sécession en Crimée' (n 872) 16:

> On peut néanmoins difficilement imaginer comment les pays occidentaux qui ont fait des déclarations aussi fortes sur le fait qu'ils ne 'reconnaîtront jamais' l'annexion de la Crimée par la Russie accepteront que leurs entreprises explorent ou exploitent les ressources pétrolières situées dans les zones maritimes de la Crimée en partenariat avec la Russie … .

6.143 In sum, given the fact that corporations can be considered as partial (and limited) subjects of international law in the specific context of State contracts, it would seem rather logical to also assume that they have obligations under international law. Corporations should indeed be obliged to respect the most fundamental of such obligations, that is, those considered as customary rules. They have thus the obligation not to recognize the new situation resulting from the illegal annexation of Crimea. In my view, this obligation should prevent them from continuing contracts with Russia when the contract had originally been signed with Ukraine. Yet, I have found no example in the past where a non-recognition obligation had been *directly* imposed on corporations. This is clearly an area where international law needs improvement. At the end of the day, while one may argue in favour of the existence of such a global non-recognition obligation, for now it will remain up to each State to decide when and how to concretely implement sanctions against corporations doing business under State contracts in Crimea.

6.3.2 The effect of the annexation on investment treaties

6.144 This section will first examine the legal consequences that the annexation has had on the BITs to which Ukraine and Russia were a party before the events (Section 6.3.2.1).[1025] I will then examine the specific fate of the Ukraine-Russia BIT (Section 6.3.2.2).

6.3.2.1 The application in Crimea of BITs to which Ukraine was a party

6.145 This section will explain the reasons why BITs to which Ukraine was a party will continue to apply to the territory of Crimea after the annexation, even if it is now under Russian control. I will then examine the practical consequences of such a unique situation.

6.3.2.1.1 The MTF rule for transfer of territory should not apply to the case of Crimea

6.146 As mentioned above, at first sight, the annexation of Crimea has all the signs (from a technical stand point) of a 'transfer' of territory (Crimea) from one State (Ukraine) to another (Russia). Article 29 VCLT and Article 15 VCST provide for the application of the MTF rule. The application of this principle to the case of Crimea would result in two consequences: on the one hand, the treaties of the predecessor State (Ukraine) would cease to be in force from the date of the annexation on the territory of Crimea. On the other hand, the successor State's treaties (Russia) would come into force with respect to that territory from that date. In other words, if the MTF rule was applied, the BITs

1025 As of 1 January 2017 Ukraine had signed 75 BITs, 65 of which were in force. See list: UNCTAD, http://investmentpolicyhub.unctad.org/IIA/CountryBits/219.

entered into by Russia with other States would apply in Crimea. Ukrainian BITs would simply no longer apply to this territory.

However, as noted above,[1026] there is one fundamental reason why the case of Crimea should not be considered as one of a transfer of territory.[1027] Since the 'transfer' was the result of the illegal use of force by Russia, one should instead speak of the 'annexation' of Crimea, which is illegal under international law. Article 6 of the Convention indicates that the MTF rule set out at Article 15 VCST *does not* apply to situations that do not occur 'in conformity with international law'.[1028] The logical consequence of that finding would be that the MTF rule *does not* apply to the annexation of Crimea.[1029] **6.147**

While admitting this limitation, two writers seem to somehow doubt the application of this general rule when stating that 'it would nonetheless be an oversight not to notice that the VCST, unlike the VCLT, has only been ratified by a handful of States'.[1030] These writers also noted that Ukraine was a party to the 1978 Convention, but not Russia. The fact that Ukraine ratified the Vienna Convention in 1992 is quite relevant here. It means that Ukraine has specifically agreed to the general principle embodied at Article 6. It also means that Ukraine agreed, more generally under Article 7 of the Convention,[1031] that the principles contained in the instrument would apply to any *future* situation (i.e., post-1992) involving matters of State succession. When signing the Convention, Ukraine therefore consented, inter alia, for the MTF rule set out at Article 15 VCST to *not* apply in the event that its territory would be subject to an illegal transfer of territory under international law.[1032] **6.148**

Another writer has argued that if Articles 29 VCLT and 15 VCST do *not* apply to the situation of annexation, 'the customary equivalent to the rule reflected in [these provisions] applies by default'.[1033] According to this author, 'a treaty could arguably apply with respect to [a] territory that a State controls and over which it claims sovereignty, *even if unlawfully*'.[1034] It is true that the **6.149**

1026 See, Chapter 6, Section 6.2.1.

1027 Costelloe (n 368) 348.

1028 Tanzi and Iapichino (n 366) 554–5.

1029 Costelloe (n 368) 348: noting that the MTF rule under Arts 29 VCLT and 15 VCST 'does not extend to territory over which a State party cannot claim title, such as annexed territory. A separate, supplementary rule, if any, would regulate the applicability of a treaty to such territory'.

1030 Repousis and Fry (n 90) 447.

1031 For an analysis of this provision, see Kaboré (n 17) 227ff.

1032 See, discussion above at Chapter 6, Section 6.2.6.

1033 Costelloe (n 368) 358.

1034 Ibid. (emphasis added). See also 359:

> A territory that a State controls and over which it claims sovereignty could conceivably include one that a State has forcibly acquired and annexed. The point to note, as the Singapore High Court did in

rules of State succession that reflect customary law will continue to apply to a situation of illegal annexation.[1035] It is also true (as mentioned above[1036]) that the *Sanum* Arbitral Tribunal, the Singapore High Court, and the Court of Appeal of Singapore have considered that the MTF rule contained at Articles 29 VCLT and 15 VCST is reflective of a rule of custom.[1037] It should therefore logically follow that the MTF rule should after all apply to the situation of Crimea. This would mean that the BITs entered into by Russia with other States would now apply to the territory of Crimea.

6.150 However, as noted by Gaggioli, all will depend on how other States *react* to a claim in favour of the application of these treaties to the territory of Crimea.[1038] States may indeed oppose such a claim by invoking a violation of a *jus cogens* norm.[1039] There are good reasons for arguing that, as a matter of principle, the MTF rule simply cannot apply to an illegal annexation of territory. The goal of Article 6 of the Convention is to prevent giving any *legal* effect to an *illegal* situation.[1040] In the context of Crimea, the aim is to *prevent* the 'normal' application of the MTF rule under which Russia's treaties would simply apply in Crimea. This is because the annexation of Crimea is anything but a 'normal' situation whereby Russia could benefit from the rights existing under rules of State succession in its newly acquired territory. In my view, the application of the MTF rule to the specific situation of Crimea (based on the ground that it is a rule of custom) would clearly undermine the purpose of Article 6 of the Convention. Moreover, any such application of the MTF rule should be considered as an implicit recognition by other States of the *effectivité* of an illegal action under international law.[1041] This is all the more true given the fact that the application of the MTF rule in this specific case would be contrary to the objective of *another rule of custom*: the non-recognition of unlawful situations arising from the use of force. The annexation of Crimea

government of *Laos v. Sanum*, is that neither Article 29 VCLT nor Article 15 VCST is absolute. Both by their terms allow for departures from the default position on territorial application. Moreover, Articles 29 VCLT and 15 VCST, and the rule of general international law they reflect, generate a presumption in favour of a treaty's application to a party's entire territory, but do not necessarily create a presumption that a treaty's application is limited to a party's territory.

1035 Gagglioli (n 941) 218–20.

1036 See, Chapter 5, Sections 5.2.2.2., 5.2.3.2., and 5.2.4.1.

1037 *Sanum*, Award, 2013 (n 370) [221] (see, also [222]–[224]); *Sanum*, Judgment, Singapore of Court of Appeal, 2016 (n 365) [47]. The same position has also been taken by many writers, including Gagglioli (n 941) 220. See, Chapter 5, Section 1.1.1.

1038 Gagglioli (n 941) 220.

1039 Ibid., 220–21.

1040 Ibid., 223. See also: Ofilio, 'Occupants, Beware of BITs (n 977), fn 19: 'The application of the moving treaty-frontier rule to an illegally annexed territory – i.e., occupied territory – would result in the protection of foreign investments at the expense of the sovereignty of the ousted government.'

1041 Ibid.

should be considered as a case of 'illegal' succession which 'devrait être considérée comme nulle et non avenue et comme ne produisant pas d'effets juridiques'.[1042] For all of these reasons, States should strongly reject the application of Russia's BITs to the territory of Crimea (even if the MTF rule is considered as custom).

While recognizing that the MTF rule set out at Article 15 VCST does not apply to the case of the illegal annexation of Crimea, two writers have recently stated that Article 29 VCLT could find application.[1043] They have highlighted the fact that the provision refers to a treaty being binding upon each party in respect of its '*entire* territory'.[1044] In fact, in their view, some examples of State practice 'might further support the argument of a broad reading of Article 29 VCLT that would also encompass annexed territories'.[1045] According to them, such an interpretation would be in accordance with the purpose of BITs, which is to protect investors and that, logically, more investors would be covered in the event that the Russian BITs were to apply to Crimea.[1046] In my view, without any evidence to the contrary, Article 29 VCLT would normally solely apply to situations in conformity with international law. Thus, the expression '*entire* territory' should be considered as a reference to a State's *de jure* territory. The ordinary meaning of the term 'territory' found in a fundamental multilateral treaty such as the VCLT should not be understood as including a territory under occupation which has been illegally annexed by the use of force.[1047] **6.151**

1042 Ibid., 224.

1043 Richard Happ and Sebastian Wuschka, 'Horror Vacui: Or Why Investment Treaties Should Apply to Illegally Annexed Territories', (2016) 33(3) *J Int Arb* 255ff.

1044 Ibid., 258.

1045 The argument is developed more generally (i.e., without referring to the situation in Crimea) in: ibid., 259, see also at 260ff.

1046 Ibid., 259, see also at 260. Another argument put forward by them is that 'the rationale of the decision in *Sanum v. Laos* validly supports the idea of extending the protection of an annexing State's investment treaties to annexed territories, at least as long as the treaty's wording does not provide to the contrary' (at 259, see also at 262).

1047 Costelloe (n 368) 358:

> Neither Article 29 nor its commentary mentions territory over which a State exercises *de facto* authority, yet which is not legally part of that State's territory. However, the use of the term 'territory of each party' in Article 29 seems to reflect the understanding that only territory which is *de jure* part of a State is included. The same holds true for the term 'territory of another State' in Article 15 VCST. Here, too, the obvious implication is that the provision applies only to *de jure* territory. These unqualified provisions simply do not address a situation of extraterritorial application, though they do not exclude such a possibility. It would be straining the text to an impermissible extent to read into these provisions an exception to the otherwise only *de jure* character of 'territory', since that term cannot by itself sustain a reading that includes annexed territory and, in fact, that is not what these provisions were designed for.

See also at 378:

> The moving treaty-frontiers rule is itself formulated by reference to 'territory'. The rule, however, may not permit a reading of the term 'territory' in such a way that includes annexed territory, which is *ex*

6.152 In sum, as a matter of principle, the MTF rule should not apply to the case of Crimea and, consequently, treaties to which Russia is a party should not find application on this territory. As further discussed below,[1048] there is one specific exception to that general principle allowing for the extension of human rights treaties from the occupying power to the occupied territory. In that case, the goal is to provide basic human rights protection *to the local population* living in the territory controlled by a foreign power, *despite* the illegality of its presence there. Clearly, the same logic cannot apply to BITs whose purpose is to provide legal protections to *foreign* investors.

6.3.2.1.2 The effect of an armed conflict and the possibility of the termination/ suspension of BITs

6.153 The effect of an armed conflict on treaties is a complicated question, which has recently been examined by scholars in light of the events in Crimea.[1049] Importantly, the question is not limited to the Crimean situation, but also, more generally, to the conflict in Eastern Ukraine since a portion of that territory is occupied by Russian troops. The VCLT does not cover the subject of armed conflict.[1050] Under Article 39 of the Vienna Convention, its provisions 'shall not prejudge any question that may arise in regard to the effects of a succession of States in respect of a treaty from (…) the outbreak of hostilities between States'.[1051] This means that any question of State succession in the context of a war between two States must necessarily take into account existing rules dealing specifically with the effect of hostilities on treaties.[1052] The ILC has recently adopted its 'Draft Articles on the Effects of Armed Conflict on Treaties' ('AREAC') with the aim of codifying customary

---

hypothesi not part of the annexing State's de jure territory. The same holds true for an unqualified reference to 'territory' in a treaty's provisions (…).

1048 See, Chapter 6, Section 6.3.2.1.4.

1049 Repousis and Fry (n 90) 424ff; See also Josef Ostfansky, 'The Termination and Suspension of Bilateral Investment Treaties due to an Armed Conflict', (2015) 6 *J Int'l Disp Settl* 145–55 (2015); Christoph Schreuer, 'The Protection of Investments in Armed Conflict', in Freya Baetens (ed), *Investment Law Within International Law* (CUP 2013) 3, 5 (see also: Christoph Schreuer, 'The Protection of Investments in Armed Conflict' (2012) 3 TDM); Arnold Pronto, 'The Effect of War on Law What Happens to Their Treaties When States Go to War?' (2013) 2 *Cambridge JICL* 227, 233; Daniel Joyner, 'Termination and Suspension of Investment Treaties as a Consequence of Armed Conflict', *International Investment Law & the Law of Armed Conflict*, 5–6 October 2017, Athens Colloquium; Danae Azaria, 'Foreign investment treaties and the ILC Draft Articles on the Effect of Armed Conflicts on Treaties', ibid; Gabriele Gagliani, 'Supervening Impossibility of Performance and the Effect of Armed Conflict on Investment Treaties: What Room for Manoeuvre?', ibid; Michail Risvas, 'Non-Discrimination and the Protection of Investments during and after Armed Conflict', ibid.

1050 Thus, Art. 73 indicates that the VCLT does not prejudice questions that 'may arise in regard to a treaty (…) from the outbreak of hostilities between States'.

1051 Vienna Convention on Succession to Treaties (n 5).

1052 On this question, see: O. Corten, 'Article 39' in Distefano, Gaggioli and Hêche (n 4), 1316, 1320, 1323–6.

international law on the matter.[1053] Under the AREAC, the general principle of the effects of armed conflict on treaties is the continued operation of those treaties.[1054] As a matter of principle, the armed conflict in Crimea does not affect the continuing operation of Ukrainian BITs on that territory.[1055]

6.154 The AREAC provides a number of exceptions to the general principle of the continued operation of treaties. The first is when a treaty contains an express provision regarding its operation in situations of armed conflict (Art. 4), which is rarely the case for BITs.[1056] Some BITs include so-called 'security clauses' under which the host State may take safety measures in situations of armed conflict.[1057] BITs also contain 'war clauses', which provide compensation for losses arising from such a conflict.[1058] The Ukraine-Russia BIT contains this clause.[1059] The full protection and security standard is also relevant when it comes to the protection of investments in situations of armed conflict.[1060]

1053 ILC, Draft Articles on the Effects of Armed Conflict on Treaties, with Commentaries, UN Doc. A/66/10, *Yearbook ILC*, Vol. II (part 2) (2011) (hereinafter 'AREAC'). The Articles were subsequently adopted by the UN General Assembly in 2011.

1054 AREAC, ibid, Art. 2 provides that: 'The existence of an armed conflict does not *ipso facto* terminate or suspend the operation of treaties: (a) as between States parties to the conflict; (b) as between a State party to the conflict and a State that is not.'

1055 See, more generally (and not taking position on the Crimea situation): Schreuer, 'The Protection of Investments in Armed Conflict' (n 1049) 5 ('as a rule, treaties dealing with the protection of foreign investment, such as bilateral investment treaties, continue to apply after the outbreak of armed hostilities').

1056 Repousis and Fry (n 90) 427.

1057 Ibid.; Schreuer, 'The Protection of Investments in Armed Conflict' (n 1049) 16ff. See also: William Burke-White and Andreas Von Staden, 'Investment Protection in Extraordinary Times: The Interpretation and Application of Non-Precluded Measures Provisions in Bilateral Investment Treaties', (2008) 48 *Virgina JIL* 324–37; Diane Desierto, *Necessity and National Emergency Clauses: Sovereignty in Modern Treaty Interpretation* (Brill 2012) 9 17, 145–50; Merryl Lawry-White, 'International Investment Arbitration in a Jus Post Bellum Framework', (2015) 16 *J World Inv and Trade* 633, 651.

1058 Schreuer, 'The Protection of Investments in Armed Conflict' (n 1049) 12; Lawry-White, ibid.; Suzanne Spears and Maria Fogdestam-Agius, 'Protection of Investments in War-Torn States: A Practitioner Perspective on War Clauses in Bilateral Investment Treaties', *International Investment Law & the Law of Armed Conflict*, 5–6 October 2017, Athens Colloquium; Gabriel Bottini, 'Reflections on the Origins and Evolution of War and Civil Disturbance Clauses', ibid; Athina Fouchard Papaefstratiou, 'Armed Conflicts Clause in Investment Treaties: Minimum Protection or lex specialis?', ibid.

1059 Agreement Between the Government of the Russian Federation and the Cabinet of Ministers of the Ukraine on the Encouragement and Mutual Protection of Investments, 27 November 1998, available at: http://investmentpolicyhub.unctad.org/Download/TreatyFile/2233 [hereinafter 'Ukraine-Russia BIT'], Art. 6 reads as follows:

> The investors of one Contracting Party whose investments suffered damage on the territory of the other Contracting Party as a result of war, civil disturbances or other similar circumstances, shall be granted a regime no less favorable than the one which the latter Contracting Party is granting to investors of any third state with respect to any measures which it undertakes in connection with such damage.

1060 Repousis and Fry (n 90) 431; Schreuer, 'The Protection of Investments in Armed Conflict' (n 1049) 3, 5ff. See also: Gleider I. Herández, 'The Interaction Between Investment Law and the Law of Armed Conflict in the Interpretation of Full Protection and Security Clauses', in Baetens (n 1049), 21, 33, 45; Sébastien Manciaux, 'The Full Protection and Security Standard in Investment Law: An Obligation of Result or an Obligation of Conduct?', *International Investment Law & the Law of Armed Conflict*, 5–6 October 2017,

These clauses are applicable during an armed conflict[1061] and do not affect the continuous operation of BITs during that time.[1062]

6.155 In the event that the BIT does *not* contain a specific clause on the issue at hand, the AREAC provides under Article 6 for the application of a test to determine whether a treaty is susceptible to termination, withdrawal, or suspension in the event of an armed conflict. This test requires the examination of both:

(a) the nature of the treaty, in particular its subject matter, its object and purpose, its content and the number of parties to the treaty; and
(b) the characteristics of the armed conflict, such as its territorial extent, its scale and intensity, its duration and, in the case of non-international armed conflict, also the degree of outside involvement.

6.156 With respect to point (a), Article 7 of the AREAC and its Annex include an indicative list of treaties whose 'subject matter implies that they continue to operate during an armed conflict'.[1063] The list does *not* specifically refer to BITs, but mentions, inter alia, treaties of friendship, commerce and navigation (FCNs) and human rights treaties. The ILC Commentary states that while the 'friendship' element of FCNs 'are unlikely to survive to an armed conflict opposing the Contracting States', it also adds that this 'does not mean that provisions relating to the status of foreign individuals do not continue to apply, that is, provisions regarding their "private rights"'.[1064] A number of passages from the Commentary suggest that the ILC considered BITs as 'agreements concerning private rights' falling under the category of FCNs treaties.[1065]

Athens Colloquium; Eric De Brabandere, 'The Subjectivity of Full Protection and Security and the Due Diligence Standard', ibid; Ira Ryk-Lakhman, ''Reasonable' Protection and Security of Foreign Investments in Armed Conflicts', ibid; Merryl Lawry-White, 'International Investment Arbitration and Standards Applicable in Conflict: Parallel or Merging Worlds?', ibid; Catharine Titi, 'The Life Cycle of Investment Protections in Times of Armed Conflict: Survival and Revival in *Ius in Bello* and *Ius Post Bellum*', ibid.

1061 Ostfansky (n 1049) 143–4.

1062 Repousis and Fry (n 90) 432; ibid., 145.

1063 AREAC (n 1053) 21.

1064 Ibid., 28.

1065 Thus, with respect to 'Treaties relating to the international settlement of disputes by peaceful means, including resort to conciliation, mediation, arbitration and judicial settlement treaty' the Commentary indicates that this category of treaties is between States and added that 'it does not include treaty mechanisms of peaceful settlement for the disputes arising in the context of private investments abroad which may, however, come within group (e) as "agreements concerning private rights"' (section (e) deals with *Treaties of friendship, commerce and navigation and agreements concerning private rights*, see, ibid., 38). In the section dealing with the category of 'Treaties for the international protection of human rights', the Commentary mentions that 'the use of the category of human rights protection may be viewed as a natural extension of the status accorded to treaties of FCN and analogous agreements concerning private rights, including bilateral investment treaties' (ibid., 33).

Based on these comments, it has been argued that BITs should also continue to operate during an armed conflict because their aim is to protect private rights.[1066] This view has been contested by others[1067] who have argued that under Article 11 of the AREAC while some BIT provisions may be suspended/terminated as a result of an armed conflict, others (such as the full protection and security and the fair and equitable treatment clause) would remain in force.[1068]

In any event, other provisions of the AREAC could apply to the Crimean situation. Article 14 suggests that Ukraine may be entitled to suspend the operation of a BIT, at least with respect to part of its territory under Russian occupation (Crimea and part of Eastern Ukraine), because it is in a situation of self-defence against the Russian aggression.[1069] It could be argued that the 'operation' of the BIT (i.e., providing legal protection to foreign investors in the territory of Crimea) is indeed 'incompatible with the exercise' of Ukraine's self-defence. In other words, Ukraine cannot simultaneously provide full protection and security to foreigners in the territory of Crimea and part of Eastern Ukraine while fighting an armed aggression against Russia. Article 14 could have been invoked by Ukraine regarding the Ukraine-Russia BIT. It would indeed seem illogical that Russia, having committed an aggression against Ukraine in the territory of Crimea, could argue at the same time that Ukraine is under the obligation under the BIT to continue to provide protection (such as full protection and security) to Russian investors doing business in Crimea.[1070] In contrast, it would seem that under Article 15 of the AREAC, Russia would not be allowed to terminate or withdraw from the BIT or suspend its operation because it committed an act of aggression.[1071] **6.157**

1066 Repousis and Fry (n 90) 430; Schreuer, 'The Protection of Investments in Armed Conflict' (n 1049) 7; Happ and Wuschka (n 1043) 248.

1067 Ostfansky (n 1049) 148ff.

1068 Ibid., 155–6.

1069 AREAC (n 1053), Art. 14:

> A State exercising its inherent right of individual or collective self-defence in accordance with the Charter of the United Nations is entitled to suspend in whole or in part the operation of a treaty to which it is a Party insofar as that operation is incompatible with the exercise of that right.

1070 See, ibid., 18, indicating the rationale behind this provision which:

> aims at preventing impunity for the aggressor and any imbalance between the two sides, which would undoubtedly emerge if the aggressor, having disregarded the prohibition on the use of force set out in article 2, paragraph 4, of the Charter, were able, at the same time, to require the strict application of the existing law and thus deprive the attacked State, in whole or in part, of its right to defend itself.

1071 Ibid., Art. 15:

> A State committing aggression within the meaning of the Charter of the United Nations and resolution 3314 (XXIX) of the General Assembly of the United Nations shall not terminate or withdraw from a treaty or suspend its operation as a consequence of an armed conflict that results from the act of aggression if the effect would be to the benefit of that State.

6.158 In any event, the present author is not aware of any party to a BIT entered into by Ukraine having notified the other of the suspension or the termination of the treaty. If that were the case, it remains that the 'survival clause' contained in the BIT would take effect and would protect the investors.[1072] As noted by one writer, 'the survival provisions appear to be a major obstacle to a successful termination of a BIT due to an armed conflict'.[1073] Thus, Articles 70 and 72 VCLT makes it clear that, as put by two writers, 'termination and suspension do not have a retroactive effect and do not affect rights created while the treaty was in force'.[1074] For instance, under Article 14(2), the Ukraine-Russia BIT which came into force on 27 January 2000 was 'valid for a term of ten years' and after that it 'automatically extended each time for another five years' until either party had notified the other of its intention to terminate the Agreement. Article 14(3) explains that 'with respect to the investments which were carried out before the termination of this Agreement and are subject to it, the provisions of all other Articles of this Agreement shall remain valid within the next ten years after that date of termination'.[1075] As a result, a termination of the treaty would not affect the rights of investors to start arbitration proceedings for ten years after this termination.

6.159 Finally, it should be added that while the AREAC provides for specific rules, the more general grounds for termination and suspension in the VCLT remain applicable in time of armed conflict.[1076] Two of them may be relevant in the present case. First, Ukraine could invoke Article 61 VCLT and argue for the 'impossibility of performing a treaty' which results from the 'permanent disappearance or destruction of an object indispensable for the execution of the treaty'. According to one writer, this ground is, however, unlikely to be

1072 Repousis and Fry (n 90) 434. More generally, on survival clauses, see: J. Harrison, 'The Life and Death of BITs: Legal Issues Concerning Survival Clauses and the Termination of Investment Treaties' (2012) 13 *J World Invest & Trade* 928; T. Voon, A. Mitchell and J. Munro, 'Parting Ways: The Impact of Mutual Termination of Investment Treaties on Investor Rights' (2014) 29 *ICSID Rev* 2, 451; A. Tzanakopoulos, 'Denunciation of the ICSID Convention under the General International Law of Treaties' in R. Hofmann and C.J. Tams (eds), *International Investment Law and General International Law: From Clinical Isolation to Systemic Integration?* (Nomos 2011) 75.

1073 Ostfansky (n 1049) 145.

1074 Repousis and Fry (n 90) 435.

1075 Ukraine-Russia BIT (n 1059).

1076 Ostfansky (n 1049) 139, describing the interaction between the VCLT and the AREAC as follows:

> The ILC Draft Articles, therefore, aspire to complement the VCLT by providing for additional grounds for termination or suspension during an armed conflict. However, this does not mean that Article 73 excludes the use of VCLT during the time of armed conflict; it only suggests that the armed conflict may create additional legal repercussions. In this sense, the grounds for termination and suspension in the VCLT certainly remain applicable, as far as their conditions are met. Two of the VCLT grounds are relevant during the time of war or insurrection: the supervening impossibility of performance under Article 61, and the fundamental change of circumstances (rebus sic stantibus) under Article 62.

successful given the fact that the provision connotes 'material impossibility'.[1077] Second, Ukraine could argue under Article 62(1) VCLT that a 'fundamental change of circumstances' (i.e., the annexation of Crimea by Russia) 'has occurred with regard to those existing at the time of the conclusion of a treaty, and which was not foreseen by the parties'. It has been noted that this argument also has a limited chance of success.[1078] In any event, this discussion remains rather theoretical at this stage. To the present author's best knowledge, Ukraine or any of its BIT treaty partners have not notified their intention to suspend or terminate any BITs because of the war in Crimea.

6.3.2.1.3 In practical terms, foreign investors benefit from no BIT protection in Crimea

The conclusion I have reached in the previous sections is that the BITs to which Ukraine was a party should continue to apply to the territory of Crimea after the annexation. As a matter of principle, these Ukrainian BITs continue to offer legal protection to the foreign investors of the other contracting parties doing business in Crimea. This means, in turn, that Ukraine remains, as a matter of principle, responsible under these BITs for any violation of the treaty committed in Crimea *after* the date of annexation. Ukraine remains, for instance, responsible for the obligation to provide foreign investors with full protection and security, a fair and equitable treatment, and legal protection against acts of expropriation. **6.160**

1077 Ostfansky (n 1049) 140–41. For him, 'as long as foreign investors have investments in the country, the impossibility does not come in question', adding that 'even their disappearance, with a stretch of imagination, cannot ever be claimed as permanent, making the invocation of the impossibility, simply, impossible'. Costelloe (n 368) 374–5 takes a different position:

> The general consequence of these rules is termination, which may well be an appropriate result if the treaty was *intuitu personae* and related specifically to the territory in question. Termination would seem particularly appropriate where the annexing State's effective control over the territory endures or is anticipated to endure indefinitely or for a very long period of time.

1078 It is not clear to what extent 'the existence of those circumstances' (i.e., the fact that Crimea was part of the territory of Ukraine when the treaty was signed) 'constituted an essential basis of the consent of the parties to be bound by the treaty'. Thus, any BIT signed by Ukraine apply to its *entire* territory and none of them were specifically designed to apply only to Crimea. See, discussion in: Ostfansky (n 1049) 139–40. See, however, Costelloe (n 368) 374 taking a different position:

> That doctrine, which in practice is limited to exceptional circumstances and finds application only in exceptional cases, seems, however, to have be designed precisely for changes as fundamental as the identity of the State in control of a certain territory. Consequently, it is conceivable that if a treaty was *intuitu personae* and related specifically to certain territory, an annexation of that territory by a third State could conceivably lead to the treaty's termination or suspension under the doctrine of *rebus sic stantibus*.

In any event, it is also not clear to what extent 'the effect of the change' (i.e., the fact that Crimea is no longer part of the territory of Ukraine) is 'radically to transform the extent of obligations still to be performed under the treaty'.

6.161 Yet, the question of the application of Ukrainian BITs to Crimea will only have any real and concrete implications in the event that a foreign investor starts a claim against Ukraine alleging violations of the BIT in the territory of Crimea. Ukraine's line of defence in any such proceedings would certainly centre around the fact that while it has sovereignty over Crimea, the territory is nevertheless presently under foreign occupation by Russia. The reality is that Ukraine has effectively *no control* over what is happening on the ground in Crimea since its annexation by Russia. Even if Ukraine is, as a matter of principle, still responsible to continue to offer legal protection to foreign investors, the fact of the matter is that it simply *cannot.*

6.162 The following paragraphs tentatively explore some of the arguments which could be raised by Ukraine in the context of any such proceedings.[1079] For instance, Ukraine could invoke the argument of *force majeure* and its impossibility to provide legal protections existing under BITs after the annexation.[1080] The ILC Commentary to Article 23 of the ILC Draft Articles on State responsibility[1081] specifies that a situation of *force majeure* precluding wrongfulness only arises when three elements are met. The first two elements require that an act 'must be brought about by an irresistible force or an unforeseen event' which is 'beyond the control of the State concerned'.[1082] The third element requires that the situation 'makes it materially impossible in the circumstances to perform the obligation'.[1083] The ILC Commentary further specifies that such 'material impossibility of performance giving rise to *force majeure* may be due to a natural or physical event (…) or to human intervention'.[1084] One of the examples referred to in the ILC Commentary is the 'loss of control over a portion of the State's territory as a result of an insurrection or devastation of an area by military operations carried out by a third State'.[1085] Without going into detail, it would seem that the events in Crimea fulfil the conditions for the application of Article 23 of the ILC Draft

1079 This analysis is meant to be preliminary and does not in any way intend to cover all possible arguments. See, discussion in: Costelloe (n 368) 373–4; Jure Zrilic, '*Force majeure* as a Defence against Conflict-Related Investment Claims', *International Investment Law & the Law of Armed Conflict*, 5–6 October 2017, Athens Colloquium.

1080 Costelloe (n 368) 375. More generally, Schreuer, 'The Protection of Investments in Armed Conflict' (n 1049) 18ff.

1081 ILC Draft Articles on State Responsibility (n 923), Art. 23 reads as follows:

> The wrongfulness of an act of a State not in conformity with an international obligation of that State is precluded if the act is due to *force majeure*, that is the occurrence of an irresistible force or of an unforeseen event, beyond the control of the State, making it materially impossible in the circumstances to perform the obligation.

1082 ILC Commentary on Articles on State Responsibility (n 927) 76, 170.

1083 Ibid.

1084 Ibid.

1085 Ibid.

Articles. Ukraine could indeed argue that the Russian occupation of the territory of Crimea makes it 'materially impossible in the circumstances to perform' in Crimea the obligation contained in BITs.

In reality, it is Russia which exercises *de facto* authority over the territory of Crimea since the annexation. It is therefore Russia which should be responsible for the actions that have taken place in Crimea since its annexation. But, as noted by one writer, 'the annexing State, even though it effectively controls the annexed territory, cannot be deemed to have succeeded to any obligations the original or *de jure* sovereign had entered into in relation to that piece of land'.[1086] Regardless, as further explained below,[1087] there are good reasons to argue that Crimea should not be considered as part of the territory of Russia under BITs entered into by Russia with other States. This is especially the case for States which have not recognized the annexation of Crimea by Russia.[1088] **6.163**

In practical terms this means that foreign investors doing business in Crimea would benefit from *none* of the protection existing either under Ukraine's BITs or Russia's BITs. The situation can be summarized as follows: **6.164**

- the legitimate authority in Crimea (Ukraine) *cannot* effectively provide legal protection to investors on the ground;
- the only State which could provide legal protection to investors (Russia) is *prevented* from doing so because the authority it exercises in Crimea is illegal.[1089]

1086 Happ and Wuschka (n 1043) 253.

1087 See, Chapter 6, Section 6.3.2.2.2.

1088 Jones Day (n 975):

> On the other hand, the tribunal's jurisdiction under BITs is based on consent, and even if Russia consents that its territory includes Crimea, this may be insufficient because it would be important how the other Contracting State to the relevant BIT interprets the term 'territory' of the Russian Federation in the BIT. For example, as France, the Netherlands, UK and Germany have not recognized Russia's annexation of Crimea as lawful under international law, there would appear to be no consent for the arbitration of disputes arising out of investments made in Crimea under Russia's BITs with these countries.

1089 See, more generally (i.e., without referring to the situation in Crimea): Happ and Wuschka (n 1043) 255:

> In relation to our hypothetical investors' claims, a tribunal might, in light of the above, feel tempted to read the applicable territorial requirements *stricto sensu*. This, in turn, would exclude any protection under either of the two potentially relevant investment treaties (assuming the investors are nationals of a third state). The investors could not rely on an investment treaty between their home state and the state that lost the territory, because that state cannot be considered responsible. They also could not rely on an investment treaty between their home state and the annexing state, because the tribunal, reading the applicable territorial requirements *stricto sensu*, would not consider the annexed area to be part of that state's territory.

6.165 It has been argued by some writers that Russia could somehow be under an obligation to provide legal protection to foreign investors doing business in Crimea which are available under the BITs to which *Ukraine* (… not Russia) was a party.[1090] One obvious objection that Russia would certainly raise in the context of any claim submitted by an investor under such circumstances is the fact that it is not a party to these Ukrainian BITs.

6.166 In sum, as noted by two writers, 'no attribution to the original or *de jure* sovereign of acts committed on that territory can be established' regarding the territory of Crimea.[1091] It has been pointed out by them that the result 'would leave investors in a legal vacuum' as no BIT protection would apply.[1092] Whether or not such a legal vacuum truly exists for them will be examined in the next section.

6.3.2.1.4 The legal protections that Russia must provide to foreign investors as the occupying force in Crimea

6.167 International law imposes important obligations and responsibilities *on Russia*, as the force occupying Crimea.[1093] The applicable rules in the field of

---

1090 Reznik (n 967) 46:

> Though the maxim of *ex injuria jus non oritur* holds that an illegal take-over cannot produce a legally valid outcome the fact that there is no legal title to the territory 'does not release (the occupant) from its obligations and responsibilities under international law towards other states in respect of the exercise of its powers' [citing the ICJ *Namibia* Advisory Opinion]. As a general principle of international law, the occupant has an obligation to care for the 'interests' of the 'nation as represented by the ousted government' and keeping obligations to foreign nationals, as BITs, could be argued an interest of the ousted government. Also, the Principle of Good Administration of the Economy could affect the obligations of an occupant. Where the effect of not complying with a BIT has negative effects on the local economy this principle should obligate the occupant to abide to the provisions of the BIT.

See also at 53:

> an occupant is obligated to comply with a BIT as long as it does not impede with the occupant's security needs nor with the occupant's possibility to achieve the goals of the LOO. As Crimea currently is not affected by hostilities Russia should have far going possibilities to comply with BITs signed by Ukraine, which consequently makes it an obligation for Russia as an occupant.

For the same view, see: Ofilio, 'Occupants, Beware of BITs' (n 977), 4:

> Thus, foreign investors who suffer losses in occupied territories should not bring their claims under BITs between the occupant and the investor's home country. Rather, foreign investors should invoke BITs between the occupied State and their home country. To illustrate, if Russia unlawfully seizes the assets of a German investor in Crimea, the investor should file her claim under the Germany-Ukraine BIT instead of the Germany-Russia BIT. It could be argued that the occupant is not bound by the BITs of the displaced sovereign because it is not a party to any of them. To be sure, States are not bound by obligations to which they have not consented. But in times of occupation, the occupants' consent to comply with BITs in force in occupied territories is expressed 'indirectly' or 'derivatively' in Article 43 of the Hague Regulations. This form of consent not only includes the occupant's submission to the substantive guarantees of the applicable BIT, but also to its dispute resolution provisions.

1091 Happ and Woschka (n 1043), 253.

1092 See, more generally (i.e., without referring to the situation in Crimea): ibid., 255.

1093 See, discussion, Reznik (n 967) 29ff.

humanitarian law continue to apply independently of the BIT.[1094] Without going into the details, suffice it to say that the general protections are contained in the Hague Conventions of 1899 and 1907,[1095] the Fourth Geneva Convention of 1949,[1096] and the Additional Protocol I to the Fourth Geneva Convention of 1949.[1097] Yet, while the definition of 'protected persons' under these instruments is wide enough to cover foreign nationals doing business (and whom have been physically present at a given point) in Crimea after the annexation,[1098] it is true that these rules do not provide much of a detailed guidance as to the exact protection that is actually offered to foreign investors.[1099] In any event, one can agree that they 'do not provide for any kind of protection that would be equivalent to that under international investment law'.[1100] Specifically, they will benefit from no access to international arbitration (unless consent to arbitration can be found in a contract or the host State's laws).

As the occupying force in Crimea, Russia will be bound, on that territory, by the fundamental human rights treaties to which it is a party. This is the conclusion reached by the ICJ in the context of Palestine[1101] and Russia's occupation of part of the territory of Georgia.[1102] Russia is a party to the European Convention of Human Rights, which includes important property rights protection, and must apply it in Crimea.[1103] The reason for applying such treaties in Crimea is to avoid a vacuum whereby individuals would otherwise be left with no legal protection and no State would assume any **6.168**

1094 On this question, see Hernández (n 1060) 24ff.

1095 Convention (IV) respecting the Laws and Customs of War on Land and its annex: Regulations concerning the Laws and Customs of War on Land. The Hague, 18 October 1907.

1096 Convention (IV) relative to the Protection of Civilian Persons in Time of War. Geneva, 12 August 1949.

1097 Protocol Additional to the Geneva Conventions of 12 August 1949 and relating to the Protection of Victims of International Armed Conflicts (Protocol I), 8 June 1977.

1098 Protected persons under the Geneva Conventions is defined at Common Art. 4: 'those who, at a given moment and in any manner whatsoever, find themselves, in case of a conflict or occupation, in the hands of a Party to the conflict or Occupying Power of which they are not nationals'. (with the exceptions for those nationals of states who are not parties to the convention).

1099 Reznik (n 967) 35ff.

1100 Happ and Wuschka (n 1043) 251.

1101 Thus, in its Advisory Opinion in *Wall in the Occupied Palestinian Territory* (n 926) [112], the ICJ held that Israel had to apply in the Palestinian occupied territories the provisions of the International Covenant on Economic, Social and Cultural Rights.

1102 In *Application of the International Convention on the Elimination of all Forms of Racial Discrimination* (n 649) [109], the ICJ concluded that the provisions of the International Convention on the Elimination of All Forms of Racial Discrimination (which entered into force on 4 January 1969) 660 UNTS 195 'generally appear to apply, like other provisions of instruments of that nature, to the actions of a State party when it acts beyond its territory'. This meant that this Treaty, to which Russia was a party, continue to apply during the Russian occupation of part of the territory of Georgia.

1103 European Convention for the Protection of Human Rights and Fundamental Freedoms (in: 213 UNTS 222, see, Art. 1 of Additional Protocol 1.

responsibility.[1104] For this reason, it has been suggested that a human rights treaty 'would apply to a State's entire territory by default' and 'would not be limited to a party's *de jure* territory'.[1105] One can indeed acknowledge the applicability in Crimea of human rights treaties while 'at the same time maintaining a position of non-recognition towards the purported change to the status' of Crimea.[1106] Finally, it has been advanced that some human rights treaties to which the *ousted States* (i.e., Ukraine) was a party to should also continue to apply in a situation of occupation.[1107]

6.169 As a matter of principle, foreign investors will also be protected by rights contained in contracts. The controversial question of 'acquired rights' is further discussed below (in Part D). The issue becomes even more complex when these contracts have been entered into by a company (or an individual) with Ukraine. It is also further complicated by the fact that the economic sanctions imposed by States on Russia may have rendered such contracts void and unenforceable.[1108] Investors will also find legal protections under Russian laws which are concretely applied in the territory of Crimea.

6.170 Finally, as the occupying force in Crimea, Russia must also apply the minimum standard of treatment ('MST') under custom.[1109] This obligation applies to *all States*, including those that have not entered into any BITs. Moreover, it means that this standard of protection can be invoked by *any*

1104 Costelloe (n 368) 361:

> One need only consider the alternative hypothetical in annexed territory to realize its absurdity. In the alternative scenario, the annexing State's treaty obligations would not apply, yet at the same time the dispossessed State could likely plead the non-attribution of a relevant act to it for the purposes of responsibility, or could invoke a circumstance precluding wrongfulness, with the result that effectively no treaty protections remain in place. The position is particularly acute with respect to treaties for the protection of individual rights, the object and purpose of which is to regulate the parties' conduct generally rather than in a territorially limited sense. Something has gone amiss if an individual were not legally in a position to invoke a treaty based right under either instrument even on the strength of an otherwise well-founded claim, simply by virtue of a strict interpretation of the general rule reflected in Article 15 VCST and Article 29 VCLT. It seems an intuitively implausible conclusion that this territory would become a legal vacuum for the purposes of treaty commitments and protections.

1105 Ibid., 362, adding that 'such a determination would be without prejudice, however, to the lawfulness of the exercise of authority over the territory and the question of title'.

1106 Ibid., 375.

1107 Reznik (n 967) 46, indicating that 'except for the application of certain human rights treaties it is all but clear to what extent an occupant must comply with treaties signed by the ousted government'. He is referring to the Venice Commission in 2009 holding that Russia, in the Georgian territories under Russian occupation, should comply with the 1951 Geneva Convention on the Status of Refugees, to which Georgia was a party (Venice Commission, 'Opinion on the law on Occupied territories of Georgia', Final Opinion on the Draft Amendments to the Law on Occupied Territories of Georgia adopted by the Venice Commission at its 81st Plenary Session (Venice 11–12 December 2009).

1108 See, Chapter 6, Section 6.3.1.2.

1109 Reznik (n 967) 39ff, 44.

foreign investor regardless of whether or not its State of origin has entered into a BIT with Russia. The MST is an *umbrella concept*, which *itself* incorporates different elements. The present author has examined the scope and content of the MST elsewhere.[1110] Suffice it to say (in the context of this book) that the MST encompasses (at the very least) an obligation for host States to prevent denial of justice in the administration of justice and to provide due process, an obligation to prevent arbitrary conduct, and an obligation to provide investors with 'full protection and security'.[1111] One of the most controversial questions in the field of investor-State arbitration is whether the fair and equitable treatment standard is one of the elements *encompassed* within the larger umbrella concept of the MST or whether it is an autonomous standard.[1112]

In sum, foreign investors doing business in Crimea will benefit from none of the protections offered under BITs entered into by Russia or Ukraine. While such an outcome is clearly regrettable for investors, they are nonetheless not in a situation of a total legal vacuum. Thus, they will remain protected by certain legal norms but not to the extent they would be expecting under a typical BIT. **6.171**

The next section examines specifically the fate of the Ukraine-Russia BIT after the annexation. **6.172**

6.3.2.2 Arbitration claims filed by Ukrainian investors against Russia under the Ukraine-Russia BIT

A number of claims have recently been filed by Ukrainian investors against Russia for breach of the Russia-Ukraine BIT committed in the territory of Crimea after the annexation.[1113] These claims have been the subject of much **6.173**

1110 See, the analysis of the concept in Dumberry, *Formation and Identification of Rules of Customary International Law* (n 286) 61ff, 94ff.

1111 On this question, see: Kong Soon Lim, 'Armed Conflicts and Customary Law on Investment Protection: Codification and Fragmentation of Protection and Security', *International Investment Law & the Law of Armed Conflict*, 5–6 October 2017, Athens Colloquium.

1112 The present author has examined the question in some detail elsewhere: See, Patrick Dumberry, *The Fair and Equitable Treatment Standard: A Guide to NAFTA Case Law on Article 1105* (Wolters Kluwer 2013) 37ff. Suffice it to say (in the context of the present book) that the fair and equitable treatment standard should be interpreted *in general* as an *independent* treaty standard with an autonomous meaning from the MST. This is certainly the case when a fair and equitable treatment clause is *unqualified* and contains *no* reference whatsoever to international law. The situation is clearly different whenever the FET clause (such as NAFTA Art. 1105) indicates specifically that it is one element of the MST.

1113 Ukraine-Russia BIT (n 1059).

discussion lately.[1114] As of May 2017, the following eight claims had been filed against Russia:[1115]

- *Aeroport Belbek LLC and Mr Igor Valerievich Kolomoisky v. Russia*, PCA Case No 2015–07;
- *PJSC CB PrivatBank and Finance Company Finilon LLC v. Russia*, PCA Case No 2015–21;
- *PJSC Ukrnafta (Ukraine) v. Russia*, PCA Case No 2015–34;
- *(i) Stabil LLC, (ii) Rubenor LLC, (iii) Rustel LLC, (iv) Novel-Estate LLC, (v) PII Kirovograd-Nafta LLC, (vi) Crimea-Petrol LLC, (vii) Pirsan LLC, (viii) Trade-Trust LLC, (ix) Elefteria LLC, (x) VKF Satek LLC, (xi) Stemv Group LLC v. Russia*, PCA Case No 2015–35;
- *Everest Estate LLC et al v. Russia*, PCA Case No 2015–36;
- *(1) Limited Liability Company Lugzor, (2) Limited Liability Company Libset, (3) Limited Liability Company Ukrinterinvest, (4) Public Joint Stock Company DniproAzot, (5) Limited Liability Company Aberon Ltd v. Russia*, PCA Case No 2015–29;
- *NJSC Naftogaz of Ukraine, PJSC State Joint Stock Company Chornomornaftogaz, PJSC Ukrtransgaz, Subsidiary Company Likvo, PJSC Ukrgasvydobuvannya, PJSC Ukrtransnafta, and Subsidiary Company Gaz Ukraiiny v. Russia*, SCC Arbitration Rules;
- *Oschadbank v. Russia*, UNCITRAL.

6.174 The *Aeroport Belbek* and the *PJSC CB PrivatBank* cases are being heard before the same tribunal (consisting of Pierre-Marie Dupuy, Daniel Bethlehem, and Vaclav Mikulka) and the hearing on jurisdiction was held together. The same situation applies to both the *PJSC Ukrnafta* and the *Stabil et al* cases (with the same tribunal consisting of Gabrielle Kaufmann-Kohler, Daniel Price, and Brigitte Stern). The Everest case is examined by a different tribunal (consisting of Andres Rigo Sureda, Michael Reisman, and Rolf Knieper). The *Ludzor* case also has a different panel (Don McRae, Bruno Simma and Eduardo Zuleta). It has been reported that these five separate claims were filed by members of the business empire of the Ukrainian oligarch, Mr. Igor

1114 See, story reported in Iareporter, 'Russia Disputes Round-Up: Updates On Status Of 11 Known Investment Treaty Claims', 19 Jan. 2016, available at: http://www.iareporter.com.proxy.bib.uottawa.ca/articles/first-uncitral-arbitral-tribunal-is-finalized-to-hear-claim-that-russia-is-liable-for-harm-befalling-investments-in-annexed-crimean-peninsula/. See also: Yarik Kryvoi, 'Annexation of Crimea and International Investment Law', *International Investment Law & the Law of Armed Conflict*, 5–6 October 2017, Athens Colloquium; Laura Rees-Evans, 'Litigating the Use of Force: Reflections on the Interaction between Investor-State Dispute Settlement and Other Forms of International Dispute Settlement in the Context of the Conflict in Ukraine', ibid.

1115 See, story reported in Iareporter, available at: http://www.iareporter.com/articles/russia-disputes-round-up-updates-on-status-of-11-known-investment-treaty-claims/.

Kolomoisky.[1116] Another interesting aspect is the fact that both the *NJSC Naftogaz* and the *Oschadbank* cases have been filed by Ukrainian State-owned companies (a point further discussed below[1117]). Since the commencement of the *PrivatBank v. Russia* proceedings, Ukraine has nationalized PrivatBank.

6.3.2.2.1 *Tribunals have to determine their jurisdiction over these claims, even if its uncontested by the parties*

The first obvious and fundamental question which each of these tribunals will have to determine is whether they have jurisdiction over the disputes. In fact, in the *Aeroport Belbek*[1118] and *Everest* cases[1119] the tribunals have decided to bifurcate the proceedings and to address the issues of jurisdiction and admissibility in a preliminary procedure. At the time of writing, the tribunals in the *Everest*,[1120] *Belbek*,[1121] *PJSC CB PrivatBank*,[1122] *Ukrnafta*,[1123] and *Stabil*[1124] cases had rendered their decisions on jurisdiction (to this list should be added the *Lugzor* case). All awards are confidential. The very limited information which has been released (as of December 2017) in the press about these awards will be discussed below. **6.175**

One particular aspect of these proceedings is the fact that the parties do not seem (at first) to deny the jurisdiction of the tribunals and do not appear (at first) to be contesting the application of the BIT to investments made by Ukrainian investors in the territory of Crimea. Thus, in these cases, the investors have argued that the territory of Crimea is now part of Russia because otherwise the BIT simply does not apply to them. Russia is also of the view that Crimea is now part of its territory (Russia has decided not to participate in these proceedings, as further explained below).[1125] It has been argued that since none of the parties to the proceedings is formally contesting the application of the BIT to these disputes, tribunals may not have to decide **6.176**

1116 See, story reported in: Iareporter, 'Russia Disputes Round-Up' (n 1114).

1117 See, Chapter 6, Section 6.3.2.3.1.

1118 *Aeroport Belbek LLC and Mr. Igor Valerievich Kolomoisky v. Russia*, PCA Case No 2015–07, see, PCA Press Release, 6 January 2016.

1119 *Everest Estate LLC et al v. Russia*, PCA Case No 2015–36, see, PCA Press Release, 9 August 2016.

1120 Ibid., Decision on Jurisdiction, 20 March 2017. See, PCA Press Release, 9 August 2016, available at: http://www.italaw.com/sites/default/files/case-documents/italaw8625_0.pdf.

1121 *Aeroport Belbek* (n 1118), Interim Award Addressing Certain Issues of Jurisdiction and Admissibility, 24 February 2017, PCA Press Release, 9 March 2017, available at: https://pcacases.com/web/sendAttach/2090.

1122 *PJSC CB PrivatBank and Finance Company Finilon LLC v. Russia*, PCA Case No 2015–21, Interim Award Addressing Certain Issues of Jurisdiction and Admissibility, 24 February 2017, PCA Press Release, 9 March 2017, available at: https://pcacases.com/web/sendAttach/2093.

1123 *PJSC Ukrnafta (Ukraine) v. Russia*, PCA Case No 2015–34, Awards on Jurisdiction, 26 June 2017, PCA Press Release, 4 July 2017.

1124 *Stabil LLC et al v. Russia*, PCA Case No 2015–35, Awards on Jurisdiction, 26 June 2017, PCA Press Release, 4 July 2017.

1125 Jones Day (n 975).

the controversial question of whether Crimea should be considered as part of the territory of Russia.[1126] Others have suggested that this situation could be considered as an implicit ad hoc submission agreement between the parties in giving jurisdiction to the tribunals over the disputes.[1127]

6.177 In my view, an arbitral tribunal *necessarily* has to decide *ex officio* the question of its jurisdiction *notwithstanding* the position of the parties on the matter. This is based on the principle *iura novit curia*, which has been recognized by tribunals in the context of investment disputes.[1128] As noted by one writer, 'investment tribunals generally consider that they are entitled to and even obliged to conduct an *ex officio* review of their jurisdiction'.[1129] This is because 'arbitrators have a duty to render an enforceable award that is, at the same time, also not prone to challenges'.[1130] In my view, this duty is all the more apparent given the very controversial and highly politically sensitive nature of these proceedings. The question of the legality of the annexation *must* be addressed by them from the outset of the proceedings.[1131]

1126 Repousis and Fry (n 90) 449:

> Could it then be argued that Russia's conduct leads to the conclusion that there is in fact no disagreement between Russia and the disputing investors over the application of the Russia-Ukraine BIT to Crimea? If this were so, an investment tribunal would not have to determine whether it has jurisdiction over the dispute in hand, since the parties would not oppose the application of the Russia-Ukraine BIT to Crimea. There is however one major complication that blocks such an escape route: Russia's non-participation in the proceedings. This is not the first time Russia has not participated in proceedings brought before her. In the cases that are however brought under the Russia-Ukraine BIT, such abstinence is a major complication inasmuch as it shows that investment tribunals will have a difficult task in interpreting the impact of Russia's abstinence to the establishment of their jurisdiction.

See also: Repousis, 'Why Russian Investment Treaties Could Apply to Crimea' (n 880) 12. The same position is also taken by Peter Tzeng, 'Sovereignty over Crimea: a Case for State-to-State Investment Arbitration', (2016) 41(2) *Yale JIL* 462 ('if both parties indeed agree that Crimea constitutes a part of Russia, the tribunals could avoid making a formal determination on the question').

1127 Happ and Wuschka (n 1043) 265: 'this illustrates the possibility of the creation of an ad hoc agreement both for jurisdiction as well as regarding the merits of the dispute. Not only could the annexing state be deemed to have consented to the arbitration procedure by way of non-objection. It might also be deemed to have accepted the investment treaty in question generally to be applicable law between the two parties to the proceedings. Notwithstanding the question whether or not the annexed territory could be considered the territory of the annexing state under international law, the substantive protections of the treaty would then apply by way of an implicit agreement between the parties that their disputes shall be decided according to the terms of the treaty'.

1128 *Metal-Tech Ltd. v. Uzbekistan*, ICSID Case No. ARB/10/3, Award, 4 October 2013 [123] indicating that it 'is the duty of a tribunal established on the basis of a treaty to verify its jurisdiction under that treaty, even if the parties have not objected to it'. See also: *Wintershall Aktiengesellschaft v. Argentina*, ICSID Case No. ARB/04/14, Award, 8 December 2008 [68]; *Gustav F W Hamester GmbH & Co KG v. Ghana*, ICSID Case No. ARB/07/24, Award, 18 June 2010, [94] *Ioan Micula, Viorel Micula, SC European Food S, S.C. Starmill S.R.L. and S.C. Multipick SRL v. Romania*, ICSID Case No. ARB/05/20, Decision on Jurisdiction and Admissibility, 24 September 2008 [65].

1129 Happ and Wuschka (n 1043) 254.

1130 Ibid.

1131 More generally, on this question, see: Sebastian Wuschka, 'The Obligation of Non-Recognition of Situations Created by an Illegal Use of Force before International Investment Tribunals', *International*

In any event, Russia decided to not participate in these proceedings.[1132] Tribunals have nevertheless ordered the continuation of these proceedings.[1133] They have also granted an application from Ukraine to make submissions as a non-disputing party to the BIT in all six cases (a point further discussed below).[1134] It has been suggested by one writer that 'had Russia participated in the proceedings it would have most likely accepted the application of Articles 15 or 31 VCST, but would have raised one of the exceptions to this article'.[1135] But, since Russia is not participating in the proceedings, the same writer then asked the question as to how a tribunal should determine what could have been Russia's approach to the matter.[1136] It may be difficult to infer *anything* from Russia's decision not to participate in the proceedings. What matters is that an arbitral tribunal has to decide the question of jurisdiction *ex officio* in default proceedings (this is what ICSID Arbitration Rule 42(4) provides for, although it does not apply to these cases filed under the UNCITRAL Rules). The question of the legality of the annexation should not be discarded by a tribunal. **6.178**

Investment Law & the Law of Armed Conflict, 5–6 October 2017, Athens Colloquium. *Contra*: Repousis and Fry (n 90) 447 (basing their argument on the 'consensual nature of international arbitration'). See also: Repousis, 'Why Russian Investment Treaties Could apply to Crimea' (n 881) 8. Another argument examined by the author (20ff) is whether a tribunal constituted under the Russia–Ukraine BIT could invoke the *Monetary Gold* principle to deny the vesting of jurisdiction.

1132 In the *Aeroport Belbek* case (n 1118), the tribunal noted that Russia had not appointed any representatives and referred to letters dated 16 June 2015 and 1 July 2015 in which Russia indicated that the '[Ukraine-Russia BIT] cannot serve as a basis for composing an arbitral tribunal to settle [the claimants' claims]', that it 'does not recognize the jurisdiction of an international arbitral tribunal at the [PCA] in settlement of the [claimants' claims]' and, finally, that nothing in its correspondence 'should be considered as consent of the Russian Federation to constitution of an arbitral tribunal, participation in arbitral proceedings, or as procedural actions taken in the framework of the proceedings.' (see, PCA Press Release, 6 January 2016, available at: http://www.pcacases.com/web/sendAttach/1553. The same letters have also been filed by Russia in other cases.

1133 See, *Aeroport Belbek* case (n 1118), Procedural Order No. 3, 30 November 2015; see, PCA Press Release, 6 January 2016. The same orders have been adopted by tribunals in other cases (available at the PCA site).

1134 See, for instance, *Aeroport Belbek* (n 1118), PCA Press Release, 15 August 2016.

1135 Repousis, 'Why Russian Investment Treaties Could apply to Crimea' (n 880) 12. Thus, by relying on the exceptions contained in these provisions, Russia could argue that the BIT does not apply *specifically* to these disputes while being consistent with its basic *general* position that Crimea is now part of the Russian territory. The same writer also suggests (at 13) that Russia could oppose the application of the BIT based on the ground of jurisdiction *ratione temporis*.

1136 Ibid., 13:

> However, Russia is not participating in the proceedings. Should the tribunal then infer that Russia's approach is the one offered above, or should it examine the application of Article 15 or 31 VCST at face value? As already noted, the difference between the two is of fundamental importance. For if Russia's abstinence is read as an acceptance of the application of Article 15 or 31 VCST, then the tribunal has a way out since the tribunal would not have to examine the presupposed legitimacy of the succession. On the contrary, it would need to accept the applicability of Article 15 or 31 VCST at face value and examine whether any of the exceptions to this article are potentially met. In light of this analysis, one may wonder whether Russia's decision not to participate in the proceedings is eventually to the benefit of her expressed position.

6.179 Finally, it should be added that there is an additional complication regarding the proceedings in two of these claims, which have been filed by Ukrainian State-owned enterprises.[1137] The companies are controlled by the government of Ukraine. They certainly have filed such politically sensitive claims with the approval of the appropriate authority from the government of Ukraine. If this is the case (and there is limited information available to assess whether it is the case), this would suggest that Ukraine is of the view that Crimea should be considered *as a part of Russia* for the application of this BIT. This is indeed the only way for Ukrainian investors to claim the benefit of the BIT before these tribunals. This position would be rather strange given the fact that Ukraine has thus far maintained strongly and continuously that its territorial integrity had been breached by Russia as a result of the illegal annexation of Crimea. In my view, this position would seriously undermine Ukraine's claim that Crimea remains part of its territory.[1138] It may be that these proceedings are part of a broader strategy by Ukraine to fight on all possible legal fronts the illegal annexation of Crimea. In any event, such a surprising position by Ukraine will certainly influence tribunals having to decide the question of their jurisdiction over these cases.

6.180 As further examined in the following two sections, in my view, tribunals in the above-mentioned eight cases should, logically, only have jurisdiction over these disputes if they come to the conclusion that Crimea is part of the territory of Russia.[1139]

6.3.2.2.2 The BIT should logically not apply to these disputes because Crimea is not part of the territory of Russia

6.181 The Ukraine-Russia BIT only covers 'Investments' made by 'Investors' of 'one Contracting Party *on the territory* of the other Contracting Party (...)' (Art. 1(1)). Let us assume for the sake of argument that the Ukrainian claimants

1137 One claim has been filed by NJSC Naftogaz of Ukraine and six of its subsidiaries (See, press release, available at: http://www.italaw.com/sites/default/files/case-documents/italaw7648.pdf). The other claim has been filed by the Ukrainian State-owned bank, Oschadbank (see: Iareporter, 'As Yukos Enforcement Grabs Headlines, Russia Has Faced At Least 10 New Treaty Arbitrations Since 2012, With Others Threatened', 14 July 2015, available at: http://tinyurl.com/oytv3av.

1138 See discussion: Repousis, 'Why Russian Investment Treaties Could apply to Crimea' (n 880) 18ff. Relying on the reasoning of the Tribunal in *CSOB v. Slovakia* which focused on the nature rather than the purpose of the activities discharged by the State-owned enterprise, he concluded that 'there are good reasons to assert that claims by state-owned enterprises should not necessarily be regarded as claims filed by the contracting parties to an investment treaty'. If this is the case, he argued that 'the claims of Ukrainian state-owned enterprises would not necessarily reflect Ukraine's position on the territorial application of the Russia–Ukraine BIT to Crimea' (19–20).

1139 Whether or not investment arbitration is the best venue to determine this controversial issue is another question. One writer has expressed doubt about these tribunals' 'legitimacy' to decide the question and has argued that State-to-State arbitration under the Ukraine-Russia BIT would be a more appropriate forum: Tzeng (n 1126) 466ff. This mechanism is examined below at Chapter 6, Section 6.3.2.4.

have made an 'investment' in accordance with the BIT and that they fulfill the *ratione personae* requirements under Article 1(2)b).[1140] The fundamental question remains whether any such investment can be considered as being made 'on the territory of the other Contracting Party', that is, Russia. Thus, in the context of claims filed by Ukrainian claimants, the BIT only provides them with protection if they have made an investment *in Russia.* The problematic aspect of these claims is that claimants alleged violations of the Ukraine-Russia BIT by Russia for actions which have taken place on the territory of *Crimea.* Tribunals therefore have to determine whether Crimea can be considered as part of the territory of Russia at the date of the commencement of the proceedings.[1141] This is the inescapable question that each tribunal needs to address from the outset of the proceedings. That question must be answered by examining the definition of 'territory' in the BIT at Article 1(4): 'the territory of the Russian Federation or the territory of the Ukraine and also their respective exclusive economic zone and the continental shelf as defined in conformity with the international law'.

Three observations can be made about this clause. First, the definition does not refer specifically to the territory of Crimea. This is a rather obvious observation from which not much can be deducted. Thus, the definition of the term 'territory' contained in the BIT does not refer to any specific territories as being part of either State. In any event, such absence is logical given the fact that at the time when the treaty was signed, Crimea was considered by both States as being part of Ukraine. Second, the clause explicitly defines the territories of both States as including their respective exclusive economic zones and continental shelf. As noted by one writer, 'where such territorial restrictions are present, support for arguing that the treaty extends protections beyond *de jure* territory is fairly thin'.[1142] That may be true, but this definition is not unique and is often found in BITs. As such, a reference to the exclusive economic zone and continental shelf does not in itself indicate much as to whether the parties intended for the BIT to cover only *de jure* territory. **6.182**

Third, the clause contains an explicit reference to 'international law'. The use of the words 'as defined in conformity with the international law' were most likely meant to qualify only the territorial scope of the 'exclusive economic zone and the continental shelf'. In other words, the extent of each State's **6.183**

1140 That is, that they are 'legal entity' which have been 'set up or instituted in conformity with the legislation prevailing' in Ukraine and that they are 'legally capable' under Ukrainian legislation 'to carry out investments on the territory of the other Contracting Party'.

1141 On this question, more generally (i.e., without referring to the situation in Crimea), see, Happ and Wuschka (n 1043) 251ff.

1142 Costelloe (n 368) 365.

exclusive economic zone and continental shelf should be in accordance with international law. Another possible interpretation would be that these words were meant to qualify, more generally, the expression 'territory of the Russian Federation'. Thus, the 'territory' of Russia would have to be 'as defined in conformity with the international law'. Under such an interpretation, the 'territory' of Russia would *not* include those parts which were integrated in *violation* of international law. This is in fact the position which has been adopted by certain writers. For Costelloe, 'qualifying words such as "in conformity with international law" limit a treaty's application in certain territories or areas by explicit reference to the international lawfulness of a State's exercise of rights over such territories or areas'.[1143] The question of the *legality* of the annexation of Crimea by Russia is not to be determined under the domestic laws of Russia, but under international law.[1144] As mentioned above,[1145] the annexation of territories by the use of force is illegal under international law. The tribunals in the *Ukrafta* and *Stabil* cases apparently came to the opposite conclusion that the term 'territory' was not limited only to the territory under a State's lawful occupation.

6.184 I have argued above that the only logical way for tribunals to conclude that they have jurisdiction over these claims under the Ukraine-Russia BIT is to consider that the territory of Crimea is now part of Russia under the Ukraine-Russia BIT. This is because the BIT only applies to Ukrainian investors making an investment *in Russia*. Given the BIT's specific features regarding the definition of 'territory', there are good reasons for arguing that a tribunal should *not* come to the conclusion that Crimea is part of Russia for the application of the treaty. Given that under international law Crimea is still part of the territory of Ukraine,[1146] tribunals should, in my view, logically, conclude that they have *no jurisdiction* over disputes submitted by Ukrainian

1143 Ibid., 365. See also, at 366: 'where the exercise of territorial or maritime rights is qualified by words such as "in accordance with international law" the conclusion that the geographic scope of the treaty or an obligation under it is restricted to de jure territory or maritime areas is impossible to overcome'. See also: Rees-Evans (n 1114) 7.

1144 The reason why a tribunal ruling on this question must apply international law is simple. The Ukraine-Russia BIT does not contain a choice of law clause indicating the law applicable to settle disputes under the instrument. When this is the case, under Art. 35 of the UNCITRAL Rules (applicable in the above-mentioned disputes) the tribunal 'shall apply the law which it determines to be appropriate'. The question of the interpretation of the term 'territory' under the BIT will have to be determined under the *Vienna Convention on the Law of Treaties*, 1155 UNTS 331 (to which both Russia and Ukraine are parties). Arts 31 and 32 of the Convention are generally recognized as rules of customary international law on matters of treaty interpretation. Under Art. 31(3)(c), a tribunal should take into account, together with the context of the treaty, 'any relevant rules of international law applicable in the relations between the parties'. The prohibition of annexation of territories by the use of force under custom is clearly one such applicable 'relevant rules of international law'.

1145 See, Chapter 6, Section 6.2.4.

1146 See, Chapter 6, Section 6.2.7.

nationals against Russia under the BIT for events which took place in Crimea after the annexation. At least, this is the solution which would seem to be the most coherent from a 'pure' international law perspective.

Yet, it seems that things are not as 'simple' in the specific context of these claims. Six tribunals (*Belbek*; *Everest*; *PJSC CB PrivatBank*; *Ukrnafta*; *Stabil*; *Lugzor*) have held that they have jurisdiction over these claims. The awards remain confidential. Very limited information is currently available regarding the actual reasoning of these tribunals. The limited information available suggests that the tribunals' decisions may have been influenced by very specific factors and circumstances arising in these claims. **6.185**

It has been reported that the tribunals have held in the *Belbek* and *PJSC CB PrivatBank* cases that Russia 'had obligations to protect Ukrainian investors in Crimea under the Ukraine-Russia BIT from the date of 21 March 2014 onward' (i.e., the date of the formal incorporation of Crimea into the Russian Federation).[1147] The news report on the cases further added that 'it appears that the arbitrators have sidestepped the thorny question as to the lawfulness of the Russian occupation and annexation of Crimea, instead zeroing in on the effectiveness of the occupation and the consequent finding that Russia should be liable for protection of Ukrainian investors in that territory'.[1148] This would suggests that the tribunals have interpreted the expression 'territory of the Russian Federation' solely based on the *de facto* situation on the ground without examining the question of the legality of annexation. The tribunals' decision to (apparently) focus on the effectiveness of the occupation in Crimea may, at first, seems surprising. Yet, their decision was certainly influenced by the position adopted by Ukraine itself, which intervened as a non-disputing party in the arbitration proceedings. Thus, it has been reported that Ukraine 'portrayed the occupation as unlawful, but ultimately effective (such that Russia should subsequently bear the responsibility of protecting Ukrainian investors under the BIT).'[1149] Very limited information is currently available regarding the position which was adopted by Ukraine in these proceedings. Little is also known about the reasoning of the tribunals in the *Ukrnafta* and *Stabil* cases apart from the fact that they upheld their jurisdiction over the **6.186**

1147 IAReporter, 'In Jurisdiction Ruling, Arbitrators Rule That Russia Is Obliged Under Bit To Protect Ukrainian Investors In Crimea Following Annexation', 9 March 2017, available at: https://www-iareporter-com.proxy.bib.uottawa.ca/articles/in-jurisdiction-ruling-arbitrators-rule-that-russia-is-obliged-under-bit-to-protect-ukrainian-investors-in-crimea-following-annexation/. See also: Global Arbitration Review On-line, 'Crimea cases against Russia to proceed', 9 March 2017.

1148 Ibid.

1149 Ibid.

disputes.[1150] The same is true for the *Everest* and *Lugzor* cases in which the tribunals also took the same decisions.[1151] In all of these cases, the awards are confidential.

6.187 The next section examines one additional reason which, in my view, militates in favour of concluding that tribunals should have declined to exercise jurisdiction over disputes submitted by Ukrainian nationals against Russia under the BIT for events which took place in Crimea after the annexation.

6.3.2.2.3 The obligation under custom not to recognize the illegal annexation of Crimea should apply to tribunals

6.188 It should be recalled that General Assembly Resolution 68/262 calls for 'all States, international organizations and specialized agencies' not to recognize any 'alteration of the status' of Crimea and 'to refrain from any action or dealing that might be interpreted as recognizing any such altered status'.[1152] In my view, a tribunal concluding that Crimea is part of Russia for the application of the Ukraine-Russia BIT would undoubtedly fly in the face of both the letter and the spirit of the Resolution. The next paragraphs explain the reasons why.

6.189 It is true that unlike Security Council Resolutions, those adopted by the General Assembly are not mandatory under international law. But, it is also well-known that 'the obligation and content of non-recognition do not depend upon any action by the appropriate political organs of the United Nations'.[1153] In that sense, it does not matter that the obligation of non-recognition was affirmed by the General Assembly, and not by the Security Council. In fact, as noted by Talmon, the fact that 'the obligation arises directly under customary international law is also shown by the fact that, in several cases, the call for non-recognition has been contained in a non-binding resolution of the General Assembly or in a statement of the President of the Security Council,

---

1150 IAReporter, 'An Update on Disputes Under the Russia-Ukraine Bit' 6 July 2017, available at: https://www-iareporter-com.proxy.bib.uottawa.ca/articles/an-update-on-disputes-under-the-russia-ukraine-bit/. See also: IAReporter, 'Investigation': Further Russia Investment Treaty Decisions Uncovered, Offering Broader Window Into Arbitrators' Approaches To Crimea Controversy' 17 Nov. 2017.

1151 IAReporter, 'Russia BIT Claims: Recent Developments in Arbitrations against the Russian Federation', 13 April 2017, available at: https://www-iareporter-com.proxy.bib.uottawa.ca/articles/russia-bit-claims-recent-developments-in-arbitrations-against-the-russian-federation/. A more detailed account of the *Everest* award is found in: IAReporter, 'Investigation: Full Jurisdictional Reasoning Comes To Light In Crimea-Related Bit Arbitration vs. Russia', 9 Nov. 2017. In the *Lugzor* case, the tribunal upheld its jurisdiction but will only provide reasoning in its final award. See, IAReporter, 'Crimea-related Lugzor v. Russia arbitration clears jurisdictional hurdles', 13 December 2017.

1152 GA Res. 68/262.

1153 Talmon (n 925) 113; Dugard, *Recognition and the United Nations* (n 916) 135: resolution 'confirm an already existing duty on States not recognize such situations'.

which do not create any obligation'.[1154] The authoritative value of the obligation of non-recognition of the annexation of Crimea is therefore a consequence of its status as a rule of custom, not by the fact that it was affirmed by one organ of the UN or another.

It is also true that GA Resolution 68/262 is only addressed to 'all States, international organizations and specialized agencies', and not to any other actors.[1155] Yet, as just mentioned, the obligation not to recognize an illegal annexation of territory that occurred in violation of the prohibition of the use of force is largely recognized as a *rule of custom*.[1156] Arbitral tribunals *must* apply rules of custom when deciding disputes under BITs. This is because tribunals will apply international law to solve disputes under BITs. This is the case whether or not the BIT contains a choice of law clause and even in cases where that choice of law does not refer to international law.[1157] At the end of the day, international law will always find application in BIT disputes.[1158] Therefore, when a tribunal is applying international law in these circumstances, it will *necessarily* have to take into account relevant rules of customary international law.[1159] Under Article 31(3)(c) of the Vienna Convention, a tribunal should take into account 'any relevant rules of international law applicable in the relations between the parties', which certainly includes rules of customary international law.[1160] In sum, a tribunal established under the Ukraine-Russia BIT *must* apply the customary obligation of non-recognition of illegal annexation of territories when deciding whether it has jurisdiction over a dispute under this treaty. 6.190

This is *a fortiori* the case given the fact that the illegal annexation of Crimea was in violation of the prohibition of the use of force, which is considered as one of the few existing *jus cogens* norms. There is no doubt that a tribunal must apply *jus cogens* norms. 6.191

1154 Talmon, ibid.

1155 Happ and Wuschka (n 1043) 255–6.

1156 See, Chapter 6, Section 6.2.5.

1157 Dumberry, *Formation and Identification of Rules of Customary International Law* (n 286) 376ff.

1158 The question as to whether or not the same conclusion can also be reached regarding disputes arising from State contracts or the host State's laws is examined ibid., 369ff.

1159 *LG&E Energy Corp., LG&E Capital Corp., and LG&E International, Inc. v. Argentina*, ICSID Case No. ARB/02/1, Decision on Liability, 3 October 2006 [89] ('applying the rules of international law is to be understood as comprising the general international law, including customary international law, to be used as an instrument for the interpretation of the [BIT]'). See also: *ADC Affiliate Ltd & ADC & ADMC Management Ltd v. Hungary*, ICSID Case No. ARB /03/16, Award, 2 October 2006 [290].

1160 The question is examined in detail in Dumberry, *Formation and Identification of Rules of Customary International Law* (n 286) 380ff (examining the position of writers). See: *Saluka Investments BV v. Czech Republic*, UNCITRAL, Partial Award, 17 March 2006 [254]: 'In interpreting a treaty, account has to be taken of "any relevant rules of international law applicable in the relations between the parties" – a requirement which the [ICJ] has held includes relevant rules of general customary international law'.

6.192 The *Methanex* Tribunal made it clear that 'as a matter of international constitutional law a tribunal has an independent duty to apply imperative principles of law or jus cogens and not to give effect to parties' choices of law that are inconsistent with such principles'.[1161] Tribunals established under the Ukraine-Russia BIT therefore have an 'independent duty' to apply *jus cogens* norms, including the prohibition of the use of force.

6.193 According to the ILC, the non-recognition obligation under Article 41(2) of the Draft Articles on State Responsibility does not only cover *formal* recognition 'but also prohibits acts which would imply such recognition'.[1162] In the *Namibia* opinion, the court also affirmed that any dealings with South Africa which may 'imply a recognition that South Africa's presence in Namibia is legal' would be inconsistent with the Security Council's declaration of illegality and as such proscribed.[1163] In my view, an award concluding that the territory of Crimea is part of Russia under the Ukraine-Russia BIT is *implying* a recognition of the annexation of that territory by Russia. Such an award is in fact giving legal effect to a situation in violation of a *jus cogens* norm.

6.194 Even if one were to consider that this non-recognition obligation is formally imposed only on States[1164] (the question as to whether it imposes any obligations on corporations was examined above[1165]), it remains that a tribunal should be particularly sensitive about deciding to exercise its jurisdiction over a dispute under the specific circumstances previously described. This decision could be considered as contrary to international or transnational public policy.[1166] Recent ICSID Tribunals have held that they either lack jurisdiction or that a claim was inadmissible when faced with the illegal conduct of an investor, such as misrepresentations made by the claimant,[1167] fraud,[1168] or bribery/corruption.[1169] In the *World Duty Free*

1161 *Methanex Corporation v. United States*, UNCITRAL, Award, 3 August 2005, Part IV, Chap. C, 11 [24].

1162 ILC Commentary on Draft Articles on State Responsibility (n 927) 114.

1163 *Namibia* Advisory Opinion, 1971 (n 1008) [121, 133].

1164 Milano (n 928) 51:

> A comprehensive approach to non-recognition is not limited to the formal recognition of the legality of the situation as such, such as an act of annexation, but it also extends to all relations, of an economic, political, diplomatic, commercial nature which imply recognition of the illegal situation. In broad terms, and with regard to the application of the doctrine of non-recognition to the situation in Crimea, States and international organizations shall refrain from any formal act of recognition of Russia's legal authority over Crimea and from any act which implies recognition of such authority.

He provides a number of examples of policy measures which could be adopted.

1165 See, Chapter 6, Section 6.3.1.2.

1166 Jones Day (n 975).

1167 *Plama Consortium Ltd. v. Bulgaria*, ICSID Case No ARB/03/24, Award, 27 August 2008 [130–146].

1168 *Inceysa Vallisoletana, S.L. v. El Salvador*, ICSID Case No ARB/03/26, Award, 2 August 2006, [248]–[252].

case, the tribunal mentioned that the concept of 'international or transnational public policy' as 'signifying an international consensus as to universal standards and accepted norms of conduct that must be applied in all fora'.[1170] In that case, the tribunal concluded that it was 'convinced that bribery is contrary to the international public policy of most, if not all, States or, to use another formula, to transnational public policy'.[1171] It is true that in these cases, tribunals dealt with illegal acts committed *by investors*, rather than by the respondent State as in the present case. Yet, it remains that an annexation of territory in violation of a *jus cogens* norm should certainly be considered as contrary to the 'transnational public policy' of all States. At any rate, any award which implies the recognition of an illegal annexation of territory in violation of a *jus cogens* norm could be open for a challenge, an annulment procedure and may also be unenforceable.[1172] At the time of writing, Russia (which did not participate in the arbitral proceedings) started set aside proceedings against the award in Switzerland in the *Ukrnafta* and *Stabil* cases.

For all of these reasons, in my view, tribunals should have concluded that they had no jurisdiction under the Ukraine-Russia BIT over claims filed by Ukrainian investors against Russia for investments made in Crimea. This would mean, in practical terms, that these Ukrainian claimants (as well as all Ukrainian nationals) will be left with no recourse under this BIT for measures taken in Crimea after the annexation. The consequences of such a unique situation are further discussed in the next section. **6.195**

It may be surprising that six tribunals came to the opposite conclusion and held that they in fact had jurisdiction over these claims. Yet, as mentioned above,[1173] the tribunals' decision to (apparently) focus on the effectiveness of **6.196**

1169 *World Duty Free Company Ltd. v. Kenya*, ICSID Case No ARB (AF)/00/7, Award, 4 October 2006 [123, 157]; *Metal-Tech v. Uzbekistan* (n 1128). More generally: Aloysius P. Llamzon, *Corruption in International Investment Arbitration* (OUP 2014). As explained by the Tribunal in *Gustav F W Hamester GmbH & Co KG v. Ghana*, ICSID Case No ARB/07/24, Award, 18 June 2010 [123], 'an investment will not be protected if it has been created in violation of national or international principles of good faith; by way of corruption, fraud, or deceitful conduct; or if its creation itself constitutes a misuse of the system of international investment protection under the ICSID Convention' and 'It will also not be protected if it is made in violation of the host State's law'.

1170 *World Duty Free*, ibid., [139].

1171 Ibid., [157].

1172 Happ and Wuschka (n 1043) 255. While recognizing that an arbitral tribunal would not be 'bound directly nor indirectly by the [non-recognition] obligation', they also added that tribunals 'will presumably be reluctant to make any finding that could be interpreted as recognizing unlawful acquisition of territory as legitimate and thus render their award subject to challenge or annulment or even unenforceable'. But their general conclusion (at 264) is that 'a tribunal, as a consequence, could feel comfortable to apply the principle of non-recognition in a manner that would not allow the annexing state to escape the obligations it had if the acquisition of territory had been lawful'.

1173 See, Chapter 6, Section 6.3.2.2.2.

the occupation in Crimea rather than its illegality was certainly influenced by the position adopted by Ukraine (intervening as a non-disputing party in the arbitration proceedings) which apparently argued that Russia should 'bear the responsibility of protecting Ukrainian investors under the BIT'.[1174] Very limited information is actually available regarding Ukraine's position in these proceedings. Yet, any such position focusing on the effectiveness of the occupation on the ground would be peculiar. In my view, the position (apparently) adopted by Ukraine gives legal effect to the annexation of Crimea, a situation in violation of a *jus cogens* norm. It is therefore rather surprising for Ukraine to have adopted such a position in these proceedings. As mentioned above, it may be that these proceedings filed by Ukrainian investors are in fact encouraged by Ukraine as part of a broader strategy to fight on all possible legal fronts the illegal annexation of Crimea.[1175]

6.3.2.3 Conclusion: should a 'pragmatic' approach be adopted instead?

6.197 Some writers have been critical of the position taken in the previous sections in favour of adopting a '*stricto sensu* interpretation' of the definition of the term 'territory' under Russian BITs and its consequence that investors would no longer benefit from any BIT protection in Crimea. They have argued for the adoption of a 'pragmatic approach' in order to free 'investors from the legal vacuum an annexation might put them in'.[1176] One easy solution to prevent any such 'vacuum' would be to extend Russian BITs to the territory of Crimea. Thus, for some authors in order to determine the territorial scope of a BIT under Article 29 VCLT, what matters is not a State's *de jure* sovereignty over a given territory, but rather whether it exercises *control* over that territory.[1177] While acknowledging that 'the obligation not to recognize illegally acquired territory is said to be well-regarded in general international law', they add that 'there is obviously no clear path, yet, in a situation where non-recognition

1174 IAReporter, 'In Jurisdiction Ruling, Arbitrators Rule That Russia Is Obliged Under Bit' (n 1147).

1175 Rees-Evans (n 1114) 5:

> It would appear that Ukraine has expressly encouraged such claims as part of its 'lawfare' strategy in responding to events in Crimea and beyond. For example, commenting on a dispute between Oscadbank (a Ukrainian State-owned bank) and Russia, the Ukrainian Prime Minister stated that the claim was to compensate for 'the damage and loss inflicted by the Russian Federation's illegal annexation of Crimea and the consequent losses by Oschadbank of revenue and property in Ukrainian territory'. He called onother State-owned companies to bring similar proceedings against Russia to 'recover losses caused by the illegal annexation of Crimea'

(referring to Yatseniuk, *Interfax-Ukraine*, 8 July 2015, <http://en.interfax.com.ua/news/economic/276618.html>, last accessed 15 August 2017).

1176 See, more generally (i.e., without referring to the situation in Crimea): Happ and Wuschka (n 1044) 268, see also 255.

1177 Ibid., 259:

benefits the occupying power'.[1178] Thus, in their view, Russia would benefit from the application of the principle of non-recognition because it would not be responsible under Russian BITs for actions taken place in Crimea. For them, it would result in providing 'for a lesser degree of obligations on the part of the annexing State as if that State had lawfully acquired the territory and the investment treaty was to apply'.[1179] Since this situation 'would contravene the object and purpose of the sanction and frustrate the application of the *ex injuria jus non oritur* principle', these two writers have argued that 'as a matter of policy, the principle of non-recognition cannot be applied strictly to illegally annexed territory' and 'it must be applied in a modified way'.[1180] Tribunals should therefore 'limit the application of the respective treaty only to the annexing State's obligations' without granting Russia any rights under the BITs.[1181] This is, in their view, 'precisely what the obligation of non-recognition and its underlying principle *ex injuria non oritur jus* mandate'.[1182]

6.198 The next paragraphs will briefly examine the arguments put forward by these two writers. The starting point is their affirmation that the goal of the principle of non-recognition 'is that the [annexing] state should not benefit from illegal conduct' and that 'non-recognition serves the purpose of a sanction'.[1183] This is no doubt true. Lauterpacht noted that 'no recognition is based on the view that acts contrary to international law are invalid and cannot become a source of rights for the wrongdoer'.[1184] As a matter of principle, the wrongdoer should not benefit from the annexation. Whether or not non-recognition should be considered as a 'sanction' is controversial. Some writers have endorsed this position.[1185] Yet, as noted by Crawford, non-recognition 'is

---

> As long as the annexing state excludes the former sovereign on the annexed territory from the exercise of any rights on that territory, thereby exercising *de facto* sovereignty, it cannot be decisive whether it exercises *de jure* sovereignty, as well. Any other approach would frustrate both the obligation of non-recognition as well as the effective implementation of obligations under a treaty. Accepting the state's exercise of control as sufficient to satisfy the territorial requirement of a treaty could, from a policy perspective, be the way to grant the provisional recognition required to deny benefits.

See also: 'The exercise of de facto sovereignty, accordingly, could be sufficient to establish 'territory' in cases where the de jure sovereign is completely deprived of the exercise of its rights'. See also at 263–4.

1178 Ibid., 262–3 (emphasis added).

1179 Ibid., 263.

1180 Ibid.

1181 Ibid., 264. For this reason, they believe that a tribunal could apply the principle of non-recognition 'in a manner that would not allow the annexing state to escape the obligations it had if the acquisition of territory had been lawful'.

1182 Ibid.

1183 Ibid., 262–3.

1184 H. Lauterpacht, *Recognition of States in International Law* (CUP 1947) 420.

1185 See, Surya Prakash Sharma, *Territorial Acquisition, Disputes, and International Law* (Brill 1997) 158. See also, the comment made by Talmon (n 925) 125: 'the obligation of non-recognition does have real substance and may prove a powerful sanction by the international community against the responsible State'.

not as such either a method of enforcement *or a sanction*'.[1186] For him, non-recognition is 'a precondition for other enforcement action' such as sanctions.[1187] In other words, non-recognition is not a sanction *in itself*. It is rather the legal foundation upon which States can individually (or collectively) set up economical, political, and diplomatic sanctions against the wrongdoer.

6.199 In any event, even if one considers that the obligation of non-recognition encompasses a sanction dimension, it is clearly not only limited to that aspect. According to one writer:

> at a minimum, the rationale of the obligation of non-recognition is to prevent, in so far as possible, the validation of an unlawful situation by seeking to ensure that a fait accompli resulting from serious illegalities do not consolidate and crystallize over time into situations recognized by the international legal order (…).[1188]

The same rational has been explained by the ICJ in the *Wall* case.[1189] Milano has also well-explained that the aim of the principle of non-recognition is 'the protection of subjective rights of the injured party; the affirmation of a community interest in the protection of fundamental norms; and the need to enforce the legal norms which are being breached'.[1190] Thus, it seems that the basic reason behind the adoption of the non-recognition principle is to ensure that *fundamental* norms of international law are respected by States.[1191] As noted by Dugard, the practice of non-recognition is confined to those situations 'which most seriously offend international law and public policy'.[1192] The principle of non-recognition is aimed at preventing to give any *legal effect* to any violations of those principles; it has a 'status-denying effect'.[1193] As noted by Crawford, 'non-recognition helps to prevent the consolidation of unlawful situations'.[1194] Lauterpacht also believes that it fulfils 'an important

1186 Crawford, *The Creation of States* (n 115) 159 (emphasis added), see also, at 173.

1187 Ibid., 160. See also: Vera Gowlland-Debbas, *Collective Responses to Illegal Acts in International Law: United Nations Action in the Question of Southern Rhodesia* (Martinus Nijhoff 1990) 278.

1188 Dawidowicz (n 925) 683.

1189 *Wall in the Occupied Palestinian Territory* (n 926) [121]: 'The Court considers that the construction of the wall and its associated régime create a "*fait accompli*" on the ground that could well become permanent, in which case, and notwithstanding the formal characterization of the wall by Israel, it would be tantamount to a de facto annexation.'

1190 Milano (n 928) 54–5.

1191 Crawford, *The Creation of States* (n 115) 160.

1192 Dugard, *Recognition and the United Nations* (n 916) 163. Thus, for him, the 'violation of an ordinary rule of international law could not possibly result in so drastic a sanction as the collective non-recognition of a State or territorial acquisition', and, consequently, only the 'norm essential to the maintenance of the prevailing international public order could possibly warrant collective actions of this kind' (at 153–4).

1193 Stefan Talmon, 'The Constitutive versus the Declaratory Theory of Recognition: Tertium Non Datur?', (2004) 75 *British YIL* 180.

1194 Crawford, *The Creation of States* (n 115) 159.

function in the maintenance of the authority of the law' and the 'vindication of the legal character of international law as against the 'law-creating effect of fact'.[1195]

In the context of Crimea, the ultimate goal is to prevent the illegal annexation from gaining any legal recognition and from bearing any legal effect. In my view, extending Russian BITs to the territory of Crimea would amount to recognizing the annexation on the ground and to give legal effect to an unlawful action. In this context, 'sanctioning' the action of Russia seems to be just part of the overall intention of non-recognition. This is why the position adopted by Ukraine in these on-going arbitration proceedings (discussed above) is rather surprising. **6.200**

One reason the writers mentioned above have argued for the application of a 'modified' non-recognition obligation is because they say that Russia will *benefit* from the non-application of its BITs to the territory of Crimea insofar as it will not have to provide any BIT protection to foreign investors doing business there. It may very well be that Russia would be better off under this scenario when compared to the situation which would prevail had it legally incorporated Crimea (in which case Russian BITs would have applied to that territory under the MTF principle). Yet, any such 'benefit' enjoyed by Russia may only be in the short term. This is because foreign investors may be under the obligation to not continue doing business in Crimea under sanction regimes imposed by many States. In any event, given the great uncertainty regarding their legal situation (including the lack of BIT protection), investors may be reluctant to maintain their investments very long in a post-annexation Crimea. One can logically predict an important reduction in foreign direct investments (FDI) in that region. At the end of the day, Russia may *not* benefit at all from the non-application of its BITs to the territory of Crimea because of a potential FDI exodus. **6.201**

In my view, the better solution remains adopting the strict application of the non-recognition principle and, consequently, refusing to extend Russian BITs to the territory of Crimea. This seems like the most efficient way to 'sanction' the illegal action of Russia. The practical outcome of the solution is admittedly not ideal insofar as it results in foreign investors no longer benefiting from any BIT protection in that territory. Yet, as noted above, this does not necessarily **6.202**

1195 Lauterpacht, *Recognition* (n 1184) 431. According to him, in an international society where:

> there is a natural tendency to regard successful breaches of the law as a source of legal rights (...) non-recognition obliviates that danger to a large extent' as it is 'the minimum of resistance which an insufficiently organized but law-abiding community offers to illegality; it is a continuous challenge to a legal wrong.

mean that investors get no legal protection at all. They will, for instance, continue to benefit from the MST under custom which includes due process, protection against arbitrary conduct, and denial of justice. Ultimately, as noted by two writers, not extending Russian BITs to the territory of Crimea leads to a clash of divergent interests: 'the interest of the international community to sanction illegal acquisition of territory by means of annexation clashes with the investors' individual interest to have their investment protected under international law'.[1196] This is a classic case where one needs to basically choose between the lesser of two evils. In my view, the Crimean crisis and its aftermath is a situation where the interest of the international community as a whole should supersede those of a few foreign investors. As guardians of the international legal order, tribunals must not recognize (even implicitly) an illegal annexation of territory and should not render awards giving any legal effect to such a basic violation of international law. This is a fundamental duty. But, it comes at an important cost for foreign investors who will benefit from no BIT protection in Crimea. I would argue that this is (sadly) the price to pay for fundamental norms of international law to have any meaning in the realm of investor-State arbitration.

6.203 Yet, as mentioned above,[1197] the six tribunals in the *Everest*; *Belbek*; *PJSC CB PrivatBank*; *Ukrnafta*; *Stabil* and *Lugzor* cases have taken a different view on the matter. While the tribunals' decisions were certainly influenced by the surprising position adopted by Ukraine intervening in the arbitration proceedings,[1198] they nevertheless seem to have followed the 'pragmatic approach' put forward by Happ and Wuschka.

6.3.2.4 The possibility of State-to-State arbitration

6.204 In March 2014, Ukraine lodged an inter-State application under Article 33 of the European Convention of Human Rights against the Russian Federation.[1199] Ukraine also filed a claim against Russia before a tribunal constituted

1196 See, more generally (i.e., without referring to the situation in Crimea): Happ and Wuschka (n 1044) 255. See also, at 267: 'allowing a state to enter a legal black hole and putting investors in the annexed territory in a legal vacuum clashes with the rationale behind the obligation of non-recognition of illegal acquisition of territory'.

1197 See, Chapter 6, Section 6.3.2.2.2.

1198 IAReporter, 'In Jurisdiction Ruling, Arbitrators Rule That Russia Is Obliged Under Bit' (n 1147).

1199 European Convention of Human Rights, No. 20958/14, *Ukraine v. Russia*. See: Marko Milanovic, 'Ukraine Derogates from the ICCPR and the ECHR, Files Fourth Interstate Application against Russia' EJIL Talk!, 5 October 2015, available at: http://www.ejiltalk.org/ukrainederogates-from-the-iccpr-and-the-echr-files-fourth-interstate-application-against-russia/ (last accessed on 22 March 2016); Philip Leach, 'Ukraine, Russia and Crimea in the European Court of Human Rights', EJIL Talk! 19 March 2014, available at: http://www.ejiltalk.org/ukraine-russia-and-crimea-in-the-european-court-of-human-rights/; Tzeng (n 1126) 463; Thomas D. Grant, 'Crimea after Cyprus v. Turkey: Just Satisfaction for Unlawful

under the United Nations Convention on the Law of the Sea[1200] and before the ICJ.[1201] The ramifications of these cases have been examined by other scholars.[1202] The present section examines another related question: whether the inter-State dispute settlement clause contained in the Ukraine-Russia BIT could be relevant regarding the legal status of Crimea after the annexation.[1203] Article 10 of the BIT provides as follows:

> 1. Disputes between the Contracting Parties as to the interpretation and application of this Agreement, shall be resolved by way of negotiations.
>
> 2. In the event, a dispute cannot be resolved through negotiations within six months as of the notification in writing of the origin of a dispute, then at the request of either Contracting Party, it shall be passed over for consideration, to the arbitration tribunal.

The question is whether Ukraine could start arbitration proceedings invoking a 'dispute' between the parties as to the 'interpretation and application of this Agreement'.[1204] The dispute would concern the *interpretation* of one clause contained in the BIT: Article 1(4) dealing with the definition of 'territory', and, specifically, whether Crimea is part of the 'territory' of Ukraine or of Russia. The dispute between the parties would also be in relation to the *application* of the BIT. Thus, many clauses in the BIT refer to legal protection being applicable in the 'territory' of the other Contracting Party. The question which could be asked is which States must provide protection to investments **6.205**

Annexation?' 19 May 2014, EJIL Talk!, available at: http://www.ejiltalk.org/crimea-after-cyprus-v-turkey-just-satisfaction-for-unlawful-annexation/. This case is somehow similar to that of Cyprus v. Turkey, 2001 -IV Eur. Ct. H.R. 1 4, decided by the ECHR in the context of the illegal 'secession' of the 'Turkish Republic of Northern Cyprus' from Cyprus. Rees-Evans (n 1114) indicates that more than 3,000 individual applications were made against either or both of Ukraine and/or Russia relating to the events in Crimea and Eastern Ukraine.

1200 *Dispute Concerning Coastal State Rights in the Black Sea, Sea of Azov, and Kerch Strait* (*Ukraine v. the Russian Federation*), UNCLOS, PCA case no. 2017–06.

1201 *Terrorism Financing and Racial Discrimination in Ukraine (Ukraine v. Russian Federation)*, Application Instituting Proceedings, 16 January 2017, referring to violation of the International Convention for the Suppression of the Financing of Terrorism (adopted on 9 December 1999, entered into force on 10 April 2002) 2178 UNTS 197 and the International Convention on the Elimination of All Forms of Racial Discrimination (adopted on 21 December 1965, entered into force on 4 January 1969) 660 UNTS 195. See, discussion in: Rees-Evans (n 1114); Gaiane Nuridzhanyan, 'Ukraine vs. Russia in International Courts and Tribunals', EJIL Talk!, 9 March 2016, available at: http://www.ejiltalk.org/ukraine-versus-russia-in-intemational-courts-and-tribunals/.

1202 Rees-Evans (n 1114), referring to other cases, including four proceedings between Russia and Ukraine at the WTO.

1203 Tzeng (n 1126) 459–68; Grant, 'International Dispute Settlement' (n 862) 27ff. The question is also mentioned in: Repousis and Fry (n 90) 449.

1204 See: Tzeng (n 1126) 467ff.

made in Crimea. As noted by one writer, the concept of 'territory' is central for the *application* of the BIT.[1205]

6.206 For Grant, 'it may seem exotic to the BIT system to seek to adjudicate a dispute as to the scope of a State's territorial and maritime entitlement under the inter-state dispute settlement provision of a BIT'.[1206] This is because a BIT is clearly not an instrument signed by the parties for purposes of settling territorial disputes between them. The preamble to the Ukraine-Russia BIT thus indicates that 'in pursuance of their intention to create and maintain favorable conditions for mutual investments' and 'in the desire to create favourable conditions for the expansion of economic cooperation between the Contracting Parties' the parties have agreed to a series of protections that are to be given to the investors of the other State. While it is true that 'it can hardly be claimed that the current situation between the Contracting Parties is conducive to that purpose',[1207] the fact of the matter is that the preamble refers to *investment* protection. Interestingly, Article 10 of the Ukraine-Russia BIT does not explicitly limit the scope of jurisdiction only to the disputes arising out of alleged breaches of the substantive protections accorded by the treaty to investors. For this reason, some writers have argued that a tribunal would have jurisdiction over a claim for the interpretation of the term 'territory'.[1208] Yet, the more prudent view is probably that it remains 'doubtful whether a dispute having no connection at all to an investment problem – that is, a dispute decoupled from the investment purposes of the BIT – would readily be entertained by a BIT tribunal'.[1209] In any event, the question remains open for the moment.

1205 Grant, 'International Dispute Settlement' (n 862) 35:

> Far from being extraneous to the BIT, a dispute as to the meaning of 'territory' is integral to it. The 'geographical scope of an investment agreement' is 'determined by the territorial limits of the states concerned.' Without a definition of the territory-that is, without a shared understanding of where one party's territory ends and the other's begins-it would be difficult, perhaps impossible, to apply a treaty which defines the scope of its application by reference to the territory of its parties. The treaty system as a whole could not function without that definition.

1206 Grant, 'International Dispute Settlement' (n 862) 33.

1207 Ibid., 34.

1208 Tzeng (n 1126) 466.

1209 Grant, 'International Dispute Settlement' (n 862) 36–7.

Part C

STATE SUCCESSION TO MULTILATERAL TREATIES

INTRODUCTION

This Part examines the following question: is a new successor State automatically bound by the *multilateral* treaties to which the predecessor State was a party at the date of succession? In order to answer this question, it is necessary to critically assess the continuity principle that was adopted under the Vienna Convention for cases of secession and dissolution (Chapter 7).[1] The present author has found no precedent where the issue of succession to a multilateral treaty has arisen in the context of investment arbitration. For that reason, an illustration of the type of legal issues that could potentially arise has been provided based on the arguments put forward by States and scholars in the context of a hypothetical case: the secession of Quebec from Canada and its succession to the NAFTA (Chapter 8). Finally, the question of State succession to the ICSID Convention will be examined (Chapter 9). The Convention is an example of a special category of treaties creating international organizations. In this section, it will be shown that there is no succession to the membership of an international organization and that, accordingly, the practice of new States has been to adhere to the Centre via a formal application (rather than by way of succession).

1 Vienna Convention on Succession of States in Respect of Treaties, signed on 23 August 1978 and entered into force on 6 November 1996, 1946 UNTS 3, in: 17 ILM 1978, 1488 [hereinafter 'Vienna Convention on Succession to Treaties'].

7

THE CONTINUITY PRINCIPLE ADOPTED UNDER THE VIENNA CONVENTION FOR SECESSION AND DISSOLUTION

I have briefly already examined in the previous chapter the regime set out regarding multilateral treaties for different types of successions.[2] This section will focus on secession and dissolution. This is because these are the types of succession which have been the most common since the end of the Cold War. **7.01**

Article 34 of the Vienna Convention indicates the regime applicable to cases of 'separation' of States. This provision uses the term 'separation' to refer to the different concepts that are 'secession' and 'dissolution' of States.[3] It provides for the application of the principle of *automatic* succession whereby the successor State is *ipso facto* bound by treaties entered into by the predecessor State without the requirement of any notification by that State. However, this rule of continuity bears two exceptions where the principle of *tabula rasa* applies: when the implicated parties have specifically agreed on the application of the *tabula rasa* rule, and where the automatic application of the treaty to the successor State would be 'incompatible with the object and purpose of the treaty or would radically change the conditions for its operation'.[4] As mentioned above (in the context of bilateral treaties), the final wording of Article 34 (which applies to *both* bilateral and multilateral treaties) is the result of several developments, and can be succinctly summarized in three phases.[5] **7.02**

As previously mentioned, the Vienna Convention has been widely criticized by the majority of authors.[6] The following paragraphs examine how scholars have assessed the principle of continuity set out at Article 34 for multilateral treaties in the context of dissolution and secession. The question was at the **7.03**

2 See, Chapter 5, Section 1.

3 On the distinction between these two concepts, see, Chapter 5, Section 1.5.

4 Vienna Convention on Succession to Treaties (n 1), Art. 34(2). These exceptions have been examined above in the context of bilateral treaties, see, Chapter 5, Section 2.4.

5 See, Chapter 5, Section 1.5.1.ff.

6 See, Chapter 5, Section 2.5.

heart of three cases before the ICJ,[7] but the court decided not to take position on the matter.[8]

7.04 Authors do *not* generally condemn the application of the principle of continuity of treaties for instances of *dissolution* insofar as it corresponds to State practice.[9] As explained elsewhere by the present writer, the principle of continuity of treaties has been adopted by several States in the context of dissolutions in Eastern Europe in the 1990s such as Czechoslovakia and Yugoslavia.[10] Third-party States, such as the member States of the European Union[11] and the United States,[12] have also adopted the general position of

---

7 *Case Concerning the Gabčíkovo-Nagymaros Project* (*Hungary v. Slovakia*), Judgment of 25 September 1997, ICJ Reports 1997, 3; *Application of the Convention on the Prevention and Punishment of the Crime of Genocide,* (*Bosnia-Herzegovina v. Yugoslavia*), Preliminary Objections, Judgment of 11 July 1996, ICJ Reports 1996, 596; *Application of the Convention on the Prevention and Punishment of the Crime of Genocide* (*Croatia v. Serbia*), Preliminary Objections, Judgment, ICJ Reports 2008, 412.

8 A. Zimmermann, 'The International Court of Justice and State Succession to Treaties: Avoiding Principled Answers to Questions of Principle', in Christian J. Tams and James Sloan (eds), *The Development of International Law by the International Court of Justice* (OUP 2013) 59–61.

9 Z. Meriboute, *La codification de la succession d'États aux traités: décolonisation, sécession, unification* (PUF 1984) 216; D.P. O'Connell, *State Succession in Municipal Law and International Law*, vol II (CUP 1967) 164–78; P. Cahier, 'Quelques aspects de la Convention de 1978 sur la succession d'États en matière de traités', in B. Dutoit and E. Grisel (eds), *Mélanges Georges Perrin* (1984) 75; Andreas Zimmermann and James G. Devaney, 'Succession to Treaties and the Inherent Limits of International Law' in Christian J. Tams, Antonios Tzanakopoulos, and Andreas Zimmermann (eds), *Research Handbook on the Law of Treaties*, (Edward Elgar 2014) 525; A. Zimmermann, 'La Convention de Vienne sur la succession d'États en matière de traités: codification réussie ou échouée?, in G. Distefano, G. Gaggioli and A. Hêche (eds), *La Convention de Vienne de 1978 sur la succession d'États en matière de traités: Commentaire article par article et études thématiques*, (Bruylant 2015) 1558–9, 1564; Gerhard Hafner and Gregor Novak, 'State Succession in Respect of Treaties' in Duncan B. Hollis (ed), *The Oxford Guide to Treaties* (OUP 2012) 416; M. Maloney, 'State Succession in Respect of Treaties: The Vienna Convention of 1978' (1978–79) 19 *Virginia JIL* 913; J. Klabbers, M. Koskenniemi and A. Zimmermann (dirs), *Pilot Project on Documentation concerning State Practice relating to State Succession and Recognition*, (Council of Europe 1999) 117; R. Szafarz, 'Succession of States in Respect of Treaties in Contemporary International Law', (1983) 12 *Polish YIL* 104; P. Caggiano, 'The ILC Draft on the Succession of States in Respect of Treaties: A Critical Appraisal', (1975) 1 *Italian YIL* 75.

10 P. Dumberry and D. Turp, 'State Succession with Respect to Multilateral Treaties in the Context of Secession: From the Principle of Tabula Rasa to the Emergence of a Presumption of Continuity of Treaties', (2013) 13 *Baltic YIL*. See also P. Dumberry and D. Turp, 'La succession d'États en matière de traités et le cas de la sécession: du principe de la table rase à l'émergence d'une présomption de continuité des traités', (2003) 36(2) RBDI 377.

11 P.J. Kuyper, 'The Community and State Succession in Respect to Treaties', in D. Curtin and T. Heukels (eds), *Institutional Dynamics of European Integration, Essays in Honour of Henry G. Schermers*, vol. II (Martinus Nijhoff, 1994) 640; G. Clariana, 'La succession dans les Communautés européennes', in G. Burdeau and B. Stern (eds), *Dissolution, continuation et succession en Europe de l'Est* (Cedin-Paris I 1994) 132. States' individual position on the matter is however not uniform. See, for instance, Austria's position in favour of the principle of *tabula rasa:* G. Hafner and E. Kornfeind, 'The Recent Austrian Practice of State Succession: Does the Clean Slate Rule Still Exists?' (1996) 1 *Austrian RIEL* 1.

12 See: P.R. Williams, 'The Treaty Obligations of the Successor States of the Former Soviet Union, Yugoslavia and Czechoslovakia: Do They Continue in Force?' (1994) 23 *Denver J Int Law Pol* 9–10; E.D. Williamson and J.E. Osborn, 'A U.S. Perspective on Treaty Succession and Related Issues in the Wake of the Break-up of the U.S.S.R. and Yugoslavia', (1992) 33 *Virginia JIL* 264; E.D. Williamson, 'State Succession and Relations with Federal States', (1992) 86 *ASIL Proc* 12.

continuity of treaties.[13] While the vast majority of authors recognize that the post-Cold War practice of new States *generally* follows the principle of continuity of treaties,[14] only a few have argued in favour of the existence of a customary rule to that effect.[15] For Judge Kreca, in his dissenting opinion in the *Case concerning the application of the Convention on the prevention and punishment of the Crime of Genocide*, Article 34 should be considered as a mere 'progressive development of law', and not as a codification of customary international law.[16]

One important point to mention is that the post-Cold War practice of new States in the context of dissolution of States is not perfectly in line with the solution set out in Article 34 of the Convention.[17] Thus, successor States have generally given notifications of their will to 'succeed' to the treaties of the predecessor State or to 'continue' to be a party to them. As a matter of principle, the very fact that a new State notifies others of its intention to be bound by a treaty is proof in itself that there is no 'automatic' succession to treaties. Thus, no such notification should logically be required if any principle of *truly* automatic succession were to exist. But the situation is slightly more complicated than that. Some States, for instance, have sent a notification precisely in order to express their desire to be *automatically* bound by a treaty.[18] In these cases, the aim of the notification must be understood as proof of continuity of treaty application rather than discontinuity. In this respect, reference should be made to the attitude of depositary States of multilateral treaties. Thus, the practice of the UN Secretary-General has been to expect receiving formal **7.05**

13 Zimmermann and Devaney, 'Succession to Treaties' (n 9) 529.

14 Brigitte Stern, 'La succession d'États' (1996) 262 Rec. des Cours 291–5; Hafner and Novak (n 9) 416; P. Pazartzis, *La succession d'États aux traités multilatéraux à la lumière des mutations territoriales récentes* (Pedone 2002) 143–211, 158–9; International Law Association, *Rapport final sur la succession en matière de traités*, Committee on Aspects of the Law of State Succession, New Delhi Conference 2002, 14–15 [hereinafter 'ILA, Rapport final']; H. Bokor-Szego, 'Continuation et succession en matière de traités internationaux', in Burdeau and Stern (n 11) 54; V. Degan, 'La succession d'États en matière de traités et les États nouveaux (issus de l'ex-Yougoslavie)' (1996) 42 AFDI 222; Zimmermann and Devaney, 'Succession to Treaties' (n 9) 528–30; V. Bilkova, 'La succession aux traités internationaux suite à la dissolution des fédérations ex-socialistes après 1990', in Distefano, Gaggioli and Hêche (n 9) 1807, 1851; Zimmermann, 'La Convention de Vienne' (n 9) 1564–5.

15 See, discussion in Pazartzis (n 14) 212. One writer who affirms the customary status of Art. 34 is: Zimmermann, 'La Convention de Vienne' (n 9) 1559. In fact, a number of authors have, on the contrary, argued in favour of the application of the rule of *tabula rasa*: P.M. Eisemann, 'Rapport du Directeur de la section de langue française du Centre', in Pierre Michel Eisemann and Martti Koskenniemi (dir), *State Succession: Codification Tested Against the Facts* (Martinus Nijhoff Publ. 2000) 48–54; T. Langstrom, 'The Dissolution of The Soviet Union in the Light of the 1978 Vienna Convention on Succession of States in Respect of Treaties', in Eisemann and Koskenniemi, ibid., 775.

16 *Genocide case*, 1996 (n 6) 779. See also: Caggiano (n 9) 76.

17 See, Dumberry and Turp (n 10).

18 Stern (n 14) 291–5; Pazartzis (n 14) 191–200, 206, 209–13.

'confirmations' from States wishing to succeed to the treaties of their predecessors.[19] A number of other States have adopted the same position.[20]

7.06 In sum, the practice of States in the context of dissolution supports the principle of the continuity of multilateral treaties, but *not* 'automatically' as envisaged at Article 34 of the Convention.[21]

7.07 Authors are very critical regarding the application of the principle of continuity in the different context of *secession*. Many writers have pointed out that the actual practice of secessionist States supports, on the contrary, the *tabula rasa* rule.[22] According to the work of the ILC,[23] as well as that of the International

---

19 UN, Treaty section, UN Office of Legal Affairs, Summary of Practice of the Secretary-General as Depositary of Multilateral Treaties, UN Doc Srr/LEG/7/Rew, 90. See, International Law Association, *Conclusions of the Committee on Aspects of the Law on State Succession*, Resolution no. 3/2008, adopted at the 73rd Conference of the International Law Association, held in Rio de Janeiro, Brazil, 17–21 August, 2008, at point no. 6:

> The UN Secretary-General has requested to every successor State –no matter the type of State succession concerned- to produce specific declarations of succession to each multilateral treaty to which the UN is the depositary. This practice is also being followed by other depositaries, either States or international organizations. Remarkably, this practice corresponds to that set up by Article 22 to the 1978 Vienna Convention, only related to newly independent States. According to UN practice, the successor State must satisfy the conditions provided for by the treaty for becoming party to it.

See also: Degan (n 14) 225.

20 See, the analysis in: Pazartzis (n 14) 210; examining the position of Switzerland, France, UK.

21 Ibid., 209–213; Stern (n 14) 294.

22 Thus, for Szafarz (n 9) 104–5:

> It seems that the practice of States in this respect has been sufficiently extensive, consistent and sustained, and that the *opinio juris* of States and the opinion of the legal doctrine sufficiently concordant to warrant the conclusion that a customary rule emerged according to which the succession of treaties of separated States is governed by the clean slate rule.

See also: Meriboute (n 9) 162; Cahier (n 9) 76; R. Mullerson, 'Law and Politics in Succession of States: International Law on Succession of States', in Burdeau and Stern (n 11) 34; I. Brownlie, *Principles of Public International Law*, 5th edn (Clarendon 1998) 663–4; M.N. Shaw, *International Law* 6th edn (CUP 2008) 689–90; American Law Institute, *Restatement of the Law Third, the Foreign Relations Law of the United States*, vol. I (American Law Institute Publ. 1987) § 210, 'Reporters' Notes' no. 4 (113); Williamson and Osborn (n 12) 263; S.A. Williams, *International Legal Effects of Secession by Quebec* (York University Centre for Public Law and Public Policy 1992) 33; D.B. Majzub, 'Does Secession Mean Succession? The International Law of Treaty Succession and an Independent Quebec', (1998) 24 *Queen's LJ* 429, 432, 434; A. Berbner, 'Things Fall Apart? NAFTA After Quebec', (1997) 6 *Dalhousie J Legal Stud* 294ff; Caggiano (n 9) 76; Szafarz (n 9) 104–5, 108; Zimmermann, 'La Convention de Vienne' (n 9) 1558–9. See, however, the different conclusion reached by V. Mikulka, 'Article 34', in Distefano, Gaggioli and Hêche (n 9) 1196:

> La pratique internationale de la fin du 20e siècle relative aux cas de désintégration d'Etats en Europe Centrale et de l'Est a connu une nette tendance vers le maintien des traités, comme certains auteurs l'ont sitôt remarqué. Les Etats successeurs de l'ancienne Yougoslavie et, en particulier, ceux de la Tchécoslovaquie ont favorisé la continuité des traités et invoquaient les principes du droit international en vigueur ou le droit coutumier à l'appui de leurs positions. Pareils renvois apparaissent souvent aussi dans la correspondance des autres Etats avec les Etats successeurs. La pratique qui a prévalu a conduit certains Etats à réévaluer leur position traditionnelle en la matière.

23 Report of the International Law Commission on the work of its 24th session, 2 May–7 July 1972, A/8710/Rev.1, in: *Yearbook ILC*, 1972, vol. II [hereinafter 'ILC Report, 24th Session, 1972'] 295ff. This is also the position of Judge Kreca in his dissenting opinion in the *Genocide case*, 1996 (n 6) 779.

Law Association,[24] the practice of secessionist States *prior* to the adoption of the 1978 Vienna Convention reveals that there was no automatic succession to treaties concluded by the predecessor State. My own examination of three cases of secession that have occurred since the creation of the United Nations (Pakistan in 1947, Singapore in 1965 and Bangladesh in 1971) shows that successor States have generally applied the rule of *tabula rasa*.[25] As mentioned above,[26] the break-up of the USSR has been considered by all actors involved as a series of 'secessions' by the former Soviet Republics (except for the three Baltic States[27]).[28] Under the Minsk Agreement and the Alma Ata Declaration, all successor States agreed to respect obligations arising from treaties to which the USSR was a party.[29] In spite of this general statement of continuity, the practice of these secessionist States has been anything but uniform.[30] While some new States have become parties to the multilateral treaties of the USSR by way of accession,[31] others have declared themselves to be automatically bound by these treaties.[32] The practice of third States has also not been uniform.[33] Overall, this inconsistent practice does not support the principle of 'automatic' succession to treaties.[34] In the context of the secession of Eritrea from Ethiopia in 1993, the new State has acceded to treaties previously entered into by Ethiopia but rarely by way of succession.[35] In fact, the Eritrea-Ethiopia Claims Commission rejected the claim that the new State had become automatically party to the 1949 Geneva Convention (which had been signed by Ethiopia).[36] The position adopted by South Sudan on succession to treaties is ambiguous and in many ways still uncertain.[37] On the

---

24 ILA, Rapport final (n 14) 3.

25 Dumberry and Turp (n 10).

26 See, Chapter 3, Section 2.4.

27 L. Mälksoo, *Illegal Annexation and State Continuity: The Case of the Incorporation of the Baltic States by the USSR (A Study of the Tension between Normativity and Power in International Law)* (Martinus Nijhoff 2003) 255–6.

28 Pazartzis (n 14) 56; I. Ziemele, 'Is the Distinction between State Continuity and State Succession Reality or Fiction? The Russian Federation, the Federal Republic of Yugoslavia and Germany', (2001) 1 *Baltic YIL* 194.

29 Article 22, Agreement Establishing the Commonwealth of Independent States ('Minsk Agreement'), 13 December 1991, UN Doc. A/46/771, in (1992) 31 ILM 138; Declaration of Alma Ata, 21 December 1991, UN Doc. A/46/60, in (1992) 31 ILM 147.

30 Pazartzis (n 14) 78; ILA, Rapport final (n 14) 14.

31 A. Zimmermann, 'Secession and the Law of State Succession', in M.G. Kohen (ed), *Secession: International Law Perspectives* (CUP 2006) 215.

32 Pazartzis (n 14) 78–80.

33 Zimmermann and Devaney, 'Succession to Treaties' (n 9) 526.

34 Pazartzis (n 14) 78–80. See also: Zimmermann and Devaney, 'Succession to Treaties' (n 9) 526.

35 Zimmermann and Devaney, ibid., citing one example of succession.

36 Eritrea-Ethiopia Claims Commission, 'Prisoners of War', Eritrea's claim no. 17, Partial Award, in (2003) 35 ILR, 212; 'Central Front', Ethiopia's claim no. 4, Partial Award, in ibid., 261.

37 J. Moussa, 'L'indépendance du Soudan du Sud et la Convention de Vienne sur la succession d'États en matière de traités', in Distefano, Gaggioli and Hêche (n 9) 1933–5; Zimmermann and Devaney, 'Succession to Treaties'
(n 9) 527; A. Genest, 'Sudan Bilateral Investment Treaties and South Sudan: Musings on State Succession to Bilateral Treaties in the Wake of Yugoslavia's Breakup' (2014) 3 TDM.

contrary, Montenegro adopted a clear position in favour of succession to multilateral treaties to which Serbia-Montenegro had been a party before the date of succession.[38] The same position in favour of continuity of multilateral treaties is also privileged by potential candidates for secession (such as Quebec and Scotland[39]).

7.08 In sum, given such diverse practice, it is premature to discuss the emergence of any *customary rule* of international law according to which the secessionist State would *automatically* succeed to the multilateral treaties concluded by the predecessor State.[40]

7.09 As explained by the ILC,[41] *multilateral* treaties are clearly different from bilateral treaties for which the 'personal equation' and the identity of the parties is fundamental.[42] I have argued elsewhere that there should be a *presumption* whereby a new State (in the context of *both* dissolution and secession) would be bound by all *multilateral* treaties to which the predecessor State was a party at the date of succession.[43] Such succession would, however,

---

38 See, the analysis in Dumberry and Turp (n 10).

39 Ibid.

40 R.J. Zedalis, 'An Independent Quebec: State Succession to NAFTA', (1996) 2(4) *NAFTA: Law & Bus Rev Am* 27; 'It seems that a strong case can be made that it is unclear whether customary international law provides to separating parts of a state a rule of continuation through which they can claim to succeed to treaties of the predecessor state'; Shaw (n 22) 977; 'it is far too early to be able to declare that continuity or a presumption of continuity is now the established norm'; Zimmerman (n 31) 214–15, 230:

> With regard to cases of secession arising outside the context of decolonisation, State practice, in particular that of the last fifteen years, is significantly less uniform ... Given this ambiguity, one must question whether it is safe enough to state that the rule contained in Article 34 of the 1978 Vienna Convention – which at least at the time it was drafted may be considered more of a progressive development than a codification of international law – has really crystallized into a rule of positive customary international law.

Zimmermann and Devaney, 'Succession to Treaties' (n 9) 526:

> it continues to remain somewhat unclear to what extent the rules in Article 34 VCSST apply in such situations and to what extent these rules are declaratory of customary international law due to such inconsistent practice, but also due to the silence of the International Court of Justice on the matter

Zimmermann, 'La Convention de Vienne' (n 9) 1565.

41 ILC, Fourth Report on Succession in Respect of Treaties, prepared by the Special Rapporteur, Sir Humphrey Waldock, A/CN.4/249, 24 June 1971, A/8410/Rev.1, in: *Yearbook ILC*, 1971, vol. II (Part One) [hereinafter ILC Report, Fourth Report, 1971] 146 [2]; ILC, Report of the International Law Commission on the Work of its 26th Session, 6 May to 26 July 1974, A/9610/Rev.1, in: *Yearbook ILC*, 1974, vol. II (Part One)) [hereinafter 'ILC Report, 26th Session, 1974'] 237 (see also at 169).

42 See, Chapter 5, Section 2.2.

43 Dumberry and Turp (n 10). This approach in favour of a presumption of continuity of multilateral treaties appears justified by the necessity to preserve a minimum of stability in international relations. See Mullerson (n 14) 44; Pazartzis (n 14) 154; Shaw (n 22) 690. See: D.P. O'Connell, 'Reflections on the State Succession Convention', (1979) 39(4) ZaöRV 736:

> We have set up a system for successor States to avoid maintaining treaties and then an elaborated machinery, which is time-consuming and administratively debilitating, to enable them to avoid the consequences of avoidance of the maintenance of treaties, that is, to enable them to continue treaties which

not be 'automatic' as set out in Article 34 of the Vienna Convention. Thus, a new State would not *ipso facto* succeed to all existing treaties of the predecessor State. The new State would have to 'confirm' its succession by notifying the depository of the treaty of its willingness to be a party to a particular treaty (or a group of treaties). The practical effect of the presumption of continuity is that in the interim period between the date of succession and the confirmation by the State of its intention to succeed or not to a specific treaty, that treaty *should continue to apply* to the new State.[44] In other words, there should be a presumption that the treaty continues to apply to the new State until that State has expressly taken position on the matter. A new State's decision to succeed to a treaty would have a retroactive effect to the date of succession. However, this presumption is rebuttable. Thus, the logical corollary of any such presumption of continuity is that a successor State is always free to decide to not be bound by a treaty to which the predecessor State was a party.[45] At the end of the day, actual State consent remains *central* to the question as to whether or not a new State is bound by treaties.

I have not found any example of succession to a multilateral treaty in the context of investment arbitration disputes. The next chapter examines one hypothetical scenario which has been much discussed by scholars. 7.10

they want to continue while adhering to the general idea of not being bound to do so. … I wonder whether there would be any practical difference if we reverse the matter, beginning with supposition that treaties remain in force for successor States, without distinction between the types of succession, and then leave the successor State to terminate them under the renunciation clauses.

44 Pazartzis (n 14) 212.

45 ILA, Rapport final (n 14) 22.

8

ONE (HYPOTHETICAL) ILLUSTRATION OF SUCCESSION TO MULTILATERAL TREATIES: THE CASE OF NAFTA AND QUEBEC'S SECESSION

8.01 More than a decade ago, a debate about succession to the NAFTA[46] emerged in the context of the potential secession of Quebec.[47] Once elected into government in 1994, the Parti Québécois (pro-independence) proposed a Draft Bill on the Sovereignty of Quebec as a platform of the position of an independent Quebec in matters of foreign policy and negotiations with Canada.[48] It indicates the position of the government of Quebec in favour of continuity of treaties.[49] The same position was reflected in *An Act Respecting the Future of Quebec* adopted in 1995 by the National Assembly of Quebec, which specifically refers to NAFTA.[50]

---

46 North American Free Trade Agreement, signed on 17 December 1992 and came into force on 1 January 1994.

47 This question is examined in Dumberry and Turp (n 10). In the 1998 *Quebec Secession* case (*Reference re Secession of Quebec*, [1998] 2 SCR 217 [83]) the Supreme Court of Canada considered this hypothetical case as one of secession. See, P. Dumberry, 'Lessons Learned from the *Quebec Secession Reference* before the Supreme Court of Canada', in M.G. Kohen (ed), *Secession: International Law Perspectives* (CUP 2006) 416–52.

48 *Draft Bill on the Sovereignty of Quebec*, tabled at the National Assembly on 6 December 1994 [hereinafter referred to as the *Draft Bill*], published in D. Turp, *Le droit de choisir: Essais sur le droit du Quebec à disposer de lui-même / The Right to Choose: Essays on Quebec's Right of Self-Determination* (Thémis 2001) 895. For an in-depth analysis of the *Draft Bill*, see, D. Turp, *L'Avant-projet de loi sur la souveraineté du Québec: texte annoté* (ed. Yvon Blais 2001).

49 Art. 7: 'Quebec shall assume the obligations and enjoys the rights arising out of the treaties to which Canada is party and in the international conventions to which Canada is a signatory, in accordance with the rules of international law.' See also, Commission nationale sur l'avenir du Québec, *Rapport*, 19 April 1995 (Gouvernement du Québec 1995) 75:

> The Government of Quebec chose to conform to the practice of continuity of treaties. It intends to continue to apply the treaties concluded by Canada and the international conventions adhered to or ratified by Canada, and which remain applicable to the territory of Quebec in accordance with the rules of international law. This decision, rendered consecutively to the achievement of sovereignty, expresses Quebec's clear will to fully participate in the international community's life and relations. (translation by the authors)

50 Bill 1, *An Act Respecting the Future of Quebec*, 1st Sess., 35th Leg., Quebec (in Turp (n 48) 901), Art. 15:

> In accordance with the rules of international law, Quebec shall assume the obligations and enjoy the rights set forth in the relevant treaties and international conventions and agreement to which Canada or Quebec is a party on the date on which Quebec becomes a sovereign country, in particular in the North American Free Trade Agreement.

Before the referendum on Quebec's independence (which was held in October 1995) took place, a debate opposed the two primary political parties of the Province regarding its eventual succession to NAFTA.[51] Scholars have also examined this question.[52] At the heart of the debate was the question as to whether or not the principle of continuity set out at Article 34 of the Vienna Convention should be considered as reflecting a rule of customary international law in the context of secession.[53] As mentioned above, the better position is that this provision does not reflect custom. Scholars have therefore concluded that Quebec would not *automatically* become party to the NAFTA.[54] Some writers have also noted that recent State practice has shown the application of the principle of non-succession in the context of multilateral treaties entered into by a limited number of States,[55] which is certainly the case of NAFTA (comprised of only three States).[56] While Quebec would not automatically succeed to the NAFTA, there seems to be no doubt that Quebec would eventually become a party to the agreement.[57] This could be done in two different ways. **8.02**

First, the *Draft Bill on the Sovereignty of Quebec* provides that any formal proclamation of the independence of Quebec by the National Assembly 'must be preceded by a formal offer of economic and political partnership with **8.03**

51 B. Landry, 'GATT et ALÉNA: un simple changement de statut pour le Québec après l'indépendance', *La Presse*, 2 February 1995, B-3; J. Ciaccia, 'Adhésion du Québec à l'ALÉNA: il ne faut pas trop se fier à la Convention de Vienne', *La Presse*, 11 February 1995, B-3. See also the legal opinions requested by different political parties: D.W. Bernstein and W. Silverman, 'Avis sur les conséquences de l'indépendance du Québec en ce qui a trait aux traités et accords conclus avec les États-Unis d'Amérique', 7 March 1995; C.N. Brower, 'Advisory Memorandum Regarding the Effect of Independence of Quebec Upon Treaties and Agreements with the United States of America', 21 March 1995 (later published as C.N. Brower and A.C. Smutny, 'The Effect of the Independence of Quebec upon Treaties and Agreements with the U.S.A.' (1997) 27(1) ARCS 52–4).

52 See: A. Grabell, 'New Northern Neighbor? An Independent Quebec, the United States and the NAFTA', (1995) 2(1) *Sw J L & Trade Americas* 281, 283, 290; F. Crépeau, 'The Law of Quebec's Secession', (1997) 27(1) ARCS 27; C.E. Roh Jr., 'The Implication for U.S. Trade Policy of an Independent Quebec' (Center for Strategic and International Studies 1995); J. Kasku-Jackson, 'Can Quebec Succeed at Secession?', (1998) 4 NEICLA 19; Majzub (n 22) 437–9; S. Dycus, 'Quebec Independence and United States Security: A Question of Continuing Rights and Duties', (1998) 15 *Ariz J Int Comp Law* 187, 200; V. Loungnarath, 'Quelques réflexions d'ordre juridique sur la clause d'adhésion de l'ALENA', (1994) 40 *McGill LJ* 1.

53 The most comprehensive analysis of the question in the context of NAFTA is found in: Zedalis (n 40) 8–9, 27.

54 Ibid.; Berbner (n 22) 297, 304ff; Ivan Bernier, 'Le maintien de l'accès aux marchés extérieurs: certaines questions juridiques soulevées par l'hypothèse de la souveraineté du Québec' (1991) 7(1) RQDI 80; Brower and Smutny (n 51) 52–4; Majzub (n 22) 429; Williams (n 22) 33; Grabell (n 52) 281; Kasku-Jackson (n 52) 19; Crépeau (n 52) 27–50. See, however, a different position in favor of the general application of a presumption of treaty continuity (dealing specifically with security issues): Dycus (n 52).

55 Pazartzis (n 14) 183–5; Bokor-Szego (n 14) 54–5; Adriana Di Stefano, 'Article 24' in Distefano, Gaggioli and Hêche (n 9) [22].

56 Crépeau (n 52) 27–50, referring to the '*intuitu personae* nature' of the NAFTA and concluding that Quebec would not automatically become party to the treaty.

57 Bernier (n 54) 80–81; Berbner (n 22) 291.

Canada'.[58] Another provision contained in the Bill indicates that the Government of Quebec would be 'bound to propose to the Government of Canada the conclusion of a treaty of economic and political partnership'.[59] The so-called 'tripartite agreement' specified that such a new partnership would be aimed at, inter alia, 'consolidat[ing] the existing economic space', which would include maintaining a custom union.[60] Based on the formal offer that could be made by Quebec, it is not impossible to imagine that Quebec and Canada could enter into some sort of economic partnership agreement whereby they would maintain a custom union. It has been argued that if this were to be the case, Quebec and Canada could be considered as a 'single unit' for the purpose of custom tariffs.[61] As a result, it has been suggested that the territory of an independent Quebec would still be considered as 'remaining' part of that of Canada for the specific application of the NAFTA.[62] Thus, NAFTA Annex 201.1 (entitled 'Country-Specific Definitions') provides that the definition of the 'territory' of Canada is 'the territory to which its customs laws apply'. As a result of an eventual agreement between Quebec and Canada, it could therefore be envisaged that the 'customs laws' of Canada would continue to apply to the territory of Quebec after its secession. Under this hypothetical scenario, the NAFTA would simply apply to the territory of Quebec (after its secession) without any requirement of a formal accession to the agreement.[63] In any event, whether or not any such agreement could be reached between Canada and Quebec is pure speculation. The most likely scenario (discussed in the next paragraph) is that of accession to the treaty.

8.04 Second, Quebec could become a party to the agreement through the mechanism of *accession* set out in the NAFTA. NAFTA contains a specific clause that must be respected by Quebec if it were to wish to become a party to the treaty (which would certainly be the case). Article 2204 (on 'accession') reads as follows:

> 1. Any country or group of countries may accede to this Agreement subject to such terms and conditions as may be agreed between such country or countries and the Commission and following approval in accordance with the applicable legal procedures of each country.

58 *Draft Bill: An Act Respecting the Future of Quebec* (n 48), Art. 1.
59 Ibid., Art. 3.
60 Ibid., Art. 3 referring to the Tripartite Agreement of June 12, 1995.
61 Majzub (n 22) 437.
62 Grabell (n 52) 282; Majzub (n 22) 437.
63 Grabell (n 52) 282; Bernier (n 54) 80–81; Majzub (n 22) 437; Kasku-Jackson (n 52) 14–15.

> 2. This Agreement shall not apply as between any Party and any acceding country or group of countries if, at the time of accession, either does not consent to such application.[64]

The main objective of this clause is evidently to deal with the situation of *already* existing States wanting to join the treaty. The clause was not specifically designed to address the situation of a *new State* seceding from a State that is *already* a NAFTA party. Since the NAFTA already applies to the territory of Quebec (as a Province of the federal State of Canada), the question of accession becomes whether the agreement should *continue* to apply after secession. In any event, Article 2204 would apply to the case of Quebec. What is also clear is that from the mere presence of a clause dealing with 'accession' in a treaty, it simply cannot be concluded that the parties wanted to *prevent* a *new* State to become a party.[65] In other words, the mere existence of Article 2204 cannot be interpreted as meaning that Quebec *cannot* accede to the treaty.[66] Moreover, certain comments made by representatives of the NAFTA parties before the 1995 referendum suggest that they believed that the question of Quebec's accession to the NAFTA would have to be decided under Article 2204.[67] This being said, NAFTA parties have not supported the automatic succession of Quebec to the agreement. **8.05**

At the end of the day, Quebec would have to negotiate the terms and conditions of its accession to NAFTA.[68] One writer described the process as taking place in three distinct phases. The first phase of the accession procedure is related to the decision by the member States to determine whether or not to start any negotiation with Quebec regarding its formal accession to the Treaty.[69] The second phase concerns the negotiation of the terms and conditions of such accession.[70] Article 2204 refers to the role of the Free Trade Commission in this matter. The Commission is composed of 'cabinet-level **8.06**

---

64 The most comprehensive analysis of this clause is found in: Loungnarath (n 52) 1.

65 Zedalis (n 40) 22:

> Nor does it seem acceptable to infer that the presence of an accession provision in a treaty means succession is incompatible therewith. The presence of such a provision can be explained as allowing nations not controlling territory under the sovereign authority of extant states party to commit themselves to the treaty's terms. It need not be understood as having but a single meaning – succession is inoperative.

See also Berbner (n 22) 300.

66 Berbner, ibid., 300–301.

67 Ibid., 292.

68 Brower and Smutny (n 51) 55; Grabell (n 52) 281; Majzub (n 22) 438–9; Kasku-Jackson (n 52) 19.

69 Loungnarath (n 52) 33.

70 Finally, the third phase of the accession process concerns the result of the negotiation between the NAFTA parties and Quebec which would have to be approved by each State in accordance with its own domestic legal procedures.

representatives of the Parties or their designees'.[71] Accession negotiation will therefore involve all NAFTA States. Under Article 2001, 'all decisions of the Commission shall be taken by consensus, except as the Commission may otherwise agree'. This means that the accession of Quebec to the Treaty would have to be agreed by all three NAFTA States.[72] Some writers have argued that accession requires unanimity and therefore gives each State effectively a right to veto.[73] Others have denied the existence of any such veto based on the inclusion of the second paragraph of Article 2204.[74] In any event, it has been argued that in both the first and second phases of the procedure, the negotiation would have to be based on the principle of good faith.[75]

8.07 Finally, what is also clear is that none of the three NAFTA parties could simply reject Quebec's candidacy on the grounds (mentioned at Art. 34 of the Vienna Convention) that it 'appears from the treaty or is otherwise established' that the application of the NAFTA to the territory of Quebec 'would be incompatible with the object and purpose of the treaty or would radically change the conditions for its operation'. Zedalis (like other scholars[76]) has convincingly shown that any such 'incompatibility' does not arise from the mere accession of a new State to a treaty when the instrument was already applicable to the territory concerned.[77] Thus, considering that an independent Quebec would be liberal democracy strongly supporting free trade, it is difficult to see how its accession to the NAFTA could fulfill any of the exceptions set out at Article 34.[78]

---

71 NAFTA Art. 2001.

72 Brower and Smutny (n 51) 55.

73 Ibid.

74 Loungnarath (n 52) 53.

75 Ibid., 24ff.

76 See, Berbner (n 22) 303. It should be added that other writers have taken a different position on whether the argument of 'incompatibility' could be raised against Quebec becoming a party to the agreement: Williams (n 22) 36; Bernier (n 54) 80. It is important to note that these two writers made these observations before the NAFTA entered into force in 1994 at the time when only a *bilateral* FTA existed between the US and Canada.

77 Zedalis (n 40) 22–6, 27. See also: Berbner (n 22) 303.

78 For an analysis of these exceptions in the context of bilateral treaties, see: Chapter 5, Section 2.4.

9

STATE SUCCESSION TO THE ICSID CONVENTION

The question addressed in this chapter is whether a *new* successor State can **9.01** *automatically* become a party to the ICSID Convention as a result of the predecessor State's membership.[79]

1. THE SPECIAL CATEGORY OF TREATIES CREATING INTERNATIONAL ORGANIZATIONS

The ICSID Convention is a multilateral treaty. Yet, one fundamental feature **9.02** of the Convention is the fact that it created an international organization, the International Centre for the Settlement of Investment Disputes (hereinafter 'the Centre'), which is considered to have 'full international legal personality'.[80] Thus, States adhere to the Convention not only as parties to a multilateral treaty (the ICSID Convention), but also as members of an international organization (the Centre).[81]

Article 4 of the Vienna Convention deals with the specific situation of 'treaties **9.03** constituting international organizations and treaties adopted within an international organization'.[82] It provides that the rules contained in the Convention

79 See, C.J. Tams, 'State Succession to Investment Treaties: Mapping the Issues', (2016) 31(2) *ICSID Rev* 321ff.

80 Art. 18, Convention on the Settlement of Investment Disputes between States and Nationals of Other States (18 March 1965, entered into force on 14 October 1966), 575 UNTS 160; (1965) 4 ILM 532 [hereinafter 'ICSID Convention'].

81 Tams (n 79) 321.

82 See: P. Palchetti, 'Article 4' in Distefano, Gaggioli and Hêche (n 9) 141ff.

apply to the effect of succession of States in respect of 'any treaty which is the constituent instrument of an international organization'.[83] This provision also indicates that this is 'without prejudice to the rules concerning acquisition of membership and without prejudice to any other relevant rules of the organization'.[84] In other words, the question of succession to a treaty constitutive of an international organization is essentially governed by the specific rules of that organization regarding membership.[85] These rules prevail over the more general provisions contained in the Vienna Convention.[86] In fact, the specific rules existing for each organization have been applied in virtually all cases. Article 4 of the Convention is almost never applied in this context.[87] This situation led the ILC Commentary to conclude that the rules of succession of States 'frequently do not apply in respect of a constituent instrument of an international organization'.[88] In fact, Bühler believes that the question of membership to international organizations is *not* a question of State succession per se, but rather one concerning the law of international organizations.[89]

83 Vienna Convention on Succession to Treaties (n 1).

84 Ibid.

85 On this provision, see: Palchetti (n 82) 147–8.

86 K. Bühler, *State Succession and Membership in International Organizations: Legal Theories Versus Political Pragmatism* (Brill 2001) 30.

87 Ibid., 290; Palchetti (n 82) 146–7.

88 ILC Report, 26th Session, 1974 (n 41) 178. See also at 180:

> In the light of the foregoing, the question may even be asked whether the law of succession applies to constituent instruments of international organizations at all. For example, the right of participation of a newly independent State in multilateral treaties in force by a notification of succession cannot normally extend to constituent instruments of an international organization because participation in those instruments is generally governed, as indicated in the preceding paragraphs, by the rules of the organization in question concerning the acquisition of membership. On the other hand, there are certain international organizations, such as some unions, which do not have, properly speaking, specific rules for acquisition of membership. In those organizations the law of succession in respect of treaties has at times been applied, and may be applied, to participation of a newly independent State in their respective constituent instruments. Furthermore, there have been cases in connection with the separation from a union of States in which the question of the participation in the organization of the separated States has been approached from the standpoint of the law concerning succession in respect of treaties. In addition, succession in respect of a constituent instrument is not necessarily linked to matters relating to membership. For instance, the 'moving treaty-frontiers' rule applies in the case of treaties constituting an international organization. In short, while the rules of succession of States frequently do not apply in respect of a constituent instrument of an international organization, it would be incorrect to say that they do not apply at all to this category of treaties. In principle, the relevant rules of the organization are paramount, but they do not exclude altogether the application of the general rules of succession of States in respect of treaties in cases where the treaty is a constituent instrument of an international organization.

89 Bühler (n 86) 291.

2. THERE IS GENERALLY NO SUCCESSION TO THE MEMBERSHIP OF AN INTERNATIONAL ORGANIZATION

With a few exceptions[90] (including in the context of financial institutions,[91] such as the IMF[92]), constitutive instruments of international organizations do *not* specifically provide for a new State to become member of an organization by way of *succession* to treaties.[93] The ILC also recognized that succession to an organization is possible in the situation where the instrument does *not* contain any formal process of admission to membership: 'when a multilateral treaty creates a weaker association of its parties, with no formal process of admission, it seems that the general rule prevails and that a new State may become a party and a member of the association by transmitting a notification of succession to the depositary'.[94] Apart from these rare situations, there is no succession to the membership of an international organization for a new State by the mere fact that the predecessor State was a member of such organization before the date of succession.[95] Thus, as noted by the ILC, 'the practice excluding succession is clearest in cases where membership of the organization is dependent on a *formal process of admission* (... .)'.[96] In other words, automatic transmission of membership status 'is excluded in all cases where acquisition of membership is made dependent on a formal process of admission'.[97] **9.04**

For the vast majority of international organizations, the question of membership is governed by the rules contained in the constitutive instrument on how States (both new and 'old' States) can become members by way of *accession*.[98] As noted by Tams, 'new States have regularly been expected to go through the organization's admissions process and join as new members.'[99] There is a **9.05**

90 See, a number of examples mentioned in: Bühler, ibid., 299ff.

91 See, A. Goia, 'State Succession and International Financial Organizations', in Pierre Michel Eisemann and Martti Koskenniemi (dir), *State Succession: Codification Tested Against the Facts* (Martinus Nijhoff Publ. 2000) 331; L. Forget 'La succession d'États en Europe de l'Est et les organisations financières internationales: l'expérience de la Banque Mondiale', in G. Burdeau and B. Stern (eds), *Dissolution, continuation et succession en Europe de l'Est* (Cedin-Paris I 1994) 106–15; I. Shihata 'Matters of State Succession in the Practice of the World Bank', in P.B. Casella (ed), *Dimensão internacional do direito: estudos em homenagem a GE do Nascimento e Silva* (Ed LTR 2000) 453–72; P.R. Williams, 'State Succession and the International Financial Institutions: Political Criteria v. Protection of Outstanding Financial Obligations', (1994) 43 ICLQ 776.

92 Bühler (n 86) 288, 297ff.

93 Ibid., 31. Tams (n 79) 12 also refers to other situations where a more flexible approach has been adopted by international organizations, including the World Band and the IMF. On this question, see: Goia (n 91) 327ff.

94 ILC Report, 26th Session, 1974 (n 41) 178. See also: H.G. Schermers and N.M. Blokker, *International Institution Law*, (4th ed., Nijhoff 2003) 90–91.

95 Karl Zemanek, 'State Succession after Decolonization' (1965–III) 116 Rec. des cours 253.

96 ILC Report, 26th Session, 1974 (n 41) 178 (emphasis in the original). See also: Schermers and Blokker (n 94) 90–91.

97 Goia (n 91) 341.

98 Buhler (n 86) 31.

99 Tams (n 79) 322; Schermers and Blokker (n 94) 90–91.

consensus on that point amongst scholars.[100] This is also the conclusion reached by the ILC.[101]

3. THE PRACTICE OF STATES REGARDING SUCCESSION TO INTERNATIONAL ORGANIZATIONS

9.06 This section briefly examines whether the practice of States has been in line with the general principles set out above. The first point to mention is that the question of succession to the membership of international organizations is only relevant when a *new* State is created. Therefore, the question does not arise in the context of a cession of territory or the integration of an entire State into an already existing State.[102]

9.07 In the context of secession, the question of membership will only concern the new secessionist State.[103] The continuator State will logically continue to be a member of the organizations to which it was a member before the date of succession.[104] A good example is the situation of Pakistan.[105] In the context of the 'partition' of British India into two distinct States (India and Pakistan), India has generally been considered as the continuing State of the British Indian Empire, while Pakistan was viewed as having seceded from India in

---

100 Bühler (n 86) 32–5, 291, referring to many writers. See also: H.M. Schermers, 'International Organizations, Membership', in R. Bernhardt (ed), *Max Planck Encyclopedia of Public International Law* (Max Planck Institute 1984) 1321; O'Connell (n 9) 183; Andreas Zimmermann, 'State Succession in Treaties', in *Max Planck Encyclopedia of Public International Law* (OUP, online edn, 2006) [16].

101 ILC Report, 26th Session, 1974 (n 41) 177–8:

> International organizations take various forms and differ considerably in their treatment of membership. In many organizations, membership, other than original membership, is subject to a formal process of admission. Where this is so, practice appears now to have established the principle that a new State is not entitled automatically to become a party to the constituent treaty and a member of the organization as a successor State, simply by reason of the fact that at the date of the succession its territory was subject to the treaty and within the ambit of the organization. (…) New States have, therefore, been regarded as entitled to become Members of the United Nations only by admission, and not by succession. The same practice has been followed in regard to membership of the specialized agencies and of numerous other organizations.

102 Bühler (n 86) 285–7, 127–51. In the context of the 'unification' of Germany, no question of admission to any international organization arose: the membership of the GDR elapsed at the date of succession when it ceased to exist, while the FRG continued its membership to such organizations without any interruption. See: Schermers and Blokker (n 94) 82; Buhler (n 86) 148, 296–7.

103 Bühler (n 86) 287–8.

104 Ibid., 285–7; A. Zimmermann, 'Continuity of States', in *Max Planck Encyclopedia of Public International Law* (n 100) [7]; Zimmermann, 'State Succession in Treaties' (n 100) [16]; Zemanek (n 95) 253.

105 See, 'The Succession of States in relation to Membership in the United Nations – Memorandum prepared by the Secretariat', UN Doc. A/CN.4/149 and Add.1, in (1962) II *Yearbook ILC*, 101ff. See also: Bühler (n 86) 42ff.

1947 right after its independence.[106] Pakistan wanted to automatically become a member of the UN.[107] The United Nations rejected such a claim and held that India simply continued the membership of British India to the organization.[108] Pakistan was later admitted to the UN as a *new* member.[109] Since then, the practice of the UN in the context of secession has been that the new State does not automatically succeed to the organization.[110]

---

106 Legal Department of the United Nations, UN Press Release, UN Doc PM/473 (12 August 1947). This question is examined in T.S.N. Sastry, *State Succession in Indian Context* (Dominant Publ. 2004) 77ff. This qualification is rather superficial, as both India and Pakistan actually became independent States *at the same time* as a result of the adoption of a law by the British Parliament Indian Independence Act (1947), 10 & 11 Geo. VI, c 30. On this point see: O'Connell (n 9, vol. I) 8.

107 UN Doc. S/498; Security Council, Official Records, 1947, No. 78, 2027–8.

108 UN Press Release (n 106) containing the legal opinion prepared by Assistant Secretary-General Kerno, dated 8 August 1947:

> From the viewpoint of international law, the situation is one in which a part of an existing State breaks off and becomes a new State. On this analysis, there is no change in the international status of India; it continues as a State with all the treaty rights and obligations, and consequently, with all the rights and obligations of membership in the United Nations. The territory which breaks off, Pakistan, will be a new State; it will not have the treaty rights and obligations of the old State, and it will not, of course, have membership in the United Nations. (...) Apart from the question of separation, the Independence Act has effected a basic constitutional change in India. The existing State of India has become a Dominion, and consequently, has a new status in the British Commonwealth of Nations, independence in external affairs, and a new form of government. It is clear, however, that this basic constitutional change does not affect the international personality.

The conclusion reached in the legal opinion was that:

> 1. The new Dominion of India continues as an original Member State of the United Nations with all rights and obligations of membership. 2. Pakistan will be a new non-member State. In order for it to become a Member of the United Nations, it would have to apply for admission pursuant to Article 4 of the Charter, and its application would be handled under the pertinent rules of procedure of the General Assembly and the Security Council. (...)

See also: K.P. Misra, 'Succession of States: Pakistan's Membership in the United Nations', (1965) *Canadian YIL* 281–9.

109 See: GA Res. 108 (II), 30 September 1947. See also: 186th meeting; Security Council, Official Records, Second Year, No. 78, 2027–31, 2052–5; 190th meeting; Security Council, Official Records, Second Year, No. 81, 2136–41; A/350; General Assembly, Official Records, Second Session, First Committee, 529, annex 1.

110 See, Bühler (n 86) 294–5. The position is explained as follows in: 'Letter from the Chairman of the Sixth Committee to the Chairman of the First Committee', 8 October 1947, UN Doc A/C.I/212 in UN Doc A/CN.4/149:

> After having considered the problem, the Sixth Committee agreed on the following principles:
>
> 1. That, as a general rule, it is in conformity with legal principles to presume that a State which is a Member of the Organization of the United Nations does not cease to be a Member simply because its Constitution or its frontier have been subjected to changes, and that the extinction of the State as a legal personality recognized in the international order must be shown before its rights and obligations can be considered thereby to have ceased to exist.
>
> 2. That when a new State is created, whatever may be the territory and the populations which it comprises and whether or not they formed part of a State Member of the United Nations, it cannot under the system of the Charter claim the status of a Member of the United Nations unless it has been formally admitted as such in conformity with the provisions of the Charter.
>
> 3. Beyond that, each case must be judged according to its merits.

9.08 In the context of dissolution, the question of succession to the membership of an international organization is relevant for *all* new States. There is no automatic succession to an international organization. A new State has to be admitted by way of accession.[111] A problematic situation arises when one of these States claims to be the continuator of the predecessor State and for that reason, argues that it continues its membership in the international organization. This question arose in the 1990s with the claim of the FRY to be the continuator of the former SFRY.[112] Another exceptional situation mentioned by Bühler in his book is that of the 'revived' membership in the case of short-lived union of States.[113] This was the situation of Syria in 1961.[114]

9.09 As a matter of principle, the question of succession to membership of an international organization should arise in the context of the *unification* of two States where, as a result of the merger, a *new* State is created. Yet, examples of unification of States (such as those of Yemen (1990),[115] the United Arab Republic (1958),[116] Tanzania (1964)[117] and Vietnam (1976))[118] show that a different approach has generally been taken, whereby the new entity has *not* been considered to be a *new* State in a number of international organizations.[119] In fact, that new State simply *continued* the membership of the predecessor State(s) to such organizations.[120]

4. THERE IS NO AUTOMATIC SUCCESSION TO THE ICSID CONVENTION

9.10 The ICSID Convention contains no provision addressing the question of the acquisition of membership by way of succession. The Convention does,

111 See, Bühler (n 86) 294–5.

112 See, Chapter 3, Section 2.1.

113 Bühler (n 86) 287–8.

114 Ibid., 50ff. The United Arab Republic was created as a result of the unification of Egypt and Syria in 1958. The State ceased to exist in 1961, with both Egypt and Syria considered as new States. Yet, the United Nations considered Syria *not* as a new State in 1961 but as an 'old' State which was simply readmitted to the organization and reinstalled in its seat as if its membership had simply been 'suspended' during the three years during which it had merged with Egypt to form the United Arab Republic. See: Habib Guerari, 'Quelques observations sur les Etats éphémères', (1994) AFDI 426–9; Richard Young, 'The State of Syria: Old or New?', (1962) 56 AJIL 482–8.

115 Bühler (n 86) 115ff, and 125.

116 Ibid., 295–6.

117 Ibid., 62ff.

118 Ibid., 68ff.

119 Schermers and Blokker (n 94) 82–3; Bühler (n 86) 295.

120 Bühler (n 86) 289, 296, distinguishes cases of *substitution* of membership when *only one* of the predecessor State was a party to an organization before the date of succession and other situations of *amalgamation* of membership when *both* predecessor States were members. He speaks of the '*substitution* of membership of unified Yemen for the membership of either one, or the *continuation* of membership of both of its component State' (at 126, emphasis in original).

however, contain a specific rule (Arts 67 and 68) as to how a State can become a party to the Convention.[121] These specific features of the ICSID Convention strongly suggest that there is *no* automatic succession to the membership to the Centre. In other words, a new State *must* apply to become a member of the Centre and a party to the Convention.[122] However, this position remains 'untested'. Thus, the present author is not aware of any case where a claim was brought forward against a successor State that had not already acceded to the ICSID Convention. Therefore, no tribunal has tested the possibility for a new State to be considered as a party to the Convention by way of succession simply as a result of the predecessor State's membership to the organization.

In any event, the actual practice of States regarding the question of membership to the Centre in situations involving State succession has been rather straightforward.[123] From the combined works of Tams and Schreuer, the following relevant points can be highlighted:[124] **9.11**

- the CSFR became a contracting State in August 1992 (before the date of dissolution). The Czech and Slovak Republics joined as new parties in 1993 and 1994, respectively.[125]
- the SFRY was a member since 1967. The successor States all became members as new States (Slovenia in 1994, Bosnia and Herzegovina in 1997, Croatia in 1998, Macedonia in 1998).[126] Serbia joined as a new member in 2007 after the secession of Montenegro from Serbia-Montenegro (2006).[127] Montenegro joined in 2013 as a new member. Kosovo did the same thing in 2009.[128]
- Timor-Leste became a member in 2002 as a new State even though Indonesia (the colonial predecessor State) had been a member since 1968.[129]

121 ICSID Convention (n 80). See, generally, Christoph Schreuer et al. (eds), *The ICSID Convention: A Commentary* 2nd edn (CUP 2009) 1267ff.

122 Tams (n 79) 323.

123 Ibid.:

> Although ICSID aspires to universal membership and allows World Bank members to join without undergoing any admissions procedure, it has clearly followed the orthodox approach precluding succession to membership. Invariably, new States that have joined the ICSID Convention have done so as new members, even though this opened up a time-gap in the application of the ICSID regime.

124 For information regarding ICSID Membership, see: https://icsid.worldbank.org/apps/ICSIDWEB/about/Pages/MembershipStateDetails.aspx?state=ST300.

125 Schreuer et al (n 121) 169 (fn 401).

126 Ibid.

127 Ibid.

128 Tams (n 79) 323.

129 Schreuer et al (n 121) 169 (fn 401).

- South Sudan joined as a new party in 2012.[130]
- The USSR and Ethiopia were not parties to the Convention and the issue of succession simply did not arise in the context of the 'secession' of the former republics and Eritrea, respectively.

9.12 As mentioned above,[131] the question of the application of Chinese BITs to Macao and Hong Kong is controversial. Article 70 provides that the Convention 'shall apply to all territories for whose international relations a Contracting State is responsible, except those that are excluded by such State by written notice to the depositary of this Convention either at the time of ratification, acceptance or approval or subsequently'. China has neither excluded nor extended the application of the ICSID Convention to these territories.[132] Consequently, as noted by one writer, 'the default position is that the Convention applies in respect of both Hong Kong and Macao'.[133] It should be added that since Russia signed the Convention in 1992, but has not ratified it, the application of Article 70 to the situation in Crimea does not arise.[134]

5. THE QUESTION OF CONSENT IN THE CONTEXT OF THE ICSID CONVENTION

9.13 In the context of the ICSID Convention, another issue that is likely to arise is that of consent to arbitration. Under the ICSID arbitration, *both* parties' consent, evidenced in writing, is required (the investor and the host State) in order for a dispute to be settled by an arbitral tribunal established under the ICSID Convention. Another important point is that the consent to the jurisdiction of the Centre by a State needs to be found at two different places.

9.14 First, in order for an ICSID tribunal to have jurisdiction over a dispute, the basic requirement is that the 'successor State be a Contracting State at the time proceedings are instituted'.[135] Secondly, the fact that the host State of the investment has ratified the Convention does not, in and of itself, constitute consent to the Centre's jurisdiction over a dispute. A more specific type of

---

130 Tams (n 79) 323.

131 See, Chapter 6, Section 5.

132 Odysseas G. Repousis, 'On Territoriality and International Investment Law: Applying China's Investment Treaties to Hong Kong And Macao' (2015) 37(1) *Michigan JIL* 156.

133 Ibid. See also: Schreuer et al (n 121) 1276, fn. 7: 'Hong Kong became a special administrative region of China on 1 July 1997 and is now covered by China's ratification of the Convention. Macao, which was covered by Portugal's participation in the Convention, is covered by China's ratification since 19 December 1999.'

134 See, Chapter 6, Section 6.

135 Schreuer et al (n 121) 170.

consent is required. This consent may be found, inter alia, in a direct agreement (a State contract) between the investor and the host State (it can also be found in a provision of that State's domestic legislation or in a BIT). The issue can become problematic when the consent is found in a State contract that was entered before the date of succession by *another State* than the respondent new State. Would a tribunal have jurisdiction in such a given case? It has been suggested that the answer to the question should be positive. Thus, as explained by Schreuer, 'consent to the Centre's jurisdiction may be given before the host State becomes a Contracting State'.[136] In fact, such consent would be valid even if it was given by *another State* (the predecessor State) before that new State became an independent State.[137] What matters is the nexus between that new State and the territory where the investment was made under the contract:[138]

> Consent to jurisdiction under the ICSID Convention is intimately linked to the host State's status as a Contracting State. Where the State continues its predecessor's treaty relationships by virtue of a universal succession, any agreements of consent to the Centre's jurisdiction contracted by the predecessor State would seem to become automatically applicable to the successor State. It would be difficult to argue universal succession and continuity with regard to the Convention and other treaties and at the same time discontinuity with regard to agreements under the Convention. If the new State continues its status as a Contracting State under the Convention on the basis of a selective declaration of continuation without universal succession, the situation is not so clear. But the better view would still be that a continuing participation in the Convention also implies continuity with regard to consent agreements. If the investment in question relates to a particular part of the predecessor State's territory, this would only apply if the new State succeeds the old one with respect to that territory.[139]

Authors also refer to the situation where a *new* State ratifies the Convention **9.15**
by way of accession (not succession).[140] They mention that the consent to the

---

136 Ibid.

137 Ibid. A different position is adopted by Chittharanjan Felix Amerasinghe, *Jurisdiction of Specific International Tribunals* (Brill 2008) 444:

> There is one circumstance where the particular consent given under Article 25(1) of the Convention may become ineffective, not because the consent of the state party to the Convention is withdrawn impliedly but because of other circumstances. Where a state party to the Convention ceases to exist without state succession taking place, the consent given by it to being a party to the Convention terminates and any particular consents to arbitration given by it pursuant to Article 25 would cease to be enforceable or, indeed, valid, because it is no longer a party to the Convention. Its agreement to the Convention system has come to an end. Similarly, its former nationals would not be able to take advantage of particular consents given by them or to them, because they have ceased to be nationals of a state party to the Convention as required by Article 25. They no longer have a national state which has agreed to the arbitration system of the Convention by being a party to it.

138 Schreuer et al (n 121) 170.

139 Ibid., 169.

140 Ibid., 170.

jurisdiction of the Centre over arbitration dispute may be given *before* a State becomes a party to the ICSID Convention:

> The situation is less clear where the new State ratifies the ICSID Convention subsequent to its independence or its merger with another State. Since consent to the Centre's jurisdiction may be given before the host State becomes a Contracting State (...), such a situation would not automatically invalidate consent. Consent to jurisdiction may be passed on to the new State regardless of whether it has succeeded the old State as a Contracting State to the Convention and indeed regardless of whether the predecessor State ever was a Contracting State. It is suggested that in this case too the solution must lie in the question of territorial nexus. If the investment is linked to territory that is part of the new State, the presumption is that rights and duties arising from the investment relationship, including the consent to the Centre's jurisdiction, will pass to the successor State.[141]

9.16 One concrete example of such a situation is mentioned by Dupont regarding Kosovo.[142] He refers to the Law regarding foreign investment that was passed by the Assembly of Kosovo in November 2005, which contains 'Mechanisms for the Resolution of Investment Disputes' (Art. 16). Through this instrument, Kosovo consented to arbitration under the ICSID Convention. Therefore, Kosovo provided such consent before its accession to the ICSID Convention in 2009 (and even *before* its unilateral declaration of independence in February 2008).

141 Ibid.

142 Pierre-Emmanuel Dupont, 'Foreign Investment and the Status of Kosovo in International Law', (2009) 10 *J World Invest & Trade* 26.

Part D

STATE SUCCESSION TO STATE CONTRACTS

INTRODUCTION

Parts B and C focused on bilateral and multilateral investment treaties which are currently considered to be the most important sources of foreign investors' rights and protections. It is under these treaties that claimant investors start arbitration proceedings in most investment arbitration disputes. Thus, according to one recent estimate, 61.8 per cent of cases conducted under the ICSID Convention (and the ICSID Additional Facility Rules) were filed under BITs (10 per cent were filed under plurilateral treaties, 18.3 per cent under State contracts and 9.4 per cent under the investment law of the host-State).[1] These figures illustrate that State contracts remain relevant today as they provide an important source of rights (and obligations) for foreign investors.

This Part focuses on the question of State succession to State contracts. The question being addressed is whether a successor State is bound by the obligations resulting from a contract (including an arbitration clause) that had been signed by the predecessor State with a foreign company before the date of succession. In order to answer this question, it is first and foremost necessary to determine (more generally) whether the successor State is bound by the

1 *ICSID Caseload, Statistics*, Issue 2015–1, 10.

predecessor State's commercial obligations[2] and whether it must respect the acquired rights of foreign investors existing before the date of succession. This question will be examined in Chapter 10. The following chapters will apply the findings on succession to acquired rights regarding the specific problem of rights and obligations that result from one special type of instrument: State contracts. Chapter 11 will begin by examining the concept of a State contract and its unique characteristics. This will be followed by an analysis of the issue of succession and will conclude by showing that the successor State can modify a State contract after the date of succession, but that it must do so while respecting basic principles of international law (Chapter 12). Yet, in my view, the matter is more complex than that. This chapter puts forward a new framework of analysis with regards to the question of succession to State contracts. I will show, on the one hand, that the solution to the problem of succession to State contracts will depend on the different type of succession that is involved (Chapter 13). On the other hand, the question as to whether or not a successor State is bound by a State contract signed by the predecessor State will also depend on a number of specific factors and circumstances, which should be taken into account by a tribunal. These different factors and circumstances will be examined in Chapter 14.

2 On this question, see: Tai-Heng Cheng, *State Succession and Commercial Obligations* (Transnational Publ. 2006).

10

STATE SUCCESSION TO ACQUIRED RIGHTS UNDER CONTRACTS

INTRODUCTION

The question of State succession to acquired rights has not been codified by the ILC. The question was initially included among the issues to be examined by the ILC Special Rapporteur on matters other than succession to treaties,[3] and was discussed in some detail in Bedjaoui's Second Report (further discussed below).[4] The Report received mixed reviews from ILC members.[5] Since the question of acquired rights was considered by them as 'extremely controversial' and that no consensus had emerged, it was decided that the matter should be excluded from codification at this stage.[6] While the Vienna Convention on Succession of States in Respect of State Property, Archives and Debts includes a provision on 'State debt' (Art. 33), it does not cover per se rights of individuals. This is evident from Article 6 indicating that 'Nothing in **10.01**

3 ILC, Working Paper submitted by M. Lachs, A/5509, in (1963) II *Yearbook ILC*, Annex II, 298.

4 ILC, Second Report on Succession of States in Respect of Matters Other Than Treaties by Mr. Mohammed Bedjaoui, Special Rapporteur – Economic and Financial Acquired Rights and State Succession, A/CN.4/216/Rev.1, in (1969) II *Yearbook ILC* [hereinafter ILC, Second Report Bedjaoui, 1969].

5 Maria Isabel Torres Cazorla, 'Rights of Private Persons on State Succession: An Approach to the Most Recent Cases', in: Pierre Michel Eisemann and Martti Koskenniemi (dir), *State Succession: Codification Tested Against the Facts* (Martinus Nijhoff Publ. 2000) 678.

6 ILC, Report of the International Law Commission on the Work of its 21st Session, 2 June – 8 August 1969, Official Records of the General Assembly, 24th Session, Supplement No. 10 (A/7610/Rev.1), A/CN.4/220, in (1969) II *Yearbook ILC* 228.

the present articles shall be considered as prejudging in any respect any question relating to the rights and obligations of natural or juridical persons'.[7]

10.02 In one recent article published on the question of acquired rights, the author concluded that 'there is no general rule providing for the way in which the rights of private persons should pass from the predecessor State to the successor State', adding that 'international law imposes very few limitations upon successor States in regard to the rights of private persons'.[8] The following sections will examine some of the most important aspects of the controversial question of State succession to acquired rights.

1. A SUCCESSOR STATE'S SOVEREIGNTY DERIVES FROM INTERNATIONAL LAW, WHICH MAY IMPOSE RIGHTS AND OBLIGATIONS UPON IT

10.03 While the successor State is often a 'new' entity,[9] it is a 'sovereign' State as much as any other already existing States. As such, it benefits from rights and obligations that are attached to its status as an independent State,[10] including the principle of the equality of States. Importantly, the successor State does not derive its sovereignty from the predecessor State, but from international law.[11] This is reflected in the definition of State succession found in the

7 See, Torres Cazorla (n 5) 678.

8 Ibid., 717, also noting that 'the complexity of international trade, the existence of different economic systems and the absence of agreement regarding the definition of "acquired rights" seem to remain intractable problems'.

9 The successor State is, however, not a new State in instances of integration of a State and cession of territory.

10 O. Schachter, 'International Law in Theory and Practice: General Course in Public International Law' (1982) 178 Rec des Cours, 34; T.M. Franck, 'Fairness in the International Legal and Institutional System: General Course on Public International Law', (1993) 240 Rec des Cours 60.

11 ILC, Second Report Bedjaoui, 1969 (n 4) 76–7:

> The successor State does not derive its sovereignty from the predecessor State, but from international law and from its own statehood. In other words, there is not a *transfer* of one sovereignty, but a *substitution* of sovereignties by the extinction of one and the creation of another. The successor State possesses its own sovereignty because it has acceded to the dignity of statehood. (…) Sovereignty is an attribute of public international law which attaches to statehood. The new State does not derive its sovereignty from the predecessor State, but from international law. Furthermore, if sovereignty is necessarily derived only from a predecessor, from whom then did the very first sovereign, at the beginning of a long chain of succession, derive his sovereignty? (emphasis in the original).

See also: Mohammed Bedjaoui, 'Problèmes récents de succession d'États dans les États nouveaux', (1970–II) 130 Rec des Cours 537; Brigitte Stern, 'La succession d'États' (1996) 262 Rec des Cours 117–8:

> lorsqu'un nouvel État apparaît sur la scène internationale, à la suite d'un processus de succession d'États, c'est un État souverain différent de l'État souverain prédécesseur. Cette souveraineté lui est reconnue par le droit international, et ne lui vient évidemment pas de l'État prédécesseur.

Erik Castren, 'Aspects récents de la succession d'États', (1951–I) 78 Rec des Cours 388.

codification instruments adopted by the ILC[12] (and the Institut in 2001[13] and in 2015[14]). Indeed, all these instruments refer to the 'replacement of one State by another' in the responsibility for the international relations in a territory rather than to the 'transfer' of any such responsibility between them. In the words of O'Connell, 'the successor State in no sense "continues" the sovereignty of its predecessor'.[15] Consequently, the rights and the obligations of the predecessor State before the date of succession cannot *automatically* be 'transferred' to the new State.[16]

However, given the fact that a new State is 'sovereign', should it be concluded that such rights and obligations should never be imposed on that entity? While such a conclusion would undoubtedly be logical,[17] it remains, as noted by Bedajoui, that such a 'mechanical' application of the principle of the equality and sovereignty of States would not take 'any account of the special situation of the successor State'.[18] For him, such an approach 'would be more **10.04**

12 Art. 2(1)b) of the Vienna Convention on Succession of States in Respect of Treaties, signed on 23 August 1978 and entered into force on 6 November 1996, 1946 UNTS 3, in: 17 ILM 1978, 1488 [hereinafter 'Vienna Convention on Succession to Treaties']; Art. 2(1)a) of the Vienna Convention on Succession of States in Respect of State Properties, Archives and Debts, in: (1983) 22 ILM 306 [hereinafter 'Vienna Convention on Succession to State Properties, Archives and Debts']. The same definition can also be found at Art. 2 of the Draft Articles on Nationality of Natural Persons in Relation to the Succession of States, adopted by the ILC on second reading in 1999, ILC Report, UN Doc. A/54/10, 1999, chp. IV [44]–[45], in: (1997) II *Yearbook ILC* 13.

13 Institut de Droit international, *State Succession in Matters of Property and Debts*, Session of Vancouver, 2001, in (2000–2001) 69 Annuaire I.D.I., 713ff [hereinafter 'IDI, State Succession in Matters of Property and Debts, Resolution, 2001'].

14 Institut de Droit international, *State Succession in Matters of State Responsibility*, 14th Commission, (Rap. M.G. Kohen), Resolution, 28 August 2015, Art. 1 [hereinafter 'IDI, State Succession to Responsibility, Resolution, 2015'].

15 D.P. O'Connell, *State Succession in Municipal Law and International Law* vol I (CUP 1967) 26.

16 Bedjaoui, 'Problèmes récents de succession d'États' (n 11) 537.

17 Stern, 'La succession d'États' (n 11) 118:

> Sur le plan de la théorie du droit, l'idée même d'une succession est considérée par certains comme incompatible avec le concept de souveraineté. La succession d'États s'analysant en une substitution d'une souveraineté à une autre, on ne peut imaginer grever la souveraineté nouvellement apparue d'une obligation juridique de reprise des droits et obligations de l'État prédécesseur. Il devrait en résulter en bonne logique qu'un État souverain ne devrait être tenu d'aucune des obligations de son prédécesseur, et que devrait donc s'appliquer ce que l'on a appelé le principe de la '*table rase*'.

18 ILC, Second Report Bedjaoui, 1969 (n 4) 75–6:

> As a first approach, it may be argued that in the matter of acquired rights nothing should be imposed on the successor State that would not be imposed on any other State. The emphasis is on statehood, which the successor State possesses like any other State. If we stopped at this concept, however, the principle of the equality and sovereignty of States would be applied mechanically, without taking any account of the special situation of the successor State. That would be tantamount to denying the existence not only of acquired rights but also of all State succession. The successor State would be merely a State, no different from the other members of the international community and not governed by a special regime, that of State succession, which would cease to exist in public international law.

idealistic than realistic'[19] given the fact that 'the successor State has not been established *ex nihilo*, any more than it has come from outer space to lodge in a corner of the Earth'.[20] Thus, because the new State derives its sovereignty from international law, 'it cannot disengage itself from pre-existing rules and situations, or at least it cannot do so immediately and forever'.[21] As rightly noted by O'Connell, 'one may subscribe to the view that changes of sovereignty is not a transfer of sovereignty (…) and still reach the conclusion that the successor State is entitled to exercise the predecessor's rights and is obliged to discharge the predecessor's duties, *because international law so directs.* (…)'.[22] As explained by Bedjaoui, 'the obligation of the predecessor State does not survive, but is replaced by an international duty deriving solely from international law'.[23]

10.05 O'Connell identifies the 'ultimate question' as being 'whether international law contains rules for regulating the disposition of public rights and duties as a consequence of a succession of States, and how these rules are to be established'.[24] Indeed, he believes that international law does impose *some* obligations upon the new successor States regarding different aspects of State succession. However, he rejects the extreme approaches that have been adopted in the past by writers whereby the new State is either bound by *all* rights and obligations or by *none* of them. The basic assumption of his work is that 'the solution lies in a presumption of continuity which concrete analysis may rebut (…) and not in a universal touchstone of succession or non-succession'.[25]

10.06 For Stern, international law imposes obligations upon the successor States based on the application of the principle of 'coherence' of the international legal order.[26] New States are indeed *automatically* bound by rules of customary

---

19 Ibid., 76.

20 Ibid.

21 Ibid., 6.

22 O'Connell, *State Succession*, 1967 (n 15) 32–3 (emphasis added). See also: Annie Gruber, *Le droit international de la succession d'États* (Bruylant 1986) 97:

> on ne voit pas pourquoi il faudrait évacuer le principe d'une norme juridique qui imposerait ce respect au successeur en vertu du droit international. Ce n'est pas en tant qu'obligation dérivée et personnalisée qu'il convient en effet de traiter le respect des droits acquis, mais en tant que norme du droit international public.

23 ILC, Second Report Bedjaoui, 1969 (n 4) 100 (emphasis in the original). It should be added that he is critical regarding the existence of any such duties.

24 O'Connell, *State Succession*, 1967 (n 15) 32–3.

25 Ibid., 35.

26 Stern, 'La succession d'États' (n 11) 119:

> Ce que j'appelle ici le principe de cohérence est le principe selon lequel un État successeur en accédant au statut d'État devient partie intégrante du système international préexistant, dont il doit respecter l'intégrité et la cohérence. De même qu'un individu entrant dans une maison doit en respecter l'agencement, un État

international law.[27] Thus, allowing new States to simply reject the generally accepted rules would amount to 'deny[ing] the existence of a general international legal order'[28] and would 'create unacceptable disorder'.[29] While the ICJ has never had the opportunity to deal with this issue directly,[30] a passage taken from the *Case Concerning the Frontier Dispute* suggests that the court supports the automatic application of custom to new States.[31] The opposite position seems to be upheld by only a few writers.[32] One ICJ judge in the *North Sea Continental Shelf Cases* expressly endorsed a similar position in his separate opinion.[33]

2. THE LEGAL ORDER OF THE PREDECESSOR STATE DOES NOT SUDDENLY DISAPPEAR AS A RESULT OF A CHANGE OF SOVEREIGNTY AND PRIVATE RIGHTS REMAIN UNAFFECTED

The direct consequence of the fact that a new State's sovereignty does not derive from the predecessor State but rather from international law, is that 'the sovereignty of the [new] State *displaces* that of the [predecessor] State in the territory in question'.[34] For Bedjaoui, this means that, as a matter of principle, 'the political organization, the public law and the public policy of the new **10.07**

successeur en entrant dans la communauté internationale doit en reconnaître l'ordonnancement. En d'autres termes, la table rase n'est pas un corollaire incontournable du principe de souveraineté, si l'on veut bien ne pas oublier qu'en accédant au statut d'État souverain le nouvel État s'insère dans une société internationale qui précisément lui confère une souveraineté, telle que définie par le droit international, c'est-à-dire soumise par exemple au respect des règles coutumières existantes.

27 ILA, *Rapport Final sur la succession en matière de traités*, New Delhi Conference 2002, Committee on Aspects of the Law of State Succession, 24.

28 H. Waldock, 'General Course on Public International Law' (1962) 106 Rec des Cours 52.

29 L. Henkin, 'International Law: Politics, Values and Function: General Course on Public International Law' (1989) 216 Rec. des Cours 57; G.M. Danilenko, *Law-Making in the International Community* (Martinus Nijhoff, 1993) 115.

30 The United Kingdom in the *Fisheries Jurisdiction case* (*United Kingdom v. Iceland*) ICJ Reports 1974, Pleadings, vol II, (Reply submitted by the Government of the United Kingdom) took the view that 'there is universal agreement that a new state has no option but to adhere to generally accepted customary law'.

31 *Case Concerning the Frontier Dispute* (*Burkina Faso v. Mali*) ICJ Reports 1986 568, where the Chamber decided that customary law (in this case the principle of *uti possidetis*) would apply to new States 'immediately and from that moment onwards'.

32 H. Thierry, J. Combacau, S. Sur, and C. Vallee, *Droit international public*, (Montchrestien 1985) 119; G.J.H. Van Hoof, *Rethinking the Sources of International Law* (Kluwer 1983) 77–8; Danilenko (n 29) 113–18.

33 *North Sea Continental Shelf Cases* (*Federal Republic of Germany v. Denmark / Federal Republic of Germany v. Netherlands*) ICJ Reports 1969 38, Judge Ammoun (at 130) for whom a rule of customary law:

> does not require the consent of all States, (…) but at least the consent of those who were aware of this general practice and, being in a position to oppose it, have not done so. (…) Thus the right of countries becoming independent, which have not participated in the formation of rules which they consider incompatible with the new state of affairs, is preserved.

34 ILC, Second Report Bedjaoui, 1969 (n 4) 76 (emphasis in the original).

State supersede those of the former one'.[35] But, as noted by O'Connell, 'change of sovereignty does not occasion the total and automatic collapse of the internal legal order' of a State.[36] In other words, the laws of the predecessor State generally remain in place after that date;[37] they 'continue to govern the life of the community despite changes in the sovereign authority'.[38]

10.08 Such a situation may seem perplexing at first glance given the fact that, as noted by Bedjaoui, 'the free formulation of municipal law is the unmistakable mark of a country's internal sovereignty' and that 'just as the demands of economic sovereignty impose non-succession, those of political sovereignty, which are here brought into play, call for a break with the former juridical order'.[39] For him, however, while 'it may be said that the principle of non-succession to the municipal law of the predecessor State is incontestable', it remains that 'in practice the principle of continuity remains in force for a period whose duration varies according to the country, the era and the sectors of juridical life involved'.[40] Clearly, any decision by the successor State to maintain the legislation of the predecessor State for a transitional period is not the result of the application of any principle of international law.[41] While some writers have put forward philosophical reasons to explain this phenomenon,[42] new States generally do this for practical reasons: to 'avoid the instant disturbance of the legal order by the territorial change'.[43] Bedjaoui thus admits

---

35 Ibid., 76.

36 O'Connell, *State Succession*, 1967 (n 15) 31.

37 S. Rosenne, 'The Effect of Change of Sovereignty upon Municipal Law', (1950) 27 *British YIL* 267.

38 D.P. O'Connell, *The Law of State Succession* (CUP 1956) 215.

39 ILC, First Report on Succession of States in respect of rights and duties resulting from sources other than treaties, by Mr. Mohammed Bedjaoui, Special Rapporteur Topic: Succession of States in respect of matters other than treaties, A/CN.4/204 and Corr.1 (French only), in (1968) *II Yearbook ILC* 94, at 110 [hereinafter 'ILC, First Report Bedjaoui, 1968'].

40 Ibid.

41 D.P. O'Connell, 'Recent Problems of State Succession in Relation to New States', (1970–II) 130 Rec des Cours 127: 'this continuity is not the contrivance of international law, which certainly cannot direct any State as to which legal system it shall utilize, and which, as a positive legal system itself, cannot project the law from one sovereignty to another.'

42 Ibid., 127:

> The law derives from the community, and if the community survives the change of sovereignty, so does the legal system which regulates it, and in virtue of which it coheres. The transfer of sovereignty involves the substitution of one source of legislative authority for another, but only in the derivatives of the Hegelian theory of the State does it connote translation of the legal system into an expression of will of the successor State. The law does, indeed, become the law of the successor State, but this is in virtue of a proposition of philosophy, and not only in virtue of a positive creative act of that State.

43 J.H.W. Verzijl, *International Law in Historical Perspective*, Vol VII (Sijthoof 1974) 23, referred to in: Torres Cazorla (n 5) 664.

that it is the 'exigencies of life [that] will oblige' the new State to start its existence by using the legislation of the predecessor State.[44]

It is precisely because the legal order of the predecessor State does not disappear as a result of a change of sovereignty that the 'relationships which have arisen under private law are equally unaffected by changes of sovereignty'.[45] Put differently, 'rights acquired under the predecessor State survive [a] change of sovereignty because the law that created them survives'.[46] For O'Connell, the conclusion to be reached from this situation is that 'the successor State must respect' the existing rights under private contracts that are not affected by an event of succession.[47] He considers such rights as 'acquired rights', which he defines as including any rights, corporal or incorporeal, properly vested in a natural or juridical person, and of an assessable monetary value.[48] Yet, as noted by O'Connell himself, the very concept of 'acquired rights' is peculiar since 'all rights are in some sense acquired'.[49] Moreover, the affirmation of their existence is somewhat tendentious.[50] In fact, this has been one of the most controversial questions of international law for decades. The whole debate (which was the object of an entire Report by ILC Special Rapporteur Bedjaoui in 1969[51]) is beyond the scope of this book. Suffice it to say that the doctrine of acquired rights, which was formulated, **10.09**

44 ILC, Second Report Bedjaoui, 1969 (n 4) 76. See also: Bedjaoui, 'Problèmes récents de succession d'États' (n 11) 519–20:

> *En droit*, on l'a dit, il ne saurait y avoir de succession à l'ordre juridique colonial, en dehors de l'oeuvre volontaire du nouveau souverain. (...) *En fait*, comme on le sait déjà, les structures en place ainsi que divers facteurs extérieurs agissent dans le sens de la continuité. Par ailleurs le souci de ne pas laisser se créer un vide juridique dès l'accession à l'indépendance impose à l'Etat nouveau de reconduire provisoirement la législation antérieure au moins pour le temps nécessaire à l'élaboration d'une législation nouvelle plus appropriée. Ce temps peut se révéler long', emphasis in the original.

45 O'Connell, *The Law of State Succession*, 1956 (n 38) 216; Rosenne (n 37) 267; Jacques Barde, *La notion de droit acquis en droit international public* (PUP 1981) 22ff; ILC, Second Report Bedjaoui, 1969 (n 4) 76: 'all private law relations of individuals are left unaffected by the change of sovereignty.'

46 O'Connell, 'Recent Problems of State Succession' (n 41) 139.

47 O'Connell, *The Law of State Succession*, 1956 (n 38) 216; O'Connell, *State Succession*, 1967 (n 15) 237–9. See also: A. Zimmermann, 'State Succession in Other Matters than Treaties' in: *Max Planck Encyclopedia of Public International Law* (OUP, online edn, 2006) [31]; Gruber (n 22) 109 111.

48 O'Connell, *State Succession*, 1967 (n 15) 245.

49 O'Connell, 'Recent Problems of State Succession' (n 41) 135.

50 Ibid.:

> The expression 'acquired rights' has been employed now for nearly a century to designate the rights which are alleged to subsist after change of sovereignty, and it has an inherently tendentious quality, so that the proposition that acquired rights are unaffected by change of sovereignty tends to validate itself rather than to derive its validity from an external source.

See also: Bedjaoui, 'Problèmes récents de succession d'États' (n 11) 533.

51 ILC, Second Report Bedjaoui, 1969 (n 4).

inter alia, by the PCIJ,[52] and endorsed by ILC Special Rapporteur Garcia-Amador,[53] is clearly no longer recognized as an *absolute* principle[54] (a point further discussed in the next section).

3. THE SUCCESSOR STATE CAN MODIFY ACQUIRED RIGHTS, BUT MUST DO SO BY RESPECTING PRINCIPLES OF INTERNATIONAL LAW

10.10 While the legal order of the predecessor State does not disappear as a result of a change of sovereignty and the private rights of individuals generally remain unchanged, it is clear that *after* the date of succession the matter becomes one that is governed by the laws of the successor State.[55] In other words, the laws of the predecessor State generally continue to apply *until* they are modified or abolished *by the successor State*.[56] For that reason, Shaw speaks of a 'presumption' of the 'continuation of foreign acquired rights' until they are modified by the successor State.[57] Thus, while a successor State may decide to preserve

52 *Advisory Opinion No. 6, Certain Questions Relating to Settlers of German Origin in the Territory Ceded by Germany to Poland*, PCIJ, 10 Sept. 1923, (ser. B) No. 6, at 36.

53 ILC, Fourth Report on State Responsibility by Mr. F.V. Garcia-Amador, Special Rapporteur, A/CN.4/119, in (1959) II *Yearbook ILC* [hereinafter 'ILC, Fourth Report Garcia-Amador, 1959'] 3: 'respect for private rights of a patrimonial nature constitutes one of the principles of international law governing the treatment of aliens.'

54 Pierre Lalive, 'The Doctrine of Acquired Rights', in M. Bender (ed), *Rights and Duties of Private Investors Abroad* (International and Comparative Law Centre 1965) 167:

> The principle of respect for rights acquired prior to the change of sovereignty is limited also in scope in an – other way because of its purpose and by the nature of things. Stability of legal relationships does not and can – not mean a final status quo, the eternal and absolute permanence of established situations. It has never been contended that the principle deprives the acquiring state of its power to legislate for the future. The state keeps its competence to enact legislation affecting acquired rights, to adapt those rights to its own legal system. This is understood, of course, without prejudice to any 'obligations assumed by treaty and to the general guarantees offered by the law of nations, to be specified below, concerning the status of aliens and the international responsibility of states'.

55 Torres Cazorla (n 5) 664; O'Connell, *State Succession*, 1967 (n 15) 264; Barde (n 45) 100ff; Malcolm Shaw, *International Law* (8th ed. CUP 2008) 1001–2; ILC, Fourth Report Garcia-Amador, 1959 (n 53) 3: 'Under international law, the acquisition of private rights of a patrimonial nature is governed entirely by municipal law'; G. Kaeckenbeeck, 'La protection international des droits acquis', (1937–1) 59 Rec des Cours 412:

> La reconnaissance et le respect des droits privés acquis avant la cession n'entrave pas plus la liberté législative de l'État cessionnaire qu'elle ne l'aurait fait pour l'État cédant. Le fait que la souveraineté de l'État cessionnaire s'est substituée dans le territoire cédé à la souveraineté de l'État cédant implique sa compétence pour légiférer souverainement dans ce territoire, et il en résulte que la question de décider avec quels effets les lois nouvelles doivent être introduites rentre entièrement dans la compétence de l'État cessionnaire.

56 O'Connell, *The Law of State Succession*, 1956 (n 38) 215; Gruber (n 22) 109–11.

57 Shaw (n 55) 1003. See also: O'Connell, *The Law of State Succession*, 1956 (n 38) 215; O'Connell, *State Succession*, 1967 (n 15) 265.

such acquired rights,[58] it remains that 'there are no inviolable acquired rights which can be enforced against the new sovereign State' based on a rule of international law or one of State succession.[59] To argue otherwise would be contrary to the principle of sovereignty.[60]

Imposing an absolute obligation upon new States to maintain acquired rights would also be contrary to the principle of the equality of States. Such equality requires 'that no more obligations shall be imposed on the successor State than on the predecessor State as concerns respect for the same rights'.[61] *The Declaration on the Rights and Duties of States* proclaims that all States have the right to decide freely of their political, economic, and social system,[62] which means that all of them (both 'old' and 'new') possess the 'inviolable right to change existing economic institutions and create new ones'.[63] It is precisely because the successor State is equal to the predecessor State that the former is not obliged to maintain the legal order of *another* State (the latter) and preserve all rights (including the so-called 'acquired rights') that existed under that order. For Bedjaoui, 'that acquired rights should be respected to exactly the same extent as they were by the predecessor State may seem to be in conformity with the principle of equality of States, since the successor [State] does not have to assume more obligations than its predecessor'.[64] **10.11**

According to O'Connell, if it is generally recognized that *all States* (including the predecessor State) have the right to expropriate the property of a foreign investor (with compensation), why should the situation be any different for *new* States?[65] For him, 'there is no reason why a successor State should be in any less strong [of] a position in this respect than any other States, or why acquired rights should be invested after a change of sovereignty with a "sanctity and permanence" greater than they had before'.[66] Thus, in the words of Bedjaoui, 'if the predecessor State can free itself from rights which it has itself created, why should those rights be binding upon the successor, which **10.12**

58 Torres Cazorla (n 5) 664; O'Connell, *State Succession*, 1967 (n 15) 266; Stern, 'La succession d'États' (n 11) 115, 309: Ko Swan Sik, 'The Concept of Acquired Rights in International Law: A Survey', (1977) 24 *Netherlands ILR* 129; J. Crawford, *Brownlie's Principles of Public International Law* 8th edn (OUP 2012) 429.

59 ILC, Second Report Bedjaoui, 1969 (n 4) 78.

60 Ibid., 99.

61 Ibid., 76.

62 *Draft Declaration on the Rights and Duties of States* with commentaries, text adopted by the International Law Commission at its first session, in 1949, and submitted to the General Assembly as a part of the Commission's report covering the work of that session, in (1949) *Yearbook ILC*.

63 ILC, Second Report Bedjaoui, 1969 (n 4) 75.

64 Ibid., 76. See also: 'The successor State cannot be held to have more obligations than the predecessor State in relation to acquired rights recognized by the latter.'

65 O'Connell, *State Succession*, 1967 (n 15) 265; Swan Sik (n 58) 129.

66 O'Connell, ibid.

has had no part in their creation?'[67] Any other solution would be contrary to the principle of the equality of States[68] insofar as 'international law does not reduce the successor State to an inferior status'.[69] Ultimately, for Bedjaoui the whole question of whether or not the new State should respect acquired rights of foreigners is 'to decide whether the will of the successor State must be respected by virtue of the equality and sovereignty of States, because the successor State is a State like any other, or whether it is to be limited, precisely because it is a successor State'.[70]

10.13 These considerations have implications that are important in terms of what States can (and cannot) do regarding acquired rights of foreigners. For O'Connell, at the end of the day, the principle of the respect of acquired rights 'is no more than a principle that change of sovereignty should not touch upon the interests of individuals more than is necessary'.[71] He adds that 'this does not mean that these interests may not be interfered with at all'.[72] The same idea is set out at Article 25 of the Resolution adopted by the Institut regarding 'State Succession in Matters of Property and Debts' providing that 'successor States shall in so far as is possible respect the acquired rights of private persons in the legal order of the predecessor State'.[73] Ultimately, what the principle of the respect of acquired rights provides for is to 'indemnif[y] the titleholders from complete and arbitrary destruction of their interests, and secure for them an impartiality on the part of the successor State in the exercise of its discretion'.[74] Thus, while a new State can change its own law (and therefore affect the acquired rights of foreigners), it must do so in an impartial, non-arbitrary, and non-discriminatory manner. In other words, any such changes must be in accordance with a number of legal obligations existing for all States under international law.[75] In fact, as mentioned by O'Connell, this is

67 ILC, Second Report Bedjaoui, 1969 (n 4) 99. For him: 'The change of sovereignty, which has given rise to discontinuity by the very fact of the existence of two different, independent juridical orders where there was previously only one, results in a hiatus and the extinction of pre-existing rights.'

68 Olugbenga Shoyele, 'State Succession and Governmental Contracts in African States', (1997) 9 *Sri Lanka JIL* 248–50.

69 ILC, Second Report Bedjaoui, 1969 (n 4) 76. See also: Yilma Makonnen, 'State Succession in Africa: Selected Problems', (1986–V) 200 Rec des Cours 126.

70 ILC, Second Report Bedjaoui, 1969 (n 4) 76.

71 O'Connell, *State Succession*, 1967 (n 15) 266.

72 Ibid.

73 IDI, State Succession in Matters of Property and Debts, Resolution, 2001 (n 13).

74 O'Connell, *State Succession*, 1967 (n 15) 266.

75 Stern, 'La succession d'États' (n 11) 115:

> l'État successeur devra mettre sur pied un nouvel ordre juridique, dans le respect des normes coutumières internationales en vigueur, concernant par exemple le respect des droits de l'homme ou des minorités, ou le respect de la propriété privée – je ne parle pas de droits acquis, cette expression étant un peu datée, et la norme internationale actuelle ne s'énonçant pas en termes de respect absolu des droits acquis.

the only issue where international law plays a role: it determines 'the extent to which rights created under the predecessor's law may be terminated by the successor State'.[76] Even Bedjaoui admits that international law imposes certain limits on a new State's freedom of action in this respect.[77]

What are these obligations imposed to a State under international law? There is no doubt, as noted by the Badinder Commission,[78] that the successor State must respect the *jus cogens* norms when modifying acquired rights.[79] The same is true for obligations contained in the umbrella concept of the Minimum Standard of Treatment ('MST') under custom.[80] While this proposition has been contested in the past by certain writers,[81] it seems undeniable today (as examined above[82]) that a new State must act in accordance with the MST. This includes (at the very least) an obligation to prevent denial of justice and arbitrary conduct as well as an obligation to provide investors due process and 'full protection and security'.[83] Indeed, some arbitral tribunals have concluded that the respect of acquired rights was protected under the MST.[84] **10.14**

See also: Shoyele (n 68) 253; Lalive (n 54) 192:

> The conclusion is, thus, inescapable: If the notion of acquired rights or of pecuniary rights depends upon municipal law as a general principle, it does not follow that each state enjoys a discretionary power in respect of such rights belonging to aliens. The exercise of this power is limited by the law of nations.

76 O'Connell, *State Succession*, 1967 (n 15) 32.

77 ILC, Second Report Bedjaoui, 1969 (n 4) 100:

> Hence, acquired rights are respected only if the successor State so wishes, or if its competence is limited by treaty. (…) However, the competence of the successor State is clearly not unlimited. Its actions should always be consistent with the rules of conduct that govern any State; for it is, first and foremost, not a successor State, but a State—in other words, a subject having, in addition to its rights, international obligations the violation of which would engage its international responsibility.

78 In the context of the break-up of Yugoslavia, the First Opinion of the Arbitration Commission of the European Community Conference on Yugoslavia (also known as the 'Badinder' Commission) of 29 November 1991 noted that 'the peremptory norms of general international law and, in particular, respect of the fundamental rights of the individual and the rights of people and minorities, are binding on all the parties to the succession'. (Art. 1(e), First Opinion, in (1993) 92 ILR 164.

79 Torres Cazorla (n 5) 667–70.

80 Ibid., 667–8; Kaeckenbeeck (n 55) 412; Lalive (n 54) 200ff; O'Connell, *State Succession*, 1967 (n 15) 266.

81 ILC, Second Report Bedjaoui, 1969 (n 4) 82, for whom the power of a new State to legislate 'cannot be limited in practice by a principle as vague as that of an international minimum, which employs such hazy criteria as the demands of civilization'. He further argues that 'it is neither sound doctrine nor in conformity with practice and judicial precedent to assert that aliens should be treated better than nationals (or even, as will be seen, to argue that they are in fact simply treated in the same way as nationals)' (at 83).

82 See, Chapter 6, Section 6.3.2.1.4.

83 See P. Dumberry, *The Fair and Equitable Treatment Standard: A Guide to NAFTA Case Law on Article 1105* (Wolters Kluwer 2013).

84 *Oko Pankki Oyj Vtb Bank (Deutschland) AG Sampo Bank PLC v. Estonia*, ICSID Case No. ARB/04/6, Award, 19 November 2007 [238]:

> According to the minimum standard under customary international law, an investor is protected against the host state's fraud, bad faith, capricious and wilful discrimination or where the host state "deprives an investor of acquired rights in a manner that leads to the unjust enrichment of the State.

10.15 Another question is whether a new State is also automatically bound by the human rights obligations contained in a treaty to which the predecessor State was a party before the date of succession.[85] It is increasingly recognized in doctrine,[86] by State practice,[87] and by certain judges at the ICJ,[88] that international human rights treaties to which the predecessor State was party are opposable to successor States because of their attachment to the population living in that State. In other words, the successor State would be automatically bound by the human rights instruments ratified by the predecessor State. Whether or not this is the case is a question beyond the scope of this book.

10.16 For O'Connell, when a successor State (like any other State) decides to terminate rights of a *foreign* person it must do so in accordance with international law and provide compensation.[89] But, for him, this is a question that has nothing to do with rules of State succession per se.[90] Thus, the

---

See also: *Hassan Awdi, Enterprise Business Consultants, Inc. and Alfa El Corporation v. Romania*, ICSID Case No. ARB/10/13, Award, 2 March 2015 [298]; 'Under international law, the doctrine of acquired or vested rights is well-established as a customary norm.'

85 On this question, see the analysis in M. Belkahla, 'La succession d'États en matière de traitées multilatéraux relatifs aux droits de l'homme' in G. Distefano, G. Gaggioli and A. Hêche (eds), *La Convention de Vienne de 1978 sur la succession d'États en matière de traités: Commentaire article par article et études thématiques* (Bruylant 2015) 1661; Torres Cazorla (n 5) 671ff.

86 See, inter alia: Menno T. Kamminga, 'State Succession in Respect of Human Rights Treaties', 1996 7(4) EJIL 469–84; Isabelle Poupart, 'Succession aux traités et droit de l'homme: vers la reconnaissance d'une protection ininterrompue des individus', in Eisemann and Koskenniemi (n 5), 465–90.

87 UN, 'Succession of States in Respect of International Human Rights Treaties', Report of the Secretary-General, Commission on Human Rights, ECOSOC, UN Doc. No. E/CN.4/1995/80 (1995); Human Rights Committee, 'General Comment 26 (61)', General Comments under article 40, paragraph 4, of the International Covenant on Civil and Political Rights, Adopted by the Committee at its 1631st meeting, UN doc. No. A/53/40, Annex VII [40]; UN, 'Status of the International Covenants on Human Rights; Succession of States in Respect of International Human Rights Treaties', Report of the U.N. Secretary-General, UN Doc. E/CN.4/1996/76, 9 January 1996.

88 See, the Separate Opinion of Judge Weeramantry in *Application of the Convention on the Prevention and Punishment of the Crime of Genocide, Preliminary Objections* (*Bosnia-Herzegovina v. Yugoslavia*), Judgment, 11 July 1996, ICJ Reports 1996, 596, for whom there is 'a principle of contemporary international law that there is automatic State succession to so vital a human rights convention as the Genocide Convention'.

89 O'Connell, *State Succession*, 1967 (n 15) 266. See also: Stern, 'La succession d'États' (n 11) 309:

> Mais l'on sait les contestations soulevées par le principe classique de la protection des droits acquis, souvent considérés comme des droits injustifiés, dont l'existence peut porter atteinte au droit souverain de l'Etat de légiférer; on sait aussi que cette théorie, même si elle était admise comme représentant le droit positif d'aujourd'hui, a ses limites, et qu'un Etat peut toujours porter atteinte aux droits acquis s'il indemnise les détenteurs de ces droits,

Georges Kaeckenbeeck, 'The Protection of Vested Rights in International Law', (1936) 17 *British YIL* 17:

> We come, therefore, to the conclusion that the principle that a cession of territory does not affect private rights is valid only as long as new legislation is not introduced which affects them; that the introduction of such legislation is not prohibited by international law, and is not in particular made by it dependent on payment of compensation.

90 O'Connell, 'Recent Problems of State Succession' (n 41) 139:

'juridical justification for the obligation to pay compensation is to be found in the concept of unjust enrichment'[91] (the concept is further discussed below[92]). Bedjaoui, on the contrary, believes that there exists no such obligation to provide compensation in the context of acquired rights.[93] At the heart of the debate is the value that should be given to the principle of property.[94] However, the question as to whether or not there exists any such obligation to provide compensation for expropriation under custom (and, most importantly, under which circumstances and what is the proper level of compensation that must be provided) is beyond the scope of this book.[95] In any event, it seems undeniable today that international law requires the host State to provide some form of compensation to an investor in the event of expropriation of private rights.

The next chapter examines the situation of State contracts following an event of State succession. **10.17**

This is, indeed, the only relevance to the problem of State Succession that the doctrine of acquired rights would appear to have, and up to this point the doctrine plays no greater role than to act as a logical derivative of the theory of continuity of laws. International law enters the discussion only in its usual role of protecting alien private rights, and only to the extent to which such rights are ordinarily protected by it.

91 O'Connell, *State Succession*, 1967 (n 15) 266, adding 'if a successor State legislated to abrogate the interest of a private person, the latter has suffered a detriment and the former is enriched at his expenses' (at 267).

92 See, Chapter 14, Section 4.

93 ILC, Second Report Bedjaoui, 1969 (n 4) 100. See also: Bedjaoui, 'Problèmes récents de succession d'États' (n 11) 539.

94 Gruber (n 22) 105:

A une conception d'un droit de propriété ayant valeur absolue, correspond la règle de respect des droits acquis et leur indemnisation intégrale en cas de nationalisation. A la remis en cause de la valeur absolue du droit de propriété, correspond inévitablement un assouplissement de la formule indemnitaire qui introduit l'idée d'équité.

95 These questions are briefly examined in P. Dumberry, *The Formation and Identification of Rules of Customary International Law in International Investment Law* (CUP 2016) 110.

11

THE CONCEPT OF STATE CONTRACTS AND ITS UNIQUE CHARACTERISTICS

11.01 A State contract is a binding legal instrument between a foreign company and a State.[96] However, this does not mean that all contracts concluded between a private foreign entity and a State are necessarily considered as 'State contracts'. Thus, ordinary commercial contracts are generally excluded from the analysis because they lack some of the fundamental characteristics of these contracts (as further examined below).[97] State contracts will typically involve an 'investment' made by a foreign party in the host State.

11.02 State contracts do not necessarily need to be concluded with the host State per se in order to be qualified as such. It has long been recognized that they may also be concluded with a State-owned company (which has a separate legal personality).[98] In fact, modern State contracts are often entered into by such entities.[99] State-owned companies are characterized by the control or ownership that the State exercises over them.[100] Several ICSID tribunals have concluded that a State is responsible for the acts committed by State-owned companies.[101] A State contract requires the other party to meet two conditions. First, it must be a physical or legal person (such as a corporation). Contracts entered into between a State-owned entity and a State (or between two State-owned entities) are generally not considered as State contracts. Second, the physical or legal person must originate from a country other than

96 P. Dumberry, 'International Investment Contracts', in T. Gazzini and E. de Brabandere (eds), *International Investment Law. The Sources of Rights and Obligations* (Martinus Nijhoff 2012) 215–43; UNCTAD, *State Contracts*, UNCTAD Series on Issues in International Investment Agreements (2004), 4; J.O. Voss, *The Impact of Investment Treaties on Contracts between Host States and Foreign Investors* (Martinus Nijhoff 2010) 15–16.

97 UNCTAD, ibid., 4.

98 J.-F. Lalive, 'Contrats entre États ou entreprises étatiques et personnes privées. Développements récents', (1983–III) 181 Rec des Cours 28–9; Ch. Leben, 'La théorie du contrat d'État et l'évolution du droit international des investissements", (2003) 302 Rec. des Cours 236. *Contra*: Maurice Kamto, 'La notion de contrat d'État: une contribution au débat', (2003) *Rev Arb* 722–9.

99 Voss (n 96) 25.

100 Under Art. 8 of the ILC Draft Articles on State Responsibility for Internationally Wrongful Acts, the conduct of an entity (or person or group of persons) is considered an act of a State under international law if the entity 'is in fact acting on the instructions of, or under the direction or control of, that State in carrying out the conduct (*Titles and Texts of the Draft Articles on Responsibility of States for Internationally Wrongful Acts Adopted by the Drafting Committee on Second Reading*, 26 July 2001, UN Doc. A/CN.4/L.602/Rev.1 [hereinafter 'ILC Draft Articles on State Responsibility'].

101 For instance, *Emilio Agustín Maffezini v. Spain*, ICSID Case No. ARB/97/7, Award, 25 January 2000.

that of the State party in order for the contract to achieve an international character.[102]

Traditionally, State contracts were typically entered into between a company originating from a developed country and a developing State. They often involved concession agreements that entitled a Western company to extract natural resources in poorer, newly-independent countries at a low cost and for a long period of time.[103] These contracts were one-sided and reflected the balance of power and politics of the time.[104] Modern State contracts are different insofar as they contain more balanced rights and obligations, reflecting the fundamental changes in North-South relations since the 1960s and the increased bargaining power of developing States.[105] These modern contracts take many forms and are no longer limited to concession agreements for the extraction of natural resources. They include lease agreements, supply or service agreements, labour contracts, loan agreements, trade or exchange agreements and financing or commercial partnerships, such as joint ventures.[106] Another noteworthy development is that these contracts are no longer confined to the North-South axis, and are increasingly 'South-South'. **11.03**

The nature of the parties involved in State contracts necessarily distinguishes them from other types of contracts. At least four characteristics are particularly significant for the purpose of the present chapter. **11.04**

First, State contracts are characterized by a unique asymmetry in bargaining power between parties that sets them apart from other types of agreements. Prior to the conclusion of the contract, this imbalance in bargaining power is in favour of the foreign private party. During contractual negotiations, this party often finds itself in both an economically and technologically superior position to the State in terms of its ability to finance and technically execute the contract.[107] At this stage, the investor's aim is to capitalize on the unequal power that it enjoys by negotiating favourable contractual terms.[108] This serves to offset the unequal power that the State might otherwise enjoy after the **11.05**

102 Jean-Michel Jacquet, 'Contrat d'État', *Jurisclasseur Droit international*, fasc. 565, 11/ 98 [1].

103 Voss (n 96) 17–25.

104 Ibid., 19.

105 This era was fundamentally marked by Newly Independent States' claims to sovereignty over their natural resources. See: Resolution on Permanent Sovereignty over Natural Resources, GA Res. 1803 (XVII), 14 December 1962; Charter of Economic Rights and Duties of States, GA Res. 3281 (XXIX), 12 December 1974.

106 UNCTAD, *State Contracts* (n 96) 4.

107 Jacquet (n 102) [5]–[8]; Nagla Nassar, 'Internationalization of State Contracts: ICSID, The Last Citadel', (1997) 14(3) *J Int Arb* 190.

108 Nassar, ibid.

contract is concluded, by which time the foreign private party's leverage will have been exhausted. Once the contract is concluded, it is indeed the State that will enjoy unequal power because of its ability to unilaterally change its legislation and impact the contract.[109]

11.06 Second, while a State contract is clearly *not* a treaty (which is concluded between *States*[110]), it is, at the same time, also not a 'simple' contract either. It is true that a State contract, like any other contract, contains binding legal obligations that must be respected by both parties. However, what makes State contracts special is that they can engender the host State's responsibility *under international law.* That does not mean that a breach of contract is a violation of international law per se, as explained by the *SGS v. Pakistan* Tribunal.[111] According to the ILC Commentaries, a breach of contract may amount to an internationally wrongful act by a State and engage its responsibility on the international plane.[112] Although State contracts are *not* a formal source of international law (under Art. 38 of the ICJ Statute), some scholars have suggested that they are true 'international legal acts'.[113] Thus, contracts create

---

109 This scenario, though common, is of course not always prevailing. The asymmetry in bargaining power may in some circumstances be in favour of the host State during negotiation. This is, for instance, the case of powerful States fortunate enough to benefit from abundant and highly sought after natural resources that foreign companies are particularly eager to exploit. In this context, the State can simply play each contractual offer off others in order to secure the best possible deal.

110 Vienna Convention on the Law of Treaties, 1969, 1155 UNTS, 331. See: *Anglo-Iranian Oil Company case* (*United Kingdom v. Iran*), preliminary objection, Judgment of 22 July 1952, ICJ Reports 1952 112, where the court refused to qualify a contract that had been entered into between Iran and a British investor as a treaty. It should be noted that in the past some authors have considered that, in some circumstances, these contracts were to some extent 'equivalent' to international treaties: A. Verdross, 'Quasi-International Agreements and International Economic Transactions', (1964) 18 *Yearbook of World Affairs* 231; I. Seidl-Hohenveldern, 'The Theory of Quasi-international and Partly International Agreements' (1975) 11 RBDI 567.

111 *SGS Société Générale de Surveillance SA v. Pakistan,* ICSID Case No. ARB/01/13, Award on Jurisdiction, 6 August 2003 [167]. See also: Voss (n 96) 33, 223. However, there are situations where there will be some overlaps and where a simple breach of contract will also constitute a breach of a BIT provision. See, discussion in: Dumberry, 'International Investment Contracts' (n 96).

112 Commentaries to the Draft Articles on Responsibility of States for Internationally Wrongful Acts Adopted by the International Law Commission at its 53rd Session (2001), November 2001, Report of the ILC on the work of its 53rd Session, Official Records of the General Assembly, Fifty-sixth Session, Supplement No. 10 (A/56/10), chp.IV.E.2) [hereinafter 'ILC Commentaries on *Draft Articles on State Responsibility*'], Art. 4 [6]:

> It is irrelevant for the purposes of attribution that the conduct of a State organ may be classified as 'commercial' or '*acta iure gestionis*'. The breach by a State of a contract clearly does not as such entail a breach of international law. Something further is required before international law becomes relevant, e.g., a denial of justice by the courts of the State in proceedings brought by the other contracting party. But the entry into or breach of a contract by a State organ is nonetheless an act of the State for the purposes of article 4, and it may amount to an internationally wrongful act.

113 P. Weil, 'Droit international et contrat d'Etat' in *Mélanges offerts à Paul Reuter. Le droit international: unité et diversité* (Pedone 1981) 562:

> Le contrat enraciné dans l'ordre juridique international doit être regardé comme un *véritable acte juridique international*: ceux des contrats d'Etats qui sont fondés dans l'ordre international constitueraient ainsi une

international legal obligations for the State party.[114] It is therefore important to note that State contracts are, indeed, a source of rights and obligations for the host State under international investment law. This is undoubtedly one of the most unique features of these contracts.

Third, under a State contract, a corporation possesses not only substantive rights, but also the ability to bring a claim against the host State on the basis of those rights before an international tribunal. As further argued above,[115] the combination of substantive and procedural rights found in such contracts is an indication that corporations possess in this specific context a *limited* international legal personality.[116] **11.07**

Fourth, State contracts invariably contain three clauses that set them apart from other types of contracts: the arbitration clause; the stabilization clause; and the applicable law clause. They are meant to address the 'concern over the impartiality of domestic courts and the objective to neutralize the in-built superiority of host country institutions, because of their sovereign powers of legislation abrogating or interfering with contracts'.[117] The goal is to set the parties on an equal footing in terms of avoiding a breach of contract and, failing that, to provide for the neutral resolution of disputes.[118] **11.08**

---

catégorie spécifique d'actes juridiques internationaux, à côté des traités, des actes unilatéraux des Etats et des organisations internationales et des actes judiciaires et arbitraux (emphasis added).

See also: C. Leben, 'Retour sur la notion de contrat d'État et sur le droit applicable à celui-ci', in *L'évolution du droit international: Mélanges offerts à Hubert Thierry* (Pedone 1998) 248, speaking of 'acte juridique international' and Leben, 'La théorie du contrat d'État' (n 98) 264ff., referring to 'un contrat situé dans l'ordre juridique international'.

114 J. Arato, 'Corporations as Lawmakers', (2015) 56 *Harv Int'l L J* 232–3, 237ff.

115 See, Chapter 6, Section 6.3.1.1.

116 See P. Dumberry, 'L'entreprise, sujet de droit international? Retour sur la question à la lumière des développements récents du droit international des investissements' (2004) 108(1) RGDIP 103–22; P. Dumberry and E. Labelle Eastaugh, 'Non-State Actors in International Investment Law: The Legal Personality of Corporations and NGOs in the Context of Investor-State Arbitration', in Jean d'Aspremont (ed), *Participants in the International Legal System: Multiples Perspectives on Non-State Actors in International Law* (Routledge-Cavendish 2011), 360–71.

117 UNCTAD, *State Contracts* (n 96) 5.

118 Leben, 'La théorie du contrat d'État' (n 98) 258.

12

MODIFICATION OF STATE CONTRACTS BY THE SUCCESSOR STATE

12.01 As mentioned above,[119] the general conclusion I have reached regarding contracts signed between *private* entities is that the successor State is free to adopt legislative changes which may affect these rights. But, importantly, it must do so by respecting a number of fundamental rights of foreign investors existing under international law. The question is whether the solution should be any different in the specific context of a State contract, which involves a State as one of the parties. One important aspect, of course, is the fact that succession will sometimes directly affect the identity of that State party to the contract. In some instances (dissolution, integration, and unification), the predecessor State will cease to exist as an independent State as a result of the changes affecting its territory. In such cases, the question becomes whether the successor State should be bound by the rights and obligations that are contained in a contract that was signed by *another* State (the predecessor State) that no longer exists. As further discussed below,[120] the question of succession is also complex when the predecessor State continues to exist (such as in cases of secession).

12.02 This important question of State succession to State contracts has surprisingly not been examined by many scholars. Thus, on the one hand, those scholars interested in State contracts and matters related to investment arbitration simply do not address the specific (and rather lateral) question of State succession. On the other hand, authors focusing on questions of State succession only address the specific issue of acquired rights without taking position on the fate of State contracts. In fact, the most detailed account of the question of State succession to State contracts remains to this day that of O'Connell, which was published more than 50 years ago. The following section will expose the interesting evolution of his position on the matter over

119 See, Chapter 10, Section 3.
120 See, Chapter 13, Section 1.

the 30 years he devoted to problems of State succession (Section 1). I will then put forward a new framework of analysis which, in my view, will provide better guidance to solve this complex question (Section 2).

1. THE THEORY DEVELOPED BY O'CONNELL

O'Connell first examined the specific question of State succession to 'concession agreements' in an article published in 1950.[121] The conclusion he reached regarding these contracts is no different than the one mentioned above for contracts signed by private persons: **12.03**

> Upon [a] change of sovereignty the successor state does not automatically inherit the rights and duties comprised in the contract of concession. These come to an end with the extinction of the personality of one of the parties to the contract, or the obliteration of its sovereignty in the territory which is subject to the operations of the concession. To admit the contrary would be to admit the doctrine of universal succession with all its implications. The treatment of the problem of concessions in the law of State succession is not exhausted, however, by an analysis of the effect of the change on the concessionary contract. Consideration must be given to the question whether the successor State incurs an obligation towards the concessionaire on a basis other than contractual. The latter has invested money and performed work, and thus brought into being a certain state of facts. To this extent the concession constitutes more than a mere *vinculum juris* between him and the State. Apart from his contractual rights, the concessionaire has an equitable interest in his investment and labour. The contractual duty expires with the change of sovereignty, but the equitable interest in the factual situation survives. This interest is described variously as an 'acquired right', 'property right', or 'vested right'.[122]

In other words, according to O'Connell, the successor State is *not* bound by contracts that were signed by *another* State (that often ceased to exist). This is because the obligations created under a contract signed by one State (the predecessor) are *not transmitted* to another (the successor State). The same conclusion is reached by Bedjaoui for whom 'acquired rights do not exist in the case of State succession' because 'a right can be claimed only from the entity which created it – in this case, the predecessor State, which has disappeared', **12.04**

121 D.P. O'Connell, 'Economic Concessions in the Law of State Succession' (1950) 27 *British YIL* 94, defining the concept of 'economic concession' as follows:

> An economic concession thus embodies the following characteristics: It is a contract between a public authority and the concessionaire. It involves the investment of capital by the latter in an undertaking for the erection of public works or the exploitation of the public domain. The reward which the concessionaire expects to derive is usually in the form of profits which the public authority, under the terms of the contract, permits him to make.

122 Ibid., 95.

adding that 'subrogation of obligations is not a principle that is clearly applicable in relations between States'.[123] But, for O'Connell, while it is undeniable that the successor State does not have any formal obligation to respect the rights and obligations contained in a contract signed *by another State*, he nevertheless believes that the other party to the original contract still has (after the date of succession) an 'interest' arising out of that contract. For O'Connell, such an 'interest' constitutes an 'acquired right' 'which the successor State is obliged by international law to respect'.[124] In fact, in his 1950 article, he argued that the doctrine of acquired rights 'has long been accepted in international law, and has been sanctioned by a considerable body of decisions of international and municipal tribunals'[125] and is, in fact, 'perhaps one of the few principles firmly established in the law of State succession'.[126] O'Connell then explained the different options a successor State is faced with in order to respect the 'interest' of a foreign investor.

12.05 One option is for the successor State to 'subrogate itself in the terms of the concession by novation of the contract'.[127] In his 1967 book (at the very end of one chapter dealing with 'governmental contracts') he developed the argument further.[128] He believes that 'perhaps the most scientifically correct scheme of rules to solve the problem of the effect of change of sovereignty on contracts' is to look at the *proper law of that contract* (which is often that of the State party to the contract[129]) in order to 'ascertain if the contract has expired from frustration'.[130] For him, such a situation of 'frustration' would occur whenever 'one of the parties to the contract has disappeared from the place of performance' and that, consequently, the 'contract has lapsed'.[131] O'Connell indicates that 'in most legal systems the disappearance of the contracting State from the place of performance will have the effect [of the frustration of the contract], but if the law of the successor State provides for complete succession the effect

123 ILC, Second Report Bedjaoui, 1969 (n 4) 74.

124 O'Connell, 'Economic Concessions' (n 121) 124.

125 Ibid., 97.

126 Ibid., 123.

127 Ibid., 124.

128 See also the analysis in: O'Connell, 'Recent Problems of State Succession' (n 41) 155ff.

129 See, Barde (n 45) 114ff, referring to many authors. Interestingly, O'Connell, *State Succession*, 1967 (n 15) 299, does not explain what to do when a State contract refers to international law as the applicable law. O'Connell simply mentions that in such a case the 'problem is very much more complex' but adds that 'such a situation is rare' in practice.

130 O'Connell, *State Succession*, 1967 (n 15) 302, see also at 298.

131 Ibid., 298. See, O'Connell, 'Recent Problems of State Succession' (n 41) 155–6:

> In the simplest case of State Succession one might say that a contract made with a predecessor State and to be performed in the territory subjected to a change of sovereignty lapses with the disappearance of one party thereto, or its incapacity to perform the contract, depending upon whether the predecessor State is totally extinguished or merely expelled.

will be negatived'.[132] When the domestic law provides for the continuation of the contract, 'a subrogation of the successor State in the contracts of the predecessor State is brought about, and, indeed, the subrogation consists of no more than a substitution of the name of the successor State for that of the predecessor State' (adding that 'everything else continues unaffected').[133] But, importantly, international law is not helpful in the event that the proper law governing the contract does *not* provide for such a subrogation.[134] In such a case, 'there is no contract to perform, for one party thereto has disappeared, and hence international law cannot enjoin performance, even when specific performance was a remedy of the proper law'.[135]

This is where the second option comes in. Thus, 'since [the successor State] is **12.06**
not bound by the terms of the contract it may expropriate the concession provided that (…) compensation is paid'.[136] He explained this solution in his classic two-volume book on State succession published in 1967 (which further analysed the issue and distinguishes between 'governmental contracts', economic 'concession agreements', and 'administrative contracts').[137] After examining numerous examples of State practice and court decisions with respect to concession agreements, he concluded that 'the generally consistent practice which has been analysed is clearly based on the principle that the acquired rights of a concessionaire must be respected by a successor State'.[138] Yet, O'Connell also admits that 'it is not immediately clear, however, in what exactly the duty of the successor State consists'.[139] As further discussed below,[140] he believes that the solution very much depends on the type of State

132 O'Connell, *State Succession*, 1967 (n 15) 302.
133 O'Connell, 'Recent Problems of State Succession' (n 41) 157.
134 Ibid., 156–7:

> It is necessary to recognize that the initial step in terminating the contract must be taken in municipal law, for international law does not, and cannot, direct as to when contracts are to be made or to terminate, unless, of course, the governing law of such contracts is international law or the general principles of law – which is a possible but exceptional situation. International law merely protects contractual performance in the case of aliens. It cannot enjoin performance when, under the governing law of the contract, there is nothing to perform, or when one of the parties has ceased to be able to perform. International law, in other words, can only endorse contracts, it cannot make, modify or terminate them. (…) International law does not guarantee the performance of all contracts made between governments and alien companies or individuals. It can, at the most, only protect the bargain to the extent to which the bargain is legally enforceable under its proper law. (…) When subrogation of the contract is achieved by its proper law, then the contract subsists, and international law guarantees the local remedies in the case where the contractor is an alien.

135 Ibid., 158.
136 O'Connell, 'Economic Concessions' (n 121) 124.
137 O'Connell, *State Succession*, 1967 (n 15) 298–303, 304–7, 345–52, 553–5.
138 Ibid., 345.
139 Ibid., 346.
140 See, Chapter 12, Section 2.

succession involved given that in the context of a cession of territory the emphasis is put on the 'legal continuity', while in the case of annexation it is focused on 'legal disruption'.[141] His general conclusion is that 'there is no justification for assuming a transmission of the contract itself'.[142] Yet, he nevertheless believes in 'the obligation of the successor State to respect the acquired rights of the contractor'.[143] Thus, while O'Connell recognized that all States (including the successor State) are 'always entitled to revoke concessions and terminate contracts in virtue of [their] general competence to expropriate against compensation',[144] they can only do so provided that the payment of a 'reasonable compensation' is given to the investor.[145] In fact, he goes as far as to say that 'compensation is the only obligation which international law imposes on the successor State'.[146] According to him, the general guiding principle is the prevention of unjust enrichment (a concept further discussed below[147]). Thus, 'as the successor is enriched by the work done it owes a duty of compensation',[148] adding that 'for the successor State to ignore this expenditure [by the concessionaire] of capital and labour, and to appropriate to itself the benefits accruing therefrom, is unjustifiably to enrich itself'.[149] O'Connell summarized his argument in his 1970 course at The Hague Academy as follows:

---

141 O'Connell, *State Succession*, 1967 (n 15) 346:

> in some case, the emphasis is thrust upon legal continuity, as in an orderly grant of independence, or a cession of territory without disruption of local administrative autonomy, or a subrogation of the successor States by treaty or contract. The successor State in these cases remains, or becomes, a party to the contract of concession, and the problem that then arises is whether the concession may, in the eyes of international law, be revoked. Where, on the other hand, the emphasis is upon legal disruption, as in the case of annexation, the subrogation of the successor state in the contract could only occur in virtue of a general devolution of rights and obligations pursuant to thesis of universal succession. If this thesis is rejected, then the successor they may not be regarded as a party to the contract which terminates with the change of sovereignty. In such a case, no question of continuing the contract for the terms of its performance can arise.

142 Ibid., 355.

143 Ibid.

144 Ibid., 347. See also:

> The argument in favor of the inherent revocability of concession agreement tends to be a fortiori in the case of successor states, which cannot be compelled to carry-on with arrangements made by their predecessor which are either contrary to their public interest or obstructive of the realization of their own ideas of social development. Change of sovereignty often involves change in the economic structure of the concrete which demand that modifications be effected in the exercise of concessionary rights.

See also: Gruber (n 22) 97–8.

145 O'Connell, *State Succession*, 1967 (n 15) 349.

146 Ibid., 351.

147 See, Chapter 14, Section 4.

148 O'Connell, *State Succession*, 1967 (n 15) 352. See also, at 298.

149 Ibid., 348–9. Thus, for him,

> The function of the concept of unjust enrichment is to restore the economic balance of the parties as at the date of termination of the contract' and therefore 'if the private contractor has created works of value for

> Suppose that a contract made with a State which loses its sovereignty is to be regarded in law, for reasons that will later be explained, as ceasing to subsist. Is there in this case any acquired right, anything for international law to protect? The answer later to be proposed is that the *equities of the factual situation brought about by the contract do subsist, even if the contract no longer does so, and that they constitute an acquired right.* The extent of the successor State's obligation towards this right is to be measured by reference to the doctrine of unjust enrichment, which creates a *vinculum juris* between the successor State and the contractor. This *vinculum* may not be recognized in the law of the successor State, which derives from that State's sovereignty, but is part of public international law as a feature of the general principles of law whereby philosophical propositions are translated into jurisprudence.[150]

Finally, it should be noted that Bedjaoui has been critical of the approach adopted by O'Connell and believes that there exists, in fact, no such right to compensation in situations *not* involving succession of States.[151] For him, 'there are strong grounds for asserting that (…) there is even less reason for recognizing acquired rights or paying compensation' in the context of State succession.[152] **12.07**

> which he has not been fully paid, the benefiting successor State is under an equitable obligation to cover his losses (…)

(O'Connell, 'Recent Problems of State Succession' (n 41) 159).

150 O'Connell, 'Recent Problems of State Succession' (n 41) 140 (emphasis added).

151 ILC, Second Report Bedjaoui, 1969 (n 4) 86:

> It is an established fact that, even where the law is amended without change of sovereignty, acquired rights are not recognized either as situations which are absolutely inviolable or as situations which can never be encroached on without compensation. This is indisputable in the case of nationals, for whom there is not – or is not yet – in international law any rule requiring compensation by their own State. Where aliens are concerned, the tendency is simply to assimilate them to nationals. Compensation is not regarded as a right.

152 Ibid.:

> *A priori*, recognizing that a State (any State) has the right, for instance, to nationalize or expropriate, means conceding the lawfulness of the action taken by that State. If the act whereby it abolishes acquired rights is regarded as lawful, how can its refusal to pay any compensation be regarded as unlawful, or, in other words, as engaging its responsibility? If the nationalization measure is conceded to be within the natural competence of the State, it is self-evident that it cannot be a wrongful act. In any event, this takes us out of the sphere of State succession into that of the international responsibility of States. (…) it is thus quite difficult to find any justification for compensation. The 'right' to compensation, once its fragile underpinning of acquired rights is removed, is seen to be unsubstantial indeed. In any event, 'acquired rights' and 'right to compensation' cannot legitimately be linked together by arguing that refusal to recognize the former gives rise to the latter. The abolition of 'acquired rights' has its basis in the exercise of a competence which international law does not take away from the successor State. It should not therefore entail the granting of compensation.

2. PROPOSAL OF A NEW FRAMEWORK OF ANALYSIS ON THE MATTER

12.08 The debate between O'Connell and Bedjaoui on this question seems less relevant these days. There is now a consensus among writers that the rights and obligations under a State contract are simply *not transferred* from one State (the predecessor) to another one (the successor State). As a matter of principle, a new State is therefore *not bound* by a State contract signed by another State.[153] According to Crawford, 'as in the case of all rights acquired under the municipal law of the predecessor State, rights deriving from State contracts and concessions are susceptible to change by the new sovereign'.[154] For him, 'territorial changes of itself neither cancels not confers a special status on private rights, they gain no regulatory or other immunity post-succession'.[155] The distinction made in the past between State contracts having a 'public' or a 'private' character does not seem to be endorsed by modern writers.[156] Yet, as

153 A different position seems to have been taken by Verzijl, t. vii (n 43) 68, stating that 'it is, and always has been, quite normal for treaties of cession to provide in general terms for the maintenance of vested rights' arising from concession contracts'. His conclusion (at 72) is that 'on the strength of the precedents quoted, the conclusion may be drawn that the principle of the maintenance of concessions and comparable State contract would seem to be an old and well-established one and to rank among the 'general principle of (international) law' adding that the existence of this principle 'cannot be destroyed by the regrettable fact that a number of, especially new, nations show an increasing tendency to deny its validity on their acquirement of independence'.

154 Crawford, *Brownlie's Principles of Public International Law* (n 58) 432. See also:

> it will be appreciated that judicial pronouncements to the effect that that mere change of sovereignty does not cancel concession rights do not give support to the acquired rights doctrine in the form that after the change of sovereignty the new sovereign must maintain the property rights of aliens acquired before the change of sovereignty (ibid.)

See also: Gruber (n 22) 97–8.

155 Crawford, *Brownlie's Principles of Public International Law* (n 58) 433.

156 Such a distinction was considered to be relevant by Kaeckenbeeck (n 89) 10–11:

> There is a substitution of one state for the other as one of the parties to the legal relation, and the principle of public international law that vested rights are unaffected by a change of sovereignty must here cover such a substitution. This is what also happens in the case of concessions granted to individuals or companies by the ceding state. It was long thought doubtful whether international law required the succeeding state to respect them. Such doubts were all the more explicable because the principle of respect for vested rights was here complicated, not only by a change in the person of the state, but also by the fact that concessions are not pure institutions of private law, but present a mixture of private and public legal characters. According as the private or the public character is thought to prevail, the application or rejection of the rule of respect for private rights appears justified. There is no doubt that the weight of opinion is at present in favour of the obligation to respect concessions, but in view of the considerable public importance which some concessions may have, it would be undue optimism to believe that the debate on this question is for ever closed. (…) But, in my opinion, the *gist* of the matter is rather that the operation of the principle of respect for vested rights is not checked by a change in the person of the state as long as the private law character of the relation prevails, but it is checked when the public character of the legal relation prevails.

See also: ILC, Fourth Report Garcia-Amador, 1959 (n 53) 10:

> Acquired or patrimonial rights are commonly classified as 'private' rights. However, the question of their true legal nature arises fairly frequently in both theory and practice because some of the rights in question

noted above, this does not mean that the successor State is entirely free to modify or annul rights and obligations contained in State contracts after the date of succession. Crawford explicitly refers to such existing limitations based on international law, including treatment of aliens (the MST) and human rights law.[157] As mentioned above,[158] the successor State should also provide compensation to a foreign investor whenever it expropriates its property.

From all of this, it may be suggested that the question of succession to State contracts is ultimately not an issue that should be resolved under any specific rule of State succession. In fact, it could be tempting to conclude that this is not even a question of State succession. Thus, after the date of succession, the matter seems to be one of general international law involving private rights. The question becomes whether or not the successor State will respect the rights contained in State contracts. If it does not, the actions may be considered as an act of expropriation. International law imposes an obligation to provide proper compensation to the investor. In that context, it could be argued that the obligations of the successor State regarding State contracts are simply not different from those of any other State having to deal with such instruments. **12.09**

Yet, in my view, it would not be appropriate to conceive this question as being completely detached from the field of State succession. In other words, the matter is not just one of expropriation and compensation. In fact, I believe that the question is much more complex than how it was described above. It cannot be reduced to a general denial of succession to contracts combined with another (also general) obligation to respect basic principles of international law. The rest of this chapter is a modest proposal by the present author putting forward a new general framework of analysis, which will help to determine when a successor State should (or should not) be bound by a State contract. **12.10**

In my view, this question of succession to State contracts cannot be answered in the abstract and in a mechanical manner. There are no black or white (or yes or no) answers applicable to all cases. As pointed out by O'Connell, 'the question whether change of sovereignty puts an end to a contract made with the predecessor States is one which can only be answered in the concrete **12.11**

are in fact of a mixed character (private and public). In particular, the question has had to be considered in the case of rights acquired under concessions granted by the State to individual aliens and the mixed character of such rights has in fact been expressly recognized in arbitral decisions. (…) In any event, the mixed character of such legal relations undeniably affects the scope of the State's obligations.

157 Crawford, *Brownlie's Principles of Public International Law* (n 58) 432.

158 See, Chapter 10, Section 3.

context'.[159] At first, this may seem like a rather obvious observation. O'Connell also adds that 'some of the arguments negating any obligation of successor States with respect to the contracts of their predecessors have been so lacking in intellectual subtlety as to be banal'.[160] What is truly interesting in this respect is his reference[161] to this passage from the *Lighthouse Arbitration* case: 'It is impossible to formulate a general, identical solution for every imaginable hypothesis of territorial succession, and any attempt to formulate such a solution must necessarily fail in view of the extreme diversity of cases of this kind.'[162] The arbitral tribunal also noted that '[i]t is no less unjustifiable to admit the principle of transmission as a general rule than to deny it. It is rather and essentially a question of a kind the answer to which depends on a multitude of concrete factors'.[163] O'Connell does not however further investigate any of these questions.

12.12 In my view, there are indeed a number of situations that can be envisaged whereby the successor State *should* be bound by a State contract. My proposal is to further develop the basic and very general idea that was briefly mentioned (*en passant*) by O'Connell and to apply it specifically to the question of State contracts. The aim is to develop a comprehensive framework of analysis that will take into account the level of complexity that surrounds this issue. This new framework is based on the following two general propositions that will be explained in Chapters 13 and 14.

12.13 First, the next chapter will explain that the issue of succession to contracts will essentially depend on the *type* of State succession at hand (Chapter 13). There is no one-fits-it-all answer. The answer to the question simply cannot be the same considering that in certain cases the predecessor State ceases to exist (dissolution) and in others it does not (secession). Evidently, the fact that, in some instances, no new State emerges (cession, integration) must have an impact on the outcome of the survival of contracts. These distinctions are examined in detail below.

12.14 Second, the answer to the question of succession to contracts may not be the same depending on a number of different circumstances and factors prevailing

159 O'Connell, *State Succession*, 1967 (n 15) 301. See also: O'Connell, 'Recent Problems of State Succession' (n 41) 155.

160 O'Connell, ibid. See also: O'Connell, ibid.

161 O'Connell, *State Succession*, 1967 (n 15) 301.

162 *Sentence arbitrale en date des 24/27 juillet 1956 rendue par le Tribunal d'arbitrage constitué en vertu du Compromis signé à Paris le 15 juillet 1932 entre la France et la Grèce*, 12 UNRIAA 155, also in (1956) 23 ILR [hereinafter '*Lighthouse Arbitration* case'] at 91. Verzijl (n 43) 223, who was acting as president of the arbitral tribunal in the *Lighthouse Arbitration* case, expressed the same opinion in subsequent writings.

163 Ibid., 91. See also: Verzijl (n 43) 223.

in each case (Chapter 14). In his book, O'Connell identified the principle of unjust enrichment as one important factor that should be taken into account when deciding whether or not the successor State (or in the case of dissolution, which of them) should be responsible for providing compensation under a State contract signed by another State. This is accurate. In fact, in Chapter 14, I will show that many different factors (including the principle of unjust enrichment) should be taken into account in order to determine whether the transfer of any rights and obligations arising from a contract to a new State is justifiable in contemporary international law.

13

SUCCESSION TO STATE CONTRACTS DEPENDS ON WHAT TYPES OF SUCCESSION IS INVOLVED

13.01 As mentioned in the previous chapter, O'Connell refers to the *Lighthouse Arbitration* award highlighting the essential distinctions between the *different types* of succession of States.[164] In my view, the principles of succession or non-succession may apply depending largely on the type of succession of

164 O'Connell, *State Succession*, 1967 (n 15) 301.

States involved for each case.[165] As such, one solution to the question of State succession to contracts may be appropriate for one type of succession of States, but not for another. Bedjaoui recognizes this context-based analysis by stating that 'if (…) politics rather than law dominates this field, it is natural also to expect different solutions according to the type of succession'.[166]

The following sections will examine the solution that should find application depending on the different types of succession. **13.02**

1. SECESSION

This section examines separately the question of whether the continuator State or the new State should be bound by a contract that had been signed by the predecessor State before the date of succession. **13.03**

1.1 The continuator State remains bound by contracts

In cases of secession, the predecessor State *continues* to exist after the date of succession and should logically, and as a matter of principle, remain bound by the obligations arising from any existing State contracts at the date of succession. This is not a matter of succession to contracts, but rather one of the continuation of the same international legal personality by that State. This basic principle is illustrated by two cases that are discussed in the following sections. **13.04**

1.1.1 Russian Federation v. Pied-Rich BV

The case of *Russian Federation v. Pied-Rich BV* involved Pied-Rich BV, a Dutch company, that had concluded a tripartite contract with the Baltic Shipping Company (BSC) and a number of Russian importers in 1989 for the delivery of women's and children's clothing.[167] Under the contract, it sold and delivered the goods to the Russian importers. Payment for the goods was guaranteed both by BSC, which transported the goods to the Soviet Union, **13.05**

165 For the same conclusion in the different context of succession to responsibility, see P. Dumberry, *State Succession to International Responsibility* (Martinus Nijhoff Publ. 2007) 6–8, 206–8. See also: IDI, State Succession to Responsibility, Resolution, 2015 (n 14). For an analysis of this Resolution, see: Marcelo G. Kohen and Patrick Dumberry, *The Institute of International Law's Resolution on State Succession and State Responsibility: Introduction, Text and Commentaries* (CUP, 2018–2019).

166 ILC, Second Report Bedjaoui, 1969 (n 4) 87.

167 *Russian Federation v. Pied-Rich BV, S & S* (1993) No. 93 (Neth. Ct. App. 1992), in (1993) 24 *Netherland ILR* 356; *Russian Federation v. Pied-Rich BV, S & S* (1993) No. 91 (Neth. Sup. Ct. 1993), in (1994) 25 *Netherlands ILR* 512. The facts of the case are summarized in: Council of Europe, Committee of Legal Advisers on Public International Law, available at http://www.cahdi.coe.int/Contribution/Details/197.

and by the Soviet Union's Ministry of Merchant Marine 'to which BSC was responsible'.[168] In other words, under these contracts, the Soviet Union's Ministry of Merchant Marine was responsible for guaranteeing the payment to Pied-Rich BV. Deliveries were made before the break-up of the USSR, but the Ministry failed to make those payments.[169]

13.06 Pied-Rich instituted arbitration proceedings in Moscow. In order to secure any payment under a future arbitral award in its favour, it applied to the District Court in Rotterdam for permission to seize the 'Kapitan Kanevsky', a vessel belonging to the Russian Federation that had been used by BSC. As mentioned by two writers, the court made certain rulings based on the assumption that the Russian Federation remained responsible for the guarantees made by the Soviet Union's Ministry of Merchant Marine.[170] The court granted Pied-Rich's request to seize the vessel. Two other judgments were rendered by the District Court in Rotterdam in relation to this case. These judgments were appealed before the Court of Appeal of The Hague. What is of importance for the present analysis is the court's remarks regarding State succession.[171] The Court of Appeal held that Russia 'should be treated as the USSR's successor'.[172] The court noted that Russia had not disputed that claim and that it had 'expressly presented itself to the international community as having succeeded to the rights and duties of the USSR'.[173] What the court likely intended to say was that Russia was the *continuing* State of the USSR (rather than its 'successor'). The court referred to the Minsk Agreement[174] and specifically noted that the guarantee, which had been made by the Ministry in June 1990 (before the break-up), was binding on the former USSR, and now on Russia.[175]

1.1.2 Republic of Serbia v. ImageSat International

13.07 The competence of a tribunal with regard to the question of State succession to a contract containing an arbitration clause was at the centre of the *Republic*

---

168 J. Klabbers, M. Koskenniemi and A. Zimmermann (dirs), *Pilot Project on Documentation concerning State Practice relating to State Succession and Recognition*, (Council of Europe 1999) 271. This formulation suggests that BSC was a State-owned company.

169 It is not too clear from the information available about the case when exactly the payments stopped and whether this occurred before or after the break-up of the USSR (which took place in December 1991).

170 J. Klabbers and M. Koseknniemi, 'Succession in Respect to State Property, Archives and Debts, and Nationality' in: Klabbers et al (n 168) 132. The decision can be found in: Klabbers et al (n 168) 269.

171 Other questions dealt with by the court, including the question of sovereign immunity, are examined in: Cheng (n 2) 362ff.

172 Klabbers et al (n 168) 272.

173 Ibid., 270, see also at 272.

174 Minsk Agreement of 8 December 1991: The Agreement Establishing the Commonwealth of Independent States, 13 December 1991, U.N. Doc. A/46/771, in (1992) 31 ILM 138.

175 Klabbers et al (n 168) 273.

of Serbia v. ImageSat International case, a decision rendered in 2009 by the High Court of England and Wales.[176] The case involved a contract concluded in June 2005 between the State Union of Serbia and Montenegro, and an Israeli company, ImageSat, for the purchase of a satellite ground control station and the exclusive usage rights of two satellites. The contract provided that disputes be referred to arbitration under the ICC Rules, with English law as the governing law and England as the default location for the arbitration. The State Union did not pay the sums that were due under the contract. In May 2006, the claimant initiated arbitration proceedings before the ICC's Court of Arbitration. Importantly, this request was filed three days *after* the referendum in Montenegro in favour of independence. On 3 June 2006, Montenegro declared its independence. As explained above,[177] Montenegro is an example of a secession with Serbia being the continuator State of the State Union.

About a month after the beginning of the proceedings, the Public Attorney of Serbia wrote to the ICC stating that the 'State Union of Serbia and Montenegro ceased to exist', and that 'certain rights, obligations and liabilities of the State Union have been undertaken by the Republic of Serbia' and that, consequently, the Republic of Serbia 'will act as the Respondent in this phase of the proceedings'.[178] The proceedings continued with the 'Republic of Serbia' acting as the respondent and the parties signed the terms of reference.[179] It was only after the statement of claim was filed by the claimant that Serbia argued, for the first time, that it 'was not an original party to the contract and had not subsequently become liable, and that the arbitrator had therefore no jurisdiction over that claim'.[180] At this stage, the arbitrator decided that the question of the proper parties to the proceedings should be determined as a preliminary issue.[181] In his partial award, he held that Serbia was the continuator of the State Union and was therefore bound by the agreement.[182] **13.08**

The award was challenged by Serbia before an English court under the Arbitration Act of 1996 seeking its setting aside on the ground that the arbitrator did not have jurisdiction to find that Serbia was the 'continuator' of **13.09**

176 *Republic of Serbia v. ImageSat International NV*, High Court of Justice, Queen's Bench Division, Commercial Court, [2009] EWHC 2853 (Comm), 16 November 2009.

177 See, Chapter 3, Section 2.5.

178 *Republic of Serbia v. ImageSat International NV* (n 176) [40].

179 Ibid., [41]–[52].

180 Ibid., [54].

181 Ibid., [57].

182 Ibid., partial award, 7 May 2008 [60]. The arbitrator subsequently issued a final award in 2009 in favour of ImageSat in the amount of euro 35 million.

the State Union and was a proper party to the proceedings. In his judgment, Justice Beatson of the High Court of Justice examined the question of whether Serbia's challenge was precluded 'by a submission to jurisdiction'.[183] He noted that the terms of reference described the respondent as: 'The Republic of Serbia, as successor to certain rights, obligations and liabilities of the former State Union of Serbia and Montenegro.'[184] Another paragraph of the terms of reference mentioned that '[Serbia] consents to its substitution in the place of' the State Union, 'without prejudice to all its rights and defences, including the right to maintain that the Agreement is not binding upon [it]'. Finally, on the question of jurisdiction, the terms contained this passage:

> *[t]he parties* agree and acknowledge that the Arbitral Tribunal is properly appointed in accordance with:
>
> (i) the dispute resolution provisions in the Agreement;
> (ii) the governing law; and
> (iii) the ICC Rules, and that the Arbitral Tribunal *shall have jurisdiction to deal with the disputes in the present arbitration. None of the parties is at present aware of any ground for challenging the jurisdiction of the tribunal* and objecting to the appointment of the Arbitral Tribunal.[185]

13.10 The court held that Serbia's challenge to the jurisdiction of the tribunal was 'precluded by its submission to jurisdiction' in the terms of reference.[186] For the court, the document granted the arbitrator 'substantive jurisdiction'[187] to deal with the question of 'whether Serbia was a party to the underlying contract which gave rise to the dispute and thus the "continuator"/"successor" point'.[188] It is also interesting to note that the court made general remarks (in the form of *obiter dicta*) on whether an arbitral tribunal (with English law as its *lex fori*) would have inherent jurisdiction over any issue of State succession.[189] The court asked the following question: 'In the absence of a contractual submission, the first question would have been whether an arbitrator is able to deal with an issue that in another context would not be justiciable in English

183 Ibid., [64].
184 Ibid., [47].
185 Ibid., [49] referring to [14] of the terms (emphasis in the original).
186 Ibid., [106]. Thus, 'Serbia contractually submitted to the arbitrator's jurisdiction by its agreement in the Terms of Reference' [112].
187 Ibid., [106].
188 Ibid., [112].
189 Ibid., [111]. These comments were made when dealing with Serbia's argument on the non-justiciability of State succession issues before English courts.

law.'[190] The reasoning of the court suggests that the answer should be in the affirmative.[191]

The court dismissed Serbia's application to set aside the award without formally taking position on the question of whether Serbia should indeed be considered as the continuator State of the State Union. Yet, it noted that 'the position taken by Serbia in its communications to the UN [[192]] and the ICJ [[193]] and the position taken by those organizations and by the Council of Europe's Committee of Ministers suggest that Serbia and those organizations regarded it as the continuator of the State Union.'[194] **13.11**

In sum, these two cases illustrate that whenever the predecessor State continues to exist, that State should normally remain bound by the obligations arising from any existing State contracts at the date of succession.[195] The **13.12**

---

190 Ibid., [113].

191 Ibid., [123]:

> it would be striking if the arbitrator is not able to make a ruling as to whether Serbia was to be treated as a party to the agreement. It would be particularly striking if an arbitrator was not entitled to investigate and could not determine even on the provisional section 30 basis whether a person or entity that has raised an objection is a party to the underlying contract and the arbitration agreement.

See also at [126]:

> Serbia's position on non-justiciability also involves both the arbitrator and the court having to accept its assertion that it was not a party to the underlying contract and the arbitration agreement. There is also force in the response (see ImageSat's skeleton argument, para. 118(5)) that it would be wrong to 'allow a State to escape liability under a commercial contract merely by pronouncing that it was not an original party to the contract, and then sheltering behind a cloak of non-justiciability in order to prevent an arbitration or adjudication based on the true legal position'.

192 Ibid., [22], referring to a letter of 3 June 2006 of the President of Serbia to the Secretary General of the United Nations stating:

> The membership of the State Union Serbia and Montenegro in the United Nations, including all organs and organisations of the United Nations system, is continued by the Republic of Serbia on the basis of Article 60 of the Constitutional Charter of Serbia and Montenegro, activated by the declaration of independence adopted by the National Assembly of Montenegro on June 3 2006. Therefore, please note that in the United Nations the name 'Republic of Serbia' is to be henceforth used instead of the name 'Serbia and Montenegro'.

193 Ibid., [37], referring to *Case Concerning Application of the Convention on the Prevention and Punishment of the Crime of Genocide, (Croatia v. Serbia)* Preliminary Objections, Judgment, 18 November 2008, where the court stated: 'Serbia has accepted "continuity between Serbia and Montenegro and the Republic of Serbia" and that Montenegro was "a new State admitted as such to the United Nations" which did "not continue the international legal personality of the State union of Serbia and Montenegro".'

194 Ibid., [135].

195 A different question arose in the case of *Compagnie Noga d'Importation et d'Exportation SA v. Russian Federation*, appeal judgment, 361 F.3d 676 (2d Cir. 2004), ILDC 840 (US 2004), 16 March 2004, which did not involve any State succession issue per se. The question was whether the Russian Federation could be held responsible for breach of contracts signed by the Russian Government. The case involved a Swiss company which had signed three contracts with different governmental entities both before and after the break-up of the USSR. *Before* the break-up of the USSR, Noga entered into in December 1990 supply contracts to provide US$550 million worth of food and consumer goods to foreign trade agencies of both the USSR and

reason is simple: the contract was signed by one State before the date of succession, who continues to exist after that date. There is no logical reason to support the opposing point, where that State should not continue to be bound by contracts it has *itself* signed in the past. The next section examines whether there should be some situations where this proposition should, in fact, *not* apply.

1.2 The new State is generally not bound by contracts, however, certain situations may require otherwise

13.13 The new secessionist State is clearly not a party to a contract signed by the predecessor State and, consequently, should not be bound by it (as mentioned in the previous section, the continuator State should remain bound by such a contract). I have found a limited number of examples of case law and State practice involving contractual claims against a new secessionist State. The examples found strongly support the principle of non-succession.

13.14 The legal qualification of the break-up of the Austria-Hungary Dual Monarchy after the First World War is controversial since it is not entirely clear whether it should be understood as an example of a dissolution of a State or

the Federative Socialist Soviet Republic of Russia ('RSFSR'), a constituent republic of the USSR; *Before* the break-up of the USSR, in April 1991, Noga entered into a US$422.5 million loan agreement with the Government of the RSFSR, which was represented by its Council of Ministers; *After* the break-up of the USSR, in January 1992, Noga and the Government of the Russian Federation entered into a US$400 million loan agreement. Both loan agreements provided for binding arbitration regarding any disputes between the parties and their successors before the Chamber of Commerce of Stockholm, Sweden, and for Swiss law to apply to resolve disputes. A dispute eventually arose regarding the performance of the Loan Agreements and Noga started arbitration proceedings against the 'Government of the Russian Federation' before the Chamber of Commerce of Stockholm. The Tribunal rendered two awards in 1997 awarding approximately US$50 million to the claimant against the 'Government of the Russian Federation (Russia)' (the Tribunal also rendered a third award in 2001 in favour of Noga in a amount of some US$25 million). The Government appealed one of the awards before the District Court of Stockholm, which dismissed the appeal. This decision was affirmed by the Svea Court of Appeal. In 2000, Noga filed two actions against the Russian Federation before United States Courts (in Kentucky and New York) seeking confirmation and enforcement of the awards. The Russian Federation objected on the ground that it had neither been a signatory to the arbitration agreement, which had been signed by the 'Russian government', nor a party to the subsequent proceedings. In a 2002 decision, the US District Court for the Southern District of New York agreed with the position of the respondent and held that the award was unenforceable against the Russian Federation (*Compagnie Noga d'Importation et d'Exportation SA v. Russian Federation*, United States District Court for the Southern District of New York, Decision, 19 Sept. 2002, briefly discussed in: (2002) 17(10) *Mealey's IAR* C-1; (2003) *Bull. ASA*, 147). Noga subsequently appealed to the Second Circuit Court. The Appeal Court concluded that: 'we hold that regardless of whether principles of Russian law, federal common law, or international law are applied, the Russian Federation and the Government are not separate "parties" for the purposes of confirming and enforcing an arbitral award under the Convention' (*Compagnie Noga d'Importation et d'Exportation SA v. Russian Federation*, Appeal judgment, 361 F.3d 676 (2d Cir. 2004), ILDC 840 (US 2004), 16 March 2004 [40]). Specifically, the court noted that under international law, all acts and omissions of a State's organs are considered as acts of that State provided that they are undertaken in their official capacity [38].

instead as a case involving the secession of Poland, Czechoslovakia, and Yugoslavia (with both Austria and Hungary being considered as the continuing States). The majority of writers are of the opinion that this is a case of dissolution.[196] Poland considered itself to be in a situation of secession when it became an independent State in 1918.[197] Polish courts have considered Austria to be the continuator State of the Monarchy and held in several cases that it should remain responsible for any international wrongful acts that had been committed prior to 1918.[198] In the *Niedzielskie v. (Polish) Treasury* case, a contract was entered into by the authorities of the former Monarchy for work to be done on certain government buildings before the War. Following the War, the territory where the buildings were situated became a part of Poland, who had taken them over. The Supreme Court of Poland came to the conclusion that 'the successor State takes over the debts of its predecessor only in so far as it has expressly accepted them'.[199] The court held that there was no obligation for the new successor State to maintain the contracts that had been signed by the predecessor State.[200] In another case, the Supreme Court held that 'there is no general international custom ordering a State which acquires property under an international treaty to respect contracts of lease concluded by the predecessor State, unless there is a special treaty stipulation to that effect'.[201] The same position of non-succession was also taken by the courts of Czechoslovakia, who considered itself to be a new secessionist State in the context of the break-up of the Dual Monarchy. One court held that the successor State was not bound by an obligation created by a private contract

---

196 An overview of the legal arguments advanced by both sides in doctrine is found in Oskar Lehner, 'The Identity of Austria 1918/19 as a problem of State Succession', (1992) 44 *Ö.Z.ö.R.V.* 63–84, 81.

197 This is the reason why the example of Poland is examined in this section under the rubric of 'secession' rather than 'dissolution' (it should be added that one case involving Austria will be discussed, for reasons explained below, in detail below in the section dealing with dissolution). See, Chapter 13, Section 3.2.

198 *Niemiec and Niemiec v. Bialobrodziec and Polish State Treasury*, Supreme Court of Poland, Third Division, 20 February 1923, in (1923–1924) 2 *Annual Digest*, at 64; *Olpinski v. Polish Treasury (Railway Division)*, Supreme Court of Poland, Third Division, 16 April 1921, in O.S.P., I, no. 15; (1919–1922) *Annual Digest* 63.

199 *Niedzielskie v. (Polish) Treasury*, Poland, Supreme Court, 13 October 1926, *in: Rw. III, 1485*/26/I; (1925–26) 3 *Annual Digest* 74.

200 O'Connell, *State Succession*, 1967 (n 15) 362.

201 *(Polish) States Treasury v. Osten*, Supreme Court of Poland, 9 June 1922 in (1919–1922) 1 *Annual Digest*, case no. 37. See also *Graffowa and Wolanowski v. Polish Ministry of Agriculture and State Lands* (1923) Supreme Court of Poland, Zb. O.S.N. 1923, No. 30; O.S.P., III., No. 230, (1923–1924) *Annual Digest* case no. 26:

> The new State is not bound by the obligations of the old State on the ruins of which it had arisen or from which it has recovered a part of its territory. It does not take over obligations of that other State either in the domain of public law or in that of private law. It is a juridical person distinct from the old State, and as such, by an act of its sovereign power, it enters into possession of the public and private property of the old State, part of the territory of which it has taken over. The new State obtains its imperium not as a result of recognition by the older State or by other States, but as a result of having gained power over the territory and having suppressed the old power and organized the new power.

signed before secession between the predecessor State and a parish under which it undertook to contribute to the costs of the maintenance of a school.[202]

13.15 After the Spanish–American War, Spain and the United States signed the Treaty of Paris (1898), by which Spain ceded Cuba, Puerto Rico, the Philippines, and Guam to the United States.[203] Cuba became an independent State in 1902. The new State of Cuba refused to be held responsible for the payment of subsidies under a State contract, which had been signed by Spain (the predecessor State) in favour of a company (the Cuba Telegraph Company). As noted by O'Connell, 'the attitude of Cuba was that an engagement contracted with Spain remained the engagement of that country, and did not pass to the successor [State]', adding that 'this conclusion is justified on the doctrine propounded by the United States that concessions not exclusively for local benefit were not binding'.[204] In fact, Cuba rejected any responsibility on the grounds that the concession granted by Spain to that company was 'a measure of war' against the Cuban people.[205] In other words, it refused any succession mainly because the obligations under the contract were considered as an odious debt. O'Connell also refers to cases decided by Israeli courts in the context of the independence of Israel in 1948. The Supreme Court held that Israel was not a 'successor State' to the United Kingdom and that it was not responsible for the concession contracts granted by the United Kingdom before 1948.[206] It should be noted that the question as to whether the case of Israel is a case of secession is controversial.[207] In any event, Israel took the view that its independence should not even be considered as one of 'State succession' and adopted a *tabula rasa* approach accordingly.

13.16 In sum, these few examples support the principle that a new secessionist State is not bound by obligations arising from contracts that were signed before the date of succession by the predecessor State. The other question is whether there are any factors and circumstances that could militate in favour of the *new* State (not the continuing State) being considered as responsible for the rights and obligations arising from a State contract. In my view, there are indeed. As further examined below,[208] this could be the case when the investment was

202 *Maintenance of a School in Slovakia Case* (1935) Supreme Court of Czechoslovakia, in Collection Vazny 14785 civ. (193821940) *Annual Digest* 102.

203 Treaty of Paris, US-Spain, 10 December 1898, in T.S. No. 343.

204 O'Connell, *State Succession*, 1967 (n 15) 315.

205 Ibid.

206 Ibid., 336–8.

207 See, Crawford, *Brownlie's Principles of Public International Law* (n 58) 421ff, concluding (at 434) that this is a case of secession.

208 See, Chapter 14, Section 2.

made on the territory of what would become the new State and where the obligations under the contract were to be performed there. In these cases, it is likely that this territory (and its population) *benefited* from the consequences of such an investment on its territory before the date of succession and that the new State would continue to do so after its independence. Such a situation may involve an unjust enrichment (a point further discussed below[209]). For Stern (in the different context of succession to international responsibility), the question remains open as to whether, in certain circumstances, the new successor State should be exempt from its responsibility for an illegal act of expropriation committed at the time it was still part of the predecessor State.[210] In fact, the existence of such a 'territorial nexus' between the contract and the territory of the new State is precisely the reason the US Restatement of the Law adopted the rule of succession in specific circumstances in the context of secession.[211] While taking the general position that rights and obligations under a contract 'remain with the predecessor State',[212] the Restatement includes an exception in the situation 'where part of a State becomes a separate State' whereby the 'rights and obligations of the predecessor State under contracts *relating to the territory of the new State*, pass to the new State'.[213] In my view (as further discussed below[214]), whenever there exists any such 'nexus' between the contract and the territory of the new State, the latter should be bound by the contract regardless of the fact that the contract was signed by the predecessor State, which continues to exist.

2. TRANSFER OF TERRITORY

This is a unique type of succession of States because it does not involve the creation of a new State, but merely the cession of territory from one existing State to another. This section examines the fate of contracts involving an investment made *on the territory that is the object of cession*. It goes without saying that contracts dealing only with parts of the territory of the predecessor **13.17**

209 See, Chapter 14, Section 4.

210 B. Stern, 'Responsabilité internationale et succession d'Etats', in Laurence Boisson de Chazournes and Vera Gowlland-Debbas (eds), *The International Legal System in Quest of Equity and Universality Liber amicorum Georges Abi-Saab* (Nijhoff 2001) 335–6. She gives the example of a wrongful nationalization of a gold mine, which would now be situated in the territory of the new successor State and ask the question whether in this situation it should still be for the continuing State to provide compensation to the injured third State.

211 American Law Institute, *Restatement of the Law Third, the Foreign Relations Law of the United States*, vol I (American Law Institute Publ., 1987) at [209(2)] dealing with both 'State Property and Contracts'.

212 See, ibid., [209(2)], adding that this is 'subject to agreement between predecessor and successor States'.

213 Ibid., [209(2)(c)] (emphasis added).

214 See, Chapter 14, Section 2.

or the successor State that have been *unaffected* by the cession of territory should be continued without any interruption.[215]

2.1 The successor State is bound by contracts

13.18 As further explained in the following sections, the practice of States and that of courts and arbitral tribunals generally supports the proposition that the successor State is bound by the State contracts signed by the predecessor State dealing with the territory over which a change of sovereignty has occurred.[216] Writers also support this position.[217] The interesting question is why the principle of succession seems to be so firmly established in the context of cession of territory. One reason may be that in such a case, the investment made under a contract and its performance is inherently linked to the territory that is the object of cession. Thus, the execution of the contract resulted in some benefit to *that* territory and its population before the date of succession. These beneficial aspects will continue after the date of cession. This is why the rights and obligations under such a contract should be binding on the State

---

215 As a matter of illustration, State contracts signed by Germany which were dealing only with activities to be performed in the city of Hamburg are simply not affected by the double cession of the territory of Alsace-Lorraine in 1871 and 1918. The same goes for contracts signed by France dealing with rights and obligations to be performed only in Paris. What matters in the context of this book is what happens to contracts performed in Alsace-Lorraine.

216 This is the conclusion reached by O'Connell, *State Succession*, 1967 (n 15) 345, examining numerous examples.

217 Lalive (n 54) 165–6:

> The [acquired rights] rule is, thus, firmly established and appears undisputed. Before trying to determine its exact scope, it may be useful to explain briefly its justification. This is easy to discover. As in the domains of intertemporal law or of conflict or laws, it is a fundamental requirement of any legal order; i.e., one of continuity and stability of legal relations and situations. In the case of *annexation or cession of territory*, these general considerations are strengthened by the acquiring state's political interest. It is in that state's interest not to antagonize the local population by all abrupt and immediate change of legal regulations or by an automatic and radical suppression of previously acquired rights. Likewise, in purely municipal situations, the legislator endeavors to avoid too brutal changes and retroactive legislation. It usually adopts transitional measures to bring about a gradual and peaceful entry into force of the new statutes. A fortiori, it would seem, the state acquiring a new territory ought to do the same, especially since it often appears as a foreign legislator to local populations (emphasis added).

See also: Kaeckenbeeck (n 55) 411:

> Le principe de respect international des droits acquis est, après la consécration que lui a donnée la Cour permanente de Justice internationale et vu la conformité de la pratique des États-Unis avec le précédent de United States versus Percheman, définitivement établi, et nous n'avons aucune hésitation à accepter comme un principe indubitable du droit international positif actuel qu'une *cession de territoire* ne rend pas caducs les droits privés valablement acquis avant cette cession. Nous avons même vu que le principe s'étend aux droits mixtes dont le caractère privé l'emporte nettement sur le caractère public et qu'il implique, dans les cas où l'État est un des sujets du rapport juridique, la subrogation de l'État cessionnaire à l'État cédant, pour autant que le caractère politique ou d'ordre public du dit rapport ne s'y oppose pas (emphasis added).

See, however, ILC, Second Report Bedjaoui, 1969 (n 4) 87, for whom 'it must be acknowledged that political considerations, rather than juridical grounds, are the deciding factor in the attitude of Governments on this question'.

that takes over that territory after the date of succession. This is indeed the solution adopted by the US Restatement of the Law.[218] While taking the general position that rights and obligations under a contract 'remain with the predecessor State',[219] the Restatement includes an exception whereby in cases of cession of territory, 'the rights and obligations of the predecessor State under contracts *relating to that territory*, are transferred to the successor State'.[220] The successor State is bound by such rights and obligations because the contract is 'related' to the territory ceded over which it is now sovereign. Succession is the result of the territorial 'nexus' established between the contract and the territory ceded to the successor State (a question further examined below[221]).

The following sections analyse the practice of successor States (Section 2.3) and that of third States whose nationals had been affected by a transfer of territory (Section 2.2). I will also examine several decisions by international courts and tribunals (Section 2.4). While such practice supports the principle of succession to contracts, it remains undeniable that judicial decisions have often been influenced by treaty provisions expressly providing for such a solution (a point further discussed below). **13.19**

2.2 Third States whose nationals had been affected by a transfer have adopted the succession principle

Many States have adopted a position in favour of succession to contracts whenever their own nationals were concerned by a cession of territory taking place elsewhere. **13.20**

One example is the position of the United States in the context of France's annexation of Madagascar in 1896[222] and the cession of the territory of Palestine after the First World War.[223] The United Kingdom also consistently took the view that the successor State was bound under international law to protect and maintain the rights which had been granted by the predecessor State to foreigners in the ceded territory before the date of succession. In the context of the cession of the Ionian Islands by the United Kingdom to Greece in 1864, the UK law officers stated that there was 'no doubt upon the general question of the continued obligation of all lawful contracts existing at the time **13.21**

218 Restatement of the Law (n 211) [209(2)].
219 Ibid., [209(2)], adding that this is 'subject to agreement between predecessor and successor states'.
220 Ibid., [209(2)(a)] (emphasis added).
221 See, Chapter 14, Section 2.
222 O'Connell, *State Succession*, 1967 (n 15) 308.
223 Ibid., 324.

of the cession of these islands to the Kingdom of Greece', and that based on 'the principles of international law (...) and the practice of all civilized States, ceded territories pass, *cum onere*, to the new sovereign'.[224] The same position was also adopted by the United Kingdom in the context of France's annexation of Madagascar in 1896[225] and the annexation of Korea by Japan in 1910.[226]

13.22 The example of the cession of Cuba and the Philippines by Spain to the United States in 1898 is intriguing.[227] In the context of negotiations preceding the signing of the peace treaty between Spain and America, one important issue concerned the fate of contracts which had been signed by Spain with foreign companies before 1898. The United States took the position that 'it does not propose to repudiate any contract found upon investigation to be binding under international law', adding that it 'would deal justly and equitably in respect of contracts that were binding under the principles of international law'.[228] In fact, the United States argued that for any contract to be respected by the successor State 'a concession must not only be related or attached to the territory ceded, but also granted for its exclusive benefit'.[229] This is a clear example of the importance of the 'nexus' between a contract and the territory ceded.[230] According to the United States, the concessions granted to a British company, Manila Railway Company, to build a railway in the Philippines was not in the exclusive interests of that territory, but had been inspired by the 'imperialistic motives of Spain'. For that reason, the United States argued that it was not obliged to respect that contract.[231] The United Kingdom (whose nationals' interests were at stake) argued that the United States contention was 'contrary to the recognized principles of international law' and that the distinction on which it was based was arbitrary because it 'leave[s] it open, in all cases of conquest and cession, to the succeeding government to repudiate the obligations of their predecessors on alleged ground motives'.[232] In fact, the United Kingdom argued that there was a 'nexus' between the contract and the territory of the Philippines:

> The obligation is one of a local nature, although contracted by the government of Spain. On the faith of it, the company has expanded a large sum of money on works

224 Ibid., 307–8, referring to a law opinion of 15 August 1863, F.O. 83/2287.
225 Ibid., 309–10.
226 Ibid., 322.
227 Ibid., 311–13.
228 Ibid., 311, referring to J.B. Moore, *History and Digest of the International Arbitrations to which the United States has been a Party*, vol I (GPO 1898) 389.
229 Ibid., 311–12
230 The question is examined below at Chapter 14, Section 2.
231 O'Connell, *State Succession*, 1967 (n 15) 312.
232 Ibid., 312, referring to a law opinion of 30 November 1900, F.O. confidential papers (7516) no.44.

> for the benefit of the Philippines and the obligation to respect the concession seems to us to belong clearly to that class of local obligations which have always been held to pass with the territory.[233]

In sum, there are several examples where the States whose own nationals' rights were affected by a cession of territory taking place elsewhere have adopted a position in favour of succession. Yet, one must be careful not to give too much weight to these precedents since the States involved may have taken this position for purely opportunistic reasons, having little to do with any legal principle. Thus, they may have favoured succession simply to protect their own nationals' interests. This is clear from the fact that the same States have sometimes taken the opposite position of non-succession whenever they were the ones that were directly involved in a cession of territory as successor State. As further examined below,[234] this is indeed the controversial position that was adopted by the United Kingdom in the context of its annexation of the Republic of South Africa. **13.23**

2.3 Successor States and their domestic courts have adopted the succession principle

When taking possession of the Philippines and Cuba from Spain in 1898, the United States respected the concessions that had been granted by Spain to foreign companies.[235] The Treaty of Peace of 1947 also recognized the validity of the contractual obligations that were undertaken by Finland with companies in the territory of Petsamo, which was ceded to the Soviet Union.[236] Many examples in the context of the unification of Italy also support the principle of succession. According to the 1866 Treaty of Vienna, the Austrian Empire ceded Venetia to the French Empire, which then ceded it to the Kingdom of Italy. Under the Treaty, Italy succeeded to the 'rights and obligations resulting from contracts regularly stipulated by the Austrian administration for [the] object of public interest specially concerning the ceded territories'.[237] The principle of the continuation of contracts was adopted by a number of Italian courts.[238] In one case, the Court of Cassation of Florence held that 'by public law the State which succeeds in a part of the territory of another State is **13.24**

233 Ibid.
234 See, Chapter 13, Section 6.2.
235 O'Connell, *State Succession*, 1967 (n 15) 311.
236 Ibid., 335.
237 Treaty of Peace, October 3, 1866, in: M.N.R.G. vol 18, 405, Art. 8.
238 O'Connell, *State Succession*, 1967 (n 15) 356.

bound, independently of special conventions, by the obligations legally contracted by the latter in relation to the territory to which it succeeds'.[239] Following this case, Italian courts have consistently adopted the principle of succession.[240]

13.25 An approach favouring the succession to contracts was also adopted by *predecessor* States whose territory was ceded to another State. One example is in the context of the cession of the territory of Alsace-Lorraine by France to Germany in accordance with the Treaty of Frankfurt (1871).[241]

13.26 The principle of succession was also adopted by a Greek tribunal in the *Nisyros* case involving the Ottoman Empire who had granted, in 1908, a concession contract to exploit a sulphur mine on the Island of Nisyros to the appellants' predecessor.[242] The Island was under Ottoman Empire sovereignty until 1912 when it fell under Italian military occupation. The Dodecanese islands (including Nisyros) were finally ceded to Italy in accordance with the Treaty of Lausanne in 1923. In 1933, the Italian Governor of the Dodecanese enacted, on the basis of an Italian Royal Decree of 1924, a Decree-Law repealing the Ottoman law of 1906 concerning mines.[243] Pursuant to Article 14 of the 1947 Paris Peace Treaty signed by, inter alia, Greece and Italy, the Dodecanesian Islands were ceded by Italy to Greece.[244] Greece passed a Royal Decree whereby holders of mining concession rights should claim the renewal of their

---

239 *Verlengo v. Finance Department*, Court of Cassation at Florence, 1878, in: Giurisprudenza Italiana, 3rd Series, vol 30, Pt. 1, Sec. 1, column 1206, referred to in 'Brief filed by Fred K. Nielsen, American Agent, Hawaiian Claims Case', in: Fred K. Nielsen, *American and British Claims Arbitration, Report* (GPO 1926) 95ff at 119–20. See also: Cecil J.B. Hurst, 'State Succession in Matters of Tort', (1924) 5 *British YIL* 175.

240 Hurst, ibid., 174ff. One example is the case of *Czario v. Valentinis* involving a contract of lease concluded between the Austrian authorities and a private party before the cession of territory. The Court of Cassation held: 'The Italian sovereignty having succeeded to the Austrian in the annexed territories by force of arms, it is to be assumed that the Italian State replaces the Austrian with regard to juridical relations of private law existing between the latter State and the private citizens.' (*Czario v. Valentinis*, Italian Court of Cassation, 15 October, 1927, in Foro delle nuove provinzie, 1927, 311–14, (1927–1928) *Annual Digest*, Case 52).

241 O'Connell, *State Succession*, 1967 (n 15) 357, referring to a decision by the Conseil d'État dated 28 April 1876, which held that according to a principle recognized under international law the successor State takes over the rights and obligations arising from contracts which had been signed by the predecessor State regarding the ceded territory.

242 *Nisyros Mines Case*, Greece, Council of State, 1952, in: (1954) 7 RHDI, 274, (1952) ILR, 135. See: Verzijl (n 43) 73.

243 Ibid., ILR, 136: The decree provided, inter alia, that:

> all concessions in favour of any person, granted whether by the Ottoman Government or the Italian Government, and relating to mines, unless it is shown that they have been regularly exploited during the period of five years immediately preceding the entry into force of this Decree, are considered null and void, without the necessity of any governmental act, and without any rights of the owners to repurchase (…).

244 Paris Peace Treaty, signed on 10 February 1947 at Paris, entered into force on 15 September 1947, in: 49 UNTS 126; (1948) UKTS, no. 50 (Cmd. 7481).

rights. The applicant made such a claim, which was decided by the Greek Administrative Tribunal for Mines. In its 1952 decision, the tribunal found that the mines in question had not been regularly exploited between 1919 and 1945 and that, therefore, the rights relating to them had ceased to exist by virtue of the Italian Governor's Decree of 1933. The Greek Council of State reversed the judgment of the administrative tribunal on the grounds that while the successor States (Italy, then Greece) had the right to pass legislation affecting the acquired rights of foreigners after the date of succession, they were nevertheless required to so in accordance with international law:

> The doctrine of international law, which has developed under the influence of Western civilization, recognizes that the sovereign right of a successor State is not limited to substituting its own legislation for that in force in the annexed territory, so far as acquired rights are concerned: for, as soon as the annexing State has established its sovereignty over the territory, it has the right to substitute its legislation in order to achieve consistency in its legislation as a whole. Nevertheless, in legislat[ion] concerning acquired rights, the successor State should deal with them on the basis of respecting them, in accordance with international agreements and with international usage. But, in any case where there is doubt on the question of the correct interpretation to be placed on a legal provision giving legislative power over annexed territory, being a doubt arising concerning the extent of such power, that provision should be construed in the light not only of the principles of public law of the State granting such power, but also subject to *the general principles of international law*.[245]

The Council of State held that the Italian Decree of 1933 was indeed in violation of international law. Specifically, Article 9 of Protocol XII of the Treaty of Lausanne, which provides that Italy, as the successor State, was subrogated in all respects with regard to the rights and obligations of Turkey vis-à-vis nationals of other signatory Powers. The Council of State reversed the judgment of the administrative tribunal. **13.27**

In sum, while the *Nisyros* decision does refer, rather vaguely, to 'general principles of international law' on the survival of acquired rights, the Council of State ultimately based its decision on the application of a treaty provision. The same observation can also be made, more generally, with respect to other judicial decisions examined in this section. Although they support the principle of succession to State contracts, the position taken by them seems to have been largely influenced by the existence of a treaty provision providing for such a solution. **13.28**

245 *Nisyros Mines Case* (n 242) 136 (emphasis added).

2.4 The limited relevance of some decisions by international courts and arbitral tribunals dealing with the matter

13.29 This section examines a number of decisions by international courts and arbitral tribunals dealing with succession to State contracts in the context of a cession of territory. These decisions generally provide limited guidance on the matter because tribunals have essentially applied treaty provisions when deciding that the successor State should be bound by obligations arising from contracts that had been signed by the predecessor State. In only one case, *Affaire des Forêts du Rhodope Central* case (1933), does the tribunal actually refer to the existence of a general principle of succession that is applicable notwithstanding the existence of any treaty provision to that effect. Yet, these decisions are important for other reasons. Indeed, some of them are frequently referred to by scholars and investors as the cornerstone of an (alleged) principle of international law whereby the successor State would have the obligation to respect all acquired rights of foreign investors. This is indeed the case for two PCIJ cases: *Questions relating to Settlers of German Origin in Poland* (1923) and *Mavrommatis Palestine Concessions* (1925). In fact, a closer analysis of these decisions will show that they do not provide much support for such a proposition. Also, while the analysis of the decisions of the PCIJ and that of the arbitral tribunal in the three *Lighthouse* cases examined below provide limited guidance on the question of succession to contracts, they will be of great assistance when the time comes to discuss the factors and circumstances that should be taken into account by a tribunal to determine the matter.[246]

2.4.1 Questions Relating to Settlers of German Origin in Poland (PCIJ, 1923)

13.30 The doctrine of acquired rights was formulated by the PCIJ in *Questions Relating to Settlers of German Origin in Poland, which dealt with the question of the eviction of German settlers by Poland* from territories which had belonged to Germany, but were ceded to Poland after the War. The court made the general proposition that private rights do not simply disappear in the event of a change of sovereignty:

> Private rights acquired under existing law do not cease on change of sovereignty. No one denies that the German Civil Law, both substantive and adjective, has continued without interruption to operate in the territory in question. It can hardly be maintained that, although the law survives, private rights acquired under it have

246 This question is examined below at Chapter 14.

> perished. Such a contention is based on no principle and would be contrary to an almost universal opinion and practice.[247]

Yet, as noted by O'Connell, the court in this case did not have to examine the general question of the survival of acquired rights by the successor State. It only had to determine the scope of one provision (Art 15 of the Minorities Treaty) under which Poland had the obligation not to terminate the rights of such minorities.[248] As noted by Bedjaoui, in that case the court 'was called upon to give an opinion on the violation of an international undertaking rather than on the existence of a principle of public international law'.[249] This is clear from these extracts of the decision: **13.31**

> The general question whether and under what circumstances a State may modify or cancel private rights by its sovereign legislative power, requires no consideration here.
>
> The Court is here dealing with private rights under specific provisions of law and of treaty, and it suffices for the purposes of the present opinion to say that even those who contest the existence in international law of a general principle of State succession do not go so far as to maintain that private rights including those acquired from the State as the owner of the property are invalid as against a successor in sovereignty.
>
> By the Minorities Treaty, Poland has agreed that all Polish nationals shall enjoy the same civil and political rights and the same treatment and security in law as well as in fact. The action taken by the Polish authorities under the Law of July 14th, 1920, and particularly under Article 5 is undoubtedly a virtual annulment of the rights which the settlers acquired under their contracts and therefore an infraction of the obligation concerning their civil rights. It is contrary to the principle of equality in that it subjects the settlers to a discriminating and injurious treatment to which other citizens holding contracts of sale or lease are not subject.[250]

Ultimately, the most that can be said is that the court supported the general proposition that private rights simply do not automatically disappear as a result of a change in sovereignty.[251] As noted by O'Connell, this statement of the court 'by itself is of minimal significance'.[252] Thus, as noted above,[253] a new State is indeed always free to adopt new legislation that can affect the rights of individuals. The same general position was taken by the PCIJ in the **13.32**

247 *Advisory Opinion No. 6* (n 52) 36.

248 O'Connell, *State Succession*, 1967 (n 15) 263–4.

249 ILC, Second Report Bedjaoui, 1969 (n 4) 74.

250 *Advisory Opinion* No. 6 (n 52) 36.

251 Swan Sik (n 58) 128.

252 O'Connell, 'Recent Problems of State Succession' (n 41) 134: 'It means that rights derived from the antecedent legal system are *ipso facto* unaffected by the change of sovereignty, but this can only be to the extent to which the law itself survives,' adding that: 'If a right derives from public law and the public law is expelled from the territory, then something additional to legal continuity is required for the right to subsist.'

253 See, Chapter 10, Section 3.

case of *German Interests in Polish Upper Silesia*,[254] as well as by some other tribunals.[255]

2.4.2 Mavrommatis Palestine Concessions (PCIJ, 1925)

13.33 The question of succession to contracts arose in the *Mavrommatis Palestine Concessions* case decided by the PCIJ in 1925. It involved a claim filed by Greece on behalf of one of its nationals against the United Kingdom.[256] The context of the claim was the end of the Ottoman Empire and the cession of several territories to the Allies, which established protectorates over them. For instance, the United Kingdom established protectorates over Mesopotamia (now Iraq) and Palestine, while France did the same regarding Syria and Lebanon. Before the War, Mr. Mavrommatis, a Greek national, had been granted by the Ottoman Empire two groups of concessions to undertake public works in the territory of Palestine (the Jaffa and the Jerusalem concessions). One question arising in this case was whether the British Government, as Mandatory of Palestine (the successor State), was under any obligation to honor these concessions granted by the Ottoman authorities.[257] The question was answered in the affirmative by Article 1 of Protocol XII of the 1923 Treaty of Lausanne which dealt explicitly with the issue.[258]

13.34 As a national of one of the 'Contracting Powers' to the Treaty (Greece), Mr. Mavrommatis was entitled to have his concession contracts (those that were signed *before* 29 October 1914, that is, the Jerusalem concession) honoured by the successor State. One group of concessions (Jaffa) had only been signed *after* that date and was therefore not covered by the treaty provision. While the court held that it did not have jurisdiction to consider these concessions, it nevertheless made this general observation:

> It will suffice to observe that if, on the one hand, Protocol XII being silent regarding concessions subsequent to October 29th, 1914, leaves intact the general principle of subrogation, it is, on the other hand, impossible to maintain that this principle falls within the international obligations contemplated in Article II of the Mandate as interpreted in this judgment. The Administration of Palestine would be bound to

---

254 *German Interests in Polish Upper Silesia, Germany v. Poland*, (1926), PCIJ Ser. A, No. 7, 22, at 31.

255 See, for instance, *Affaire Goldenberg* (*Allemagne v. Roumanie*), 27 September 1928, 2 UNRIAA 901, at 909: 'Le respect de la propriété privée et des droits acquis des étrangers fait sans conteste partie des principes généraux admis par le droit des gens.'

256 *The Mavrommatis Palestine Concessions*, 1924, PCIJ, Ser. A, No. 2.

257 O'Connell, *State Succession*, 1967 (n 15) 323.

258 Treaty of Peace of Lausanne, signed on 24 July 1923, in: UKTS 1923, No. 16 (Cmd. 1929); 28 LNTS 11; (1924) 18 *AJIL* Supp., 4. The provision reads as follows: 'Concessionary contracts and subsequent agreements relating thereto, duly entered into before the 29th October, 1914, between the Ottoman Government or any local authority, on the one hand, and nationals (including Companies) of the Contracting Powers, other than Turkey, on the other hand, are maintained'.

> recognize the Jaffa concessions, not in consequence of an obligation undertaken by the Mandatory, *but in virtue of a general principle of international law* to the application of which the obligations entered into by the Mandatory created no exception.[259]

Since the PCIJ declined its jurisdiction over the Jaffa concession claim, it did not examine the question of whether any such 'general principle of international law' exists regarding the protection of concession rights in a situation where no treaty provision provides for an express solution. With respect to the Jerusalem concession, it simply applied Protocol XII providing for the maintenance of such contractual rights. For this reason, it has been rightly highlighted that the case does not provide much support in favour of the existence of any principle of succession to contracts under general international law.[260] The court simply applied a treaty provision. **13.35**

2.4.3 Lighthouse case (PCIJ, 1934) and Lighthouse in Crete and Samos case (PCIJ, 1937)

The *Lighthouse* case involved concession rights obtained in 1860 by a French company (Société Collas et Michel) from the Ottoman Empire for the management, development, and maintenance of the system of lights on the coasts of the Ottoman Empire in the Mediterranean, the Dardanelles, and the Black Sea. The concession for the maintenance of the lighthouses on the coasts of the Ottoman Empire had been renewed many times since then.[261] At the heart of the dispute was a contract concluded in April 1913 between the Ottoman Government and the French firm for the renewal of the concession for 25 years. France and Greece disagreed on the fate of the contract after some of the territories where the lighthouses were situated had been ceded by the Ottoman Empire to Greece. France and Greece signed a special agreement in 1931 and the matter was decided by the PCIJ in 1934.[262] **13.36**

The court identified three questions to be decided: determine the intentions of the parties with regards to the scope of the contract; whether this contract was 'duly entered into' according to Ottoman law; and whether it was enforceable against Greece. Only the last question is of interest for the purpose of this book. The court examined Article 9 of Protocol XII of the Lausanne Treaty,[263] **13.37**

---

259 *The Mavrommatis Palestine Concessions* (n 256) 28 (emphasis added).

260 O'Connell, *State Succession*, 1967 (n 15) 325.

261 *Lighthouse Case between France and Greece*, Judgment, 17 March 1934, PCIJ, Ser. A/B, no. 62, at [19].

262 Ibid., [3]. An analysis of the case can be found in: J.H.W. Verzijl, *The Jurisprudence of the World Court: A Case by Case Commentary*, vol I (Sijthoff 1965) 370–82.

263 Treaty of Lausanne (n 258). The provision reads as follows:

> In territories detached from Turkey under the Treaty of Peace signed this day, the State which acquires the territory is fully subrogated as regards the rights and obligations of Turkey towards the nationals of the other contracting Powers and companies in which the capital of the nationals of the said Powers is

and concluded that it meant two different things. First, the 'succession State' (Greece) was 'subrogated as regards [to] concessionary contracts entered into with the Ottoman Government prior to October 29th, 1914, in so far as concerns the territories detached from Turkey under the Treaty of Lausanne'.[264] Second, Greece was also subrogated in regards to the concessionary contracts entered into with the Ottoman Government 'prior to the coming into force of the respective treaties of peace, in so far as concerns territories detached from Turkey after the Balkan wars'.[265] The concession rights in the present case concerned the latter situation. It is important to note that at the time the contract was concluded (in April 1913), 'the greater part of Turkey in Europe had been occupied by the Balkan Allies and, so far as concerns the Mediterranean coasts and the islands, by Greece'.[266] Yet, as the court mentioned, 'the fate of all the occupied territories was not yet decided'.[267] Regardless, certain territories where the lighthouses were situated were occupied by Greek troops at that date; they were no longer controlled by Turkey.

13.38 One of the questions raised by the parties in the proceedings was whether 'the territorial sovereign is entitled, in occupied territory, to grant concessions legally enforceable against the State which subsequently acquires the territories it occupies'.[268] Greece argued essentially that, on the one hand, the Ottoman Empire was no longer sovereign over these territories in April 1913 and therefore could not sign the renewal of the contract. On the other hand, it also argued that, as the occupying force in the territory, Greece could not either. The court did not examine this question based on the clear language contained in the Protocol.[269] The court concluded on this point that: 'The Greek Government is not therefore entitled to object to its subrogation as regards the contract of April 1st/14th, 1913, on the ground that certain territories were occupied by Greek troops at that date.'[270] The court held that the concession contract granted to the company was 'duly entered into and was

---

preponderant, who are beneficiaries under concessionary contracts entered into before the 29th October, 1914, with the Ottoman Government or any local Ottoman authority. The same provision will apply in territories detached from Turkey after the Balkan wars so far as regards concessionary contracts entered into with the Ottoman Government or any Ottoman local authority before the coming into force of the treaty providing for the transfer of the territory. This subrogation will have effect as from the coming into force of the treaty by which the transfer of territory was effected except as regards territories detached by the Treaty of Peace signed this day, in respect of which the subrogation will have effect as from the 30th October, 1918.

264 *Lighthouse Case* (n 261) [83].
265 Ibid., [83].
266 Ibid., [24].
267 Ibid., [62].
268 Ibid., [80].
269 Ibid. The question is examined in detail by Judge Séfériadès in his separate opinion.
270 Ibid., [83].

accordingly operative as regards the Greek Government in so far as concerns lighthouses situated in the territories assigned to it after the Balkan wars or subsequently'.[271] In other words, the 1913 contract was one of those contracts covered by Article 1 of Protocol XII of the 1923 Treaty of Lausanne and Greece was obligated to maintain it.

Ultimately, the court only applied the terms of the Lausanne Treaty and did not discuss the general question of whether or not a successor State was under the obligation to maintain rights that had been granted under a contract by the predecessor State before the cession of the territory. As such, the reasoning of the court provides limited guidance to the question examined in this section. **13.39**

In the subsequent *Lighthouse in Crete and Samos* case of 1937, the court simply confirmed that its ruling of 1934 extended specifically to the territories of Crete and Samos.[272] Greece had argued that the lighthouses situated in the territories of Crete and Samos 'remained outside the ambit of the contract concluded (…) as the territories in which they are situated were detached from Turkey well before that date'.[273] Thus, an autonomous Cretan State had been created before the contract was renewed in 1913.[274] The contract could therefore not apply to the territory of Crete over which Turkey could no longer exercise any rights.[275] On this point, the court identified the question as being the following: 'had every political link between the Ottoman Empire and the **13.40**

271 Ibid., [90].

272 *Lighthouses in Crete and Samos*, Judgment, 8 October 1937, PCIJ, Ser. A/B, no. 71. An analysis of the case can be found in: Verzijl (n 262) 483–95.

273 Ibid., [34].

274 Ibid. A few words should be said about the particular history of the Greek-speaking region of Crete which was under Ottoman occupation since the seventeenth century. A series of revolts against the Turks in the nineteenth century reached its climax in the insurrection of 1896–97 that led to war (in 1897) between Greece and the Ottoman Empire. The European Powers intervened in the war, forcing the Ottoman Empire to evacuate Crete in 1898. An autonomous Cretan State was formed under nominal Ottoman rule but in fact governed by a high commission of the occupying powers (England, France, Russia and Italy). Crete was in favour of its union with Greece but the occupying powers rejected its demand. The Young Turks revolution of 1908, however, enabled the Cretans to proclaim their union with Greece and in 1909 foreign occupation troops were withdrawn. In 1913, Crete was officially incorporated into Greece.

275 The court summarized that argument as follows:

> According to the contention of the Greek Government, the situation of the territories of Crete and Samos is of an entirely different order. The latter territories, which enjoyed a wide autonomy, were not and could not have been detached from Turkey by a transfer of sovereignty in from that State to Greece, seeing that in 1913 Turkey had long since lost her sovereignty in regard to them. It follows, according to this argument, that in April 1913 the Ottoman Government no longer had any title, competence or capacity to conclude the contract of April 1st/14th, 1913, and accordingly the contract, though valid in itself, was not duly entered into or validly concluded in respect of these territories (ibid., [36]).

islands of Crete and Samos disappeared at the time of the conclusion of the contract in dispute, that is to say, on April 1st/14th, 1913?'[276] The court added that:

> only if it were shown that no such link subsisted on that date, would it be possible to regard these territories as having been already detached from the Ottoman Empire before the conclusion of the contract, and to consider the latter as not having been duly entered into in regard to the aforesaid territories.[277]

The court took the view that 'notwithstanding its autonomy, Crete had not ceased to be a part of the Ottoman Empire'.[278] It is only in May 1913 (i.e., *one month after* the contract was signed in April 1913) that Crete was officially incorporated into Greece by Article 4 of the Treaty of London.[279] Article 4 of the Treaty indicates that 'His Imperial Majesty the Sultan declares that he cedes to Their Majesties the Allied Sovereigns the island of Crete and renounces in their favour all rights of sovereignty and all other rights which he possessed over that island.'[280] For the court, 'it would be difficult to find more decisive evidence of the persistence of the Sultan's sovereignty up to that date than is furnished by this formal renunciation made by the latter in an international instrument signed by Greece'.[281]

13.41 In any event, the court stated that Article 9 of Protocol XII of the Lausanne Treaty 'makes no exception or reservation' and 'applies to all the territories which were detached from Turkey after the Balkan wars, without regard to the special status possessed by some of them under the Ottoman Empire'.[282] The court further explained that under this provision 'the idea of the detachment of the territories is closely, connected with and correlated to that of their

---

276 Ibid., [37].

277 Ibid.

278 Ibid., [38]. See also at [39]:

> The Greek Government would have needed to prove that, at the time of the conclusion of the contract in dispute, the territories of Crete and Samos were already, in law, territories detached from the Ottoman Empire, in the full meaning of the word 'detached', which in the opinion of the Court connotes the entire disappearance of any political link. For, as has been already observed, it is the date of the detachment of the territories which is decisive in this case. The wide forms of autonomy conferred on the territories in question could only be taken into consideration for the solution of the present dispute, if they justified the conclusion that the autonomous territories were already, at the date of the contract, detached from the Ottoman Empire to the extent that every political link between them and the Sublime Porte had been severed, so that the Sultan had lost all power to make contracts in regard to them.

279 Treaty of London, 17–30 May 1913, in: G.FR. de Martens, *Nouveau recueil général de traités*, Gr. VII, t. 8, at 16.

280 *Lighthouses in Crete and Samos* (n 272).

281 Ibid., [41].

282 Ibid., [34].

assignment to another sovereign'.[283] Thus, this provision 'leaves no room for a break in continuity of the sovereignty over the territories referred to therein' and 'provides for the direct and immediate succession of Greece to the obligations contracted by the Ottoman Empire in respect of the territories over which Ottoman sovereignty is ceded'.[284] The court therefore concluded that the lighthouses in Crete and Samos were situated in 'territories which not only were assigned to Greece after the Balkan wars but also were not detached from the Ottoman Empire until that time'. Article 9 of Protocol XII of the Treaty of Lausanne was therefore applicable to the April 1913 contract. Consequently, the court decided that the contract 'must be considered as having been duly entered into, and as accordingly operative in regard to Greece in respect of the said territories'.[285]

Once again, in this case, the court simply applied a treaty provision to arrive to the conclusion that the successor State was bound to respect a contract which had been signed by the predecessor State. The importance of this case to the present discussion is therefore limited. **13.42**

2.4.4 The Lighthouse Arbitration case (French-Greek Arbitral Tribunal, 1956)

The *Lighthouse Arbitration* case was decided in 1956 by the French-Greek Arbitral Tribunal, which had been set up under the rules of the Permanent Court of Arbitration in The Hague.[286] The case involved several claims (contractual and delictual): France had no less than 27 claims and Greece ten counter-claims. Only a few of these claims are relevant for the present purpose. **13.43**

The *Lighthouse Arbitration* case is a good illustration of the principle that the continuing State should remain responsible for *its own* internationally wrongful acts committed before the date of succession. This is expressed by the arbitral tribunal in its reasoning concerning Claim no. 12–a, whereby France sought compensation against Greece (the successor State) for acts committed directly by the authorities of the Ottoman Empire (the predecessor State).[287] The alleged internationally wrongful act was the unauthorized removal by the Ottoman Empire of a buoy belonging to the French company Collas et Michel. The arbitral tribunal ruled that the Ottoman authorities had not committed any wrongful act in doing so and that the acts were legitimate for **13.44**

283 Ibid.
284 Ibid.
285 Ibid., [43].
286 *Lighthouse Arbitration* case (n 162), 90.
287 Ibid., 81.

reasons of security. In one *obiter dictum*, the arbitral tribunal nevertheless indicated that even if the Ottoman Empire had committed such an internationally wrongful act, Greece could not be held liable for it. It was Turkey (the continuing State of the Ottoman Empire[288]) which would be liable for its 'own' acts committed before the loss of a substantial portion of its territory. This was in accordance with Article 9 of Protocol XII of the 1923 Lausanne Peace Treaty.[289] Therefore, the *obiter dictum* by the arbitral tribunal supports the proposition that in cases of cession of territory, the continuing State should remain responsible for *its own* internationally wrongful acts committed before the date of succession.[290] The same principle was applied by the tribunal in dealing with Claim no. 11.[291]

13.45 Claim no. 4 dealt with tax exemptions granted to a Greek shipping company and its ship (the Haghios Nicolaos) by a law proclaimed by the local authorities of Crete in 1908. After 1913, when the Island became officially part of Greece, the law remained in place. This tax exemption was alleged by the French company to be in violation of its existing concession rights. Therefore, France sought reparation from Greece. Right from the outset, the arbitral tribunal indicated that the liability of Greece should not be based on the above-mentioned provision of the Lausanne Peace Treaty which dealt with the rights and obligations *of Turkey* and not those of Crete. The arbitral tribunal held that such a liability 'could result only from a transmission of responsibility in accordance with the rules of customary law or the general principles of law regulating the succession of States in general'.[292] The arbitral tribunal concluded that the tax exemption was a breach of a *contractual* obligation that had been committed by Crete. The tribunal described Crete as an 'autonomous island State the population of which had for decades passionately aspired to be united, by force of arms if necessary, with Greece, which was regarded as the mother country'.[293] Greece had also recognized that this was in violation of the concession agreement. The arbitral tribunal added that this violation by the Cretan authorities was made in favour of a Greek company and that the Greek authorities maintained the situation after 1913. The arbitral tribunal thus concluded on this point that:

288 On this question, see: P. Dumberry, 'Is Turkey the "Continuing" State of the Ottoman Empire under International Law?' (2012) 59(2) *Netherlands ILR* 235–62; P. Dumberry, 'Turkey's International Responsibility for Internationally Wrongful Acts Committed by the Ottoman Empire', (2012) 42 *Revue générale de droit* 562–89.

289 Treaty of Lausanne (n 258).

290 See, analysis in: Dumberry, *State Succession to International Responsibility* (n 165) 130ff.

291 See, analysis: ibid.

292 *Lighthouse Arbitration* case (n 162) 90.

293 Ibid., 92.

> [T]he Tribunal can only come to the conclusion that Greece, having adopted the illegal conduct of Crete in its recent past as [an] autonomous State, is bound, as [a] successor State, to take upon its charge the financial consequences of the breach of the concession contract. Otherwise, the avowed violation of a contract committed by one of the two States, linked by a common past and a common destiny, with the assent of the other, would, in the event of their merger, have the thoroughly unjust consequence of cancelling a definite financial responsibility and of sacrificing the undoubted rights of a private firm holding a concession to a so-called general principle of non-transmission of debts in cases of territorial succession, which in reality does not exist as a general and absolute principle.[294]

Therefore, the tribunal did *not* take a stance on the question of succession to contractual obligations per se. It simply held that the successor State had *continued* a breach of contract which was initially started before the date of succession and, hence, should be responsible for any damages arising from such an act (a question further examined below[295]). **13.46**

The tribunal also pointed out that the solution would have been the same even if the obligation had been regarded as *delictual* rather than contractual. There is no doubt that Greece was held responsible for its *own* internationally wrongful acts (delict of omission) committed *after* 1913 when Crete was officially ceded to Greece. Thus, Greece was responsible for *maintaining* in place the discriminatory practice *after* it had undeniable sovereignty over the Island.[296] The question remains whether Greece was also held accountable, as the successor State, for acts committed by Crete *before* 1913. This is a question of succession to State responsibility that is controversial and has been addressed by the present author elsewhere.[297] In my view, this case is an illustration that in the context of a cession of territory there is an exception to the general principle that the continuing State should be responsible for the acts committed on the ceded territory before the date of succession. The exception is when the internationally wrongful acts were committed by a largely autonomous government. At the time of the events, Crete had indeed a largely autonomous government.[298] In the award, the tribunal mentions that this was an important point that had been expressly discarded by the PCIJ in **13.47**

---

294 Ibid.

295 See, Chapter 14, Section 1.

296 *Lighthouse Arbitration* case (n 162) 92.

297 Dumberry, *State Succession to International Responsibility* (n 165) 138ff.

298 *Lighthouse Arbitration* case (n 162). The arbitral tribunal indicated about Crete (in the original French version of the award) that:

> son émancipation comme entité autonome a déja commencé en 1868 … [d]epuis lors, l'île de Crète a vécu une vie politique séparée … et mené l'existence d'un État autonome, investi de pouvoir très larges, mais sous la suzeraineté de l'Empire Ottoman.

its 1937 judgment.[299] In such a case, the successor State (i.e., the State to which the territory is ceded) should be held responsible for the consequences of obligations arising from the internationally wrongful acts that had been committed before the date of succession.[300] The Institut recently adopted the same position on the matter.[301] The question of responsibility for actions of an autonomous government in the context of State contracts is further examined below.[302]

13.48 Finally, Claim no. 27 dealt with the actions taken by Greece in 1929 (i.e., well after the event of succession) that resulted in the seizing of the lighthouse administration, without however paying compensation to the firm.[303] Importantly, the original concession contracts entered into between Turkey and Collas et Michel in 1860 provided that Turkey might take over the administration of the lighthouse, subject to the payment of compensation as agreed beforehand by the parties or as determined by arbitration. After having explained the nature of this clause,[304] the tribunal held that Greece had been subrogated into the position of Turkey under the concession contract and could therefore only take over the lighthouse administration under the same

---

The cession of territory in 1913 by the Ottoman Empire is described by the arbitral tribunal as 'sa renunciation finale à un résidu de droits de suzeraintê qu'il avait encore retenus après avoir érigé l'île en Etat autonome' (UNRIAA 181).

299 Ibid.:

> Dans son exposé des motifs, la Cour fait expressément coïncider la date de la disparition des derniers liens politiques turco-crétois avec celle de l'attribution de l'île à la Grèce, mais elle se refuse nettement à entrer dans un examen de la portée du régime de large autonomie octroyé à l'île antérieurement à 1913, sauf au point de vue de son importance pour le problème spécifique du 'détachement' final *{loco cit.*, 103). Par conséquent, les effets internationaux dudit régime de large autonomie à tous autres points de vue ont été écartés par la Cour en termes exprès, et c'est précisément ce régime d'autonomie qui joue un rôle important dans la solution des controverses soulevées par les réclamations nos 11 et 4 (UNRIAA 195).

300 Dumberry, *State Succession to International Responsibility* (n 165) 140–41.

301 IDI, State Succession to Responsibility, Resolution, 2015 (n 14), Art. 11.

302 See, Chapter 14, Section 3.

303 *Lighthouse Arbitration* case (n 162) in UNRIAA, 245.

304 Ibid.:

> La substance de la clause de reprise est, en conséquence, demeurée la même pendant toute la durée de la concession depuis 1860: l'État concédant aura le droit, à tout instant, de mettre fin unilatéralement à l'existence de la concession, mais à une condition fondamentale et stricte: de ne pas procéder à cette opération unilatérale avant d'avoir payé au concessionnaire – ou, au moins, avant de lui en avoir garanti le paiement – toutes les indemnités qui auront été préalablement fixées par les Parties elles-mêmes ou, en cas de désaccord, par des arbitres. Cette condition est, en effet, absolument essentielle et la seule efficace comme sauvegarde des droits du concessionnaire contre l'abus éventuel, par l'État concédant, de son pouvoir public, ainsi que l'histoire des concessions l'a prouvé partout et en abondance' (UNRIAA 246).

conditions and, consequently, had to pay compensation to the French company.[305] Again, the tribunal simply applied a clause within a contract without taking position on the general question of succession to contracts.

In sum, apart from the issue of a continuous breach of contractual obligations and that of breach committed by autonomous entities (further discussed below[306]), the award seems to be overall more relevant to the other question of succession to responsibility. Yet, one reason for having discussed in some detail the award is because it is one of the rare awards examining how the general question of succession to State contracts can be resolved. As further explained above,[307] the present author put forward a new framework of analysis to deal with the question and the reasoning of the arbitral tribunal (which will be exposed later) will be most useful in that respect. **13.49**

2.4.5 Affaire des Forêts du Rhodope Central (1933)

Another case involving a cession of territory is *Affaire des Forêts du Rhodope Central (Fond)*.[308] The Ottoman Empire granted to some individuals property and exploitation rights over forests situated in Central Rhodope.[309] This territory had become part of Bulgaria in 1913 as a result of the Treaty of Constantinople which was signed between the Ottoman Empire and Bulgaria after the Second Balkan War.[310] The treaty contained a provision guaranteeing the respect of 'acquired rights' existing before the cession of territory.[311] The owners of the forest company became Greek nationals as a result of the cession of territory. Bulgaria refused to recognize the concession to the owners. The fate of these concession rights was the object of a dispute between Greece and Bulgaria and an Arbitrator (Mr. Unden) was appointed by the Council of the League of Nations under Article 181 of the Treaty of Neuilly (which was signed in 1919 and under which Bulgaria had ceded some of its territories to **13.50**

305 Ibid.:

> Par sa mainmise sur le service des phares de la Société a partir du ler Janvier 1929 sans paiement – ou garantie de paiement – préalable d'une indemnité, arrêtée dans des conditions qui en assurent l'équité, le Gouvernement hellénique, en tant que successeur dans la concession par subrogation, a accompli un acte d'autorité directement contraire d'une de ses clauses essentielles (UNRIAA 246).

306 See, Chapter 14, Sections 1 and 3.

307 See, Chapter 12, Section 2. The question is further discussed below at Chapter 14.

308 *Affaire des Forêts du Rhodope Central (Fond)*, Award, 29 March 1933, in 3 UNRIAA 1389.

309 See, O'Connell, *State Succession*, 1967 (n 15) 331.

310 Treaty of Peace Between Bulgaria and Turkey, signed at Constantinople on 29 September 1913, between Bulgaria and Turkey.

311 Ibid., Art. 10: 'Les droits acquis antérieurement à l'annexion des territoires ainsi que les actes judiciaires et titres officiels émanant des autorités ottomanes compétentes, seront respectés et inviolables jusqu'à la preuve légale du contraire'; Art. 11: 'Le droit de propriété foncière dans les territoires cédés, tel qu'il résulte de la loi ottomane sur les immeubles urbains et ruraux, sera reconnu sans aucune restriction.'

its neighbouring States).[312] Article 181 provided that 'private rights' that had been guaranteed in previous treaties (including the Treaty of Constantinople) should not be affected by the transfer of territory.[313] Interestingly, in a preliminary award on the application of that provision, the arbitrator mentioned that this provision was representing a common principle of international law:

> Un principe général du droit commun international, celui du respect, sur un territoire annexé, des droits privés régulièrement acquis sous le régime antérieur, se trouve expressément sanctionné par le Traité de Neuilly, suivant l'exemple des traités de paix de 1913–1914.[314]

13.51 The same reasoning is also found later in the award on the merits:

> II est difficile, toutefois, de comprendre l'utilité d'une règle si évidente. Personne ne saurait sérieusement soutenir que la diminution ou l'accroissement des territoires acquis [aurait] pût avoir un effet quelconque sur les obligations des États quant au respect des droits privés dans ces territoires. À première vue, les termes employés par les rédacteurs de l'article semblent plutôt indiquer que; les droits privés se référant aux territoires en question doivent être respectés nonobstant la cession partielle ou intégrale de ces territoires intervenue en 1919. Ce serait là une consécration expresse du principe bien connu du respect des droits acquis dans des territoires cédés, c'est-à-dire le renouvellement, à la charge de l'État cessionnaire, d'une obligation incombant à l'État cédant.[315]

13.52 The arbitrator therefore affirmed the existence of a general principle of international law protecting acquired rights in the context of a cession of territory. This would impose such an obligation upon States independently of whether or not a treaty provision provides for such a protection (such as Art. 181 of the Treaty of Neuilly in that case).[316] In fact, of all the decisions examined in this section, this award seems to be the only one that explicitly

312 Treaty of Peace between the Allied and Associated Powers and Bulgaria, and Protocol and Declaration, signed at Neuilly-sur-Seine on 27 November 1919, in: UKTS 1920, No. 5 (Cmd. 522).

313 Ibid. The article reads as follows:

> Les transferts de territoires effectués en exécution du présent Traité ne porteront aucune atteinte aux droits privés visés dans les Traités de Constantinople de 1913, d'Athènes de 1913 et de Stamboul de 1914. Tous transferts de territoires effectués par ou à la Bulgarie en exécution du présent Traité comporteront également et aux mêmes conditions le respect de ces droits privés. En cas de désaccord relatif à l'application du présent article, le différend sera soumis à un arbitre nommé par le Conseil de la Société des Nations.

314 *Affaire des Forêts du Rhodope Central* (n 307), Award, 4 November 1931, at 1396.

315 Ibid., Award of 29 March 1933, at 1401.

316 In its award on the merits, the arbitrator came to the conclusion that Bulgaria had violated private rights guaranteed under Art. 181 of the Treaty of Neuilly. He awarded compensation to Greece for the damage suffered by its nationals.

takes a position on the question of succession to contracts. It clearly supports the principle of succession to State contracts in the context of a cession of territory.

3. DISSOLUTION OF STATE

This section will first examine the general principle of non-succession which should normally prevail as well as some situations where the opposite approach should be adopted (Section 3.1). I will then examine State practice supporting these conclusions (Section 3.2). **13.53**

3.1 While new States are generally not bound by contracts, there are situations where succession should prevail

In the context of the dissolution of a State, the question of succession to contracts becomes all the more complicated given the fact that the predecessor State no longer exists. At first, this would seem to be a straightforward situation where the new successor States should not be bound by any of the obligations arising from a contract that was signed by a State that no longer exists. In other words, if there were a type of succession that would call for the non-succession solution, it is logical to assume that it would be with regards to dissolution. This solution seems appropriate given the difficult task that a tribunal is faced with when deciding issues of succession to contracts in the context of a dissolution. Thus, not only does it have to examine whether succession is possible, but it must also, subsequently, determine which of the different successor State(s) should be responsible for the rights and obligations arising from a State contract. **13.54**

However, the question remains whether this solution of non-succession is fair and justified in all circumstances. In the different context of succession to State responsibility, I have argued that the strict and automatic application of the principle of non-succession would result in an injured third State being left with no debtor to provide compensation for the damage it suffered as a result of the commission of a wrongful act.[317] The unfairness, which would result from the application of a strict principle of non-succession in cases of dissolution, has been acknowledged by the arbitral tribunal in the *Lighthouse Arbitration* case: **13.55**

317 Dumberry, *State Succession to International Responsibility* (n 165) 104–5.

> What justice, or even what juridical logic, would there be, for example, in the hypothesis of an international wrong committed against another Power by a State which subsequently splits up into two new independent States, in regarding the later as being free from an international obligation to make compensation which would without any doubt have lain on the former, predecessor, State which had committed the wrong?[318]

The same argument has also been put forward by scholars.[319] The Institut recently adopted the solution of succession to responsibility in the context of dissolution.[320]

13.56 In my view, there are a number of different factors and circumstances that may influence whether the successor States could be considered bound by obligations arising from State contracts, even in the situation where the predecessor State has ceased to exist. As further examined below,[321] such continuity of obligations could be possible, for instance, whenever the investment was made on the specific territory of one of the successor States and where the obligations under the contract were only performed there. Whenever this is the case, it is likely that the new State *benefited* from the consequences of such an investment on its territory. The question of the 'nexus' between a contract and the territory of a new State is further examined below.[322] Under this scenario, why should the new State be exempt from their responsibility for the duties arising from the contract? As further discussed below,[323] the principle of unjust enrichment may also play an important role in this context.

3.2 Analysis of State practice

13.57 The question of succession to rights and obligations contained in a State contract was examined by an arbitral tribunal in the 1929 case of *Sopron-Koszeg Railway Company v. Austria and Hungary*.[324] In 1907, the Sopron-Koszeg Railway Company was granted a 90-year railway concession by the

318 *Lighthouse Arbitration* case (n 162) 93.

319 According to Verzijl (n 43) 219–20, in the situation where a 'State responsible for such a wrong splits into two before the reparation due is adjusted', 'it would really be absurd to assume that the successor State can nevertheless take shelter behind the argument put forward by the dominant doctrine, according to which the offences of its predecessor(s) do not regard it'. Georg Schwarzenberger, *International Law as Applied by International Courts and Tribunals* vol I, 3rd edn (Steven & Sons 1957) 175–6, is of the view that whenever a State 'split into two States' after the commission of an 'international tort', the successor States should be held responsible for that internationally wrongful act 'based on ground of estoppel' and 'on the rules governing the principle of good faith'.

320 IDI, State Succession to Responsibility, Resolution, 2015 (n 14), Art. 15.

321 See, Chapter 14, Section 2.

322 Ibid.

323 See, Chapter 14, Section 4.

324 *Sopron-Koszeg Railway Company v. Austria and Hungary*, in 2 UNRIAA 961; (1930) 24 AJIL 164.

Royal Hungarian Government. As a result of the territorial changes brought about by the treaties of St. Germain and Trianon after the First World War, the middle section of the railway now passed through Austria and the two ends remained in Hungary. The fate of the railways of the former Austro-Hungarian Monarchy which now passed through the territory of different States was decided under Article 320 of the Treaty of St. Germain[325] and Article 304 of the Treaty of Trianon.[326] These provisions provided that an agreement on the administrative and technical reorganization would have to be reached by these companies with each State. Having reached an agreement with Hungary but failing to do the same with Austria, the company brought the dispute before the Council of the League of Nations, which appointed an arbitral tribunal to decide the case.

From the outset, it should be mentioned that even though Austria was clearly the continuator State of the Monarchy under the Treaty of St. Germain, which the arbitrators had to apply to resolve the dispute, the tribunal seems to have nevertheless considered it as a *new State* (and the break-up of the Monarchy as a case of *dissolution*).[327] The same position was adopted at around the same time by the Tripartite Claims Commission.[328] As mentioned above,[329] the legal qualification of the break-up of the Austria-Hungary Dual Monarchy after the War is controversial. The 'Allied and Associated Powers' (the British Empire, France, Italy, Japan, United States, etc.) took the view that this was not a case of a dissolution of a State. They believed that post-War Austria and Hungary were in fact *identical* with the now extinct Dual Monarchy.[330] They insisted on both States being considered as continuing States in order to ensure that they would be held responsible for the internationally wrongful acts that had been committed by the Dual Monarchy during the War.[331] The Peace Treaty of St. Germain (entered into by the Allied Powers and Austria) thus contained a clause providing for Austria's responsibility for the loss and damages resulting from the War.[332] Austria took the opposite position that it **13.58**

325 Treaty of Peace between the Allied and Associated Powers and Austria; Protocol, Declaration and Special Declaration, St. Germain-en-Laye, 10 September 1919, entered into force on 16 July 1920, in UKTS 1919 No. 11 (Cmd. 400).

326 Treaty of Peace between the Allied and Associated Powers, and Hungary, Protocol and Declaration (Treaty of Trianon), 4 June 1920, in: 6 LNTS 187; (1920) UKTS No. 10 (Cmd. 896).

327 O'Connell, *State Succession*, 1967 (n 15) 330.

328 *Administrative Decision no. 1*, 25 May 1927, Tripartite Claims Commission, 6 UNRIAA 203, at 209–10.

329 See, Chapter 13, Section 1.2.

330 *See* the discussion in Krystyna Marek, *Identity and Continuity of States in Public International Law* (Droz 1968) 220ff.

331 Verzijl (n 43) 126.

332 Treaty of Peace of St. Germain (n 325), Art. 177. The United States also considered Hungary as the continuing State of the Monarchy and signed with it a separate peace treaty in 1921: Treaty Establishing Friendly Relations between the United States of America and Hungary, signed in Budapest on 29 August

was a *new* State in 1918. Accordingly, the Austrian Constitutional Court decided that Austria was not responsible for the obligations of the Monarchy and for claims that were filed against it.[333]

13.59 It is in this context that the tribunal made a number of remarks on the fate of private rights when State succession occurs. The tribunal first highlighted the fact that a change in sovereignty over a given territory does not automatically lead to the disappearance of all private rights of persons that existed under the laws of the predecessor State:

> (…) en principe, les droits tenus par une compagnie privée, d'un acte de concession, ne sauraient être mis à néant ou lésés du seul fait que le territoire sur lequel est assis le service public concédé a changé de nationalité; … la majorité des auteurs et les solutions de la pratique internationale les plus conformes à la conception moderne du droit des gens sont en ce sens.[334]

13.60 Yet, the tribunal also mentioned that existing contractual rights do not necessarily remain intact after the date of succession and that a State has the freedom to make changes to these instruments:[335]

> Les dispositions contractuelles qui régissaient la Compagnie … avant la guerre ne peuvent être déclarées ni totalement invalides par l'effet des changements de souveraineté qui ont affecté les territoires sièges de son entreprise, ni davantage totalement valides et exécutoires dans leur lettre et teneur jusqu'à la fin de la concession.[336]

13.61 In another case decided by the same arbitral tribunal dealing with the claim of the Zeltweg-Wolfsberg and Unterdrauburg-Woellan Railway Company against Austria and Yugoslavia, it was held that Article 320 of the Treaty of St. Germain reflected a general principle of international law:

> (…) l'article 320 se borne à confirmer, ainsi que l'a reconnu la jurisprudence antérieure, ce principe du droit public international que les droits tenus par une compagnie privée,

---

1921, in USTS, no. 660; in (1922) 16 AJIL 13–16. The United States also ratified a treaty in 1924 with Hungary and Austria dealing with the determination of the amounts to be paid by these two States as a result of the previous separate treaties it had entered into with them in 1921: The Agreement of 26 November 1924 can be found in 48 LNTS 70; 6 UNRIAA 199.

333 *Military Pensions (Austria) Case*, Austrian Constitutional Court, 7 May 1919, case no. 126, in *Sammlung der Erkenntniss des österreichischen Verfassungsgerichtshofes*, vol I (1919), no. 9, 17, in (1919–1922) *Annual Digest* 66. See also, other cases decided by the Austrian Constitutional Court: case no. 253–254, 20 October 1919, in ibid., no. 18–19, at 36–7 (in (1919–1922) *Annual Digest* 67); case no. 18, 11 March 1919, in ibid., no. 2, at 5 (in (1919–1922) *Annual Digest*).

334 *Sopron-Koszeg Railway Company* (n 324) 967.

335 O'Connell, *State Succession*, 1967 (n 15) 330.

336 *Sopron-Koszeg Railway Company* (n 324) 969. See also: *Barcs-Pakrac Railway Case*, 2 UNRIAA 1569, at 1575–6.

> d'un acte de concession, ne sauraient être mis à néant ou lésés du seul fait que le territoire sur lequel est assis le service public concédé a changé de nationalité (...).[337]

The reasoning of both tribunals favours the principle of succession to State contracts. However, it is true that in both cases the tribunals were merely applying treaty provisions which specifically provided for such a solution regarding railway companies. Both tribunals seem to have nevertheless considered this solution of succession as being in accordance with international law. One reason which may explain why they took this position is because of the territorial nexus that existed between the contract and specific successor States.[338] Thus, after the dissolution of the Empire, the different railway tracks continued to exist and were now located in the territories of new States. It seems logical that a State should continue to be bound by contracts relating to railways that were located on its territory. These two cases tend to support the proposition (mentioned above) that there are situations where the principle of succession should apply, even in the context of a dissolution. **13.62**

4. UNIFICATION AND INCORPORATION OF STATES

This section will first examine the general principle of succession which applies in the context of unification and incorporation (Section 4.1), which will be then followed by an analysis of State practice (Section 4.2). **13.63**

4.1 The successor State is bound by the contracts

In the different context of succession to State responsibility, the solution of succession is favoured by scholars for unification[339] as well as for incorporation of States.[340] The Institut also adopted that approach in its recent Resolution.[341] The same position was also adopted by ILC Special Rapporteur Bedjaoui.[342] It has been argued that in the event that the new unified State found it desirable to exercise the rights that belonged to its predecessor States, **13.64**

337 *Affaire des chemins de fer Zeltweg-Wolfsberg et Unterdrauburg-Woellan (Autriche et Yougoslavie)*, October 1933, 6 August 1934, 12 May 1934 and 29 June 1938, in 3 UNRIAA 1795–815, at 1803.

338 The question is examined below at Chapter 14, Section 2.

339 See the analysis in: Dumberry, *State Succession to International Responsibility* (n 165) 93ff.

340 See the analysis in: ibid., 83–4.

341 IDI, State Succession to Responsibility, Resolution, 2015 (n 14), Arts 13, 14.

342 ILC, First Report Bedjaoui, 1968 (n 39) 101 [47]: 'The two merging States have decided to join forces in the future and the liabilities of each are fully assumed by the new political entity they have created.'

it should equally have to fulfill their responsibilities and obligations.[343] The same is true for cases of incorporation.

13.65 A similar outcome should also prevail regarding State contracts. Underlying this principle is the fact that the States involved in these two types of succession usually had a comparable level of economic development, and common views and interests.[344] ILC Special Rapporteur Bedjaoui, who generally rejects the survival of acquired rights, admits that it 'is natural' to 'expect different solutions according to the [different] type of succession'.[345] He explains as follows why the solution of maintaining acquired rights should be adopted in the context of merger and incorporation of States:

> Acquired rights in the case of merger or integration of States do not appear in the same light as in the case of colonization or decolonization, for instance. When a voluntary merger of two States occurs, the States in question are, by construction, aiming at common objectives and share the same views concerning the development of the community which they are forming. Consequently, it must be anticipated that acquired rights will be respected, or even that the question will not arise. By construction, so to speak, integration implies the pre-existence of two juridical orders which are fairly near (otherwise there would probably not be a merger) and in any event are not mutually antagonistic. The operation will have been facilitated, or even dictated, by an identity of present interests and the prospect of a common political and juridical future. It is obvious that one State does not merge with another if its rights and interests or those of nationals would suffer as a result. It is for this reason that, *ex hypothesi*, the problem of acquired rights in this case takes on a special one. It is true that the integration creates a new State which legally replaces the other two, but – to use a metaphor – it may safely be asserted that the 'substance' of the two components continues to exist therein. The new State is in this case almost the arithmetical sum of the other two, so far as rights and obligations are concerned, and if it should refuse to recognize acquired rights it would be despoiling itself, as it were, in seeking to despoil the two States to whose disappearance it owes its existence.[346]

13.66 The explanation given by Bedjaoui clearly emphasizes the existing 'territorial nexus' between the acquired rights of persons and the territory of the predecessor State which has now become that of the successor State.[347] Thus, for Bedjaoui, in the context of unification, the 'substance' of the two components continues to exist in the personality of the new State. As he notes, 'the

343 Michael John Volkovitsch, 'Righting Wrongs: Toward a New Theory of State Succession to Responsibility for International Delicts', (1992) 92(8) *Colum L Rev* 2206; Wladyslaw Czaplinski, 'State Succession and State Responsibility', (1990) 28 *Canadian YIL* 357.

344 Gruber (n 22) 98.

345 ILC, Second Report Bedjaoui, 1969 (n 4) 87.

346 Ibid.

347 The concept of territorial 'nexus' is further explained below, See Chapter 14, Section 2.

new State is in this case almost the arithmetical sum of the other two'.[348] This is indeed the reason why the new State should continue to be held responsible for the rights and obligations existing under contracts which were binding on either of the predecessor States before the unification. The same principle should apply for incorporation. In fact, the US Restatement has adopted this solution of succession in that context: 'where a State is absorbed by another State, (…) rights and obligations under contracts of the absorbed State, pass to the absorbing State'.[349]

4.2 State practice and decisions by courts and tribunals support the succession principle

I have found one example of State practice, one arbitration award and one domestic court decision in the context of unification and incorporation. They all support the application of the succession principle. **13.67**

The creation of the United Arab Republic (UAR) in 1958 was the result of the unification of Egypt and Syria.[350] This unification lasted for only three years. The UAR respected the concession contracts which had been granted by Egypt and Syria before the unification.[351] One illustration is the nationalization of the *Société Financière de Suez* by Egypt in July of 1956.[352] The question of the actual nationality of the company was quite controversial and different approaches were put forward (French and/or Egyptian nationality, even 'international').[353] What is clear is that it was not a 'purely' Egyptian company. Before the nationalization, the relationship between this company (and its predecessors) and the State of Egypt was governed by a series of concession contracts.[354] The nationalization was therefore, inter alia, a breach of contract committed by the predecessor State. An agreement was entered into on 13 July 1958 (i.e., *after* the unification) between the UAR and the corporation under which the former undertook, inter alia, to pay some EGY£28.3 million to the shareholders of the latter.[355] This is clearly a case of a new State being held liable for the obligations arising from internationally **13.68**

348 ILC, Second Report Bedjaoui, 1969 (n 4) 87.

349 Restatement of the Law (n 211) [209(2)(b)].

350 The Proclamation of 1 February 1958 makes it clear that this is not merely a 'union of States'; it expressly mentioned that the two States were uniting 'into one State'.

351 O'Connell, *State Succession*, 1967 (n 15) 344; Eugene Cotran, 'Some Legal Aspects of the Formation of the United Arab Republic and the United Arab States', (1959) 8 ICLQ 368, adding that the UAR had an obligation under international law to do so.

352 L. Focsaneanu, 'L'accord ayant pour objet l'indemnisation de la compagnie de Suez nationalisée par l'Égypte', (1959) AFDI 161–204.

353 Ibid., 171ff.

354 Ibid.

355 UN Doc. A/3898, S/4089, September 23, 1958.

wrongful acts committed by the predecessor State.[356] This is also a good example of a succession to the obligations arising from a State contract which had been signed by one of the predecessor States before the unification.

13.69 Another relevant case is *Compagnie d'Enterprises CFE SA v. Yemen*. This case involved a contract for the construction and maintenance of the Al Mukalla Harbour, which was signed in 1981 between Compagnie d'Enterprises CFE SA ('CFE'), a Belgian company, and the Yemen Port Authority, a State-owned company of the People's Democratic Republic of Yemen ('PDRY'). The contract provided that any arising disputes would be settled by arbitration under the ICC's Rules of Conciliation and Arbitration. On 9 December 1992, CFE filed such a request with the ICC and arbitration proceedings were set up to take place in Nicosia, Cyprus. In November 1993, the parties signed the Terms of Reference and agreed that the party described in both the contract and the arbitration request as 'the Government of the People's Democratic Republic of Yemen' would now be identified as 'the Government of the Republic of Yemen, comprising inter alia the former Government of the People's Democratic Republic of Yemen'.[357] The reason behind such a change was to take into account the merger of the PDRY with the Yemen Arab Republic on 22 May 1990 to create a new State, the 'Republic of Yemen'.

13.70 The central preliminary issue before the arbitrator was whether the Republic of Yemen succeeded to the PDRY in its rights and obligations arising from the contract. In the proceedings, Yemen claimed that it was 'not the proper party to the proceedings and that it had no relationship with the contract' that was signed by the PDRY, which no longer existed when the arbitration proceedings were initiated in December 1992.[358] In an interim decision, the arbitrator rejected Yemen's claim and decided to proceed with the merits of the case.[359] The Yemeni Government appealed against the decision before a court in Aden, which allowed the appeal and annulled the arbitrator's decision in

356 See, Dumberry, *State Succession to International Responsibility* (n 165) 95. It should be added that two separate treaties were also signed *after* the unification by the UAR with France and the United Kingdom under which the former provided compensation to the nationals of the latter for actions which had been taken by Egypt in 1956: *Accord général entre le gouvernement de la République française et le gouvernement de la République arabe unie*, in: La documentation française, 18 October 1958, no. 2473; (1958) RGDIP 738ff; Agreement between the Government of the United Kingdom of Great Britain and Northern Ireland and the Government of the United Arab Republic Concerning Financial and Commercial Relations and British Property in Egypt, in: (1959) UKTS no. 35 (Cmd. 723); 343 UNTS 159; (1958) 14 Rev. égyptienne d.i., 364; (1960) 54 AJIL 511–519.

357 See, *Yemen v. Compagnie d'Enterprises CFE SA*, Appeal judgment, No 10717, ILDC 630 (CY 2002), 28 June 2002, Cyprus Supreme Court. See, analysis in: *Oxford Rep IL* [F2].

358 Ibid., *Oxford Rep IL* [F3].

359 *Compagnie d'Enterprises CFE SA v. Yemen*, ICC Case no 7748/BGD/OLG, Interim Decision, 30 June 1995, see, ibid., [F4].

October 1996. Meanwhile, the arbitration proceedings on the merits continued in Nicosia. Yemen did not appear at the merits stage of these arbitration proceedings. The final award was issued in default of appearance ordering Yemen to pay US$32.5 million to CFE.[360] Yemen filed an application to annul this award before the District Court of Nicosia, Cyprus. The district court rejected Yemen's application and upheld the arbitration award.[361] Yemen then brought an appeal before the Supreme Court of Cyprus.[362]

The Supreme Court held that the new State of Yemen was bound by the contract which had been signed by one of the predecessor States based on the doctrine of acquired rights. This is the summary of the reasoning of the court on the matter: 13.71

> Acquired rights remain in force, regardless of the prevailing legal situation in the successor state. Such rights are transferred to the new state, insofar as the (original) contracting state continued to exist or, at least, retained sovereignty over the geographical area wherein the contractual right was granted or pertained and wherein the (original) contracting state has already benefited from the performance of the contract, especially when works have been done in its territory that remain in the same geographical area; this is so even if the political situation has changed or the government or the (original contracting) state was transformed into a new entity in international law.
>
> The right to resort to arbitration was an 'acquired right' arising from the contract and could not be rejected by Yemen as the successor State that was created by the unification of the two predecessor States. There was no change in the geographical area covered by the two predecessor States, nor did the political system change fundamentally, so as to support the argument that the People's Democratic Republic of Yemen had been forced to sign the contract. The new State was created in conditions of absolute calm and peace, following an agreement by the two predecessor States to merge in a complete union wherein the international personalities of the predecessor States merged in a single international entity, the Republic of Yemen. The latter benefited from the works done in the People's Democratic Republic of Yemen, and she possesses them now.
>
> If the new State has benefited from the works of the predecessor State, then it has to bear responsibility for them. 'The better view is that he (sic) who takes the benefit must take the burden. So where an identifiable region has benefited by public expenditure to an ascertainable extent, then whoever takes over that part of the territory takes over part of the public debt which corresponds to the benefit. The

360 *Compagnie d'Enterprises CFE SA v. Yemen*, ICC Case no 7748/BGD/OLG, Final Award, 26 September 1997. See, analysis in: *Oxford Rep IL* [F4].

361 *Yemen v. Compagnie d'Enterprises CFE SA*, District Court of Nicosia, Application for annulment, 12 December 1999.

362 Ibid. *Oxford Rep IL* [F5].

corollary to this is that no debt is assumed if no benefit attaches, even if the territory is expressly charged with the debt'.[363]

13.72 While the decision of the Supreme Court seems to be based generally on the doctrine of acquired rights,[364] it is noteworthy that it considered the arbitration clause contained in the contract as binding on the successor State. One factor that was considered to be important by the court was the fact that the contract had been performed on the territory of the predecessor State which was now that of the new successor State as a result of the unification. The existence of such a nexus between the contract and the territory of the new State is indeed one important factor that should be taken into account by a tribunal.[365] The court also explicitly used the concept of unjust enrichment (a point further discussed below[366]).

13.73 The question of succession to contracts also arose in one ICC arbitration award rendered in 1994.[367] It involved a contract signed by some high-ranking officials from East Germany's Ministry of Defence[368] with a US company (CIC International Ltd.). The contract was signed just a few days (on 28 September 1990) before the incorporation of East Germany within West

---

363 *Yemen v. Compagnie d'Enterprises CFE SA*, Cyprus Supreme Court. 8 June 2002, No 10717, Oxford RIL, case analysis [H1]–[H3], referring to [12]–[14] of the decision (citing Max Sørensen, *Manual of Public International Law* (McMillan & Co 1968) 292–4).

364 Ibid. See *Oxford RIL*, case analysis by A. Constantinides [A.4]–[A.5]:

> Another interesting, albeit less clear, point in the decision is the parallel discussion of the doctrine of acquired rights and the question of state succession in respect of debt. In particular, the court made use of the 'final beneficiary rule' ('he who takes the benefit must take the burden'), which is usually applied to allocated or localized public debts in case of state dissolution, in order to justify the continued validity of acquired rights. Such merging is at odds with state practice, which differentiates between public debts and (private) acquired rights. On a second reading, however, it could denote that the doctrine of acquired rights can be imbued with the more sophisticated principles applied to state succession in respect of public debt. Thus, instead of an automatic transfer of acquired rights to the successor state (as favoured by the traditional rule), the decision could be read as implying a balancing of interests and the taking into account of, for example, the local or final beneficiary. Under this reading, the decision suggests a welcome qualification to the doctrine of acquired rights, which (even if still predominant) has repeatedly come under attack as illegitimate due to its colonial origins. Be that as it may, in the circumstances of this case, the court could hardly have reached any different conclusion.

365 See, Chapter 14, Section 2.

366 See, Chapter 14, Section 4.

367 The case is discussed in: B. Leurent and J.C. Holet, 'Les incidences politiques de la souveraineté sur l'arbitrage: reconnaissance et continuité des Etats' (2003) *Rev arb* 787–8, referring to a non-published award which was subject to annulment proceedings before French courts: *Société CIC International Ltd. v. Ministre de la Défense de la République d'Allemagne*, Cour d'appel de Paris (1Ch. C), 19 January 1999, in (1999) *Rev. arb.* 601, note by Ch. Jarrosson.

368 Case summary (1999) *Rev. arb.* 601 referring to the 'Chef du département des achats et le Sous-Secrétaire pour le désarmement du ministère pour le Désarmement et la Défense de l'ex-République Démocratique d'Allemagne.'

Germany (3 October 1990). Under the contract, which contained an arbitration clause, the company bought 25 per cent of the military assets of East Germany. After the date of succession, the company claimed that the successor State (Germany) was responsible for the execution of the contract and started ICC arbitration proceedings against that State.

Germany did not contest the jurisdiction of the tribunal based on the fact that the arbitration clause was contained in a contract involving another State. Germany apparently signed the terms of reference without raising the issue of its own succession to the arbitration clause.[369] It however contested its responsibility for the execution of the contract based on contractual grounds that were unrelated to the issue of succession per se. The arbitrator rejected the claim on the ground, inter alia, that the contract specifically included a clause whereby the contract had to be ratified by West Germany, which never happened. In one *obiter*, the arbitrator mentioned that, in any event, succession to the contract would not have been possible because the treaty of unification between East Germany and West Germany did not provide for any universal succession of the goods, assets, and liability of the predecessor to the successor State.[370] Importantly, the contract had been signed *after* the treaty of unification. This solution has been endorsed by writers considering the specific aspects of the case and the fact that German law was applicable to solve the dispute.[371] It has also been suggested that a different solution of succession would have applied had the contract been signed *before* the treaty of unification.[372] What matters for the purpose of this book is that Germany did not contest the jurisdiction of the arbitrator on the ground that there could be no 13.74

369 In the context of annulment proceedings which took place after the award was rendered, the Paris Court considered that Germany had *itself* consented to arbitration when it signed the Terms of Reference: 'à défaut d'être insérée dans un contrat, la convention d'arbitrage peut aussi résulter d'un accord conclu par les parties postérieurement à la naissance du litige tel celui concrétisé, comme en l'espèce, par la signature d'un acte de mission' (in: ibid.).

370 Case summary (ibid.) referring to this passage from the Paris Court:

> Considérant que pour statuer comme il l'a fait, l'arbitre a retenu successivement: – que la République Fédérale d'Allemagne était un tiers au contrat; – qu'elle n'aurait pu être obligée par le dit contrat que si elle l'avait approuvé, ce que n'ignorait pas la société CIC International Ltd., ce qui précisément n'avait jamais été le cas; – que la théorie de l'unification des États ne pouvait pas être invoquée pour obliger la République Fédérale d'Allemagne à exécuter le contrat conclu; – que les dispositions légales en matière de contrôle des armements interdisaient en tout état de cause à la République Fédérale d'Allemagne d'approuver le marché litigieux, les ventes d'armement étant soumises à des restrictions légales et ces ventes étant notamment interdites à des marchands travaillant pour leur propre compte sans qu'aucun contrôle des destinataires réels ne puisse être exercé; – que le contrat était nul pour avoir été signé au nom de la République Démocratique d'Allemagne par des personnes dépourvues de pouvoir pour l'engager; Qu'il a en conséquence rejeté l'intégralité des prétentions de la société CIC International Ltd.

371 Leurent and Holet (n 367) 789.

372 Ibid.

succession to an arbitration clause contained in a State contract signed by another State.

5. NEWLY INDEPENDENT STATES

13.75 This section will first examine the general principle of non-succession which should normally prevail for Newly Independent States as well as some situations where the opposite approach could be adopted (Section 5.1). I will then examine some examples of State practice in this context (Section 5.2).

5.1 Generally, new States are not bound by contracts, but there may be some exceptions

13.76 From a technical standpoint, the situation of a Newly Independent State is comparable to that of a secessionist State since in both cases, the predecessor State continues to exist despite the emergence of a new State on what used to be its territory. As mentioned above, in the context of a secession, the continuator State remains bound by any existing State contracts at the date of succession. There is no reason why the situation should be any different for Newly Independent States. Yet, I have argued (and will further discuss below[373]) that, in the context of secession, and only in certain situations, the successor State should be responsible for the obligations arising from contracts.[374] For instance, this is the case when there is a nexus between the contract and the territory of the new State. Another relevant factor is when there is a situation of unjustified enrichment. These factors and circumstances will be further discussed below.[375] The question addressed in this section is whether the same solution of succession should also prevail for Newly Independent States given their particular status under international law. In other words, should a Newly Independent State *ever* be held responsible for any obligation arising from State contracts that was signed by the colonial power?

13.77 One of the most controversial questions of the last decades has been whether or not the 'traditional' rules of State succession should apply to the specific case of Newly Independent States emerging from decolonization. One of the strongest voices in favour of adopting different rules for this particular group of new States was ILC Special Rapporteur Bedjaoui. In his First and Second

373 See, Chapter 14, Section 5.
374 See, Chapter 13, Section 1.2.
375 See, Chapter 14, Sections 2 and 4.

Reports (published in 1968 and 1969), he explained that 'Decolonization does not involve a mere nominal change of sovereignty, as in cases of traditional succession where one monarch replaced another in a given territory.'[376] He draws the following differences between what he calls a 'traditional State succession' from new types of succession:

> Generally speaking, it [i.e., cases of traditional State succession] does not involve the establishment of a new State – although the plebiscite, for example, may have that result – but the redistribution of territory within a region. Usually, too, the region itself is one that can be considered relatively 'homogeneous' in levels of living and civilization (as in the case of the succession of States in Europe, for instance). Without necessarily being identical, the juridical orders of the countries concerned are substantially the same. The inhabitants of the piece of territory affected by succession were citizens of one country and become *citizens* of the same class of the other country (subject to various option rights). In principle, acquired rights are respected (...). It is one of the hypothetical cases relating to the *past*, when State succession, although regulated in some areas by the principle of *tabula rasa*, was governed mainly by the principle of legal continuity and stability.[377]
>
> The hypothetical cases relating to the *present*, on the other hand, are regulated by the opposite principle of *rupture and change*, except for some important nuances. These cases of succession result from decolonization and, unlike the previous cases, involve the creation of a State. The new entity is under-developed; its level of living and degree of civilization differ from those of the former metropolitan country, and it seeks to become stronger. The juridical orders of the two countries are not identical and are sometimes not even comparable, although the former metropolitan country may have introduced some similarities, especially in former settler colonies. The legal status of the inhabitants of the new State changes from that of colonized persons to that of citizens. The relationship based on domination is dissolved, and the principle of succession does not apply to those components of the former juridical order which reflect that relationship. Since emancipation *ex hypothesi* involves a change in political, economic and social aims within the territory, it normally constitutes a hiatus, a break in continuity, especially since in many cases independence is achieved after a long period of very tense relations with the colonial Power.[378]

---

376 ILC, Second Report Bedjaoui, 1969 (n 4) 90.

377 ILC, First Report Bedjaoui, 1968 (n 39) 100 (emphasis in the original).

378 Ibid., 101 (emphasis in the original). See also: Bedjaoui, 'Problèmes récents de succession d'États' (n 11) 545:

> Contrairement à ce qui se passait pour les successions classiques, la décolonisation pose, pour la première fois sans doute, le problème des distorsions économiques entre États. Et dès lors que l'État prédécesseur et l'État successeur accusent, contrairement à la forme classique de succession, des niveaux économiques différents, *le problème des droits acquis prend tout son relief économique.* C'est pourquoi, si le respect des droits acquis peut dans d'autres types de succession s'imposer pour des raisons d'équité, il apparaît ici au contraire comme mettant en échec tout un devenir national (emphasis in the original).

13.78 Similarly, Makonnen provides five reasons why new States emerging from decolonization are of a fundamentally different nature than other types of succession:

> State succession in the event of decolonization is a new phenomenon which is different in many ways from the traditional theories and practices of State succession. The characteristics differentiating this new phenomenon, at least at the theoretical level, from the traditional forms of State succession are numerous, but the few most important ones will be dealt with here. First, unlike most cases of traditional State succession, those which arise from decolonization do not aim merely at the change of sovereignty in a territory. The main objective of this event is rather the creation of new sovereignty over a territory by totally displacing the old sovereignty over that territory. The newly created international legal personality starts its life as nothing more or less than a full-fledged independent and sovereign State, with all the inherent and inalienable rights of a sovereign State. Second, State succession arising from decolonization has clear goals and purposes and invokes well-defined legal and political principles which govern the consequences of succession. The consequences of such succession are prejudged by these principles even before the event takes place. Therefore, the rules governing the conduct of succession are to be derived from the purposes and goals of decolonization. Third, State succession arising from decolonization presupposes (as a matter of fact but not as a matter of law) the existence of a stronger predecessor and a weaker successor. Therefore, upon the event of succession, the transaction is possibly conducted between unequal parties (again in fact, not in law). Fourth, unlike the traditional European cases of State succession, in the event of decolonization, the 'relational-complex' and the geographical, cultural, etc., differences between the predecessor and the successor States are decisive factors which strongly promote disruption of the *status quo* relations rather than safeguard their continuity. Fifth, owing to the nature of earlier relationships (colonial) between the predecessor and the pre-natal successor State, the period of succession tends to be a matter of at least a decade rather than just a five minute 'one-shot deal'.[379]

13.79 The distinctive nature of Newly Independent States has a concrete impact on whether the 'traditional rules' of succession should apply to them.[380] According to Bedjaoui, 'en droit … il ne saurait y avoir de succession à l'ordre colonial, en dehors de l'œuvre volontaire du nouveau successeur'.[381] Similarly, for Makonnen:

> Decolonization is the opposite of colonization and its purpose is to undo what has been done through colonization (…). The guiding principles governing the consequences of State succession are the complete elimination of 'colonialism in all its forms and manifestations' and creating the condition for the realization of the right to self-determination by the newly emerging successor State. Hence, the rules of State

379 Makonnen (n 69) 130–31.

380 ILC, First Report Bedjaoui, 1968 (n 39) 101.

381 Bedjaoui, 'Problèmes récents de succession d'États' (n 11) 520.

> succession cannot be neutral in cases of succession arising from decolonization owing to such prejudgment with regard to the results of the succession.[382]

This issue was debated by scholars in the context of the question whether or not Newly Independent States should, upon their independence, respect the 'acquired rights' which had been granted during colonial time. In his First Report, Bedjaoui noted that the principle of the respect for rights acquired by individuals in good faith 'correspond very little or not at all to the situation resulting from decolonization'.[383] For him, in the context of decolonization 'there are no rules of international law providing for continuity of the former juridical order *ipso jure*' and, as a result, 'concessions granted under the legislation of the predecessor State should not necessarily be binding on the new State'.[384] In this context, 'the governing factor is not [a] general obligation to respect acquired rights *but the sovereign will of the new State*'.[385] Bedjaoui further examined the question in his Second Report, noting that the principle of the respect for acquired rights was 'developed largely on the basis of the similarity of economic conditions in the two States, whereas the situation is radically different in the case of decolonization'.[386] In fact, one fundamental reason for treating acquired rights differently in the context of new States emerging from decolonization is directly linked to how these rights were acquired during the colonial period: **13.80**

> Having been subjected to a period of domination during which its own property and that of its nationals were not consistently or completely protected, but were, on the contrary, often confiscated at the time of conquest by the colonial Power and its nationals, the new State tries to translate into legal terms its need to recover fully everything it considers it lost through colonization, and usually refuses to grant any indemnity or assume responsibility for any liabilities.[387]

For Bedjaoui, 'while in the case of other types of succession respect for acquired rights may be necessary for reasons of equity, in this case it clearly frustrates the whole development of the nation'.[388] He further explained the reasons why respecting acquired rights in the context of new States emerging from decolonization would have such a negative impact on their development: **13.81**

382 Makonnen (n 69) 131.
383 ILC, First Report Bedjaoui, 1968 (n 39) 101.
384 Ibid., 115.
385 Ibid. (emphasis in the original).
386 ILC, Second Report Bedjaoui, 1969 (n 4) 90. See also: Bedjaoui, 'Problèmes récents de succession d'États' (n 11) 528; Gruber (n 22) 98–9.
387 ILC, First Report Bedjaoui, 1968 (n 39) 101.
388 ILC, Second Report Bedjaoui, 1969 (n 4) 90.

> Rather than the 'renewing function' (*function reconductive*) of decolonization, it is its 'reversing function' (*fonction inversive*) that necessarily takes precedence, in order to put an end to the relationships based on domination. And these relationships are not just political; indeed, it may be said that they are primarily economic. Consequently, the process of decolonization is inevitably a process of gradual destruction of certain types of economic and financial relationships which helped to maintain those relationships based on subordination. The relationship between the metropolitan country and its overseas possessions was nothing more than a particular system of exploitation known as the 'colonial compact' regime.
>
> If the colonial system cannot operate without a hierarchical economic order, characterized by the predominance of the interests of the metropolitan country and of its nationals and by the existence of a structural imbalance between the colony and the metropolitan country, conversely decolonization can only be the restoration of egalitarian structures, which implies the rejection of certain economic situations resulting from the colonial regime. *Thus, it is clear that decolonization and the renewal of acquired rights are contradictory.* Either decolonization or acquired rights must be sacrificed. (...) The fundamental incompatibility between decolonization and acquired rights derives from the fact that the successor State is confronted with a choice, over which it cannot hesitate, between the *possible* equity which requires it to respect private rights and the *real* necessity which forces it to consider the public interest and national development.[389]

13.82 The same conclusion regarding the non-maintenance of acquired rights in the specific context of decolonization has been reached by other scholars, such as Lalive[390] and Crawford.[391] For all of these reasons, Bedajoui (having noted the rather hypocritical position taken by Western Powers in the 1960s on this question[392]) has argued that not only should the new State not have to respect

---

389 ILC, Second Report Bedjaoui, 1969 (n 4) 90–91 (emphasis in the original). See also: Bedjaoui, 'Problèmes récents de succession d'États' (n 11) 550–51.

390 Lalive (n 54) 169, also noting that in the context of new States emerging from decolonization 'the holders of acquired rights in many cases are citizens of the former colonial power' whose 'rights well may have been acquired in extremely favourable, though formally regular, conditions'. For him, maintaining after independence 'such established and often privileged positions is likely to appear to local public opinion as an intolerable survival of the former colonial regime and as an unbearable restriction of the new sovereignty.'

391 Crawford, *Brownlie's Principles of Public International Law* (n 58) 429: 'the continuation of the pre-independence economic structure, which commonly involves extensive foreign ownership of major resources, would produce a situation in which political independence and formal sovereignty were not matched by a normal competence to regulate the national economy.'

392 ILC, Second Report Bedjaoui, 1969 (n 4) 87:

> Yet it is ironical to see how the same imperial Powers of the nineteenth century which, in their colonial policies, vigorously denied the existence of any rule affording protection to acquired rights – or shrugged it off in order to practice the principle of *tabula rasa* in this matter – have felt able, in connexion with the reverse modern phenomenon of decolonization, to demand the application of the same 'traditional rules' that they once sought to emasculate. It is child's play for the student of politics to note that one and the same Power has shifted its position, according as it was involved in the capacity of successor State (repudiating all acquired rights in the colonial territory which it had just conquered), of third State (conversely demanding respect for acquired rights, in the context of the colonial rivalries of the time) or of

acquired rights, but it should also not be obligated to compensate for any expropriation because of the unfair manner that such rights and properties were acquired in the first place:

> There are no grounds for agreeing to pay compensation on the attainment of independence, because colonization has enriched the metropolitan country and made a substantial historical contribution to the industrialization, power and prosperity of the conquering State. Consequently, according to this view, the latter has no acquired right to compensation but, on the contrary, has incurred a debt to its former overseas possession. (…) It is thus difficult to see how equity or the principle of unjustified enrichment could be applied in the case of such property, which is simply being returned through decolonization to the original owners who were dispossessed.[393]

It should be added that this radical position whereby Newly Independent States should never be obligated to compensate for expropriation has been rejected by many others writers.[394] O'Connell, for instance, rejects the very idea that a specific regime should prevail for these States regarding acquired 13.83

> predecessor State (claiming in the case of decolonization the protection of rights similar to those which it had itself previously repudiated, since in some cases it was the same territory that was involved). But to pass on from the student of politics, however, the jurist can only be taken aback and voice serious doubts concerning the soundness, or even the existence, of rules that come and go according to circumstances.

On this argument, see the comments of Gruber (n 22) 99–101, arguing, on the contrary, that 'la pratique des puissances pendant la colonisation ne permet pas de conclure au rejet des droits acquis'. See also, more generally, Makonnen (n 69) 128–9:

> The newly independent African countries are justified in contending that since there was no continuity of rights and obligations of the predecessor nations (the African peoples and nations) when colonization took place, there could be no automatic continuity of rights and obligations in the event of decolonization. The clean slate doctrine should then, by parity of reasoning equally apply to both events of State succession (State succession arising from colonization and State succession arising from decolonization).'

393 ILC, Second Report Bedjaoui, 1969 (n 4) 93–4. See also: ILC, First Report Bedjaoui, 1968 (n 39) 116:

> But many jurists who still subscribe to the concept of acquired rights contend that the successor State cannot retroactively annul the advantages granted to foreigners without paying the latter monetary compensation. They tend to consider that the validity of the nationalization of industries engaged in exploiting natural wealth (petroleum, mineral ores, etc.) depends on the payment of 'fair, effective and prompt compensation'. However, others will certainly deem the very concept of compensation 'unfair' within the colonial context, or will at least consider that it is of no real significance unless it is held to apply to both parties. This approach to the question would make it necessary for all profits earned by concessionary enterprises, the reinvestment of which outside the territory was prejudicial to the latter, to be taken into account in any dispute concerning compensation. It has also been pointed out that a country whose economy has long been dominated by foreign owners cannot seriously contemplate developing its economy and raising the level of living of its inhabitants if it is forced to reimburse the total value of installations left behind by concessionary companies. Hence, the idea of fair compensation would not call for repayment of the value of industrial installations, but would imply that all the elements of a situation characterized by the transfer of profits and the total or partial amortization of the investments made should be taken into account.

394 Gruber (n 22) 101–2, 105ff. See also, more generally, O'Connell, *State Succession*, 1967 (n 15) 266–7.

rights.[395] In any event, the special situation of Newly Independent States emerging from decolonization seems to have had an impact on the drafting of the 1962 GA Resolution 1803 on the permanent sovereignty over natural resources.[396] Paragraph 4 of the Resolution provides that when nationalizing a foreign investor's interests, a new State must pay the owner an 'appropriate compensation'. Yet, one of the preambular paragraphs of the Resolution makes a reservation 'in respect of property acquired before the accession to complete sovereignty of countries formerly under colonial rule'. Bedjaoui argued that this paragraph excludes these States from having to pay compensation.[397]

13.84 In sum, there are convincing reasons for recognizing that former colonies should not, as a matter of principle, be held responsible for obligations arising from contracts which were signed by the colonial power. Similarly, as examined elsewhere by the present author,[398] writers largely support the principle of non-succession to responsibility for Newly Independent States whereby it should be for the colonial power, which continues its existence, to provide reparation for the consequences of its own internationally wrongful acts committed before the date of succession.[399] Indeed, this is the solution

---

395 O'Connell, 'Recent Problems of State Succession' (n 41) 140, arguing (at 142ff) that Newly Independent States have in general respected the acquired rights of foreigners and adding:

> This factual survey is not intended to lay the basis for a rule of positive law (…) but to demonstrate the fallacy of the suggestion that there are irresistible sociological pressures directed either to the repudiation altogether of the concept of international law protection of private rights, or to the distinguishing of the cases of decolonization from other types of State Succession. Only a minority of new States has experienced such pressures, and in each case the dominant element in the situation has been political (…). The argument, then, that there is a juristic basis for treating acquired rights in decolonized countries as a special case appears to lack cogency (…).

396 GA Res. 1803 (n 105).

397 ILC, Second Report Bedjaoui, 1969 (n 4) 90–91:

> There is incompatibility between the concept of acquired rights and the affirmation of the *inalienable* and *permanent* right of peoples to dispose of their natural resources. If such a right is inalienable, it is inconceivable that rights belonging to anyone other than the people can arise, much less that they can have the status of inviolable acquired rights' (emphasis in the original).

Gruber (n 22) 102–9 takes a different position on the matter.

398 Dumberry, *State Succession to International Responsibility* (n 165) 168ff.

399 Volkovitsch (n 343) 2201; D.P. O'Connell, 'Independence and Problems of State Succession', in W. O'Brien (ed), *The New Nations in International Law and Diplomacy* (Stevens & Sons 1965) 31; M. Shaw, 'State Succession Revisited', (1994) 5 *Finnish YIL* 58; Hazem M. Atlam, *Succession d'Etats et continuité en matière de responsabilité internationale* (Ph.D. Thesis, Université de droit, d'économie et des sciences d'Aix-Marseille 1986) 258; F. Okoye, *International Law and the New African States* (Sweet & Maxwell 1973) 178ff; Sir Robert Jenning and Sir Arthur Watts, *Oppenheim's International Law*, vol I, 9th edn (Longman 1996) 233–4; Zyade Motala, 'Under International Law, Does the New Order in South Africa Assume the Obligations and Responsibilities of Apartheid Order? An Argument for Realism over Formalism', (1997) 30 *Comp & Int'l L J S Afr* 291.

recently adopted by the Institut in its Resolution on State succession to responsibility.[400]

13.85 The question remains whether or not there are some situations where, on the contrary, the Newly Independent States should be held responsible for the obligations arising from State contracts. Interestingly, the Resolution of the Institut on State succession to responsibility provides (in the specific context of Newly Independent States) that 'the conduct, prior to the date of succession of States, of a national liberation movement which succeeds in establishing a newly independent State shall be considered the act of the new State under international law'.[401] For reasons further discussed below,[402] the use of the concept of unjust enrichment (which is relevant for other types of succession) may, however, not be appropriate in the specific context of Newly Independent States.[403] Similarly, the existence of a nexus between the performance and execution of a contract and the territory of the Newly Independent States should not necessarily lead to the application of the solution of succession. The specific nature of Newly Independent States should be carefully considered in such a case.[404]

5.2 State practice is ambiguous

13.86 As mentioned above, Bedjaoui is of the view that in the context of decolonization 'private rights, concessionary or other, cannot be regarded as acquired rights' insofar as they 'are protected only if the new sovereign consents'.[405] He refers to a number of examples where the new States have indeed consented to the protection of private rights under concession agreements in the context of the independence of the Philippines, Algeria, and Indonesia.[406] While the principle of the respect of private rights was contained in an agreement signed between Indonesia and the Netherlands,[407] he noted that Indonesia subsequently repudiated all such private rights.[408] For him, while some new States may have agreed to protect such rights, their actual practice supports the

400 IDI, State Succession to Responsibility, Resolution, 2015 (n 14), Art. 16(1): 'When the successor State is a newly independent State, the obligations arising from an internationally wrongful act committed by the predecessor State shall not pass to the successor State.'
401 IDI, State Succession to Responsibility, Resolution, 2015 (n 14), Art. 16(3).
402 See, Chapter 14, Section 4.
403 This is the position of Bedjaoui, 'Problèmes récents de succession d'États' (n 11). *Contra*: Gruber (n 22) 108–9, for whom the question whether the principle should apply depends on the circumstances of each case.
404 The question is examined below, see Chapter 14, Section 2.2.
405 ILC, First Report Bedjaoui, 1968 (n 39) 115.
406 Ibid., 115.
407 Draft Agreement on Transitional Measures, 2 Nov. 1949, Art 4, 272 UNTS, 1950, 200.
408 ILC, Second Report Bedjaoui, 1969 (n 4) 97.

principle of non-succession.[409] There are indeed many examples supporting this conclusion. Thus, several provisions of the *Déclaration de principes relative à la coopération économique et financière* (dated 19 March 1962), which is part of the *Evian Accords* that ended the war, indicate that Algeria (the successor State) would protect the rights of French companies after its independence.[410] At the time, France took the position that this was in accordance with international law.[411] Yet, despite these assurances, Algeria did not provide such protection to foreign nationals in practice.[412] Other writers have interpreted the overall picture of State practice differently as generally respecting the acquired rights of foreign companies by providing compensation after expropriation.[413] Gruber admits, however, that there are a number of important cases where this tendency was not followed,[414] including the famous example of the expropriation of the company Union Minière du Haut-Katanga in the context of the independence of Congo.[415]

13.87 The situation that followed the independence of Congo (1960) is indeed rather confusing.[416] While some writers have referred to it as supporting the principle of the respect of acquired rights,[417] most of them have used it to

409 Ibid., 97–8.

410 See, analysis in O'Connell, *State Succession*, 1967 (n 15) 344; Gruber (n 22) 113. The text of the Agreement is found in: JORF, 20 March 1962, 3019–32. Art. 18 reads as follows: 'Algeria shall assume the obligations and enjoy the rights contracted on behalf of itself or of Algerian public establishments by the competent French authorities.'

411 Statement of the Minister of Foreign Affairs, in 'Chronique de jurisprudence française' (1970) AFDI 903:

> Les Accords d'Évian ne font, en matière d'intérêts privés, que confirmer une des règles s'inscrivant dans les principes généraux du droit valables en matière de succession d'États, règle dite du respect international des droits acquis et selon laquelle les droits privés doivent être respectés en cas de changement de souveraineté.

For an analysis of case law in relation to Algeria regarding the question of succession to responsibility, See, Dumberry, *State Succession to International Responsibility* (n 165) 177.

412 Evelyne Lagrange, 'Les successions d'États: pratiques françaises', (2003) 63 *La L Rev* 1235ff; Maurice Flory, Bruno Etienne, Gérard Fouilloux and Jean-Pierre Santucci, *La succession d'États en Afrique du Nord* (CNRS 1968) 84–5.

413 Gruber (n 22) 112–17. See also: Karl Zemanek, 'State Succession after Decolonization', (1965–III) 116 Rec des cours 288; 'no new State [in the context of decolonization] appears to have argued that acquired rights (...) lapsed *eo ipso* through state succession'; O'Connell, 'Recent Problems of State Succession' (n 41) 142:

> In fact, only two of all the newly independent States have pursued a policy of expropriation of foreign property, Algeria and Guinea, and the situation of the former, with a large alien population, could hardly be regarded as an ordinary one. All other new States have managed to adjust themselves satisfactorily to the inherited institutions of capitalist exploitation, and indeed to profit by them.

414 Gruber (n 22) 114–15. See also: O'Connell, 'Recent Problems of State Succession' (n 41) 142: 'To argue from these instances to a general denial of acquired rights is clearly to argue from the exceptional instead of from the normal, and hence to lose perspective.'

415 Gruber, ibid.

416 For an analysis of case law in relation to Congo regarding the question of succession to responsibility, See: Dumberry, *State Succession to International Responsibility* (n 165) 173.

417 See, analysis in: O'Connell, 'Recent Problems of State Succession' (n 41) 343.

illustrate the rejection of such rights by the new State.[418] Belgium's courts have rendered several decisions dealing with different problems of State succession arising from the independence of Congo.[419] One interesting case is that of *Crépet v. État belge et Société des forces hydro-électriques de la colonie*.[420] In 1958 (i.e., before the independence of Congo), the plaintiff filed a suit against the colonial Belgian Congo and a company for the non-payment of public work that he had performed under a contract that was signed with the colonial Belgian Congo. After the independence of Congo, the action was subsequently filed against the new State of Congo before a Belgian court. Deciding without the appearance of Congo, the Civil Tribunal of Brussels refused to hold the new State responsible for the obligations arising from the internationally wrongful acts on the ground that, as a matter of principle, these acts do not automatically devolve to the new State without any specific agreement to that effect between the predecessor State and the successor State. The court also held that the new State of Congo should, however, be responsible for the *contractual* breach which had been committed before its independence. The court considered it as a 'local debt' dealing with work undertaken only in this region of Africa which should, therefore, automatically be transferred to the successor State.[421] The court ordered Congo to act as the respondent in these proceedings. The court seems to have based its reasoning on the existence of a nexus between the territory of the new State and the contract where it was performed entirely.[422] The reasoning of the court also suggests that the concept of unjust enrichment may have played a role in determining that the

---

418 Gruber (n 22) 114–15.

419 These court cases are discussed in: Paul de Visscher, 'Le problème de la succession d'Etats envisagé dans l'histoire diplomatique du Congo', (1960–1962) 11 *Comunicazioni e studi* 75–85; Jean-Victor Louis, 'L'accession du Congo belge à l'indépendance, problèmes de succession d'États dans la jurisprudence belge', (1966) AFDI 731–56; Jean-Pierre de Brandt, 'De quelques problèmes de succession d'États à la suite de l'accession à l'indépendance de la République du Congo (Léopoldville)', (1965) RBDI 497–523; M. Waelbroeck, 'Arrêt no. 8160 du Conseil d'État Belge, note d'observations', (1961) 1 RJDA 1961 34ff; L.F. Ganshof, 'Les dettes de l'ex-colonie du Congo belge', (1964) *Revue juridique du Congo* 9; M. Rougevin-Baville, 'Le sort des droits et obligations de l'ancienne 'Colonie du Congo belge' d'après la jurisprudence des juridictions de Belgique', (1963) 2(1) *Revue judiciaire congolaise* 1.

420 Civil Tribunal of Brussels, 30 January 1962, in: (1962) *Journal des tribunaux* 242, extracts in: De Brandt, ibid., 514–16.

421 *Journal des tribunaux*, ibid.:

> Attendu qu'il y a lieu, pour décider de la recevabilité de l'action à l'égard de la République du Congo, de déterminer si les obligations de la ci-devant colonie du Congo belge dont se prévaut le demandeur sont passées à la charge du nouvel État; Attendu qu'il ressort de l'examen des faits de la cause que le premier chef de demande concerne des travaux qui devaient être exécutés exclusivement en Afrique, aux confins du Congo ex-belge et du Ruanda-Urundi dans l'intérêts de ces territoires. Qu'il s'agit dès lors d'une dette locale, en principe transférée ipso facto à l'État successeur, même en l'absence de traité avec l'État prédécesseur.

See also, for a similar reasoning: *Demol v. Etat belge*, in (1964) *Journal des tribunaux* 603.

422 This question examined at Chapter 14, Section 2.

new State should be responsible for the obligations arising from a contract that was initially signed by the colonial power.[423]

13.88 Another relevant example of State practice is in the context of the independence of Namibia. Article 140(3) of the Namibian Constitution provides that the acts of the South African Government (which illegally occupied Namibia for decades) should be deemed those of the new Namibian State:

> Anything done under such laws prior to the date of Independence by the Government, or by a Minister or other official of the Republic of South Africa shall be deemed to have been done by the Government of the Republic of Namibia or by a corresponding Minister or official of the Government of the Republic of Namibia, unless such action is subsequently repudiated by an Act of Parliament, and anything so done by the Government Service Commission shall be deemed to have been done by the Public Service Commission referred to in Article 112 hereof, unless it is determined otherwise by an Act of Parliament.[424]

13.89 The case of *Mwandinghi v. Minister of Defence, Namibia*[425] before the High Court of Namibia and that of *Minister of Defence, Namibia v. Mwandinghi*[426] before the Supreme Court of Namibia involved damages arising from the shooting of Mr. Mwandinghi, a Namibian national, by forces operating for the South African Defence Forces in 1987.[427] Before independence, the plaintiff submitted a claim for damages against the Minister of Defence of South Africa. Upon independence, he sought to substitute the Minister of Defence of Namibia as the defendant based on Article 140(3) of the new Namibian Constitution. He applied to the High Court by notice of motion for an order to allow the substitution. The Minister of Defence of Namibia opposed the motion on the ground that the Namibian Constitution did not make the new State responsible for the obligations arising from the internationally wrongful acts that had been committed by the predecessor State. The argument was based on the fact that, on the one hand, Article 140(3) would not cover 'delicts' (i.e., internationally wrongful acts) and, on the other hand, that Article 145 of the Constitution contains a disclaimer according to which an obligation may

423 This question examined at Chapter 14, Section 4.

424 Constitution of Namibia, adopted by the Constituent Assembly of Namibia on 9 February 1990, entered into force on 21 March 1991, UN Doc. S/20967/Add.2. Importantly, this provision also reserves the right for the new State to repudiate (by an act of legislation) acts of South Africa.

425 *Mwandinghi v. Minister of Defence, Namibia*, 14 December 1990, in: 1991 (1) SA 851 (Nm), in: 91 ILR 343.

426 *Minister of Defence, Namibia v. Mwandinghi*, 25 October 1991, in: 1992 (2) SA 355 (NmS), in: 91 ILR 358.

427 On these two decisions, see: Neville Botha, 'To Pay or Not to Pay?: Namibian Liability for South African Delicts', (1990–1991) 16 *South African YIL* 156–62; Neville Botha, 'Succession to Delictual Liability: Confirmation', (1991–1992) 17 *South African YIL* 177–9; Hercules Booysen, 'Succession to Delictual Liability: A Namibian Precedent' (1991) 24 *Comp & Int'l L J S Afr* 204–14.

be accepted by Namibia only to the extent that it is recognized as binding under international law.[428]

13.90 The present author has examined elsewhere the reasoning of the court dealing with the issue of succession to international responsibility.[429] For the purpose of the present book, only the part of the decision concerning contractual obligations will be examined. In its judgment, the High Court (comprised of one sitting judge) referred to writers indicating that private property rights do not lapse automatically when a territory is transferred, but added that this principle was 'not always followed' by States and that 'to a great extent the continuance of vested private rights depended on the attitude of the successor State'.[430] He added that 'in the field of contractual succession of one State to the rights and obligations of its predecessor, writers on international law are not unanimous as to the basis on which such liability exists'.[431] The judge also noted that all parties to the proceedings agreed that Namibia was bound by the contracts, including the concession contracts, as a result of Article 140(3) of the Namibian Constitution:

> As far as the position regarding Namibia after 21 March 1990 is concerned, it seems that the parties are at least *ad idem* that not only personal rights between private persons *inter se* survived the change, but also previous contracts of the predecessor government, concessions granted by it as well as licenses, etc. This unanimity derives from the interpretation of the parties of art 140 of the Constitution. (…) In general I think it can be said that art 140 not only accomplishes a complete transfer of powers from the previous Government, but also an acceptance by the new Government of all that was previously done under those laws in the exercising of the powers conferred thereby. There are further many other sections contained in the Constitution whereby rights acquired before independence are protected and retained.[432]

---

428 Art. 145 of the Namibian Constitution reads as follows:

> (1) Nothing contained in this Constitution shall be construed as imposing upon the Government of Namibia:
>
> (a) any obligations to any other State which would not otherwise have existed under international law;
> (b) any obligations to any person arising out of the acts or contracts of prior Administrations which would not otherwise have been recognised by international law as binding upon the Republic of Namibia.
>
> (2) Nothing contained in this Constitution shall be construed as recognising in any way the validity of the Administration of Namibia by the Government of the Republic of South Africa or by the Administrator-General appointed by the Government of the Republic of South Africa to administer Namibia.

429 Dumberry, *State Succession to International Responsibility* (n 165) 191ff.

430 *Mwandinghi v. Minister of Defence* (n 425) at 345.

431 Ibid.

432 Ibid.

13.91 This is also the interpretation that writers have given to this provision.[433] For the judge, Article 140(3) was 'an acceptance by the new State of the rights and obligations in existence prior to 21 March 1990'.[434] He went on to explain that the words 'anything done under such laws' at Article 140(3) should be given their ordinary meaning and should therefore not be limited to the lawful acts performed by the previous government. He concluded that the expression used was general enough to cover the claim of the plaintiff for 'delicts' committed by the South African Defense Forces.[435] Therefore, the judge decided that the Minister of Defence of Namibia was substituted as the defendant in the present case to the Minister of Defence of South Africa.[436]

13.92 In sum, while this case may be more relevant to the analysis of the question of succession to State responsibility, it is noteworthy that the court recognized the principle of succession to contracts even if Namibia was clearly a case of a Newly Independent State. Such an outcome may be surprising considering that these States have been largely considered as exempt from any succession to the obligations of their colonial powers. Yet, the reasoning of the court was essentially based on the specific provision contained in the Constitution providing for the general principle of succession.

13.93 Overall, the practice of Newly Independent States is rather confusing with examples supporting both the solution of succession and that of non-succession.

6. ANNEXATION OF STATES IN THE CONTEXT OF COLONIZATION

13.94 As mentioned above, annexation is not a recognized type of succession in modern international law because of the illegality of the use of force.[437] I have nevertheless decided to examine relevant State practice arising in the context of annexation. This is because these cases and examples of practice are often referred to by the very few scholars who have examined the question of succession to State contracts in the past. They are also often mentioned by the parties in arbitration proceedings. While there is no doubt that these examples

433 H.A. Strydom, 'Namibian Independence and the Question of the Contractual and Delictual Liability of the Predecessor and Successor Governments', (1989–1990) 15 *South African YIL* 113–14.

434 *Mwandinghi v. Minister of Defence* (n 425) 349.

435 Ibid., 351–2.

436 Namibia appealed this decision before the Supreme Court, which dismissed the appeal and confirmed the decision of the lower court.

437 See, Chapter 6, Sections 6.2.4. and 6.2.6.

are an interesting source of information, it should be kept in mind that they arose in a very specific context and, therefore, have a less significant impact today.

6.1 Colonial successor States have rejected succession to contracts

In his book, O'Connell identified a significant number of cases in the context of annexation where successor States have systematically refused to be held responsible for any obligations under contracts which had been signed by the predecessor State. Bedjaoui explained that 'in the case of colonization, political considerations took precedence over the juridical approach to the principle of acquired rights'.[438] He highlighted the fact that 'the political position of refusing to take account of acquired rights was justified by one weak argument after another, all of them based on the inapplicability of the principle of acquired rights'.[439] Thus, the first argument that was used by Western colonial States was that 'the vast areas conquered by [them] were not organized into States, so that the non-existence of a State in the colonized territory justified the metropolitan country's rejection of any claim to acquired rights: no State, therefore no succession, therefore no acquired rights'.[440] The second argument used by Western colonial States to deny any succession to contracts was that 'a more or less feeble sovereignty existed before the colonization but that the territory was still too backward for the rules of the international law of the time to be applied to it'.[441] Thus, the colonial State took this position of non-succession because they considered the predecessor State to be backwards and believed that they should, therefore, not assume any liabilities arising from the contracts that were signed by such regimes. **13.95**

This was clearly the position taken by the United Kingdom after its annexation of Burma in 1886: 'when a civilized Government succeeds a Government like that of the Kingdom of Upper Burma, it is under no obligation to accept and to discharge, subject to the conditions imposed by civilization and good Government, the obligations incurred by its predecessor under entirely unlike conditions'.[442] Thus, since Upper Burma was 'an uncivilized country', the United Kingdom believed that it was therefore 'possible that in dealing with such a State rules more favourable to the succeeding Government could be applied than to the case where two civilized States have been incorporated **13.96**

438 ILC, Second Report Bedjaoui, 1969 (n 4) 90.

439 Ibid., 88.

440 Ibid.

441 Ibid.

442 O'Connell, *State Succession*, 1967 (n 15) 358–60, referring to a letter from the Secretary for Upper Burma to the Secretary to the Government of India, dated 8 June 1886.

with Her Majesty's Dominions'.[443] The same position was adopted by Italy following its annexation of Ethiopia in 1935.[444] A similar argument was advanced in the 1920s by Sir Cecil Hurst in the different context of succession to State responsibility. He argued that the imposition of a rule of succession to the obligations arising from internationally wrongful acts upon the 'better governed and more advanced' States would have the effect of discouraging them from intervening in 'backward States' to put an end to the 'anarchy and misrule' existing in such countries, and that this situation would result in setting a 'premium on misgovernment'.[445] Sir Cecil, who acted as Counsel to Great Britain, used the same argument in the *R.E. Brown* case (further discussed below[446]).[447]

13.97 Finally, Bedjaoui refers to a third argument used by colonial successor States, which was to 'accept more or less explicitly the existence of a State and of a succession and to recognize the principle of acquired rights, but at the same time to reduce the field of application of that principle to cases of succession

443 Ibid., 360, referring to Opinion of 30 Nov. 1900, FO Confidential papers (7516) no. 22A.

444 Ibid., 332.

445 Hurst (n 239) 178:

> A principle which would render a conqueror liable for damages for all the unliquidated claims based on wrongful acts of the State he is driven to subdue would be neither just nor reasonable, and would entail consequences which would be fruitful of mischief. Such a principle would enable a small and backward State to withstand all pressure from a better governed and more advanced neighbour, and would act as a direct encouragement to any such backslider among the family of nations to render itself secure from intervention and absorption by perpetuating anarchy and misrule within its borders. The more the condition of such a State cried aloud for intervention for the sake of the inhabitant of the country, whether native of foreign, the more would neighbouring Governments be held back for necessary action by the contemplation of the burdens it might entail. In short, if there were any such rule of international law, it would merely set a premium on misgovernment.

446 See, Chapter 13, Section 6.2.

447 'Brief filed by Fred K. Nielsen, American Agent, R.E. Brown Case', in: Nielsen (n 239) 165ff, at 184. In relation to the possibility he raised during the pleading that European Powers could invade newly Communist Russia to stop the atrocities committed there at that time, he stated that any rule of succession to obligations arising from the commission of internationally wrongful acts would make 'Governments hesitate long before they set out to redress very grievous wrongs that may be committed in any particular part of the world.' In its pleading in the *R.E. Brown* case, Great Britain provides this other example:

> Supposing the Ruler of Government of a country is grossly extravagant, is wasting the substance of the people in some riotous form of spending, and it is creating trouble and the Government of one of the big Powers says: This must stop, we cannot allow this to go on, it is a danger to civilization and we are going to stop it, if, in such circumstances, a country or several countries in alliance, stepped in and tried to provide good and decent and proper Government in that particular State that was behaving wrongly, can it be said that they would have to pay all the damages that had been wrongfully incurred by the country that, at the time they took it over, had rendered itself bankrupt and helpless so far as money matters are concerned? I submit that would be wrong; I submit it would not be in the interests of civilization, and certainly it would not be moral in the circumstances. If one comes to deal with the subject, and think it out, I submit there can obviously be no general rule regard to State succession.

in: 'Answer of His Britannic Majesty's Government in the Robert E. Brown Claim' 253–6, quoted in: 'Brief filed by Fred K. Nielsen, American Agent, Hawaiian Claims Case', in: Nielsen (n 239) 95ff, 97.

other than colonization'.[448] In other words, the non-application of the principle of acquired rights in the case of colonization 'was an exception to a rule that was otherwise considered to be well established'.[449]

6.2 State practice supports the principle of non-succession

The position of non-succession was, for instance, taken by France when annexing Madagascar in 1896.[450] This was also the position adopted by Italy after annexing Ethiopia in 1935[451] and that of the United Kingdom after its annexation of Burma in 1886.[452] Another clear example (examined in the next paragraphs) of this non-succession approach regarding State contracts is the one adopted by the United Kingdom when the Boer Republic of South Africa was annexed to the British Empire in 1902 at the end of the Boer War (1899–1902).[453] It is interesting to note that the position adopted by the United Kingdom in this specific case was contrary to its position taken in the past (as mentioned above[454]), for example when the interests of its own nationals were at stake in the context of the annexation of Madagascar by France and the cession of the Philippines and Cuba to the United States.[455] **13.98**

The general position of Great Britain was to reject any responsibility for wrongful actions taken by the Boer Republic before the date of succession.[456] Great Britain also rejected having the obligation to automatically respect and maintain all acquired rights detained by individuals. In this context, the High Commission announced that it would consider all concession rights on its merits.[457] Great Britain set up the Transvaal Concession Commission to examine the concession contracts which had been signed by the Boer Republic. The Commission published a report containing some recommendations **13.99**

448 ILC, Second Report Bedjaoui, 1969 (n 4) 89.

449 Ibid.

450 O'Connell, *State Succession*, 1967 (n 15) 309. See the analysis in: ILC, Second Report Bedjaoui, 1969 (n 4) 89; Lagrange (n 409) 1211ff; D. Bardonnet, *La succession d'Etats à Madagascar: succession au droit conventionnel et aux droits patrimoniaux* (LGDJ 1970); G. Gidel, *Les effets de l'annexion sur les concessions* (Larose 1904) 247–8.

451 O'Connell, *State Succession*, 1967 (n 15) 332.

452 Ibid., 358–60.

453 Ibid., 316–22, 360–62.

454 See, Chapter 13, Section 2.2.

455 O'Connell, *State Succession*, 1967 (n 15) 318–20.

456 See many examples cited in Dumberry, *State Succession to International Responsibility* (n 165) 71ff.

457 O'Connell, *State Succession*, 1967 (n 15) 316–17. He also mentions that the Colonial Office was informed by the legal adviser to the High Commission that it could treat all concessions granted by the Boer Republics as having expired on annexation. However, he notes that the Colonial Office also received at around the same time a more balanced legal opinion from the Law Officers rejecting this view.

regarding 27 concessions.[458] The Report contains the following nuanced position on the fate of acquired rights:

> It is clear that a State which has annexed another State is not legally bound by any contract made by a State which has ceased to exist, and that no court of law has jurisdiction to enforce such contracts if the annexing State refuses to recognize them, see *Cook v. Sprigg* (1899) A. C. 572. But the modern usage of nations has tended in the direction of the acknowledgment of such contracts. After annexation, it has been said the people change their allegiance, but their relations to each other and their rights of property remain undisturbed, *U.S. v. Pencheman*, 7 Pet. 51; and property includes rights which lie in contract, *Soulard v. U.S.*, 4 Pet. 54. (...) Concessions of the nature of those which were the subject of enquiry presented examples of mixed public and private rights; They probably continue to exist after annexation until abrogated by the annexing State, and, as a matter of practice in modern times, where treaties have been made on cession of territory, have been often maintained by agreement. (...) Though we doubt whether the duties of an annexing State towards those claiming under concessions or contracts granted or made by the annexed State have been defined with such precision in authoritative statements or acted upon with such uniformity in civilized practice, we are convinced that the best modern opinion favours the view that as a general rule the obligations of the annexed State towards private persons should be respected. Manifestly the general rule must be subject to qualification, as that an insolvent State could not by aggression which practically left to a solvent no other course than to annex it, convert its worthless into valuable obligations; again an annexing State would be justified in refusing to recognize obligations incurred by the annexed State for the immediate purposes of the war against itself; and that probably no State would acknowledge private rights the existence of which caused or contributed to cause the war which resulted in annexation.[459]

13.100 Interestingly, while the Commission stated that the United Kingdom was not bound under international law by such contracts, it nevertheless mentioned the existence of a 'general rule' under which 'the obligations of the annexed State towards private persons should be respected'.

13.101 Courts of the Union of South Africa (which had the status of a Dominion of Great Britain) have repeatedly rejected claims based on private rights that had been granted by the South African Republic before the annexation.[460] The

---

458 Ibid., 317.

459 Report of the Transvaal Concessions Commission; see Parl. Pap. South Africa, 1901 [Cd. 623], 5–7. The Report also mentioned that: 'The acceptance of this principle clearly renders it necessary that the annexing Government should in each case examine whether the rights which it is asked to recognize have, in fact, been duly acquired.' The Report refers to situation when a concession may properly be cancelled: '(a) the grant of the concession was not within the legal powers of the late Government, or (b) was in breach of a treaty with the annexing State, or (c) when the person seeking to maintain the concession acquired it unlawfully or by fraud, or (d) has failed to fulfil its essential conditions without lawful excuse.'

460 *Vereeniging Municipality v. Vereeniging Estates Ltd.* 1919, Supreme Court of South Africa, Transvaal Provincial Division, (1919) South African LR 159; (1919/1922) *Annual Digest* Case 33, at 60.

question of the survival of the acquired rights was also decided by English courts. In the case of *West Rand Central Gold Mining Co. Ltd. v. The King*, the High Court of Justice of England dealt with a case where, before the outbreak of the Boer War, a gold mine in the Republic of Transvaal owned by the claimant was confiscated by officials acting on the behalf of the Government of that Republic.[461] The claimant argued that the Republic was liable to return the gold or its value. It further claimed that, as a result of the conquest and annexation of the territories by Great Britain, the *contractual* obligation was now binding upon the successor State based on a presumption in favour of a transfer of liabilities.[462] Counsel for Great Britain argued, on the contrary, that there was 'no principle of international law by which a conquering State becomes *ipso facto* liable to discharge all the contractual obligations of the conquered State'.[463]

Lord Alverstone CJ, writing for the court, rejected the claim of the claimant. **13.102**
He indicated that the proposition submitted by the claimant 'that by international law the conquering country is bound to fulfill the obligations of the conquered, could not be sustained'.[464] He added that 'when making peace the conquering Sovereign can make any conditions he thinks fit respecting the financial obligations of the conquered country, and it is entirely at his option to what extent he will adopt them'.[465] The Lord Justice also indicated that there was no 'reason at all why silence should be supposed to be equivalent to a promise of universal novation of existing contracts with the Government of the conquered State'.[466] The decision was summarized as follows in the headnote of the case:

---

461 *West Rand Central Gold Mining Company Ltd. v. The King*, King's Bench, (1905) 2 K.B. 391, in Clive Parry, *British International Law Cases*, vol II (Stevens 1965) 283. This case is discussed in: Hurst (n 239) 173; 'Answer of His Britannic Majesty's Government in the Robert E. Brown Claim' 13 (quoted in: Nielsen (n 239) 95ff, 113–14).

462 Ibid. This is the full quotation of the argument developed by Counsel for the claimant:

> The Sovereign has, it is admitted, power when annexing a conquered State to impose what terms and conditions he pleases as to the taking over of the obligations of the conquered State; but if nothing is said about a particular obligation then it must be deemed to have been taken over, and it can be enforced in the municipal Courts of the conquering State.

Counsel for the claimant also submitted that:

> by international law, where one civilized State after conquest annexes another civilized State, the conquering State, in the absence of stipulations to the contrary, takes over and becomes bound by all the contractual obligations of the conquered State, except liabilities incurred for the purpose of or in the course of the particular war.

463 Ibid.

464 Ibid.

465 Ibid.

466 Ibid.

> There is no principle of international law by which, after annexation of conquered territory, the conquering State becomes liable, in the absence of express stipulation to the contrary, to discharge financial liabilities of the conquered State incurred before the outbreak of war.[467]

13.103 Another illustration of the manner in which the protection of acquired rights was decided in the context of the annexation of the Boer Republic is the *R.E. Brown* case,[468] decided by the US-Great Britain Arbitral Commission in 1923. This award is known for being the first statement of an international tribunal in support of the (alleged) principle of non-succession to obligations arising from the commission of internationally wrongful acts.[469] The Commission indicated, in an *obiter dictum*, that it could not endorse a doctrine based on 'an assertion that a succeeding state acquiring a territory by conquest without any undertaking to assume such liabilities is bound to take affirmative steps to right the wrong by the former state'.[470] For the present section, what is of importance is the fact that the case also involved (alleged) *contractual* rights detained by a foreigner.

13.104 The *R.E. Brown* case involved a US national who had 'pegged out' in 1895 some 1,200 mining claims for gold mining concessions in the Boer Republic of South Africa at the time it was still considered to be an 'independent' republic. The Government of the Boer Republic of South Africa later made three proclamations by which it rejected Mr. Brown's applications for these concessions. Mr. Brown alleged that he was deprived of his license rights to which he believed he was entitled. He subsequently brought an unsuccessful lawsuit before the High Court of the Boer Republic of South Africa.[471] All these events took place *before* change affecting the sovereignty of the Boer

467 Ibid.

468 *R.E. Brown* (*United States v. Great Britain*), Award, 23 November 1923, 6 UNRIAA 129. A brief reference should be made to another case: *Union Bridge Co. (United States) v. Great Britain*, US-Great Britain Arbitral Tribunal, Award, 8 January 1924, in: 6 UNRIAA 138; (1925) 19 AJIL 215; (1923–1924) *Annual Digest* 170. This case is commented in: Verzijl (n 262) 221. This case dealt with the internationally wrongful acts committed by officials of the Orange Free State against a US company. The company sold materials for steel bridge to the Orange Free State, which refused to pay. After these events, the annexation of the Orange Free State by Great Britain took place. At first, the United States invoked diplomatic protection for the company on the ground of the succession of Great Britain to contractual liability of the Orange Free State. This position was soon abandoned. The United States pursued its claim instead on the ground of Great Britain's direct liability for acts committed *after* the annexation. The tribunal therefore did not discuss any issues of State succession.

469 See analysis in: Dumberry, *State Succession to International Responsibility* (n 165) 73.

470 *R.E. Brown* (n 468) 130.

471 Ibid., 120–21. The summary of the case described these events as follows:

> Proclamation issued on June 18, 1895, by President of South African Republic designating certain tract of land, called Witfontein, as public gold field beginning July 19, 1895. Suspension of proclamation on July 18, 1895, by Executive Council at Pretoria. Application for 1,200 prospecting licences, made under the proclamation by Mr. Robert E. Brown, United States citizen, on July 19, 1895. Licences refused on the

Republic. The United States presented a claim in 1903 on behalf of its national to Great Britain. Great Britain refused to take responsibility for the alleged wrongful acts. Indeed, in a letter addressed to the US Ambassador, Lord Lansdowne, Chief of the British Foreign Office, noted that he was not aware of any rule of international law whereby 'the conquering State takes over liabilities for wrongs which have been committed by the Government of the conquered country and any such construction appears to be unsound in principle'.[472] In the proceedings, the United States took the general position that Great Britain should take responsibility for what took place in the Boer Republic before the date of annexation:

> [I]nasmuch as Great Britain has acquired the entire and complete territory of the South African Republic by conquest, and has succeeded to and holds the full and entire sovereignty thereof, thereby replacing and substituting itself for the South African Republic which has by such acts wholly ceased to exist, Great Britain is bound to pay the debts of the defunct Republic, and especially so when such debts are in the nature of judgement debts.[473]

The United States based its argumentation on Mr. Brown's 'acquired rights'. Indeed, in its pleading, it refers to Mr. Brown as having 'acquired valuable mining rights under the legislation of the South African Republic of which he was deprived by authorities of that Republic'.[474] The United States argued that Great Britain had an obligation to respect such rights after its annexation of the Boer Republic: **13.105**

ground of suspension of proclamation. Pegging out of 1,200 mining claims by Brown who, notwithstanding refusal of licences, asserted title. Second proclamation issued on July 20, 1895, by State President adjourning opening of Witfontein until August 2, 1895. Suit brought on July 22, 1895, before High Court of the South African Republic by Brown demanding licences to cover 1,200 claims already pegged off. Resolution adopted on July 26, 1895, by Second Volksraad approving withdrawal of first proclamation and issuance of second one, and declaring that no person who had suffered damage should be entitled to compensation. Third proclamation issued on July 31, 1895, by State President further adjourning opening until August 30, 1895. New government regulations for distributing mining claims by lot drawn up on August 15, 1895, and made applicable to Witfontein on August 20, 1895. Alternative claim for damages in the original action filed by Brown in October, 1895. Judgment in Brown's favour on January 22, 1897, the Court setting aside resolution of July 26, 1895 as unconstitutional, ordering issuance of licences, and inviting Brown to pursue alternative claim for damages by motion in the event of his being unable to peg off 1,200 mining claims. Licences for 1,200 mining claims of no practical value issued on February 9, 1897. Damages sought by Brown by motion, notice of which given on December 10, 1897. Chief Justice dismissed from office by State President on February 16, 1898, under so-called testing law of February 26, 1897. Judgment delivered on March 2, 1898, denying motion, with leave to start new action. No further attempt by Brown to get relief in Courts.

472 Letter of Lord Lansdowne, Chief of the British Foreign Office, to the US Ambassador, in: Nielsen (n 239) 197.

473 'United States' Memorial', quoted in: Hurst (n 239) 164.

474 'Brief filed by Fred K. Nielsen, American Agent, R.E. Brown Case', in: Nielsen (n 239) 165.

> International law requires that, when a nation absorbs another nation through conquest, the absorbing State shall respect and safeguard rights of person and of property in the conquested State.[475]
>
> ... it is well-established that appropriate judicial acts of an extinguished State, defining such rights, should not be disregarded by the absorbing State.[476]

13.106 The United States also maintained that Great Britain should be liable for acts committed *after* the annexation by its own officials against Mr. Brown.[477] Great Britain's contention was that Mr. Brown had never acquired such rights.[478] While this situation was no doubt the result of the actions of the local authorities of the Boer Republic, Great Britain maintained that it had no control over the authorities at that time and, therefore, should not be held responsible for the obligations arising from such acts.[479]

13.107 The Arbitral Commission came to the conclusion that Mr. Brown had indeed acquired a right and that the authorities of the Boer Republic denied it. However, the Arbitral Commission followed Great Britain's line of argumentation and decided that Mr. Brown had suffered a 'denial of justice' from the Government of the Boer Republic.[480] In fact, the Commission referred, more

---

475 Ibid., 167.

476 Ibid., 180.

477 Ibid. Finally, the United States also argued that Great Britain should be held accountable for acts committed by the local authorities of the Boer Republic because of the peculiar relation of suzerainty which it maintained in the region at the time of the commission of the illegal acts.

478 Ibid., 183.

479 Ibid.:

> During the period in which Brown was engaged in difficulties with authorities of the South African Republic, that country was a free and independent State. To establish Brown's right to compensation as against Great Britain, it is necessary for the United States to show not only that there was an obligation on the part of the South African Republic to pay compensation in respect to the injury suffered by Brown, but also that liability for such failure of duty on the part of the Government of a conquested State passed to the conqueror upon annexation of the conquested State.

480 *R.E. Brown* (n 468) 128–9:

> We are of opinion that Brown had substantial rights of a character entitling him to an interest in real property or to damages for the deprivation thereof, and that he was deprived of these rights by the Government of the South African Republic in such manner and under such circumstances as to amount to a denial of justice within the settled principles of international law. We fully appreciate the force of the argument to the contrary which has been made on technical grounds. It may well be said that at no time did Brown acquire and hold any title or right to specific mining claims; that at most he was entitled to a licence under which he might have located and become the owner of particular claims; that the actual pegging of claims in his behalf on July 19, 1895, was unsupported by any licence, and therefore had no legal effect; that the judgment of January 22, 1897, established merely his right to a licence and gave him no title to particular claims; that the alternative demand for damages was never liquidated; and that his legal remedies were not completely exhausted inasmuch as he never followed up the claim for damages by taking out a new summons in accordance with leave granted by the order of March 2, 1898. Notwithstanding these positions, all of which may, in our view, be conceded, we are persuaded that on the whole case, giving proper weight to the cumulative strength of the numerous steps taken by the

broadly, to an 'amazing controversy between the Court and the Executive' which resulted in the 'virtual subjection of the High Court to the executive power'.[481] It also mentioned that the 'obedient legislature immediately enact-[ing], at the demand of the Executive, a new law in February 1897' which 'was the prelude of the state of so-called legal anarchy, which endured for approximately a year, and eventually led to the armed intervention of Great Britain and the ultimate annexation of the South African Republic'.[482] For the Commission, 'throughout this controversy the Brown case was referred to as the turning point, and the 1897 law as the actual instrument by which the independence of the High Court was destroyed'.[483] Thus, 'effective guarantees of property rights had disappeared' and the 'capricious will of the Executive had become the sole authority in the land'.[484] According to the Commission, 'these intolerable conditions led directly to the war, in which the independence of the State itself was suppressed.'[485] The Commission concluded on this point that:

> Growing out of this very transaction, a system was created under which all property rights became so manifestly insecure as to challenge intervention by the British Government in the interest of elementary justice for all concerned, and to lead finally to the disappearance of the State itself. Annexation by Great Britain became an act of political necessity if those principles of justice and fair dealing which prevail in every country where property rights are respected were to be vindicated and applied in the future in this region.[486]

For the Commission, this case was a 'real denial of justice', adding that 'if there had never been any war, or annexation by Great Britain, and if these proceedings were directed against the South African Republic, we should have no difficulty in awarding damages on behalf of the claimant'.[487] Yet, the Commission concluded that Great Britain should nevertheless not be held responsible for such a denial of justice for the following reasons: 13.108

Government of the South African Republic with the obvious intent to defeat Brown's claims, a definite denial of justice took place. We can not overlook the broad facts in the history of this controversy. All three branches of the Government conspired to ruin his enterprise. The Executive Department issued proclamations for which no warrant could be found in the Constitution and laws of the country. The Volksraad enacted legislation which, on its face, does violence to fundamental principles of justice recognized in every enlightened community. The judiciary, at first recalcitrant, was at length reduced to submission and brought into line with a determined policy of the Executive to reach the desired result regardless of Constitutional guarantees and inhibitions.

481 Ibid., 124–5.

482 Ibid.

483 Ibid., 126.

484 Ibid.

485 Ibid.

486 Ibid., 129.

487 Ibid.

> We are equally clear that this liability never passes to or was assumed by the British Government. Neither in the terms of peace granted at the time of the surrender of the Boer Forces, nor in the Proclamation of Annexation, can there be found any provision referring to the assumption of liabilities of this nature. It should be borne in mind that this was simply a pending claim for damages against certain officials and had never become a liquidated debt of the former State.[488]

13.109 The Commission therefore denied the claim. The case is clearly more significant to the analysis of the different question of succession to State responsibility rather than that of succession to acquired rights per se. Thus, while contractual rights under a State contract were at the origin of the case, the question decided by the Commission was essentially whether the successor State should be responsible for an internationally wrongful act (a denial of justice) committed by the predecessor State against a foreign national, before the annexation.[489] Yet, the case is interesting because of the position adopted by the parties in the proceedings with regards to the survival of acquired rights after the annexation took place. The United States clearly supported the principle of succession. On the contrary, the United Kingdom argued that no such principle existed. It is noteworthy that this position was the exact opposite to the one it had previously taken when the interests of its own nationals were at stake in other instances of cession of territories (a point discussed above[490]).

488 Ibid.

489 Ibid. Yet, it should be added that the Commission admitted that in fact the claim did *not* 'properly speaking' involve 'any question of State succession'. This is because the United States did not base its argumentation on the existence of any doctrine of succession to international responsibility: 'The United States plants itself squarely on two propositions: first, that the British Government, by the acts of its own officials with respect to Brown's case, has become liable to him; and, secondly, that in some way a liability was imposed upon the British Government by reason of the peculiar relation of suzerainty which is maintained with respect to the South African Republic'. Both arguments were rejected by the Commission. This point is examined in: Hurst (n 239) 165.

490 See, Chapter 13, Section 2.2.

14

SUCCESSION TO STATE CONTRACTS DEPENDS ON WHETHER A NUMBER OF FACTORS AND CIRCUMSTANCES ARE INVOLVED

I examined in the previous chapter that the type of succession involved is important to determine whether or not there should be any succession to State contracts. Thus, succession to contracts seems to be well established in the context of cession of territory, unification and incorporation of States. On the contrary, in the context of Newly Independent States, it is the *tabula rasa* principle which should normally find application (even though State practice is rather ambiguous and does not fully support the principle of non-succession). The solution of non-succession also seems to be logical for new secessionist States. Thus, in that context, the continuing State should normally continue to be bound by the rights and obligations arising from the contract *it had itself* signed before the date of succession. Finally, the fact that the predecessor State ceases to exist in the context of a dissolution militates in favour of applying the solution of non-succession. Yet, in the previous chapter, I also mentioned that there are *particular circumstances* where the solution of **14.01** non-succession would not be appropriate in the context of a secession, Newly Independent States, and dissolution. The present chapter examines specifically a number of different *factors and circumstances* that should be taken into account to determine whether or not there should be succession to State contracts.

14.02 The method of analysis used here is not entirely novel. In fact, some of its basic features have already been examined by the present author when addressing the question of succession to State responsibility.[491] In fact, it corresponds to what the arbitral tribunal in the *Lighthouse Arbitration* case (examined above[492]) mentioned in its award about the importance of taking into account not only the different types of State succession involved, but also a number of different factors and circumstances. O'Connell was the first scholar to recognize this important fact.[493] In his 1970 Hague Academy course, he explained the essence of the problem of State succession and the importance of addressing it with flexibility. More precisely he stated:

> The law of State Succession must thus centre upon one basic concept, namely the reconciliation of the independence of successor States with the expectations of other States and peoples. Looked at from another point of view, this central principle might be described as one of minimal disturbance of existing legal situations, consistent with the actual state of affairs resulting from a succession of States. This may not appear to be saying much, but it at least suggests that there will be a range of practical solutions, as the test of disruption is applied to a variety of situations. No unique rule is therefore likely to be discoverable that will suit all occasions of change of sovereignty, and the function of the jurist will be to apply in each case of State succession such rules as are discernible in legal tradition by reference to the standard of continuity or discontinuity. (...) [a] philosophy of State Succession must therefore centre upon the question of the continuity of law.[494]

14.03 When addressing the issue of succession to international responsibility, O'Connell elaborated on the importance of taking into account different factors and circumstances:

> It is exasperating not to be able to propose a synthetic structure of State succession doctrine which can accommodate the problem of torts, but the truth is that the matter cannot be brought to any finer focus than in Verzijl's conclusion in the *Lighthouse case* that *many concrete factors*, including the continuing nature of the wrong, and its

491 See Dumberry, *State Succession to International Responsibility* (n 165) 207ff.
492 *Lighthouse Arbitration* case (n 162). See, analysis at Chapter 13, Section 2.4.4.
493 O'Connell, *State Succession*, 1967 (n 15) 301.
494 O'Connell, 'Recent Problems of State Succession' (n 41) 120–21.

liquidated or unliquidated character, *are to be taken into account, and the factors may require different evaluation in different types of successions of States.*[495]

The question as to which factors and circumstances are relevant was recently addressed in the Resolution adopted by the Institut de Droit international on the question of 'State Succession in Matters of State Responsibility'.[496] I believe that the solution adopted by the Institut is perfectly applicable to the different context of succession to State contracts. Under the Resolution, whenever the predecessor State continues to exist, that State should continue to enjoy rights and to assume obligations arising from the internationally wrongful acts in which it was involved before the date of State succession.[497] This is the solution adopted at Articles 4 and 5 of the Resolution. Yet, the Resolution also provides for two exceptions where the rights and obligations may be transferred to the successor State in the following circumstances: **14.04**

- the existence of a *direct link* between the wrongful act and the territory and/or the population of that successor State;
- when the author of the wrongful act was an organ of the predecessor State which has later become an organ of that successor State.

The Final Report also indicates that 'the acceptance by a successor State of the obligations stemming from a wrongful act committed by the predecessor State (or even endorsing its responsibility) may constitute another exception to the non-succession rule in case of subsistence of the predecessor State after the date of State succession'.[498] It should be noted that 'the need to avoid unjust enrichment' is also mentioned at Article 7 of the Resolution dealing with the allocation of rights and obligations in the context of a plurality of successor States. **14.05**

In my view, these factors and circumstances should also apply to determine the question of succession to contracts. In the following sections, I will examine the four different factors that may have an impact on whether or not a successor State should be bound by a State contract signed by the predecessor State before the date of succession: **14.06**

- the position taken by the successor State (after the date of succession) regarding the issue of succession to contracts;

495 Ibid., 164 (emphasis added).

496 IDI, State Succession to Responsibility, Resolution, 2015 (n 14). For an analysis of this Resolution, see: Kohen and Dumberry, *State Succession and State Responsibility* (n 165).

497 Institut de Droit international, *State Succession in Matters of State Responsibility*, 14th Commission, Rapporteur Marcelo G. Kohen, Final Report, 28 June 2015, 27.

498 IDI, State Succession in Matters of State Responsibility, Final Report (n 497) 31.

- the existence of a 'nexus' between a contract and the territory of the successor State;
- whether the contract was signed by an organ of a territorial unit of the predecessor State that has a structural continuity with the successor State;
- the need to avoid any unjust enrichment.

1. THE POSITION TAKEN BY THE SUCCESSOR STATE REGARDING THE ISSUE OF SUCCESSION TO CONTRACTS

14.07 The most basic criterion that should be taken into account when determining whether a successor State should be responsible for the rights and obligations arising from a State contract is the position actually taken by that State regarding the contract after the date of succession. Thus, it is important to analyse the reaction of the successor State with regards to the contract that was signed by the predecessor State. There are indeed a number of situations (examined in the next paragraphs) where it would be logical for the succession solution to apply.

14.08 The successor State is always free to recognize its responsibility for the rights and obligations arising from a State contract which was signed by the predecessor State. In the previous sections, many situations were examined where the successor States affirmed that they would respect the acquired rights of foreigners. Such a position may, for instance, be taken in the domestic law of that State. One such example is the Namibia Constitution.[499] As numerous examples examined above have shown,[500] another common option is for the successor State to recognize such obligations in the context of a treaty. The successor State may also recognize its responsibility for any obligation arising from a *breach* of a State contract which was committed by the *predecessor* State before the date of succession. In such a case, the solution of succession should obviously prevail. The successor State may also decide after the date of succession to continue to perform the terms of a contract, even if that contract was originally signed by another State (the predecessor State). In such a case, there is no doubt that the successor State is bound by the rights and obligations arising from that contract. In the event that the successor State continues to perform the terms of a contract, it should evidently be responsible for any breach of the contract it commits *after* the date of succession. In fact,

499 See, Chapter 13, Section 5.2.

500 See, for instance, several examples in the context of cession of territory at Chapter IV, Section 4.2.

this is not even a question of State succession, but rather one of State responsibility for wrongful acts.

Another possibility is when the successor State (after the date of succession) *continues a breach* of a State contract which was originally committed by the *predecessor* State before the date of succession. When this is the case, *two different* breaches will co-exist. The first breach is committed by the predecessor State and ends at the date of succession. The second breach commences at that very moment and is imputable to the successor State. The fact that the new successor State is responsible for the acts it has *itself* committed after its independence is uncontroversial. This is not even a question of State succession. The issue is covered by Article 11 of the ILC Articles on State Responsibility.[501] In its commentary on Article 11, the ILC specifically refers to the position of the successor State in that context: '[I]f the successor State, faced with a continuing wrongful act on its territory, endorses and continues that situation, the inference may readily be drawn that it has assumed responsibility for it.'[502] **14.09**

The more complicated question is to determine whether the successor State should *also* be responsible for breaches committed *before* the date of succession. As examined elsewhere by the present author in the context of succession to State responsibility,[503] certain scholars have argued that if the new State continues the internationally wrongful act that was originally committed by the predecessor State, the new State should be held accountable not only for *its own* act committed after the date of succession *but also* for the damage that was caused by the predecessor State *before* that date. In other words, the new State should take over the obligations arising from internationally wrongful acts that were committed by the predecessor State *before* its independence *because* of its continuation of the original wrongful act.[504] It has been suggested that the solution to this problem may depend on whether the predecessor State continues its existence as a result of the events affecting its territorial integrity.[505] Thus, when the predecessor State continues to exist after the **14.10**

501 ILC Draft Articles on State Responsibility (n 100), Art. 11: 'Conduct which is not attributable to a State under the preceding articles shall nevertheless be considered an act of that State under international law if and to the extent that the State acknowledges and adopts the conduct in question as its own.'

502 ILC Commentaries on Draft Articles on State Responsibility (n 112), 119 [3]. See also: James Crawford, *State Responsibility: The General Part* (CUP 2013) 182–3.

503 Dumberry, *State Succession to International Responsibility* (n 165) 218ff.

504 Ibid., referring to the position of a number of writers and that of ILC's Special Rapporteur Crawford in: 'First Report on State Responsibility (*addendum* no. 5)', by James Crawford, Special Rapporteur, 22 July 1998, UN Doc. A/CN.4/490/Add.5. [281]–[283]; ILC Commentaries on *Draft Articles on State Responsibility* (n 112) 119–20.

505 Dumberry, *State Succession to International Responsibility* (n 165) 220.

changes affecting its former territory have occurred, that State should, in principle, remain responsible for *its own* internationally wrongful acts that were committed *before* the date of succession. As recognized by the Institut in its above-mentioned Resolution, a distinction should also be made between wrongful acts having a continuing character and those having a composite character.[506] Thus, when a successor State *continues* the breach of an international obligation committed by an act of the predecessor State 'having a continuing character', Article 9 indicates that 'the international responsibility of the successor State for the breach extends over the entire period during which the act continues and remains not in conformity with the international obligation'. The second paragraph of this provision deals with wrongful acts having a *composite* character, which is defined as 'when a successor State completes a series of actions or omissions initiated by the predecessor State defined in the aggregate as a breach of an international obligation'.[507] In such a case under Article 9(2), 'the international responsibility of the successor State for the breach extends over the entire period starting with the first of the actions or omissions of the series and lasts for as long as these actions or omissions are repeated and remain not in conformity with the international obligation'. In my view, these solutions developed in the different context of succession to State responsibility could serve as useful guidelines to solve issues of succession to State contracts.[508] In fact, as mentioned above,[509] in the *Lighthouse Arbitration* case, the tribunal held that the successor State (Greece) had continued a breach of contract which was initially committed before the date of succession (by the autonomous authorities of Crete) and should, therefore, be responsible for any damages arising from such act.[510]

2. THE EXISTENCE OF A 'TERRITORIAL NEXUS' BETWEEN A CONTRACT AND THE SUCCESSOR STATE

14.11 I have previously mentioned several situations highlighting the importance of the existence of a 'nexus' between the territory of a successor State and the place where a contract was performed. In my view, such a 'territorial nexus' is one of the most important criterion that should be taken into account when

506 IDI, State Succession to Responsibility, Resolution, 2015 (n 14), Art. 9.

507 Ibid.

508 The scope and content of Art. 9 is examined in: Kohen and Dumberry, *State Succession and State Responsibility* (n 165).

509 See, See, Chapter 13, Section 2.4.4.

510 *Lighthouse Arbitration* case (n 162) 92: '[T]he Tribunal can only come to the conclusion that Greece, having adopted the illegal conduct of Crete in its recent past as autonomous State, is bound, as successor State, to take upon its charge the financial consequences of the breach of the concession contract.'

deciding whether a successor State (and in the context of dissolution, which one) should be bound by the obligations arising from a State contract to which the predecessor State was a party. This concept of 'territorial nexus' is mentioned by Schreuer and others in the context of their analysis of whether *consent to the jurisdiction* of the ICSID Centre, which was given by the predecessor State, could pass to the new successor State who becomes a party to the Convention by way of *accession* after the date of succession:

> It is suggested that in this case too the solution must lie in the question of territorial nexus. If the investment is linked to territory that is part of the new State, the presumption is that rights and duties arising from the investment relationship, including the consent to the Centre's jurisdiction, will pass to the successor State.[511]

In my view (as further explained in the next sections), the remarks by these authors about the 'territorial nexus' (i.e., the identification of the actual territory where an investment is made) is of great importance to the present discussion regarding succession to contracts. The first part of this section examines the solutions put forward in the different context of State succession to responsibility and to property (Section 2.1). I believe that the same solutions could be used by analogy to solve issues arising in the context of succession to contracts (Section 2.2). **14.12**

2.1 Overview of the solutions adopted in the context of succession to State responsibility, property and State debts

The question of the importance of the 'territorial nexus' was recently addressed by Rapporteur Kohen in the context of the Resolution adopted by the Institut de Droit international on 'State Succession in Matters of State Responsibility'.[512] As highlighted in his Final Report, the question of where a wrongful act took place is, in general, not 'necessarily decisive'.[513] The report explains the reason for this.[514] What is important (apart from the special case of 'territorial regimes') is not *where* a wrongful act takes place, but rather where the *consequences* of such an act are felt. In other words, what is relevant is the 'existence of a direct link between the consequences of the internationally **14.13**

511 Christoph Schreuer et al. (eds), *The ICSID Convention: A Commentary* 2nd edn, (CUP 2009) 170.
512 IDI, State Succession to Responsibility, Resolution, 2015 (n 14).
513 IDI, State Succession in Matters of State Responsibility, Final Report (n 497) 28.
514 Ibid.:

> Acts committed within or in relation to a given territory can be the result of centrally controlled organs, and not necessarily those of the territorial unit in which those acts were performed. Moreover, internationally wrongful acts can be committed inside or outside the territory of the author or the injured State, and the place where the acts were committed is irrelevant, unless the spatial element forms part of the elements of the primary obligation that has been violated.

wrongful act and the territory or the population that becomes part of the territory or the population of the successor State'.[515] Thus, in his Final Report, Rapporteur Kohen refers to the existence of a 'direct link of the consequences of the wrongful act with the territory or the population concerned' as one *exception* to the 'general non-succession rule in cases in which the predecessor State continues to exist after the date of State succession'.[516]

14.14 In fact, the expression 'direct link' between a wrongful act and a territory is expressly used in a number of provisions of the Resolution dealing with situations where the predecessor State continues to exist after the date of succession.[517] Under these provisions, the *rights* arising from an internationally wrongful act committed by a State *against* the predecessor State pass to the successor State if there exists a 'direct link' between the consequences of this act and the territory or the population of that successor State.

14.15 Let us take the example of a wrongful act committed in the context of a secession. Article 12(2) of the Resolution allows the secessionist State to claim reparation to the State that committed the wrongful act against the predecessor State before secession. This is possible for the secessionist State provided that there exists a 'direct link' between the consequences of this wrongful act and its own territory (or its population). This would be the case, for instance, if the acts committed destroyed property or infrastructures situated in the territory over which the new State is now sovereign. The same should prevail if the act damaged the environment or natural resources in that territory. Under this scenario, while the acts were undoubtedly committed against the predecessor State, it remains that, after the date of succession, the real and lasting consequences of such acts are clearly suffered by the new State (not the continuing State). Put differently, after the date of succession, the 'victim' of such acts is the new State, and not the continuing State. It should consequently be for the new State to claim reparation to the perpetrator of these acts.

14.16 The same logic should also apply to the reverse situation of a wrongful act committed by the predecessor State against another State. Whenever there is a 'direct link' between the consequences of this act and the successor State, the obligations arising from this act should be transferred to that State.

515 Ibid., 29.

516 Ibid., 28.

517 See, IDI, State Succession to Responsibility, Resolution, 2015 (n 14), Art. 11(2) (transfer of territory), Art. 12(2) (separation), Art. 16(2) (Newly Independent States).

In the context of dissolution (Art. 15(2)), the existence of a 'direct link between the consequences of the internationally wrongful act committed against the predecessor State and the territory or the population' of the successor State(s) is also a 'relevant factor' to determine which of the different successor States should possess the right to claim reparation against the perpetrator. The provision reads as follows: **14.17**

1. When a State dissolves and ceases to exist and the parts of its territory form two or more successor States, the rights or obligations arising from an internationally wrongful act in relation to which the predecessor State has been the author or the injured State pass, bearing in mind the duty to negotiate and according to the circumstances referred to in paragraphs 2 and 3 of the present Article, to one, several or all the successor States.
2. In order to determine which of the successor States becomes bearer of the rights described in the preceding paragraph, a relevant factor will in particular be the existence of a direct link between the consequences of the internationally wrongful act committed against the predecessor State and the territory or the population of the successor State or States.
3. In order to determine which of the successor States becomes bearer of the obligations described in paragraph 1, a relevant factor will in particular be, in addition to that mentioned in paragraph 2, the fact that the author of the internationally wrongful act was an organ of the predecessor State that later became an organ of the successor State.[518]

The second paragraph of the provision makes it clear that any successor State has the *right* to claim reparation against the perpetrator when there exists a 'direct link' between the consequences of a wrongful act and the territory or the population of that State. Article 15(3) provides that the existence of any such a 'direct link' is also relevant to determine which of the successor States should be responsible for *obligations* arising from the commission of an internationally wrongful *by* the predecessor State against another State. **14.18**

The 'nexus' between a successor State and its territory is also central to determine other questions of State succession. Thus, the rules contained in the Vienna Convention on Succession of States in Respect of State Property, Archives and Debts regarding succession to State property are based on the fundamental factor of *where* the property is located after the date of succession.[519] Zimmermann provides the following summary of the different solutions adopted under the Convention regarding succession to property: **14.19**

518 IDI, State Succession to Responsibility, Resolution, 2015 (n 14).

519 Vienna Convention on Succession to State Properties, Archives and Debts (n 12).

> [T]he convention is largely based on the distinction between instances of succession relating to Newly Independent States and those relating to other States. Yet, in all different types of State succession immovable property is considered to be automatically transferred to the respective successor State. Besides, in cases of cession of territory, according to the convention, the successor State acquires that movable property which was connected with the activities of the predecessor State in the ceded territory. In the case of a unification of States, the convention provides that the successor State acquires the whole property of both predecessor States. Under the convention, where a State separates or where a complete dismemberment of a State takes place, the successor State, apart from acquiring the immovable property located in its territory, as well as the movable property related to the activities of the predecessor State in said territory, shall also receive an equitable share of the remaining movable property, as well as of the property of the predecessor State located abroad. Art. 15 Vienna Convention on Succession of States in Respect of State Property, Archives and Debts specifically addresses the legal situation of newly independent States, which, under the convention, are supposed not only to receive the whole property of the predecessor State located in the territory of the Newly Independent State, but also a share of the remaining property.[520]

14.20 Thus, the Convention gives to the successor State (in the context of a cession of territory, a dissolution, or a secession) the right to take over the 'movable property' that was connected with the activities of the predecessor State in what is now its territory.[521] The Convention clearly establishes a link between succession to property and the question of where (i.e., in which territory) the activities related to that property were connected. The Institut's Resolution regarding 'State Succession in Matters of Property and Debts' also adopted the same basic principles.[522] In fact, Article 16 is quite suggestively entitled 'Allocation of Property in Accordance with the Principle of Territoriality'. It provides that 'State property that is closely connected to a territory passes with that territory to the successor State'.[523] Similarly, Article 20 deals with 'Movable Property and other State Property' and provides that 'Movable property of the predecessor State connected to the activity of the predecessor State in relation to the territory to which the succession relates, passes to that successor State'.[524] Again, succession under these provisions is dependent on the existence of a territorial nexus between the property and the successor State.

---

520 A. Zimmermann, 'State Succession in Other Matters than Treaties' in: *Max Planck Encyclopedia of Public International Law* (OUP, online edn, 2006) [8].

521 See, for instance, Art. 17(1)(c), Vienna Convention on Succession to State Properties, Archives and Debts (n 12).

522 IDI, State Succession in Matters of Property and Debts, Resolution, 2001 (n 13).

523 Ibid.

524 Ibid.

The existence of a 'nexus' between a successor State and its territory is also central to determine the question of State succession to 'State debts' under the Vienna Convention on Succession of States in Respect of State Property, Archives and Debts.[525] The term 'State debts' is defined at Article 33 as including 'any financial obligation of a predecessor State arising in conformity with international law towards another State, an international organization or any other subject of international law'.[526] Scholars have recognized the existence of different categories of debts.[527] A distinction is made between a so-called 'localized debt', which was contracted by the central government, but used specifically by the State in a clearly defined portion of a territory'[528] and a 'local debt', which is contracted not by the central government, but by a local government. According to Menon, to be qualified as a 'localized debt', a debt must fulfill the following three criteria: (1) 'the State must have intended the corresponding expenditures to be effected for the territory concerned'; (2) 'the State must actually have used the proceeds of the loan in the territory concerned'; and (3) 'the expenditure must have been effected for the benefit and in the actual interest of the territory in question'.[529] Both 'local' and 'localized' debts are intrinsically linked to a specific territory. This aspect has an important impact on the allocation of responsibility for the debts between the different States concerned. **14.21**

In the context of a transfer of territory, Article 37 of the Convention provides for the general solution whereby 'the State debt of the predecessor State shall pass to the successor State in an equitable proportion, taking into account, in particular, the property, rights and interests which pass to the successor State in relation to that State debt'.[530] The Convention provides for the same solution regarding secession (Art. 40) and dissolution (Art. 41). Yet, a specific solution should prevail for those debts which are closely connected with the territory transferred. Thus, for O'Connell, 'local debts follow the political fortunes of the territory with which they are concerned'.[531] Thus, if the local government (responsible for that debt) was located in the territory which has been transferred to another State, the successor should be held responsible for such debts after the date of succession. Similarly, since 'a localized debt is contracted by the central government but intended particularly to benefit a **14.22**

525 Vienna Convention on Succession to State Properties, Archives and Debts (n 12).

526 Ibid.

527 See: P.K. Menon, 'The Succession of States and the Problem of State Debts', (1986) 6 BC *Third World L J* 111.

528 ILC, 'Ninth Report on Succession of States in Respect of Matters Other Than Treaties', A/CN.4/301l1981/Add.l of 13, in (1981) 2 *Yearbook ILC* UN Doc. [29].

529 Menon (n 527) 114, referring to: ILC, ibid., [22].

530 Vienna Convention on Succession to State Properties, Archives and Debts (n 12).

531 O'Connell, *The Law of State Succession*, 1956 (n 38) 182, citing many examples of State practice, at 174–82.

specified locality', it follows that 'if that locality is transferred to the successor state, it is generally agreed that the successor state shall be responsible for local debts'.[532] In my view, the same principle should also apply in the context of secession and dissolution. In the context of unification and integration of States, the entire territory of the predecessor State is now considered to be that of the successor State. In this context, Article 39 provides that all State debt of the predecessor States will pass to the successor State.[533] One exception would be Newly Independent States, where Article 38 established a general rule of non-succession to debts (with the possibility of an agreement between the States concerned).[534]

14.23 In sum, the existence of a territorial nexus between a localized debt and the successor State is an important factor to be considered under the 1983 Vienna Convention.

14.24 The following section examines the extent to which these findings can apply to solve issues of succession to State contracts.

2.2 Concrete application of these solutions to the issue of succession to State contracts

14.25 In my view, the existence of a 'territorial nexus' is important in the context of succession to contracts. Thus, it matters *where* an investment was made under a contract and where the contract was performed. This is because the contract in question has a direct impact on a specific territory. It is the territory where the investment was made which will benefit (or suffer) from the implementation and the performance of the contract. To put it simply, this is the place where the contract will create jobs and will have an impact on the local economy and the population. Thus, as noted by O'Connell (in the context of 'administrative' contracts) 'the more locally identified is the contract the greater is the presumption that it has benefited the absorbed territory'.[535] In fact, authors in the past have argued that a successor State should only be bound by concession contracts that have had a 'positive' impact on its

532 Menon (n 527)126.

533 Vienna Convention on Succession to State Properties, Archives and Debts (n 12). See also: Menon (n 527) 136ff.

534 Vienna Convention, ibid. See, Menon (n 527) 129ff.

535 O'Connell, *State Succession*, 1967 (n 15) 367.

territory.[536] As further examined below,[537] the question of the territorial nexus is closely related to the principle of unjust enrichment.

It is interesting to note (as mentioned before) that the existence of a 'territorial nexus' is at the centre of the analysis of the US Restatement of the Law on the question of succession to State contracts.[538] Paragraph 209(2) deals with both 'State Property and Contracts' and mentions that 'subject to agreement between predecessor and successor States, (…) rights and obligations under its contracts, remain with the predecessor State'. Yet, paragraph 209(2)(a) provides an exception to the rule of non-succession whereby in cases of cession of territory, 'the rights and obligations of the predecessor State under contracts relating to that territory, are transferred to the successor State'. In such a case, the successor State is bound by all rights and obligations because the contract is 'related' to the territory ceded over which it is now sovereign. In fact, as mentioned above,[539] this solution of succession corresponds to State practice in the context of a cession of territory. Paragraph 209(2)(c) of the Restatement also provides for the same solution in the context of a secession. Thus, normally, rights and obligations under contracts signed by the predecessor State (which continue to exist after the secession) 'remain with' that State. Yet, one specific exception is mentioned whereby 'rights and obligations of the predecessor State under contracts relating to the territory of the new State, pass to the new State'.[540] Again, what is of importance is the fact that the contract, which was signed by the predecessor State, is 'related' to the territory over which the new secessionist State is now sovereign. The Restatement also provides for the same rule of succession in the context of incorporation.[541] Rather strangely, the Restatement does not provide the same rule in the context of a dissolution. Yet, there is no reason it should not also apply in that situation. Thus, the rights and obligations under a contract (signed by the 14.26

536 See the comment by Kaeckenbeeck (n 55) 348–9, referring to Francis B. Sayre, 'Change of Sovereignty and Concessions', (1918) AJIL 705. For a different theory based on the benefit of contracts to the *population* of a State, see: Alfred R. Cowger Jr., 'Rights and Obligations of Successor States: An Alternative Theory', (1985) 17 *Case West Res J Int L* 301:

> Under this theory, the population that is transferred to the successor nation is the focus of the succession analysis, and the determination of which rights and obligations are to be succeeded turns on which of these rights and obligations are based on some benefit to the populace. Simply put, any rights which benefit the transferred citizenry and any obligations which are the result of or the precursor to benefits acquired for the citizenry are succeeded to by the successor nation.

He argues that this theory apply to 'the undertaking of the preexisting contractual and legal obligations of the state to its people which resulted in a benefit to its people' (at 312).

537 See, Chapter 14, Section 4.

538 Restatement of the Law (n 211) [209(2)].

539 See, Chapter 13, Section 2.

540 Restatement of the Law (n 211).

541 Ibid., [209(2)(b)]: 'where a State is absorbed by another State, (…) rights and obligations under contracts of the absorbed State, pass to the absorbing State.'

predecessor State) which are specifically 'related' to the territory of one of the successor States should pass to *that* State. One situation where the territorial nexus may not find application is regarding Newly Independent States. Thus, while a contract may have been performed in the territory of that State, it should not necessarily follow that it has benefited in any way from it. In fact, colonization has provided many illustrations where such contracts have had (to say the least) a negative impact on the territory of these new States. Succession should not find application whenever this is the case.

14.27 In sum, the existence of a 'nexus' between a contract and the territory of the successor State is an important criterion that should be taken into account when deciding whether that State should be bound by the rights and obligations arising from a State contract that was signed by the predecessor State. The following section examines another relevant criterion.

3. CONTRACTS SIGNED BY AN ORGAN OF A TERRITORIAL UNIT OF THE PREDECESSOR STATE WHICH HAS A STRUCTURAL CONTINUITY WITH THE SUCCESSOR STATE

14.28 Another important criterion that should be taken into account when determining which State(s) should be held responsible for the rights and obligations arising from a State contract is the question of who actually signed the contract (and who eventually breached it) *before* the date of succession.

14.29 The first part of this section examines the solution adopted in the different context of State succession to State responsibility (Section 3.1). I believe that the same solution could be used by analogy to solve issues of succession to contracts (Section 3.2).

3.1 The solution adopted in the context of succession to State responsibility

14.30 In his Final Report on State succession to international responsibility, Rapporteur Kohen refers to one 'possible' exception to the non-succession rule: whenever the wrongful act was committed before the date of succession by the composing entity of the predecessor State (for example, a federated entity or an autonomous government) which later becomes an independent State (or part of another State in the context of a transfer of territory).[542] In these

542 IDI, State Succession in Matters of State Responsibility, Final Report (n 497) 30.

specific circumstances, that successor State could assume the *obligations* arising from that act. This type of 'special connection' between one successor State and a wrongful act is expressly mentioned in Article 11(3) (transfer of territory) and Article 12(3) (separation).[543] Under these provisions, the obligations arising from an internationally wrongful act committed by the predecessor State pass to the successor State 'when the author of that act was an organ of a territorial unit of the predecessor State that has later become an organ of the successor State'.[544] In the context of a dissolution, the fact that the author of the internationally wrongful act was an organ of the predecessor State that later became an organ of the successor State is also a 'relevant factor' to determine which State is the bearer of the obligation to repair.[545]

It should be recalled at this juncture that under international law, the acts of a federated entity or any other political subdivisions are regarded as those of the State. This is clear from the reading of Article 4 of the ILC Articles on Responsibility of States for Internationally Wrongful Acts.[546] A State would therefore have to compensate another State for the acts committed by any of its political subdivisions, including a breach of contract. This is the prevailing situation *before* this political entity becomes an independent State. The question is what should happen after the date of succession. **14.31**

In the context of succession to State responsibility, the present writer has argued that the principle established in Article 10(2) of the ILC Draft Articles for acts committed by *insurrectional movements* in their armed struggle for independence may be used, by analogy, more generally in other situations involving State succession.[547] Thus, the reason for a new State to be held responsible for the acts committed by an insurrectional movement is because of the *structural continuity* between the new State and the actual wrongdoer.[548] This is clear from the ILC Commentary on that provision.[549] Thus, according **14.32**

---

543 IDI, State Succession to Responsibility, Resolution, 2015 (n 14).

544 Ibid., Art. 16(3) provides for the same general principle in the context of Newly Independent States but refers specifically to the 'conduct' of a national liberation movement which succeeds in establishing the new State.

545 Ibid., Art. 15(3).

546 ILC Draft Articles on State Responsibility (n 100), Art. 4: 'The conduct of any State organ acting in that capacity shall be considered an act of that State under international law ... whatever its character as an organ of the central government or of a territorial unit of the State.'

547 Dumberry, *State Succession to International Responsibility* (n 165) 259ff.

548 Ibid., 224ff.

549 ILC, Report of the International Law Commission on the Work of its 27th Session, 5 May to 25 July 1975, Draft Articles on State Responsibility, UN Doc. A/10010/Rev.1, in: (1975) II *Yearbook ILC* 101 [6]:

> The attribution to the new state of the acts of the organs of the insurrectional movement which preceded it, and of such acts only, is then justified by virtue of the continuity between the organisation of the insurrectional movement and the organisation of the state to which it has given rise. From being only an

to the ILC, it is the 'structural' continuity between the organization of the insurrectional movement and the organization of the new State, which explains why the responsibility should be transferred to the latter for the acts committed by the former.[550] Thus, 'the same entity which previously had the characteristics of an insurrectional or other movement has become the government of the State it was struggling to establish'.[551] This is indeed the position supported by many writers,[552] including myself.[553] The Resolution adopted by the Institut also includes a provision (Article 12(6)) to the same effect as Article 10(2) of the ILC Articles.[554]

14.33 I have argued elsewhere that the same solution should apply to other cases (not involving any insurrectional movement) where there is also a structural continuity between a new State and an autonomous political entity that committed an internationally wrongful act before independence.[555] The new successor State should thus be held responsible for obligations arising from internationally wrongful acts committed before its independence by an autonomous government (or by any other political entity clearly identifiable) with which the new State has an *organic and structural continuity*. The present author has found two cases that have endorsed this principle, including the *Lighthouse Arbitration* case (mentioned above[556]).[557] One recent case supporting this proposition is the case of *Bijelic v. Montenegro* decided by the European Court of Human Rights.[558]

> embryo State, the insurrectional movement has become a State proper, without any break in the continuity between the two. It is in fact the same entity which previously had the characteristics of an insurrectional movement and which now has those of a State proper.

Very similar wording is used in: ILC Commentaries on Draft Articles on State Responsibility (n 112) 114 [6]. See also in: ILC, 'Fourth Report on State Responsibility of the Special Rapporteur', Mr. Roberto Ago, 24th session of the ILC, 1972, UN Doc. A/CN.4/264 and Add.1, ILC Report, A/8710/Rev.1 (A/27/10), 1972, chp. IV(B) [72]–[73] in: (1972) II *Yearbook ILC* 71, at 131 [159], [194].

550 ILC, 'Report of the International Law Commission on the work of its 53d session', Official Records of the General Assembly, 56th session, Supplement No. 10, UN doc. A/56/10, ch. IV.E.2, 2001, 114 [6].

551 Ibid.

552 Crawford, *State Responsibility* (n 502) 178–9; G. Cahin, 'Attribution of Conduct to a State: Insurrectional Movements', in: J. Crawford, A. Pellet and S. Olleson (eds) *The Law of International Responsibility* (CUP 2010) 249.

553 P. Dumberry, 'New State Responsibility for Internationally Wrongful Acts by an Insurrectional Movement', (2006) 17(3) EJIL 611ff.

554 IDI, State Succession to Responsibility, Resolution, 2015 (n 14).

555 Dumberry, *State Succession to International Responsibility* (n 165) 259ff.

556 See, Chapter 13, Section 2.4.4.

557 Dumberry, *State Succession to International Responsibility* (n 165) 136, 141, 196–200, 261, referring to *Lighthouse Arbitration* case (n 162) 81; *Samos (Liability for Torts) Case*, Greece, Court of the Aegean Islands, 1924, no. 27, in: 35 Thémis 294; (1923–1924) *Annual Digest* 70.

558 *Bijelic v. Montenegro and Serbia*, ECtHR, Application no. 11890/05, Judgment, 18 April 2009. The case is examined in: B.E. Brockman-Hawe, 'Succession, the Obligation to Repair and Human Rights; The European Court of Human Rights Judgment in the Case of Bijelic c/Montenegro and Serbia', (2010) 59 ICLQ 845–67. See also: Marcel Szabó, 'State Succession and the Jurisprudence of the European Court of

The next section examines the extent to which these findings can apply to the different issue of succession to contracts. **14.34**

3.2 Concrete application of this solution to the issue of succession to State contracts

In my view, the solution developed by the Institut (and by myself in previous writings[559]) in the context of succession to State responsibility should apply (with necessary adaptation[560]) to the problem of succession to State contracts. Thus, it is necessarily important whether a contract was signed by an organ of a territorial unit of the predecessor State that later became an organ of the successor State. The successor State should indeed be bound by the rights and obligations arising from a State contract which was signed before the date of succession by an organ of a territorial unit of the predecessor State with which the new State has an *organic and structural continuity*. **14.35**

Let us take a simple example of a State contract signed by the government of the Province of Quebec in relation to an investment performed on its territory before its (hypothetical) independence. After the secession of Quebec, the question becomes who should be responsible for the rights and obligations arising from that contract: the new State or the continuator State (Canada). Aside from the important aspect of the existence of any 'nexus' between that contract and the territory of Quebec (a point already examined above[561]), it would seem logical that the new State of Quebec should continue its responsibility for a contract that was signed by the government of Quebec before the date of succession. This is indeed a situation where, to paraphrase the Institut's Resolution, 'the author of [an] act' (here, signing a contract) 'was an organ of a territorial unit of the predecessor State that has later become an organ of the successor State'.[562] Such a situation calls for the application of the rule of succession. The same solution should also find application in the context of a dissolution. The hypothetical situation in relation to a contract signed by the Province of Quebec in the context of secession should certainly apply in the event of a dissolution. In other words, the same logic should apply independently of whether Canada continues to exist after secession or whether **14.36**

Human Rights', in Christina Binder and Konrad Lachmayer (eds) *The European Court of Human Rights and Public International Law Fragmentation or Unity?* (Nomos 2014) 143; P. Dumberry, 'La succession d'États en matière de responsabilité internationale et ses liens avec la responsabilité des États en matière de traités', in Distefano, Gaggioli and Hêche (n 85), 1581–608.

559 Dumberry, *State Succession to International Responsibility* (n 165) 259ff.

560 Thus, in the context of State contracts, it is hard to see how an organ of a territorial unit can (before the date of succession) breach a contract to which it is not a party.

561 See, Chapter 14, Section 2.

562 IDI, State Succession to Responsibility, Resolution, 2015 (n 14), Art. 12(3).

it completely disintegrates (and is replaced by many new States). In both situations, the contract was signed by an organ of a territorial unit of Canada that has later become an organ of the successor State. Both situations call for the new State to be bound by such contracts. Logically, that State should be held accountable for any breach of contract committed by the organ of an entity which later becomes independent.

14.37 One recent case where the issue arose is that of *Active Partners Group v. South Sudan*.[563] The case involved a claim by a company registered in the Republic of Sudan against the Republic of *South* Sudan. The award explains as follows the instrument at the heart of the arbitration proceedings:

> A dispute has arisen between the Parties concerning alleged breaches by the Respondent of the Financial Agreement between the Claimant and the Ministry of Finance and Economic Planning on behalf of the Respondent dated November 18, 2008 (the 'Finance Agreement') and under the Contract for Construction of Electric Power Infrastructure between the Claimant and the South Sudan Electricity Corporation on behalf of the Respondent dated October 5, 2008 (the 'Technical Contract' and together with the Finance Agreement, the 'Contract').[564]

14.38 Later in the award, the tribunal indicates that both contracts were signed by the 'Government of South Sudan'.[565] The award also explains the background of the case: 'In 2007, the autonomous government of South Sudan invited interested qualified parties to participate in a tendering process for the construction of electric power infrastructure (…)'.[566] Importantly, in 2007, South Sudan was not an independent State. It became an independent State four years later after a referendum and was admitted to the United Nations on 9 July 2011.[567] Thus, at the time when the tender process was launched and the contract was eventually signed, South Sudan was, as explained by the tribunal, an 'autonomous government'.[568] The independence of South Sudan is considered to be an example of secession.[569]

14.39 It should be recalled that in 2005 the 'Government of the Republic of the Sudan' and 'The Sudan People's Liberation Movement/Sudan People's Liberation Army' signed a Comprehensive Peace Agreement ('CPA'). The CPA

563 *Active Partners Group Ltd. v. Republic of South Sudan*, PCA Case no 2013/4, Award, 27 January 2016.
564 Ibid., [5].
565 Ibid., [122]–[123].
566 Ibid., [114].
567 GA Res. 65/308, 9 July 2011.
568 *Active Partners* (n 563) [114].
569 For an analysis of the reasons why it should be considered as an example of secession, see: J. Moussa, 'L'indépendance du Soudan du Sud et la Convention de Vienne sur la succession d'États en matière de traités', in Distefano, Gaggioli and Hêche (n 85) 1933–5.

consists of a series of six agreements, among which is the Power Sharing Agreement ('PSA'),[570] indicating that in accordance with the Machakos Protocol,[571] during the 'Interim Period'[572] the 'Southern Sudan level of Government' (i.e., the autonomous government of South Sudan before its independence) 'shall exercise authority in respect of the people and States in the South'.[573] While signing treaties remained, in general, under the exclusive authority of the central government (Sudan),[574] the 'Government of Southern Sudan' nevertheless had the authority during that 'Interim Period' to sign investment agreements with other States,[575] and the power to enter into contracts with foreign companies for the construction of an electric power infrastructure (such as in the instant case).[576] Thus, the *Active Partners Group* award is a good illustration of an agreement before independence whereby an autonomous government would have the power to sign contracts with foreign companies. Naturally, once the autonomous government becomes an independent State, these contracts are considered to be binding on that entity. In fact, this point was probably considered so 'obvious' by the tribunal that the award contains no explanation whatsoever on these questions.

Finally, a few words should be said about the consequences arising from the fact that an autonomous government played an important role in the *negotiation* of a contract that was signed by the predecessor State. In my view, this aspect should be taken into account by a tribunal when determining whether a State contract is binding on a new State. This question was in fact mentioned by the ICJ in the *Gabcikovo-Nagymaros Project* case (in the different context of succession to a bilateral treaty). In this case, Slovakia argued that 'while still a constituent part of Czechoslovakia, it played a role in the development of the Project, as it did later, in the most critical phase of negotiations with Hungary **14.40**

570 PSA, Chapter II of the CPA, signed in May 2004.

571 Machakos Protocol, signed on 20 July 2002, Chapter I of the CPA.

572 That is, from 9 January 2005 to 9 January 2011.

573 PSA, Art. 1.3.2.

574 The 'signing of International Treaties on behalf of the Republic of Sudan' is listed as one of the 'exclusive legislative powers of the National Legislature', i.e., the central Sudan Government (PSA, Art. 2.2.9, Schedule A, Point 25).

575 Thus, both the 'National Government' and the 'Government of Southern Sudan' had 'Concurrent Powers' and had 'legislative and executive competencies' with respect to inter alia 'the initiation, negotiation and conclusion of International and Regional Agreements on, inter alia, investment'. See, Art. 3.3 (the 'powers of the Government of Southern Sudan shall be as set forth in Schedules B and D (…)', Schedule D, Point 19.

576 Thus, other such 'Concurrent Powers' included 'Economic and Social Development in Southern Sudan', 'Trade, commerce, industry and industrial development', 'Electricity generation and water and waste management', etc. It should be added that the 'Government of Southern Sudan' did not have exclusive authority regarding signing oil contracts. Thus, the National Petroleum Commission (consisting of representative of both the National Government and Government of Southern Sudan) had power to 'Negotiate and approve all oil contracts for the exploration and development of oil in the Sudan, and ensure they are consistent with the NPC's principles, policies and guidelines'. See, PSA, Arts 3.3. and 3.4.4.

about the fate of the Project'.[577] While the court decided that it was 'not necessary, in the light of the conclusions [it had] reached (...) to determine whether there are legal consequences to be drawn from the prominent part thus played by the Slovak Republic', it nevertheless added that 'its role does, however, deserve mention'.[578]

4. THE NEED TO AVOID UNJUST ENRICHMENT

14.41 Another relevant circumstance, which has been previously mentioned, is the need to avoid situations of unjust enrichment that could result from the application of the principle of non-succession to State contracts. This section will first define the concept and its status under international law (Sections 4.1 and 4.2). I will then briefly examine how the concept has been used in the past to solve issues of State succession (Section 4.3) and how it could be useful specifically regarding matters of State contracts (Section 4.4).

4.1 The concept of unjust enrichment

14.42 The concept of unjust enrichment (*enrichissement sans cause*) is intrinsically ambiguous and imprecise.[579] By its very nature, one needs to 'take into account all the circumstances of each specific situation' to determine whether unjust enrichment has occurred.[580] The obligation to compensate for any unjust enrichment does not arise directly from the commission of an act but derives from a *state of fact*, which may be caused by a legal or an illegal act.[581] The concept has thus often been used in instances involving the infringement of property rights of foreigners in cases where the acts *did not* amount to an internationally wrongful act.[582] As one writer puts it, 'the basis of liability for

577 *Case Concerning the Gabčíkovo-Nagymaros Project* (*Hungary v. Slovakia*), Judgment, 25 September 1997, ICJ Reports 1997 [124].

578 Ibid.

579 O'Connell, *The Law of State Succession*, 1956 (n 38) 274.

580 This is specifically mentioned in the case of *Sea-Land Service, Inc. v. Iran, et al.*, Iran-US Claims Tribunal, Award No. 115–33–1, 22 June 1984, in: 6 Iran-US CTR 168–169. See also: E. Jiménez de Aréchaga, 'International Law in the Past Third of a Century', (1978-I) 159 Rec. des Cours 299–300.

581 G.C. Rodriguez Iglesias, 'El enriquecimiento sin causa como fundamento de responsabilidad internacional' (1982) 34 REDI 389.

582 Christoph H. Schreuer, 'Unjustified Enrichment', in R. Bernhardt (ed), *Encyclopedia of Public International Law*, vol 9 (North Holland 1986) 382. This was explained as follows by the Iran-US Claims Tribunal in *Sea-Land Service* (n 580) 169:

> [The concept of unjust enrichment] involves a duty to compensate, which is entirely reconcilable with the absence of any inherent unlawfulness of the acts in question. Thus the principle finds an obvious field of application in cases where a foreign investor has sustained a loss whereby another party has been

unjust enrichment is not necessarily linked with any delictual responsibility as such but is predicated on an injustice which must be remediated'.[583]

In order for a State's action to qualify as an unjust enrichment, not only does the consequence of such an act need (i) to result in its enrichment, but also such enrichment needs (ii) to be 'unjust' and, finally, (iii) to be detrimental to another party.[584] These three conditions will be briefly examined in the following paragraphs. **14.43**

The first fundamental requirement is that a situation of enrichment has occurred.[585] The Iran-US Claims Tribunal determined that 'where there is no "beneficial gain" to the party allegedly enriched, the remedy of unjust enrichment is not available'.[586] The notion of a 'beneficial gain' has been the object of controversy in the context of the Iran-US Claims Tribunal. Certain decisions came to the conclusion that the State needs to make *actual use* of the property for an unjust enrichment to arise.[587] On the contrary, it has been argued by one judge in his dissenting opinion that such a benefit 'occurs when goods are available for use by a State, regardless of whether the claimant can show particular instance of such use'.[588] In the context of expropriation, some tribunals have required that the expropriating State *make actual use* of the property.[589] However, the expropriated property does not necessarily need to **14.44**

---

enriched, but which does not arise out of an internationally unlawful act which would found a claim for damages.

583 Charles M. Fombad, 'The Principle of Unjustified Enrichment in International Law', (1997) 30 *Comp & Int'l L J S Afr* 124.

584 These different requirements were identified by the Iran-US Claims Tribunal in *Sea-Land Service* (n 580) 168–9:

> There are several instances of recourse to the principle of unjust enrichment before international tribunals. There must have been an enrichment of one party to the detriment of the other, and both must arise as a consequence of the same act or event. There must be no justification for the enrichment, and no contractual or other remedy available to the injured party whereby he might seek compensation from the party enriched.

585 Fombad (n 583) 123.

586 *Flexi-Van Leasing, Inc. v. Iran*, Iran-US Claims Tribunal, Award no. 259–36–1, 13 October 1986, in: 12 Iran-US CTR 353.

587 *Sea-Land Service* (n 580) 171–2; *Flexi-Van Leasing*, ibid., 353–5.

588 *Flexi-Van Leasing*, ibid., Dissenting Opinion of Judge Holtzmann, 363. See also, the separate opinion of Judge Holtzmann, *Sea-Land Service* (n 580) 213–16.

589 In the case of *Thomas C. Baker Arbitration*, in: J.B. Moore, *History and Digest of the International Arbitrations to which the United States has been a Party*, vol IV (GPO 1898) 3668, compensation was awarded as a result of the use by the Mexican army of materials belonging to an American national. In the case of *Sucrerie de Roustchouk v. État Hongrois*, Belgian-Hungarian Mixed Arbitral Tribunal, Award, 29 October 1925, in: 5 *Recueil des décisions des tribunaux arbitraux mixtes* 772, at 776, it was the refloating by the Hungarian military authorities of one barge belonging to a Belgian company that the army had previously sunk which led to compensation.

result in any *financial* benefits for that State; an *advantage* or a *benefit* is sufficient.[590]

14.45 The second requirement is that the enrichment be 'unjust'. The concept is 'used in its broadest sense to cover all instances of illegitimate, unconscionable, inequitable and unfair acquisition of wealth'.[591] The Iran-US Claims Tribunal also vaguely defines the notion by stating that 'there must be no justification for the enrichment'.[592] International practice has considered specific situations to be 'unjust', for instance, the fact that one company had not paid the balance due to another company for the work performed under a contract,[593] the use of materials belonging to a foreign national by the army of a State,[594] and the use of property by the host State for which no compensation had been given to the foreign national.[595]

14.46 The third requirement is that the enrichment is not only 'unjust', but also to 'the detriment of the other'.[596] In other words, the enrichment needs to be 'directly linked with and result in an impoverishment on the other side'.[597] One international arbitral decision speaks of the condition of simultaneity of the enrichment and the detriment.[598] Another decision by the Iran-US Claims Tribunal mentions that both the enrichment of one party and the detriment of another party must 'arise as a consequence of the same act or event'.[599]

14.47 Finally, the Iran-US Claims Tribunal stated that 'the damage for unjust enrichment should be measured in terms of the extent to which that State has been enriched'.[600] Thus, what is sought as a remedy to unjust enrichment is the 'achievement of an acceptable economic equilibrium' between the two parties.[601] Such a goal is reached by the reestablishment of the previous

---

590 *Contra*: Fombad (n 583) 123, for whom the increase of wealth is necessary.

591 Ibid.

592 *Sea-Land Service* (n 580) 168–9.

593 *Schlegel Corp. v. National Iranian Copper Industries Co.*, Iran-US Claims Tribunal, Award No. 295–834–2, 27 March 1987, in: 14 Iran-US CTR 176, 181–3; *Burroughs Wellcome & Co. v. Chemische Fabrik auf Actien*, Great-Britain-Germany Mixed Arbitral Tribunal, Award, 19 January 1926, in: 6 *Recueil des décisions des tribunaux arbitraux mixtes*, 13.

594 *Thomas C. Baker* (n 589) 3668; *Sucrerie de Roustchouk* (n 589) 772.

595 *William A. Parker (United States) v. Mexico*, US-Mexico General Claims Commission, Award, 31 March 1926, in: 4 UNRIAA 35.

596 *Flexi-Van Leasing* (n 586) 353.

597 Fombad (n 583) 123.

598 *Dickson Car Wheel Co. (United States) v. Mexico*, US-Mexico General Claims Commission, Award, July 1931, in: 4 UNRIAA 676.

599 *Sea-Land Service* (n 580) 168–9.

600 *Flexi-Van Leasing* (n 586) 353–5.

601 Schreuer, 'Unjustified Enrichment' (n 582) 381.

economic position of the enriched party.[602] Thus, the 'acceptable economic equilibrium' is sought not by simply compensating the victim of the internationally wrongful acts, but by first 'depriving the enriched party of its unjustly gained benefits, which are then awarded to the other party'.[603] The amount of compensation 'will not exceed the amount by which the defendant's wealth has been increased or that by which the claimant has been impoverished'.[604]

4.2 Unjust enrichment is a general principle of law

The principle of unjust enrichment is frequently used in domestic law.[605] It is recognized as a 'principle of law' under both Civil Law[606] and Common Law.[607] According to the Iran-US Claims Tribunal, the concept 'is codified or judicially recognized in the great majority of the municipal legal systems of the world, and is widely accepted as having been assimilated into the catalogue of general principles of law available to be applied by international tribunals'.[608] **14.48**

One of the first international tribunals to refer to the concept was in the *Lena Goldfields* case.[609] This case has been described by one writer as 'the fountainhead of all unjust enrichment claims in investment disputes'.[610] The US-Mexico General Claims Commission in the 1931 *Dickson Car Wheel Co.* case stated that the concept had 'encountered serious difficulties in its practical application in municipal law' and that it had 'not yet been transplanted to the field of international law'.[611] However, this statement is not representative of contemporary international law since international tribunals have often used the principle of unjust enrichment in many different areas of international **14.49**

602 Christoph H. Schreuer, 'Unjustified Enrichment in International Law', (1974) 22 *Am J Comp L* 300.

603 Schreuer, 'Unjustified Enrichment' (n 582) 381.

604 Fombad (n 583) 125.

605 For a municipal law comparative perspective on the concept, see: Paolo Gallo, 'Unjust Enrichment: A Comparative Analysis' (1992) 40 *Am J Comp L* 431ff; John A. Dawson, *Unjust Enrichment: A Comparative Analysis* (Brown & Company 1951); David Johnston and Reinhard Zimmermann (eds), *Unjustified Enrichment: Key Issues in Comparative Perspective* (CUP 2002).

606 See, inter alia: E. Clive, 'Unjustified Enrichment', in: A. Hartkamp, M. Hesslink, E. Hodius, C. Joustra, E. Du Perron and M. Veldmann (eds), *Towards a European Civil Code*, 3rd edn (Nijmegen, Aspen 2004) 585; Reinhard Zimmermann, 'Unjust Enrichment: The Modern Civilian Approach', (1995) 15 *Oxford J Legal Stud* 403ff.

607 D.P. O'Connell, 'Unjustified Enrichment', (1956) 5(1) *Am J Comp L* 3.

608 *Sea-Land Service* (n 580) 168–9.

609 *Lena Goldfields Ltd. v. USSR*, Award of 1930, in: *The Times*, 3 September 1930, 7. See also: A. Nussbaum, 'The Arbitration the Lena Goldfields Ltd. and the Soviet Government' (1950) 36 *Cornell LQ* 31.

610 Ana Vohryzek, 'Unjust Enrichment Unjustly Ignored: Opportunities and Pitfalls in Bringing Unjust Enrichment Claims under ICSID', (2009) 31 *Loy LA Int'l & Comp L Rev* 520.

611 *Dickson Car Wheel* (n 598) 676.

law.[612] For instance, the concept was used to settle outstanding business transactions in the context of World War I arising from contracts between business partners who had subsequently become enemy nationals and had seen their contracts invalidated pursuant to the Versailles Treaty.[613] The concept has also been frequently used in awards of the Iran-US Claims Tribunal, who described it as a 'general principle of law'[614] and 'an important element of State responsibility'.[615] In his dissenting opinion in the *Ambatielos Claim* case, Judge Spiropoulos stated that it 'forms part of the general principles of law applicable in international relations'.[616]

14.50 Many scholars recognize the concept of unjust enrichment as a 'general principle of law' (in the sense of Art. 38 of the Statute of the ICJ).[617] O'Connell is one of the most fervent supporters of the concept (specifically in

612 See, for instance: *Thomas C. Baker* (n 589); *Sucrerie de Rustchuk* (n 589) 92; *Sudden & Christenson, Inc. v. US* (1940) 34 *AJIL* 737; *Spanish Zone Morocco* Case (*Great Britain v. Spain*), 2 UNRIAA 616; Parker (n 595) 36–41; Landreau Arbitration (*US v. Peru*), (1948) 1 UNRIAA 347, 347–67. A review of international judicial decisions is found in: Schreuer, 'Unjustified Enrichment', 1974 (n 602) 281–301; Rodriguez Iglesias (n 581) 120–30.

613 See Arts 296, 299 and 304 of the Versailles Treaty, Paris, signed on 28 June 1919, entered into force on 10 January 1920, in: *The Treaties of Peace 1919–1923* (Carnegie Endowment for International Peace 1924); (1919) UKTS No. 8 (Cmd. 223). See: *Arnold & Foster Ltd. v. J.W. Erkens*, U.K.-Germany Mixed Arbitral Tribunal, 13 and 20 October 1926, in: 6 *Recueil des décisions des tribunaux arbitraux mixtes*, 606. The concept was also used in situations where transfer of assets took place under putative agreement which later turned out to be invalidly concluded due to lack of authority of State-agents: *Parker* (n 595) 35.

614 *Sea-Land Service* (n 580) 168–9; *Schlegel Corp* (n 593) 181–3.

615 *Benjamin R. Isaiah v. Bank Mellat*, Iran-US Claims Tribunal, Award No. 35–219–2, 30 March 1983, in: 2 Iran-US CTR 232, 236–7. For an analysis of the use of this concept by the Iran-US Claims Tribunal, see: G.H. Aldrich, *The Jurisprudence of the Iran-United States Claims Tribunal* (Clarendon 1996) 396–411.

616 *Ambatielos Claim* (*Greece v. United Kingdom*), Award, 6 March 1956, in: 12 UNRIAA 83, 129, Judge J. Spiropoulos.

617 Elio Fanara, *Gestione di affari e arricchimento senza causa nel diritto internazionale* (Giuffrè 1966) 241; Wolfgang Friedmann, *The Changing Structure of International Law* (Columbia UP 1964) 206; Detlev Chr. Dicke, 'Unjustified Enrichment and Compensation', in: Detlev Chr. Dicke (ed), *Foreign Investment in the Present and a New International Economic Order*, (Fribourg UP 1987) 273; Wilfred Jenks, *The Prospects of International Adjudication* (Oceana Publ. 1964) 417; André Goncalves Pereira, *La succession d'États en matière de traités* (Pedone 1969) 190; O'Connell, 'Unjustified Enrichment' (n 607) 34; Nussbaum (n 609) 41; O'Connell, *The Law of State Succession*, 1956 (n 38) 273; Manlio Udina, 'La succession des États quant aux obligations internationales autres que les dettes publiques', (1933-II) 44 Rec des Cours 769–70; Schwarzenberger (n 319) 579; Jiménez de Aréchaga (n 580) 299–300; Paul Guggenheim, *Traité de Droit international public*, t. I, (Librairie de l'Université 1953) 155; Volkovitsch (n 343) 2210–11; Fombad (n 583) 123, 129; Hanoch Dagan, *Unjust Enrichment: A Study of Private Law and Public Values* (CUP 1997) 155; Louis B. Sohn, 'The Iran-United States Claims Tribunal: Jurisprudential Contributions to the Development of International Law', in R.B. Lillich (ed), *Iran-United States Claims Tribunal* (Seven Sokol Colloquium 1984) 102; John R. Crook, 'Applicable Law in International Arbitration: The Iran-US Claims Tribunal Experience, (1989) 83(2) AJIL fn 70; Christina Binder and Christoph Schreuer, 'Unjust Enrichment' in *Max Planck Encyclopedia of Public International Law* (OUP, online edn, 2006) [10]; Aldrich (n 615) 398; Werner Lorenz, 'General Principles of Law: Their Elaboration in the Court of Justice of the European Communities', (1964) 13(1) *Am J Comp L* 12, 27; Wilfred Jenks, *The Prospects of International Adjudication* (Oceana Publ. 1964) 417; Vohryzek (n 610) 507ff; L. McNair, 'The General Principles of Law Recognized by Civilized Nations' (1957) 33 *British YIL* 15–16.

the context of State succession, as further discussed below[618]). He has described the principle as follows:

> Unjust enrichment as a concept stands or falls with the general principles of law as a jurisprudential category. It is, like other general principles which mediate between positive law and justice, derived from the nature of law itself and given existential significance inasmuch as it is embodied in many positive legal systems. It is, like some other principles of *jus gentium*, at once a philosophical derivative and a common practice of nations. Because it is a general principle it is part of the substructure of international law, and hence it is available to create a legal situation where none previously existed in municipal law, and so to attract to the solution of international problems the positive law rules of international law as a system of diplomatic protection.[619]

A few writers have expressed doubt as to whether the concept was at all a general principle of law.[620] This is, for instance, the position of Bedjaoui (further discussed below[621]).[622] For Schreuer, the sporadic use of this principle in practice does not permit one to conclude that it is 'firmly embedded in international law'.[623] However, he does add that 'the concept might be usefully applied in certain areas of international law if appropriately developed'.[624] In a recent article on the topic, Schreuer concluded that 'unjust enrichment may be no more than a remedy, which leaves the concept's scope of application to be determined by international practice'.[625] **14.51**

Interestingly, a number of writers have recognized the principle of unjust enrichment as a 'general principle of law' in the specific context of investment **14.52**

618 See, Chapter 14, Section 4.3.2.

619 O'Connell, 'Recent Problems of State Succession' (n 41) 159.

620 For instance, see: Charles Rousseau, *Droit international public*, vol I, (Sirey 1977) 380–81; Paul Reuter, *Droit International Public* (PUF Thémis 1958) 90; Georges Ripert, 'Les règles du droit civil applicables aux rapports internationaux', (1933-II) 44 Rec. des Cours 631–2.

621 See, Chapter 14, Section 4.3.2.

622 Bedjaoui, 'Problèmes récents de succession d'États' (n 11) 555:

> La notion d'enrichissement sans cause paraît devoir ne pas dépasser l'horizon du droit privé et interne. On n'est même pas assuré qu'elle soit connue de tous les systèmes nationaux. En tout cas elle n'est pas une notion, et encore moins une règle du droit international public. On peut certes, çà et là, relever quelques rares cas de jurisprudence où l'on semble admettre le principe de l'enrichissement sans cause se. Mais d'autres décisions repoussent énergiquement ce principe.

623 Schreuer, 'Unjustified Enrichment' (n 582) 382.

624 Ibid. In previous writing (Schreuer, 'Unjustified Enrichment', 1974 (n 602) 301), the author concluded that 'with international law in the present stage of development, restitution for unjustified enrichment can be considered hardly more than a decision-technique to be applied once that basic policy decisions have been made, and not a normative principle or general rule from which specific "correct" decisions can be logically derived.' Rodriguez Iglesias (n 581) 387, 396–7, believes that the concept is a general principle of international law that can be used in settling international legal disputes, but states that there is no norm in international law *prohibiting* unjust enrichment *as such*. See also: Friedmann (n 617) 206.

625 Binder and Schreuer (n 617) [11].

arbitration.[626] While a comprehensive analysis of all investment arbitration cases where the principle has been invoked and dealt with by tribunals is beyond the scope of this book,[627] suffice is to mention that a number of tribunals have come to the conclusion that unjust enrichment is a 'general principle of law'. This is, for instance, the position adopted by the *Saluka* Tribunal.[628] In *Occidental*, the Tribunal referred to 'unjust enrichment and to those principles contained in the Chorzow Factory case' as 'the principles of public international law to be applied when determining damages'.[629] In her dissenting opinion in this case, Stern also used the expression 'violation of the international principle against unjust enrichment'.[630] The concept has also been examined by the *Azurix* and *Amco* tribunals.[631]

14.53 In sum, the principle of unjust enrichment is largely recognized as a 'general principle of law' and can therefore be used by tribunals in the context of investment disputes.

4.3 The application of the principle to resolve State succession issues in general

4.3.1 Judicial decisions

14.54 The principle of unjust enrichment was referred to by at least two international tribunals and two national court decisions deciding issues involving questions of State succession.

626 Vohryzek (n 610) 507ff. In fact, she goes much further and affirmed at 503, in my view wrongly, that it is 'a general principle of customary international law'; Yaraslau Kryvoi, 'Counterclaims in Investor-State Arbitration' (2012) 21(2) *Minnesota JIL* 250; Dana H. Freyer, 'Recovering Damages for Unjust Enrichment in International Arbitration' (2007) 1(1) *World Arb & Med Rep* 21–2.

627 For such an analysis, see: Vohryzek (n 610) 536ff: concluding her analysis by stating that 'while an entryway remains for unjust enrichment as a cause of action and a measure of damages, ICSID Tribunals have not employed it' (at 546).

628 *Saluka Investments Bv (The Netherlands) v. Czech Republic*, Partial Award, 17 March 2006 [449]: 'The concept of unjust enrichment is recognised as a general principle of international law', adding at [450]: 'If it is assumed that the "fair and equitable treatment" standard also includes the general principle of unjust enrichment, an investor would therefore also be protected by this standard against unjust enrichment by the host State.'

629 *Occidental Exploration and Production Company v. Ecuador*, ICSID Case No. Arb/06/11, Award, 5 October 2012 [653].

630 Ibid., dissenting opinion of Brigitte Stern [132, 137, 144].

631 *Azurix Corp. v. Argentina*, ICSID Case No. ARB/01/12, Award, 14 July 2006 [436ff]; *Amco Asia Corp. and others v. Indonesia* [Resubmitted Case], ICSID Case No ARB/81/1, Award, 5 June 1990 [156]. It has been argued by Vohryzek (n 610) 529ff that the case of *ADC Affiliate Ltd. v. Hungary*, ICSID Case No. ARB/03/16, Award, 2 Oct. 2006 [497] also supports the application of the principle of unjust enrichment.

In the *Emeric Koranyi* case, the Hungary-Romania Mixed Arbitral Tribunal first determined that the outstanding debt was of an administrative character.[632] The tribunal used the concept of unjust enrichment to decide the question of the successor State's responsibility. Thus, the tribunal indicated that for the successor State (Romania) to be held liable for the outstanding debt, it would need to have been contracted in the 'interest' of the territory subsequently transferred and the money received or to be received, would allow that territory 'to obtain some improvement or benefit'. However, the tribunal came to the conclusion that this sum of money deposited was for the exclusive use of the plaintiffs and Romania, therefore, had not 'profited' from it. Accordingly, the tribunal decided that Romania should not be held responsible for the reimbursement of the sum of money deposited. **14.55**

As mentioned above,[633] the *Lighthouse Arbitration* case, which was decided by the French-Greek Arbitral Tribunal,[634] involved several French claims and Greek counter-claims. Two of them concerned the concept of unjust enrichment. In Claim no. 13, France requested the reimbursement for some work conducted by a French company, which occurred prior to the cession of the territory of Crete (at the time a territory formally under the control of the Ottoman Empire) to Greece in 1913. France based its claim on the grounds that Greece (as the successor State) had enriched itself by the increase in value of the property resulting from the repair of a light by the French company. The tribunal found that the repair work undertaken by the French company was within the normal scope of contractual obligations of the concessionaire.[635] It therefore rejected the claim without pronouncing itself on the validity of the concept of unjust enrichment. In its analysis of Greece's counter-claim no. 9, the tribunal was called to decide on the costs of a port beacon which had been erected by the French concessionaire during the military occupation, and had been subsequently maintained by Greece. The tribunal decided that there had been no enrichment. Interestingly, the tribunal used the words 'supposed **14.56**

632 *Emeric Koranyi and Mme. Ernest Dengcjel (née Koranyi) v. Romanian State*, Hungary-Romania Mixed Arbitral Tribunal, Award, 27 February 1929, in: *8 Recueil des décisions des tribunaux arbitraux mixtes* 980; (1929–1930) *Annual Digest* 64. In this case, the plaintiffs (apparently Hungarian nationals) had deposited in 1918–1919 a sum of money (8,000 Hungarian crowns) in a tax-collector office of the city of Maromarossziget, which was then part of the Austria-Hungary Dual Monarchy. By a decision of the Hungarian District Court of Maromarossziget the tax-collector office was ordered to return the money (with interests) to the plaintiffs. In the meantime, and before the office could effect the payment, the territory of Transylvania (where the city of Maromarossziget was situated) was ceded to Romania after the break-up of the Dual Monarchy pursuant to the Trianon Treaty (n 324). The Romanian office which took over the assets of the plaintiff refused to return the money on the ground that the deposit had been made before the territory was ceded to Romania.

633 See, Chapter 13, Section 2.4.4.

634 *Lighthouse Arbitration* case (n 162).

635 Ibid., 209.

principle' suggesting that there is a doubt as to whether the concept should be considered a general principle of law.[636]

14.57 In the *Zilberszpic* case, a private contractor had concluded an agreement with the Russian Orthodox Charitable Society of Kielce, which was at the time situated in Polish territory under Russian ruling.[637] The agreement for the construction of an apartment house for the Society was partially performed by the contractor. But, as a result of World War I, the money due to him remained unpaid. Under Article XII of the Peace Treaty of Riga of 18 March 1921, Poland was recognized as the owner of all former Russian State property in its territory. This included property rights that had been given up by the former Russian Tsars, such as the property of the Society. The Supreme Court of Poland concluded that the building had never been a Russian State property before the date of succession. In the absence of any contractual relationship between the plaintiff and Poland regarding the building of the apartment, the court concluded that the plaintiff could claim part of his expenditures for the increase in value of the land resulting from its investment (with the deduction of the sum already paid for this construction). The court specifically made reference to the notion of unjust enrichment. However, it did so solely on the ground that this concept existed under Polish municipal law, without any discussion as to whether it was also embodied in international law.

14.58 Finally, the *Niedzielskie* case involved a contract signed by the authorities of the Austria-Hungary Dual Monarchy for work done on certain government buildings before the outbreak of the First World War.[638] In dealing with the property at stake, the Supreme Court of Poland referred to the concept of unjust enrichment, but concluded that in the present case, no such enrichment occurred.[639]

14.59 In sum, the analysis of these cases illustrates that even though courts have referred to the principle of unjust enrichment, the concept was actually never used to decide any of these cases on the merits.

636 Ibid., 241 (referring to 'prétendu principe général de droit').

637 *Zilberszpic v. (Polish) Treasury*, Supreme Court of Poland, First Division, 14 December 1928, Zb. O.S.N., 1928, no. 190; (1927–1928) 4 *Annual Digest* 82.

638 After the end of the War, the territory where the buildings were situated was ceded to Poland, and the buildings taken over by the latter.

639 *Niedzielskie* case (n 199) 75:

> It is true that Poland took over all the immovable property of the Austrian State, but no question of unjustified enrichment arises seeing that, apart from school buildings, hospitals, and state forests, Poland had to pay for the properties taken over by a contribution to the cost of war to be paid to the Allied Powers.

4.3.2 Scholarship

As mentioned above, one of the most vocal advocates of the use of the principle of unjust enrichment to deal with questions of State succession is O'Connell.[640] As noted above, for him, the principle is in fact central to the whole question of succession, noting that it has a 'special significance in the solution of problems of State succession when one of the party to a legal relationship has disappeared'.[641] In his view, 'the juridical justification for the obligation to pay compensation is to be found in the concept of unjustified enrichment.'[642] Writers are generally favourable to the use of the principle of unjust enrichment to solve problems of State succession. **14.60**

As explained by the present author elsewhere,[643] this is also the case regarding the specific question of State succession to State responsibility.[644] In fact, some of the writers who reject the possibility of any succession to international responsibility make an exception for the special situation when such acts result in the unjust enrichment of the successor State. In this context, they believe that the successor State should be held responsible for the acts that took place before the date of succession.[645] One example is the work of Drakidis, who applied this principle specifically in the context of the cession of the Dodecanesian Islands to Greece in 1947.[646] Other scholars have been more **14.61**

640 O'Connell, *State Succession*, 1967 (n 15) 266–7, 348–9, 352; O'Connell, 'Recent Problems of State Succession' (n 41) 140.

641 O'Connell, *State Succession*, 1967 (n 15) 34, see also: 266–7, 348–9, 352; O'Connell, 'Recent Problems of State Succession' (n 41) 140.

642 O'Connell, *The Law of State Succession*, 1956 (n 38) 273. He also mentions that this principle 'is the norm behind the doctrine of respect for acquired rights in the law of State succession'.

643 Dumberry, *State Succession to International Responsibility* (n 165) 263. P. Dumberry, 'The Use of the Concept of Unjust Enrichment to Resolve Issues of State Succession to International Responsibility' (2006) 39(2) RBDI 506–28.

644 Volkovitsch (n 343) 2210–11; Pierre Michel Eisemann, 'Emprunts russes et problèmes de succession d'États', in: P. Juillard and B. Stern (eds), *Les emprunts russes et le règlement du contentieux financier franco-russe* (Cedin Cahiers internationaux no. 16, 2002) 62.

645 Udina (n 617) 769–70; Oscar Schachter, 'State Succession: the Once and Future Law' 1993 33(2) *Va J Int'l L* 256; Ivan A. Shearer, *Starke's International Law* 11th edn (Butterworths 1994) 303; A. Verdross, *Völkerrecht* 4th edn (Springler Verlag 1959) 198; A. Verdross and B. Simma, *Universelles Völkerrecht, Theorie und Praxis* (Dunker & Humblot 1984) 633–4; Restatement of the Law (n 211) [209(g)], 105 and also Reporters' notes no. 7, at 107; Waelbroeck (n 419) 35; Lynn Berat, 'Genocide: The Namibian Case Against Germany', (1993) *Pace Int'l L Rev* 165, 193. This is also the position of Natalino Ronzitti, *La successione internazionale tra stati* (Giuffrè 1970) 220–21, who, however, is of the view that the obligation of the new successor State is a *new obligation*, which does not arise from the previous obligations of the predecessor State.

646 Philippe Drakidis, 'Succession d'Etats et enrichissements sans cause des biens publics du Dodécanèse' (1971) 24 RHDI 109–10. He is of the view that, in principle, in the context of a cession of territory it should be for the continuing State (Italy) to compensate the victim of expropriation acts, but that whenever the successor State (Greece) has unjustly enriched itself as a result of the acts, it should be for that State to compensate its nationals.

prudent in their appraisal of the application of this principle in the context of State succession to State responsibility.[647]

14.62 Certain authors have clearly rejected the proposition that the concept could be helpful to solve problems of State succession. For Bedjaoui, the principle should not find application in the context of decolonization.[648] As mentioned above, he rejects the arguments put forward in support of the existence of an obligation for Newly Independent States to provide compensation to Western companies resulting from acts of nationalization.[649] In any event, in this situation Bedjaoui affirms that it would be 'difficult, if not impossible' to prove that the successor State has been enriched, that the enrichment took place at the expense of the claimant, and that the enrichment is unjustified.[650] The basic reason behind his belief that the principle of unjust enrichment should not apply in a case of nationalization is because the property is simply returned to its original owner (the State) whose goods had been *illicitly* taken by the Colonial power in the first place.[651] Thus, for him, the theory of unjustified enrichment 'is completely inapplicable because enrichment can be considered legitimate in the case of decolonization; it is not unjustified, since it constitutes compensation for the exploitation of the territory during the preceding decades'.[652] In fact, if the principle of unjust enrichment were to apply, it should be *against the foreign company*, rather than against the new State.[653]

647 Jean Philippe Monnier, 'La succession d'Etats en matière de responsabilité internationale' (1962) 8 AFDI 89–90; Louis Henkin, Richard Crawford Pugh, Oscar Schachter and Hans Smit, *International Law, Cases and Materials*, 3rd edn (West Publ. Co. 1993) 293.

648 Bedjaoui, 'Problèmes récents de succession d'États' (n 11) 554ff. See also, ILC, First Report Bedjaoui, 1968 (n 39) 101 [43].

649 Bedjaoui, ibid., 550: '[l]es raisons morales de l'indemnisation en droit international général comme en matière de succession d'Etats, ont pris chaque fois le pas d'autant plus aisément que le fondement juridique de l'indemnisation restait encore à trouver'; ILC, Second Report Bedjaoui, 1969 (n 4) 9:

> It has been pointed out that the acquired right to compensation is very fragile, since a solid foundation has still not been found for it. It was believed that the duty to pay compensation could be justified by the doctrine of unjustified enrichment. This doctrine, which has been carried over from municipal private law, is open to methodological objections based on the principle of such transposition. Above all, however, it is largely inapplicable in the case of succession resulting from decolonization.

650 ILC, Second Report Bedjaoui, 1969 (n 4) 95.

651 Bedjaoui, 'Problèmes récents de succession d'États' (n 11) 550:

> il n'y a pas lieu de consentir à une indemnisation lorsque survient l'indépendance, car la colonisation a enrichi la métropole et a rempli une fonction historique considérable dans l'industrialisation, la puissance et la prospérité de l'Etat conquérant.

See also (at 551):

> On s'aperçoit donc pas comment l'équité ou le principe de l'enrichissement sans cause pourraient recevoir application dans le cas de ces biens qui font tout simplement retour, par la décolonisation, à leur propriétaire d'origine qui en avait été dépossédé.

652 ILC, Second Report Bedjaoui, 1969 (n 4) 96.

653 Bedjaoui, 'Problèmes récents de succession d'États' (n 11) 556.

This is especially the case when rights were given to a foreign company by the colonial power during the 'suspicious period', that is, just before the proclamation of independence.[654] Needless to say that his position has been rejected by a number of other writers.[655]

Finally, it should be added that the Institut's Resolution on 'State Succession in Matters of Property and Debts' refers to the principle of unjust enrichment.[656] Thus, Article 8 of the Resolution indicates that the result of the apportionment of property and debts should be equitable and that 'unjust enrichment shall be avoided'.[657] As mentioned above, the Institut has also recently adopted a resolution on State succession to State responsibility in which the principle of unjust enrichment also plays a role.[658] **14.63**

4.4 The application of the principle in the context of succession to State contracts

Elsewhere, I have argued that the principle of unjust enrichment should be used to resolve issues of State succession to State responsibility.[659] I believe that the principle should also play a central role in solving issues of succession to State contracts. As previously observed, the principle of unjust enrichment is a remedy used in judicial practice to 'reverse accretions of wealth under circumstances in which contractual or delictual principles would have been unable to reach this result'.[660] As O'Connell puts it, the function of the principle of unjust enrichment 'is to mitigate the hardship which would result in certain cases from an application of strict law by applying principles of **14.64**

654 Ibid., 557:

> Comment enfin indemniser des 'droits acquis' pendant la 'période suspecte', c'est-à-dire des droits certes régulièrement acquis conformément à la législation de l'État prédécesseur, mais obtenus à la hâte à la veille de l'indépendance grâce à une réglementation de circonstance et dans le but manifeste de diminuer ou *d'appauvrir* le patrimoine de l'État successeur. Si la théorie de l'enrichissement sans cause devait s'appliquer, elle serait dans ce cas opposable non pas à l'État successeur mais à l'État prédécesseur qui a tenté d'appauvrir le premier. Un cas typique de droits acquis pendant la 'période suspecte' est celui de l'Union minière du Haut-Katanga [in the context of the independence of Congo, 1960] (emphasis in the original).

Elsewhere he also explained that 'If the theory of unjustified enrichment were to be applied, it would in this case be applicable not to the successor State but to the predecessor State, which had tried to impoverish its successor' (ILC, Second Report Bedjaoui, 1969 (n 4) 96).

655 See, for instance, Gruber (n 22) 108–9.

656 IDI, State Succession in Matters of Property and Debts, Resolution, 2001 (n 13) 713ff.

657 Ibid., see also, Arts 11 and 13.

658 IDI, State Succession to Responsibility, Resolution, 2015 (n 14), Art. 7(2), 12(5).

659 Dumberry, *State Succession to International Responsibility* (n 165) 263.

660 Schreuer, 'Unjustified Enrichment' (n 582) 289. See also: *Sea-Land Service* (n 580) 169, which indicated that for the concept of unjust enrichment to apply 'there must be no (…) contractual or other remedy available to the injured party whereby he might seek compensation from the party enriched'.

justice and equity'.[661] It has rightly been argued that the usefulness of this concept in the context of State succession is that it 'entirely sidesteps the question of whether international law includes a specific "legal" rule as a "general principle" imposing a fiscal obligation upon successor states in cases of state succession'.[662] Therefore, the principle plays a 'mediating role between the categories of justice and of law';[663] it is 'on the borderland of law and ethics'.[664]

14.65 The principle of unjust enrichment is indeed closely related to the notion of equity. Equity has been described as 'the key ... to the entire problem of State succession',[665] and is referred to in the Vienna Convention on Succession of States in Respect of State Properties, Archives and Debts[666] as well as in the work of the Institut on 'State Succession in Matters of Property and Debts'.[667] There is some support to apply the concepts of equity and fairness to solve issues of State succession. For instance, the Badinter Arbitration Commission in its *Opinion no. 1* stated that 'the outcome of succession should be equitable, the States concerned being free to settle terms and conditions by agreement'.[668] Equity plays an important role in the allocation of rights and obligations between the continuator and the successor State or amongst the successor States themselves.[669]

14.66 One situation where the concept of unjust enrichment could play an important role is in the context of succession to contracts involving a contract that is performed by an investor *specifically in one part* of the territory of the predecessor State which later becomes an independent State (such as in cases of secession, and dissolution), or is ceded from one State to another. The fact that the contract is executed in one specific part of the country is important insofar as it provides benefits to that territory and its population.[670] One clear example of such a situation is when the contract involves the construction of

661 O'Connell, 'Unjustified Enrichment' (n 607) 16.

662 M.H. Hoeflich, 'Through a Glass Darkly: Reflections upon the History of the International Law of Public Debt In Connection With State Succession', (1982) 1 *Univ Illinois LR* 39, 46.

663 O'Connell, *State Succession*, 1967 (n 15) 34. See also in: O'Connell, *The Law of State Succession*, 1956 (n 38) 273. See also the analysis of the author of the concept under English Law: O'Connell, 'Unjustified Enrichment' (n 607) 2–17.

664 O'Connell, 'Unjustified Enrichment' (n 607) 4.

665 O'Connell, *The Law of State Succession*, 1956 (n 38) 268.

666 See Arts 37, 40 and 41, Vienna Convention on Succession to State Properties, Archives and Debts (n 12).

667 IDI, State Succession in Matters of Property and Debts, Resolution, 2001 (n 13) 713ff, at Art. 8.

668 *Opinion no. 1*, 29 November 1991, in: (1993) 92 ILR 166 (under letter 1)e).

669 Sandrine Maljean-Dubois, 'Le rôle de l'équité dans le droit de la succession d'États', in Pierre Michel Eisemann and Martti Koskenniemi (dir), *State Succession: Codification Tested Against the Facts* (Martinus Nijhoff Publ. 2000) 149. See also: Dumberry, *State Succession to International Responsibility* (n 165) 279ff.

670 O'Connell, *State Succession*, 1967 (n 15) 367: 'the more locally identified is the contract the greater is the presumption that it has benefited the absorbed territory.'

infrastructures, such as roads, bridges, airports, etc. These infrastructures will stay in place in the given territory following the date of succession.

Problems may arise in the event that certain obligations under the contract have not been completely fulfilled at the date of succession. It may be that the work has not been entirely performed. One especially complicated situation is when the State has not fulfilled all of its payment obligations under the contract at that date. The event of State succession may result in some confusion regarding the fate of the contract under which these infrastructures were built. The most problematic situation arises in the context of a dissolution, where the State party to the contract ceases to exist as an independent State. What happens to the contract in this situation? Should any of the new successor States continue to execute the contract (and, if so, which one?)? There is also confusion in the context of secession. Should the new State or the continuing State continue to execute the contract? **14.67**

The important first step is to determine whether this is a situation where the principle of unjust enrichment should find application. It should be recalled that a situation of unjust enrichment requires that a State 'has benefited from [a] measure and the foreign interest involved has suffered a loss as a direct result'.[671] In the example examined, the new State (where the contract was performed before the date of succession) will undoubtedly benefit after its independence from such a situation. Thus, the government and its population will continue using the infrastructures that were built on its territory under the contract. This benefit is all the more evident in the event that the contractor has not been entirely paid for the work performed at the date of succession. In such a case, the benefit gained by the new State is directly linked to the loss suffered by the contractor, which has performed work under a contract and has not been paid. This is a classic situation of unjust enrichment. Under this scenario, in my view, the new State should be considered bound by the obligations arising from that contract (even though it was signed before the date of succession by another State, the predecessor State). The new State should accordingly provide payment for the work performed. This is indeed the solution put forward by O'Connell some 50 years ago: **14.68**

> The middle-way solution seems to have been to admit that upon a change of sovereignty of one the parties to the contract has disappeared from the place of performance, and that the contract as such lapses from 'frustration', but to argue that the benefit to the private contractors under the contract, in so far as it has been performed, must be satisfied under the doctrine of unjust enrichment. The solution is

671 Fombad (n 583) 125.

> suggested by the comparable problem under both English law and civil law. The result is that the government is released under the contract, but must pay the contractor whatever is due to him at the date of change of sovereignty if the benefits of his work accrue to the territory affected. If the contract is totally executory the matter is at an end altogether.[672]

14.69 In fact, the unilateral cancellation of a contract by one party is a frequent situation resulting in an unjust enrichment.[673] A party refusing to pay the other party for work performed under a contract is also a classic case of unjust enrichment.[674] There is no reason the same basic solution should not apply in the context of State succession. Apart from the obvious (and complicated) fact that one of the parties to the contract has disappeared (such as in a case of dissolution), this is still a situation of unjust enrichment. As noted by Schreuer (who, as noted above, is sceptical about the concept being considered a general principle of law) 'where improvement has been made by private contractors on land which has subsequently passed to a different sovereign, national courts have sometimes awarded the contractors compensation to the extent of the actual value of the improvement to the new sovereign'.[675] In fact, the situation just described is not significantly different from the classic unjust enrichment example where a State expropriates an investor's property without providing any compensation in return.[676] In both situations, the State enriches itself at the detriment of the investor.

14.70 In the scenario described in the previous paragraph, the new State (where the contract was performed before the date of succession and which, consequently, benefited from such an investment) may refuse to take over any obligations arising from the contract. One obvious ground for refusal would be to argue that it is a new entity that is entirely distinct from the predecessor State. As such, the new State is clearly not an original party to the contract and, consequently, cannot be bound by its terms. Thus, given the fact that the new State has no formal obligation to make any payment under the contract (to which it is not a party), any such refusal cannot be considered as a *breach* of the contract. In other words, one cannot breach a contract to which one is not a party. As mentioned above,[677] there is now a consensus among writers that the rights and obligations under a State contract are simply *not transferred* from

672 O'Connell, *State Succession*, 1967 (n 15) 298, 302; See also: J. Crawford, 'The Contribution of Professor D.P. O'Connell to the Discipline of International Law' (1980) 51 *British YIL* 30.

673 Fombad (n 583) 126ff; Binder and Schreuer (n 617) [18].

674 *Schlegel Corp* (n 593) 181–3 [14]–[17].

675 Schreuer, 'Unjustified Enrichment' (n 582) 382, citing the *Zilberszpic* case (n 637). See also: Schreuer, 'Unjustified Enrichment', 1974 (n 602). 292; Binder and Schreuer (n 617) [16].

676 Fombad (n 583) 125; Jiménez de Aréchaga (n 580) 299–300.

677 See, Chapter 12, Section 2.

one State (the predecessor) to another one (the successor State). As a matter of principle, a new State is therefore *not bound* by a State contract signed by another State. The question is whether this undeniably forceful argument is fatal to a contractor's claim for payment based on the doctrine of unjust enrichment. In other words, should the contractor get paid by the new State for the work performed *even if* there is, as a matter of principle, no succession to State contracts?

It should be recalled here that an entity does not have to formally be a party to a contract to be considered as having benefited from it.[678] Thus, in the context of the Iran-US Claims Tribunal, authors have noted that 'when work was performed without a contract, but in promise of a future contract, the tribunal awarded unjust enrichment'.[679] What matters is that an enrichment has occurred. This is the case when a new State gets infrastructures 'for free'; when the investor has not been fully paid for such work. The nonexistence of a formal contract binding on the new State is therefore *not* a fatal hurdle for the application of the doctrine of unjust enrichment. In fact, two writers went even further in affirming that the principle only applies when *no contract* exists.[680] In any event, the existence of an unjust enrichment is a factual situation which is not related to the commission of any breach of law. No wrongful act needs to be demonstrated for an unjust enrichment to exist.[681] What matters is that an enrichment 'has occurred and that it is without legal justification under international law'.[682] Thus, as noted by two writers, unjust enrichment is 'designed to redress undesirable shifts of control over assets which are not covered by other areas of the law', adding that 'typically, a situation giving rise to liability for unjust enrichment would therefore be covered neither by responsibility for a wrongful act nor by an underlying valid agreement'.[683] In fact, these two writers affirm that 'the remedies for an internationally wrongful act and for unjust enrichment are mutually exclusive' and that 'a remedy for unjust enrichment is available only where no other remedies, and in particular no claim to damages for a wrongful act, are available'.[684] **14.71**

In sum, the situation described in the previous paragraphs is, in my view, one of unjust enrichment where the new State should be under the obligation to **14.72**

678 Schreuer, 'Unjustified Enrichment' (n 582) 290.
679 Binder and Schreuer (n 617) [22] referring to several cases.
680 Binder and Schreuer (n 617) [27]–[28]: 'International arbitral practice overwhelmingly supports the opinion that a claim based on unjust enrichment can only be pursued in the absence of a claim based on a contract.'
681 *Sea-Land Service* (n 580).
682 Fombad (n 583) 123.
683 Binder and Schreuer (n 617) [2].
684 Ibid., [30].

provide compensation for the work performed. This is so even if, as a matter of principle, a new State is *not bound* by a State contract signed by another State before the date of succession. It should be added that the situation described in the previous paragraphs could also qualify as one where the new State 'continues' a wrongful act initially committed by the predecessor State[685] and should, consequently, be responsible for obligations under the contract.

14.73 Finally, a few words should be said about the possible use of the concept of unjust enrichment for different types of succession of States. In a case where the predecessor State *does not* cease to exist as a result of the events affecting its territorial integrity (such as in the case of secession), the relevant question will be which (if any) of the continuing State or the new State has enriched itself after the date of succession. The same type of question will arise in the context of a dissolution: which of the new States has enriched itself from the execution of the contract? In the context of a cession of territory, since the contract is specifically linked to the territory ceded it would seem obvious that the successor State should be responsible for any situation of unjust enrichment.[686] For reasons explained above,[687] the particular context of colonization should be carefully analysed when determining whether the principle should find application for Newly Independent States. The case of *Compagnie d'Enterprises CFE SA v. Yemen* (already mentioned above[688]) provides an illustration of how the principle should be used in the context of a unification of States. The decision of the Supreme Court of Cyprus took into account the principle of unjust enrichment to determine the issue of succession to State contracts:

> Acquired rights remain in force, regardless of the prevailing legal situation in the successor state. Such rights are transferred to the new state, insofar as the (original) contracting state continued to exist or, at least, retained sovereignty over the geographical area wherein the contractual right was granted or pertained and wherein the (original) contracting state has already benefited from the performance of the contract, especially when works have been done in its territory that remain in the same geographical area; this is so even if the political situation has changed or the government or the (original contracting) state was transformed into a new entity in international law. (...) If the new state has benefited from the works of the predecessor state, then it has to bear responsibility for them.[689]

14.74 The Supreme Court held that the new State of Yemen was bound by an arbitration clause contained in a State contract that had been signed by one of

685 See, Chapter 14, Section 1.
686 For a detailed analysis of the question in the context of cession/transfer, see: Drakidis (n 646) 109–10.
687 See, Chapter 13, Section 5.1.
688 See, Chapter 13, Section 4.2.
689 *Yemen v. Compagnie d'Enterprises CFE SA* (n 361) [H1]–]H3], referring to [12]–[14] of the decision.

the predecessor States. One factor that was considered important by the court was the fact that the contract had been performed on the territory of one of the predecessor States, which had since then become the territory of the new successor State as a result of the unification. Thus, the court refers to the fact that the new State had *benefited* from the performance of the contract for the construction and maintenance of a harbour on what is now its territory and should, accordingly, be responsible for the obligations arising from that contract. This example seems to perfectly illustrate how the concept of unjust enrichment can be helpful to solve succession issues involving State contracts.

Part E

SPECIFIC PROBLEMS ARISING WHEN STATE SUCCESSION OCCURS DURING ARBITRATION PROCEEDINGS

INTRODUCTION

Thus far, the question of State succession has been examined from the perspective of what happens *after* the events leading to changes in the identity and territory of a State have occurred. In other words, I have explored and provided a framework as to how a tribunal should consider the different issues that may arise in cases of succession, once this succession has *already occurred*. The question is slightly more complicated when the events leading to this change in sovereignty over a given territory happen *during* arbitration proceedings. The fact that succession takes place after a request for arbitration has been filed by a claimant investor is likely to have an impact on the on-going proceedings. This Part will examine the consequences that succession may have on the different actors involved in the proceedings as well as the challenging legal issues with which tribunals will be faced.

First, as further analysed in Chapter 15, the event may have (depending on the type of succession involved) an impact on the core question of the identity of the respondent State in the proceedings. Certain States will cease to exist during the proceedings (such as in situations of dissolution, unification, and integration), while others will simply lose part of their territory (in the cases of a cession of territory and secession). A tribunal will be faced with the basic (yet complicated) question as to whether or not it still has jurisdiction over a given dispute. Another closely-related difficulty for the tribunal will be to identify the State that will act as the respondent for the remainder of the proceedings. Major difficulties will arise if a State concerned refuses to participate in such proceedings. I will examine the limits of the tribunals' powers in this respect.

Second, as further analysed in Chapter 16, the event of succession may result in territorial modifications and/or a change in identity of the *home State* of the claimant investor. This may have an impact on the nationality of the claimant investor. Thus, an investor may have started BIT arbitration proceedings as a national of one State and could, during the proceedings, lose that nationality and become a national of another State. The central question examined below is whether an arbitral tribunal should continue to have jurisdiction over a dispute when a claimant involuntarily changes its nationality during the proceedings as a result of succession. This question, in turn, raises the other controversial issue of whether or not the rule of 'continuous nationality' should find application in the context of investment arbitration cases involving matters of State succession.

15

SUCCESSION AFFECTING THE RESPONDENT STATE

This chapter examines what happens *after* a request for arbitration has been filed by an investor when the State (respondent in the arbitration proceedings) ceases to exist such as in the case of dissolution, unification, and integration. The chapter will analyse a number of legal issues arising from such a dramatic situation, including whether a tribunal should continue to have jurisdiction over the dispute and, if so, more practically, which States should be acting as the respondent for the rest of the proceedings. **15.01**

1. A TRIBUNAL SHOULD CONTINUE TO HAVE JURISDICTION OVER A CASE DESPITE THE CHANGES AFFECTING THE RESPONDENT STATE DURING THE PROCEEDINGS

In my view, in a situation like the one described above, an arbitral tribunal should continue to have jurisdiction over the case despite the changes affecting the identity of the respondent State.[1] The question of a tribunal's jurisdiction over a given dispute is determined at the moment when the arbitration claim is filed. Under the ICSID Convention, the requirement is that the respondent **15.02**

1 The question is discussed in Justin A. Fraterman, 'Secession, State Succession and International Arbitration' (paper, SSRN, 2013) 18–19.

State be a party to the Convention.[2] The critical date for the status of a State as a contracting party to the Convention is the date of the registration of the request for arbitration by the Secretary-General of ICSID.[3] Therefore, the critical date is *not* the date when the State *consented* to arbitration. In fact, a State may consent to the jurisdiction of the Centre (and such consent can be found, for instance, in a State contract or in a BIT) *before* it becomes a contracting party to the Convention.[4] This situation has occurred in a number of cases.[5] In the context of this book, what matters is that at the time that the request for arbitration is filed, the respondent is an existing sovereign State having the status of a party to the Convention.

15.03 This is indeed the conclusion that was reached by the tribunal in the *Mytilineos* case (further discussed in detail below[6]). The tribunal examined the effects of the secession of Montenegro, an event that took place during arbitration proceedings. The tribunal referred to the 'well-established principle that jurisdiction is to be determined in light of the situation as it exists on the date the judicial proceedings are instituted'.[7] The events following the institution of judicial proceedings are therefore, strictly speaking, irrelevant as to a tribunal's jurisdiction over a given case. In support of this affirmation, the tribunal cited the ICJ's *Arrest Warrant* decision stating that:

> The Court recalls that, according to its settled jurisprudence, its jurisdiction must be determined at the time that the act instituting proceedings was filed. Thus, if the Court has jurisdiction on the date the case is referred to it, it continues to do so regardless of subsequent events. Such events might lead to a finding that an application has subsequently become moot and to a decision not to proceed to judgment on the merits, but they cannot deprive the Court of jurisdiction.[8]

15.04 The same solution was adopted by the *Mytilineos* Tribunal dealing with succession occurring after the start of the arbitration proceedings:

---

2 Art. 25, Convention on the Settlement of Investment Disputes between States and Nationals of Other States (March 18, 1965) (entered into force Oct. 14, 1966), 575 UNTS 160; (1965) 4 ILM 532 [hereinafter 'ICSID Convention'].

3 C. Schreuer and R. Dolzer, *Principles of International Investment Law*, (OUP 2008), 11–12; 234; Christoph Schreuer et al. (eds), *The ICSID Convention: A Commentary* 2nd edn (CUP 2009) 144–5.

4 Schreuer, ibid., 145.

5 Ibid.

6 See, Chapter 15, Section 2.2.

7 *Mytilineos Holdings SA v. State Union of Serbia & Montenegro and Republic of Serbia*, UNCITRAL, Partial Award on Jurisdiction, 8 September 2006 [159].

8 *Case Concerning the Arrest Warrant of 11 April 2000 (Democratic Republic of Congo v. Belgium)*, 14 February 2002, ICJ Reports 2002, 1 [26].

> The Tribunal finds that the same rule [i.e., the one mentioned by the *Vivendi II* Tribunal] also applies with regard to possible changes in the personality of respondents in investment cases. Though changes in the 'identity' of States occur less frequently than changes of the nationality of natural or legal persons, there is no reason why the two should not be treated in the same way.[9]

In sum, once a tribunal has established its jurisdiction over a dispute, to paraphrase the *Vivendi II* Tribunal, such a fact 'cannot be defeated' and is 'simply not affected by subsequent events',[10] even if the event involves changes in the *identity* of a State. This being said, when these dramatic changes take place, the rest of the proceeding is greatly impacted (a question examined below). As further discussed in the next section, the practical consequences of such an event, affecting the identity of the respondent State during arbitration proceedings, will differ depending on the type of succession involved. **15.05**

2. THE PRACTICAL CONSEQUENCES OF CHANGES AFFECTING THE RESPONDENT STATE ARE DIFFERENT DEPENDING ON THE TYPE OF SUCCESSION INVOLVED

2.1 Incorporation and unification of States

Let us take the example of proceedings instituted by an investor against the predecessor State (East Germany) before its integration with an already existing State (West Germany). While there is no automatic continuation of BITs which had been entered into by the predecessor State with other States,[11] the successor State may not necessarily object to act as the respondent in such proceedings. Zimmermann's examination of State practice in the context of the 'unification' of Germany is that the overall debt of East Germany passed to the successor State.[12] This is in accordance with Article 39 **15.06**

---

9 *Mytileneos* (n 7).

10 *Compañiá de Aguas del Aconquija SA and Universal v. Argentina (Vivendi II)*, ICSID Case No. ARB/97/3, Decision on Jurisdiction, 14 November 2005 [63].

11 See, Chapter 5, Section1.2. As mentioned above (at Chapter 13, Section 4.1), in the context of integration, the successor State should be bound by obligations arising from contracts signed by the predecessor State before the date of succession.

12 A. Zimmermann, 'State Succession in Other Matters than Treaties' in *Max Planck Encyclopedia of Public International Law* (OUP, online edn, 2006) [13]:

> State practice with regard to Germany and Yemen has confirmed that in cases of both a merger of two States to form a new State or the absorption of one State by another, it is the united successor State which not only inherits the overall assets of the respective predecessor State or States, but that the successor State is also responsible for the overall debts of its predecessors State or States, such principle already being reflected in Art. 39 Vienna Convention on Succession of States in Respect of State Property, Archives and Debts.

of the Vienna Convention on Succession of States in Respect of State Property, Archives and Debt (which applies not only to cases of unification, but also to those of integration[13]) providing that 'the State debt of the predecessor States shall pass to the successor State'.[14] It is true that the term 'debts' in the Vienna Convention does not cover, per se, pending arbitration claims where the predecessor State is acting as a respondent. Yet, Article 33 defines the term 'State debt' as 'any *financial obligation* of a predecessor State arising in conformity with international law towards another State, an international organization or *any other subject of international law*'.[15] It is not clear whether a pending arbitration claim is covered by the definition of a 'financial obligation'. Yet, as mentioned above,[16] there are convincing arguments in favour of classifying corporations and individuals as partial and limited subjects of international law in the specific context of when they are parties to arbitration proceedings initiated under State contracts or BITs. In this context, it seems plausible that the successor State could decide not to object to its status as the respondent in arbitration proceedings. In fact, as mentioned above,[17] this is exactly the position which was taken by Germany in the *CIC International Ltd.* case. This case involved arbitration proceedings that were started *after* unification by an investor. It dealt with Germany's non-fulfillment of obligations arising from a contract signed by East Germany in the days preceding the date of succession.[18] In this case, Germany did not contest the jurisdiction of the tribunal on the ground that the contractual obligations were those undertaken by a different State (East Germany). In all likelihood, Germany's position would have been no different had the proceedings been instituted *before* the unification.

15.07 In sum, the impact of changes affecting the respondent State in the context of the incorporation of a State is unlikely to be fatal regarding the continuation of the proceedings.

15.08 The same solution should also apply in the context of unification of States. Thus, it would seem logical for the new successor State to consider itself to be the respondent in the context of proceedings which started before the unification against one of the predecessor States. Such an outcome is likely considering that the successor State is responsible for the overall debts of the

13 P.K. Menon, 'The Succession of States and the Problem of State Debts' (1986) 6 *B.C. Third World LJ* 137.

14 Vienna Convention on Succession of States in Respect of State Property, Archives and Debts, in (1983) 22 ILM 306.

15 Ibid. (emphasis added).

16 See, Chapter 6, Section 6.3.1.1.

17 See, Chapter 13, Section 4.2.

18 *Société CIC International Ltd. v. Ministre de la Défense de la République d'Allemagne*, Cour d'appel de Paris (1Ch. C), 19 January 1999, in (1999) Rev. arb. 601, note by Ch. Jarrosson.

predecessor States under Article 39 of the Vienna Convention.[19] As mentioned above,[20] a similar issue arose in the context of the case of *Compagnie d'Enterprises CFE SA v. Yemen* involving a claim which was started *after* the unification of Yemen.[21] While in this case the successor State objected to the jurisdiction of the tribunal over a contractual dispute involving obligations undertaken by one of the predecessor States, both the tribunal and the Supreme Court of Cyprus concluded that Yemen should be considered as the respondent State in these proceedings. In my view, these judicial bodies would have come to the same conclusion had the proceedings been started *before* the date of succession against one of the predecessor States. This conclusion is reinforced by the fact that, as mentioned above,[22] the successor State should be considered bound by obligations arising from contracts which were signed by a predecessor State before the unification. Moreover, under Article 31 (al. 1) of the Vienna Convention, the successor State becomes automatically party to all BITs which had been entered into by the predecessor States before the date of unification[23] (although, as noted above, the application of such a principle of automatic continuation is problematic in the context of unification).

2.2 Secession

In the context of a secession, the predecessor State continues to exist and its status as a respondent in any on-going proceedings is therefore unaffected. A good illustration is the *Mytilineos* case that involved a Greek claimant who instituted arbitration proceedings in 2004 under the 1997 Greece-FRY BIT against *two* respondents: The 'State Union of Serbia & Montenegro' and the 'Republic of Serbia'.[24] In its award rendered in September 2006, the tribunal noted that since the claim had been filed, 'Montenegro, a constituent unit of the State Union of Serbia and Montenegro, declared its independence'.[25] The tribunal added that this event was, however, not problematic here because it was 'uncontroversial that the Republic of Serbia will continue the legal identity of the State Union of Serbia and Montenegro on the international level'[26] and should therefore be considered as the respondent in the proceedings. While it is indeed logical for the continuing State to maintain its status as the respondent in such proceedings, one can envisage that a different solution may be adopted under certain circumstances (examined in the next paragraphs). **15.09**

19 Vienna Convention on Succession of States in Respect of State Property, Archives and Debts (n 14).
20 See, Chapter 13, Section 4.2.
21 *Yemen v. Compagnie d'Enterprises CFE SA*, Cyprus Supreme Court. 8 June 2002, No 10717.
22 See, Chapter 13, Section 4.1.
23 Vienna Convention on Succession of States in Respect of State Property, Archives and Debts (n 14).
24 *Mytileneos* (n 7) [7].
25 Ibid., [158].
26 Ibid.

15.10 As mentioned above,[27] a new State could be bound by contracts signed by the predecessor State when the investment was made and performed uniquely on that territory. When this is the case, it is likely that the new State *benefited* from the consequences of such an investment on its territory and will continue to do so after independence. The continuing State may refuse to take part in proceedings arising in these circumstances on the ground that the successor State should be responsible for the proper execution of these contracts, including any liabilities that may result. It would indeed seem logical for the successor State to be considered as the respondent in the context of such proceedings. In fact, the successor State may consider such an arbitration claim as a portion of the 'debt' of the predecessor State for which it should be responsible after the date of succession.[28] But, what happens if the new State (just like the continuing State) refuses to do so? This is a situation where there would simply be no State acting as the respondent in the proceedings. Could the tribunal simply decide that the new secessionist State should now be considered as the proper respondent in these ongoing proceedings? In other words, can a tribunal, *during* the proceedings, simply 'replace' the State formally designated as the respondent with another State? In my view, a tribunal does not have the power to do that (as further examined below,[29] the answer may be different in the context of commercial arbitration involving private companies).

15.11 The question seems even more problematic in the context of allegations of BIT violations which entirely took place on the territory of what is now the secessionist State. As mentioned above,[30] the new State is not automatically bound by the BITs signed by the predecessor State. In the absence of any consent to treaty continuation by the home State of the investor and the new State, that State is not a party to the BIT under which the investor filed a claim. Any decision by the new State to nevertheless participate as a respondent in such on-going proceedings would have some rather peculiar consequences. The new successor would thus be the respondent State in proceedings involving allegations of a violation of a treaty to which it *is not a party* and which were in fact committed by *another State* (the predecessor State) at a time when it did not even exist as a sovereign State. For these reasons, a new State

---

27 See, Chapter 14, Section 2.

28 Some support for this position can be found under Art. 40 of the Vienna Convention on Succession of States in respect of State Property, Archives and Debts (n 14). Under this provision, 'unless the predecessor State and the successor State otherwise agree, the State debt of the predecessor State shall pass to the successor State in an equitable proportion, taking into account, in particular, the property, rights and interests which pass to the successor State in relation to that State debt'.

29 See, Chapter 15, Section 2.5.

30 See, Chapter 5, Section 2.5.

may refuse to participate in such proceedings. On the contrary, by participating in the proceedings, a new State could signal its intention to be bound by that BIT.[31] In any event, what is clear is that without the consent of the new State, a tribunal does not have the power to *replace* the predecessor State by the secessionist State as the respondent in such proceedings.

2.3 Dissolution of States

15.12 In the context of dissolution, the situation also seems very problematic. The respondent State against which the investor has filed a claim no longer exists as a sovereign State. This State therefore cannot participate in the proceedings. Evidently, one option is for one of the successor States to decide to act as the respondent in such proceedings. In the context of State contracts, the analysis mentioned above[32] shows that, in general, new States are not bound by obligations arising from such contracts signed by the predecessor State. Yet, I have also referred to a number of relevant factors and circumstances where one of the successor States should be considered bound by such obligations.[33] Thus, it would seem logical for a new State to act as the respondent in an on-going proceeding whenever allegations are specifically linked to a contract that was entirely performed on what is now its territory. The new State could consider any such pending arbitration claim as a portion of the debt of the predecessor State for which it should assume responsibility.[34]

15.13 But what happens if none of the successor States accept acting as the respondent in such proceedings? Ultimately, the question comes back to whether a tribunal would have the power in such a situation to simply 'replace', during the proceedings, the predecessor State (which no longer exists) by one of the successor States as the proper respondent, and if so, which one. As mentioned above, in my opinion, a tribunal would not have the power to do so. The outcome does not differ in the context of BIT violations considering that there is no principle of automatic continuation of BITs in the context of dissolution.[35]

31 As noted in Chapter 4, Section 2.2, the continuation of a BIT requires not only the consent of the new State, but also that of the other State party to the treaty (i.e., the home State of the claimant investor).

32 See, Chapter 13, Section 3.1.

33 See, Chapter 14.

34 Support for such a solution can be found under Art. 41 of the Vienna Convention on Succession of States in Respect of State Property, Archives and Debts (n 14):

> When a State dissolves and ceases to exist and the parts of the territory of the predecessor State form two or more successor States, and unless the successor States otherwise agree, the State debt of the predecessor State shall pass to the successor States in equitable proportions, taking into account, in particular, the property, rights and interests which pass to the successor States in relation to that State debt.

35 See, Chapter 5, Section 2.5.

2.4 Transfer of territory

15.14 In the context of a cession of territory, the situation is complicated when on-going proceedings concern contractual breaches or violations of a BIT specifically related to the territory that was ceded/transferred from one State to another. Importantly, the identity of the predecessor State, as a sovereign State, is *not affected* by the cession of part of its territory. Logically, it should continue to be acting as the respondent in any on-going proceedings. Yet, that State may refuse to take part in such proceedings on the grounds that the successor State now has sovereignty over that territory and, consequently, should assume all liabilities and responsibilities related to it. Such refusal may not be fatal in the event that the successor State decides to take over the responsibilities. That position would indeed be logical in that context.[36] But, if it were to refuse, there would simply be no respondent in such proceedings. A tribunal would not have the power in such a situation to simply 'replace' the predecessor State by the successor State as the proper respondent in the proceedings.

15.15 The situation is all the more complicated when the on-going proceedings concern allegations of BIT violations in relation to the territory transferred. Let us take the hypothetical example of Crimea being in a situation of a *legal* cession of territory by Ukraine to Russia (and therefore, solely for the sake of argument, *not* involving any *illegal* annexation) and a French investor having started proceedings under the France-Ukraine BIT before the date of succession. In accordance with the 'moving treaty frontiers' rule, Ukraine's BITs would cease to apply in Crimea, and Russia's BITs would now take effect on that territory after the cession.[37] Which of the States, either the predecessor State (Ukraine) or the successor State (Russia), should be acting as the respondent in these proceedings? One simple option would be for the predecessor State to agree to continue acting as the respondent in the proceedings. This would be logical given the fact that the claim concerns allegations of a breach committed by Ukraine (not Russia) under a treaty to which it is a party. Yet, Ukraine may refuse to take part in these proceedings since it is now Russia who has sovereignty over that territory and should, accordingly, take over all liabilities and responsibilities related to it.

---

36 As mentioned above (see, Chapter 13, Section 2.1), the successor State should be considered bound by obligations arising from contracts which were signed by the predecessor State before the cession whenever these contracts are linked to the ceded territory. I have also examined above (see, Chapter 14, Sections 2 and 4) a number relevant factors and circumstances which could further strengthen this conclusion, including the concepts of the territorial 'nexus' and unjust enrichment.

37 See, Chapter 5, Section 1.1.1.

15.16 Indeed, Russia may agree to act as the respondent in such proceedings. Russia could consider any such pending arbitration claim as a portion of the 'debt' of the predecessor State for which it should be responsible after the cession of territory.[38] However, in this situation, Russia would be the respondent State in proceedings involving allegations of violations of a treaty to which it *is not a party* (the France-Ukraine BIT) and which were in fact committed by *another State* (Ukraine) at a time when it exercised *no sovereignty* over that given territory. For all these reasons, it may be that the successor State would simply refuse to act as the respondent in such proceedings. Such an outcome would be highly problematic since no State would be the respondent in the proceedings. As mentioned above, a tribunal does not have the power to 'replace' the predecessor State by the successor State. In any event, what is clear is that a tribunal only has jurisdiction over that specific claim filed by that French investor under the France-Ukraine BIT. It does not have jurisdiction over any other BITs to which *Russia* is a party. Evidently, the tribunal cannot decide to apply the Russia-France BIT to a claim filed under a *different* treaty (France-Ukraine BIT).

2.5 One illustration in the different context of commercial arbitration: the *Société des Grands Travaux de Marseille* case

2.5.1 Introduction

15.17 In the context of contracts signed between *private entities*, an arbitration clause is, in principle, binding only on the parties to the contract. One exception is in the context of a legal succession. As noted by Born, one of the consequences of a legal succession is that the succeeding company 'will be the owner of all assets and liabilities (including contract rights and obligations) of the previously-existing entities'.[39] He also added that 'most national laws provide that the merged or surviving entity succeeds by operation of law as a party to the contracts, including the arbitration agreements, of the previously-existing entities'.[40]

15.18 The *Société des Grands Travaux de Marseille v. East Pakistan Industrial Development Corporation* case deals with the slightly different question as to whether

38 In this respect, the successor State could rely on Art. 37 of the Vienna Convention on Succession of States in Respect of State Property, Archives and Debts (n 14). Under this provision while 'the passing of the State debt of the predecessor State to the successor State is to be settled by agreement between them', when no such agreement is concluded 'the State debt of the predecessor State shall pass to the successor State in an equitable proportion, taking into account, in particular, the property, rights and interests which pass to the successor State in relation to that State debt'.

39 Gary B. Born, *International Commercial Arbitration* 2nd edn (Kluwer 2014) 1462–3.

40 Ibid.

an arbitration clause contained in a contract signed by a company with a Bangladeshi *State-owned* company can extend to *another* non-signatory State-owned company of that State. The award also addresses the other more difficult question of whether the State of Bangladesh could be considered bound by the arbitration clause contained in the original contract. The question as to whether a State is bound by an arbitration clause contained in a contract signed by one of its State-owned companies is controversial. It has been suggested that while it should generally not be the case,[41] certain exceptions exist, including one based on the doctrine of corporate-veil piercing.[42] In the *Société des Grands Travaux de Marseille* case, the sole arbitrator extended the arbitration agreement signed by one Bangladeshi *State-owned* company to *another* non-signatory Bangladeshi State-owned company as well as to the *Government* of Bangladesh, who was joined to the arbitration proceedings. Authors have generally endorsed the solution reached in this award, given the very special circumstances of the case.[43]

15.19 It is true that the question examined in this section is different from the one decided by the sole arbitrator in the *Société des Grands Travaux de Marseille* case. Thus, this section examines the question of the replacement of *one State by another*. Yet, the case is interesting because the issues tackled in the award may have certain implications in the context of State succession. Thus, although the award does not address the issue of State succession per se, the origin of the dispute concerns the consequences of the secession of Bangladesh from Pakistan in 1971. Taken from that broader temporal perspective, this is a case involving the extension of an arbitration clause contained in a contract signed by a State-owned company *from Pakistan* (the predecessor and continuing State) to another non-signatory *Bangladeshi* State-owned company as well as to the *new secessionist State* of Bangladesh. Yet, it should be noted that although the reasoning of the award may be interesting, it remains that it should not be considered as an endorsement to the powers of a tribunal to

---

41 Georgios Petrochilos, 'Extension of the Arbitration Clause to Non-Signatory States or State Entities: Does it Raise a Difference?' in Bernard Hanotiau and Eric A. Schwartz (eds), *Multiparty Arbitration* (ICC Institute of World Business Law, Kluwer 2010) 120, referring to *Svenska Petroleum Exploration AB v. Lithuania* [2006] EWCA Civ 755 [81], but also to different conclusions reached by other tribunals, for instance: *Zeevi Holdings v. Bulgaria and the Privatization Agency of Bulgaria*, UNCITRAL Case No UNC 39/DK, Final Award, 25 October 2006; *Elf Aquitaine Iran v. National Iranian Oil Company*, Preliminary Award, 14 January 1982.

42 Ibid., 123: 'there are two circumstances where the effects of an arbitration agreement may be extended to a non-signatory state or state entity in the absence of substantive liability on the basis of ordinary private law principles'. According to him, an arbitration agreement can be extended to a non-signatory on the basis of an implicit intent of the State to be bound and the doctrine of corporate-veil piercing.

43 See, Karl-Heinz Böckstiegel, *Arbitration and State Enterprises: A Survey on the National and International State of Law and Practice*, (Kluwer 1984) 45–6; P. Lalive, 'Arbitrage international et ordre public suisse: Une surprenante décision du Tribunal fédéral: l'arrêt SGTM/Bangladesh' (1978) 98 *Revue de droit Suisse* 529.

'replace' *one State by another* as the proper respondent during ongoing proceedings. Ultimately, the circumstances of this case are truly unique and exceptional. The conclusion reached by the sole arbitrator simply cannot be extended more generally to State succession questions in investment arbitration disputes.

2.5.2 The facts of the case

The case involved the East Pakistan Industrial Development Corporation (EPIDC), a corporation founded and wholly owned by the Pakistan Government.[44] In 1965, EPIDC concluded a contract with the French company Société des Grands Travaux de Marseille (SGTM). Under this contract, SGTM was to construct a pipeline for the transport of gas in the Eastern part of Pakistan. Importantly, this territory seceded from Pakistan when the People's Republic of Bangladesh declared its independence in 1971. The contract provided for arbitration in Geneva under the ICC Rules and for Pakistani law to govern the contract. Two years *before* Bangladesh's independence, SGTM filed an arbitration claim in the amount of FF12 million. The parties subsequently designated Mr. Andrew Martin as sole arbitrator and agreed that arbitration would take place in Geneva under the arbitration law of the Canton of Geneva. In 1972, approximately one year *after* Bangladesh declared its independence, the terms of reference were signed by the parties (EPIDC and SGTM). **15.20**

A mere *two days* after the signing of the terms of reference, the President of Bangladesh passed a decree, Order No. 39, providing for the establishment of the Bangladesh Industrial Development Corporation (BIDC), which was to replace the EPIDC.[45] Importantly, Order No. 39 also provided that all assets of EPIDC were transferred to and vested in BIDC, and that all debts and liabilities incurred were 'unless the Bangladesh Government otherwise directed' deemed to have been incurred by BIDC. The Order also contained the following clause (clause (e) of sect. 4) specifically dealing with arbitration proceedings to which EPIDC had been a party: **15.21**

44 *Société des Grands Travaux de Marseille v. East Pakistan Industrial Development Corporation*, ICC Case No. 1803, reported in *Collection of ICC Arbitral Awards, 1974–1985*, 40ff.

45 Ibid. Order No. 39, 'The Bangladesh Industrial Development Corporation Order 1972', which came into force on 9 May 1972, but which had a retroactive effect and was deemed to have had effect on 26 March 1971 (i.e., the date of the declaration of independence). According to the case report (ibid., 41), 'The Order provided that subscriptions for the shares of EPIDC were automatically transferred to BIDC, that the board of directors of EPIDC was deemed to be the board of directors of BIDC, and that all officers, advisers and other employees of EPIDC were automatically transferred to BIDC.' It should be added that the President of Bangladesh subsequently decreed the dissolution of EPIDC (Order No. 78, 'The Bangladesh Industrial Development Corporation (Amendment) Order 1972', with effect from 4 July 1972).

> All arbitration proceedings to which, immediately before the commencement of this Order, the East Pakistan Development Corporation was a party shall be deemed to have abated and no award or decision made or given in such proceedings shall have any effect or be binding on, or enforceable against, the East Pakistan Industrial act on behalf of the East Pakistan Industrial Development Corporation in any such proceedings shall be deemed to be revoked and cancelled with effect from the 26th day of March, 1971, and any provision in the contract or agreement providing for the settlement by arbitration of the disputes in respect of which such proceedings were instituted, shall be deemed to be of no legal effect; Provided that the disputes in respect of which such arbitration proceedings were instituted may be settled by such means as may be determined by an agreement between the Bangladesh Industrial Development Corporation and the party concerned.[46]

15.22 *At this stage* (in September 1972), SGTM requested from the arbitrator that BIDC be substituted as the respondent for EPIDC, or alternatively, that BIDC be added as the respondent in the arbitration proceedings. One month later, the President of Bangladesh decreed a new order ('Disputes Debts Order') which provided:

> Any debt, liability or obligation incurred by the erstwhile East Pakistan Industrial Development Corporation arising out of or in connection with any contract shall be deemed not to have been incurred, undertaken, entered into or made by the Bangladesh Industrial Development Corporation if such debt, obligation, liability or contract is or was the subject matter of any dispute.[47]

15.23 It should be noted that at that time, SGTM was the only creditor of EPIDC and this Order was clearly aimed at impacting the present arbitration dispute.[48] Four days later, the President decreed Order no. 140 providing for the dissolution of BIDC and that all of its assets were to be vested in the Bangladesh Government.[49] Importantly, the Order indicated that '[t]he Government shall consider any representations which may be made to it by or on behalf of persons claiming to be creditors of BIDC or of any predecessor in title thereof' and that it had the 'power to make ex gratia payment of compensation in respect of any such claim', but only 'if and to the extent that the same shall to it appear to be just'.

---

46 Ibid.

47 Ibid.

48 P. Lalive, 'Jurisprudence de droit international privé', (1978) ASDI 393.

49 Order 140, 'The Bangladesh Industrial Development Corporation (Dissolution) Order 1972', 15 November 1972.

2.5.3 The arbitrator's procedural order

The tribunal issued a procedural order on 15 December 1972 ordering that: (1) BIDC be substituted as the respondent to replace EPIDC; and (2) the Government of Bangladesh be joined as the second respondent in the arbitration proceedings.[50] **15.24**

The arbitrator first examined Order No. 39. He considered that the order was a 'universal succession' within the meaning of Article 17 of the Swiss Federal CCP.[51] Accordingly, BIDC 'must be deemed to have been, *ab initio*, a party to the contract in question' and it must be 'substituted for EPIDC in the arbitration proceedings'.[52] He also considered the effect of one passage contained in Order No. 39 indicating that debts and liabilities of EPIDC would not be transmitted to BIDC if the Government decided so. Indeed, this was what the President did by subsequently issuing the Disputes Debts Order. Yet, for the Arbitrator, it was 'equally, and painfully, clear' that the Disputes Debts Order had been issued 'for the sole purpose of being injected as a spoliatory measure into the present arbitration'.[53] For him, the order was a 'discriminatory and confiscatory measure directed exclusively against the present Claimant and the present arbitration'.[54] He also concluded that the 'tenor and intended effect' of the order was 'wholly repugnant to Swiss conceptions of natural justice, fair dealing and the standards of morality binding upon sovereign Governments'.[55] He added that: **15.25**

> the notion that a debt should become void and indeed nonexistent *ab initio* for no better reason than that the debtor has chosen to put it in dispute is an extreme example of what natural justice abhors – the person or the public authority setting itself up as judge of its own cause.[56]

In sum, the order was 'a flagrant abuse of right and a measure which is quite irreconcilable with Swiss "ordre public"; it should not be recognized or applied by any Swiss judge or in any arbitration which is proceeding in Switzerland and is governed by Swiss procedural law'.[57]

---

50 *Société des Grands Travaux de Marseille* (n 44), Procedural Order, 15 December 1972. The reasons for such order were given by the arbitrator in a document dated 8 January 1972.

51 The arbitrator held that the law governing the effect of the dissolution of EPIDC was the Swiss Concordat on Arbitration. In accordance with Art. 24 of the Swiss Concordat, the arbitrator applied 'by analogy' the Swiss Federal Code of Civil Procedure (Art. 17(3)) providing that 'Succession on the ground of universal succession or as a result of specific provisions of the law is not to be regarded as a change of a party.'

52 *Société des Grands Travaux de Marseille* (n 44), 44.

53 Ibid.

54 Ibid.

55 Ibid.

56 Ibid.

57 Ibid.

15.26 The arbitrator went on to examine the effect of clause (e) of sect. 4 of Order No. 39 regarding the arbitration proceedings. He concluded that its purpose was to 'deprive any award in the present arbitration of its effect, not only in Bangladesh but also in the outside world at large'.[58] He considered that 'as a matter of public international law the Bangladeshi legislator cannot validly interfere with arbitral proceedings which are pending in a foreign country to which his territorial jurisdiction does not extend'.[59] He described the purpose of the clause as 'by any acceptable standard of international law and State practice a most reprehensive interference with the functioning of the judicial machinery (including arbitration) of a foreign country', which was contrary to Swiss public order 'by reason of its discriminatory and confiscatory nature'.[60]

15.27 The arbitrator finally considered the legal effects of Order No. 140 which dissolved BIDC and transferred to the Government of Bangladesh all of its assets and liabilities. He emphasized on one 'irregularity' contained in the Order: 'the Government makes no promise to settle the debts, and notably the foreign debts as a matter of legal duty; it promises no more than to consider presentations and, at its discretion, to make ex gratia payments'.[61] For the arbitrator, this 'irregularity' was in violation of international law and was a 'clear breach of the Bangladesh Government's duty under customary international law to pay prompt, effective and adequate compensation'.[62] The arbitrator also stated that 'it is right and proper for a judge or arbitrator to refuse to accept the destruction of a foreign juristic person' because in this case it 'shocked the conscience of the community' and it was contrary to the Swiss's 'ordre public'.[63] Consequently, the arbitrator decided to wipe out the 'irregularity' and to give effect to the universal succession under Order No. 140.

15.28 The arbitrator concluded that 'the Bangladesh Government must be deemed to have been an original party to the arbitration clause of the Principal Agreement which is at issue in these proceedings' and consequently, had it joined as a defendant in the proceedings.[64] It should be added that in 1973 the arbitrator rendered his final award holding that BIDC and the Government of Bangladesh were jointly and severally liable to pay SGTM approximately FFR11.8 million, plus interest.

---

58 Ibid., 45.
59 Ibid.
60 Ibid.
61 Ibid., 46.
62 Ibid. The arbitrator considered that under the relevant Swiss conflict rule, the legality of this 'irregularity' had to be determined by to the law of the seat, i.e., the law of Bangladesh, but only insofar as that law was compatible with public international law.
63 Ibid., 47.
64 Ibid., 46–7.

2.5.4 Annulment proceedings before Swiss courts

The arbitrator's procedural order was subject to annulment proceedings commenced by the two defendants before the Cantonal Court of Geneva. The court dismissed the action instituted by BIDC on the ground that it no longer existed, but admitted the action instituted by the Bangladesh Government. The court therefore annulled the award on the ground that the arbitrator lacked competence to force the Government of Bangladesh to be a defendant in the proceedings, and to substitute EPIDC (which had been dissolved) with BIDC (a non-existing legal entity). This decision was appealed by SGTM. The Supreme Court (*Tribunal Fédéral*) upheld the decision of the lower court.[65] **15.29**

The court was of the view that the Orders of the State of Bangladesh did not amount to a universal succession under Swiss law. Nevertheless, the court recognized that the effect of these orders was 'to deprive the appellant from the possibility of presenting his claims' in conformity with the contract and they therefore had a 'discriminatory character because the appellant is practically the only one aimed at by these Orders'.[66] The court also noted that 'the fact that a State appropriate[s] to itself the assets of a corporation governed by its law, without having regard to the corresponding debts and liabilities, is incompatible with Swiss ordre public'.[67] Yet, for the court there was 'no mandatory and well established rule of Swiss legal order which obliges a party to submit itself to an arbitral procedure against its will' and therefore concluded that Swiss public order could not be the basis for compelling Bangladesh to be a party to the proceedings.[68] This specific aspect of the court's decision has been criticized by writers.[69] **15.30**

---

65 *Société des Grands Travaux de Marseille v. East Pakistan Industrial Development Corporation*, Swiss Federal Supreme Court (Tribunal Fédéral), Decision, May 5, 1976, in: (1980) *Yearbook Commercial Arbitration* 217. See also, analysis in Lalive (n 48) 387.

66 Ibid., 219.

67 Ibid.

68 Ibid.

69 Lalive (n 48) 387; Lalive (n 43) 529–51.

16

SUCCESSION AFFECTING THE HOME STATE OF THE CLAIMANT INVESTOR AND RESULTING IN CHANGES OF NATIONALITY

INTRODUCTION

16.01 The previous chapter examined the situation when the events of succession have an impact on the respondent State in on-going proceedings. This chapter focuses on the different situation when events affect the *home State* of the claimant investor which may result in changes of nationality *during* arbitration proceedings.[70] To take a simple illustration, what happens to the claim of an investor from Sarajevo against the Netherlands under the Netherlands-SFRY

70 On this question, see: Belén Olmos Giupponi, 'Exploring the Links Between Nationality Changes and Investment Claims Arising out of Armed Conflicts', *International Investment Law & the Law of Armed Conflict*, 5–6 October 2017, Athens Colloquium. It is important to note that I will only examine the question of what happens when succession occurs *after* the request for arbitration has been filed by the claimant investor, not the reverse situation where a request for arbitration is submitted after such an event.

BIT if Bosnia becomes an independent State *during* the arbitration proceedings. In such a case, the person who started the arbitration claim as a Yugoslav national has now become a national of the new State of Bosnia. Should the tribunal seized under the Netherlands-SFRY BIT still have jurisdiction over that claim given the fact that the claimant is no longer a Yugoslav national? Is there a rule of international law requiring that a claimant remains, throughout the arbitration proceedings, a national of the home State party to a BIT under which a claim was filed? I will answer these two questions in Sections 2.2 and 2.3 respectively. Before doing so, a few words should be said about the rules of State succession regarding changes in nationality (Section 2.1).

Questions of State succession affecting the home State of the claimant investor and resulting in changes of nationality are especially relevant in the context of arbitration claims filed under a BIT. As noted by one writer, nationality is the gateway to legal protection under an investment treaty.[71] Thus, a tribunal's jurisdiction over a dispute is based, inter alia, on whether the claimant qualifies as an 'investor' of one of the contracting parties under the BIT. BITs require that an 'investor' have the nationality of that contracting party. As further explained below, in the context of an ICSID arbitration, the Convention requires that strict nationality requirements be fulfilled. In contrast, the question of the nationality of a claimant filing a request for arbitration under a State contract is generally *not* relevant to determine a tribunal's jurisdiction over a dispute.[72] **16.02**

1. OUTLINE OF THE BASIC RULES REGARDING ACQUISITION/LOSS OF NATIONALITY IN THE CONTEXT OF STATE SUCCESSION

This section will distinguish the existing rules regarding the acquisition/loss of nationality in the context of State succession depending on whether the claimant in the arbitration proceedings is a *natural* person (an individual) (Section 1.1) or a *legal* person (corporation, company) (Section 1.2). **16.03**

---

71 Anthony C. Sinclair, 'The Substance of Nationality Requirements in Investment Treaty Arbitration', (2005) 20 *ICSID Rev*; Pia Acconci, 'Determining the Internationally Relevant Link between a State and a Corporate Investor, Recent Trends Concerning the Application of the 'Genuine Link Test', (2004) 5 *World Inv & Trade* 139.

72 Thus, no consequences are likely to arise in the event when an individual or a corporation changes his/her/its nationality during the arbitration proceedings. The situation is entirely different, of course, if the claimant has initiated proceedings under the ICSID Convention where strict nationality requirements must be fulfilled.

1.1 Individuals

16.04 Let us take the example of Mr. Smith being a national of State A and having filed an arbitration claim against State B under the BIT entered into by States A and B. What would happen if, *during* the proceedings, a given event causes a change in the identity of State A? Specifically, what would be the consequences for Mr. Smith regarding his nationality? Different questions will arise depending on the types of succession involved.[73] Indeed, different solutions have been adopted under the Draft Articles on the Nationality of Natural Persons in Relation to State Succession (the 'Draft Articles'). Although the Draft Articles are non-binding, they nevertheless provide useful guidelines regarding changes of nationality affecting natural persons (the Draft Articles do not apply to legal persons[74]). The following paragraphs summarize the solutions which should prevail depending on the different types of succession involved:

- unification between State A and another State to create new State C: after the unification, Mr. Smith will no longer be a national of State A since it has ceased to exist. He will acquire the nationality of State C if he is now (i.e., after the date of succession) habitually residing in the territory of that new State. The principle is now well-established under State practice,[75] and it is reflected at Article 21 of the Draft Articles.[76]
- incorporation of State A within State C: after the integration, Mr. Smith will no longer be a national of State A since it no longer exists. He will acquire the nationality of State C if he is habitually residing in the territory of that State. The principle is now well-established under State practice,[77] and it is reflected at Article 21 of the Draft Articles.
- dissolution of State A leading to the creation of several new States (C, D, E): after the dissolution, Mr. Smith will no longer be a national of State A since it no longer exists. He will normally acquire the nationality of

73 These questions are examined in Fraterman (n 1) 20ff.

74 The reasons for excluding legal persons from the work of the ILC are explained in ILC, 'First Report by the Special Rapporteur V. Mikulka on State Succession and Its Impact on the Nationality of Natural and Legal Persons', UN A/CN.4/467, (1995) II(1) *Yearbook ILC* 18–19 [hereinafter 'ILC, First Report, Mikulka, Succession to Nationality'].

75 A. Zimmerman, 'State Succession and the Nationality of Natural Persons Facts and Possible Codification' in P.M. Eisemann and M. Koskenniemi (eds), *State Succession: Codification Tested against the Facts* (Martinus Nijhoff 2000) 618, 651; Zimmermann (n 12) [26]. See also: ILC, 'Draft Articles on Nationality of Natural Persons in relation to the Succession of States with commentaries', 1999, 51st session, (1999) II(2) *Yearbook ILC* 42 [hereinafter 'ILC, Commentary on Draft Articles on State Succession to Nationality']: 'The Commission is of the view that Article 21 embodies a rule of customary international law.'

76 ILC, Draft Articles on the Nationality of Natural Persons in relation to State Succession, UN GAOR 54th Sess. Supp. No. 10, UN Doc. A/54/10, 12 Dec. 1999, [hereinafter 'ILC, Draft Articles on State Succession to Nationality'], Art. 21.

77 Zimmerman (n 75) 618, 651; Zimmermann (n 12) [26].

one of the new States (say, State C) if he is, after the date of succession, habitually residing in the territory of that new State.[78] This is the solution provided for under Article 22 of the Draft Articles.[79]

- secession of State C from State A. If Mr. Smith is habitually residing in the territory which seceded from State A to become State C, he would normally acquire the nationality of the new State C. This is the solution adopted at Article 24 of the Draft Articles.[80] On the contrary, if Mr. Smith is habitually residing in the territory which remained part of State A (after the secession of State C) he will keep the nationality of State A.
- Newly Independent State: same solution as secession.[81]
- transfer of territory, whereby the territory where Mr. Smith was habitually residing is ceded by State A to State C. After the cession, Mr. Smith will no longer be a national of State A, and will normally acquire the nationality of State C if he is habitually residing in that territory.[82] This is the solution adopted under Article 20 of the Draft Articles,[83] which is 'based on the prevailing State practice'.[84] Yet, as noted by one writer, there is no automatic rule affirming the acquisition of one nationality (that of the successor State) and the loss of another (that of the predecessor State).[85]

---

78 ILC, Commentary on Draft Articles on State Succession to Nationality (n 75) 43 indicating that the criterion of habitual residence 'is consistent with the presumption in article 4', that it is 'widely accepted by publicists' and 'was used on a large scale' (for instance, in the context of the dissolution of the Austro-Hungarian Monarchy). The ILC Commentary also noted that in more recent cases of dissolution (Yugoslavia and Czechoslovakia), some successor States used the 'citizenship' of the former Republics as the main criterion for determining which individuals should be considered as their nationals. The ILC decided to 'resort to "citizenship" of a constituent unit of a State only with respect to persons residing outside the territory of a particular successor State' (ibid., 44).

79 ILC, Draft Articles on State Succession to Nationality (n 76), Art. 22. Art. 22(b) (i) also provides for the same solution regarding other persons living *outside* the territory of the new State, but who have 'an appropriate legal connection with a constituent unit of the predecessor State that has become part of that successor State'. See also, another category mentioned at Art. 22(b)(ii).

80 Ibid., Art. 24(a). The ILC Commentary on Draft Articles on State Succession to Nationality (n 75) explains that the criterion of habitual residence was applied in many cases of secession, but that other criteria (such as citizenship, place of birth) were used also in other instances. Art. 24(b)(i) also provides for the same solution regarding other persons living *outside* the territory of the new State, but who have 'an appropriate legal connection with a constituent unit of the predecessor State that has become part of that successor State'.

81 ILC, Commentary on Draft Articles on State Succession to Nationality (n 75) 46.

82 Zimmerman (n 75) 651; O. Dorr, 'Cession', in *Max Planck Encyclopedia of Public International Law* (n 12) [23]–[26].

83 ILC, Draft Articles on State Succession to Nationality (n 76), Art. 20.

84 ILC, Commentary on Draft Articles on State Succession to Nationality (n 75) 41.

85 Zimmermann (n 12) [27]:

> State practice confirms that, absent a treaty-based rule to the contrary, a transfer of territory does not, as such, involve an automatic change of the nationality of the inhabitants of the territory ceded. Yet, the acquiring State may under international law grant its nationality to those persons being domiciled in the ceded territory, regardless of whether they had previously lost the nationality of the ceding State. On

16.05 In all cases examined above, the question as to whether Mr. Smith becomes a national of the successor State (State C in all examples) is one to be determined under the domestic law of that State.[86] International law does not impose any strict obligations upon the successor State:

> According to the predominant opinion, the role of international law with respect to nationality is very limited. The function of international law is at the most to delimit the competence of the predecessor State to retain certain persons as its nationals and of the successor State to claim them as its own. International law cannot prescribe that such persons change their nationality, either automatically or by submission. (…) The necessary conclusion is that the function of international law with respect to nationality is, in principle, a negative function. In any event, international law cannot directly remedy the flaws of internal legislation, that is to say it cannot substitute for internal legislation indicating who are and who are not nationals of the State.[87]

16.06 The ILC Draft Articles only go so far as to establish a 'presumption' of nationality. Thus, Article 5 indicates that 'persons concerned having their habitual residence in the territory affected by the succession of States are presumed to acquire the nationality of the successor State on the date of such succession'.[88] The provision thus refers to the 'habitual residence' as being the relevant factor in this respect.[89] In other words, in all the examples examined above, Mr. Smith is simply *presumed* to have acquired the nationality of State C (the successor State). However, this is just a presumption. As explained in the ILC Commentary, it was meant to 'address the problem of the time-lag between the date of the succession of States and the adoption of legislation or, as the case may be, the conclusion of a treaty between States concerned on the question of the nationality of persons concerned following the succession'.[90] Mr. Smith's nationality remains a question to be determined under the

---

> the other hand, absent a treaty obligation, the State part of whose territory was ceded, is not under a customary law obligation to withdraw its nationality from the inhabitants of the territory concerned.

See also: Zimmerman (n 75) 623.

86 As noted in ILC, First Report, Mikulka, Succession to Nationality (n 74) 167, there is a 'broad consensus in both the literature and the practice of the courts in favor of recognizing that nationality is governed essentially by internal law'. See also: *Autopista Concesionada de Venezuela, C.A. v. Venezuela*, ICSID Case No. ARB/00/5, 27 Sept. 2001 [61].

87 ILC, First Report, Mikulka, Succession to Nationality (n 74) 167.

88 ILC, Draft Articles on State Succession to Nationality (n 76).

89 ILC, Commentary on Draft Articles on State Succession to Nationality (n 75) 29, noting that 'habitual residence is the test that has most often been used in practice for defining the basic body of nationals of the successor State, even if it was not the only one' (referring to D.P. O'Connell, *State Succession in Municipal Law and International Law* (vol. I, CUP 1967) 518. Art. 8 of the ILC, Draft Articles on State Succession to Nationality (n 76) deals with the different situation of persons concerned having their habitual residence *in another State* and provides that 'a successor State does not have the obligation to attribute its nationality to persons concerned if they have their habitual residence in another State and also have the nationality of that or any other State'.

90 ILC, Commentary on Draft Articles on State Succession to Nationality (n 75) 28.

domestic law of each successor State.[91] Article 6 of the Draft Articles calls upon States to 'enact legislation on nationality and other connected issues arising in relation to the succession of States consistent with the provisions of the present draft articles'. Importantly, Article 4 of the Draft Articles calls upon States to 'take all appropriate measures to prevent' situations where individuals would become stateless as a result of the combination of the application of the domestic laws of the different States involved. Yet, as noted by one writer, 'States seem to have no customary law obligation to avoid causing statelessness.'[92]

The question as to whether Mr. Smith will *lose* the nationality of the predecessor State (State A in all examples above) in the context of a secession, a Newly Independent States, or of a transfer of territory is a matter to be determined by the domestic law of that State. The Draft Articles indicate that in the case of secession, the 'predecessor State shall withdraw its nationality from persons concerned qualified to acquire the nationality of the successor State' (but not before the person has effectively acquired the nationality of the new State).[93] Some States may provide individuals a 'right of option' regarding nationality.[94] Thus, under Article 26 of the Draft Articles, the continuing State and the new State shall grant a right of option to persons 'who are qualified to have the nationality' of both States. Similarly, in the context of a dissolution, the Draft Articles indicate that the new State should grant a right of option to those 'who are qualified to acquire the nationality of two or more successor States'.[95] Yet, there exists no general 'right of option' for individuals under international law.[96] States are free to offer such an option or not. The only limitation which seems to be imposed on States under the Draft Articles **16.07**

---

91 Ineta Ziemele, *State Continuity and Nationality: The Baltic States and Russia: Past, Present and Future as Defined by International Law* (Martinus Nijhoff 2005) 258.

92 Zimmerman (n 75) 651, 658.

93 ILC, Draft Articles on State Succession to Nationality (n 76) Art. 25(1).

94 Ibid., Art. 11. See: Gibran Van Ert, 'Nationality, State Succession, and the Right of Option: The Case of Quebec', (1998) 36 *Canadian YIL* 151.

95 Ibid., Art. 23(1).

96 Zimmermann (n 12) [22]:

> Generally speaking, it must be assumed that States involved in a process of succession should take into account the wishes of the people concerned, as well as existing family links and that they should avoid creating situations of statelessness (…) It is also doubtful whether, as of today, an individual right of option, which is frequently provided for in treaties, has also already become part of customary international law.

See also: Zimmerman (n 75) 651, 658: 'This lack of uniform State practice as to whether an option should be granted at all and the diversity of the solutions adopted forces one to doubt the customary nature of the obligation to grant a right of option.'

is that such a 'right of option' should be granted to individuals if they 'would otherwise become stateless as a result of the succession of States'.[97]

16.08 Ultimately, as explained by Zimmerman, there is nothing 'automatic' about the question of acquisition and loss of nationality in the context of State succession:

> In the past, it had been asserted that a succession of States automatically leads to the loss of the nationality of the predecessor State and to the automatic acquisition of the nationality of the respective successor State. Yet, a careful analysis of State practice proves that such an assumption is not warranted. Instead one may only assume that States concerned might, under certain circumstances, be under an obligation respectively to grant or to withdraw their nationality from the population living in the territory which is subject to the process of succession. In particular, the question arises as to what are the criteria for the respective successor State in order to be in a position to grant its nationality on the one hand and on the other hand, who may be considered to have retained the nationality of the respective predecessor State, where indeed such predecessor State continues to exist.[98]

16.09 The lack of strict rules regarding the question of the acquisition/loss of nationality resulting from State succession makes it difficult to draw any general conclusions.[99] In other words, whether or not Mr. Smith will lose his State A nationality and acquire that of State C will depend on the type of succession involved and, ultimately, on the solution adopted under the domestic laws of the States concerned.

1.2 Legal persons

16.10 Legal persons (including corporations) also have a nationality.[100] Each State is entirely free to determine under its own domestic law the criteria under which legal persons are considered to have its nationality.[101] In general terms, as noted by Judge Jessup in his separate opinion in the *Barcelona Traction* case, 'there are two standard tests of the nationality of a corporation':[102] the

97 ILC, Draft Articles on State Succession to Nationality (n 76) Art. 11(2). See also, Arts 1 and 4.

98 Zimmermann (n 12) [22].

99 Ziemele (n 91) 258–9, 65.

100 I. Seidl-Hohenveldern, *Corporations in and under International Law* (Grotius 1987) 8; ILC, First Report, Mikulka, Succession to Nationality (n 74) 166.

101 Peter Muchlinski, 'Corporations in International Law', in *Max Planck Encyclopedia of Public International Law* (n 12) [7]; Okan Beygo, 'Nationality of Corporations in International Claims Arising Out of Foreign Investment Disputes', (1993) 46 RHDI 34, 36ff; F.A. Mann, 'The Effect of State Succession upon Corporations', (1972) 88 LQR (also in F.A. Mann, *Studies in International Law* (OUP 1973) 526).

102 *Case Concerning the Barcelona Traction, Light and Power Co. Ltd. (Second Phase)* (Belgium v. Spain), Judgment of 5 February 1970, ICJ Reports 1970, Separate opinion, Judge Jessup [34].

principle of 'incorporation' which is generally prevailing under the domestic laws of countries of Common Law tradition and the concept of '*siège social*' or seat of the business (head office) which is favoured by States of Civil Law tradition.[103] Whether a State adopts one approach or another (or a combination of different criteria) is a matter of domestic law.[104]

A State can offer diplomatic protection to a legal person having its 'nationality'.[105] As noted by the ICJ in the *Nottebohm case*, while it is 'for every sovereign State, to settle by its own legislation the rules relating to the acquisition of its nationality' for both natural and legal persons, it remains that it is 'international law which determines whether a State is entitled to exercise protection and seize the Court'.[106] In this context, different tests have been applied under international law to determine the nationality of a legal person.[107] In the *Barcelona Traction case*, the court opted for one variant of the incorporation test: 'the traditional rule attributes the right of diplomatic protection of a corporate entity to the State under the laws of which it is incorporated and in whose territory it has its registered office'.[108] The ILC Draft Articles on Diplomatic Protection adopted a test referring first to incorporation, but also to the seat of business in the event where there is an insufficient connection.[109] **16.11**

103 Lucius Caflisch, 'La nationalité des sociétés commerciales en droit international privé', (1967) 24 ASDI 119ff. See also: ILC, 'Second report on State Succession and its impact on the nationality of natural and legal persons, by Mr. Vaclav Mikulka', UN A/CN.4/474, (1996) II(1) *Yearbook ILC* [hereinafter 'ILC, Second Report on State Succession to Nationality, Mikulka'] [144]:

> The nationality of legal persons is normally established by reference to one or more elements such as actual place of management, incorporation or formation, centre of operations and, sometimes, control or dominant interest. While in some legislations of the European continent reference is made to incorporation – formation – and the actual place of management as alternative criteria for determining the nationality of a legal person, under Anglo-American law, the norms relating to the legal status of commercial corporations do not include nationality as a point of attachment, but go directly to incorporation or formation.

104 L.C. Caflisch, 'The Protection of Corporate Investments Abroad in the Light of the *Barcelona Traction Case*', (1971) 31 ZaöRV 179.

105 Seidl-Hohenveldern (n 100) 7.

106 *Nottebohm Case*, ICJ Reports 1955, 20–21.

107 Beygo (n 101) 34, 54ff.

108 *Barcelona Traction Case* (n 102) [70].

109 ILC, Draft Articles on Diplomatic Protection with Commentaries, Text adopted at its 58th session, 2006, (2006) II(2) *Yearbook ILC*, Art. 9:

> For the purposes of the diplomatic protection of a corporation, the State of nationality means the State under whose law the corporation was incorporated. However, when the corporation is controlled by nationals of another State or States and has no substantial business activities in the State of incorporation, and the seat of management and the financial control of the corporation are both located in another State, that State shall be regarded as the State of nationality.

16.12 The question of the use of standard tests to determine the nationality of a corporation is more complex under BITs. States are indeed free to adopt whatever tests they want in their BITs, even standards that differ from those used under their own domestic law.[110] In the context of BIT arbitration proceedings, a tribunal will have to apply the criteria mentioned in that treaty. These instruments vary with respect to how they specifically define 'investor' and the nationality of corporations.[111] For instance, a study of BITs entered into by countries of the Americas found five different definitions of corporate nationality.[112] The same assessment can also be made for the rest of the world.[113] Some treaties require that a corporation be not only incorporated in a party State, but that its effective management (such as its headquarters) also be located there.[114] Other treaties further require that a corporation be controlled by nationals of the State of incorporation or have substantial business activities in that State.[115] Finally, at the other extreme of the spectrum, some BITs entered into by the Netherlands extend protection to legal entities not even incorporated in that country provided that they are controlled by Dutch nationals.[116] It is also not uncommon for States to adopt themselves different tests in their BITs depending on which State they are contracting with.[117]

16.13 Whether or not a State adopts under its own domestic law one standard test or another to determine corporate nationality will have some important consequences in the context of State succession.[118] As noted by Fraterman, 'since

110 Piero Bernardini, 'Nationality Requirements under BITs and Related Case Law', in F. Ortono et al. (eds) *Investment Treaty Law, Current Issues II, Nationality and Investment Treaty Claims* (BIICL 2007) 18.

111 See: Tarcisio Gazzini, 'The Role of Customary International Law in the Protection of Foreign Investment' (2007) 8 *J World Inv & Trade* 709; Rudolf Dolzer and Margrete Stevens, *Bilateral Investment Treaties*, 58 (Martinus Nijhoff Publ. 1995) 34.

112 Lawrence Jahoon Lee, 'Barcelona Traction in the 21st Century: Revisiting its Customary and Policy Underpinnings 35 Years Later', (2006) 42 *Stan JIL* 272. Out of 40 BITs examined, the author found no less than five different definitions of 'investor': five treaties defined nationality of a corporation solely based on incorporation; 15 required incorporation plus the seat of management; nine required incorporation, seat of management, *and* effective economic activities; ten allowed claims based on incorporation plus the seat of management *or* economic activities; and finally, only one treaty required incorporation and control.

113 K.J. Vandevelde, *Bilateral Investment Treaties: History, Policy and Interpretation*, (OUP 2010) 158ff; Bernardini (n 110) 20ff; Norah Gallagher, 'The Requirement for Substantive Nationality', in F. Ortono et al. (eds) *Investment Treaty Law, Current Issues II, Nationality and Investment Treaty Claims* (BIICL 2007) 31ff.

114 Sinclair (n 71) 374, discussing examples and referring specifically to the UK-Philippines BIT and the Italy-Libya BIT.

115 See, e.g., US Model BIT; Canada Model BIT.

116 For instance, the Netherlands-Bulgaria BIT, discussed in Sinclair (n 71) 368.

117 See examples in Beygo (n 101) 65ff.

118 It should be added here that (in context *other* than State succession) a legal person can change its nationality *voluntarily* by deciding to incorporate in a different State. In such a case, the company would first have to be dissolved under the law of the State of the original incorporation: Schereuer (n 3) 294 (quoting Broches). See also: M. Mendelson, 'The Runaway Train: the Continuous Nationality Rule from the Panevezys-Saldutiskis Railway Case to Loewen', in T. Weiler (ed), *International Investment Law and Arbitration: Leading Cases from*

legal persons are, by their very nature, constructs of the legal system of the State in which they are constituted, the particular rules of that State will be highly determinative of what happens to such entities after State succession'.[119] In other words, it is of great importance whether one State adopts the test of incorporation or that of the seat of management when examining the question of a corporation's change of nationality resulting from State succession. The point has been well-summarized by ILC Special Rapporteur Mikulka:

> The impact of State succession on these criteria for attachment is prima facie obvious. The criterion of actual place of management can give rise to attachment to the successor State in the case of unification, to one of the successor States in the case of dissolution, or, in the case of partial succession, to either the successor State or the predecessor State. The criterion of incorporation, on the other hand, can produce much more varied results: in cases in which the predecessor State ceases to exist, such as cases of unification through absorption, the legal order of the predecessor State may simply disappear. In cases of dissolution, the regime may be taken over – maintained – by all the successor States. In cases of separation of part of a territory, the legal order of the predecessor State continues to exist in that State and may at the same time be taken over – maintained – by the successor State.[120]

In the next paragraphs, I will briefly outline the impact that State succession could have on the nationality of corporations, distinguishing between situations where the home State of an investor adopted the seat of management or the incorporation approach.[121] **16.14**

The seat of management of a corporation will remain in the same place, notwithstanding the events of succession. In other words, while State borders may change, the seat will remain fixed in one location. In the context of a unification, an integration, or a transfer of territory, the seat of management of a corporation, which was located in the territory of the predecessor State (before the date of succession), will now be on the territory of the successor State. In the context of a dissolution, the seat will now be on the territory of *one* of the new successor States. In these cases, a corporation will very likely be considered as having the nationality of the successor State where its seat of management is now located after the date of succession. Each successor State can, of course, adopt whatever solution it considers appropriate to determine corporate nationality. Yet, it would appear logical for a successor State to **16.15**

---

the ICSID, NAFTA, Bilateral Treaties and Customary International Law (Cameron May 2005) 32, 34. The situation is different in the context of State succession where any change of nationality is *involuntary*.

119 Fraterman (n 1) 21.

120 ILC, Second Report on State Succession to Nationality, Mikulka (n 103) [151].

121 See, Fraterman (n 1) 21–2.

consider a corporation that has its seat on its territory as one of its nationals.[122] In the context of secession (or Newly Independent States), the nationality of the corporation will depend on whether the seat of management is (after the date of succession) located on the territory of the secessionist new State or on that of the continuing State.[123] Indeed, this is the conclusion reached by Mann, for whom corporations will normally become 'inhabitants of the successor State'.[124] However, the situation becomes more complicated when a company having its seat in a new State after the date of succession decides to register in *another* State.[125] This situation raises the potential issue of the 'competition' of two legal orders over one corporation and the possibility that they *both* consider it as having its nationality.

16.16 The situation is more problematic in the event that the home State has adopted incorporation as the relevant criteria to determine corporate nationality. The incorporation of a corporation is performed in accordance with a specific law of the home State. In situations where the predecessor State ceases to exist after succession (such as in situations of unification, integration, or dissolution), the legal order of that State also ceases to exist. In that case, a company incorporated under that law would, logically, be considered as dissolved. This is because the law under which that corporation was incorporated is simply no longer applicable. Whether or not some aspects of the legal order of the predecessor State (including its laws on incorporation of corporations) will remain in place after the date of succession is a matter to be determined by each successor State. In this context, a corporation would not automatically acquire the nationality of the successor State. This is ultimately a

---

122 Mann (n 101) 530.

123 E. Wyler, *La règle dite de la continuité de la nationalité dans le contentieux international*, (PUF 1990) 112:

> Pour ce qui a trait aux personnes morales, il convient de préciser qu'en l'absence de toute stipulation conventionnelle – cas fort rare – on admet l'application du droit de l'État prédécesseur à titre provisoire. Si cette législation a retenu le critère du siège administratif réel en matière d'attribution de nationalité, le fait que la société a maintenant son siège sur le territoire de l'État successeur conduit à considérer qu'elle a acquis la nationalité de celui-ci et perdu celle de l'État prédécesseur.

124 Mann (n 101) 530:

> It is submitted that a combination of three circumstances is required to bring about a change of domicile and nationality. These are the creation of the corporation under the law of the predecessor State, the present of the corporation itself in the transferred territory and the continuation of its presence after the transfer. Presence, for this purpose, (...) in the sense of the existence of both the registered office, the corporate home and the head office, the *siège administratif*, the center of control. It is in such circumstances that it is reasonable to regard the corporation as an 'inhabitant' who has elected to remain.

125 Ibid., 535. He refers to many cases, including one in the context of the independence of Algeria in which a company having its seat of business in Algiers decided to transfer its seat to Paris after independence. French courts have considered the company to now be French, but at the same time Algerian courts have considered it as an Algerian company. See: *Caisse centrale de réassurance des mutuelles agricoles*, in : *Clunet* (1967) 874, *Rev crit*, 1971, 451 (see also: 41 ILR, 369, 384).

matter to be decided by the successor State under its own legal order. The same situation would, in fact, prevail in the context of a transfer of territory.

In the context of a dissolution, the situation is also very complicated if more than one successor State decides to maintain the legal order of the predecessor State. This would lead to an awkward situation where one corporation could potentially be considered to be incorporated in more than one country and, consequently, have more than one nationality. The possibility for a corporation to have more than one nationality is a matter of controversy. It has been suggested that this may indeed be the case (in situations *not* involving State succession) when two States are using *different* tests to determine the nationality of an entity.[126] What could be peculiar in the specific setting of succession is the possibility for a corporation to have multiple nationalities while States are using the *same* test. One may think, for instance, of a situation in the context of a dissolution where a corporation could be considered to be 'incorporated' under the laws of two (or more) successor States at the same time. The same situation could also occur in the context of a secession. Since the legal order of the continuous State is not altered by secession, the identity and nationality of a company incorporated under such a law would also remain unaffected by the territorial changes.[127] In the event that the new State were to maintain the legal order of the predecessor State, a corporation could also be considered to have the nationality of both the continuator and the successor State at the same time. 16.17

126 Schreuer (n 3) 292:

> Juridical persons may be treated as having multiple nationalities where the criteria of incorporation, seat and control do not coincide. A company may be incorporated in State A, have its main seat of business in State A or B and may be controlled by nationals of State C. Additionally, if control is an admissible criterion for nationality, it may be shared by nationals of several States.

The same conclusion is reached by Wyler (n 123) 104:

> Ainsi, les États peuvent choisir souverainement les critères pertinents pour décider de l'attribution de leur nationalité à une personne morale. Ce choix témoigne d'une certaine diversité, d'où la possibilité de conflits, deux États pouvant prétendre chacun qu'une même entité jouit de sa nationalité en vertu d'un critère de rattachement différent (several examples are mentioned at 105ff).

See also: Caflisch (n 103) 150–51; Dorr (n 82) [27]. See, however, Mendelson, (n 118) 32, indicating that a 'company can of course have only one nationality'. For him, the passage from Schreuer's book (n 3) just quoted (see n 126) 'seems to confuse difficulties in determining what *is* the nationality of a company with the possibility of its holding multiple nationalities' (emphasis added), adding that 'in principle, it should not be possible for a company to hold more than one nationality or, at any rate, for a court or tribunal so to find in respect of any given matter' (see fn 88).

127 Mann (n 101) 530ff; Caflisch (n 103) 155–6; Wyler (n 123) 112:

> Mais au cas où le droit de l'État prédécesseur aurait opté pour le critère du lieu d'incorporation, l'État successeur accordera sa nationalité à l'entité dans l'hypothèse où l'État prédécesseur aurait disparu. Si ce dernier subsiste, l'application de ce même critère fait que la société conservera en principe la nationalité de l'État prédécesseur.

16.18 Having examined the basic rules of State succession regarding changes of nationality, the next section will focus on what a tribunal should do when such changes occur during the arbitration proceedings.

2. A TRIBUNAL SHOULD CONTINUE TO HAVE JURISDICTION OVER A CASE DESPITE A CLAIMANT CHANGING ITS NATIONALITY AFTER THE COMMENCEMENT OF THE PROCEEDINGS

16.19 The fundamental question examined in this section is whether or not a tribunal should *continue* to exercise jurisdiction over a dispute when an event of succession affects a claimant's nationality during the proceedings. The analysis begins by examining how tribunals should deal with such a situation when a claim has been initiated under a BIT (Section 2.1). I will then examine the specific conditions prevailing for ICSID arbitration claims (which could be filed under a BIT or a State contract) (Section 2.2).

2.1 The situation under BITs in general

16.20 In the context of an arbitration claim filed under a BIT, a tribunal will have to determine whether it has jurisdiction *ratione personae* over the dispute by applying the relevant provisions contained in the BIT.[128] Under BITs, the claimant needs to fulfill the nationality requirements under the definition of 'investor'. BITs' definition of 'investor' (almost always) refer to each State's domestic law on nationality.[129] The question of whether an investor can be considered as a 'national' of one of the parties to the BIT (and therefore have access to arbitration under the instrument and benefit from the substantive protections it contained) is therefore a matter of the domestic law of that State.[130] For this reason, tribunals will often have to analyse a State's domestic laws defining what is a 'national'.[131]

---

128 L.F. Reed and J.E. Davis, 'Who is a Protected Investor?' in Bungenberg, J. Griebel, S. Hobe and A. Reinisch (eds), *International Investment Law: A Handbook* (C.H. Beck, Hart, Nomos 2015) 619ff.

129 Vandevelde (n 113) 157.

130 Schreuer (n 3) 265; Schreuer and Dolzer (n 3) 47.

131 *Tza Yap Shum v. The Republic of Peru*, ICSID Case No. ARB/07/6, Decision on Jurisdiction and Competence, 19 June 2009 [67]–[77]. A good illustration of these basic principles is the reasoning of the tribunal in *Ioan Micula, Viorel Micula, S.C. European Food SA, S.C. Starmill S.R.L. and S.C. Multipack S.R.L v. Romania*, ICSID Case No. ARB/05/20, Decision on Jurisdiction and Admissibility, 24 September 2008 [86]:

> It is not disputed by the Parties that as a general principle it is for each State to decide in accordance with its law who is its national. This is a well established principle of international law and, as just recalled, is consistent with the provision of Article 1(2)(a) of the [Sweden-Romania] BIT [defining investors as 'any natural person who is a citizen of a Contracting Party in accordance with its Laws']. It is also well established in ICSID jurisprudence that the domestic laws of each Contracting State determine

While the question of the attribution of nationality is clearly one within the '*domaine réservé*' of each State,[132] an arbitral tribunal retains the authority to investigate claims of nationality when it is challenged.[133] This was indeed the conclusion reached by the *Soufraki* Tribunal: 16.21

> It is accepted in international law that nationality is within the domestic jurisdiction of the State, which settles, by its own legislation, the rules relating to the acquisition (and loss) of its nationality. Article 1(3) of the BIT reflects this rule. But it is no less accepted that when, in international arbitral or judicial proceedings, the nationality of a person is challenged, the international tribunal is competent to pass upon that challenge. It will accord great weight to the nationality law of the State in question and to the interpretation and application of that law by its authorities. But it will in the end decide for itself whether, on the facts and law before it, the person whose nationality is at issue was or was not a national of the State in question and when, and what follows from that finding. Where, as in the instant case, the jurisdiction of an international tribunal turns on an issue of nationality, the international tribunal is empowered, indeed bound, to decide that issue.[134]

Importantly, BITs generally do not indicate the specific moment in time when a claimant must satisfy that nationality requirement to have access to arbitration under the treaty.[135] In the context of disputes initiated under the UNCITRAL Rules (or any mechanism other than the ICSID Convention[136]), tribunals have often remained rather vague as to what they consider to 16.22

nationality. Thus, in this case, the Tribunal must determine the nationality of Messrs. Micula under the national law of the State whose nationality they claim to have, i.e., Swedish law.

132 *Nationality Decrees in the Tunis and Morocco Case*, PCIJ Series B, no. 4, 1923, 24.

133 *Ioan Micula* (n 131), [87]:

> The Parties disagree as to the role of international law in the Tribunal's interpretation of Article 1 of the BIT with respect to nationality. The Tribunal is of the opinion that in interpreting the BIT, i.e., an instrument between two sovereign States, it may take into account, as directed by Article 31(3)(c) of the Vienna Convention on the Law of Treaties, any relevant rules of international law. The Tribunal is also mindful of the role of international law when nationality is acknowledged for international purposes. Indeed, it is well established that the acquisition of nationality must not be inconsistent with international law. The burden of proving that nationality was acquired in a manner inconsistent with international law lies with the party challenging the nationality. In that respect, there exists a presumption in favour of the validity of a State's conferment of nationality. The threshold to overcome such presumption is high.

134 *Soufraki v. United Arab Emirates*, ICSID Case No. ARB/02/07, Award, 7 July 2004 [55], [63]. In *Soufraki v. United Arab Emirates*, ICSID Case No. ARB/02/07, Decision on Annulment, 5 June 2007 [64], the *ad hoc* Committee came to the same conclusion:

> the principle is in fact well established that international tribunals are empowered to determine whether a party has the alleged nationality in order to ascertain their own jurisdiction, and are not bound by national certificates of nationality or passports or other documentation in making that determination and ascertainment.

135 Reed (n 128) 633.

136 As further explained in next section, the ICSID Convention contains specific requirements on the critical date which has to be applied by an arbitral tribunal.

be the critical date.[137] Yet, it seems clear that the claimant must be a national of one of the parties to the BIT at the time that the request for arbitration is filed. BITs are however silent regarding the length of time a claimant should keep that nationality.[138] The question remains whether a claimant is required to retain the *same* nationality *after* the request for arbitration has been filed, and maintain that status up for the rest of the proceedings until the award is rendered by the tribunal. Some writers have argued that there exists no such requirement.[139] The *Yukos* award, decided under the Cyprus-Russia BIT and applying the UNCITRAL rules, also came to the conclusion that a change of nationality subsequent to the date the filing of the claim was not relevant for jurisdictional purposes.[140] The question is further examined in the next section in light of the specific rules existing under the ICSID Convention.

2.2 The specific criteria under the ICSID Convention

16.23 In order for an ICSID tribunal to exercise jurisdiction over a dispute it must meet the *ratione personae* and *ratione temporis* requirements of *both* the ICSID Convention *and* the investment protection instrument (which can be either a contract or an investment treaty).[141] Yet, since BITs generally provide no indications as to the timing of nationality, ICSID tribunals constituted under such treaties will focus on the specific requirements contained in the Convention. Under Article 25(1), tribunals have jurisdiction over legal disputes arising directly out of an investment between a 'Contracting State' (i.e., a State which is a party to the Convention) and a 'national of another Contracting State', which is almost always the claimant.[142] Article 25 imposes both a positive and

---

137 Reed (n 128) 633.

138 Ibid., 634.

139 Mendelson (n 118) 37; 'there is nothing in the language to suggest that the same nationality has to be held *continuously* between these two points [i.e. between the time of injury and filing the claim], and still less that a change of nationality subsequent to the institution of proceedings will affect standing' (emphasis in original). In the context of his analysis of the *Loewen* award (further examined below), he concludes that (at 38):

> there is nothing in the NAFTA itself to support the extension of the *dies ad quem* beyond the date of registration of the claim. Unless, therefore, such a requirement can be found in the applicable rules of the dispute-settlement mechanisms, it does not exist. As we have seen from the analysis above, of the rules of ICSID and its Additional Facility, there is no such requirement in the case of the former, and probably not in the case of the latter either.

140 *Hulley Enterprises Ltd. (Cyprus) v. Russia*, UNCITRAL, PCA Case No. Aa 226, Interim Award on Jurisdiction and Admissibility, 30 November 2009, [550]–[551].

141 Reed (n 128) 615.

142 Gustavo Laborde, 'The Case for Host State Claims in Investment Arbitration', (2010) 1(1) *J Int Disp Settl* 102. Thus, to the best of my knowledge, no BIT claim has ever been commenced by a host State against an investor under the ICSID Convention. The situation is different under State contracts where both parties have rights and obligations. Yet, it is only in rare situations that corporations are acting as respondents in claims submitted by States (or State-owned entities) alleging violation of their rights under a contract.

a negative requirement for investors (both natural and legal persons) to submit a claim under the Convention. First, the investor needs to be a 'national of another Contracting State', that is, a national of a State party to the Convention. Second, at the same time, the investor must *not* have the nationality of the host State against which the claim is filed. The Convention therefore excludes dual nationals if one of the nationalities is that of the host State. Most importantly, Article 25 deals with the relevant timing of such a nationality. Here, a distinction must be drawn between natural and legal persons.

With respect to a *legal* person,[143] Article 25 requires that it holds the nationality of a Contracting State (other than the host State) at *one moment only*:[144] 'on the date on which the parties consented to submit such dispute to ... arbitration'.[145] Article 25 does *not* require that the claimant have the nationality of a Contracting State at the moment when the alleged breach is committed. In the context of a BIT claim, the effective date of consent will often be the date when the investor started the proceedings.[146] The filing of the request for arbitration (and its registration with the Centre) is therefore the critical date when a claimant must satisfy the nationality requirement under a BIT in order to have access to ICSID arbitration. This is the important date for a tribunal when considering its jurisdiction over a dispute.[147] Changes of nationality occurring *after* that date are *not relevant* for jurisdictional purposes.[148] The point is well-explained by Schreuer: 16.24

> Any change in the juridical person's nationality after the date of consent is immaterial for jurisdiction. Subsequent to consent, a juridical person may lose the nationality of the original Contracting State and may acquire the nationality of a non-Contracting State or that of the host State without losing access to ICSID. As the Tribunal in

According to one estimate (M. Toral and T. Schultz, 'The State, a Perpetual Respondent in Investment Arbitration? Some Unorthodox Considerations', in Michael Waibel, Asha Kaushal, Kyo-Hwa Liz Chung, and Claire Balchin (eds), *The Backlash Against Investment Arbitration: Perceptions And Reality* (Kluwer 2010) 589) only five such claims have been identified under ICSID.

143 For Schreuer (n 3) 278, such an entity must have the legal personality under Art. 25 of the ICSID Convention.

144 Ibid., 294.

145 According to Schreuer ibid., 279ff, the determination of the nationality of a 'juridical' person should be based on the test of 'incorporation' and '*siège social*'.

146 Ibid., 294–5.

147 *Ceskoslovenska Obchodni Banka, a.s. v. The Slovak Republic*, ICSID Case No. ARB/97/4, Decision on Objections to Jurisdiction, 24 May 1999 [31]: 'It is generally recognized that the determination whether a party has standing in an international judicial forum for purposes of jurisdiction to institute proceedings is made by reference to the date on which such proceedings are deemed to have been instituted.'

148 C. McLachlan, L. Shore and M. Weiniger, *International Investment Arbitration: Substantive Principles* (OUP 2007) 153–4, 161; Zachary Douglas, *The International Law of Investment Claims* (CUP 2009) 291; Mendelson (n 118) 32.

Vivendi v. Argentina II observed: 'once established, jurisdiction cannot be defeated. It simply is not affected by subsequent events'.[149]

16.25 Article 25 requires that a *natural* person holds the nationality of a contracting State at *two different dates*: the date on which the parties consented to submit such a dispute to arbitration, and, on the date on which the request for arbitration is registered by the Centre. Importantly, natural persons must *not* have the nationality of the host State against which the claim is filed at these two dates.[150] Accordingly, it has been suggested that an individual investor could change his/her nationality between the two dates.[151] The Convention therefore does *not* require the natural person to have the nationality of a contracting State at the time of the commission of the internationally wrongful act and the alleged breach of the BIT.[152]

16.26 In any event, the Convention does not require the claimant to remain a national of that State *after* the request for arbitration has been registered by the Centre. This is indeed the position adopted by writers.[153] The *Siag* Tribunal clearly stated that 'the ICSID Convention does not require a party to hold

149 Schreuer (n 3) 295, referring to *Compañiá de Aguas del Aconquija SA and Vivendi Universal SA v. Argentina*, ICSID Case No. ARB/97/3, Decision on Jurisdiction, 14 November 2005 [63]. They also refer to the *Loewen* case (further discussed below) and the conclusion reached by the tribunal that a judicial person must have a continuous nationality until the date when the award is rendered by the tribunal noting (at 295) that this 'is certainly not a requirement of the ICSID Convention', adding that 'Art. 25 spells out the applicable rules on nationality for the purposes of ICSID's jurisdiction'.

150 Schreuer and Dolzer (n 3) 237. As noted by Schreuer (n 3) 276, 'the Convention only states that the positive and negative nationality requirements must be met at two discrete dates, that of consent and that of registration (...) it is silent on the intervening period'.

151 Schreuer (n 3) 276: 'The individual investor may change his or her nationality between the two critical dates, without affecting jurisdiction, as long as he or she has the nationality of some Contracting State other than the host State at both dates.' See also: Reed (n 128) 632–3.

152 It is noteworthy that in the case of *Victor Pey Casado and President Allende Foundation v. Chile*, ICSID Case No. ARB/98/2, Award, 8 May 2008 [414], the ICSID Tribunal stated that in the absence of any indication in the Spain-Chile BIT on the critical date, the nationality requirement had to me meet at the time of consent to arbitration *and* at the time when the alleged damage took place. Writers have generally endorsed this position: Reed (n 128) 633–4, 637; Mendelson (n 118) 123; Douglas (n 148) 292; the requirement is implicit in the architecture of the investment treaty and exists independently of the ICSID Convention'.

153 While discussing the different question of changes of nationality during the intervening period (i.e., between consent to arbitration and registration of the request for arbitration), Schreuer (n 3) 276, states that:

> In the traditional law of diplomatic protection, a requirement of continuous nationality is often asserted from the time the claim arises up to the date it is taken up by the State of the injured person's nationality *or even up to the date of a decision.* The Convention *does not require continuity of nationality.* Its wording is directed at distinct points in time and not at a continuous period of time, which could have been expressed quite easily by 'from' and 'to', or 'continuously until', rather than by 'as well as' and 'on either date' (emphasis added).

This passage was endorsed by the tribunal in *Waguih Elie George Siag and Clorinda Vecchi v. Egypt*, ICSID Case No. ARB/05/15, Decision on Jurisdiction, 11 April 2007 [205]–[206]. See also: McLachlan et al (n 148) 153–4, 161; Douglas (n 148) 291; Mendelson (n 118) 32: 'there is no requirement for the individual to continue to hold the same nationality *after* instituting proceedings', emphasis in the original.

constant nationality until the date an award is rendered' and that 'the only dates of relevance to Article 25 of the ICSID Convention are those of consent and registration'.[154] In light of this, the fact that a natural person *involuntarily* changes nationality as a result of State succession after the request for arbitration has been registered by the Centre is simply *not* relevant in terms of an ICSID tribunal's jurisdiction over a dispute.[155] A tribunal should therefore continue to exercise jurisdiction over such a dispute in these circumstances.

2.3 The controversial question of the application of the rule of continuous nationality

At the heart of the question as to whether a tribunal should continue to exercise jurisdiction over a dispute when succession affects the claimant's nationality during the proceedings is the debate regarding the existence of a rule requiring a claimant to have a 'continuous' nationality. The question came into the spotlight for the first time in the field of investment arbitration when the *Loewen* Tribunal applied the rule (or at least one version of the rule) to deny its jurisdiction over a claim. Although the *Loewen* award did not involve any issue of State succession, the reasoning of the Tribunal could certainly apply (at least in theory) to cases where a claimant's nationality changes during the proceedings. In the following sections, I will first critically examine the *Loewen* case (Section 2.3.1), which will be followed by an assessment of the rule of continuous nationality and its discontent in the field of diplomatic protection (Section 2.3.2). I will then argue that the rule should not find application in situations involving involuntary change of nationality such as State succession (Section 2.3.3) and that, in any event, it has no place in the specific context of BIT investor-State disputes (Section 2.3.4). **16.27**

2.3.1 The origin of the controversy: the Loewen *case*

Loewen Group Inc. ('TLGI'), a Canadian funeral services company, and its founder (and main shareholder and Chief Executive Officer) Raymond L. Loewen, a Canadian national, filed a claim in 1998 against the United States alleging breaches of several NAFTA provisions. The tribunal held that, on the merits, the claim would have been dismissed based on its conclusion (in the form of a very long *obiter dictum*) that Loewen had failed to exhaust local remedies because it did not appeal to the US Supreme Court against a decision **16.28**

154 *Siag* (n 153) [499].

155 Mendelson (n 118) 33: 'continuous nationality is *not* generally required under ICSID. (…) A change of nationality subsequent to registration but prior to the handing down of the award would therefore seem, in all cases, to be immaterial' (emphasis in the original).

previously rendered by a Mississippi Court.[156] The present author has discussed elsewhere in some detail the reasoning of the tribunal regarding the specific allegation of denial of justice.[157] For the purpose of the present book, the focus will be put on the grounds for which the tribunal rejected its jurisdiction over the dispute. The tribunal held that it did not have jurisdiction over the claim because TLGI had not maintained a 'continuous' Canadian nationality throughout the entire proceedings as a result of a corporate reorganization plan of the company (which had been approved by Canadian and US bankruptcy courts) that took place during the proceedings.[158] Under that reorganization plan, TLGI ceased to exist as an independent company and transferred its assets and obligations to its former American subsidiary, the Loewen Group International Inc. ('LGII', which later changed its name to Alderwoods Group). Just before going out of business, TLGI assigned all of its rights, titles, and interest to the NAFTA claim to a newly created Canadian corporation called Nafcanco. After the reorganization, the United States filed a jurisdictional objection arguing that TLGI was no longer a Canadian company, but now a US-based one (Alderwoods). The United States' objection to the jurisdiction of the tribunal over the claim was twofold: on the one hand, a US company cannot file under international law a claim against its own home State (the United States); and, on the other hand, the rule of continuous nationality requires that the claimant maintain its Canadian nationality throughout the proceedings until the award is rendered by the tribunal.

16.29 In its award, the tribunal upheld the United States' objection to its jurisdiction based on the claimant's lack of continuous nationality. The tribunal stated that 'in international law parlance, there must be continuous national identity from the date of the events giving rise to the claim, which date is known as the *dies a quo*, through the date of the resolution of the claim, which date is known as the *dies ad quem*'.[159] The tribunal examined NAFTA Articles 1116 and 1117 and concluded that 'those articles deal only with nationality requirements at the *dies a quo*, the beginning date of the claim' and were silent on 'the question of whether nationality must continue to the time of resolution of the claim'.[160] According to the tribunal, such 'silence' would 'require the application of customary international law to resolve the question of the need for continuous

156 *The Loewen Group, Inc and Raymond L. Loewen v. United States of America*, ICSID case No. ARB (AF)/98/3, Award, 26 June 2003 [217].

157 Patrick Dumberry, *The Fair and Equitable Treatment Standard: A Guide to NAFTA Case Law on Article 1105* (Wolters Kluwer 2013); Patrick Dumberry, 'Denial of Justice under NAFTA Article 1105: A Review of 20 Years of Case Law', (2014) 32(2) *ASA Bull.* 145–63.

158 *Loewen* (n 156) [240].

159 Ibid., [225].

160 Ibid., [226].

national identity'.[161] The reasoning of the tribunal on this point has been rightly criticized. Thus, the fact that these two provisions only mention a nationality requirement when the claim is filed could logically indicate that this is the only relevant date.[162] In other words, NAFTA was *not* silent on the issue and there was therefore no need to look at custom. In any event, it has been rightly noted that 'there is no basis for applying a presumption that the continuous nationality rule applies in the context of such treaties' (a point further examined below).[163]

While the tribunal's (very limited) analysis of the question of continuous nationality was largely based on diplomatic protection, it nevertheless noted that '[a]s claimants have been allowed to prosecute claims in their own right more often, [a] provision has been made for amelioration of the strict requirement of continuous nationality'.[164] But, the tribunal concluded that there was no such 'specific provision' in the NAFTA.[165] At this stage of the reasoning of the tribunal, it is quite apparent that it had failed to explain why, in the first place, 'a rule developed in one context (diplomatic protection) necessarily carried over into another area (investor claims)'.[166] **16.30**

The tribunal concluded that 'claimants have not shown that international law has evolved to the position where continuous nationality to the time of resolution is no longer required'.[167] This affirmation is somewhat ironic given the fact that the Tribunal did not provide *a single* reference supporting the existence of any such a 'rule' which would require continuous nationality until **16.31**

---

161 Ibid.

162 Mendelson (n 118) 44:

> The *dies a quo* must be the date of the injury. The date of the submission is therefore the *dies ad quem*. That does not, as a matter of logic (and leaving aside interpretation), wholly exclude the possibility that nationality has to continue unchanged beyond that date, but if a *dies ad quem* is (by necessary implication) provided for by the treaty, then there is no lacuna that needs to be filled from (alleged) customary law (…).

See also, at 52:

> the argument that, because the NAFTA contained no express provisions on the subject, the alleged customary rule had to be imported, was contrary to well-established principles of treaty interpretation. The correct application of those principles would not have led to the conclusion that continuous nationality up to the date of award was required by the NAFTA or the ICSID Additional Facility.

163 Mendelson (n 118) 29, see also, at 46–7.

164 *Loewen* (n 156) [229].

165 Ibid., see also, at [230]:

> As international law relaxed to allow aggrieved parties to pursue remedies directly, rather than through diplomatic channels, the need for a rigid rule of *dies ad quem* also was relaxed. But as was previously noted, such relaxations came about specifically in the language of the treaties. There is no such language in the NAFTA document and there are substantial reasons why the Tribunal should not stretch the existing language to affect such a change.

166 Mendelson (n 118) 45.

167 *Loewen* (n 156) [235].

the time of the resolution of the dispute.[168] Mendelson speaks of a 'thin and perhaps even tendentious' analysis.[169] The ILC Special Rapporteur, in his Seventh Report of 2006, stated that the reasoning of the tribunal on the question of *dies ad quem* was 'seriously flawed' and 'disposed of in a manner which gives no indication that the tribunal applied its mind to the matter at all'.[170] For him, the tribunal 'simply asserts, without any examination whatsoever of authority (despite the fact that counsel referred the tribunal to the relevant authorities)' the existence of a rule of customary international law requiring continuous nationality until the date of the resolution of the claim.[171] In fact, one of the very few references provided in the award is the following paragraph dealing with the work of the ILC on diplomatic protection:

> TLGI further contends that the International Law Commission issued a report which proposed eliminating the continuous nationality rule even in cases of diplomatic protection, a field that would seem more nationality oriented than the protection of investors. The report itself met with criticism in many quarters and from many points of view. In any event, the ILC is far from approving any recodification based on the report.[172]

16.32 It is quite surprising that the tribunal seems to have barely noticed *en passant* the work of the ILC and its strong criticism of the rule of continuous nationality.[173] Thus, ILC Special Rapporteur Dugard not only noted the 'dubious' status of the 'rule' of continuous nationality as custom (since support for the rule was far from being unanimous[174]), but he was in fact in favour of

---

168 M.S. Duchesne, 'The Continuous Nationality of Claims Principle: Its Historical Development and Current Relevance to Investor-State Investment Disputes', (2004) 36 *Geo Wash Int'l L Rev* 809:

> Whatever other reaction the Loewen tribunal's decision might invite, its discussion on the continuous nationality 'rule' was, if not cursory, then at least conclusory (...) the tribunal's discussion of the continuous nationality issue simply asserts the existence of a rule without citation or even discussion (...) [The Tribunal] approached the issue with a preconceived notion of customary international law and felt little need to put that notion to the test of careful examination.

169 Maurice Mendelson, 'The Requirement for Continuous Nationality', in F. Ortono et al. (eds) *Investment Treaty Law, Current Issues II, Nationality and Investment Treaty Claims* (BIICL 2007) 48. See also: Mendelson (n 118) 51 noting that 'the panel did not make a particularly impressive job of it' in the context of its analysis of the objections raised by the respondent based on the continuous nationality rule and that 'no authority was cited, and unsupported assertions were made'.

170 ILC, 'Seventh Report on Diplomatic Protection by John Dugard, Special Rapporteur', 58th Session, UN Doc. A/CN.4/567, 7 March 2006 [41]. [hereinafter 'ILC, Seventh Report on Diplomatic Protection, Dugard'].

171 Ibid., [41].

172 *Loewen* (n 156) [236].

173 Mendelson (n 118) 27.

174 ILC, 'First Report on Diplomatic Protection, by John Dugard', 52d Sess., UN Doc. A/CN.4/506, 2000 [hereinafter 'ILC, First Report on Diplomatic Protection, Dugard'] [9]: 'The continuity of nationality rule is

abandoning the rule altogether (a point further explained below).[175] Most importantly, for the present discussion, the Report also noted the evident lack of common agreement regarding the *dies ad quem*.[176] The tribunal simply decided not to take into account the view expressed by the ILC Special Rapporteur on this important point.

Many scholars have rejected the *Loewen* Tribunal's affirmation that such a 'rule' exists under custom.[177] According to one writer, 'the Tribunal totally disregarded the fact that contemporary investment treaties, either bilateral or multilateral, and the recent works of the International Law Commission do not include the requirement of continuous nationality through the resolution of the claim'.[178] For Mendelson, 'the assertion that there is a rule of customary international law requiring continuous nationality up to the time of the award or judgment is in fact unsupported by sufficient authority, and there is authority, as well as arguments of principle, against it'.[179] The comprehensive analysis undertaken by Duchesne also shows that there is very limited support for the tribunal's finding about the existence of any such a rule.[180] **16.33**

---

supported by *some* judicial decisions, *some* State practice, some codification attempts and *some* academic writers. On the other hand, there is strong opposition to it' (emphasis added).

175 Ibid., [21]–[22].

176 Ibid., [16]: 'The absence of agreement over the content of the continuity rule is nowhere more apparent than in the dispute over the meaning to be given to the *dies ad quem*, the date until which continuous nationality of the claim is required.'

177 J. Paulsson, *Denial of Justice in International Law* (CUP 2006) 183–4; J. Paulsson, 'Continuous nationality in Loewen' (2004) 20 *Arb Int* 214; Alexandra Diehl, *The Core Standard of International Investment Protection: Fair and Equitable Treatment*, (Wolters Kluwer 2012) 482–3; Duchesne (n 168) 801–2: P. Acconci, 'The Requirement of Continuous Corporate Nationality and Customary International Rules on Foreign Investment: the Loewen Case', (2005) 14 *Italian YIL* 195–223; Mendelson (n 118) 97–149; F. Orrego Vicuña, 'Changing Approaches to the Nationality of Claims in the Context of Diplomatic Protection and International Dispute Settlement', in S. Schlemmer-Schulte and K.-Y. Tung (eds), *Liber amicorum Ibrahim F.I. Shihata: International Finance and Development Law* (Kluwer 2001) 503–25; R. Wisner and N. Gallus, 'Nationality Requirements in Investor-State Arbitration', (2004) 5 *J World Invest & Trade* 927–45; N. Rubins, 'Loewen v. United States: The Burial of an Investor-State Arbitration Claim', (2005) 21 *Arb Int* 23–36; D. Wallace, 'Fair and Equitable Treatment and Denial of Justice: Loewen v. US and Chattin v. Mexico', in Weiler (n 118) 669; Dirk Pulkowski, 'The Final Award in Loewen v. United States', in Aguilar Alvarez and W. Michael Reisman (eds), *The Reasons Requirement in International Investment Arbitration: Critical Case Studies* (Nijhoff 2008) 300–309.

178 Pia Acconci, 'Is There Room For Customary Law in International Law on Foreign Investments? The Requirement of Continuous Corporate Nationality in the *Loewen* Case', (2005) 3 TDM.

179 Mendelson (n 118) 51–2. See also: Mendelson (n 169) 45.

180 Duchesne (n 168) 801:

> The bottom line is this: If there is no common practice among states, much less agreement among states, tribunals, or legal scholars as to the date until which original nationality must be maintained, then there is no basis on which a rule of customary international law can be founded. Thus, even if continuous nationality were a rule, it would be a meaningless one, for there is no agreement on how long after the date of injury the claimant's nationality must remain unchanged.

16.34 The tribunal then applied these principles to the facts of the case. The tribunal noted that TLGI assigned to Nafcanco (a Canadian company) only the NAFTA claim, while '[a]ll of the assets and business of TLGI have been reorganized under the mantle of an American corporation'.[181] As a result, the tribunal reasoned that '[a]ll of the benefits of any award would clearly inure to the American corporation' and that '[s]uch a naked entity as Nafcanco, even with its catchy name, cannot qualify as a continuing national for the purposes of this proceeding'.[182] These findings have been criticized by writers.[183]

16.35 Another feature of the award that has been subject to criticism is the tribunal's approach regarding Mr. Loewen who was also a claimant in his personal capacity as an investor.[184] This issue was important since he had remained a Canadian national at all relevant times, including when the award was rendered. The United States argued that the tribunal had no jurisdiction over the claim given the fact that he no longer had control over his stock in the company. In the award, the tribunal noted that it had 'allowed [him] to continue in the proceeding[s] to determine whether he in fact continued any stock holding in the company', but that now (at the end of the proceedings) '[n]o evidence was adduced to establish his interest and he certainly was not a party in interest at the time of the reorganization of TLGI'.[185] For one writer, 'this seems an extraordinary piece of reasoning' considering that Mr. Loewen had lost control of his stock as a result of the misdemeanours and the denial of justice committed by the Mississippi court.[186]

16.36 The following sections will explain the reasons why any so-called 'rule' requiring continuous nationality until the award is rendered should not find application in the context of investment arbitration disputes involving changes of nationality resulting from State succession. The analysis will be divided in the following three propositions:

---

181 *Loewen* (n 156) [237].

182 Ibid.

183 Acconci (n 178) 6; Mendelson (n 118) 47:

> As far as the Tribunal should have been concerned, the Agreement is silent on this subject [i.e., transferability of claims]. Arguably, in such cases, the object of the Agreement in protecting investors against unfair and illegal treatment, and in providing them with a remedy of their own, should have militated in favour of respecting the assignment. And the instinctive reaction of the private lawyer, to which allusion had already been made, might have also come in here: assignment of claims is certainly known to domestic law, and also to international law. If this was a way of avoiding a great injustice, what was wrong with it?

184 Rubins (n 177) 29; Pulkowski (n 177) 309–11; Mendelson (n 118) 48–9.

185 *Loewen* (n 156) [239].

186 Mendelson (n 118) 49, see also 49ff, 52.

- the existence of a rule of continuous nationality is contested in the context of diplomatic protection, and regardless, there is very limited support for applying it until the date of the award (Section 2.3.2);
- in any event, it is generally recognized that the rule does not apply in the context of diplomatic protection when changes of nationality are involuntary, such as in cases of State succession (Section 2.3.3);
- moreover, the rule should not apply in the context of BIT investment arbitration disputes (Section 2.3.4).

2.3.2 The existence of the rule is contested in the context of diplomatic protection

It is a well-known principle of international law that, by the mechanism of diplomatic protection, a State can offer to pursue, at international level, the claim of one of its nationals who has suffered injuries as a consequence of the commission of an act by another State. By doing so, the PCIJ has affirmed that the State 'is in reality asserting its own rights, its right to ensure, in the person of its subjects, respect for the rules of international law'.[187] Since a State is 'asserting its own right' when protecting one of its nationals by exercising diplomatic protection, it is evident that this person must qualify as being one of its nationals.[188] **16.37**

It is often said that the 'traditional' rule of diplomatic protection concerning the nationality of claims is the principle of 'continuous nationality'.[189] A first essential condition for a State to exercise diplomatic protection on behalf of a person is that he/she must have the nationality of that State at the time of the *commission* of the internationally wrongful act by another State. The second condition is that such person remains a national of that State at least until that State *takes up his/her claim*.[190] For Mendelson, 'there is a fairly consistent practice both of international and of domestic tribunals, and of governments, of requiring a link of nationality to exist both at the time of the injury, and (at any rate) at the time of the presentation of the claim'.[191] **16.38**

187 *Mavrommatis Palestine Concessions* case *(Jurisdiction)*, 30 August 1924, PCIJ Series A, no. 2.

188 *Panevezys-Saldutiskis Railway* case, Judgment of 28 February 1939, PCIJ Series A/B, no. 76, 16–18:

> This right is necessarily limited to the intervention on behalf of [a State's] own national because, in the absence of a special agreement, it is the bond of nationality between the State and the individual which alone confers upon the State the right of diplomatic protection, and it is as a part of the function of diplomatic protection that the right to take up a claim and to ensure respect for the rules of international law must be envisaged.

189 The historical developments of the 'rule' are examined in Duchesne (n 168) 793ff.

190 Ibid.

191 Mendelson (n 118) 15ff examining many cases.

16.39 Yet, it should be pointed out that the recognition of the existence of such a rule is far from being unanimous.[192] It has been suggested in doctrine that it is not a rule of international law.[193] This is, for instance, the position of Umpire Parker in *Administrative Decision No. V*,[194] the view adopted by some members of the Institut de Droit international,[195] as well as the position defended by Judge van Eysinga in his dissenting opinion in the *Panevezys-Saldutiskis Railway* case.[196] Some authors have suggested that the rule should be dropped altogether.[197] These criticisms are also echoed in the work of ILA's Rapporteur Orrego Vicuña, for whom the rule does not take into account the 'new approach to diplomatic protection, where it is increasingly the right of the individual and not that of the State acting on its behalf the one that is upheld and enforced'.[198] For him, '[t]he retention of the rule of continuance of nationality does not seem to find any longer justification in the light of the changing role of nationality as a requirement of diplomatic protection'.[199] Similarly, ILC's Special Rapporteur Dugard is of the view that '[t]he traditional "rule" of continuous nationality has outlived its usefulness' and 'has no place in a world in which individual rights are recognized by international law and in which nationality is not easily changed'.[200] He further explains that the rule does not make much sense in some areas of international law where the individuals are exercising their own rights, referring specifically to the situation under investment treaties:

---

192 Duchesne (n 168) 797ff.

193 I. Sinclair, 'Nationality of Claims: British Practice', (1950) 27 *British YIL* 130; J.H.W. Verzijl, *International Law in Historical Perspective*, (vol 6 A.W. Sijthoff 1973) 723; Duchesne (n 168) 799ff.

194 *Administrative Decision No. V*, United States-German Mixed Claims Commission, 31 October 1924, in 7 UNRIAA 143:

> Those decisions which have adopted [the rule of continuous nationality] as a whole have recognized it as a mere rule of practice. Usually they have been rendered by divided commissions, with one member vigourously dissenting. When the majority decisions in these cases come to be analyzed, it is clear that they were in each case controlled by the language of the particular protocol governing the tribunal deciding them (…).

195 See, the position of N. Politis, in (1933) *Annuaire IDI* 487–8, challenging the proposal of the Institut's Rapporteur Borchard endorsing the rule of continuous nationality.

196 *Panevezys-Saldutiskis* case (n 188) 34–5.

197 Wyler (n 123) 133–4; M. Bennouna, 'La protection diplomatique, un droit de l'État?' in *Boutros Boutros-Ghali Amicorum Discipulorumque Liber. Paix, Développement, Démocratie* (vol. I, Bruylant 1998) 245.

198 ILA, 'The Changing Law of Nationality of Claims, Interim Report', Francisco Orrego Vicuña, Committee on Diplomatic Protection of Persons and Property, (2000) 35–6 (also in 'Changing Approaches to the Nationality of Claims in the Context of Diplomatic Protection and International Dispute Settlement', (2000) 15(2) *ICSID Rev.* 350.

199 Ibid., 37.

200 ILC, 'Addendum to First Report on Diplomatic Protection, by Mr John R. Dugard, Special Rapporteur', 20 April 2000, UN Doc. A/CN.4/506/Add.1 [hereinafter 'ILC, Addendum to First Report on Diplomatic Protection, Dugard'] [24]. He makes reference to the 'dubious status of the requirement of continuity of nationality as a customary rule' (ibid., [12]) which is 'emphasized by the uncertainties surrounding the content of the alleged rule' and in particular the question of the 'date until which continuous nationality of the claim is required' (ibid., [16]).

> Developments in international human rights law, which elevate the position of the individual in international law, have further undermined the traditional doctrine [of the continuous nationality]. If an individual has the right under human rights instruments to assert his basic human rights before an international body, against his own State of nationality or a foreign State, it is difficult to maintain that when a State exercises diplomatic protection on behalf of an individual it asserts its *own* right. Investment treaties which grant legal remedies to natural and legal persons before international bodies raise similar difficulties for the traditional doctrine.[201]

It should be added that some scholars have argued that the rule of continuous nationality is based on the 'false assumption' (affirmed by the PCIJ in the *Mavrommatis Palestine Concessions* case[202]) that an injury caused directly to a national of a State is deemed to be an injury to *that State* rather than to the *individual him/herself*. Several writers[203] and ICJ judges[204] have criticized this assumption as being a legal fiction in the context of changes of nationality.[205] As observed by O'Connell, 'if the State were really injured the only relevant point in time would be the moment of the injury; thereafter the State would be able, logically, to seek redress even if the injured individual died or changed his nationality'.[206] It has been suggested that the right to claim belongs to the *individual* injured by the act (not the State)[207] and is therefore not affected by **16.40**

201 ILC, First Report on Diplomatic Protection, Dugard (n 174) [66].

202 *Mavrommatis Palestine Concessions* case (n 187).

203 Brigitte Bollecker-Stern, *Le préjudice dans la théorie de la responsabilité internationale* (Pédone 1973) 99; Philippe Cahier, 'Changements et continuité du droit international, Cours général de droit international public', 1985-VI 195 Rec. des Cours, 315: '[s]i en effet c'est l'Etat qui est atteint en la personne de son ressortissant, alors seule la nationalité au moment du fait illicite doit entrer en ligne de compte'; Sir Robert Jenning, 'General Course on Principles of International Law', 1967-II 121 Rec. des Cours 475–6:

> The rule of nationality of claims, indeed, is illogical on any view. Thus, as generally stated, it provides that the individual in question must have possessed that link of nationality continuously from the time of injury up to the time *of the presentation* of the claim and even, according to *some* authorities, up to the time of an award; though it is true that there may be some mitigation of this rule … But both the requirement and the mitigation are surprising because, if the theory is that the injury to the individual national is what creates the injury to the State, it should follow that the existence of a nationality link at the moment of the injury would suffice (emphasis in the original).

See also: Louis Dubouis, 'La distinction entre le droit de l'Etat réclamant et le droit du ressortissant dans la protection diplomatique', (1978) LXVII *Rev. crit. d.i. privé* 623; Charles de Visscher, *Théories et réalités en droit international public* 2nd edn (Pedone 1955) 342; Charles de Visscher, 'Cours général de droit international public', (1972-II) 136 Rec des Cours 165.

204 In the words of Judge Fitzmaurice in his individual opinion in the *Barcelona Traction* case (n 102) 100, if 'the wrong done to the State in the person of its national arises … *at the moment of injury*, the claims then becomes indelibly impressed *ab initio* with the national character concerned' and therefore the 'injury to the claimant State is not, so to speak, "*de*-inflicted" by the fact that the individual claimant or company ceases to have its nationality' (emphasis in the original).

205 This is also the position taken in ILC, First Report on Diplomatic Protection, Dugard (n 174) [67].

206 D.P. O'Connell, *International Law* (vol. II Stevens & Sons 1970) 1034.

207 O'Connell (n 89) 540, proposing two alternative theoretical foundations upon which may be based his proposition that the rule of continuous nationality should not apply when changes of nationality result from succession of States:

the fact that he/she later changes nationality[208] (that right would 'follow' the injured individual through his/her changes of nationality).[209]

16.41 In sum, support for the rule of continuous nationality is far from being unanimous in the context of diplomatic protection. There is limited support in doctrine,[210] as well as in case law,[211] for requiring continuous nationality *beyond* the moment of the presentation of the claim and extending such a requirement (as the *Loewen* Tribunal did) until *the date the award is rendered.* For Mendelson, 'courts and tribunals have not, as a rule, required the link to exist continuously up to the time of *award*'.[212] As explained below, the ILC Draft Articles rejected extending the continuous nationality requirement until that date.

2.3.3 The rule does not apply in the context of diplomatic protection when changes of nationality are involuntary, such as in situations of State succession

16.42 The application of the rule of continuous nationality is all the more problematic in the context of diplomatic protection when a change of nationality results from State succession. The application of this rule limits the possibility for both the predecessor State and the successor State to submit claims on

---

> Assuming the rule of continuous nationality to exist as one of substantive law, there are two ways of avoiding its operation in cases of State succession. The first way, dependent on the view that the claim is primarily that of the individual and only secondarily that of the State, is to argue that the rationalization of the rule excludes its operation when the change of nationality occurs through change of sovereignty, and that the successor State is competent to claim on his behalf. The second way, dependent on the alternative view that a claim is always that of the State, is that the successor State inherits the claim, so that it is asserting its predecessor's rights by transmission, and not protecting an individual previous susceptible of protection by another State.

208 Orrego Vicuña (n 198) 36: 'if the right of the individual is affected the relevant critical date is that of the wrong, and the situation should not change simply because there has been a change of nationality intervening thereafter; the wrong follows in this perspective the affected individual.'

209 Ibid., 43, for whom the 'wrong follows the individual in spite of changes of nationality and so does his entitlement to claim'. This is also, for instance, the position held by H. Rolin, in (1933) *Annuaire IDI* 519–20.

210 Sir R. Jenning and Sir A. Watts, *Oppenheim's International Law* 9th edn, vol. I (Longman 1996) 512–13; I. Brownlie, *Principles of Public International Law* 5th edn (OUP 1998) 484: 'the majority of governments and of writers take the date of the award or judgment as the critical date.'

211 *Affaire des biens britanniques au Maroc Espagnol (Great-Britain v. Spain)*, case no. 36 'Benchiton', Award of Umpire Huber, 29 December 1924, in 2 UNRIAA 706.

212 Mendelson (n 118) 15 (emphasis in the original). See also, his conclusion (at 27):

> It is, on the other hand, by no means settled that the victim needs to possess the claimant State's nationality at any later stage in the proceedings. The practice, the case-law and the opinions of the most highly qualified specialists are insufficiently consistent to require such an extension of the time period; and there are good reasons of theory and policy as to why it should not be extended.

behalf of persons injured as a result of internationally wrongful acts committed before the date of succession.[213]

As mentioned above, nationals of the predecessor State will 'normally' become nationals of the successor State where they have their habitual residence after the date of succession. Since at the time of the commission of the internationally wrongful act by another State, the individual injured possessed the nationality of the predecessor State (and not that of the successor State), the rule of continuous nationality would prevent the successor State from exercising its diplomatic protection on behalf of its 'new' national. They are sometimes referred to as 'late' nationals. This reality is largely acknowledged in doctrine.[214] This is indeed the conclusion reached by the PCIJ in the *Panevezys-Saldutiskis* case.[215] In that case, Estonia (a new State since 1918) exercised diplomatic protection in 1937 on behalf of an Estonian railway company which had been expropriated by Lithuania in 1919. The problem was that at the time that the act was committed, the company was still a Russian company and only became Estonian several years later. The court therefore rejected the claim by applying the rule of continuous nationality. **16.43**

It has been suggested in doctrine that in such cases where the predecessor State continues to exist, it should be the one exercising diplomatic protection.[216] Indeed, this is true when there exists a right of option of nationality, and when the person injured before the date of succession decided to keep the nationality of the predecessor State. In such a case, the continuing State may espouse the claim of such person since there is no break in the chain of nationality. However, such a right of option is not always available, and even in cases where it does exist, a person may decide not to exercise it. In this last scenario, the individual injured before the date of succession would become a national of the successor State at the date of succession. The predecessor State could not exercise diplomatic protection for such person for the simple reason that he/she would no longer be its national at the time the claim is submitted.[217] Thus, the rule of continuous nationality would prevent the predecessor **16.44**

---

213 See, the analysis in P. Dumberry, *State Succession to International Responsibility* (Martinus Nijhoff 2007) 340ff; P. Dumberry, 'Obsolete and Unjust: the Rule of Continuous Nationality in the Context of State Succession', (2007) 76(2) *Nordic JIL* 153–83.

214 B. Stern, 'Responsabilité internationale et succession d'États' in L. Boisson de Chazournes and V. Gowlland-Debbas (eds), *The International Legal System in Quest of Equity and Universality. Liber amicorum Georges Abi-Saab* (Nijhoff 2001) 354; P.-M. Dupuy, *Droit international public* 4th edn (Dalloz 1998) 54; P. Guggenheim, *Traité de Droit international public*, (vol. I Librairie de l'Université 1953) 474.

215 *Panevezys-Saldutiskis* case (n 188) 16–17. See, Dumberry (n 213) 390ff.

216 See, Dumberry (n 213) 356.

217 A good illustration of this last principle is the *Henriette Levy* case, French-US Commission, 1881, in J.B. Moore, *History and Digest of the International Arbitrations to which the United States has been a Party*, vol. III, (GPO 1898) 2514ff.

State from exercising diplomatic protection for their former nationals, who have since the date of succession become nationals of the successor State. In sum, the application of the rule of continuous nationality in the context of State succession would result in *neither* the predecessor State nor the successor State being able to exercise diplomatic protection on behalf of an individual injured as a result of an internationally wrongful act committed before the date of succession.[218]

16.45 Many scholars believe that the application of the rule of continuous nationality may lead to unjust results when changes of nationality are *involuntary*, such as in cases of State succession.[219] It would result in nationals of the successor State being left without any possible redress for internationally wrongful acts suffered at the time when they were nationals of another State.[220] The fact that the application of this rule, in the context of State succession, would ultimately deprive 'large numbers and extensive categories of persons' of a remedy, has been described as 'offensive to the modern conception of the role of international law in protecting the individual'.[221] Other writers have maintained that the application of the rule in the context of State succession, in fact, rewards the wrongdoer State, as its 'wrongs' go unpunished.[222] For all of these reasons, many authors believe that the rule of continuous nationality should not apply in the context of changes of nationality resulting from State

218 Dumberry (n 213) 408. Thus, on the one hand, the rule prevents the *successor State* from exercising diplomatic protection on behalf of its *new nationals* because they were not its nationals at the time the internationally wrongful act was committed. On the other hand, the rule also prevents the *predecessor* State from exercising diplomatic protection on behalf of its *former nationals* because they are no longer its nationals at the time a claim is presented to the State responsible for the act.

219 C. Rousseau, *Droit international public* (vol. 5 Sirey 1983) 119 : 'il est parfaitement inique de refuser toute réparation aux particuliers en raison de changements accidentels (décès) ou imposés (mutations territoriales) affectant leur statut juridique'; A. de Lapradelle and N. Politis, *Recueil des arbitrages internationaux*, vol. III, 1872–1875 (Pedone 1954) 99–100 (fn 1); Mendelson (n 118) 19; John Dugard, 'Continuous Nationality', in *Max Planck Encyclopedia of Public International Law* (n 12) [11]; Verzijl (vol 5, n 193) 449; O'Connell (n 89) 537–9; U. Fastenrath, 'Der deutsche Einigungsvertrag im Lichte des Rechts der Staatennachfolge', (1992) 44 ÖZöRV 39; R. Donner, *The Regulation of Nationality in International Law* 2nd edn (Transnational Publ. 1994) 252.

220 This is, for instance, the position of O'Connell (n 206) 1035–6, expressing doubts that the rule of continuous nationality 'has or should have a place among the established rules of international law' partially based on the ground that 'the wholesale change of nationality forced upon peoples in this century' would 'leaves a substantial body of alien rights without a practical remedy if the rule of continuous nationality [was] rigorously applied'. This is also the position of de Visscher (n 203) 166.

221 O'Connell (n 89) 538–9.

222 G. Salvioli, 'Les règles générales de la paix', (1933-IV) 46 Rec. des Cours 125–7; D.C. Ohly, 'A Functional Analysis of Claimant Eligibility', in R. Lillich (ed), *International Law of State Responsibility for Injuries to Aliens* (UP Virginia 1983) 286.

succession.[223] The work of the Institut de Droit international,[224] and the ILA,[225] also support the proposition that the rule is not appropriate in the context of State succession. The same position has been adopted by several ICJ judges in their individual and dissenting opinions,[226] including Judge van Eysinga in the *Panevezys Saldutiskis Railway* case,[227] and also by arbitral tribunals in the *Pablo Nájera*[228] and *Administrative Decision No. V* cases.[229]

---

223 E.J.S. Castren, 'Aspects récents de la succession d'Etats', (1951-I) 78 Rec. des Cours 487–8; O'Connell (n 88) 538–9; W. Wengler, *Völkerrecht*, vol. I (Springler 1964) 602; Brownlie (n 210) 483: for whom the principle of continuous nationality 'may be modified in cases of State succession'; J.H.W. Verzijl, *The Jurisprudence of the World Court: A Case by Case Commentary*, vol. I (A.W. Sijthoff 1965) 567–8. *Contra*: H.F. Van Panhuys, *The Role of Nationality in International Law: An Outline* (A.W. Sythoff 1959) 91, indicating that 'international judicial bodies show little inclination to adopt [the] view' that any exception should be made to the rule of continuous nationality in the context of State succession.

224 Institut de Droit international, 'La protection diplomatique des individus en droit international. La nationalité des réclamations', Session of Warsaw, 1965, in (1965) 51-II *Annuaire IDI* 157ff. It should be added that an exception was made only for Newly Independent States. See also, the same position defended by several members of the Institut de Droit international at its 1931 and 1932 sessions. See, the analysis in Dumberry (n 213) 352ff., 357 (fn 81).

225 Orrego Vicuña (n 198) 35–6.

226 *Barcelona Traction* case (n 102), individual opinion of Judge Fitzmaurice, 100–101: 'Thus a rigid application [of the rule of continuous nationality], though justified where necessary to prevent abuses, should be eschewed where it would work injustice … A clear case of this would be where the change in nationality was involuntary, e.g., because of a re-alignment of State boundaries … ' See also: 'too rigid and sweeping an application of the continuity rule can lead to situations in which important interests go unprotected, claimants unsupported and injuries unredressed, not on account of anything relating to their merits, but because purely technical considerations bring it about that no State is entitled to act.' The same position was also taken by Judge Jessup in his individual opinion, at 203:

> Sir Gerald Fitzmaurice makes a forceful argument against any 'too rigid and sweeping' application of the continuity rule, but I believe his illustrative situation in paragraph 62 of his separate opinion may be covered by another rule deriving from the law of State succession, and on that basis would escape the application of the continuity rule for international claims which I consider to be generally binding – *specialia generalibus derogant*.

227 *Panevezys-Saldutiskis* case (n 188) 16, 35:

> the question arises whether it is reasonable to describe as an unwritten rule of international law a rule which would entail that, when a change of sovereignty takes place, the new State or the State which has increased its territory would not be able to espouse any claim of any of its new nationals in regard to injury suffered before the change of nationality. It may also be questioned whether indeed it is any part of the Court's task to contribute towards the crystallization of unwritten rules of law which would lead to such inequitable results.

See also, at 16–17:

> [it] is difficult to see why a 'claim' against a third State arising out of an unlawful act should not also pass from the old to the new State. Regarded from this aspect of the law of State succession – there is nothing surprising in the fact that Estonia should have had the right to take up a case which previously only Russia could have espoused. Such a 'succession' is an absolutely characteristic and even essential feature of the law of State succession. The successor State is continually exercising rights which previously belonged exclusively to the old State, and the same holds good as regards obligations. Accordingly it would be quite normal that in this case the successor State should have protected both diplomatically and before the Court a company the diplomatic protection of which formerly fell to Russia alone.

See, the analysis in Dumberry (n 213) 401ff.

228 *Pablo Nájera (France) v. United Mexican States*, France-Mexico Claims Commission, Decision no. 30-A, 19 October 1928, *obiter dictum* by President Verzijl, in 5 UNRIAA 488, (1927–1928) *Annual Digest* 52:

16.46 The work of the ILC Special Rapporteur on diplomatic protection has adopted the firm position that the rule of continuous nationality should not be applied in the context of changes to nationality resulting from State succession.[230] For Special Rapporteur Dugard, the rule 'may cause great injustice where the injured individual has undergone a *bona fide* change of nationality, unrelated to the bringing of an international claim, after the occurrence of the injury, as a result, inter alia, of ... [a] cession of territory or succession of States'.[231] For this reason, the ILC decided that the rule of continuous nationality should have a 'basic exception' dealing with cases of 'involuntary changes of nationality of the protected person, arising from succession of States' and another one for 'situations where it would be impossible to apply the rule of continuity owing to, for example, the disappearance of the State of original nationality through dissolution or dismemberment'.[232] The ILC therefore adopted Article 5(2) providing an exception to the rule of continuous nationality in the context of changes of nationality resulting from State succession.[233]

16.47 The Institut de Droit international recently adopted a Resolution on State succession to State responsibility which includes one provision whereby a successor State may exercise diplomatic protection in respect of a person or a

---

> Le cas présent diffère essentiellement des hypothèses dans lesquelles un individu, ressortissant de l'Etat A à l'époque des dommages, devient après cette époque et avant la date de la réclamation, ressortissant de l'Etat B de son propre fait. *Dans le cas de changements collectifs de nationalité en vertu d'un titre de succession d'Etats, la situation juridique doit être appréciée d'une manière beaucoup moins rigide* que ne le fait généralement la pratique arbitrale dans les hypothèses normales de changement individuel de nationalité par le fait volontaire de l'intéressé (emphasis added).

229 *Administrative Decision No. V* (n 194) 141–3:

> The general practice of nations not to espouse a private claim against another nation that does not in point of origin possess the nationality of the claimant nation has not always been followed. And that phase of the alleged rule invoked by the German Agent which requires the claim to posses continuously the nationality of the nation asserting it, from its origin to the time of its presentation or even to the time of its final adjudication by the authorized tribunal, is by no means so clearly established as that which deals with its original nationality. Some tribunals have declined to follow it. Others while following it, have challenged its soundness. The application in all of its parts of the rule invoked by the German Agent to a privately-owned claim in which the nationality has changed by voluntary or involuntary transfer since the right accrued would deprive the claimant of all remedy for its enforcement through diplomatic intervention. The practical effect would frequently be to deprive the owner of his property. *As the rule in its application necessarily works injustice, it may well be doubted whether it has or should have a placed among the established rules of international law.* Those decisions which have adopted it as a whole have recognized it as a mere rule of practice (emphasis added).

230 See, the analysis in Dumberry (n 213) 348ff.

231 ILC, Addendum to First Report on Diplomatic Protection, Dugard (n 200) [1].

232 ILC, 'Report of the International Law Commission on the Work of its Fifty-Third Session', 23 April to 1 June and 2 July to 10 August 2001, ILC Report, A/56/10, 2001, chp. VII, 507ff [177].

233 ILC, Draft Articles on Diplomatic Protection (n 109), Art. 5(2): 'A State may exercise diplomatic protection in respect of a person who is its national at the date of the official presentation of the claim but was not a national at the date of injury, provided that the person had the nationality of a predecessor State (...).'

corporation who is its national at the date of the official presentation of the claim, but was not at the date of the injury.[234] This situation covers, inter alia, *involuntary* changes of nationality, such as in the context of State succession. The position adopted by the Institut is supported by many scholars.[235] I have examined elsewhere four examples of international judicial decisions where the rule of continuous nationality was not applied in the specific context of State succession to responsibility.[236] I have also found several examples of State practice where reparation was provided in an agreement to the successor State for its nationals, which did not have its nationality at the time the damage occurred.[237] In these cases, the State responsible for the internationally wrongful act committed before the date of succession did not raise any objection based on the continuous nationality rule to the claims submitted by a successor State on behalf of its new nationals.

In sum, the rule of continuous nationality does not apply in the context of diplomatic protection when changes of nationality are involuntary, such as in situations of State succession. In my view, as further explained in the next section, the same solution should prevail in the context of arbitration claims filed directly by individuals/corporations under BITs. **16.48**

2.3.4 The rule does not apply in the context of investment arbitration

Article 17 of the ILC Draft Articles on diplomatic protection specifically indicates that its provisions 'do not apply to the extent that they are inconsistent with special rules of international law, such as treaty provisions for the protection of investments'. The ILC Commentaries expressly referred to investment treaties which 'contain special rules on the settlement of disputes which exclude or depart substantially from the rules governing diplomatic protection', adding that 'such treaties abandon or relax the conditions relating **16.49**

---

234 Institut de Droit international, State Succession in Matters of State Responsibility, 14th Commission, (Rap. M.G. Kohen), Resolution, 28 August 2015, Art. 10(1):

> A successor State may exercise diplomatic protection in respect of a person or a corporation that is its national at the date of the official presentation of the claim but was not a national at the date of injury, provided that the person or the corporation had the nationality of the predecessor State or lost his or her previous nationality and acquired, for a reason unrelated to the bringing of the claim, the nationality of the successor State in a manner not inconsistent with international law.

For an analysis of this Resolution, see: Marcelo G. Kohen and Patrick Dumberry, *The Institute of International Law's Resolution on State Succession and State Responsibility: Introduction, Text and Commentaries*, (CUP 2018–2019).

235 See, analysis in Dumberry (n 213) 355.

236 Ibid., 367ff, referring to: *Pablo Nájera* (n 228) 487–8; *Claim of Finnish Shipowners against Great Britain in respect of the Use of Certain Finnish Vessels During the War* (*Finland v. United Kingdom*), Award of Dr. Bagge, 9 May 1934, in 3 UNRIAA 1481. I have also examined other examples in the context of Mixed Arbitral Tribunals established after the First World War (ibid., 370) and the United Nations Compensation Commission (UNCC) set up after the Gulf War (1990–1991) (ibid., 379).

237 Ibid., 382ff.

to the exercise of diplomatic protection, particularly the rules relating to the nationality of claims and the exhaustion of local remedies'.[238] Thus, contrary to the position adopted by the *Loewen* Tribunal, the ILC recognized that the solutions existing in the field of diplomatic protection cannot be automatically replicated in the different context of investment arbitration.

16.50 There are many reasons for rejecting the application of the rule of continuous nationality in the context of investor-State disputes.[239] First, as noted by one writer, the 'policy reasons for conditioning diplomatic protection on continuous nationality do not apply in the context of a direct investor-State arbitration'.[240] Judge Jessup explained in the *Barcelona Traction* case that the rule was adopted in the context of diplomatic protection to prevent a person who is a national of a 'weaker' State to change his/her nationality to that of a more powerful State in terms of representation against the State responsible for the wrongdoing.[241] Clearly, the danger of any such 'nationality-shopping' *does not exist* when the change of nationality is *involuntary*, as in cases of State succession.[242] In any event, this argument is simply not relevant in the context of investment arbitration where a claim is filed by an investor directly.[243]

16.51 Second, the direct investor-State dispute resolution mechanisms which exist under BITs 'are not only different from, but were specifically designed to displace, the traditional diplomatic-protection regime'.[244] Indeed, one of the

238 ILC, Draft Articles on Diplomatic Protection (n 109) 89. See also at 90:

> The dispute settlement procedures provided for in BITs and ICSID offer greater advantages to the foreign investor than the customary international law system of diplomatic protection, as they give the investor direct access to international arbitration, avoid the political uncertainty inherent in the discretionary nature of diplomatic protection and dispense with the conditions for the exercise of diplomatic protection.

239 Duchesne (n 168) 802–15; Reed (n 128) 636; Mendelson (n 118) 124–6, 141; McLachan et al. (n 148) [5.68]; Accondi (n 177) 225–36, 228–31; Douglas (n 148) 291.

240 Duchesne (n 168) 804.

241 *Barcelona Traction Case* (n 104) 189, separate opinion of Jessup [48]. See also: *Administrative Decision No. V* (n 194) 141:

> any other rule would open wide the door for abuses and might result in converting a strong nation into a claims agency in behalf of those who after suffering injuries should assign their claims to its nationals or avail themselves of its naturalization laws for the purpose of procuring its espousal of their claims.

242 Mendelson (n 118) 9.

243 Duchesne (n 168) 806–7:

> Even at a glance, it seems obvious that these traditional concerns have no relevance to a treaty creating an individual right of access to international arbitration. In that context, there is no possibility of protection or claim 'shopping' because, beyond the point at which the injury occurs, nationality becomes irrelevant and there is no advantage in changing it. So long as both the right and the duty to prosecute the resulting claim are vested in the investor, a subsequent change in nationality does not alter this fact of self-reliance.

See also: Douglas (n 148) 291.

244 Duchesne (n 168) 806–7. As noted by Dugard (n 219) [14] (who was the ILC Special Rapporteur on Diplomatic Protection):

aims of BITs is to recognize the right of individuals to have direct access to international tribunals. In the context of this evolution, as noted by one writer, 'it would be ironic at best if the institutions created to correct the deficiencies of diplomatic protection were automatically saddled with the same practices and rules that often contributed to making diplomatic protection ineffective and inequitable in the first place'.[245] It has been argued that, in fact, the importation of the continuous nationality principle into BITs would 'likely undermine the very objectives those agreements were designed to achieve'.[246]

Finally, importing the rule of continuous nationality into the field of investment arbitration seems contrary to the approach adopted by many writers to consider investors as having direct *procedural* rights under BITs.[247] Indeed, in the words of Mendelson, 'fundamentally, the traditional continuous nationality rule can have no application' in investor-State disputes.[248] Thus, in the context of a direct claim filed by an investor invoking a breach of substantive investment protections contained in a BIT, one simply cannot consider such a claim as that of the home State of the investor. Thus, 'the fiction that the injury was done to the State has no application once it is recognized that the investor has his own rights that he is entitled to vindicate without the assistance of his national State'.[249] In this sense, there seems to be no reason to require that a claimant possesses the nationality of the home State beyond the date when the request for arbitration is filed. In fact, it is not entirely clear why the *home State* of the investor would insist on a claimant having its nationality continuously after that date. After all, it is not that State's claim, but rather one of its nationals. In general, the home State has nothing to do with claims filed by its own nationals, and it should therefore not be concerned about changes of nationality occurring after that date.[250] In any event, such concerns do not **16.52**

some decisions, notably *Loewen Group Inc v. USA* have found the rule of continuous nationality to be applicable to investment treaties, but the better view is that the rule is inapplicable to investment treaties as the whole purpose of such treaties is to replace the regime of diplomatic protection with one more friendly to investors and less governed by conditions for the bringing of claims.

245 Duchesne (n 168) 808.

246 Ibid., 804.

247 Ibid.:

> Moreover, once a state has breached a private investor's rights under an investment treaty or other investment agreement, the separate right to recover damages for that breach is really a property right vested in the claimant. As such, any subsequent change in the investor's nationality, or even subsequent transfer of the claim, should be irrelevant. These changes do not affect the fact that the respondent state breached its obligations under a binding agreement, and so should not affect the state's liability for that breach.

248 Mendelson (n 118) 28.

249 Ibid.

250 Ibid., 29: Thus, home States 'have less interest in whether, subsequent to the making of the investment, there has been a change in any *particular* investor's nationality, especially since they will not be called upon to

arise in the context of State succession where changes of nationality are *involuntary*. In fact, as noted by one writer, emphasis on the continuous nationality of the claimant (in the non-succession context) could be considered as in the *host* State's interest since it has agreed to give protection specifically to nationals of the other contracting party to the BIT, and not to nationals of any other States.[251]

16.53 For all of these reasons, no investment tribunal has followed the interpretation adopted by the *Loewen* Tribunal on the question of continuous nationality.[252] In fact, in the *Yukos* award, the tribunal explicitly endorsed the date of the start of the proceedings as the relevant date for the question of jurisdiction in a case involving a *voluntary* change of nationality (and therefore not involving any State succession issue):

> Because the dates on which some of the 'oligarchs' moved to Israel were not clearly established, this confrontation raises the question of whether the rule of nationality of claims in international law means that nationality is adjudged as of the date of the filing of the claim, or as of a later date, such as that of the judgment. The Award in the NAFTA case of *Loewen v. United States of America* accepted the judgment day standard. That holding has been the subject of criticism. It is not generally sustained by the study of diplomatic espousal undertaken in recent years by the International Law Commission of the United Nations, whose Special Rapporteur, Professor John Dugard, has concluded that the date of the filing of the claim should govern rather than the judgment day. This Tribunal is not disposed to apply the judgment day standard in the light of the authorities and considerations assembled by Dugard, and in view of the fact that this proceeding in any event is not an exercise in the diplomatic espousal by a State of the claims of its national but a Treaty-authorized proceeding brought directly against a State by an entity which qualifies as an Investor of another Contracting Party. Thus the pertinence of rules of diplomatic protection to these proceedings is not to be assumed. The Tribunal must therefore consider the nationality of the 'oligarchs' as of the date of the filing of the claim, namely February 2005.[253]

---

present or conduct that investor's claim' (emphasis in the original). It should be added however that any question of change of nationality would be crucial in the event that the home State were to exercise diplomatic protection *after* the proceedings if the host State fails to comply with an award. See Art. 27, ICSID Convention. In such a situation, the application of the continuous nationality rule would prevent both the predecessor State (if it continues to exists) and the successor State to exercise diplomatic protection on behalf of the investor.

251 Ibid.

252 Reed (n 128) 636. It should be added that in *EnCana Corporation v. Republic of Ecuador*, LCIA Case No. UN3481, UNCITRAL, Award, 3 February 2006 [128], the tribunal did not take position on the issue:

> EnCana's nationality has not changed and there has been no subrogation of claims into the ownership of any third State national. It is accordingly unnecessary to deal with the question whether and how far international law rules in the field of diplomatic protection such as the rule of continuous nationality apply to direct claims by investors under BITs, and if they do, to identify the terminus ad quem for the purposes of that rule.

253 *Hulley Enterprises* (n 140) [550]–[551].

Similarly, in its award, the *Siag* Tribunal noted that 'the Loewen decision has been the subject of intense scrutiny and criticism by international law scholars and investment arbitration practitioners'.[254] The tribunal referred specifically to the *Loewen* Tribunal's 'cursory treatment of customary international law on a subject' and the fact that the award 'did not cite a single authority in support of any of its propositions with regard to continuous nationality'.[255] It also mentioned that commentators had 'stigmatized the Tribunal's application of a rule developed in one particular context (diplomatic protection) to another area (investment treaty claims)'.[256] The *Siag* Tribunal concluded that 'the ICSID Convention does not require a party to hold constant nationality until the date an award is rendered'.[257] **16.54**

In sum, while the scope of the continuous nationality rule is still debated among writers, to the best of the present author's knowledge, no one is suggesting that such continuity be required for claimant investors in the context of BIT arbitration *beyond* the moment of the start of the arbitration proceedings. Ultimately, what matters is to have the 'right' nationality at that moment. Changes of nationality occurring after that date should not be relevant once a tribunal has decided that it has jurisdiction over a dispute. **16.55**

254 *Siag* (n 153) [498].
255 Ibid.
256 Ibid.
257 Ibid., [499].

Part F
GENERAL CONCLUSION

17

GENERAL CONCLUSION

This book has provided readers with an analysis of the interaction between two fields of international law: State succession and international investment law. Two main questions were examined: the question of succession to BITs and to State contracts.[1] **17.01**

The first question examined in Part B was whether or not a successor State is bound by the BITs entered into by the predecessor State with other States. I began by analysing the practice of States (both successor States and other States parties to BITs) on the matter.[2] My investigation (and that of other writers as well) has shown that it is in fact very common for States to reach an agreement on this question. Indeed, the States concerned have either signed new BITs with each other or have expressly agreed upon the continuation of the old BIT to which the predecessor State was a party. My analysis has furthermore illustrated that there are many situations where (depending on the specific circumstances of each case) the continuation of a specific BIT can be inferred from the behaviour of the States in question or from a tacit agreement. **17.02**

One central question examined in this book (and certainly the most controversial) is what happens to a BIT of the predecessor State when the States concerned have *not* agreed on its continuation. The starting point of my analysis was a critical assessment of the different solutions adopted under the 1978 Vienna Convention for specific types of State succession. I have argued that it is incoherent for the ILC to apply, on the one hand, the solution of automatic continuity for bilateral treaties in the context of secession and dissolution of States, while adopting, on the other hand, the solution of *tabula rasa* for Newly Independent States. In any event, there are no logical reasons to apply the principle of automatic continuity to bilateral treaties given the **17.03**

---

1 I have also examined in Part C the question of succession to multilateral treaties. The issue has in fact not arisen in the field of investment arbitration. The question of succession to the ICSID Convention is quite straightforward and has not been the object of much controversy.

2 I have also critically analysed all (publically-available) investment arbitration cases involving BITs in the context of State succession. This analysis has shown that tribunals increasingly have to decide cases involving matters of State succession, including a number of pending proceedings arising from the annexation of Crimea by Russia.

particular nature of these instruments. In my view, bilateral treaties do not automatically continue to be in force as of the date of succession unless *both* States concerned (the successor State and the other State party) have explicitly (or tacitly) agreed on such a continuation. This basic solution should apply to *all new States* rather than exclusively to those emerging from the process of decolonization.

17.04 A few words should be said here about an argument developed by Tams in his groundbreaking article. Tams believes that 'the argument for automatic succession to bilateral treaties meets with considerable obstacles'[3] and that 'as long as these are seen as one category, and viewed as inter-party bargains of an "essentially voluntary" character, the case for automatic succession is weak'.[4] However, while admitting that 'there is force' to the approach (adopted in the present book) which rejects that a new State is automatically bound by BITs, he nevertheless adds that 'perhaps it does not do full justice to arguments in favour of automatic succession to BITs'.[5] The argument is tentatively (in the words of Tams himself[6]) laid down as follows:

> If that case were made, it would need to be based on analysis that looks beyond the number of parties, and that takes issue with the characterisation of BITs as 'essentially voluntary' inter-State arrangements. An argument for automaticity could instead emphasise that, while concluded between States, BITs establish substantive rights of investors, which are directly enforceable in arbitral proceedings. While formally bilateral, it does indeed seem overly restrictive to view BITs merely as inter-State bargains. Yet once the focus is broadened to include the interests of foreign investors, two related arguments in favour of automaticity could be advanced.
>
> *First*, treaty-based investor rights could be likened to 'vested' or 'acquired' rights, which occupied a prominent place in traditional debates about State succession – and which were claimed by many to survive instances of State succession. Applied to the present context, one could perhaps argue that foreign investors making an investment when a BIT applies should acquire the right to have that investment protected by the BIT after the State succession has taken place.
>
> *Second*, pressing the point in light of recent arguments about automatic succession to particular categories of treaties, there might be room for a 'human rights analogy':

---

3 C.J. Tams, 'State Succession to Investment Treaties: Mapping the Issues', (2016) 31(2) *ICSID Rev.* 334.

4 Ibid.

5 Ibid., 335.

6 Ibid., 336:

> These points are purposively put tentatively, as the debate is at an early stage – and as quite often, the parties have determined the fate of their BITs explicitly or implicitly. It must be recognised that the case argument for automatic succession to BITs is anything but straightforward. It depends on a particularly investor-friendly reading of those treaties, which – given recent backlashes against investment arbitration – may have lost some of its appeal. However, the brief sketch of potential arguments suggests that the matter is at least open to argument.

adapting a prominent dictum by the UN Human Rights Committee, one could indeed argue that, as rights under BITs 'belong [to foreign investors] ..., once [foreign investors] are accorded the protection of the rights under the [treaty], such protection devolves with territory and continues to belong to them, notwithstanding ... State succession'.[7]

One of the most controversial questions in the field of investment arbitration is whether an investor has a 'direct' or a 'derivative' right under a BIT. The question is beyond the scope of this book. Suffice it to say that there are many reasons to favour the direct rights theory over the derivative approach.[8] As noted by Douglas, '[t]he functional assumption underlying the investment treaty regime is clearly that the investor is bringing a cause of action based upon the vindication of its own rights rather than those of its national State'.[9] Without going into further detail, it should be noted that Douglas has developed a theory slightly different from the 'direct' model by distinguishing between procedural and substantive rights contained in BITs.[10] In essence, if one were to take the position that BITs establish *direct substantive rights* to investors, it is theoretically possible to envisage the existence of an argument in favour of automatic succession. The argument would be that if these substantive rights are indeed *those of investors* (and not those of States under the 'derivative' theory), they should exist *notwithstanding* the will of the States parties to the BIT. In other words, these rights would 'survive' the disintegration (and even the extinction) of one of the parties to the BIT. **17.05**

In my view, the fact of the matter is that even under the strict 'direct' model, investors are *clearly not parties to the BIT*; they only receive legal protection if **17.06**

7 Ibid., 335–6.

8 Zachary Douglas, *The International Law of Investment Claims* (CUP 2009), 30ff; See: Tillmann Rudolf Braun, 'Globalization-driven Innovation: The Investor as a Partial Subject in Public International Law – An Inquiry into the Nature and Limits of Investor Rights', Jean Monnet Working Paper Series, JMWP 04/13, 29ff.

9 Zachary Douglas, 'The Hybrid Foundation of Investment Treaty Arbitration' (2003) 74 *British YIL* 151, 182. See also: Campbell McLachlan, Laurence Shore and Matthew Weiniger, *International Investment Arbitration: Substantive Principles* (OUP 2007), 61–5.

10 Douglas (n 8), 35. For him, while 'the procedural right to assert claims against the host state in arbitration is vested directly in the investor', the other question is whether 'the substantive investment protection obligations are owed directly to investors that qualify as such under the investment treaty'. He supports the view that substantive investment protection obligations are *not* owed directly to investors:

> Upon the claimant's filing of a notice of arbitration, the claimant investor perfects the host state's unilateral offer to arbitrate, and the two parties thus enter into a direct legal relationship in the form of an arbitration agreement. At the same time, the claimant becomes a counterparty to the host state's obligation to submit to international arbitration for an assessment of its conduct towards the claimant's investment on the basis of the norms of investment protection set out in the treaty. This obligation encompasses the duty of the host state to pay compensation if the international tribunal adjudges its conduct to be violative of these norms. The minimum standards of investment protection could thus be characterised as the applicable adjudicative standards for the claimant's cause of action rather than binding obligations owed directly to the investor.

they fulfil certain conditions, such as being an 'investor' who makes an 'investment' under the definition of the scope of the BIT. Moreover, even if one adopts the 'direct' theory, it remains that the parties to a treaty are free to terminate the instrument according to the general rules of the law of treaties.[11] It should be added, importantly, that the rights of investors are nevertheless protected under clauses in the BIT providing for a minimum period of application and the presence of a 'survival clause'.[12] Yet, importantly, these provisions provide protection to the investors in the context of the *termination* (unilateral by one State, or by agreement by both States[13]) of the BIT. In my view, a survival clause does not apply in the extraordinary situations of State succession, such as when, for instance, one of the parties to the instrument no longer exists as a sovereign State.[14] In such a case, the BIT will simply *cease to have any application*. The survival clause cannot have any effect in such a situation and does not offer any protection to foreign investors of the other contracting party. The survival clause cannot find application in the event that one of the parties *does not itself survive* the event leading to a State succession.

17.07 In sum, even if one endorses the view that investors have 'direct' rights under a BIT, it remains that no such rights can 'automatically' survive the dramatic event of a State succession affecting the very existence of one of the contracting parties. In other words, the 'direct' rights theory does *not* support the application of any principle in favor of automatic succession to BITs.

17.08 The second question examined in Part D of this book concerned State contracts: whether or not a successor State is bound by the obligations contained in a contract (which includes an arbitration clause) signed by the predecessor State with a foreign company before the date of succession. Based on my analysis of the more general issue of succession to acquired rights, I have reached the conclusion that the successor State is always free, under international law, to modify the terms of a State contract after the date of succession. Yet, any such changes must be done by respecting principles of

---

11 Braun (n 8) 1; Tania Voon, Andrew Mitchell and James Munro, 'Parting Ways: The Impact of Investor Rights on Mutual Termination of Investment Treaties', (2014) 29(2) *ICSID Rev* 451–73.

12 See, J. Harrison, 'The Life and Death of BITs: Legal Issues Concerning Survival Clauses and the Termination of Investment Treaties' (2012) 12(6) *J World Invest and Trade* 933ff.

13 The question of the protection of investors' rights in the context of the termination of the BIT by mutual consent of the contracting parties is examined in: Harrison, ibid., 941ff; Braun (n 8) 55ff; Voon et al. (n 11).

14 Harrison indicates that 'there are situations in which a survival clause will not have its desired effect due to rules which are external to the BIT' (ibid., 939), referring to rules and principles regarding the validity of treaties (error, fraud, corruption, coercion of a representative of a State, etc.) and *jus cogens* rules whereby a treaty automatically becomes void and is terminated when it conflicts with an emerging peremptory rule of international law (ibid., 940).

international law, including the MST and an obligation to provide compensation in the event of expropriation.

Even if, as a matter of principle, the successor State is not bound by State contracts, I have also argued that the matter is in fact more complex than that simple proposition would suggest. As a result, I have put forward a modest proposal for a new framework of analysis concerning the question of succession to State contracts. The issue was examined based on a first hypothesis: the solution to the problem of succession to State contracts depends on the different types of succession involved. Thus, I have shown that State practice and court decisions have applied the principle of succession for certain types of succession (cession of territory, unification and integration of States), but not for others (secession and dissolution). This book further discussed whether there should be particular circumstances where the principle of succession should apply in the context of secession (where the predecessor State continues to exist) and dissolution (where it ceases to exist). In my view, this is indeed the case based on the second hypothesis I have put forward: the solution to the question of succession to State contracts depends on a number of factors and circumstances which may exist in a given case. My assessment of State practice and court decisions shows support for the importance of such elements. Some of the most important factors that should be taken into account include the existence of a 'territorial nexus' between a contract and the successor State, as well as the need to avoid any unjust enrichment. These relevant elements should always be considered when determining whether the predecessor or the successor State (and in the context of dissolution, which of the new States) should be responsible for rights and obligations contained in State contracts. **17.09**

Finally, I have explored a number of specific problems that may arise when the event of State succession occurs during the arbitration proceedings. For example, a succession occurring during arbitration proceedings may affect the identity of the respondent State or that of the home State of the claimant investor. The latter example would result in a change in nationality for the claimant investor. Through my analysis, I have argued that a tribunal should continue to have jurisdiction over a case in these circumstances, despite the changes affecting the respondent State or the home State of the claimant. **17.10**

BIBLIOGRAPHY

All websites listed were active at February 2018, the date of the submission of the manuscript.

BOOKS

Akcam, T., *A Shameful Act: The Armenian Genocide and the Question of Turkish Responsibility* (Metropolitan Books 2006).

Aldrich, G.H., *The Jurisprudence of the Iran-United States Claims Tribunal* (Clarendon 1996).

Amerasinghe, C.F., *Jurisdiction of Specific International Tribunals* (Brill 2008).

Barde, J., *La notion de droit acquis en droit international public* (Publ. univ. de Paris 1981).

Bardonnet, D., *La succession d'Etats à Madagascar: succession au droit conventionnel et aux droits patrimoniaux* (LGDJ 1970).

Basdevant, J., *Dictionnaire de la terminologie du droit international* (Sirey 1960).

Bernhardt, R. (ed.), *Encyclopedia of Public International Law* (North Holland 1986).

Böckstiegel, K-H., *Arbitration and State Enterprises: A Survey on the National and International State of Law and Practice* (Kluwer 1984).

Bollecker-Stern, B., *Le préjudice dans la théorie de la responsabilité internationale* (Pédone 1973).

Born, B.G., *International Commercial Arbitration*, 2nd edn (Kluwer 2014).

Brossard, J. and D. Turp, *L'accession à la souveraineté et le cas du Québec*, 2nd edn (PU Montréal 1995).

Brownlie, I., *Principles of Public International Law*, 4th edn (Clarendon Press 1990).

Brownlie, I., *Principles of Public International Law*, 5th edn (Clarendon Press 1998).

Brownlie, I., *Principles of Public International Law*, 6th edn (OUP 2003).

Bühler, K., *State Succession and Membership in International Organizations: Legal Theories Versus Political Pragmatism* (Brill 2001).

Cheng, T.-H., *State Succession and Commercial Obligations* (Transnational Publishers 2006).

Christakis, T., *Le droit à l'autodétermination en dehors des situations de décolonisation* (LGDJ 1999).

Clapham, A., *Human Rights Obligations of Non-State* (OUP 2006).

Craven, M., *The Decolonization of International Law: State Succession and the Law of Treaties* (OUP 2007).

Crawford, J., *State Responsibility: The General Part* (CUP 2013).

Crawford, J., *Brownlie's Principles of Public International Law*, 8th edn (OUP 2012).

Crawford, J., *The Creation of States in International Law*, 2nd edn (OUP 2006).

Dagan, H., *Unjust Enrichment: A Study of Private Law and Public Values* (CUP 1997).

Danilenko, G.M., *Law-Making in the International Community* (Martinus Nijhoff 1993).

Dawson, J.A., *Unjust Enrichment: A Comparative Analysis* (Little, Brown & Co 1951).

de Lapradelle, A. and N. Politis, *Recueil des arbitrages internationaux*, vol. III, 1872–1875 (Pédone 1954).

De Visscher, C., *Théories et réalités en droit international public*, 2nd edn (Pédone 1955).

Delbez, L., *Principes généraux du droit international public*, 3rd edn (LGDJ 1964).

Desierto D., *Necessity and National Emergency Clauses: Sovereignty in Modern Treaty Interpretation* (Brill 2012).

Diehl, A., *The Core Standard of International Investment Protection: Fair and Equitable Treatment* (Wolters Kluwer 2012).

Dolzer, R. and M. Stevens, *Bilateral Investment Treaties* (Martinus Nijhoff 1995).

Donner, R., *The Regulation of Nationality in International Law*, 2nd edn (Transnational Publ. Inc. 1994).

Douglas, Z., *The International Law of Investment Claims* (CUP 2009).

Dugard, J., *Recognition and the United Nations* (Grotius Publ. 1987).

Dumberry, P., *State Succession to International Responsibility* (Martinus Nijhoff 2007).

Dumberry, P., *The Fair and Equitable Treatment Standard: A Guide to NAFTA Case Law on Article 1105* (Wolters Kluwer 2013).

Dumberry, P., *The Formation and Identification of Rules of Customary International Law in International Investment Law* (CUP 2016).

Dupuy, P.-M., *Droit international public*, 4th edn (Dalloz 1998).

Fanara, E., *Gestione di affari e arricchimento senza causa nel diritto internazionale* (Giuffrè 1966).

Flory, M., *La succession d'Etat en Afrique du Nord* (CNRS 1968).

Friedmann, W., *The Changing Structure of International Law* (Stevens and Sons 1964).

Fricker, C.V., *Gebiet und Gebietshoheit* (Tübingen 1901).

Gidel, G., *Les effets de l'annexion sur les concessions* (Larose 1904).

Goncalves Pereira, A., *La succession d'États en matière de traités* (Pédone 1969).

Gowlland-Debbas, V., *Collective Responses to Illegal Acts in International Law: United Nations Action in the Question of Southern Rhodesia* (Martinus Nijhoff 1990).

Gruber, A., *Le droit international de la succession d'Etats* (Bruylant 1986).

Guggenheim, P., *Traité de Droit international public*, vol. I (Librairie de l'Université 1953).

Hall, W.E., *A Treatise on International Law*, 8th edn (Clarendon 1924).

Hamant, H., *Démembrement de l'URSS et problèmes de succession d'États* (Bruylant 2007).

Henckaerts, J.M. and L. Doswald-Beck (eds), *Customary International Humanitarian Law*, vol 1 (CUP 2005).

Henkin, L., R. Crawford Pugh, O. Schachter and H. Smit, *International Law, Cases and Materials*, 3rd edn (West Publ. Co. 1993).

Ijalaye, D.A., *The Extension of Corporate Personality in International Law* (Oceana Publ. 1978).

Jellinek, G., *L'Etat moderne et son droit*, vol II (Panthéon-Assas 2004).

Jenks, W., *The Prospects of International Adjudication* (Oceana Publ. 1964).

Jenning, Sir R. and Sir A. Watts, *Oppenheim's International Law*, vol. I: Peace: Introduction and Part 1, 9th edn (Longman 1996).

Johnston, D. and R. Zimmermann (eds) *Unjustified Enrichment: Key Issues in Comparative Perspective* (CUP 2002).

Karavias, M., *Corporate Obligations under International Law* (OUP 2013).

Kelsen, H., *Principles of International Law*, 2nd edn (Holt, Rinehart and Winston 1966).

Klabbers, J., M. Koskenniem, O. Ribbelink and A. Zimmermann (eds), *State Practice Regarding State Succession and Issues of Recognition* (Council of Europe 1999).

Kohen, M.J. (ed.), *Secession: International Law Perspectives* (CUP 2006).

Kohen, M.J. and P. Dumberry, *The Institute of International Law's Resolution on State Succession and State Responsibility: Introduction, Text and Commentaries* (CUP forthcoming 2018–19).

Lauterpacht, H., *Recognition of States in International Law* (CUP 1947).

Llamzon, P.A., *Corruption in International Investment Arbitration* (OUP 2014).

Mälksoo, L., *Illegal Annexation and State Continuity: The Case of the Incorporation of the Baltic States by the USSR (A Study of the Tension between Normativity and Power in International Law)* (Martinus Nijhoff 2003).

Mann, F.A., *Studies in International Law* (OUP 1973).

Marcoff, M.G., *Accession à l'indépendance et succession d'États aux traités internationaux* (Fribourg 1969).

Marek, K., *Identity and Continuity of States in Public International Law* (Droz 1968).

McLachlan, C., L. Shore and M. Weiniger, *International Investment Arbitration: Substantive Principles* (OUP 2007).

Meriboute, Z., *La codification de la succession d'États aux traités: décolonisation, sécession, unification* (PUF 1984).

Moore, J.B., *History and Digest of the International Arbitrations to which the United States has been a Party*, vol. III (GPO 1898).

Moore, J.B., *Digest of International Law*, vol. I (GPO 1906).

Nielsen, K., *American and British Claims Arbitration* (Washington, G.P.O. 1926).

O'Connell, D.P., *The Law of State Succession* (CUP 1956).

O'Connell, D.P., *State Succession in Municipal Law and International Law*, vol. I (CUP 1967).

O'Connell, D.P., *International Law*, vol. II (Stevens & Sons 1970).

Okoye, F., *International Law and the New African States* (Sweet & Maxwell 1973).

Paulsson, J., *Denial of Justice in International Law* (CUP 2006).

Pazartzis, P., *La succession d'États aux traités multilatéraux à la lumière des mutations territoriales récentes* (Pédone 2002).

Quoc Dinh, N., P. Daillier and A. Pellet, *Droit international public*, 6th edn (LGDJ 1999).

Reuter, P., *Droit International Public* (PUF Thémis 1958).

Rigaux, F., *Droit public et droit privé dans les relations internationales* (Pédone 1977).

Ronzitti N., *La successione internazionale tra stati* (Giuffrè 1970).

Rousseau, C., *Droit international public* (Sirey 1953).

Ruzie, D., *Droit international public*, 14th edn (Dalloz 1999).

Sastry, T.S.N., *State Succession in Indian Context* (Dominant Publ. & Dist., New Delhi 2004).

Schermers, G. and N.M. Blokker, *International Institution Law*, 4th edn (Martinus Nijhoff 2003).

Schreuer, C. and R. Dolzer, *Principles of International Investment Law* (OUP 2008).

Schreuer, C., L. Malintroppi, A. Reinisch and A. Sinclair (eds), *The ICSID Convention: A Commentary*, 2nd edn (CUP 2009).

Schrijver, N.J., *Sovereignty over Natural Resources: Balancing Rights and Duties in an Interdependent World* (Groningen 1995).

Schwarzenberger, G., *International Law as Applied by International Courts and Tribunals*, vol. I, 3rd edn (Steven & Sons 1957).

Seidl-Hohenveldern, I., *Corporations in and under International Law* (Grotius 1987).

Sharma, S.P., *Territorial Acquisition, Disputes, and International Law* (Brill 1997).

Shaw, M.N., *International Law*, 4th edn (CUP 1997).

Shearer, A.I., *Starke's International Law*, 11th edn (Butterworths 1994).

Sørensen, M., *Manual of Public International Law* (McMillan & Co 1968).

Thierry, H., J. Combacau, S. Sur and C. Vallee, *Droit international public* (Montchrestien 1985).

Toriguian, S., *The Armenian Question and International Law*, 2nd edn (Univ. La Verne Press 1988).

Turp, D., *L'Avant-projet de loi sur la souveraineté du Québec: texte annoté* (Yvon Blais 2001).

Turp, D., *Le droit de choisir: Essais sur le droit du Québec à disposer de lui-même/ The Right to* Choose: Essays on Québec's Right of Self-Determination (Thémis 2001).

Udokang, O., *Succession of the New States to International Treaties* (Oceana Publ. 1972).

Vandevelde, K.J., *Bilateral Investment Treaties: History, Policy and Interpretation* (OUP 2010).

Van Hoof, G.J.H., *Rethinking the Sources of International Law* (Kluwer 1983).

Van Panhuys, H.F., *The Role of Nationality in International Law: An Outline* (A.W. Sythoff 1959).

Verzijl, J.H.W, *The Jurisprudence of the World Court: A Case by Case Commentary*, vol. I (A.W. Sijthoff 1965).

Verzijl, J.H.W., *International Law in Historical Perspective* (A.W. Sijthoff 1973).

Villiger, M.E., *Customary International Law and Treaties* (Kluwer 1985).

Villiger, M.E., *Commentary on the 1969 Vienna Convention on the Law of Treaties* (Martinus Nijhoff 2009).

Voss, J.O., *The Impact of Investment Treaties on Contracts between Host States and Foreign Investors* (Martinus Nijhoff 2010).

Wang, G., *International Investment Law: A Chinese Perspective* (Routledge 2014).

Wengler, W., *Völkerrecht*, vol. I (Springler 1964).

Weston, B.H and R.B. Lillich, *International Claims: Their Settlement by Lump Sum Agreements* (UP Virginia 1975).

Williams, S.A., *International Legal Effects of Secession by Quebec* (York University Centre for Public Law and Public Policy 1992).

Wyler, E., *La règle dite de la continuité de la nationalité dans le contentieux international* (PUF 1990).

Wyler, E., *Théorie et pratique de la reconnaissance d'État: Une approche épistémologique du droit international* (Bruylant 2013).

Ziemele, I., *State Continuity and Nationality: The Baltic States and Russia: Past, Present and Future as Defined by International Law* (Martinus Nijhoff 2005).

Zimmermann, A., *Staatennachfolge in völkerrechtliche Verträge – zugleich ein Beitrag zu den Möglichkeiten und Grenzen völkerrechtlicher Kodifikation* (Springer 2000).

ARTICLES IN BOOKS

Belkahla, M., 'La succession d'États en matiere de traitées mulitatereux relatives aux droit de l'homme', in G. Distefano, G. Gaggioli and A. Hêche (eds), *La Convention de Vienne de 1978 sur la succession d'États en matière de traités: Commentaire article par article et études thématiques* (Bruylant 2015).

Bennouna, M., 'La protection diplomatique, un droit de l'État?' in *Boutros Boutros-Ghali Amicorum Discipulorumque Liber. Paix, Développement, Démocratie*, vol. I (Bruylant 1998).

Bernardini, P., 'Nationality Requirements under BITs and Related Case Law', in F. Ortono et al. (eds) *Investment Treaty Law, Current Issues II, Nationality and Investment Treaty Claims* (BIICL 2007).

Berezowski, C., 'Les problèmes de la subjectivité internationale', in V. Ibler (ed.), *Mélanges offerts à Juraj Andrassy* (Martinus Nijhoff 1968).

Bilkova, V., 'La succession aux traités internationaux suite à la dissolution des fédérations ex-socialistes après 1990', in G. Distefano, G. Gaggioli and A. Hêche (eds), *La Convention de Vienne de 1978 sur la succession d'États en matière de traités: Commentaire article par article et études thématiques* (Bruylant 2015).

Binder, C. and C. Schreuer, 'Unjust Enrichment', in *Max Planck Encyclopedia of Public International Law* (OUP, online edn, 2006).

Bokor-Szego, H., 'Continuation et succession en matière de traités internationaux', in G. Burdeau and B. Stern (eds), *Dissolution, continuation et succession en Europe de l'Est* (Cedin-Paris I 1994).

Bühler, K.G., 'State Succession, Identity/Continuity and Membership in the United Nations', in P.M. Eisemann and M. Koskenniemi (eds), *Codification Tested against the Facts* (Martinus Nijhoff 2000).

Cahier, P., 'Quelques aspects de la Convention de 1978 sur la succession d'États en matière de traités', in B. Dutoit and E. Grisel (eds), *Mélanges Georges Perrin* (Payot 1984).

Cahin, G., 'Attribution of Conduct to a State: Insurrectional Movements', in J. Crawford, A. Pellet and S. Olleson (eds), *The Law of International Responsibility* (CUP 2010).

Cheng, T-H., 'State Succession and Commercial Obligations: Lessons from Kosovo', in Mahnoush Arsanjani et al. (eds), *Looking to the Future: Essays on International Law in Honor of W. Michael Reisman* (Martinus Nijhoff 2010).

Christakis, Ch., 'L'obligation de non-reconnaissance des situations créées par le recours illicite à la force ou d'autres actes enfreignant des règles fondamentales', in Ch. Tomuschat and J.-M. Thouvenin (eds), *The Fundamental Rules of the International Legal Order: Jus cogens and Obligations Erga Omnes* (Martinus Nijhoff 2005).

Clariana, G., 'La succession dans les Communautés européennes', in G. Burdeau and B. Stern (eds), *Dissolution, continuation et succession en Europe de l'Est* (Cedin-Paris I 1994).

Clive, E., 'Unjustified Enrichment', in A. Hartkamp, M. Hesslink, E. Hodius, C. Joustra, E. Du Perron and M. Veldmann (eds), *Towards a European Civil Code*, 3rd edn (Nijmegen, Aspen 2004)

Corten, O., 'Article 39', in G. Distefano, G. Gaggioli and A. Hêche (eds), *La Convention de Vienne de 1978 sur la succession d'États en matière de traités: Commentaire article par article et études thématiques* (Bruylant 2015).

Dawidowicz, M., 'The Obligation of Non-Recognition of an Unlawful Situation', in J. Crawford, A. Pellet and S. Olleson (eds), *The Law of International Responsibility* (OUP 2010).

Di Stefano, A., 'Article 24', in G. Distefano, G. Gaggioli and A. Hêche (eds), *La Convention de Vienne de 1978 sur la succession d'États en matière de traités: Commentaire article par article et études thématiques* (Bruylant 2015).

Dicke, D. Chr., 'Unjustified Enrichment and Compensation', in D. Chr. Dicke (ed.), *Foreign Investment in the Present and a New International Economic Order* (Fribourg UP 1987).

Dorr, O., 'Cession', in *Max Planck Encyclopedia of Public International Law* (OUP, online edn, 2006).

Dugard, J., 'Continuous Nationality, Enrichment', in *Max Planck Encyclopedia of Public International Law* (OUP, online edn, 2006).

Dumberry, P., 'International Investment Contracts', in T. Gazzini and E. de Brabandere (eds), *International Investment Law. The Sources of Rights and Obligations* (Martinus Nijhoff 2012).

Dumberry, P., 'La succession d'États en matière de responsabilité internationale et ses liens avec la responsabilité des États en matière de traités', in G. Distefano, G. Gaggioli and A. Hêche (eds), *La Convention de Vienne de*

1978 sur la succession d'États en matière de traités: Commentaire article par article et études thématiques (Bruylant 2015).

Dumberry, P. and E. Labelle Eastaugh, 'Non-State Actors in International Investment Law: The Legal Personality of Corporations and NGOs in the Context of Investor-State Arbitration', in J. d'Aspremont (ed.), *Participants in the International Legal System: Multiples Perspectives on Non-State Actors in International Law* (Routledge-Cavendish 2011).

Dumberry, P. and G. Dumas-Aubin, 'The Doctrine of "Clean Hands" and the Inadmissibility of Claims by Investors Breaching International Human Rights Law', in U. Kriebaum (ed.), *Aligning Human Rights and Investment Protection* (2013) 10(1) *TDM Special Issue*.

Eisemann, P.M., 'Rapport du Directeur de la section de langue française du Centre', in P.M. Eisemann and M. Koskenniemi (eds), *Codification Tested against the Facts* (Martinus Nijhoff 2000).

Eisemann, P.M., 'Emprunts russes et problèmes de succession d'Etats', in P. Juillard and B. Stern (eds), *Les emprunts russes et le règlement du contentieux financier franco-russe* (Cedin Cahiers internationaux no. 16, 2002).

Fiedler, W., 'Continuity', in R. Bernhardt (ed.), *Encyclopaedia of Public International Law*, vol. 1 (North Holland 1984).

Forget, L., 'La succession d'États en Europe de l'Est et les organisations financières internationales: l'experience de la Banque Mondiale', in G. Burdeau and B. Stern (eds), *Dissolution, Continuation et Succession en Europe de l'Est: succession d'États et relations économiques internationales* (Montchrestien 1994).

Gagglioli, G., 'Article 6', in G. Distefano, G. Gaggioli and A. Hêche (eds), *La Convention de Vienne de 1978 sur la succession d'États en matière de traités: Commentaire article par article et études thématiques* (Bruylant 2015).

Gallagher, N., 'The Requirement for Substantive Nationality', in F. Ortono et al. (eds), *Investment Treaty Law, Current Issues II, Nationality and Investment Treaty Claims* (BIICL 2007).

Gammara, Y., 'Current Questions of State Succession Relating to Multilateral Treaties', in P.M. Eisemann and M. Koskenniemi (eds), *Codification Tested against the Facts* (Martinus Nijhoff 2000).

Garrido-Munoz, A., 'Article 8', in G. Distefano, G. Gaggioli and A. Hêche (eds), *La Convention de Vienne de 1978 sur la succession d'États en matière de traités: Commentaire article par article et études thématiques* (Bruylant 2015).

Goia, A., 'State Succession and International Financial Organizations', in P.M. Eisemann and M. Koskenniemi (eds), *Codification Tested against the Facts* (Martinus Nijhoff 2000).

Gradoni, L., 'Article 2', in G. Distefano, G. Gaggioli and A. Hêche (eds), *La Convention de Vienne de 1978 sur la succession d'États en matière de traités: Commentaire article par article et études thématiques* (Bruylant 2015).

Graf-Brugère, 'Article 31', in G. Distefano, G. Gaggioli and A. Hêche (eds), *La Convention de Vienne de 1978 sur la succession d'États en matière de traités: Commentaire article par article et études thématiques* (Bruylant 2015).

Hafner, G. and I. Buffard, 'Les principales différences entre les propositions de la Commission du droit international et le résultat de la Conférence des Nations Unies à Vienne sur la succession d'États en matière de traités', in G. Distefano, G. Gaggioli and A. Hêche (eds), *La Convention de Vienne de 1978 sur la succession d'États en matière de traités: Commentaire article par article et études thématiques* (Bruylant 2015).

Hafner, G., 'Austria and Slovenia: Succession to Bilateral Treaties and the State Treaty of 1955', in M. Mrak (ed.), *State Succession* (Brill 1999).

Hafner, G. and G. Novak, 'State Succession in Respect of Treaties', in D.B. Hollis (ed.), *The Oxford Guide to Treaties* (OUP 2012).

Henry, E., 'Article 16', in G. Distefano, G. Gaggioli and A. Hêche (eds), *La Convention de Vienne de 1978 sur la succession d'États en matière de traités: Commentaire article par article et études thématiques* (Bruylant 2015).

Hernández, G.I., 'The Interaction Between Investment Law and the Law of Armed Conflict in the Interpretation of Full Protection and Security Clauses', in F. Baetens (ed.), *Investment Law Within International Law* (CUP 2013).

Hofmann, R., 'Annexation', in *Max Planck Encyclopedia of Public International Law* (OUP, online edn, 2006).

Jacquet, J-M., 'Contrat d'État', *Jurisclasseur Droit international*, fasc. 565.

Jenks, W.C., 'Multinational Entities in the Law of Nations', in *Transnational Law in a Changing Society: Essays in Honor of Philip C. Jessup* (Columbia UP 1972).

Kaboré, A.P., 'Article 7', in G. Distefano, G. Gaggioli and A. Hêche (eds), *La Convention de Vienne de 1978 sur la succession d'États en matière de traités: Commentaire article par article et études thématiques* (Bruylant 2015).

Karagiannis, S., 'Article 29', in O. Corten and P. Klein (eds), *Les Conventions de Vienne sur le Droit des Traités. Commentaire Article par Article* (Bruylant 2006).

Karavias, M., 'Treaty law and Multinational Enterprises: More Than Internationalized Contracts?', in C.J. Tams, A. Tzanakopoulos and A. Zimmermann (eds), *Research Handbook on the Law of Treaties* (Edward Elgar 2014).

Klabbers, J. and M. Koskenniemi, 'Succession in Respect to State Property, Archives and Debts, and Nationality', in J. Klabbers, M. Koskenniemi, O. Ribbelink and A. Zimmermann (eds), *State Practice Regarding State Succession and Issues of Recognition* (Council of Europe 1999).

Kohen, M.G., 'Le problème des frontières en cas de dissolution et de séparation d'Etats: quelles alternatives?', in O. Corten, B. Delcourt, P. Klein and N. Levrat, *Démembrement d'Etats et délimitations territoriales: L'uti possidetis en question(s)* (Bruylant 1999).

Kohen, M.G, 'Introduction', in M.G. Kohen (ed.), *Secession: International Law Perspectives* (CUP 2006).

Kolliopoulos, A., 'Article 9', in G. Distefano, G. Gaggioli and A. Hêche (eds), *La Convention de Vienne de 1978 sur la succession d'États en matière de traités: Commentaire article par article et études thématiques* (Bruylant 2015).

Koskenniemi, M., 'Report of the Director of Studies', in P.M. Eisemann and M. Koskenniemi (eds), *Codification Tested against the Facts* (Martinus Nijhoff 2000).

Kuyper, P.J., 'The Community and State Succession in Respect of Treaties', in D. Curtin and T. Heukels (eds), *Institutional Dynamics of European Integration, Essays in Honour of Henry G. Schermers*, vol. II (Martinus Nijhoff 1994).

Lalive, P., 'The Doctrine of Acquired Rights', in M. Bender (ed.), *Rights and Duties of Private Investors Abroad* (International And Comparative Law Center 1965).

Langstöm, T., 'The Dissolution of the Soviet Union in the Light of the 1978 Vienna Convention on Succession of States in Respect to Treaties', in P.M. Eisemann and M. Koskenniemi (eds), *Codification Tested against the Facts* (Martinus Nijhoff 2000).

Leben, C., 'Retour sur la notion de contrat d'Etat et sur le droit applicable à celui-ci', in *L'évolution du droit international: Mélanges offerts à Hubert Thierry* (Pédone 1998).

Leben, C., 'Quelques réflexions théoriques à propos des contrats d'Etat', in *Souveraineté étatique et marchés internationaux à la fin du 20e siècle: Mélange en l'honneur de Philippe Kahn* (Litec 2000).

Liberti, L., 'Investissements et droits de l'homme', in P. Kahn and T. Wälde (eds), *New Aspects of International Investment Law* (Martinus Nijhoff 2007).

Maljean-Dubois, S., 'Le rôle de l'équité dans le droit de la succession d'Etats', in P.M. Eisemann and M. Koskenniemi (eds), *Codification Tested against the Facts* (Martinus Nijhoff 2000).

Marques Antunes, S., 'Acquiescence', in *Max Planck Encyclopedia of Public International Law* (OUP, online edn, 2006).

Mendelson, M., 'The Runaway Train: The Continuous Nationality Rule from the Panevezys-Saldutiskis Railway Case to Loewen', in T. Weiler (ed.), *International Investment Law and Arbitration: Leading Cases from the ICSID, NAFTA, Bilateral Treaties and Customary International Law* (Cameron May 2005).

Mendelson, M., 'The Requirement for Continuous Nationality', in F. Ortono et al. (eds), *Investment Treaty Law, Current Issues II, Nationality and Investment Treaty Claims* (BIICL 2007).

Milanovic, M., 'The Spatial Dimension: Treaties and Territory', in C.J. Tams, A. Tzanakopoulos and A. Zimmermann (eds), *Research Handbook on the Law of Treaties*' (Edward Elgar 2014).

Mikulka, V., 'Article 34', in G. Distefano, G. Gaggioli and A. Hêche (eds), *La Convention de Vienne de 1978 sur la succession d'États en matière de traités: Commentaire article par article et études thématiques* (Bruylant 2015).

Milulka, V., 'Article 35', in G. Distefano, G. Gaggioli and A. Hêche (eds), *La Convention de Vienne de 1978 sur la succession d'États en matière de traités: Commentaire article par article et études thématiques* (Bruylant 2015).

Moussa, J., 'L'indépendance du Soudan du Sud et la Convention de Vienne sur la succession d'Etats en matière de traités', in G. Distefano, G. Gaggioli and A. Hêche (eds), *La Convention de Vienne de 1978 sur la succession d'États en matière de traités: Commentaire article par article et études thématiques* (Bruylant 2015).

Muchlinski, P., 'Corporations in International Law', in *Max Planck Encyclopedia of Public International Law* (OUP, online edn, 2006).

Mullerson, R., 'Law and Politics in Succession of States: International Law on Succession of States', in G. Burdeau and B. Stern (eds), *Dissolution, continuation et succession en Europe de l'Est* (Cedin-Paris I 1994).

O'Connell, D.P., 'Independence and Problems of State Succession', in W. O'Brien (ed.), *The New Nations in International Law and Diplomacy* (Stevens & Sons 1965).

Odendahl, K., 'Commentary to Article 29', in O. Dorr and K. Schmalenbach (eds), *The Vienna Convention on the Law of Treaties* (Springer 2012).

Ohly, D.C., 'A Functional Analysis of Claimant Eligibility', in R. Lillich (ed.), *International Law of State Responsibility for Injuries to Aliens* (UP Virginia 1983).

Orrego Vicuña, F., 'Changing Approaches to the Nationality of Claims in the Context of Diplomatic Protection and International Dispute Settlement', in S. Schlemmer-Schulte and K.-Y. Tung (eds), *Liber amicorum Ibrahim F.I. Shihata: International Finance and Development Law* (Kluwer 2001).

Ortega Terol, J.M., 'The Bursting of Yugoslavia: An Approach to Practice Regarding State Succession', in P.M. Eisemann and M. Koskenniemi (eds) *Codification Tested against the Facts* (Martinus Nijhoff 2000).

Palchetti, P., 'Article 4', in G. Distefano, G. Gaggioli and A. Hêche (eds), *La Convention de Vienne de 1978 sur la succession d'États en matière de traités: Commentaire article par article et études thématiques* (Bruylant 2015).

Panoussis, I., 'La succession d'États aux traités à l'épreuve du cas kosovar', in G. Distefano, G. Gaggioli and A. Hêche (eds), *La Convention de Vienne de 1978 sur la succession d'États en matière de traités: Commentaire article par article et études thématiques* (Bruylant 2015).

Petrochilos, G., 'Extension of the Arbitration Clause to Non-Signatory States or State Entities: Does it Raise a Difference?', in B. Hanotiau and E.A. Schwartz (eds), *Multiparty Arbitration* (Kluwer ICC 2010).

Poupart, I., 'Succession aux traités et droit de l'homme: vers la reconnaissance d'une protection ininterrompue des individus', in P.M. Eisemann and M. Koskenniemi (eds), *Codification Tested against the Facts* (Martinus Nijhoff 2000).

Pulkowski, D., 'The Final Award in Loewen v. United States', in A. Alvarez and W.M. Reisman (eds), *The Reasons Requirement in International Investment Arbitration: Critical Case Studies* (Martinus Nijhoff 2008).

Reed, L.E. and J.E. Davis, 'Who is a Protected Investor?', in M. Bungenberg, J. Griebel, S. Hobe and A. Reinisch (eds), *International Investment Law: A Handbook* (C.H. Beck, Hart, Nomos 2015).

Reiner, C. and C. Schreuer, 'Human Rights and International Investment Arbitration', in P.-M. Dupuy, E.-U. Petersmann and F. Francioni (eds), *Human Rights in International Investment Law and Arbitration* (OUP 2009).

Schermers, H.M., 'International Organizations, Membership', in R. Bernhardt (ed.), *Max Planck Encyclopedia of Public International Law* (Max Planck Institute 1984).

Schreuer, C.H., 'Unjustified Enrichment', in R. Bernhardt (ed.), *Max Planck Encyclopedia of Public International Law* (Max Planck Institute 1984).

Schreuer, C.H., 'The Protection of Investments in Armed Conflict', in F. Baetens (ed.), *Investment Law Within International Law* (CUP 2013).

Shaw, M.N. and C. Fournet, in O. Corten and P. Klein (eds), *Les Conventions de Vienne sur le droit des traités – Commentaire article par article*, vol. III (Bruylant 2006).

Shihata, I., 'Matters of State Succession in the Practice of the World Bank', in P.B. Casella, *Dimensão internacional do direito: estudos em homenagem a GE do Nascimento e Silva* (Ed LTR 2000).

Sinclair, I., 'Some Reflections on the Vienna Convention on Succession of States in Respect of Treaties', in *Essays in Honour of Erik Castren* (1978).

Sohn, L.B., 'The Iran-United States Claims Tribunal: Jurisprudential Contributions to the Development of International Law', in R.B. Lillich (ed.), *Iran-United States Claims Tribunal* (Seven Sokol Colloquium 1984).

Stern, B., 'Rapport de synthèse', in G. Burdeau and B. Stern (eds), *Dissolution, continuation et succession en Europe de l'Est* (Cedin-Paris I 1994).

Stern, B., 'Responsabilité internationale et succession d'Etats', in L. Boisson de Chazournes and V. Gowlland-Debbas (eds), *The International Legal System in Quest of Equity and Universality. Liber amicorum Georges Abi-Saab* (Martinus Nijhoff 2001).

Suy, E., 'Reflexions sur la distinction entre la souverainté et la compétence territoriale', in R. Marcic, et al. (eds), *Internationale Festschrift für Alfred Verdross* (Wilhem Fink Verlag 1971).

Szabó, M., 'State Succession and the Jurisprudence of the European Court of Human Rights', in C. Binder and K. Lachmayer (eds), *The European Court of Human Rights and Public International Law Fragmentation or Unity?* (Nomos 2014).

Talmon, S., 'The Duty Not to "Recognize as Lawful" a Situation Created by the Illegal Use of Force or Other Serious Breaches of a Jus Cogens Obligation: An Obligation without Real Substance?', in Ch. Tomuschat and J-M Thouvenin (eds), *The Fundamental Rules of the International Legal Order: Jus cogens and Obligations Erga Omnes* (Martinus Nijhoff 2005).

Tams, C.J., 'The Sources of International Investment Law', in T. Gazzini and E. De Brabandere (eds), *International Investment Law: The Sources of Rights and Obligations* (Brill 2012).

Tanzi, A. and L. Iapichino, 'Article 15', in G. Distefano, G. Gaggioli and A. Hêche (eds), *La Convention de Vienne de 1978 sur la succession d'États en matière de traités: Commentaire article par article et études thématiques* (Bruylant 2015).

Toral, M. and T. Schultz, 'The State, a Perpetual Respondent in Investment Arbitration? Some Unorthodox Considerations', in M. Waibel, A. Kaushal, K.-H.L. Chung and C. Balchin (eds), *The Backlash Against Investment Arbitration: Perceptions and Reality* (Kluwer 2010).

Torres Cazorla, M.I., 'Rights of Private Persons on State Succession: An Approach to the Most Recent Cases', in P.M. Eisemann and M. Koskenniemi (eds), *Codification Tested against the Facts* (Martinus Nijhoff 2000).

Tzanakopoulos A., 'Denunciation of the ICSID Convention under the General International Law of Treaties', in R. Hofmann and C.J. Tams (eds), *International Investment Law and General International Law: From Clinical Isolation to Systemic Integration?* (Nomos 2011).

Vahlas, A., 'A Propos de Trois Questions Récurrentes en Matière de Succession d'Etats: Application au Cas Yougoslave', in P.M. Eisemann and M. Koskenniemi (eds), *Codification Tested Against the Facts* (Martinus Nijhoff 2000).

Verdross, A., *Völkerrecht*, 4th edn (Springler Verlag 1959).

Verdross, A. and B. Simma, *Universelles Völkerrecht, Theorie und Praxis* (Dunker & Humblot 1984).

Wallace, D., 'Fair and Equitable Treatment and Denial of Justice: Loewen v. US and Chattin v. Mexico', in T. Weiler (ed.), *International Investment Law and Arbitration: Leading Cases from the ICSID, NAFTA, Bilateral Treaties and Customary International Law* (Cameron May 2005).

Weil, P., 'Droit international et contrat d'Etat' in *Mélanges offerts à Paul Reuter. Le droit international: unité et diversité* (Pédone 1981).

Wyler, E., 'Le droit de la succession d'États à l'épreuve de la fiction juridique', in G. Distefano, G. Gaggioli and A. Hêche (eds), *La Convention de Vienne de 1978 sur la succession d'États en matière de traités: Commentaire article par article et études thématiques* (Bruylant 2015).

Zimmerman, A., 'State Succession and the Nationality of Natural Persons – Facts and Possible Codification', in P.M. Eisemann and M. Koskenniemi (eds), *Codification Tested Against the Facts* (Martinus Nijhoff 2000).

Zimmermann, A., 'Secession and the Law of State Succession', in M.G. Kohen (ed.), *Secession: International Law Perspectives* (CUP 2006).

Zimmermann, A., 'State Succession in Treaties', in *Max Planck Encyclopedia of Public International Law* (OUP, online edn, 2006).

Zimmermann, A., 'Continuity of States', in *Max Planck Encyclopedia of Public International Law* (OUP, online edn, 2006).

Zimmermann, A., 'The International Court of Justice and State Succession to Treaties: Avoiding Principled Answers to Questions of Principle', in C.J. Tams and J. Sloan (eds), *The Development of International Law by the International Court of Justice* (OUP 2013).

Zimmermann, A., 'La Convention de Vienne sur la succession d'États en matière de traités: codification réussie ou échouée?', in G. Distefano, G. Gaggioli and A. Hêche (eds), *La Convention de Vienne de 1978 sur la succession d'États en matière de traités: Commentaire article par article et études thématiques* (Bruylant 2015).

Zimmermann, A. and J.G. Devaney, 'Succession to Treaties and the Inherent Limits of International Law', in C.J. Tams, A. Tzanakopoulos and A. Zimmermann (eds), *Research Handbook on the Law of Treaties* (Edward Elgar 2014).

ARTICLES

Abi-Saab, G., 'The Newly Independent States and the Rules of International Law: An Outline' (1962) 8 *Howard LJ*.

Acconci, P., 'Determining the Internationally Relevant Link between a State and a Corporate Investor, Recent Trends Concerning the Application of the "Genuine Link" Test' (2004) 5 *World Inv. & Trade*.

Acconci, P., 'The Requirement of Continuous Corporate Nationality and Customary International Rules on Foreign Investment: The Loewen Case' (2005) 14 *Italian YIL*.

Acconci, P., 'Is There Room For Customary Law in International Law on Foreign Investments? The Requirement of Continuous Corporate Nationality in the *Loewen* Case' (2005) 3 TDM.

Adeyeye, A., 'Corporate Responsibility in International Law: Which Way To Go?' (2007) 11 *Singapore YBIL*.

Alvarez, J.E., 'Are Corporations "Subjects" of International Law?' (2011) 9 *Santa Clara J Int'l L*.

Alvarez, J.E., 'Bit on Custom' (2009–10) 42 *NYU J Int'l L & Pol*.

Arato, J., 'Corporations as Lawmakers' (2015) 56 *Harv Int'l L J*.

Barale, J., 'L'acquiescement dans la jurisprudence internationale' (1965) 11 AFDI.

Berat, L., 'Genocide: The Namibian Case Against Germany' (1993) 165 *Pace Int'l L Rev*.

Berbner, A., 'Things Fall Apart? NAFTA After Quebec' (1997) 6 *Dalhousie J Legal Stud*.

Bernier, I., 'Le maintien de l'accès aux marchés extérieurs: certaines questions juridiques soulevées par l'hypothèse de la souveraineté du Québec' (1991) 7(1) RQDI.

Beygo, O., 'Nationality of Corporations in International Claims Arising out of Foreign Investment Disputes (1993) 46 RHDI.

Binder, C., 'Sanum Investments Limited v. The Government of the Lao People's Democratic Republic' (2016) 17 *J World Invest. & Trade*.

Blum, Y.Z., 'Russia Takes over the Soviet Union's Seat at the United Nations' (1993) 3(2) EJIL.

Booysen, H., 'Succession to Delictual Liability: a Namibian Precedent' (1991) 24 *Comp & Int'l L J S Afr* 204–14.

Botha, N., 'To Pay or Not to Pay?: Namibian Liability for South African Delicts' (1990–1991) 16 *South African YIL*.

Botha, N., 'Succession to Delictual Liability: Confirmation' (1991–1992) 17 *South African YIL*.

Brockman-Hawe, B.E., 'Succession, the Obligation to Repair and Human Rights; The European Court of Human Rights Judgment in the Case of Bijelic c/ Montenegro and Serbia' (2010) 59 ICLQ.

Brower, C.N. and A.C. Smutny, 'The Effect of the Independence of Quebec upon Treaties and Agreements with the U.S.A.' (1997) 27(1) *American Review of Canadian Studies*.

Burke-White, W. and A. Von Staden, 'Investment Protection in Extraordinary Times: The Interpretation and Application of Non-Precluded Measures Provisions in Bilateral Investment Treaties' (2008) 48 *Virgina JIL*.

Caflisch, L., 'La nationalité des sociétés commerciales en droit international privé' (1967) 24 ASDI.

Caflisch, L., 'The Protection of Corporate Investments Abroad in the Light of the *Barcelona Traction Case*', 31 ZaöRV 179.

Caggiano, P., 'The ILC Draft on the Succession of States in Respect of Treaties: A Critical Appraisal' (1975) 1 *Italian YIL*.

Chen, A., 'Queries to the Recent ICSID Decision on Jurisdiction upon the Case of Tza Yap Shum v. Republic of Peru: Should China-Peru BIT 1994 Be Applied to Hong Kong SAR under the "One Country Two Systems"' (2009) 10 *J World Inv & Trade*.

Christakis, T., 'Les conflits de sécession en Crimée et dans l'est de l'Ukraine et le droit International' (2014) 3 *Journal du droit international*.

Christakis, T., 'Self-Determination, Territorial Integrity and *Fait Accompli* in the Case of Crimea' (2015) 75 ZaöRV.

Cohen-Jonathan, G., 'L'arbitrage Texaco-Calasiatic contre Gouvernement Libyen' (1977) 23 AFDI.

Costelloe, D., 'Treaty Succession in Annexed Territory' (2016) 65 ICLQ.

Cotran, E., 'Some Legal Aspects of the Formation of the United Arab Republic and the United Arab States' (1959) 8 ICLQ.

Cowger, A.R. Jr., 'Rights and Obligations of Successor States: An Alternative Theory' (1985) 17 *Case West. Res J Int L* 301.

Craven, M.C.R., 'The Problem of State Succession and the Identity of States under International Law' (1998) 9(1) EJIL.

Crawford, J., 'State Practice and International Law in Relation to Secession' (1998) *British YIL*.

Crawford, J., 'The Contribution of Professor D.P. O'Connell to the Discipline of International Law' (1980) 51 *British YIL*.

Crépeau, F., 'The Law of Quebec's Secession' (1997) 27(1) *American Review of Canadian Studies*.

Crook, J.R., 'Applicable Law in International Arbitration: The Iran-US Claims Tribunal Experience (1989) 83(2) AJIL.

Cwicinskaja, N., 'The Legality and Certain Legal Consequences of the "Accession" of Crimea to the Russian Federation' (2014) 34 *Polish YIL*.

Czaplinski, W., 'State Succession and State Responsibility' (1990) 28 *Canadian YIL*.

Czaplinski, W., 'La continuité, l'identité et la succession d'États-évaluation de cas récents' (1993) 26 RBDI.

d'Aspremont, J., 'Decolonization and the International Law of Succession: Between Regime Exhaustion and Paradigmatic Inconclusiveness' (2013) 12 *Chinese JIL*.

De Brandt, J-P., 'De quelques problèmes de succession d'États à la suite de l'accession à l'indépendance de la République du Congo (Léopoldville)' (1965) RBDI.

Degan, V., 'La succession d'États en matière de traités et les États nouveaux (issus de l'ex-Yougoslavie)' (1996) 42 AFDI.

Delbez, L., 'Du territoire dans ses rapports avec l'État' (1932) RGDIP.

de Visscher, P., 'Le problème de la succession d'Etats envisagé dans l'histoire diplomatique du Congo' (1960–1962) 11 *Comunicazioni e studi*.

Dominicé, C., 'L'émergence de l'individu en droit international public' (1987–1988) 16 *Annales d'études internationales*.

Douglas, Z., 'The Hybrid Foundation of Investment Treaty Arbitration' (2003) 74 *British YIL*.

Drakidis, P., 'Succession d'Etats et enrichissements sans cause des biens publics du Dodécanèse' (1971) 24 RHDI.

Dubouis, L., 'La distinction entre le droit de l'Etat réclamant et le droit du ressortissant dans la protection diplomatique' (1978) LXVII *Rev. crit. d.i. privé*.

Duchesne, M.S., 'The Continuous Nationality of Claims Principle: Its Historical Development and Current Relevance to Investor-State Investment Disputes' (2004) 36 *Geo Wash Int'l L Rev*.

Dumberry, P., 'L'entreprise, sujet de droit international? Retour sur la question à la lumière des développements récents du droit international des investissements' (2004) 108(1) RGDIP.

Dumberry, P., 'New State Responsibility for Internationally Wrongful Acts by an Insurrectional Movement' (2006) 17(3) EJIL.

Dumberry, P., 'Obsolete and Unjust: the Rule of Continuous Nationality in the Context of State Succession' (2007) 76(2) *Nordic JIL*.

Dumberry, P., 'Turkey's International Responsibility for Internationally Wrongful Acts Committed by the Ottoman Empire' (2012) 42 *Revue générale de droit*.

Dumberry, P., 'Is Turkey the "Continuing" State of the Ottoman Empire under International Law?' (2012) 59(2) *Netherlands ILR*.

Dumberry, P., 'Denial of Justice under NAFTA Article 1105: A Review of 20 Years of Case Law' (2014) 32(2) *ASA Bull.*

Dumberry, P., 'An Uncharted Question of State Succession: Are New States Automatically Bound by the BITs Concluded by Predecessor States Before Independence?' (2015) 6(1) *J Int Disp Settl.*

Dumberry, P., 'State Succession to Bilateral Treaties: A Few Observations on the Incoherent and Unjustifiable Solution Adopted for Secession and Dissolution of States under the 1978 Vienna Convention' (2015) 28 *Leiden JIL*.

Dumberry, P. and D. Turp, 'La succession d'États en matière de traités et le cas de la sécession: du principe de la table rase à l'émergence d'une présomption de continuité des traités' (2003) 36(2) RBDI.

Dumberry, P. and D. Turp, 'State Succession with Respect to Multilateral Treaties in the Context of Secession: From the Principle of Tabula Rasa to the Emergence of a Presumption of Continuity of Treaties' (2013) 13 *Baltic YIL*.

Dumberry, P. and G. Dumas-Aubin, 'How to Impose Human Rights Obligations on Corporations under Investment Treaties?' (2011–2012) 4 *Yb Int'l Invest L & Pol*.

Dumberry, P. and G. Dumas-Aubin, 'When and How Allegations of Human Rights Violations can be Raised in Investor-State Arbitration' (2012) 13(3) *J World Invest & Trade*.

Dupont, P-E., 'Foreign Investment and the Status of Kosovo in International Law' (2009) 10 *J World Invest & Trade*.

Dycus, S., 'Quebec Independence and United States Security: A Question of Continuing Rights and Duties' (1998) 15 *Ariz J Int Comp Law*.

Fastenrath, U., 'Der deutsche Einigungsvertrag im Lichte des Rechts der Staatennachfolge' (1992) 44 Ö.Z.ö.R.V.

Fecák, T., 'Czech Experience with Bilateral Investment Treaties: Somewhat Bitter Taste of Investment Protection' (2011) 2 *Czech Yearbook of Public & Private International Law*.

Focsaneanu, L., 'L'accord ayant pour objet l'indemnisation de la compagnie de Suez nationalisée par l'Égypte' (1959) AFDI.

Forteau, M., 'La contribution au développement du droit international général de la jurisprudence arbitrale relative aux investissements étrangers' (2009) 4(1) *Anuário Brasileiro de Direito Internacional*.

Fombad, C.M., 'The Principle of Unjustified Enrichment in International Law' (1997) 30 *Comp & Int'l L J S Afr*.

Freyer, D.H., 'Recovering Damages for Unjust Enrichment in International Arbitration' (2007) 1(1) *World Arb & Med Rep*.

Gallo, P., 'Unjust Enrichment: A Comparative Analysis' (1992) 40 Am JCL.

Ganshof, L.F., 'Les dettes de l'ex-colonie du Congo belge' (1964) *Revue juridique du Congo*.

Gazzini, T., 'The Role of Customary International Law in the Protection of Foreign Investment' (2007) 8 *J World Inv & Trade*.

Gdalina, A., 'Crimea and the Right to Self-Determination: Questioning the Legality of Crimea's Secession from Ukraine' (2016) 24 *Cardozo JICL*.

Geiss, R., 'Russia's Annexation of Crimea: The Mills of International Law Grind Slowly but They Do Grind' (2015) 91 *Int'l L Stud*.

Genest, A., 'Sudan Bilateral Investment Treaties and South Sudan: Musings on State Succession to Bilateral Treaties in the Wake of Yugoslavia's Breakup' (2014) 3 TDM.

Grabell, A., 'New Northern Neighbor? An Independent Québec, the United States and the NAFTA' (1995) 2(1) *Sw J L & Trade Americas*.

Grant, T.D., 'Annexation of Crimea' (2015) 109(1) AJIL.

Grant, T.D., 'International Dispute Settlement in Response to an Unlawful Seizure of Territory: Three Mechanisms' (2015) 16(1) *Chicago JIL*.

Grant, T.D., 'The Yanukovych Letter: Intervention and Authority to Invite in International Law' (2015) 2 *Indon J Intl & Comp L*.

Guerari, H., 'Quelques Observations Sur Les Etats Ephémères' (1994) AFDI.

Hafner, G. and E. Kornfeind, 'The Recent Austrian Practice of State Succession: Does the Clean Slate Rule Still Exist?' (1996) 1 *Austrian RIEL*.

Hailbronner, K., 'Legal Aspects of the Unification of the Two German States' (1991) 2(1) EJIL.

Happ, R. and S. Wuschka, 'Horror Vacui: Or Why Investment Treaties Should Apply to Illegally Annexed Territories' (2016) 33(3) *J Int Arb*.

Harrison, J., 'The Life and Death of BITs: Legal Issues Concerning Survival Clauses and the Termination of Investment Treaties' (2012) *13 J World Invest & Trade*.

Hart, N. and S. Srikumar, 'Investor-State Arbitration before the High Court of Singapore: Territoriality, Nationality and Arbitrability' (2015) 4 *Cambridge JICL*.

Hoeflich, M.H., 'Through a Glass Darkly: Reflections upon the History of the International Law of Public Debt In Connection With State Succession' (1982) 1 *Univ Illinois LR*.

Hurst, C.J.B., 'State Succession in Matters of Tort' (1924) 5 *British YIL*.

Hwang, M. and A. Chang, 'Case Comment: Government of the Lao People's Democratic Republic v. Sanum Investments Ltd: A Tale of Two Letters' (2015) 30 *ICSID Rev*.

Kaeckenbeeck, G., 'The Protection of Vested Rights in International Law' (1936) 17 *British YIL*.

Kammerhofer, J., 'Uncertainty in the Formal Sources of International Law: Customary International Law and Some of Its Problems' (2004) 15(3) EJIL.

Kamminga, M.T., 'State Succession in Respect of Human Rights Treaties' (1996) 7(4) EJIL.

Kamto, M., 'La notion de contrat d'État: une contribution au débat' (2003) Rev Arb.

Kasku-Jackson, J., 'Can Quebec Succeed at Secession?' (1998) 4 NEICLA.

Kearney, R.D., 'The Twenty-Sixth Session of the International Law Commission' (1975) 69(3) AJIL.

Keith, K.J., 'Succession to Bilateral Treaties by Seceding States' (1967) 61(2) AJIL.

Kinley, D. and J. Tadaki, 'From Talk to Walk: The Emergence of Human Rights Responsibilities for Corporations at International Law' (2004) 44(4) *Virginia JIL*.

Koskenniemi, M. and M. Lehto, 'La succession d'États dans l'ex-URSS, en ce qui concerne particulièrement les relations avec la Finlande' (1992) 38 AFDI.

Ko Swan, Sik, 'The Concept of Acquired Rights in International Law: A Survey' (1977) 24(1) *Netherlands ILR*.

Kryvoi, Y., 'Counterclaims in Investor-State Arbitration' (2012) 21(2) *Minnesota JIL*.

Kunz, J.L., 'Identity of States under International Law' (1955) 49 AJIL.

Laborde, G., 'The Case for Host State Claims in Investment Arbitration' (2010) 1(1) *J Int Disp Settl*.

Lagerwall, A., 'L'agression et l'annexion de la Crimée par la Fédération de Russie: Quels enseignements au sujet du droit international?' (2014) *Question de droit international, Zoom Out I*.

Lagrange, E., 'Les successions d'États: pratiques françaises' (2003) 63 *La L Rev*.

Lalive, P., 'Jurisprudence de droit international privé' (1978) ASDI.

Lalive, P., 'Arbitrage international et ordre public suisse: Une surprenante décision du Tribunal fédéral: l'arrêt SGTM/Bangladesh' (1978) 98 *Revue de droit suisse*.

Lawry-White, M., 'International Investment Arbitration in a Jus Post Bellum Framework' (2015) 16 J *World Inv & Trade*.

Lee, L.J., 'Barcelona Traction in the 21st Century: Revisiting its Customary and Policy Underpinnings 35 Years Later' (2006) 42 *Stan JIL*.

Lehner, O., 'The Identity of Austria 1918/19 as a problem of State Succession' (1992) 44 Ö.Z.ö.R.V.

Lehto, M., 'Succession of States in the Former Soviet Union: Arrangements Concerning the Bilateral Treaties of Finland and the USSR' (1993) 4 *Finnish YIL*.

Lester, A.P., 'State Succession to Treaties in the Commonwealth' (1963) ICLQ.

Leurent, B. and J.C. Holet, 'Les incidences politiques de la souveraineté sur l'arbitrage: reconnaissance et continuité des Etats' (2003) Rev arb.

Lim, D., 'The Virtue of Judicial Restraint: Two Comments on Laos v. Sanum' (2015) 10(2) *Global Arbitration Rep*.

Lorenz, W., 'General Principles of Law: Their Elaboration in the Court of Justice of the European Communities' (1964) 13(1) *Am J Comp L*.

Louis, J-V., 'L'accession du Congo belge à l'indépendance, problèmes de succession d'États dans la jurisprudence belge' (1966) AFDI.

Loungnarath, V., 'Quelques réflexions d'ordre juridique sur la clause d'adhésion de l'ALENA' (1994) 40 *McGill LJ*.

MacGibbon, C., 'The Scope of Acquiescence in International Law' (1954) 31 *British YIL*.

Majzub, D.B., 'Does Secession Mean Succession? The International Law of Treaty Succession and an Independent Quebec' (1998) 24 *Queen's LJ*.

Maloney, M., 'State Succession in Respect of Treaties: The Vienna Convention of 1978' (1978–79) 19 *Virginia JIL*.

Mann, F.A., 'The Effect of State Succession upon Corporations' (1972) 88 LQR.

Mayorga, O., 'Occupants, Beware of BITs: Applicability of Investment Treaties to Occupied Territories' (2017) 19 *Palestine YIL*.

McNair, L., 'The General Principles of Law Recognized by Civilized Nations' (1957) 33 *British YIL*.

Menon, P.K., 'The Succession of States and the Problem of State Debts' (1986) 6 *B C Third World L J*.

Menon, P.K., 'The Newly Independent States and Succession in Respect of Treaties' (1990) 18 *Korean JCL*.

Menon, P.K., 'The Legal Personality of Individuals' (1994) 6 *Sri Lanka JIL*.

Milano, E., 'The Non-Recognition of Russia's Annexation of Crimea: Three Different Legal Approaches and One Unanswered Question' (2014) 1 *Questions Int'l L*.

Misra, K.P., 'Succession of States: Pakistan's Membership in the United Nations' (1965) *Canadian YIL*.

Monnier, J.P., 'La succession d'Etats en matière de responsabilité internationale' (1962) 8 AFDI.

Motala, Z., 'Under International Law, Does the New Order in South Africa Assume the Obligations and Responsibilities of Apartheid Order? An Argument for Realism over Formalism' (1997) 30 *Comp & Int'l L J S Afr*.

Nassar, N., 'Internationalization of State Contracts: ICSID, The Last Citadel' (1997) 14(3) *J Int Arb*.

Nikouei, M. and Zamani, M., 'The Secession of Crimea: Where Does International Law Stand?' (2016) 85(1) *Nordic JIL*.

Nussbaum, A., 'The Arbitration the Lena Goldfields Ltd. and the Soviet Government' (1950) 36 *Cornell LQ*.

O'Connell, D.P., 'Economic Concessions in the Law of State Succession' (1950) 27 *British YIL*.

O'Connell, D.P., 'Unjustified Enrichment' (1956) 5(1) *Am J Comp L*.

O'Connell, D.P., 'Reflections on the State Succession Convention' (1979) 39 ZaöRV.

Oktem, E., 'Turkey: Successor or Continuing State of the Ottoman Empire?' (2011) 24 *Leiden JIL*.

Olson, P.M., 'The Lawfulness of Russian Use of Force in Crimea' (2014) 53 *Mil L & L War Rev*.

Orakhelashvili, A., 'The Position of the Individual in International Law' (2001) 31 *W Int'l J*.

Ostfansky, J., 'The Termination and Suspension of Bilateral Investment Treaties due to an Armed Conflict' (2015) 6 *J Int'l Disp Settl.*

Paulsson, J., 'Continuous Nationality in *Loewen*' (2004) 20 *Arb. Int.*

Pereira Fleury, R., 'State Succession and Bits: Challenges for Investment Arbitration' (2016) 27 *Am Rev Int'l Arb.*

Pilgrim, C.M., 'Some Legal Aspects of Trade in the Natural Resources of Namibia' (1990) 61 *British YIL.*

Pronto, A., 'The Effect of War on Law – What Happens to Their Treaties When States Go to War?' (2013) 2 *Cambridge J Int'l & Comp L.*

Qerimi, Q. and S. Krasniqi, 'Theories and Practice of State Succession to Bilateral Treaties: The Recent Experience of Kosovo' (2013) 14(9) *German LJ.*

Reeves, S., 'To Russia with Love: How Moral Arguments for a Humanitarian Intervention in Syria Opened the Door for an Invasion of the Ukraine' (2014–15) 23 *Mich St Int'l L Rev.*

Repousis, O.G., 'On Territoriality and International Investment Law: Applying China's Investment Treaties to Hong Kong and Macao' (2015) 37(1) *Michigan JIL.*

Repousis, O.G., 'The Application of Investment Treaties to Overseas Territories and the Uncertain Provisional Application of the Energy Charter Treaty to Gibraltar' (2016) 32(1) *ICSID Rev.*

Repousis, O.G., 'Why Russian Investment Treaties Could Apply to Crimea and What Would This Mean For the Ongoing Russo–Ukrainian Territorial Conflict' (2016) *Arb Int.*

Repousis, O.G and J. Fry, 'Armed Conflict and State Succession in Investor-State Arbitration' (2016) 23(3) *Columbia JEL.*

Rich, R., 'Recognition of States: The Collapse of Yugoslavia and the Soviet Union' (1993) 4(1) EJIL.

Rodriguez Iglesias, G.C., 'El enriquecimiento sin causa como fundamento de responsabilidad internacional' (1982) 34 REDI.

Rosenne, S., 'The Effect of Change of Sovereignty upon Municipal Law' (1950) 27 *British YIL.*

Rougevin-Baville, M., 'Le sort des droits et obligations de l'ancienne 'Colonie du Congo belge' d'après la jurisprudence des juridictions de Belgique' (1963) 2(1) *Revue judiciaire congolaise.*

Rubins, N., 'Loewen v. United States: The Burial of an Investor-State Arbitration Claim' (2005) 21 *Arb Int'l.*

Sarvarian, A., 'Codifying the Law of State Succession: A Futile Endeavour?' (2016) 27(3) EJIL.

Sayre, F.B., 'Change of Sovereignty and Concessions' (1918) AJIL.

Schachter, O., 'The Development of International Law through the Legal Opinions of the United Nations' (1948) 20 *British YIL.*

Schachter, O., 'State Succession: the Once and Future Law' (1993) 33(2) *Virginia JIL*.

Schreuer, C.H., 'Unjustified Enrichment in International Law' (1974) 22 *Am J Comp L*.

Schreuer, C., 'The Protection of Investments in Armed Conflict' (2012) 3 TDM.

Schrijver, N.J., 'The UN Council for Namibia *vs.* Urenco, UCN and the State of the Netherlands' (1988) 1 *Leiden JIL*.

Schwebel, S.M., 'International Protection of Contractual Arrangements' (1959) ASIL.

Seidl-Hohenveldern, I., 'The Theory of Quasi-International and Partly International Agreements' (1975) 11 RBDI.

Shaw, M., 'State Succession Revisited' (1994) 5 *Finnish YIL*.

Shen, W., 'Conceptuality or Textuality? Understanding the Notion of Expropriation in the Context of Tza Yap Shum v. The Republic of Peru' (2014) 7 *J East Asia & Int'l L*.

Shen, W., 'The Good, the Bad or the Ugly? A Critique of the Decision on Jurisdiction and Competence in Tza Yap Shum v. The Republic of Peru' (2011) 9 *Chinese JIL*.

Shoyele, O., 'State Succession and Governmental Contracts in African States' (1997) 9 *Sri Lanka JIL*.

Sinclair, A.C., 'The Substance of Nationality Requirements in Investment Treaty Arbitration' (2005) 20 *ICSID Rev*.

Sinclair, I., 'Nationality of Claims: British Practice' (1950) 27 *British YIL*.

Stepanowa, A., 'International Law and Legality of Secession in Crimea' (2014) *Cambridge JICL*.

Strydom, H.A., 'Namibian Independence and the Question of the Contractual and Delictual Liability of the Predecessor and Successor Governments' (1989–1990) 15 *South African YIL*.

Swan Sik, K., 'The Concept of Acquired Rights in International Law: A Survey' (1977) 24 *Netherlands ILR*.

Szafarz, R., 'Succession of States in Respect of Treaties in Contemporary International Law' (1983) 12 *Polish YIL*.

Talmon, S., 'The Constitutive versus the Declaratory Theory of Recognition: Tertium Non Datur?' (2004) 75 *British YIL*.

Tams, C.J., 'State Succession to Investment Treaties: Mapping the Issues' (2016) 31(2) *ICSID Rev*.

Tancredi, A., 'Neither Authorized nor Prohibited?: Secession and International Law after Kosovo, South Ossetia and Abkhazia' (2008) 18 *Italian YIL*.

Tancredi, A., 'The Russian Annexation of the Crimea: Questions Relating to the Use of Force' (2014) 1 *Questions of Int'l L*.

Tucker, E.W., 'Has the Individual Become the Subject of International Law?' (1965) 34 *U Cin L Rev.*

Tzeng, P., 'Sovereignty over Crimea: a Case for State-to-State Investment Arbitration' (2016) 41(2) *Yale JIL.*

Van Ert, G., 'Nationality, State Succession, and the Right of Option: The Case of Quebec' (1998) 36 *Canadian YIL.*

Vazquez, C.M., 'Direct vs. Indirect Obligations of Corporations under International Law' (2005) 45 *Colum J Transnat'l L.*

Verdross, A., 'Quasi-International Agreements and International Economic Transactions' (1964) 18 *Yearbook of World Affairs.*

Vidmar, J., 'Remedial Secession in International Law: Theory and (Lack of) Practice' (2010) 6 *St. Antony's Int Rev.*

Vohryzek, A., 'Unjust Enrichment Unjustly Ignored: Opportunities and Pitfalls in Bringing unjust Enrichment Claims under ICSID' (2009) 31 *Loy L A Int'l & Comp L Rev.*

Volkovitsch, M.J., 'Righting Wrongs: Toward a New Theory of State Succession to Responsibility for International Delicts' (1992) 92(8) *Colum L Rev.*

Voon, T., A. Mitchell and J. Munro, 'Parting Ways: The Impact of Mutual Termination of Investment Treaties on Investor Rights' (2014) 29 *ICSID Rev.*

Waelbroeck, M., 'Arrêt no. 8160 du Conseil d'État Belge, note d'observations' (1961) 1 RJDA.

Wang, H., 'The (In)applicability of Sino-Foreign BITs to Hong Kong and Macao' (2011) 8 *Manchester J Int'l Econ L.*

Weller, M., 'The International Response to the Dissolution of the Socialist Federal Republic of Yugoslavia. Current Developments' (1992) 86 AJIL.

White, T.W., 'Referendum in Crimea: Developing International Law on "Territorial Realignment" Referendums' (2016) 38(3) *Houston JIL.*

Williams, P.R., 'The Treaty Obligations of the Successor States of the Former Soviet Union, Yugoslavia and Czechoslovakia: Do They Continue in Force?' (1994) 23 *Denver J Int Law Pol.*

Williams, P.R., 'State Succession and the International Financial Institutions: Political Criteria v. Protection of Outstanding Financial Obligations' (1994) 43 ICLQ.

Williamson, E.D., 'State Succession and Relations with Federal States' (1992) 86 ASIL.

Williamson, E.D. and J.E. Osborn, 'A U.S. Perspective on Treaty Succession and Related Issues in the Wake of the Break-up of the U.S.S.R. and Yugoslavia' (1992) 33 *Virginia JIL.*

Wisner, R. and N. Gallus, 'Nationality Requirements in Investor-State Arbitration' (2004) 5 *J World Invest & Trade.*

Yasseen, M.K., 'La Convention de Vienne sur la Succession d'Etats en matière de traités' (1978) 24 AFDI.

Young, R., 'The State of Syria: Old or New ?' (1962) 56 AJIL.

Young, S.C., 'Foreign Direct Investment Disputes with Unrecognized States: FDI Arbitration in Kosovo' (2016) 22(5) *J Int Arb*.

Zadorozhnii, O., 'To Justify against All Odds: the Annexation of Crimea in 2014 and the Russian Legal Scholarship' (2015) 35 *Polish YIL*.

Zamuner, E., 'Le Rapport entre Empire ottoman et la République turque face au droit international' (2004) 6 *J Hist Int'l L*.

Zedalis, R.J., 'An Independent Quebec: State Succession to NAFTA' (1996) 2(4) *NAFTA: Law & Bus Rev Am*.

Zhang, Q., 'Are the PRC BITs Applicable to China's Special Administrative Regions? In Consideration of the Sanum v. Laos Case' (2016) 2(1) *China and WTO Review*.

Ziemele, I., 'Is the Distinction between State Continuity and State Succession Reality or Fiction? The Russian Federation, the Federal Republic of Yugoslavia and Germany' (2001) 1 *Baltic YIL*.

Zimmermann, R., 'Unjust Enrichment: The Modern Civilian Approach' (1995) 15 *Oxford J Legal Stud*.

COURSES

Barberis, J.A., 'Nouvelles questions concernant la personnalité juridique internationale' (1983-I) 179 Rec des cours.

Bedjaoui, M., 'Problèmes récents de succession d'Etats dans les Etats nouveaux' (1970-II) 130 Rec des cours.

Cahier, P., 'Changements et continuité du droit international, Cours général de droit international public' (1985-VI) 195 Rec des cours.

Cansacchi, G., 'Identité et continuité des sujets de droit international' (1970-I) 130 Rec des cours.

Castren, E.J., 'Aspects récents de la succession d'Etats' (1951-I) 78 Rec des cours.

De Aréchaga, E.J, 'International Law in the Past Third of a Century' (1978-I) 159 Rec des cours.

Degan, V., 'Création et disparition de l'État (à la lumière du démembrement de trois fédérations multiethniques en Europe)' (1999) 279 Rec. des Cours 300.

De Visscher, C., 'Cours général de droit international public' (1972-II) 136 Rec des cours.

Dinstein, Y., 'The Interaction between Customary International Law and Treaties' (2006) 322 Rec des cours.

Franck, T.M., 'Fairness in the International Legal and Institutional System: General Course on Public International Law' (1993) 240 Rec des cours.

Ferrari-Bravo, L., 'Méthodes de recherche de la coutume internationale dans la pratique des États' (1985) 192 Rec des cours.

Franck, T.M., 'Fairness in the International Legal and Institutional System: General Course on Public International Law' (1993) 240 Rec des cours.

Friedmann, W., 'General Course in Public International Law' (1969-II) 127 Rec des cours.

Henkin, L., 'International Law: Politics, Values and Function: General Course on Public International Law' (1989) 216 Rec des cours.

Jenning, R., 'General Course on Principles of International Law' (1967-II) 121 Rec des cours.

Kaeckenbeeck, G., 'La protection international des droits acquis' (1937–1) 59 Rec des cours.

Kelsen, H., 'Théorie générale du droit international public. Problèmes choisis' (1932–IV) 42 Rec des cours.

Lalive, J-F., 'Contrats entre États ou entreprises étatiques et personnes privées. Développements récents' (1983–III) 181 Rec des cours.

Lauterpacht, H., 'Règles générales du droit de la paix' (1937-IV) 62 Rec des cours.

Leben, C., 'La théorie du contrat d'État et l'évolution du droit international des investissements' (2003) 302 Rec des cours.

Makonnen, Y., 'State Succession in Africa: Selected Problems' (1986–V) 200 Rec des cours.

Mendelson, M.H., 'The Formation of Customary International Law' (1985) 192 Rec des cours.

O'Connell, D.P., 'Recent Problems of State Succession in Relation to New States' (1970–II) 130 Rec des cours.

Ripert, G., 'Les règles du droit civil applicables aux rapports internationaux' (1933-II) 44 Rec des cours.

Salvioli, G., 'Les règles générales de la paix' (1933-IV) 46 Rec des cours.

Schachter, O., 'International Law in Theory and Practice: General Course in Public International Law' (1982) 178 Rec des cours.

Schoenborn, W., 'La nature juridique du territoire' (1929-V) 30 Rec des cours.

Stern, B., 'La succession d'États' (1996) 262 Rec des cours.

Udina, M., 'La succession des États quant aux obligations internationales autres que les dettes publiques' (1933-II) 44 Rec des cours.

Waldock, H., 'General Course on Public International Law' (1962) 106 Rec des cours.

Zemanek, K., 'State Succession after Decolonization' (1965–III) 116 Rec des cours.

STUDIES/RESEARCH PAPERS/THESIS/CONFERENCE PAPERS

Ackermann, T., 'Investments Under Occupation: Belligerent Occupation and the Application of Investment Treaties', International Investment Law and the Law of Armed Conflict, 5–6 October 2017, Athens Colloquium.

Atlam, H.M., 'Succession d'Etats et continuité en matière de responsabilité internationale' (Ph.D. Thesis, Université de droit, d'économie et des sciences d'Aix-Marseille 1986).

Azaria, D., 'Foreign Investment Treaties and the ILC Draft Articles on the Effect of Armed Conflicts on Treaties', International Investment Law and the Law of Armed Conflict, 5–6 October 2017, Athens Colloquium.

Berkes, A., 'The Responsibility of the Host State for the Violations of Investors' Rights in a Part of its Territory under Occupation', International Investment Law and the Law of Armed Conflict, 5–6 October 2017, Athens Colloquium.

Bernstein, D.W. and W. Silverman, 'Avis sur les conséquences de l'indépendance du Québec en ce qui a trait aux traités et accords conclus avec les États-Unis d'Amérique', 7 March 1995.

Bottini, G., 'Reflections on the Origins and Evolution of War and Civil Disturbance Clauses' International Investment Law and the Law of Armed Conflict, 5–6 October 2017, Athens Colloquium.

de Brabandere, E., 'The Subjectivity of Full Protection and Security and the Due Diligence Standard', International Investment Law and the Law of Armed Conflict, 5–6 October 2017, Athens Colloquium.

Brower, C.N., 'Memorandum on the March 7, 1995 Advisory Memorandum Regarding the Effect of Independence of Quebec Upon Treaties and Agreements with the United States of America', 21 March 1995.

Braun, T.R., 'Globalization-driven Innovation: The Investor as a Partial Subject in Public International Law – An Inquiry into the Nature and Limits of Investor Rights', Jean Monnet Working Paper Series, JMWP 04/13.

Broude, T., 'The Protection of Investments in Occupied Territories: Some Considerations', International Investment Law and the Law of Armed Conflict, 5–6 October 2017, Athens Colloquium.

Durieux, A., 'Le problème juridique des dettes du Congo et de l'Etat du Congo', Académie Royale des Sciences d'Outre-Mer, Mémoire in-8, t. 28, fasc. 3, Brussels, 1961.

Fouchard Papaefstratiou, A., 'Armed Conflicts Clause in Investment Treaties: Minimum Protection Threshold or *Lex Specialis*?', International Investment Law and the Law of Armed Conflict, 5–6 October 2017, Athens Colloquium.

Fraterman, J.A., 'Secession, State Succession and International Arbitration', paper, SSRN, 2013.

Gagliani, G., 'Supervening Impossibility of Performance and the Effect of Armed Conflict on Investment Treaties: What Room for Manoeuvre?', International Investment Law and the Law of Armed Conflict, 5–6 October 2017, Athens Colloquium.

Giupponi, B.O., 'Exploring the Links Between Nationality Changes and Investment Claims Arising out of Armed Conflicts', International Investment Law and the Law of Armed Conflict, 5–6 October 2017, Athens Colloquium.

Joyner, D., 'Termination and Suspension of Investment Treaties as a Consequence of Armed Conflict', International Investment Law and the Law of Armed Conflict, 5–6 October 2017, Athens Colloquium.

Kryvoi, Y., 'Annexation of Crimea and International Investment Law', International Investment Law and the Law of Armed Conflict, 5–6 October 2017, Athens Colloquium.

Osmani-Sadriu, V., 'Treaty Application in Kosovo Through Rules of Succession and as Domestic Law: The Example of the CISG', University of Pittsburgh, Ph.D. Thesis 2015.

Lawry-White, M., 'International Investment Arbitration and Standards Applicable in Conflict: Parallel or Merging Worlds?', International Investment Law and the Law of Armed Conflict, 5–6 October 2017, Athens Colloquium.

Manciaux, S., 'The Full Protection and Security Standard in Investment Law: An Obligation of Result or an Obligation of Conduct?', International Investment Law and the Law of Armed Conflict, 5–6 October 2017, Athens Colloquium.

Mayorga, O., 'Arbitrating War: Military Necessity as a Defense to the Breach of Investment Treaty Obligations', Harvard University Program on Humanitarian Policy and Conflict Policy Brief, Aug. 2013.

Mayorga, O., 'Arbitration of Disputes Under State Contracts in Times of Belligerent Occupation', International Investment Law and the Law of Armed Conflict, 5–6 October 2017, Athens Colloquium.

Paparinskis, M., 'International Investment Law and Disputed Territories: A Generalist Perspective', International Investment Law and the Law of Armed Conflict, 5–6 October 2017, Athens Colloquium.

Peterson, L.E., 'Human Rights and Bilateral Investment Treaties. Mapping the Role of Human Rights Law within Investor-State Arbitration', Rights and Democracy Report (2009).

Peterson, L.E. and K. Gray, 'International Human Rights in Bilateral Investment Treaties and Investment Treaty Arbitration', Working Paper for the Swiss Ministry for Foreign Affairs (2003).

Rees-Evans, L., 'Litigating the Use of Force: Reflections on the Interaction between Investor-State Dispute Settlement and Other Forms of International Dispute Settlement in the Context of the Conflict in Ukraine', International Investment Law and the Law of Armed Conflict, 5–6 October 2017, Athens Colloquium.

Reznik, P., 'Survival of BITs and Investor Rights in Crimea – Russia's Trick or Treat(y) with investors', Thesis in International Law, Faculty of Law, Stockholm University, 2014.

Restatement (Third), Foreign Relations Law of the United States, Vol. I, St. Paul, American Law Institute Publ., 1987.

Risvas, M. 'Non-discrimination and the Protection of Investments During and After Armed Conflict', International Investment Law and the Law of Armed Conflict, 5–6 October 2017, Athens Colloquium.

Ryk-Lakhman, I., '"Reasonable" Protection and Security of Foreign Investments in Armed Conflicts', International Investment Law and the Law of Armed Conflict, 5–6 October 2017, Athens Colloquium.

Samatova, A., *Die Auswirkungen der Staatensukzession auf bilaterale Investitionsschutzabkommen* (The impact of state succession on bilateral investment agreements), Vienna University, 2017.

Schrijver, N.J., 'The Status of Namibia and of Its Natural Resources in International Law. A Report to the United Nations Council for Namibia', in: UN Doc. A/AC.131/GSY/CRP. 13 July 1984.

Soon Lim, K., 'Armed Conflicts and Customary Law on Investment Protection "Codification and Fragmentation of protection and security"', International Investment Law and the Law of Armed Conflict, 5–6 October 2017, Athens Colloquium.

Spears, S. and M. Fogdestam-Agius, 'Protection of Investments in War-Torn States: A Practitioner Perspective on War Clauses in Bilateral Investment Treaties', International Investment Law and the Law of Armed Conflict, 5–6 October 2017, Athens Colloquium.

Titi, C., 'The Life Cycle of Investment Protections in Times of Armed Conflict: Survival and Revival in *Ius in Bello* and *Ius Post Bellum*', International Investment Law and the Law of Armed Conflict, 5–6 October 2017, Athens Colloquium.

Wuschka, S., 'The Obligation of Non-Recognition of Situations Created by an Illegal Use of Force before International Investment Tribunals', International Investment Law and the Law of Armed Conflict, 5–6 October 2017, Athens Colloquium.

Zrilic, J., '*Force majeure* as a Defence against Conflict-Related Investment Claims', International Investment Law and the Law of Armed Conflict, 5–6 October 2017, Athens Colloquium.

MISCELLANEOUS

Broad, V.W., 'In taking Crimea, Putin gains a sea of fuel reserves', *New York Times*, 17 May 2014.

Ciaccia, J., 'Adhésion du Québec à l'ALÉNA: il ne faut pas trop se fier à la Convention de Vienne', *La Presse*, 11 February 1995.

'Crimea applies to be part of Russian Federation after vote to leave Ukraine', *The Guardian*, 17 March 2014.

Global Arb. Rev., 'Ukrainian Bank Claims Against Russia', 10 January 2016.

Global Arb. Rev., 'Naftogaz Threatens Treaty Claim Over Crimea', 22 February 2016.

Grant, T.D, 'Crimea after Cyprus v. Turkey: Just Satisfaction for Unlawful Annexation?', EJIL Talk!, 19 May 2014.

Iareporter, 'After failure of claim under Kazakh statute, Canadian miner hopes that USSR-Canada investment treaty permits arbitration with Kazakhstan', 18 December 2013.

Iareporter, 'In final UNCITRAL award, door left open for Greek company to bring another BIT claim against Serbia', 26 April 2013.

Jones Day, 'Crisis In Crimea: Is Your Foreign Investment There Protected By a Treaty?', April 2014.

Ku, J., 'Ukraine Prepares Even More International Lawsuits That Russia Will Ignore', Opinio Juris, 27 February 2016.

Landry, B., 'GATT et ALÉNA: un simple changement de statut pour le Québec après l'indépendance', *La Presse*, 2 February 1995.

Lim, D., 'Case Comment: Government of the Lao People's Democratic Republic v. Sanum Investments Ltd [2015] SGHC 15', Singapore Law Blog.

Mann, H., 'International Investment Agreements, Business and Human Rights: Key Issues and Opportunities', IISD, 2008.

Milanovic, M., 'Ukraine Derogates from the ICCPR and the ECHR, Files Fourth Interstate Application against Russia' EJIL Talk!, 5 October 2015.

Nuridzhanyan, G., 'Ukraine vs. Russia in International Courts and Tribunals', EJIL Talk!, 9 March 2016.

Peters, A., 'Sense and Nonsense of Territorial Referendums in Ukraine, and Why the 16 March Referendum in Crimea Does Not Justify Crimea's Alteration of Territorial Status under International Law', EJIL Talk!, 16 April 2014.

Roh, Jr. C.E., 'The Implication for U.S. Trade Policy of an Independent Quebec', Center for Strategic and International Studies.

Wisehart, D., 'The Crisis in Ukraine and the Prohibition of the Use of Force: A Legal Basis for Russia's Intervention?', EJIL Talk!, 4 March 2014.

World Bank, World Investment Report, 2014.

INDEX